The Mergers & Acquisitions Handbook

The Mergers & Acquisitions Handbook

Editors

Milton L. Rock
Chairman, MLR Enterprises Inc.
Philadelphia, Pennsylvania

Robert H. Rock
Chairman, IDD Enterprises L.P.
New York, New York

Martin Sikora
Editor, *Mergers & Acquisitions*
Philadelphia, Pennsylvania

Second Edition

McGraw-Hill, Inc.

New York   San Francisco   Washington, D.C.   Auckland   Bogotá
Caracas   Lisbon   London   Madrid   Mexico City   Milan
Montreal   New Delhi   San Juan   Singapore
Sydney   Tokyo   Toronto

Library of Congress Cataloging-in-Publication Data

The mergers & acquisitions handbook.—2nd ed. / editors, Milton L.
  Rock, Robert H. Rock, Martin Sikora.
     p.   cm.
  Rev. ed. of: The Mergers and acquisitions handbook. c1987.
  Includes index.
  ISBN 0-07-053353-9
  1. Consolidation and merger of corporations—United States—
Handbooks, manuals, etc. I. Mergers and acquisitions handbook.
II. Title: Mergers and acquisitions handbook.
HD2746.5.M465   1994
685.1′6—dc20   93-28601
                                                                                              CIP

  2 3 4 5 6 7 8 9 0   DOC/DOC   9 9 8 7 6 5

ISBN 0-07-053353-9

*The sponsoring editor for this book was Caroline Carney, the editing supervisor was
Mitsy Kovacs, and the production supervisor was Pamela A. Pelton. This book was
set in Baskerville by Carol Woolverton, Lexington, Massachusetts, in cooperation
with Warren Publishing Services, Biddeford, Maine.*

Printed and bound by R. R. Donnelley & Sons Company.

 This book is printed on recycled, acid-free paper containing
a minimum of 50% recycled, de-inked fiber.

*To Connie Benoliel, Caro Rock,
and Vivian Sikora for their great
inspiration and support.*

Contents

Part 1. Planning and Strategic Issues

Part 2. Organizing to Merge and Acquire

Part 3. Pricing, Valuation, Negotiating, and Deal Structuring

Part 4. Subsets of M&A

Part 5. Finishing Touches

Part 6. After the Merger

Part 7. The Paper Chase: Regulation, Communication, and Defenses

Part 8. International Acquisitions and Globalization

Preface

Over the last four decades, mergers, acquisitions, and the related field of divestitures have become integral elements in the strategic initiatives of well-managed businesses. By the early 1990s, the practice of mergers and acquisitions had been firmly established as a fine business art and a proven technique for seizing competitive advantage and responding to the myriad forces challenging managers in the highly charged modern world. Deftly executed mergers and acquisitions help companies deal with globalization, leapfrogging technology, industrial consolidation, economic ramifications of political change, and other pervasive trends that impact their prospects for survival. In fact, it is with these forces in mind, notably globalization, that we have developed the second edition of *The Mergers & Acquisitions Handbook.*

A compendium of state-of-the-art knowledge and practice, the *Handbook* deals with every important facet of sound and value-creating mergers, acquisitions, and divestitures in the 1990s. Subjects run across the entire scope of the M&A process including strategic planning, international dealmaking, sound valuation, optimum pricing, enhancement of shareholder value, tax implications, and the complex area of due diligence, to name some. Our authors comprise a blue-ribbon corps of experts who have honed their skills in the actual practice of M&A.

The Mergers & Acquisitions Handbook is aimed at the practicing professional who, although skilled in one discipline, may need quick access to information about complementary talents and disciplines. But it also can be used by the professional or the business executive who has increasing need for an overview of the entire M&A mosaic as a part of basic managerial decisions. The *Handbook* may be read from cover to cover by those who want to steep themselves in the romance of M&A, or each self-contained chapter may be accessed easily by those with specific needs.

Milton L. Rock
Robert H. Rock
Martin Sikora

About the Editors

MILTON L. ROCK, Ph.D., is chairman of MLR Enterprises in Philadelphia and was the publisher of *Mergers & Acquisitions, Mergers & Acquisitions International,* and many other professional financial journals. He is the former managing partner of the Hay Group, a worldwide management consulting firm. His previous books include *The Compensation Handbook,* Third Edition, and *Corporate Restructuring,* both published by McGraw-Hill.

ROBERT H. ROCK is chairman of IDD Enterprises, a New York–based publisher of business and financial newsletters and magazines, including *Mergers & Acquisitions.* He is the former chairman and CEO of the Hay Group.

MARTIN SIKORA is editor of *Mergers & Acquisitions,* and lectures on the subject at the Wharton School of the University of Pennsylvania.

Introduction

We are proud to present the second edition of the McGraw-Hill *Mergers & Acquisitions Handbook*. Its timing could not be better. While the M&A fundamentals described in our first edition have held steady over the past six years, the M&A scene has swung like a pendulum, moving across the board from carefree optimism to cautious pessimism.

Our first edition was published in 1987, near the peak of an M&A boom. In the 1980s, more than $2 trillion changed hands; in the process, U.S. firms doubled their debt, using a quarter of their cash flow to service it. Yet, by the decade's end, the pendulum was heading the other way. As noted in one of the opening chapters in this handbook, Economic Drivers of M&A, by 1990 deals were down by 20 percent in number and 50 percent in value from their 1988 record highs. United States M&A activity fell back to its 1982 level, with blockbuster deals all but disappearing.

But 1993 marks a time of centering. Although M&A activity is showing signs of revival in key industries, a boom is unlikely. We are at the start of a steadier, more balanced, more realistic era for M&A. This edition, even more than our first, shows how important it is for acquirers who are anxious to create value to view M&A as a total process, keeping the lessons of recent history in mind.

ECONOMIC CRASH

In the late 1980s, the U.S. economy had moved rapidly from a state of "everything goes" to a time when everything went. During the "green light" period, deals were obscured by dollars. A handful of huge, hostile, highly leveraged transactions got most of the ink and much of the money. The dealdoer's traditional motto, "Get cheap money," had become "Just get it." In this overheated market, economic viability was ignored in favor of transactional ease. Arbitrageurs prospered while planners starved. The question of the day was not "Should we play the game?" but, Ponzi-like, "How can I get out at the top?"

By the late 1980s the speculative bent of the M&A market was so pervasive in equity markets that the mere rumor of congressional legislation to deny interest deductions on hostile acquisition debt all but caused a crash in the stock market—the so-called Black Monday of October 19, 1987. But this decline in equity prices was nothing compared to the substantive changes that were occurring elsewhere in the economy.

During this period, economic fundamentals, often ignored during the premium-paying deals decade, were taking their inevitable toll. The high-priced buyers who had counted on being even higher-priced sellers crashed to new lows. Biggest-ever buyouts—Revco, Best Products, and Federated Department Stores—became biggest-ever bankruptcies. Nor were smaller buyers immune from the downward trend. In firms large and small, strategic synergy and operational efficiency provided little protection against the ravages of overpricing and overleverage.

M&A lenders and advisers read the handwriting (and fine print) on the wall and pulled back. In this reactive phase, those that had gambled heavily in the M&A game were too weak or too gun-shy to support even sound transactions. Funds for financing and refinancing highly leveraged transactions chilled, then froze. Investment banking commissions tumbled from $2 billion in 1988 to less than $200 million in 1991 according to data collected by IDD Enterprises. Many investment banks have dismantled or eliminated their M&A departments.

U.S. financial institutions have recovered from this overreaction. Regulatory restraints on highly leveraged transactions (HLTs) have lifted. As several of the chapters in this handbook attest, there are signs of new vitality in the merger market. Strategy-minded corporate buyers are becoming more active, favoring more realistic pricing and striking synergistic deals, large and small.

LEGAL CRACKDOWN

The legal environment has gone through similar swings since the appearance of our first edition. While the economy was moving first toward and then away from permissiveness, so, too, was the legal climate. This process was gradual, to be sure, but it seemed to happen overnight—in fact, just as we were coming out with our first edition. When the ink was barely dry on our first handbook, on an ordinary business day in February 1988, federal marshals, acting on behalf of the Securities and Exchange Commission, stormed into two old-line houses to make arrests for alleged insider trading—and arrested no less than the M&A process as we knew it then.

During John Shad's chairmanship, the SEC would expose insider trading (the purchase or sale of securities based on nonpublic information, typically about a pending M&A deal) as a symptom of a larger problem: the market for corporate control had spun out of control. For far too many, M&A had become a game. In the years since that watershed event, the SEC has made many more arrests and Congress has passed several strict white collar crime bills. Regulators and stock exchanges around the world have followed suit.

Meanwhile, subtler legal changes also have been taking place in the so-called corporate governance area. By any measure, company boards have become a much more responsible, informed, powerful force in corporate decision making. Here, too, while the change has been slow, it has been punctuated by several dramatic events.

In a series of high courtroom dramas, judges have dismantled and rebuilt the Business Judgment Rule, a judicial doctrine that protects directors' decisions from second-guessing by the courts. Although this doctrine can be invoked in judging the merits of virtually any board decision, typically it is applied in the M&A area.

At the time we went to press, corporations and their advisers were still reeling from the 1985 Delaware court decision in *Smith v. Van Gorkom* and its immediate legal aftermath. The defendants in this case lost because they failed to show that they had exercised due care in accepting a merger offer.

Decisions of comparable impact were rendered in the 1986 cases of *Revlon, Inc. v. MacAndrews & Forbes* and *Blasius Industries, Inc. v. Atlas Corp.* The *Revlon* case, also decided in Delaware, determined that if directors put their company up for sale they were bound to accept the best price offered shareholders. By the time the first *Handbook* came out, the Business Judgment Rule had weakened beyond recognition.

Since then, however, several new cases turned the *Smith v. Van Gorkom* coin to its flip side. *Paramount Communications v. Time Inc.* and *Newell Co. v. Vermont American Corp.*, both 1989 cases, proved that directors who demonstrate care in decision making can find protection under the rule. (In *Paramount*, the Delaware courts ruled that directors could reject an acquisition offer if they were executing a bona fide plan for adding shareholder value over time.) In 1992, two cases—*In Re Allegheny International* and *Stroud v. Grace*—affirmed the positive principle of the rule's protection. Legal observers are predicting a continuation of this moderate judicial climate.

BOARDROOM CHALLENGES

Not coincidentally, directors themselves during this time have moved from permissiveness toward management, to extreme independence, and now seem heading toward more dialogue. RJR Nabisco, Inc. directors, called cronies by some critics because of their perquisites, made headlines in 1988 when they turned down their own CEO in favor of a buyout fund that offered an historically high price of $25 billion. Four years later, the board of General Motors Corp., long criticized for its inaction, made history when it restructured GM's top management—and future.

Such changes are in part responses to the growing power of shareholders to vote and to sue. Institutional investors, now estimated to control over half of all outstanding equities in U.S. markets, have bigger clout not only in proxy contests but in legal contests as well. They are joined by individual investors in suing directors for decisions they make that fail to increase returns on equity. M&A decisions are particularly vulnerable to this kind of ambulance chasing. According to a recent five-year study by The Wyatt Co. of Chicago, companies with a history of merger, acquisition, or divestiture activity are more than three times as likely to experience a claim against their directors or officers than less-active companies.

In this arena, we have seen a shift in director fears from the buy side to the sell side. When dealmaking helped revitalize the world economy during the 1980s, acquisitive companies went on the offensive for properties that strengthened their competitive positions. In that environment, target company directors anguished over their fiduciary responsibilities in responding to unsolicited bids. They also agonized over their personal and professional exposure, as we saw first-hand in a series of symposia we at MLR Publishing sponsored under the rubric "The Board at Risk."

Now, following a lull in acquisitions, public company directors seem more afraid to acquire than to be acquired. Starting out in today's choppy waters, they have remained "in irons," afraid of making a big commitment that may not pay off. Their focus has been inward, on tasks like cleaning up balance sheets. Acquisitions have been "out," and risk avoidance "in." But as in other spheres, we see signs of temperance. Some directors are realizing that their fears have prevented them from approving acquisitions initiatives that would have positioned their companies for longer-term benefits.

In late 1992, the climate seemed to shift. Pennzoil Corp., after holding back on acquisitions for three years, finally moved, trading $1.2 billion in stock for some oil and gas properties owned by the stock's issuer, megacompetitor Chevron Corp. Gillette Co. proposed a $562-million purchase of Parker Pen Holdings, Ltd.; Perkin-Elmer Corp. and Applied Biosystems agreed to a $330-million stock swap; and troubled Continental Airlines had several offers from buyers. And by mid-1993 the changes were taking hold, with The New York Times/Affiliated Publications and Galen Health Care/Columbia Hopsital Corp. ranking among the megamergers.

This is occurring as economic and legal pressures on directors ease up and as more CEOs and directors seek a dialogue with the investor community. The Investor Responsibility Research Center in Washington, D.C., reports an increase in negotiations that keep proxy issues off the ballot. The same applies to individual investors. The fall 1993 "Target 50" list of the United Shareholders Association (USA) was more notable for omissions than entries.

GLOBAL PROTECTIONISM

By the late 1980s, free trade had few friends. One of the first items of business in the newly formed European Community (EC) was the crafting of a new code of merger regulations. Even the formerly laissez-faire-trade Bush administration was broadcasting a hit list (Super 301) of the most unfair of its trading partners. Congress passed a trade bill in 1988 that set forth new disclosure and reporting obligations on foreign investors.

Ongoing negotiations for the General Agreements on Tariffs and Trade (GATT) almost broke down completely at the turn of the decade as the nascent EC sought special agricultural protections. On this continent, the North American Free Trade Agreement (NAFTA) almost missed getting on track for congressional approval.

The near future promises to steer away from such extreme protectionism. There are signs of hope for balanced agreements in both GATT and NAFTA, and new or renewed national administrations are pledging a measure of support for these carefully crafted agreements.

Meanwhile, independent of national boundaries, new types of multinational buyers and sellers are emerging—companies or investment groups that take positions in foreign firms using foreign capital and adapting to foreign technological standards. This is true not only of older industries that are in the throes of consolidation, but newer industries that are in the process of expansion, such as telecommunications, health sciences, and biotechnology.

Many of these investors also are driving new ownership stakes in restructured geographic territory in a newly dispersed Commonwealth of Independent States, in a recently consolidated Europe, or in unifying the Americas—South, Central, and North.

Thus 1993 marks a centering time for M&A investment policy around the world as nations and regions, almost collectively, appear to be forging a middle course in this arena, and abandoning previous extremes of free trade or protectionism.

WHAT NEXT?

The cumulative impact of these changes—economic, legal, corporate, and geopolitical—has had a sobering, but not a dulling, effect on the M&A scene. Far from changing the fundamental realities of the M&A process, these developments have revealed even more starkly the importance of understanding that process.

We at *Mergers & Acquisitions* know better than anyone that the heartbeat of M&A is in the heartlands, where thousands of middle-market transactions are planned, financed, and closed, year after year. Strategically based and sensibly priced, these small and mid-sized transactions have always offered true value to their participants and to society at large.

These deals are the focus of this 1993 edition, as they have been in all our publications for nearly 30 years. From its founding in 1965, *Mergers & Acquisitions* has ignored the then-dominant fad of conglomeration in favor of strategic "fit." The magazine preached the same strategic message from the go-go 1960s to the sober 1970s and straight through the manic 1980s.

This same message sounded through loud and clear in the first edition of this handbook. Hitting the market just as the M&A field was supposedly collapsing, the handbook has sold over 20,000 copies, and continues to sell briskly. Nonetheless, we recommend this second edition, which captures the state of the art for the 1990s.

HOW TO USE THIS BOOK

In our first edition, we presented the M&A process as a continuum, with distinct phases from planning to postmerger integration. This edition follows this same course, but reflects a changed M&A environment.

Part 1, Planning and Strategic Issues, has been greatly expanded. If the dramatic changes of the past six years have taught us anything, it is that early M&A blueprinting cannot be safely ignored. Therefore we have added broad economic analysis and practical planning tools, among other additions.

Part 2, Organizing to Merge and Acquire, reflects some of the greater caution in the post-1980s M&A scene. There is more to forming an acquisition team or pursuing acquisition candidates than there was six years ago, say our returning authors. This section also includes a new chapter on confidentiality agreements—a must for dealmaking today.

Part 3, Pricing, Valuation, Negotiating, and Deal Structuring, contains revisions of the classic chapters that helped make our first edition such a success. It also features new solutions to solve new problems, and explains how to meet the special challenges of divestitures in this decade and how to finance in an illiquid market.

Part 4, Subsets of the M&A Market, explores special deal formats, such as LBOs and divestitures, corporate restructuring, middle-market mergers and acquisitions, and buying troubled companies.

Part 5, Finishing Touches, rolls out a number of unprecedented guides to help readers protect themselves against emerging risks. There are new chapters on how to reduce environmental and product liability as a buyer and a seller, and how to protect intellectual property on both sides. We also include a new chapter on noncompete agreements.

Part 6, After the Merger, once again offers useful guidance on integrating managements after the transaction is over and the real deal begins. This heavily revised section presents the latest scholarship on what really happens after mergers, and why. It also provides more details on merging benefits and compensation plans, now broken into two separate chapters.

Part 7, The Paper Chase, is *must* reading. It summarizes key developments in U.S. and European antitrust regulations, as well as landmark legal cases affecting today's M&A decisions.

Part 8, International Acquisitions and Globalization, new to this edition, covers critical M&A policy developments in the Pacific Rim, Europe, the Eastern Bloc, and the Americas.

WHO SHOULD READ THIS BOOK?

Judging from the response to our original edition, readers of this handbook will continue to be both corporate development and planning professionals, and their advisers. In the past six years, this group has not grown, but it has become more diverse because of the continued strong growth of the middle market.

M&A activity is still generating fees for a few large Wall Street firms, for regional banking firms, for boutiques, and, increasingly, for accounting firms—both the Big Six and regional. These organizations have geared up to take on middle-market deals ranging in price from $5 million to $250 million. With their portfolios of client relationships and their legions of professionals, the Big Six are particularly well-positioned to gain an increasing share of the middle market. At the same time, even the major investment banking firms are actively searching for middle-market transactions. The top-tier firms that once would have turned up their noses at deals priced under $50 million now readily embrace them. The same is true of major law firms.

Not every firm has maintained an M&A presence, but those that have remained committed to M&A's special professional practice will benefit from its re-emergence.

MILLENNIUM

In preparing this updated handbook for our corporate and professional reader-ship, we have aimed to preserve the bedrock fundamentals of our original edition while reflecting the dynamic new world of the 1990s. In the year 2000, when we publish our third edition, we plan to do the same. It is our fervent hope, however, that by then the "M&A game" will have disappeared from the face of the earth, leaving in its stead only the real M&A—that vital force for business and economic growth in a free and fair marketplace around a changing globe.

Milton L. Rock
Robert H. Rock
Martin Sikora

PART 1

Planning and Strategic Issues

1

Corporate Acquisitions: A Strategic Perspective

Peter Lorange
*President, International Institute
for Management Development,
Lausanne, Switzerland*

Eugene Kotlarchuk
*Former Senior Vice President, Shearson
Lehman Brothers, New York, New York*

Harbir Singh
*Associate Professor of Management, The
Wharton School, University of Pennsylvania,
Philadelphia, Pennsylvania*

The diversified company that uses strategic planning to provide for its long-term survival constantly faces the choice of acquisition versus internal development to achieve growth. The decision should be geared to the basic strategy of the concern. Long-term survival of any corporation depends on its continued ability to develop strength relative to its competitors. Success in achieving this strength depends on the ability to shift resources from well-established, mature business activities to emerging business activities with growth potential. Within this ongoing process of self-renewal, the company must decide whether, given its basic strategy, it is better off shifting these resources through acquisitions or through redistribution among existing entities.

BUSINESS STRATEGIES

A diversified firm may have a hierarchy of business strategies. The strategic self-renewal process may take place at each level within the hierarchy. Acquisitions facilitate the strategic self-renewal at the portfolio level, the business family level, and the business element level.

The Portfolio Strategy.   The philosophy at this level is to develop a set of interrelated businesses that provide reasonable balance and stability within the firm. The portfolio of businesses may be developed purely on financial bases and ignore relationships of technologies or markets among the businesses. Alternatively, the portfolio may be put together by joining businesses that are to some degree related in terms of technology, know-how, or product-market niches. The latter type of portfolio development will build an underlying theme for the interrelationships among the businesses, perhaps in the form of an essential or core skill. Planning for an acquisition in this context involves a search for business entities that will balance and strengthen the firm's overall portfolio theme.

The Business Family Strategy.   The strategic challenge at this level is to formulate a set of closely related business activities that tend to build upon a common technology or know-how base as it applies to the acquirer's business practices. The acquisition is used to develop related new business activities. The business family strategy thus yields a group of interrelated businesses that allow the firm to exploit shared resources in technology, product markets, or distribution channels, and to build new businesses from the foundations of existing units. Acquisitions may be dictated by the need to enter new growth markets that permit the firm to apply its established base. Alternatively, acquisitions might be made to absorb an existing resource base and the know-how embodied in an already well-established business.

The Business Element Strategy.   The strategic challenge at this level is to develop a competitive product/market strategy (vis-à-vis a given competitor) for capturing a particular customer. Success depends on developing competitive strength in a specific business segment. An acquisition under this strategy may be a means to a greater market share by takeover of a competitor. Such a move potentially can strengthen the firm's internal operations by broadening its product and/or service spectrum while simultaneously reducing competition.

ALTERNATIVE ACQUISITION APPROACHES

In strategic planning for acquisitions, a firm must decide which of these three strategies it is pursuing and then determine how an acquisition may, at a given strategic level, enhance its self-renewal. The essence of an acquisition, then, is to create a strategic advantage by paying for an existing business and integrating that entity with the firm's strategy at either the portfolio, business family, or business element level.

The incentive to acquire exists when acquisition is more cost-effective than is internal development. For an acquisition to be viable, these conditions must apply:

- The price that is paid must be lower than the total resources necessary for internal development of a comparable strategic position.
- The anticipated benefits must reflect a generation of future values as part of the portfolio, business family, or business element strategy.

The intelligent acquirer must consider carefully what it is buying, and how the acquisition fits into its organization. What know-how is being bought? How productive is this know-how? Can meaningful synergy be developed between existing organizational entities and the acquired entity? It is impossible to calculate the benefit from the acquisition without assessing the synergistic value of the purchase, a process that goes far beyond a simple valuation of the assets and liabilities listed on the balance sheet.

Planning can expose the variety of reasons for making a corporate acquisition as well as the variations in anticipated benefits from the combinations of two firms. Acquisition of an ongoing business implies the purchase of a set of income-generating resources. But within that guideline, there are several different types of acquisitions, just as there are different strategy approaches. The types of acquisitions may be classified as horizontal, vertical, concentric, or unrelated (conglomerate) acquisitions.

Horizontal Acquisitions.   One firm acquires another firm in the same industry. The principal anticipated benefits from this type of acquisition are economies of scale in production and distribution, and possible increases in market power in a more concentrated industry. The primary impetus for strategic analysis of a horizontal acquisition would originate at the business element level. Benefits to the acquirer would be primarily in the form of a strengthened product-market strategic position.

Vertical Acquisitions.   The acquiring and target firms are in industries with strong supplier-buyer relationships. The acquired firm is either a supplier or a customer of the acquiring firm. Vertical acquisition usually is undertaken when the market for the intermediate product is imperfect, because of scarcity of resources, criticality of the purchased products, or control over production specifications of the intermediate product, among other reasons. Strategic analysis for making vertical acquisitions could reside at the business element level or at the business family level of the acquirer. At the business element level, vertical acquisitions that narrowly affect a specific product-market might be considered. At the business family level, acquisitions that benefit a group of business elements (and have transferable and broader resources) might be proposed.

Concentric Acquisitions.   The acquirer and target firms are related through basic technologies, production processes, or markets. The acquired firm represents an extension of the product lines, market participations, or technologies of the acquiring firm. Concentric acquisitions represent an outward move by the acquiring firm from its current set of businesses into contiguous businesses. Benefits could be from economies of scope (exploitation of a shared resource) and, ideally, from entry into a related market having higher returns than the acquirer formerly enjoyed. The benefit potential to the acquirer is high, because these acquisitions offer opportunities to diversify around a common core of strategic resources. Concentric acquisitions could affect different business families in the acquiring firm. Thus, the primary planning and analysis might be at the corporate level, to promote a unifying theme among the firm's entities.

Unrelated or Conglomerate Acquisitions.   These transactions are not aimed explicitly at shared resources, technologies, synergies, or product-market strategies. Rather, the focus is on how the acquired entity can enhance the overall stability and balance of the firm's total portfolio, in terms of better use and generation of resources. Strategic analysis for conglomerate acquisitions should be done at the corporate level and be incorporated in the portfolio strategy of the acquiring firm.

VALUATION OF AN ACQUISITION CANDIDATE

After the broad strategic criteria have been developed, the potential acquirer must affix values to specific acquisition candidates in line with the basic strategy that is being pursued. These questions must be addressed:

■ *What is the strategic rationale for the acquisition?* The acquirer must determine which of the three basic strategies the transactions fits and then articulate the intended advantages the target will bring to the appropriate strategy.

■ *Is it better to buy than develop internally?* The acquirer is forced into an assessment of the costs and benefits of reaching a particular business configuration through various types of mergers, internal development, or a combination of actions. The acquisition should be evaluated in relation to alternative modes of achieving a desired strategic position.

■ *What resources does the acquisition bring beyond the financial statements?* The acquirer must assess the managerial quality of the target, the specific know-how of the target management, whether the target management will produce results after the acquisition, and whether the target management is likely to become unmotivated or leave. In addition, the acquirer should calculate its own expenditure of nonfinancial resources such as the cost of managerial time involved in making the acquisition work.

- *Are there discrepancies in the value that result from different viewpoints within the acquiring firm?* The acquirer must ask itself whether the acquisition is largely "political"—and based on the subjective judgments of some managers—or objective, and based on facts and firm criteria. If a large discrepancy between these two viewpoints exists, it is a warning that care must be taken and, if the discrepancies cannot be resolved, that the valuation procedure probably has not been sufficiently thorough.

Internal Development versus Acquisition

The choice between internal development and acquisition is determined largely by the costs and benefits, including important opportunity cost factors, which often are overlooked. These factors relate to the degree of "disturbance," or internal motivational dysfunction that might occur as a result of an acquisition.

Acquisition itself means that resources will have to be channeled from ongoing business activities to pay for the transaction. Since these resources could have been used for internal development, the existing organization might resist the use of resources for outside purchases, and managements of existing businesses could lose motivation. Another potential source of loss of motivation is the disturbance that an acquisition unavoidably creates in the ongoing business activities of the organization. New people must be integrated into the functioning of the organization, new managerial assignments made, and new relationships developed. These integration activities take time, create human tension, and expend organizational energy.

The very fact that a firm is willing to pursue its strategies through acquisitions may have dysfunctional impact on its internal operations. The commitment to pursue new business through internal means transmits an explicit message to the organization that top management has confidence in incumbent personnel. A strong negative motivational effect may be created by the firm that oscillates between internal development and acquisitions, because such a strategy may transmit mixed signals to the operating personnel. A commitment to internal excellence needs to be explicitly fostered in such an environment.

Because of these disruptions, and because strategic planning for acquisitions is highly judgmental, the relative success or advantage of an acquisition may be subject to controversy within an organization, depending on the points of view of its various elements. Management may find it advantageous to pursue an acquisition that adds know-how, develops competitive strength, or extends the scope of an existing business. These offer potential long-term payoffs, but they may create short-term problems in the form of the aforementioned internal disruptions. Therefore, members of the organization below top management might not share in the enthusiasm. Stockholders may like the acquisition if it offers long-term value to their holdings or maximization of profits. Again, however, organizational and political forces could impair the increase in value perceived by stockholders. Careful planning takes these disparate points of view into account.

Setting the Premium:
Initial Considerations

A question often asked is: "What is the appropriate premium over market price to pay for a public company?" An acquirer that owns controlling interest in a company, sets profitability goals, and actively intervenes in strategy implementation expects to receive gains and often is willing to use part of them to pay a premium above the company's market value.

Many acquirers justify their acquisitions and acquisition prices on expected synergies. Examples include a new product line that fits the acquirer's present distribution channels, a raw product supplier that assures a manufacturer's uninterrupted needs at reasonable prices, and a seasonal business that buys a counterseasonal business to smooth the revenue stream.

Premiums paid for acquisitions recently have been significant, but it is questionable whether some of the high premiums will ever be recouped in adequate returns on investment. Perhaps some acquisitions are made for other than purely financial reasons. For example, some acquirers believe that they must pay a high premium for a target to assure their own survival, even if an adequate return on investment is never realized. The buyer may have decided that internal development is not feasible or that establishing a similar set of specialized resources on its own is more expensive. Such an acquirer would be willing to pay a significant premium. Even though the deal may be perceived as overpriced, the acquirer at least may regain part of its previous competitiveness, and assure its continued viability and growth.

An acquirer may buy another company to improve its financial position, in real terms or to convey a perception of a more secure financial position to the financial markets. For example, an acquirer with intensive research and development programs that is a heavy user of cash may acquire a heavy cash generator to fund its R&D needs. Acquisition of a cash generator might favorably affect the buyer's stock price and make it easier to raise money in the public marketplace through sale of securities. If the company is private, an improved cash flow position may reduce the cost of bank debt or enhance prospects of securing funds through a private placement.

Some acquisitions are secured at high premiums because of unrealistic assessments of future events. Most key methods for evaluating purchase price offers involve discounting of future income streams, which are based on assumptions of future performance of the company, future economic expectations, and future earnings increases through synergies. If the assumptions are too optimistic, overly generous premiums may never be recouped.

If survival or competition in a set of industries over the long term is the determining factor, an acquisition premium may be justifiable to the buying management. But before paying such premiums, management would be wise to study carefully (and seek opinions from third parties) whether internal development is the better course of action.

Determinants of the Premium

The extent of the premium to be paid is a key element in the decision to acquire a business. The purchase price usually is higher than the current value of a business, primarily because stockholders of the target company need an incentive to transfer control to another owner. The acquirer should start to calculate an offer by investigating the gap between the target's current market value and the value that the target will take on when it becomes part of the purchasing company. At the very least, these gains should exceed the amount paid over current value (on the premium).

The challenge in deciding the premium arises from the fact that the gains from an acquisition are contingent upon a set of actions by the acquiring firm. The buyer's problem is compounded by the lack of perfect information on the target firm before acquisition. Further, top management of the acquiring firm should not assume that a specific premium can be decided upon before negotiation (in the case of a merger) or bidding (in the case of a tender offer) is initiated, because a hostile reaction to a particular offer could force the acquirer to raise the bid. The acquirer should be prepared with an initial price offer and a reservation (exit) price. It also would be useful to have a series of intermediate points at which to make bids. Sophisticated buyers regard the final premium as the outcome of negotiation or bidding, not as a predetermined figure. The final premium may well equal a predetermined figure. However, this would happen only if the dynamics of the negotiation or competitive bidding process went entirely as the acquirer expected.

STEPS IN THE ACQUISITION PROCESS

The acquiring corporation should prepare for the acquisition event through these four steps: identifying the acquisition strategy and screening criteria, selecting the screening approach, making the acquisition, and planning the postacquisition integration process. The acquiring corporation must decide how it will screen attractive acquisition targets. A formal acquisition screen to identify attractive companies initially subordinates their availability as takeover candidates and emphasizes other criteria. An opportunistic approach reviews only companies that are known or rumored to be available. The choice of acquisition screen will depend, in part, on whether the acquisition will be based on a portfolio, business family, or business element strategy.

Understanding Your Own Strengths and Weaknesses

Before a firm's strategy or acquisition goals can be met, top management must identify its own internal strengths and weaknesses in such areas as availability of management time to accomplish the acquisition, finances, management quality, culture, organization, research and development, marketing, reputation in the marketplace, and long-term strategy. Although this step may seem obvious, many corporations treat it lightly and, based on inadequate knowledge of their own affairs, develop acquisition criteria that can lead to failure. These evaluations may be deemed unnecessary by an acquisition team if the acquisition search follows a strategic planning study or an ongoing planning effort. But practice has shown that even if the acquisition team is the same as the planning team, some important strengths and weaknesses are overlooked, especially those pertaining to the culture of the buying firm. Many strategic plans and analyses do not include an objective recognition of a company's culture. What is "culture"? Culture can be said to embody the beliefs and values of the company's management that influence the behavior of all the employees of the company. Culture includes management's perception of its image and identity, the company's work ethic, and its attitudes toward employees, customers, and the community. If the acquirer does not explicitly identify its cultural match with the target firm, a tension-filled postacquisition period may ensue and result in the loss of management at both the acquiring and the acquired firms.

Developing Flexible Acquisition Criteria

After a firm understands its own strengths and weaknesses, and its strategic goals and alternatives, acquisition criteria can be developed. Criteria should be broad, yet specific enough to help the evaluating team recognize a potential fit. Specific criteria are especially important in reviewing opportunistic acquisition candidates. A realistic acquisition effort should not discard any leads on candidate companies. Many structured acquisition searches have become so rigid in scope that after a year or more of effort, no acquisition has resulted, or worse, a less attractive candidate is acquired because the opportunistic one was shunted aside very early.

Alternative Screening Approaches

The list of potentially attractive industries probably will be extensive even after obvious unsuitable candidates have been eliminated. To narrow the list further, the acquisition team should identify the industries with predicted favorable trends. Next, those industries that may prove synergistic to the acquirer's business should be highlighted. When a limited number of industries has been selected, companies in those industries should be examined to determine whether any are of the desired size that the buyer seeks.

The primary focus of this effort should be on the target's position in its industry segment, its perceived strengths and weaknesses compared to those of the acquirer, the target's potential financial results if it continues as an independent entity, and its positive or negative impact on the acquirer. The last factor is very important, because it will help in developing the price that realistically can be paid.

Opportunistic Approach

To reiterate, no leads on companies for sale should be discarded. One of those leads may fit the acquisition criteria better than any of the companies identified from any formal search. Thus, sufficiently specific criteria must exist so that an acquisition team readily can identify a potential fit, whether it comes in through the formal, structured acquisition program or through an outside broker network.

Analyzing Internal
Development Alternatives

Before deciding on a specific acquisition, the acquirer should analyze on a case-by-case basis whether it is better off making the deal or pursuing the same ends through internal development. This step, often bypassed by acquirers, can help set the maximum price the buyer is willing to pay and give it one more chance to weigh the alternatives. Internal development studies often do not prod managements into action unless they are presented directly with viable alternatives such as acquisitions. But when there is a clear choice, based on adequate examination of the benefits and detriments of each route, management often has opted for internal development after a long period of dragging its feet.

Accordingly, an acquisition search should be viewed not as a *fait accompli,* but as a corporate development. The search may show that it is better for the company to proceed on an internal development course as soon as possible, so that it does not miss out on an emerging industry typified by a potential acquisition target. The acquisition search and the acquisition itself are but the culminations of the corporate goal and strategy. The search should be flexible enough to allow the corporation to decide on significant internal development in place of acquisition, if warranted.

Postacquisition Integration Plans

Preliminary postacquisition integration plans should be formulated even before negotiations take place. For example, if the target is very entrepreneurial and the acquirer is a large, structured company, it might be wise to state at the initial contact that the acquirer's intent is to have a hands-off policy after the merger if it wants to preserve the target's entrepreneurial flair. More important, however, the acquirer should anticipate some of the potential problems that may occur, particularly if relocation may be involved or if overlapping functions exist between merger partners. Integration plans should take into account personnel conflicts that may result from duplicate functions. Some recent methods used by corporations to ease the transition have included establishing transition teams before the merger takes place, inviting management to social functions before and after the merger, and conducting attitude surveys on a confidential basis soon after the transaction is completed. In cases of conflicts, the acquirer should act swiftly even if the action is greeted unfavorably by some of the target company's management. Swift action may cause short-term losses, but it is better than a lingering conflict that will severely affect future performance of the company. The worst decision is to leave a conflict unresolved; this will lead to demoralized employees, lower productivity, and ultimately lower stock values if news of such problems reaches the public.

Although a single generic strategy cannot be applied to all acquisitions, certain general tasks can be prescribed:

- Establishing which managers in the target company will be directly responsible for the target company or any of its activities after the acquisition.

- Planning for possible incentive compensation programs to motivate and assure retention of key managers of the target company.
- Developing probable reporting relationships and the degree of autonomy to be given the acquisition candidate.
- Analyzing which functions probably will be integrated and which will remain separate from the acquiring firm.
- Preparing for potential personnel conflicts, and identifying areas where such conflicts may occur. This will permit swift action in cases of irreconcilable differences and conflicts.
- Identifying cultural dissimilarities, deciding whether the functions that are not integrated can or should retain their own cultures, and determining how cultural assimilation that is necessary can take place over time.

The exact recommendations for integration should depend on the type of acquisition that was consummated and on which of the three strategies the acquisition met. Table 1.1 shows some of the desirable integration approaches under the three strategies.

Integration of an acquired firm is an important factor in obtaining benefits from an acquisition. The acquired firm usually has some very desirable resources and

Table 1.1. Postacquisition Strategy Recommendations

Type of acquisition	Management integration	Functional integration	Long-term planning and control
Portfolio	Acquired firm should be autonomous.	Financial functions	Overall general plans
	Acquired firm should report to buyer's CEO or one level below CEO.		
Business family	Integrated organization and management.	Financial functions	Detailed operational plans and controls
	Reporting most appropriate at level below CEO (group vice president).	Marketing and distribution	
Business element	Integrated organization and management.	Financial functions	Most detailed operational plans and controls
	Reporting most appropriate at division level if kept unconsolidated. Most likely, target will be merged into acquirer's equivalent business.		

some resources that are less desirable, and it is not easy to separate what the buyer wants to keep or emphasize and what it wants to divest or subordinate. This problem can be aggravated by cultural mismatches and the learning time the acquiring firm needs to determine how it will really increase the postacquisition revenues of the acquired firm. The main challenges after the acquisition are the following:

- Setting a value on managerial know-how
- Determining whether to integrate the acquired firm or keep it independent
- Determining how to win commitment from the personnel of the acquired firm

An acquisition is based on the premise that some estimated gains (directly or implicitly) from the transaction will exceed the premium paid for the acquired firm. The postacquisition problems reside in the exploitation of these estimated gains. Typically, this is a considerable challenge, because interaction between the acquirer and target company's management is very delicate. Winning commitment from the target management depends on the dynamics of the acquisition transaction (unfriendly takeover or merger) and the amount of cultural mismatch between the firms.

The integration of productive assets (physical facilities, production plants, distribution channels) is also an important dimension of the postacquisition challenge. A frequent reason for acquisition is the use of shared resources and the transferability of resources between firms. However, the cost of unbundling the target firm's resources often may exceed preacquisition estimates.

The management of corporate acquisitions is a complex and multidimensional process. We have shown how decision making for corporate acquisitions interacts with strategic planning in the large, diversified corporation. We note that the relationship between corporate strategy and acquisition analysis needs to be viewed in the larger context of the strategic planning process. We also note that this relationship does not translate into a simple set of decision rules that differentiate between successful and unsuccessful acquisitions. The emphasis on the diversification decision process enables managers to evaluate acquisition candidates against alternative modes of diversification, such as *de novo* entry or joint ventures. This emphasis also enables managers to address the important managerial challenges of the postacquisition period. Although not all problems associated with a given acquisition are fully foreseeable, this approach provides managers with an opportunity to deal with the more predictable postacquisition challenges.

BIBLIOGRAPHY

Bradley, James, and Donald Korn, "The Changing Role of Corporate Acquisitions," *Journal of Business Strategy*, Spring 1982.

Lorange, Peter, *Corporate Planning: An Executive Viewpoint*, Prentice-Hall, Englewood Cliffs, N.J., 1980.

Rappaport, Alfred P., "Selecting Strategies That Create Shareholder Value," *Harvard Business Review*, May–June 1981.

Rumelt, Richard P., "Strategy, Structure and Economic Performance," Harvard University, Division of Research, Cambridge, Mass., 1974.

Salter, M. S., and W. Weinhold, *Diversification through Acquisition: Strategies for Creating Economic Value*, Free Press, New York, 1979.

Singh, Harbir, "Corporate Acquisitions and Economic Performance," University of Michigan, University Microfilms, Ann Arbor, 1984.

Steiner, Peter O., "Mergers: Motives, Effects and Policies," University of Michigan, Ann Arbor, 1975.

Yip, George S., *Barriers to Entry*, Lexington Books, Lexington, Mass., 1983.

2

Development of the M&A Market*

Geoffrey T. Boisi

Senior Partner, The Beacon Group,
New York, New York

Stuart M. Essig

Vice President, Goldman, Sachs & Co.,
New York, New York

The market for corporate control, or the merger and acquisition market, has been a part of the fabric of American business for more than a century. During the last forty years, particularly in the past decade, this market has become increasingly sophisticated and somewhat ritualized. The result has been the growth of a variety of advisers, counsels, lawyers, and expert witnesses, all of whom not only facilitate the M&A process but fuel the continued evolution of the M&A market itself.

This chapter seeks to provide a historical perspective of the growth, development, and recent decline of merger-related activity during the 1980s and 1990s, both in the U.S. market and internationally. Such a perspective requires a basic understanding of capital market theory, the roles and motivations of different participants (including investment bankers), the intricacies of the process, and the fundamental importance of the market to the efficient functioning of the American and, increasingly, the global economy. For today, it is fair to say that it is the rule, rather than the exception, that at some point in their career, most individuals will

*Special thanks to George H. Walker, Associate, Goldman Sachs & Co. for his assistance in this endeavor.

participate, either directly or indirectly, in a merger or acquisition proposal that will materially affect their economic lives.

OVERVIEW OF THE MARKET FOR CORPORATE CONTROL

The forces that drive the market for corporate control can be divided, like a balance sheet, into asset and financing-related components. Asset-related forces involve the supply and demand for scarce strategic resources, which include land, capital equipment, natural resources, intellectual property, and managerial talent. Financing-related forces include the level of real interest rates, the availability of equity and venture capital, bank liquidity and the credit environment, risk premiums, inflation and inflationary expectations, and security price volatility. Additionally, the "focus" of the market is important. Market focus refers to the methodology employed by acquirers to evaluate opportunities. In the 1960s, for example, acquirers, particularly "conglomerate builders," focused on the income statement and the earnings per share accretion of a given acquisition; in the 1970s, focus shifted to the balance sheet; while in the 1980s, it moved to cash flows with the evolution of leveraged buy-out activity. It is the ebb and flow of these forces and shifts in focus that help drive cycles in the M&A market.

Both the asset and financing-related forces are themselves the result of yet more fundamental elements of the business cycle. These macroeconomic forces include monetary and fiscal policy, various political, legal, and regulatory regimes, certain cultural forces, and technological change. Shifts in these fundamental economic factors influence the market, as broadly defined, and the business cycle, which in turn stimulates or retards the narrower asset and financing-related forces that drive mergers and acquisitions.

General Capital Market Theory and the Merger Market

To understand the fundamental rationale for merger and acquisition activity, one needs to take a short detour to consider capital market theory. Typically, abnormally large risk-adjusted profits are made either through simple good fortune or through an understanding of aberrations in the market pricing mechanism combined with sufficient capital to profit from that knowledge. The continuous updating of the pricing mechanism is accomplished through speculation and arbitrage.

In this context, arbitrage differs from the definitions used in academia and in the press. Academics consider arbitrage the risk-free, simultaneous, and profitable purchase and sale of a given asset. Meanwhile, the press has vilified "risk arbitrage"; that is, speculating in the securities of corporations (or governments, agencies, etc.) that have announced or are expected to disclose an event (e.g., an acquisition) that will dramatically change the value of the security. When the speculation is based on inside information, it is theft; if it is based on publicly available information and its interpretation, it is an important component of the market pricing mechanism.

Arbitrage, for the purposes of this examination, is defined more broadly. We consider a strategic decision by a firm to purchase a company rather than to build a comparable asset to be an arbitrage. If public market values are substantially less than replacement cost, one would expect many such strategic arbitrages. We also consider the decision by an owner of a company to increase the liquidity of his or her assets by converting equity to cash through a sale also to be the exercise of arbitrage. So, too, for purposes of this discussion, is the sale of a given security and the purchase of another because of the investor's performance expectations and relative valuation. None of these examples meets the academic definition of arbitrage since the transactions are neither simultaneous nor riskless. Furthermore, they are very different from the arbitrage transactions assailed in the press.

Implicit in financial models and in our conception of markets are two hypotheses: (1) a model of market equilibrium and (2) a notion of market efficiency. First, equilibrium in a market depends on various actions that result in a temporary state of optimization. In the case of the financial markets, issuers attempt to finance their operations at minimal cost, while investors try to maximize their risk-adjusted returns. The forces of supply and demand generally intersect, determining the quantity and value of securities, and, in the process, establishing expected returns, both absolutely and relative to all other outstanding issues.

Arbitrage, broadly conceived, is the "glue" that binds together the model of security pricing and the theory of market efficiency; namely, an assumption exists that at least a handful of individuals stand ready to profit from imperfections in the flow of information to the market or to profitably invest in the creation and/or dissemination of relevant information. These individuals buy and sell securities based on this information, thus insuring the continuous updating of prices and the efficient allocation of capital.

Arbitrage-driven equilibrium is crucially dependent, however, on the quantity and quality of information available to investors. Market efficiency refers to the way in which information is assimilated by the players in a market, and the ability of issuers and investors to communicate and comprehend the data as they are transmitted. If a market is "efficient," market values fully reflect the relevant available information regarding a given security at a particular moment in time, and the marginal cost of information-gathering equals or exceeds its marginal revenue. No market, however, is perfectly efficient. Certain players have greater information than others and have greater access to the means of profiting from that information. Nevertheless, capital markets in developed nations are generally efficient enough to prohibit the small investor from profiting on recently disseminated news, because security prices in general will have incorporated the new information with great speed.

Broadly speaking, it is possible to view the market for corporate control as a pure exercise in arbitrage. Individuals seeking to profit from imperfections in the utilization of an asset (a violation of our model of equilibrium) or from the mispricing of corporate obligations (a violation of our notion of market efficiency) take actions to benefit themselves. They are, after all, arbitrageurs seeking superior risk-adjusted profits. The actions these players take based on market imperfections, whether real or merely illusory, may vary. They may range from simply speculating in the securities of a company, on the assumption that the market ultimately will price the securities correctly, to launching a hostile tender offer for the entire corporation. The fundamental and crucial difference between these two investment/arbitrage strategies is corporate control.

The investor intent on profiting from restructuring the target company cannot be content with waiting for the market to reevaluate the security. That investor requires control of the company. Conversely, the speculator, who may seek to actively change the valuation of the firm by providing the market with information after establishing a position in the security, does not attempt to directly alter the firm's balance sheet, and therefore does not need control.

Control allows an investor access to the asset portfolio of a company, and thus provides the opportunity to "arbitrage" the left-hand side of the balance sheet. Control also provides access to the right-hand side of the balance sheet and an opportunity to reconfigure the company's capital structure. As a result, individuals and corporations engaged in mergers and acquisitions are arbitrageurs, not unlike securities speculators. The arbitrageur deals in the outstanding securities of a company, while the acquirer chooses to reconfigure at least one side of a company's balance sheet and pays a control premium for the privilege. Arbitrage, by any name, is a reaction to an imperfection in either the market equilibrium or the use of information, and functions to keep the system honest and efficient.

MERGERS AND ACQUISITIONS
ACTIVITY IN THE 1980s

The decade of the 1980s was marked by watershed growth in merger and acquisition activity in the United States and abroad. The total dollar volume of international merger and acquisition deals was about $50 billion in 1980. It gradually increased to $150 billion by 1985, plateaued at that level through 1987, and then spiked to almost $250 billion in 1988. The decline in activity was even more abrupt. Dollar volume fell to $188 billion in 1989 and fell again by more than 50 percent to $91 billion in 1990. In 1991, the dollar volume of U.S. deals fell by another 30 percent. Transaction volume fell dramatically in the early 1990s, as credit became more difficult to secure, despite low levels of real interest rates, and as recessionary influences forced many companies to focus their energies on internal operations. Furthermore, the strong stock market made the public equity offering the exit strategy of choice for many sellers seeking liquidity.

Interestingly, the trend in the number of deals during the 1980s was not nearly as dramatic as the changes in average deal-size. In fact, the number of deals in any given year remained essentially unchanged from 1980 through 1989, fluctuating at around 2500, with the noticeable exception of 1985 and 1986, which saw approximately 3500 deals each. The number of transactions in the early 1990s decreased less dramatically than did the dollar volume; thus, the rise and fall in dollar volume of merger activity were driven by dramatic changes in the average size of transactions much more than by changes in the number of deals.

International Mergers and Acquisitions

The 1980s also was a period of dramatic growth in international mergers and acquisitions. Between 1980 and 1990, the percentage of U.S. transactions in which foreign firms acquired American companies increased from 9.8 percent in 1980 to about 12 percent in 1990. Similarly, the growth in purchases of foreign companies by U.S. companies was even more substantial, growing from 5.4 percent of total announced deals in 1980 to 12.6 percent in 1990. Thus, the increase in cross-border M&A was disproportionate to the overall level of activity for the period, and, although the number has declined slightly since 1990, almost one-quarter of M&A transactions involving a U.S. corporation still are cross-border.

Cross-border transactions were by no means limited to the United States, Japan, and West Germany, as is commonly perceived. In fact, the United Kingdom and Canada have been the largest recipients of foreign bids, with the United States, Japan, and Germany far behind in terms of the relative ratios of foreign to domestic acquirers. Merger and acquisition activity in rapidly developing markets such as Hong Kong, Taiwan, Indonesia, Mexico, and Argentina also has accelerated recently.

Despite the contraction in the merger market as a whole, cross-border transactions are likely to grow both as a percentage of total transactions and in absolute terms. With the European Community (EC) emerging as the single largest consumer market, merger activity has been gradually increasing to confront the challenges of unification. A recent study of possible consolidation activity in Europe showed that there were more than five times the number of competitors in Europe as in the United States in the battery, turbine, locomotive, and tractor manufacturing industries. Most dramatically, the study also showed that there are more than 300 major appliance manufacturers in the EC compared to just four in the United States.

Cash and Financing

The transactions currency also has changed dramatically in the past decade. Cash was the most dominant form of currency in the 1980s. Even in the most highly leveraged transactions in the 1980s, stockholders frequently were bought out fully for cash, and the holders of junk bonds and commercial loans became substantial investors in the newly leveraged entity. "Paper" offers were not the norm. From 1980 through 1989, cash was the medium of currency in about 44 percent of transactions, stock in 30 percent, and some combination of cash, stock, and other securities in 26 percent.

The ability of acquirers to finance transactions with cash in the 1980s was critically dependent on four factors: the junk bond market, the highly leveraged transaction (HLT) market within banks, deregulation of the financial markets, and a favorable economic environment. The favorable environment for obtaining credit and completing transactions is illustrated especially well by the leveraged buyout (LBO) statistics for the period. The number of LBOs actually doubled every three years from 1980 through 1988, increasing from 13 to 125 in actual numbers. The value of deals increased even more dramatically, from roughly $1 billion in 1980 to a whopping $61 billion in 1988, capped by the Kohlberg, Kravis, Roberts & Co. buyout of RJR Nabisco, Inc.

Changes in fundamental economic factors, particularly the dramatic contraction of credit markets, ended the reign of the "financial buyer" in 1989. Transactions in the 1990s require significantly more equity and stronger coverage ratios than they did in the mid- to late-1980s. In mid-1992, while the high-yield markets became more active as investors sought greater returns than they could get from government bonds, virtually all new high-yield issues were refinancings rather than new leveraged acquisitions.

The decline in the number of active acquirers in the early 1990s reduced the competition for the acquisition of some companies and eliminated the possibility of accessing the merger market for certain would-be sellers that were unable to find natural strategic buyers. Consequently, transaction structures and processes have become increasingly complex and situation-specific. Negotiated transactions, joint ventures, stock deals, and tax-motivated structures have become commonplace. Efforts to "arbitrage" the balance sheets of companies continue, but the mechanisms for reallocating productive assets have changed dramatically.

Hostile Transactions

The most dramatic corporate control transaction is the "hostile" or unsolicited takeover or tender offer. The number of these contested deals fluctuated dramatically in the 1980s. Surprisingly, the number of contested transactions actually peaked in 1982 at 43 percent of total M&A volume. Since then, contested transactions have declined to less than 20 percent of total volume. While the number of billion-dollar hostile deals fell to just 18 in 1990 and 10 in 1991, these transactions remain an important subset of M&A activity.

Both financial and strategic players participated in very large unsolicited offers during the 1980s. Examples of financial offers include Campeau Corp.'s acquisition of Federated Department Stores Co., the Rales Brothers offer for Interco, Inc., the Bass family's offer for MacMillan, Inc., and William Farley's purchase of West Point-Pepperell, Inc. But, by no means were all of the hostile transactions driven by so-called financial buyers. Many respected, well-run, and prestigious corporations have made unsolicited offers. It should be pointed out that a disproportionate number of the "raiders" eventually were raided themselves. A paper published by the SEC ("Are Bad Bidders Good Targets?") pointed out that one of the best indicators of raid vulnerability is a firm's own activity in making unsolicited offers.

Hostile deals also became increasingly cross-border as the 1980s progressed. Many foreign acquirers resorted to unsolicited offers for U.S. companies. The largest of these that were consummated in the 1980s were Grand Metropolitan PLC's acquisition of Pillsbury; B.A.T. Industries PLC's purchase of Farmers Group; and Beazer PLC's acquisition of Koppers Co. In 1991, Schneider S.A. of France completed an unsolicited acquisition of electrical equipment manufacturer Square D Co.

Hostile merger activity also has emerged within Europe. Nestle S.A. bought Rowntree PLC in an unsolicited transaction, and BP made an unsolicited bid for Britoil PLC. Two Euro-giants, Siemens AG and General Electric Co. PLC, jointly acquired a competitor, Plessey PLC. In the 1990s, unsolicited United Kingdom offers, like those for Imperial Chemical Industries PLC, Racal Electronics PLC, and Hawker-Siddeley PLC have involved acquisitions by large, cash-rich, acquisitive British conglomerates of industrial targets that were at low points in their business cycles.

The decline of cash as the dominant transaction medium and the strength of the equity market in the early 1990s has had two effects on corporate acquirers. First, "strategic buyers" are frequently more cash-rich than "financial buyers," who now are unable to access the market for high-yield securities. Thus, if a strategic buyer makes a cash offer, it can seldom be topped by a financial buyer. Secondly, the strength of the equity market better enables a strategic buyer to make an acquisition today than it could in a poor equity-market environment. This further enhances strategic buyers' ability to compete successfully with financial buyers.

Depending on the identity of the corporation and the manner in which the unsolicited offer is conducted, it is possible to minimize the taint associated with raiding. In the 1990s, the diminishing stigma of unsolicited offers has left corporate acquirers still active in aggressive takeovers. Recall American Telephone & Telegraph Corp.'s successful bid for NCR Corp. and Georgia-Pacific Corp.'s acquisition of Great Northern Nekoosa Corp.

One should not limit even a brief discussion of hostile transactions to those that are completed or merely announced. Unsolicited offers have had much more far-reaching effects. Most importantly, companies showed a surprising willingness in the 1980s to take on significant debt in corporate restructurings, both in order to discourage unsolicited acquirers and to increase the present value of future tax shields associated with tax-deductible debt financing. Santa Fe Pacific Corp. and Kroger Co. each took on more than $5 billion of debt, and USG, Inc. and Owens-Corning Fiberglass, Inc. each took on more than $3 billion of debt in restructurings to repel potential acquirers. Before capitulating to Philip Morris, Kraft Inc. announced its willingness to take on more than $13 billion in debt to fight the hostile bid.

THE SOURCES OF MERGER-RELATED PROFITS IN THE 1980s

Mergers and acquisitions, like other investing and speculating activities, are grounded in attempts to profit from imperfections in the utilization of an asset—a violation of our model of equilibrium—or from the mispricing of corporate obligations—a violation of our notion of market efficiency. Both can be seen clearly in the 1980s.

The most common argument put forth by acquirers in the merger market during that period was that acquisitions allowed them to achieve "synergies." This argument typically was presented by corporate acquirers who believed that two entities, when combined, were worth more than if they had remained independent. These synergies frequently were grounded in economies of scale or scope and could occur at any stage of the so-called value chain: raw materials sourcing, production, distribution, marketing, and so on. This argument was particularly pervasive among corporate acquirers in the 1960s and 1970s. Companies thus profited from the reallocation of corporate assets to more productive uses in the combined entities.

Ironically, while the synergies case continued to be made, much of the 1980s M&A activity was a rebuttal to this argument. Through acquisition, many corporations had grown into unwieldy conglomerates manufacturing unrelated products. Wall Street came to discount the value of overly diversified firms' securities for two reasons. First, there were real diseconomies of scale and scope, particularly for managements trying to operate a multiplicity of unrelated businesses. The lessons learned in one business were often nontransferable and caused firms to unwittingly destroy the value of various subsidiaries. "Busting-up" these corporations created value through more efficient asset allocation. Secondly, investors found it difficult to value conglomerates operating several (occasionally more than thirty) different companies in unrelated industries. This produced a breakdown of information and uncertainty in the pricing mechanism. Whatever the cause, financial buyers appeared, and they were eager to arbitrage the "conglomerate discount."

Management is not explicitly listed on the balance sheet. Nonetheless, it too has been a constant ingredient in merger-related activity, because it is an important builder or destroyer of economic value. In the era of conglomerate-building, many acquirers thought that their understanding of scientific, earnings-based management would allow them to enhance the value of smaller, less sophisticated firms. This emphasis on combination a decade later would generate much of the bust-up activity associated with the 1980s. But management ability continued to be an important element in 1980s merger activity as many acquisitions were made on the basis of obtaining good management teams or replacing bad ones. Good teams, it was thought, could be leveraged to operate not only their previous firms as subsidiaries of the acquirer but also to manage related assets of the acquiring company. Likewise, poor teams destroyed shareholder value and the simple act of replacing them was supposed to produce a gain for the acquirer. Management-motivated acquisitions also fit the arbitrage model.

Other sources of arbitrage gain include revaluing the left side of companies' balance sheets. Often, the target of an acquisition would have assets that were inadequately reflected in the market valuation of the firm. Some were "hidden," such as brand names that the corporation owned and could sell but were either not on the balance sheet or had long ago been depreciated below their market values. One could argue, for example, that the Camel, Winston, and Salem cigarette brand names were the most valuable assets of R.J. Reynolds. Classic film libraries of major movie studios are another example of valuable assets that were not adequately reflected in the price of the parent firm's equity. While the real estate market boomed in the 1970s and 1980s, most real estate investments were reflected on firms' balance sheets at depreciated cost, which represented a fraction of the market value of the individual assets. In an inflationary environment, most fixed assets were valued at a fraction of their individual market values or replacement costs. Cash, marketable securities, and overfunded pension funds of a corporation were also undervalued on the corporate balance sheet. M&A allowed acquisition arbitrageurs to profit from any hidden value by obtaining corporate control.

The arbitrage opportunities on the right side of a firm's balance sheet are equally significant. As discussed earlier, many firms had capital structures with remarkably little debt, which for a time was perceived as inefficient, given the tax-advantaged status of debt financing. Merely purchasing a portion of the outstanding equity and replacing it with debt would allow one to enhance the value of a company through newly acquired future tax shields. Additional tax arbitrages were made possible by the Economic Recovery Tax Act of 1981, which allowed the buyer to write up the target's assets to acquisition-level values and then depreciate them over a reduced period of time. Since the maximum capital gains tax rate for the seller was 20 percent, both buyer and seller were able to extract additional gains from the U.S. Treasury. It should be noted that many of these subsidies have since been eliminated, particularly by the 1986 Tax Reform Act.

Shifting risk from equity holders to debtholders was a tactic prevalent in the late 1980s. Most corporate bonds were issued long before the 1980s and had antiquated covenants that allowed the acquirer, or its new parent, to lever the target without repurchasing the existing debt. After the acquisition was completed and the target was levered, the value of the previously outstanding debt immediately declined as the risk inherent in the instrument increased dramatically. These inefficient covenants, like the tax shields, could be arbitraged only by controlling the right side of a corporation's balance sheet.

Finally, management buy-outs (MBOs) illustrate yet another unique arbitrage-driven merger opportunity prevalent in the 1980s. MBOs were not unheard of in the 1970s bear market, particularly by firms that had executed initial public offerings only a short time before and had seen their equity fall to depressed trading levels. However, in the 1980s, MBOs grew in both number and size, driven by the same forces that powered leveraged buy-outs (LBOs).

Many authorities argued, quite powerfully, that MBO transactions represented a conflict of interest. Management, after all, has access to information unavailable to outside bidders or even to the corporation's other owners. Additionally, management has the power to artificially depress the firm's stock price by decreasing corporate earnings in ways that do not necessarily destroy economic value; i.e., increasing maintenance or capital expenditures, reducing the dividend, changing the firm's public relations strategy, and so on. This puts the executives in the unique position of being able both to create the market mispricing and to profit from it at the expense of the corporation's other owners. On the other hand, MBOs enriched existing shareholders and often empowered firms by creating better economic incentives for managers and employees. Ultimately, board-mandated auctions helped preserve the MBO, which is valuable to shareholders, as well as decrease the likelihood that shareholders would be disenfranchised by any given transaction.

The Changing Concept of Control

In the 1980s, as outlined in the theoretical background, investors sought to control corporations to achieve their objectives. In the 1990s, investors and potential acquirers have similar goals, but the increased complexity of the market has created less costly means of achieving them. The combination of increased institutional ownership, changing proxy rules, and the use of strategic minority stakes and joint ventures has made unsolicited offers and acquisitions less important means of achieving certain ends. This trend certainly will continue and will improve shareholder democracy and global economic restructuring.

THE DEVELOPMENT OF M&A PROFESSIONALS

As anyone who has witnessed a change in corporate control realizes, the principals comprise only a small portion of the significant participants in the transaction. Investment bankers, commercial lenders, accountants, lawyers, consultants, proxy solicitors, and public relations firms, among others, can be deeply involved in a given transaction. As the 1980s marked a dramatic increase in both the size and complexity of transactions, this change was accompanied by growth in the number and significance of these additional players. The changing competitive environment for these professionals is being shaped not only by the same macro forces driving the merger market but by additional forces unique to the merger advisory, banking, and legal environments.

Since the level of domestic merger activity has declined, competition among investment bankers and other merger-related professionals has intensified. Nonetheless, significant growth in the international mergers business, particularly in Europe, has buoyed many firms' results in the early 1990s. Compensation increasingly has become linked to the client's objective, whether it be to acquire an asset or to achieve the highest possible sale price. In the 1990s investment bankers and lawyers frequently are being asked to justify their contributions. Structuring a global joint venture is no less time-consuming or challenging than defending a domestic raid target, and the importance of advisers is no less significant.

Increased Emphasis on Relationships

Despite the historic trend towards "transaction" banking, primary emphasis on financial advisory relationships is reemerging. Most importantly, with regard to sensitive issues, clients generally look to a few advisers—financial, strategic, and legal—with whom they feel comfortable about sharing confidential information. Relationships have been a cornerstone of the recent success of boutiques, while larger investment banks are promoting the relationships of their senior bankers in marketing their services. Not surprisingly, given the strategic and often critical importance of the advice they are seeking, clients are becoming much more sophisticated and demanding in selecting their advisers.

Lowering and Eliminating Regulatory Barriers

Deregulation is occurring on a worldwide scale. Although Congress has not yet eliminated the Glass-Steagall Act, the Federal Reserve has granted selected major banks the authority to underwrite a variety of corporate securities. While commercial banks already are free to compete with investment banks in some businesses such as mergers, foreign exchange, and certain international debt and equity transactions, the result of deregulation is that competition for the issuance of domestic corporate securities, particularly debt, has intensified. Furthermore, commercial banks have begun to compete for high-margin, high-value-added merger and acquisition advisory business by leveraging their traditional lending relationships, and tying many of their services to advisory relationships.

Globalization

As a result of the deregulation and globalization of financial markets, all full-service banking competitors, including U.S. domestic investment banks, U.K. merchant banks, Japanese securities firms, and the Swiss and German universal banks are strategically positioning themselves to be international, if not global, firms. Experience has proven that entry into foreign markets is more costly and difficult than was anticipated. Realism has dictated a focus on controlled growth in selected businesses, with an emphasis on execution, profitability, and intercountry (as opposed to intracountry) transactions and flows. Eastern Europe, Latin America, and Southeast Asia are getting increased focus.

Increased Focus on Principal Investment Activity

In light of declining margins in the merger and acquisitions business, and a perceived expertise in valuation and negotiation, many firms have concluded that principal investing must become a major component of strategy. Significant competitive advantage in principal investment can be attributed to the quality and magnitude of the deal flow resulting from a firm's client base, broad marketing coverage, and significant transaction and industry-specific expertise.

INTO THE FUTURE

The volume of merger and acquisition activity has fluctuated dramatically in the United States throughout the past century. But no trend, either up or down, matched the M&A surge of the 1980s. It is unlikely that we will soon see a return to the M&A volume of the last decade. However, the market will continue to develop and evolve in response to fundamental macroeconomic changes, such as the creation of the European Common Market, the fall of communism in Eastern Europe, widespread evolutions in key industries, such as the decline of certain heavy industries and the growth of new service-sector industries, and certain merger-related developments like changes in antitrust and tax legislation.

Most importantly, the merger market will become increasingly global. While 1980s transactions were limited largely to North America, Western Europe, and Japan, the global merger market will encompass transactions for companies in Eastern Europe, Latin America, South America, and Asia. Consequently, merger professionals, whether lawyers, bankers, accountants, or consultants, not only will have to become globally competent but will have to compete globally.

For a variety of reasons, hostile tender offers are unlikely to return to their previous volume levels. First, managers and investors can better recognize the potential value of "hidden" assets. This recognition by investors decreases the value of the potential arbitrage, while management is more likely to consider ways to securitize or otherwise capture values that previously would have remained "hidden." Second, many of the potential arbitrage opportunities that existed in the early 1980s have already been affected. Few firms, for example, still have bonds outstanding with antiquated covenants that permit risk-transfers. Large conglomerates with extraordinary diseconomies of scale or scope feel under continuous pressure to reevaluate their strategies. The public's contempt for hostile transactions, government's recognition of the tax revenue lost from mergers in the 1980s, and the economic cost of its weak antitrust enforcement make it unlikely that Washington would permit many of the arbitrages that drove certain hostile transactions in the 1980s. Finally, bank credit, often extended to nearly insolvent companies in the 1980s, no longer is granted so freely.

After witnessing a decade of extraordinary levels of hostile activity, most participants are more aware of the costs inherent in such transactions. Putting a company "in play" often prohibits, rather than induces, dialogue between management and shareholders about the corporation's long-term direction. The notion of corporate democracy may be better illustrated by a proxy fight in which everyone votes in its interest but the majority wins. Today's investors, particularly institutions, if frustrated with management, are more likely to enter into a dialogue and try to change a management team or a particular strategy than to encourage a hostile tender.

These changes, among others already explored, will have a profound impact on the environment in which the merger professional operates. Merger advisory assignments will become more global, and hence, more competitive. Nontraditional competitors will continue to enter the arena, but will be increasingly hard-pressed to compete effectively, given the heightened sophistication of the market, the demand for auxiliary services, the amount of available business, and the new nature of corporate governance. Firms that enjoy relationships with both managements and shareholders will be uniquely situated to provide high-quality advice and develop state-of-the-art merger products.

Although the hectic pace of the 1980s is unlikely to return in the near future, the merger market will continue to become more sophisticated, more global, more competitive, and more important to the world economy than ever.

3

Economic Drivers of M&A

Robert H. Rock

Chairman, IDD Enterprises, L.P.,
New York, New York

For more than a century, dramatic surges in M&A activity have come and gone. What makes—and breaks—them? In my view, several principal factors come into play. Among them are the economic outlook, financing alternatives, price expectations, strategic challenges and opportunities, and, last but not least, the reputation of the M&A professional community.

A scan of the scene in the 1990s shows all of these forces at work and in sync in an M&A market that has recently reversed directions. After turning downward, it seems to have hit bottom and headed toward renewal, thanks to middle-market strength.

ECONOMIC OUTLOOK

One of the strongest forces dictating merger behavior in our era and in eras past is economic outlook. American economic history has been a continual saga of booms and busts. Cycles of public attitude mirror the economy, alternating between times of optimism and pessimism. The pessimism of the 1970s was supplanted by the optimism of the 1980s, which in turn gave way to the pessimism of the early 1990s.

These shifts in public sentiment—never occurring in neat calendar decades, but always making their mark on each—are reflected in the M&A marketplace, which

27

by the early 1990s was emerging from a brief period of severe gloom. In the 1980s, $2.2 trillion changed hands in shuffling the assets of some 25,000 companies. For the better part of the decade, this occurred through buyer-motivated acquisitions, including many large, hostile deals. Toward the end of the decade, M&A activity became more divestiture-driven. "Restructuring" by downsizing, once only a euphemism for takeover defense, had become a virtual rite of passage to market respectability.

In this process—and in buying back their own stock to reduce takeover exposure—U.S. firms doubled their debt to some $2 trillion while retiring a half billion dollars worth of equity. During this self-proclaimed decade of leverage, more than one quarter of U.S. corporate cash-flow was used to service debt. By 1990, the M&A boom was over. Deals were off that year by 20 percent in number and 50 percent in value from their 1988 record highs.

Success in M&A requires the careful identification and valuation of acquisition candidates, based on both strategic and financial criteria. For corporate acquirers, the analysis looks at a deal's potential for improving the performance of both the acquired business and the parent. Improvement often depends on merger synergies. Yet these synergies frequently fall short of expectations, particularly when the economy turns south. Consequently, a forecast for the global economy in general, and the U.S. economy in particular, is critical to M&A strategy.

In the early 1990s, the U.S. economy stumbled along, unable to shake off the look and feel of recession. Yet, as the lead-in to a feature story in a major business magazine announced at the time, "Believe it or not, the U.S. tops the industrial world in growth." Indeed, during 1992, the United States led the developed world in growth of industrial output. The United States was the only one of the seven major industrialized nations with a year-to-year improvement. Germany and Japan posted year-to-year declines projected to be 3 percent and 5 percent, respectively.

In comparison with the rest of the world, the U.S. economy wasn't too bad. The U.S. economy's estimated 2.5 percent GNP growth, 2.4 percent inflation rate, and 7.3 percent unemployment rate looked almost robust by comparison. EC economic growth slowed to 0.8 percent in 1992 from an anemic 1.4 percent the year before. European domestic economies were weighted down by large fiscal deficits and steep interest rates. Even the vaunted German economy was sagging. The 1992 jobless rate in West Germany was 6.6 percent and officially 14.5 percent in East Germany, although about one-third of the latter's workforce was without full-time employment. Unemployment in Italy, France, and the United Kingdom was in double digits.

The situation was no better in the rest of the world. Canada's GNP was flat and its unemployment rate was over 10 percent. Japan's economy was stumbling, with GNP growth only 1.5 percent in 1992. Japan's tradition of lifelong employment was being honored in the breach as companies, pushed into the red by the economic slowdown, were shedding workers.

Irrespective of considerable pessimism, the American economy was highly competitive. A 1992 McKinsey & Co. study referred to a "silent revolution" that had made many American firms first in the world. For example, comparing machine tool makers, the study found that U.S. companies had extended their productivity lead over their German counterparts.

Over the past decade, many American companies have met head-on the global competitive onslaught and are winning. Where once they saw danger in the global economy, now they see opportunity. Barring any harmful surprises, the U.S. economy has a good foundation for continued, though perhaps lackluster, growth. Little inflation, low interest rates, increasing productivity, greater exports, and rising profit margins allow for significant growth.

America's competitive renewal should lead to restored confidence in expanding through acquisitions. Mergers and acquisitions should again be a central theme of corporate strategy, provided financing is available.

FINANCING ALTERNATIVES FOR BUYERS

The deals market of the early 1990s looked a lot like the market of the late 1970s and early 1980s. For example, mezzanine financing, which had been usurped by junk bonds, has returned to more traditional private placements. The financial razzle-dazzle exemplified by pay-in-kind securities (PIKs), deferred-interest bonds (DIBs), and resets is out. As an acquisition currency, equity is in. The dealmaking flavor is again "plain vanilla." Although pressures against dealmaking and deal financing remain intense, the early 1990s decline in M&A activity does not signal the end of this vital economic process.

To be sure, financial buyers disappeared, commercial lenders retreated, foreign acquirers stepped to the sidelines, and insurers—still the principal providers of long-term financing—provided funds only to the strongest credits. All this put the brakes on many would-be acquisitions. The worldwide economic slowdown scotched many others. Few companies, regardless of size, were bold enough to commit to acquisitions when the economy was generating mixed signals as to when the marathon stagnation would finish running its course.

Where once both private and institutional investors bought junk bonds yielding 12 to 18 percent, lenders of the early 1990s demanded 25 to 30 percent through a combination of core interest rates and equity kickers. Moreover, investors required that buyers put up a bigger slug of equity money—20 to 40 percent, in contrast to the former 10 percent that had been standard in leveraged transactions, thereby adding a wider layer of protection.

Nevertheless, without much fanfare, scores of mid-sized deals, priced at $5 million to $250 million, were getting done. Corporate buyers, frequently using stock swaps, engineered most of the significant deals. In this middle market, M&A activity was particularly brisk in health care, banking, retailing, consumer products, and telecommunications.

For transactions with the right stuff, there was ample mezzanine financing and an abundance of equity capital, although prying it loose was difficult. (Financing companies, expensive sources of total deal financing with particular emphasis on the mezzanine market, were still gun-shy on M&A lending.)

But as we approached mid-decade, we began seeing a new financial conservatism that steered a middle course between frenzy and freeze. Mezzanine financing and equity, though expensive, was readily available. And while senior debt was hard to raise, given the banking industry's new-found abhorrence of extreme leverage,

banks that had stayed with asset-based lending during the 1980s were actively looking to provide acquisition financing, funding millions of dollars in middle-market
deals through new senior debt facilities.

Even more importantly, equity as an acquisition currency was back in vogue. Equity deals were being fashioned, sometimes using premium equity (e.g., PERCS and
LYONS), convertible instruments, and employee ownership (e.g., ESOPs and pension investments).

FINANCING ALTERNATIVES
FOR SELLERS

A surge in the equity market amplified the dirge heard in M&A. Noting the super-
charged initial public offering (IPO) market and the elevated stock market, many
would-be sellers were unwilling to accept the prices offered by a chastened M&A
market, and quite a few took the IPO route as an alternate exit vehicle.

Once, buyout firms counted on divesting some divisions, or selling the entire
company, to generate big returns for their investors. The recent market, however,
did not afford a suitable return for such sales, so dealmakers have turned to an
alternative exit strategy. This trend continued as long as private companies, or restructuring firms with subsidiaries for sale, were able to peddle shares at whopping
multiples through public offerings.

Companies, both private and public, recognized that they could get better value
for their assets in the public equity market than in the private M&A market. Many
recent IPOs and equity carve-outs would have been yesterday's acquisitions and divestitures. But the attractiveness of the equity alternative could wane. In 1992 stocks
were selling at an average of 23 times the previous 12-month earnings. Such heady
valuations had not been seen since 1955, except during very brief periods in 1961
and 1987.

As in the past, these lofty multiples will not last. When skyrocketing stock prices
begin to falter, and the trendy IPO market starts to evaporate, the stampede of equity
offerings will slow, putting the M&A market in a better position to compete. Indeed,
we are seeing signs of such a turn of events as we go to press with this new edition. In
any event, the recent rise in IPO activity eventually may lead to M&A deals. A public
presence gives a company a high profile and a trackable performance, both of which
can attract potential buyers. Some LBO funds and some freestanding, lightly leveraged firms may be using the IPO vehicle as a first step toward eventual merger or
acquisition; an IPO can be a way of "teeing up" a company for sale.

PRICE EXPECTATIONS
FOR BUYERS

Buyers must be cautious when setting prices, since acquisitions carry high stakes.
Good ones can enhance shareholder value by expanding geographical coverage,
broadening distribution networks, advancing technological skills, and creating operating efficiencies. Bad ones can destroy the value of healthy companies.

Companies today are making acquisitions that enhance their key market positions and are doing divestitures that extract noncore businesses. In terms of corporate development, they are sticking to their knitting. In contrast to the 1980s, buyers have the upper hand. They not only dictate price, but also can set terms and conditions. With the disappearance of most financial buyers and the reticence of many corporate ones, strategic acquirers can negotiate on a highly friendly and frequently exclusive basis. The days of so-called controlled auctions, pursued frequently in the 1980s to smoke out the highest bid, are long gone. Sellers today must work to attract and satisfy a qualified buyer.

Given the recent difficulty of financing deals, M&A valuations have dropped from their 1980s levels. In the early 1990s, good companies continued to sell at a premium, bad companies were not selling at all, and marginal properties were nearly impossible to sell. Yet many sellers had not made the psychological shift in their price expectations. Entrepreneurs with stand-alone businesses and corporations with unwanted divisions balked at recent pricing levels—in the neighborhood of 4 to 6 times cash flow versus multiples of 8 to 12 just a few years ago.

STRATEGIC CHALLENGES AND OPPORTUNITIES

Today, strategic acquirers have little trouble attracting sufficient capital to get deals done. Since recent waves of unrealistic optimism and backlash pessimism have subsided, more and more companies are doing deals that make sense in terms of their strategic purpose, business fit, and operations integration.

The current world market offers some great opportunities for strategic corporate buyers. Consolidation within industries, privatization in Europe and Latin America, globalization of markets, and standardization of M&A rules are creating many dealmaking opportunities. American companies are responding by doing deals here and abroad that extend market penetration and enhance operating efficiencies. Restructuring is popular in the United States, where firms have been freeing up capital through the sale of noncore businesses.

U.S. companies are building worldwide competitive positions through acquisitions and alliances in response to the continuing evolution of markets and competitors that are increasingly unimpeded by national boundaries. Such deals should help advance the competitiveness of U.S. businesses in increasingly global marketplaces. More and more, U.S. corporate buyers are turning their sights to Europe, to Latin America, and to neighboring Canada and Mexico—still awaiting U.S. congressional approval of the North American Free Trade Agreement signed in 1992.

Their European counterparts remain interested but cautious. In the late 1980s, a highly confident group of European business leaders were striking bold deals throughout the world. Today, because of the economic slowdown that gripped the Continent in the early 1990s, they seem more wary about their corporate development opportunities. They have been hesitant to undertake aggressive growth strategies, particularly those that require large acquisitions. As a result, dealmaking throughout Europe has dragged.

When European economies improve, M&A activity should pick up. In addition to

European-based buyers, U.S. and Japanese firms will continue to position themselves in Europe via acquisitions, as well as greenfield investments and joint ventures. The race for global advantage has been joined. Even in the period of hesitancy that marked the early 1990s, many mid-sized deals still were getting done in Europe, particularly by firms seeking to refocus and deleverage through divestiture or to expand and reposition through acquisition.

In terms of the number of completed deals, based on data from IDD Enterprises collected from 1989 to 1992, the United States continued to lead the United Kingdom and continental Europe, but its lead was shrinking. In 1989, the United States logged over 4200 deals, more than twice the combined total of the United Kingdom (which recorded over 2200) and the rest of Europe (which recorded over 1600). In 1990, U.S. activity slowed slightly, while European activity doubled and began holding steady; U.K. activity declined precipitously. In 1991, nearly 4000 companies changed hands in the United States, a total nearly matched by continental Europe, which tallied over 3800, but far greater than the United Kingdom, which completed only half that many.

In terms of the value of completed deals, the United States has continued to lead the other two M&A blocs, again with a diminishing lead when compared to a more active continental Europe. The downward U.S. trend has been precipitous. In 1989, completed U.S. transactions were worth some $326 billion. By 1992, their value had dropped to $115 billion.

All of this signals stronger middle-market activity in both the United States and Europe. The average size of transactions in the United States has decreased significantly in recent years, putting them on a par with trimmer European transactions. These, too, have decreased in average size, but by far less.

REPUTATION OF M&A PROFESSIONALS

Another motivator or inhibitor of M&A activity is the esteem in which M&A advisers are held. As recently as 30 years ago, such advisers went under the generic term of attorneys, accountants, or bankers, but the merger and acquisition boom of the 1960s gave rise to a special practice that carried the M&A name. The brief history of that practice shows the importance of the reputation factor.

In 1965 the U.S. Office of Trademarks and Patents issued a trademark on the name *Mergers & Acquisitions* to a new bimonthly trade publication. The term had not been in wide use at the time, and M&A as a profession was in its infancy. It has come a long way since then.

In 1980, MLR Publishing, a predecessor firm to IDD Enterprises, Ltd., took over *M&A* from the journal's founder, Stanley Foster Reed. Moving away from Reed's academic bent, the new owners set out to enhance the professionalism of the M&A field by convening roundtables, commissioning articles, and conducting conferences to define standards of professional conduct. From the beginning of this endeavor, MLR was encouraged in this by its editorial board, made up of corporate CEOs and other business leaders who regarded dealmaking as a professional practice similar to the practice of medicine and law.

With the acceleration of M&A activity in the mid- to late-1980s, most of *M&A*'s articles focused on the methodologies, techniques, and tactics of dealmaking. The size and complexity of transactions required ever more sophisticated know-how. Nevertheless, *M&A* continued to address ethical questions.

As the excesses of the 1980s were revealed, the professional standing of the M&A field in general, and some M&A practitioners in particular, plummeted. Investment bankers were portrayed in newspapers, books, and movies as arrogant wheeler-dealers who got obscenely rich by shuffling paper. Lawyers fared no better. Moreover, they were blamed for many of the problems afflicting corporate America. The princes of Wall Street were viewed as pirates who ushered in an era of money lust and financial abuse. Once revered as ingenious, M&A professionals now were reviled as inept; once the drivers of M&A activity, they now drove it away.

The current fall-off in M&A activity—driven not only by economic, financial, and regulatory forces, but also by the poor reputation of dealmakers—has resulted in the reassignment or dismissal of individual M&A practitioners, and the downsizing or dismantling of entire M&A departments. This reduction in M&A practice has in turn accelerated the drop in the volume of M&A deals, as fewer would-be sellers or buyers are reached or welcomed as clients. This lull provides the time to rethink and reconfirm the professionalism of the M&A field. The firms that have demonstrated technical know-how and built an ethical reputation continue to receive M&A advisory assignments. They will become the models for firms that upgrade their M&A work when M&A activity surges again, as it surely will.

THE NEXT STAGE

In summary, the bull market in highly leveraged deals is over, but strategic deals are moving ahead. When capital becomes more readily available through the reemergence of commercial bank lending and the resurgence of other lending sources, M&A activity should accelerate again.

Having traveled from optimism to pessimism, the M&A world is settling somewhere in between. As we enter the middle of the decade, all the signs—economic, financial, strategic, and professional—point toward renewed growth of M&A as a business activity and as an honorable profession.

4

Planning Models for M&A Analysis

William J. Edwards
Vice President, Arthur D. Little, Inc.,
Cambridge, Massachusetts

The more things change, the more they remain the same.
ALPHONSE KARR, 1849

The use of models for analyzing and valuing acquisitions, mergers, and diversifications is neither a new nor a precise discipline. As a tool for decision-making, modeling probably first appeared in the Stone Age, when people started to analyze and quantify the benefits to be derived from bartering for goods and services. Similarly, strategic analysis (the analysis of market demand, market share, competition, resource allocation, and so forth) is not a recent phenomenon. The British and Dutch East India companies of the early 1600s were well versed in the economic advantages of market control.

The wave of merger, acquisition, and divestiture activity that took place during the 1980s has been attributed primarily to corporate America's rush to implement strategic plans. Many authoritative observers have characterized the strong activity as the era of strategy-driven mergers and acquisitions. Yet, to those who lived during the first quarter of this century or who have studied American business history, the 1980s wave of strategic merger and acquisition activity may not have seemed so new. Certainly, the motivations behind corporate America's recent tendency toward strategic consolidations were not new. They bore a striking resemblance to economic principles embodied in the great basic-industry consolidations of the early twentieth century. The mergers and acquisitions that took place in the steel, railroad, oil, and automotive industries were implementations of ideas that focused on the objective of market control. The strategies formulated by Carnegie, Morgan, Gould, Rockefeller, Sloan, Ford, and other visionary magnates of that era were motivated by many of the same factors that drove the current wave of business consolidations.

The primary objective of the industrial scions of the early twentieth century was not significantly different from that of their modern counterparts—namely, the maximization of stockholder wealth. There are, however, significant differences between the circumstances of the early twentieth century and those of the 1980s. The early corporations were controlled by the magnates themselves. Consequently, stockholder wealth was synonymous with personal wealth. Secondly, the lack of government regulations permitted those industrialists to base their strategy on a monopolistic versus oligopolistic view of the market. But despite these differences, there are many similarities in the business and economic principles that formed the basis for a corporate strategy of consolidation then and those that formed the basis for such a strategy in the 1980s and 1990s.

Although strategic consolidation is perhaps the primary force driving merger activity, a secondary, important force is strategic diversification.

The motivational forces that determine corporate America's diversification strategies also are not new. The era of business acquisitions and mergers between World War II and the 1980s was characterized by American industry's emphasis on unrelated diversification. There were times during the heyday of the conglomerate mergers, in the mid-1960s, when it was nearly impossible for the uninformed observer to understand the business rationale underlying the corporate plans being implemented. Yet the rush to build free-form conglomerates did have strategic underpinnings. The economic concept of amassing a portfolio of businesses that could minimize cyclicality embodied a method for reducing the risk of major fluctuations in earnings. The implementation of this strategy stabilized both earnings and dividends, and was a financially motivated method for maximizing stockholders' wealth.

CREATION OF
STOCKHOLDER VALUE

Strategic consolidation and strategic diversification basically are founded on the same corporate objective: the creation of stockholder value. To explain how these strategies have been used recently, it will be beneficial to describe them and differentiate between them from a historic perspective. Table 4.1 summarizes the key factors of the strategies of the early 1900s and the 1960s.

There are major differences between past strategies' factors and the factors that drove the wave of acquisitions and mergers in the 1980s. First and foremost, the

Table 4.1. Historical Merger and Acquisition Strategies

Strategic consolidation in the early 1900s	Strategic consolidation in the 1960s
Microeconomically focused—domestic	Macroeconomically focused—domestic
Market/industry control objective	Financial control objective
Operating line management perspective	Staff management perspective
Stockholder wealth created by control of competitive environment	Stockholder wealth created by reduction in earnings cyclicality and business risk across a broader portfolio of industries
Industry growth: critical element	Industry growth: noncritical element
Operationally oriented—reduction in cost of production and distribution is a key objective	Nonoperationally oriented—reduction in overhead and financing expenses is emphasized

economic focus broadened to include international markets. Historically, corporate strategy had a domestically focused, microeconomic perspective. With the emergence of foreign competition as a significant factor in both U.S. and international markets, corporate management was forced to broaden its analysis of the competitive environment to include worldwide markets and international competitors.

In addition, strategic consolidations in the 1980s, which are continuing into the 1990s at a slower pace, were driven by survival-oriented factors. The contraction of domestic demand for products caused by economic recessionary forces, the decrease in market share of U.S. manufacturers caused by lower-priced foreign competition, and substitutions resulting from introductions of technologically superior products have dramatically affected the financial viability of many U.S. companies competing in basic industries. Whether it was because of the decrease in total market demand or the decline in percentage shares of markets, the financial performance of many historically successful industrial competitors eroded to dangerously low levels. Management took a number of tactical steps to improve financial performance. It reduced the cost of producing goods by rationalizing capacity, improving labor productivity, or reducing or stabilizing wages and benefits. It cut selling, general, and administrative expenses by reducing its workforce, trimming discretionary expenses, closing sales and distribution locations, and taking other cost-cutting steps. Such tactical actions often were not sufficient to reverse the trends when uncontrollable market forces were eroding the corporation's competitive position. Given the foregoing scenario, the strategic answer was corporate divestiture.

The strategic diversification movement of the 1960s turned into the strategic divestiture program of the 1980s and 1990s. Regardless of the strategic or economic motivation, major corporate divestitures have grown enormously over the last decade. According to statistics extracted from the Mergers & Acquisitions Data Base, in 1979 there were 37 major divestitures, including 22 with announced prices totaling $2.1 billion. This trickle of activity reached torrential proportions by 1989. There were 1,119 major corporate divestitures with an estimated transaction value of more than $60.7 billion. Even in slower-paced 1991, there were 1,007 sell-offs with identifiable values of $32.6 billion. Corporate consolidations, like the stock market, are a two-way street. For every seller, there has to be a buyer. Strategy-driven dispositions can have many motivations, but the common thread in the 1980s and 1990s trend appears to be that the divested enterprise had not added, nor was it expected to add value to stockholder wealth. Conversely, the acquiring company has appraised the enterprise as something that would enhance or preserve its stockholders' wealth. Both seller and buyer allegedly have had the same information available to them, yet they have made management decisions that can be characterized as diametrically opposite.

TECHNOLOGY BECOMES THE PARAMOUNT ATTRACTION

Strategic diversification in the 1980s and 1990s has been motivated by corporate America's desire to participate in emerging, technologically focused industrial growth. It is a commonly held belief that technological innovation is the province of small, entrepreneurially driven business enterprises, and not the large, bureaucratic corporate institutions of the *Fortune* 500. Diversification, by definition, implies a broadening of operations and scope. But unlike the diversification of the 1960s, which was financially driven, the M&A activity in the 1980s and 1990s has been market/industry-driven. The large corporations, with their huge financial resources, have sought to acquire positions in growth industries where competition is dictated not by financial or operational strength, but by technological factors. In many cases, the only rational entry strategy available to corporations wishing to enter these markets or industries is acquisition or merger.

Table 4.2 summarizes the key factors that drove the strategic consolidation and

Table 4.2. Merger and Acquisition Strategies of the 1980s and 1990s

Strategic consolidation	Strategic diversification
Microeconomically focused—international	Macroeconomically focused—international
Market/industry cost and survival objectives	Market/industry participation objectives
Marketing/production management perspective	Executive management perspective
Stockholder wealth protected by increased share of competitive environment	Stockholder wealth enhanced by participation in growth industries
Industry maturity: critical element	Industry maturity and basis of competition: critical elements
Operationally oriented—rationalization of industry capacity, sales and distribution economies	Technologically oriented—control of key factors that differentiate products

strategic divestiture of the 1980s and continues into the 1990s. In many cases, they are surprisingly similar to the factors that motivated corporate management in earlier decades of the twentieth century. Yet, in many respects they differ. No longer is it sufficient to focus strategic decision making on domestic markets. The international market has become the competitive arena. Financial strength no longer assures participation in growth industries. Technological innovation and its management increasingly are the keys to competitive position and financial strength. Strategic management of the corporate enterprise increasingly has moved from a financially focused, portfolio-oriented perspective to a market-focused, operationally oriented perspective. As a result of these shifts in strategic perspective, the analytical task of financial professionals is increasingly complex.

THE ANALYTICAL ENVIRONMENT

Beauty is in the eye of the beholder.
MARGARET W. HUNGERFORD, 1878

Like beauty, value is a very personal measure. Statistics compiled from the Mergers & Acquisition Data Base indicated that the average premium paid, above market value, for acquiring publicly held companies during the late 1970s and 1980s ranged from a high of 70 percent in 1979 to a low of about 40 percent in 1987. *The early 1990s premiums have averaged in the low- to mid-50-percent range.* This would imply that either professional analysts and their sophisticated investor clientele *historically undervalued* corporations or, alternatively, that strategic valuations by corporate management resulted in significantly higher value than traditional financial analysis would suggest.

The task of corporate executives and their staffs of financial analysts has not changed. Management must convince the board of directors, which represents the stockholders, that the corporation's proposed action will enhance or maintain stockholder wealth. Financial management's responsibility is to prove quantitatively that the sum of the parts in a proposed merger exceeds the combined value of either entity standing alone. Given that merger environment, how do financial executives convince boards of directors that

$$100 + 100 = 246 \longrightarrow 270 ?$$

Determining the Premiums

The quantitative methodology for valuing corporations has not changed significantly over the last 20 years. Whether one operates from the perspective of the external independent financial analyst or the internal corporate financial executive, one must determine the present value of the corporation, based on informed judgments of its expected future performance. Technical dissimilarities between individual, institutional, or corporate investors, such as tax considerations, do not account for the 40 to 70 percent range in premiums paid. Nor does valuation methodology account for these high premiums, because analysts tend to calculate value in an increasingly similar manner. Given that cash or cash equivalents are used to pay for investment, the cash generated while the investment is held, and the cash received from its sale or liquidation, become the principal ingredients in investment valuation.

On the surface, the analyst's tasks are simple: first, determine how much cash will be generated while the investment is held; then determine how much cash will be received when the investment is liquidated; and, finally, determine the minimum yield that stockholders will accept, given both the business and financial risks inherent in such an investment. Knowing these three things (the cash flows, the residual value at the date of liquidation, and the required yield), an investor can determine an investment's present value by using the mathematical technique of discounting future cash receipts.

On a purely pragmatic basis, the premiums paid for publicly owned corporations are influenced by many non-economic factors that may have greater impact on acquisition prices than the methods employed in the financial valuation process. An investment banker's advice on what it will take to close the deal, defensive competitive responses (such as acting to prevent a financially strong corporation from acquiring a competitively viable, but financially weak competitor), and other hard-to-quantify factors often have greater influence on acquisition pricing than either the analytical methods used or the discount (interest) rates selected. In the real world, acquisition pricing is more art than science, more driven by judgment than facts, more dependent on divergent views of markets and opportunities than differing techniques of valuation. If these observations were untrue, the market value of a corporation prior to acquisition would be closer to the price paid by the acquiring company. There would be no white knights, Wall Street arbitrage specialists would not exist, and shark repellents and golden parachutes would not be needed by corporate management to assure their continued incumbency.

Conforming to Strategic Plans

If conventional wisdom and pragmatic analysis confirm that neither the analytical framework and technical factors, nor valuation methodologies and Wall Street influences, account for the 40 to 70 percent premiums being paid in the market, then a key question remains. How do corporations quantitatively justify to themselves, and ultimately their stockholders, the prices paid for acquisitions? The answer is, strategic management of corporate resources, which impacts not only the prices paid in acquisitions but accounts for the huge increase in divestitures. Although strategic management has been around for 50 years, only in recent times has it been labeled a management style. The distinguishing feature of the 1980s and 1990s is not strategic management but the formalized strategic plan.

The strategic plan integrates marketing into the financial planning process. As a result, the plan not only establishes the basis for operational budgets and internal resource allocations, but concurrently creates the analytical framework for acquisition and divestiture decision making. A strategic plan is based on detailed analysis of the competitive environment. The plan must delineate clearly the corporation's businesses in an analytical framework which quantifies industry demand, market share, product mix, selling prices, cost of goods, operating expenses, nonoperating costs, and financial resource requirements (e.g., operating-working capital, investment-capital assets, financial obligations, debt repayment and/or stockholder dividends). This framework forms a solid foundation for analyzing the corporation's internal operations at both the business unit and consolidated levels, and concurrently permits the company to evaluate diversification and acquisition opportunities consistently. The strategic plan must be modeled knowledgeably in a computer-based environment that permits users to readily change their assumptions of the future. The strategic plan then becomes not only a dynamic framework for analyzing industry demand and industry capacity utilization, but also a structured framework for evaluating probable competitive responses to changes in forecast demand.

Interjecting the Strategic Model

Dynamic "what if" strategic models are communication tools that support executive management decisions, especially in the areas of resource allocation, divestitures, and acquisitions. The tool never should be so complex in its structure that only middle management can operate or explain it. Strategic models offer only a structure for consistent decision making. They never can become substitutes for management judgment, nor should they be constructed in a manner that attempts to quantify or integrate all possible factors that could affect operating performance. For example, knowledgeable management must appraise the competitive environment realistically when given a specific forecast of industry demand, and formulate a competitive response in quantifiable terms. The strategic planning model should be used as a means of documenting assumptions that affect corporate performance and cash flow. An attempt to integrate fully the competitive environment (e.g., current and potential competitors), the technical environment (e.g., product obsolescence and product substitution), and the bargaining environment (material purchasing, international trade barriers, noncash bartering, etc.) in a single strategic model probably will never be justifiable on a cost-benefit basis.

A CONCEPTUAL FRAMEWORK
FOR FINANCIAL MODELING

There is no universally applicable model capable of structuring the strategic plans of all corporations. Rather, the challenge to financial and planning practitioners is to construct a dynamic tool that is detailed enough to include all quantifiable variables having a material impact on either operating performance or corporate value, and at the same time simple enough so that decision makers will use it not only to evaluate alternatives but as the vehicle for communicating expected results.

Modeling in a strategic planning environment requires that corporate financial professionals must raise their sights. They no longer can focus strictly on earnings before taxes and noncash charges as the starting points for their analysis of cash flow and investment valuation. The process must begin at the level of international industry demand and proceed in an orderly manner through analyses of market shares, product mix, and product price. The foregoing variable components of revenue, and the validity of the assumptions of what creates revenue, have far greater impact on operating performance and corporate value than any other line item in a corporation's financial statement. The key to corporate performance and investment valuation lies not within the domain of financial theory, but within the microeconomic environment of both industry demand and competitive behavior. If the analysis of the factors that influence a corporation's market size and share is unsound, the resulting operating projection or investment valuation will be of little or no value.

Financial management often has admonished marketing and sales counterparts to remember that a sale is not a sale until a customer's check clears the bank. Strategic managers would be well advised to remind their financial counterparts that cash flow begins with revenue and not adjusted net income. The external economic and competitive forces that affect demand for a corporation's products are the most critical variables affecting operating cash flows. These factors simultaneously are the key influences on pricing strategy and the key determinants of productive capacity utilization. When the foregoing elements are known, it is a more or less mechanical task to determine a corporation's revenue, cost of goods, and standard gross margin.

Strategic and planning managers, on the other hand, actually must lower their sights and become more conversant with the realities of the internal environment. In the area of cost of goods, they must understand production capacity utilization issues. They must understand the impact that variations in cash flow caused by changing demand have on the fixed and variable costs of production. *Similarly, they have to realize that the cost of an outside salesperson is often more than the cost of borrowing $1 million for one year.*

Managers from all functional disciplines must focus their sights on the increasing importance of financial resource allocation. In our increasingly technologically driven economy, the ability to analyze the cash flow impact of research, development, and engineering expenditures is critical to a well-developed strategic planning framework. These off-balance-sheet investments are beginning to surpass the historic capitalized asset investment as the primary determinants of long-term competitive advantage. Being a low-cost producer no longer assures that a corporation will remain competitively strong.

Financial management has the responsibility of constructing models that are both technically sound and user-friendly. They must achieve this objective by reducing the number of financial variables and increasing the number of strategic and operating variables that can be manipulated by users. There is always a danger that models of this nature may oversimplify the financial dimension of the analysis. But one should not forget that the objective is not accounting accuracy at the level of published financial statements; it is decision accuracy at the level of materiality.

DETERMINANT OF CASH FLOW

Table 4.3 presents a schematic overview of the four primary components that, when integrated, constitute a strategic planning model. The first three components—gross margins, expenses, and resources—are the primary determinants of cash flow.

Table 4.3. Elements of a Strategic Analysis Model

Gross margin component:
Industry
Market share
Product mix
Produce price
Standard product cost
Expense component:
Manufacturing expense
R&D and engineering expense
Direct operating expense
Other operating and nonoperating expense
Resource component:
Operating requirements
Investment requirements
Financing requirements
Valuation component:
Rate matrix
Valuation matrix

Elements of Gross Margins. The gross margin component contains five matrix modules:

Industry Demand: This is expressed in dollars or units, and requires a degree of detail sufficient to illustrate both historic and future trends relating to the product categories in which the operating unit competes.

Market Share: The percentage share of industry demand accruing to the operating unit which is based on, and consistent with, the business strategies contained in the plan.

Product Mix: The historic and projected products that will be sold by the operating unit in each forecast category of industry demand.

Product Price: This details the pricing strategy on both a historic and projected basis for the operating units' products.

Product Standard Cost: In theory, this is a variable matrix when viewed in prospective terms, but in practice, it is normally a nonvariable component in strategic projections.

Factors in the Expense Component. The expense component contains four linear modules:

Manufacturing Expense: The complexity and content of this module is dictated by the information available both historically and prospectively. At minimum, noncash fixed expenses should be segregated.

R&D and Engineering Expense: A key dimension for assessing the off-balance-sheet investments in an operating unit's future competitive position.

Direct Operating Expense: These should be detailed at the levels of the market, sales, general, and administrative categories of direct expense (variable, semivariable, and fixed cost elements).

Other Operating and Nonoperating Expense: Included are noncash charges (amortization, depreciation, etc.), financing expense (interest, etc.), nonoperating expense (income), and provisions for taxes and dividends.

Composition of the Resource Component. The resource component contains three modules:

Operating Requirements: This category tends to be revenue- and expense-dependent variables, unless changed by policy or other management intervention (e.g., terms and conditions of sale). Normally included are balance sheet items such as accounts receivable, inventories, prepaid expenses, accounts payable, accrued liabilities, and current and deferred taxes.

Investment Requirements: These can be either dependent and/or independent variables, and include fixed assets, capitalized leases, amortizable noncurrent assets, and current and noncurrent contractual liabilities.

Financing Requirements: These include both short- and long-term debt obligations, which are independent variables; stockholders' equity, which is a dependent variable; and cash (surplus or shortfall), which is the slack variable.

Relating the Parts

There are 12 separate modules that can be assembled into the conventional statements of income, financial position, and cash flow. It should not surprise any reader that 4 of the 12 modules are used in determining revenue, the normal point of departure in traditional financial analysis, and that it takes 6, or half the modules, to calculate the business unit's operating gross margin. The schematic framework for constructing strategic models focuses management's attention on those factors that can truly determine the value of an operating unit or acquisition. They are the external market for a corporation's goods and services, and the competitive environment that permits the firm to share in that market at prices projected from the cost of making its products. The framework tends to emphasize the key ingredient, cash flow, which is revenue. Without revenue there can be no net income, no need for operating capital, and no cash resources to repay the corporation's obligations to creditors, debtholders, or stockholders.

VALUATION PROCESS WITH A DISCOUNTED CASH FLOW APPROACH

One objective of strategic planning is to quantify the corporate/stockholder value derived from a given strategic operating plan, and to be able to compare this expected value with that of alternative plans or operating scenarios. Quantification requires a forecast of operating cash flows, determination of a residual value, and selection of an appropriate discount rate. Finally, a method for testing alternative scenarios must exist if the process is to be efficient. This same structure of analysis also is required for valuation of either divestiture or merger opportunities.

In addition to the 12-module framework for determining operating cash flows, a forecasting model needs three major elements: the forecast's time horizon, the selection of an appropriate discount rate, and the selection of a residual value.

The Time Horizon. The easiest element to determine is the time horizon. The number of years to be forecast in a strategic plan, or for a divestiture or acquisition analysis, is strictly a function of what management is comfortable with. Most operating forecasts are in the 5- to 15-year range. The selection of the time horizon is based on the ability of the planner to convince management and the board of directors that they can forecast industry demand, technological change, and international economic environments with sufficient accuracy to assure that the forecast results are materially valid for decision making.

The Discount Rate. As for the appropriate discount rate to be used for appraisal valuation of internal capital projects and for valuation of M&A opportunities, financial theorists have suggested the corporation's "cost of capital" as the proper rate. Financial theory is founded on the work of academicians in the area of microeconomics in the mid- to late-1950s. The work of these academicians was based on research conducted by Gordon and Shapiro and their published papers relating to the required rates of profit in a corporate environment. It continued with the work of Harry Markowitz and James Tobin on the theory of portfolio selection, and was furthered by Franco Modigliani and H. M. Miller in their work on structure and valuation. The capital asset pricing model (CAPM) emerged from the pioneering work of Fisher, Fama, Jensen, Blume, and others during the 1960s. The CAPM established a framework for understanding a corporation's cost of equity capital and looked to the stock market as a key determinant in this process. Academicians have debated the concept of an efficient market, whether it be a weak, semistrong, or strong form, but perhaps one of the more relevant comments on the subject is a quote from C. W. J. Granger and O. Morgenstern in their 1970 publication *Predictability of Stock Market Prices*: "The only valid statement," they said, "is that current price embodies all knowledge, all expectations, and all discounts that infringe upon the market."[1]

Current Market Information. The statement by Granger and Morgenstern is particularly appealing to the pragmatists among us. It suggests that we are rather safe in using current market information to establish the cost of a firm's equity capital. Textbooks have taught us that the cost of equity capital is equal to the risk-free rate plus a market return plus an individual corporate return. The formula is summarized in the mathematical equation:

$$K_e = R_f + B_j(R_m - R_f)$$

where K_e = cost of equity capital
$\quad R_f$ = risk-free rate
$\quad B_j$ = the beta coefficient
$\quad R_m$ = market return
$R_m - R_f$ = market return (premium)

Alternative Rates.   What are these various components, and how are they determined? First, the alleged risk-free rate is the rate on government bonds that is observed in the market at the date of analysis. It can be found by picking up a copy of *The Wall Street Journal* and turning to the section containing the prices and yields on U.S. government bonds, then selecting the yield (rate) that matches the time horizon of the forecast being made. Second, according to the work of Roger G. Ibbotson and Rex A. Sinquefield, the forecast returns on a common stock will exceed those on long-term government debt by 5.4 percent (the observed range is 5.0 percent to 5.5 percent).[2] Finally, the risk-free premium for an individual public corporation security is the product of the market-risk premium times the individual security's systematic risk, or its beta coefficient. In actual practice, it is valuable to use not only the historic beta coefficient of the individual corporation, but the beta coefficient of the industry in which the corporation is competitively classified.

We will refrain from the necessarily long dissertation on determining the corporation's total cost of capital and whether current or future debt/equity ratios should be used to weight the various components. The mathematical procedures are well documented in many textbooks on corporate finance. From the practitioner's perspective, it is a far better technique to apply multiple discount rates to the cash flow forecasts resulting from the operating planning model. Table 4.4 outlines six primary determinants for alternative rates that can be used as the key components of the cost of capital.

Calculating Residual Value.   The determination of residual value should depend on the objective of the evaluation. Seldom does one undertake analysis with the objective of liquidating the business entity being acquired. Similarly, it is highly unlikely that one plans to resell the enterprise as a stand-alone corporation. Therefore, in most evaluations, we are dealing with an ongoing business enterprise. For that reason, and because of the selection of the discounted cash flow (DCF) methodology for evaluation, perhaps the most intuitively appealing method of determining residual value is Alfred Rappaport's suggestion that the residual value is the present value of a perpetuity. In summary, Rappaport suggests that the present value (PV) of the residual is equal to earnings after taxes (EAT) in the final year of the forecast, divided by the discount rate selected, times the discount factor at that time period. Stated mathematically:

$$\frac{\text{EAT}_N}{\text{discount rate}} \times \text{discount factor at } N = \text{PV of residual } N$$

For practitioners of the free cash flow evaluation methodologies, a slight modification of Rappaport's models suggests substitution of net cash flow in the final time period of the analysis for the earnings aftertax components in the original form. This is stated mathematically as

$$\frac{\text{NCF}_N}{\text{discount rate}} \times \text{discount factor at } N = \text{PV of residual } N$$

THE EVALUATION MATRIX

When using financial analytical models, whether for strategic planning, the evaluation of strategic plans, or the evaluation of merger and divestiture opportunities, it is extremely difficult for the analytical practitioner to assume the risk profile of executive management or boards of directors who are charged with decision making. For this reason, the use of a valuation matrix is recommended.

Figure 4.1 presents schematically the end product of the cash flow and residual valuation analysis. It combines three key pieces of information in a multidimensional matrix of information. The X axis is the time dimension, which runs from the initiation of the analysis through the time horizon selected by the analyst for presentation of the plan. The Y axis represents the present value at each point in time for which the discounted cash flows plus residual value are positive. Six separate rates are used to discount the expected cash flow. These rates are based on the cost of capital components outlined in Table 4.4. When coupled with the information and assumptions in the forecast relating to industry demand, market, share, pricing, cost of goods sold, and so on, that are contained explicitly in modules 1 to 12, the valuation matrix represents all expected present values, at varying discount rates, that are forecast in the strategic plan of operation presented. This matrix represents a framework in which the analyst does not have to select ahead of time either the appropriate discount rate or the time horizon, or interpret the motivational-risk bases of the executive managers charged with making the decision. Rather, the matrix presents management with an array of present values based on their own intuitive feelings about the strategic alternatives they are considering.

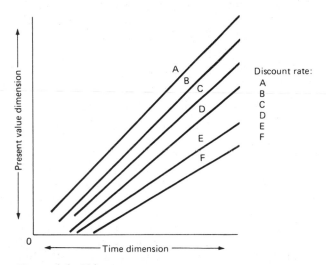

Figure 4.1. Valuation matrix.

Table 4.4. Important Elements Used by Strategic Models in Calculating Acquirer's Discount Rates

"Risk-free" rate, long-term government bonds
Industry average cost of capital rate
Corporate cost of capital rate
Internal "hurdle rate"
Internal rate at 10% risk premium
Internal rate at 25% risk premium

MODELING IN A PERSONAL COMPUTER ENVIRONMENT

Anyone who has dealt with forecasts and with management's desire to test alternative marketing or operating scenarios knows that the emergence of the personal computer (PC) as an analytical tool and the development of spreadsheet software have been blessings. Sensitivity analysis, which alters variables to obtain alternative forecasts, is a critical part of the evaluation process. Modern PC spreadsheets have replaced pencils and paper, calculators, and mainframes as the tools of the analyst. The ability to conduct factor analysis on critical assumptions and the ability to analyze the impact of alternative scenarios in a timely manner are rather recent phenomena. Understanding the impact of various possible situations on the value of the operating entity, or on the strategic acquisition opportunity, is far more relevant than selecting a "correct discount rate." The PC is the modern slide rule/calculator that permits analysts to model dynamically that "what if" framework. Strategic models must contain all relevant or material variables, and must adhere to generally accepted accounting principles.

STRATEGY-DRIVEN ANALYSIS

Strategically oriented modeling, whether for planning, diversification, or divestiture valuation, is like the fundamentals of mathematics in that it requires mastery of the basics before the application of theory. Just as mathematics requires a mastery of addition and subtraction, the strategic modeling environment requires that analysts concentrate on the external factors that drive international market demand for the corporation's goods or services, and couple this knowledge with an understanding of the competitive environment. The competitive factor includes not only current international competitors, but any reasonable expectations of future competitive constraints resulting from technical advancements in products or product substitution. Multiplication and division are analogous to the need of strategic modelers to understand how both internal corporate policies and procedures, and external environments, determined by government regulation or industry practice, affect the current and the future economic viability of the acquiring corporation or its merger target.

The financial theory of the firm is similar to the mathematical concepts in calculus and statistics. The microeconomic and operational constraints that establish the competitive positions of the various industry players must be understood before the analyst can model the corporation. The infinite set of variables that could affect a corporation's financial performance must be condensed to the point where the variables having material impact on performance have been identified. Finally, numerical analysis for the mathematician is similar to the task of the person charged with strategic modeling in a financial environment, who must provide a framework that is flexible enough to permit quantification of alternative future scenarios, whether economic, political, technological, or societal.

Strategy-driven acquisition and merger analysis is based on the fundamental premises that:

- Businesses operate in a dynamic rather than a static environment.

- Strategic consolidations and diversifications are based on a strategic operating plan.

- External forces that influence industry demand and external factors that establish competitive position have greater impact on value than the methods used to determine *the* value.

- Cash flow starts with industry demand and not adjusted net income.

- The prices paid in the market often are based on nonfinancial factors such as management's judgments and egos, the scarcity or overabundance of merger candidates, investment bankers' opinions of "what it will take to do the deal," and the personal biases of government regulators.

Strategic financial models are necessary for quantifying expected value. But reality suggests that this determined value is only one element in a much more complex framework that establishes the amount paid for an acquisition, or the amount received for a divestiture.

NOTES

1. C. W. J. Granger and O. Morgenstern, *Predictability of Stock Market Prices,* Health Lexington Books, Lexington, Mass., 1970.

2. Roger G. Ibbotson and Rex A. Sinquefield, *Stock, Bonds, Bills and Inflation: The Past (1926–76) and the Future,* Financial Analyst Research Foundation, New York, 1977.

5

The Payoff in Mergers and Acquisitions

J. Fred Weston

Cordner Professor Emeritus of Money and Financial Markets, Graduate School of Management, University of California at Los Angeles, Los Angeles, California

Growth is vital to the well-being of a business. Growth is the linchpin for programs to generate capital for financial health, upgrade technologies, strengthen market positions, enhance operating efficiencies, and recruit top-notch management talent by providing opportunities for promotions and broadened responsibilities. Without growth possibilities, most firms would lose their purposes for existing, stagnate, wither, and then die. For the soundly operated firm, restructuring and realignments frequently are necessary adjuncts of growth—either to expand the firm as a whole, or, in many cases, to cut back the overall size of the company so that emphasis can be placed on the business segments with the best growth prospects.

The many forms of adjustments that firms use to compete effectively in the financial and human resource markets have come to be known as restructuring activities, often referred to in an abbreviated way as M&A activities. The first issue is why the burst of such activity in the 1980s?

REASONS FOR THE M&A
MOVEMENT OF THE EIGHTIES

The takeover and restructuring activities beginning in the 1980s were induced by three major sets of forces. One relates to fundamental issues of corporate governance. A second involves changing economic, political, and social environments. Third are the characteristics of individual firms with respect to their product and market positions, managerial capabilities, and organization effectiveness. The interactions of these three major categories of variables have produced the takeover and restructuring movements.

Issues of Corporate Governance and Control

The takeover movement of the 1980s laid bare some fundamental problems in the governance and management of corporations. The deficiencies in effective corporate governance and control that emerged include:

- Separation of ownership and control: Management domination of board of directors which is supposed to monitor and control management on behalf of shareholders.
- Agency problems: Conflict of interest between managers and owners. Management perks. Lack of efficiency enforcement.
- Ineffective (static) planning and control systems. Slack in segment plans—easy performance targets.
- Internal cash flows not subject to capital market disciplines. Weak segments often subsidized. Some stronger segments did not perform up to their potentials or to what could be their values to other owners.
- Excessive conglomeration. Unrelated activities were difficult to manage efficiently. Aggravated by lack of incentives to stimulate segment managers to think like entrepreneurial owners.

The Changing Environments

Some of the major developments in the external environments of business firms are described briefly as follows:

Increased international competition. Geographic markets have become global in scope, and the increased worldwide competition created pressures for businesses throughout the world to undertake restructuring so they could become leaner and meaner competitors. This was the most powerful force in operation.

Changing technologies. They created competition among industries.

Changing manufacturing methods. These ranged from economies of scale to flexible manufacturing systems and economies of scope. Meanwhile, shocks from the oil markets caused repeated adjustments in the mix of production input factors.

Changed management of human resources. The shift from hierarchy to participative management.

Fluctuating exchange rates. These resulted in changing prices for buying and selling goods as well as companies.

Revised antitrust policy. Enforcement was redirected to focus on increased competition resulting from the above five factors plus reactions to other changes in government policies.

Accelerated deregulation. In the 1970s and 1980s regulation was eased in airlines, banking, the savings and loan industry and other financial services, broadcasting, cable, communications, transportation, and oil and gas. These industries accounted for almost 40 percent of all M&A activity during the 1980s.

Innovations in financial services. Deregulation stimulated new entries in a field that already was plagued with excess capacity and pressures on profit margins. Competitive responses include innovative products and speculative investments.

Government finance. Persistent U.S. government deficits. Large balance of payments deficits. Continuing uncertainty and fear of inflation and/or high interest rates.

Changes in tax policy. Four major tax revisions during the 1980s. Arbitraging of different tax opportunities became common. Further advantages to debt financing with elimination of capital gains advantage to retained earnings.

Economic growth. Long period of stable growth in 1980s further encouraged the use of tax-advantaged debt.

Recession. Recession beginning in 1990 caused firms to adjust debt to lower cash inflows.

These changes in external environments, coupled with the problems in corporate governance systems related to internal policies of firms, produced the restructuring era. Let us next consider the consequences.

MERGER AND TAKEOVER ACTIVITY

Mergers and takeovers do not represent a simple phenomenon (Table 5.1). Mergers are mostly friendly and with a single bidder. The bidder typically is in a mature industry, has surplus cash, and is seeking a target with growth opportunities that require cash.

Tender offers may be friendly or hostile. Hostile bids typically are resisted, leading to multiple bidders. Management ownership of targets is low in hostile bids, but relatively higher in friendly bids. Target firms in hostile bids typically are below the industry average in performance, and the market values of their securities are well below the replacement costs of their assets. In a friendly merger, the target is above the industry average in performance, with a market value of securities greater than the replacement cost of assets.

Table 5.1. A Taxonomy of Types of Takeover Activity

Mergers	Tender offers	
Friendly, negotiated	Friendly	Hostile
1. Not resisted	1. Not resisted	1. Resisted
2. Stock	2. Cash or stock	2. Cash
3. Single bidder	3. Single bidder	3. Multiple bidders
4. Announcement anticipated	4. Anticipated to some degree	4. Surprise
5. Management ownership higher	5. Management ownership high	5. Management ownership low
6. Bidder firm with surplus cash seeking a target with growth opportunities, needing cash	6. Target above industry average in performance	6. Target below industry average in performance
	7. Target in growth industry	7. Target in mature industry
	8. Industry and firm q-ratio equal to average and higher than q for hostile targets	8. Industry and firm q-ratios are low
	9. Bidder likely to be another firm seeking new favorable investment opportunities	9. Bidder likely to be a raider

The data on mergers and acquisitions in Table 5.2 reflect the above distinctions. The table charts the abnormal returns for parties to mergers and acquisitions—typically measured by increases in stock prices over normal trading levels; these increases are attributed by deal announcements. For acquired firms, the abnormal returns are higher for tender offers than for mergers and are quite substantial. For bidders, the returns are small and insignificant. For the acquired firms, the abnormal returns are higher when the form of payment is cash. Bidders have a small positive abnormal return when the payment is in cash and a small negative return when stock is the acquisition currency.

Panel C in Table 5.2 shows a time trend that was influenced by legal and regulatory behavior after 1968 and by the financial innovations in the 1980s. The trend of abnormal returns to targets has been upward, while the trend for buyers has been downward. Since 1980, the abnormal returns to buyers have been negative. The main force driving these negative returns is the increased frequency of competition from multiple bidders. For all the time segments, the total abnormal returns to targets plus bidders are always positive, representing a 7 to 8 percent increase in value.

Table 5.2. Variables Influencing Level of Abnormal Returns

	Acquired (%)	Buyer (%)	Frequency of multiple bids (%)
A. Method of Combining			
1. Mergers	20	+2 to 3	
2. Tender offers	35	−2 to +2	
B. Method of Payment			
1. Cash	25	+2	
2. Stock	10	−2	
C. Time Period—Regulation and Financial Innovation			
1. Pre-1968	20	+4	18
2. 1968–1980	35	+1	30
3. 1981–1984	35	−3	46
D. Number of Bidders, 1968–84			
1. Single bidder		+1	
2. Multiple bidders		−2.5	

In absolute dollar amounts, direct gains to shareholders during 1981–1986 have been estimated at or above $250 billion. Indirect gains may be even greater. These represent improvements in performance by firms to avoid takeovers, or simply because other firms demonstrated how it could be done.

The overall data suggest that value has been increased by merger and takeover activity. These large-scale studies agree that tax savings have performed a significant role in less than 10 percent of mergers or takeovers. Although tax considerations have played a large role in individual cases, they did not represent the dominant driving force in merger activity.

FORMS OF RESTRUCTURING AND THEIR RESULTS

Next, data on a wide range of different forms of restructuring are analyzed. An important objective from a public policy standpoint is to determine whether social value is enhanced by mergers. If, for example, mergers and acquisitions increase efficiency, the improvement represents a social gain regardless of the theory that explains how it is achieved.

Table 5.3 provides an overview of the many forms of restructuring activities that have taken place. In addition, it sets forth the returns, again measured by increased stock prices, from these activities. Most produced positive returns. To explain these results we need to explain each form of restructuring activity and its rationale.

Five major types of corporate change or transformation restructuring are sur-

Table 5.3. Forms of Restructuring and their Financial Results

Form of restructuring	Event returns %
I. Expansion	
A. Merger studies	
1. Acquired firms	20
2. Acquiring firms	2 to 3
B. Tender offer studies	
1. Acquired firms	35
2. Acquiring firms	+2 to −2
C. Joint ventures	
1. Absolute	2.5
2. Scaled by investment	23
II. Sell-offs	
A. Spin-offs	2 to 4
B. Divestitures	
1. Sellers	0.5 to 1
2. Buyers	0.34
C. Equity carve-outs	2
III. Changes in ownership structure	
A. Leverage and ownership adjustments by exchange offers	
1. Debt for equity	14
2. Preferred for equity	8
B. Leverage and ownership adjustments by share repurchases	16
C. Going private	20
D. Leveraged buy-outs	40 to 50
E. Leveraged cash-outs	20 to 30
F. ESOPs	?
IV. Corporate control	
A. Unequal voting rights	
1. Value of control	5 to 6
2. Dual-class recapitalizations	−1
B. Proxy contests	10
C. Premium buy-backs	
1. Greenmail	−2
2. Standstill agreements	−4
V. Merger defenses	−4 to +4

veyed. They are expansion, sell-offs, changes in ownership structure, issues of corporate control, and merger defenses.

Expansion

The preceding evidence on the first two categories of mergers and tender offers demonstrated that the returns to target firms increased over the decades as government regulation increased and as sophisticated defensive tactics by targets were developed. The returns to bidding firms decreased over the decades because for them the same influences operated in the reverse direction. But even for the most recent period of the 1980s, the total wealth increase from M&A activity is positive.

The third category under expansion in Table 5.3 is joint venture activity. When scaled to the size of investments, joint ventures appear to achieve about a 23 percent return higher than predicted by general capital market return-risk relationships.

Sell-offs

The two major types of business dispositions are spin-offs and divestitures.

A spin-off creates a separate new legal entity. Its shares are distributed on a pro rata basis to existing shareholders of the parent company. Thus, existing stockholders have the same proportion of ownership in the new entity as in the original firm. There is, however, a separation of control. In some sense, a spin-off represents a form of a dividend to existing shareholders.

In a divestiture cash comes into the firm. A divestiture involves the sale of a portion of the firm, i.e., a subsidiary, division, product line, etc., to a buyer that presumably finds it more valuable. An equity carve-out, a variation on the divestiture, involves the sale of a part interest in a subsidiary via a public stock offering to create a new stand-alone company that nonetheless remains under the parent's control.

Spin-offs.   Schipper and Smith[1] found a positive 2.84 percent abnormal return to the parent (statistically significant) on the spin-off announcement date. The size of the announcement effect is positively related to the size of the spin-off relative to the size of the parent. The average size of the spin-off is about 20 percent of the original parent. Spin-offs motivated by avoidance of regulation experienced an abnormal return of 5.07 percent as compared to 2.29 percent for the remainder of the sample. Examples of regulation avoidance include separating a regulated utility subsidiary from non-utility businesses and spinning off a foreign subsidiary to avoid restrictions by U.S. laws.

Hite and Owers[2] found abnormal returns of 3.8 percent, somewhat higher than for the full sample of Schipper and Smith. They also found a positive relationship between the relative size of the spin-off and the announcement effect. Neither study found an adverse effect on bondholders.

The Copeland, Lemgruber, and Mayers[3] study extends the earlier studies in a number of dimensions. Particularly, they test for post-selection bias. In their first sample, they did this by including announced spin-offs that were not completed (11 percent of the sample). This enabled them to study the effects of successive announcements. A second expanded sample, subject to post-selection bias, confirmed the impact of successive announcements. Additionally, they studied ex-date effects, which they found to have positive abnormal performance. Further, they found that taxable spin-offs do not have positive abnormal returns, while nontaxable spin-offs do. However, when they controlled for the size of the spin-off, the difference between the two tax categories disappeared.

For their sample with no post-selection bias, the two-day abnormal return from the first announcement was 2.49 percent; for the larger sample it was 3.03 percent. Both results are significant from a statistical standpoint. Thus, avoiding the post-selection bias makes a difference; the return is lower for the sample which includes firms with announced spin-offs that never were consummated. For the eight firms with announced spin-offs that never were made, the two-day average return was a negative (but insignificant) 0.15 percent.

Divestitures.   Event studies of divestitures have found significant positive abnormal two-day announcement-period returns of between 1 and 2 percent for selling firm shareholders. The announcement effects on returns to buyers did not appear to be statistically significant.

A study by Klein[4] looked at divestitures in depth. When firms initially announced the price, the size of effects depended upon the percentage of the firm sold, as measured by the price of the sell-off divided by the market value of the equity on the last day of the month prior to the announcement period. There was no significant price effect when the percentage of the equity sold was less than 10 percent. When the percentage of equity sold was between 10 and 50 percent, abnormal returns to the seller averaged a positive 2.53 percent. When the percentage of the equity sold was greater than 50 percent, the abnormal return was 8.09 percent. The results appear to reflect the potential impact on sellers.

When the abnormal gains to sellers from divestitures are aggregated, the totals represent substantial dollar amounts. Black and Grundfest[5] estimate that for the 1981–1986 period, the abnormal value increases to sellers in corporate divestitures could be placed conservatively at $27.6 billion.

Equity Carve-outs.   Equity carve-outs on average are associated with positive abnormal returns of almost 2 percent over a five-day announcement period. This is in contrast to findings of significant negative returns of about 2 to 3 percent when parent companies publicly offer additional shares of their own (as opposed to their subsidiary's) stock.

The main explanations for the positive returns in spin-offs and in equity carve-outs relate to management incentives. Managers may receive incentives and rewards more closely related to actual performance than when the quality of performance might have been obscured in consolidated financial statements or monitored by superiors unfamiliar with the unique problems of a disparate subsidiary. In spin-offs, the creation of a free-standing stock price, reflecting the market's assessment of management's performance on a continual basis, may help assure that management compensation plans based on stock options will more directly measure and reward performance. In addition, more homogeneous organization units may be managed more effectively.

For divestitures, the main explanation appears to be that the resources are shifted to higher-valued uses. The buying company is motivated by the expectation that it can generate greater value from the assets than the selling firm.

Changes in Ownership Structure

Share repurchases represent an alternative means of making payouts to shareholders. Cash tender offers to repurchase shares result in significant positive abnormal returns to shareholders of about 13 to 15 percent; returns are even higher when they are financed by debt than by cash. Both tendering and non-tendering share-holders benefit.

Through an exchange offer, a company can change its capital structure while holding its investment policy unchanged. Debt-for-common-stock offers have the effect of increasing leverage, and vice versa. The theory and wealth effects of exchange offers are similar to those for share repurchases. Among the characteristics that typically result in positive returns to shareholders are:

- The offer increases leverage
- The offer implies an increase in future cash flows
- The offer implies that the common stock is undervalued by the market

Leverage-increasing exchange offers, like share repurchases, often are used as an alternative means of making payouts to shareholders. When share repurchases or exchange offers are used as takeover defenses, returns to shareholders are likely to be negative.

Going Private and Leveraged Buyouts

"Going private" refers to the transformation of a public corporation into a privately held firm. A leveraged buyout (LBO), financed largely by borrowing, is the acquisition of the stock or assets of a public company by a small group of investors. The buying group may be sponsored by buyout specialists (for example, Kohlberg, Kravis, Roberts & Co.) or by investment bankers. A variant of the LBO going-private transaction is the management buyout (MBO) in which a segment of the company is sold to its managers. Since 1981, unit MBOs have represented more than 10 percent of total divestitures.

Increased leverage does not seem to have been a dominating motive in LBOs. While leverage is increased at the formation of the LBO, it is sharply reduced in successive years. Muscarella and Vetsuypens[6] present data showing the pattern of leverage for a sample of 72 firms that were taken private in LBOs and returned to public ownership through stock offerings about three years later. The debt-to-equity ratio before the LBO was 78 percent, rose to 1,415 percent at the time of the LBO (on a market basis), dropped to 376 percent before the offering, and declined to 150 percent after selling shares to the public. Since equity values are increased, the ending leverage ratios at market could be below 100 percent. Thus, super-leverage does not appear to be a lasting consequence of LBOs. The initial financing is designed to facilitate higher management participation in the equity, which is associated with subsequent operating improvements, value increases, and leverage reductions.

There is an important economic perspective to bring to LBOs. They were a unique and valuable economic innovation in combining four important elements. First, was the use of high leverage so that the equity segment was reduced in size. Key management personnel could be provided with a significant equity ownership either through their own investments or the improvements they achieve in operating performance. The gains to managers would have significant impact on their wealth positions. Second, there was always a turnaround element involved in the

LBO, based on highly qualified management either already on board or available for recruitment. Third, the management possessed the power of unrestricted decision making; they could utilize their knowledge, could be flexible, and could make prompt decisions without several layers of hierarchical review. Fourth, the rewards of successful operations were large and significant; they provided strong motivation to key managers and employees in the new firm.

This innovative concept was sound. Returns to the original shareholders on the initiation of an LBO or MBO were at least on the order of magnitude of 40 to 50 percent. Successful LBOs could go public again. In the so-called reverse LBOs, returns to the shareholders (who now included the key personnel) were in the 50 to 60 percent range.

To understand the subsequent history of LBOs, we must view it in an economic perspective. Significantly high returns attract additional investment. LBOs began to total $20 billion annually by the early 1980s and had reached $61 billion per year in 1988. The data clearly illustrate the operation of the fundamental economic principle that high returns attract the flow of additional economic resources for investment. But LBO activity fell off greatly in 1989 and 1990.

By 1988 there was enough LBO money to finance an additional $250 to $300 billion of LBO transactions. But by 1989 some LBO funds were reporting that they hadn't done a deal for two years because many proposals made no business sense or were overpriced. When they did bid on attractive deals, the winning bid was often 50 to 75 percent higher than the second highest bid.

Leveraged cash-outs (or defensive recapitalizations) are a relatively new technique of financial restructuring first developed by Goldman, Sachs & Co. for Multimedia, Inc. in 1985. It is considered to be a defensive tactic, because in most cases leveraged cash-outs (LCOs) have been responses to takeover bids. In a typical LCO, outside shareholders receive a large one-time cash dividend, and insiders (managers) and employee benefit plans receive new shares instead of cash. The cash dividend is financed mostly by newly borrowed funds, both senior bank debt and mezzanine debt, i.e., subordinated debentures. As a result, the firm's leverage is increased to an abnormally high level and the proportional equity ownership of management significantly rises through the recapitalization. LCOs are associated with a positive 20 to 30 percent abnormal return at the announcement time. But financial difficulties often were encountered after the recaps when cash flows were not large enough to pay down debt.

ESOPs.   An employee stock ownership plan (ESOP) is a type of stock bonus plan that invests primarily in the securities of the sponsoring employer firm. A dramatic increase in the use of ESOPs as a takeover defense occurred in 1989. For example, in response to a tender offer by Shamrock Holdings, the investment vehicle for the family of Roy E. Disney, Polaroid established an ESOP that held 14 percent of Polaroid's common stock. Like most large corporations, Polaroid is chartered in Delaware. The Delaware antitakeover statute forbids hostile acquirers from merging with a target for at least three years unless 85 percent of the company's voting shares are acquired in a tender offer.

ESOPs have been used in a wide variety of corporate restructuring activities. Fifty-nine percent of leveraged ESOPs were the vehicles used to buy private companies from their owners. This enabled the owners to reap tax-free gains by investing the funds they received in a portfolio of securities. ESOPs also have been used in buyouts of large private companies as well.

Thirty-seven percent of leveraged ESOPs were employed in divestitures. In one of the biggest ESOP transactions, Hospital Corp. of America sold more than 100 of its hospitals to HealthTrust Inc.—The Hospital Co., a corporation created and owned by a leveraged ESOP.

Leveraged ESOPs have been used as rescue operations. An ESOP was formed in 1983 to avoid the liquidation of Weirton Steel Co., and it subsequently became a profitable, publicly owned company. However, ESOPs used in attempts to prevent the failures of Rath Packing, McLean Trucking, and Hyatt Clark Industries did not succeed and were followed by bankruptcies.

A number of leveraged ESOPs were formed as takeover defenses to hostile tender offers. ESOPs were established as takeover defenses by Dan River Corp. in 1983, Phillips Petroleum Co. in 1985, and Harcourt Brace Jovanovich, Inc. in 1987.

The Tax Reform Act of 1986 also permits excess pension assets to be shifted into an ESOP tax-free. Ashland Oil reverted $200 million and Transco Energy Co. $120 million into new ESOPs to take advantage of that shield.

ESOP transactions may represent economic dilution. Potentially, they transfer shareholders' wealth to employees. ESOPs represent a form of an employee pension program. If the ESOP contribution is not offset by a reduction in other benefit plans or in the direct wages of workers, employees gain at the expense of shareholders. The argument has been made that any borrowing by the ESOP uses some of the debt capacity of the firm. It also could be argued that such borrowing substitutes for other forms of debt that the firm otherwise would use. To the extent that there is a valid belief that ESOP transactions represent economic dilution to the original shareholders, the price charged the ESOP for the company stock transferred to the plan may contain a premium to compensate for economic dilution. Since the U.S. Department of Labor reviews such transactions, this may be a source of its disagreements about the fairness of the price charged the ESOP by management. The impact of moving equity shares to the ownership of the employees is a disadvantage of ESOPs.

The broader economic consequences of ESOPs have been analyzed. If managements also control the ESOPs that are created, there is no increase in employee influence on the company. While employees may receive stock that can be sold, the additions to their wealth may be relatively small, and may not be sufficient to foster motivation for increased efforts by workers or harmonious relations between workers and management.

On the other hand, if workers do receive substantial increases in control over the company through ESOPs, other harmful results might follow. Workers might use their increased ownership powers to redistribute wealth away from the original shareholders and other shareholders in the firm. The view has been expressed that market forces can be relied on to produce employee ownership where it is appropriate, without the necessity of tax subsidies, and that the subsidies may cause a misallocation of resources.

ESOPs have provided some participation to workers. However, the motivational influences do not appear to have been sufficient to truly affect company performance. In addition, the ESOPs appear often to be controlled by managements and used by them as instruments of policy. It has been estimated that the federal revenue losses from ESOPs for the 1977–1983 period were about $13 billion, an average of $1.9 billion per year.[7] Questions have been raised about whether these tax subsidies really serve a useful purpose.

Corporate Control Issues

The fourth set of restructuring formats deals with corporate control issues. We first consider *unequal voting rights* such as a Class A and a Class B stock. Typically the Class A stock has superior rights to dividends but inferior rights to vote. The Class B stock has superior voting rights but limited dividends. One study shows that in dual-class companies, management's voting rights ownership was almost 60 percent, but their claims to cash flow were only 24 percent.[8] Often two classes of stock appear in corporations where the family founders seek to maintain or increase their control positions.

A strong motive for superior voting rights is that they enable the management control group to achieve continuity of future plans and operating programs. Some argue that the superior voting rights are likely to receive higher benefits in a merger or takeover. Empirical studies indicate that securities with superior voting rights sell at a premium of 5 to 6 percent.

One way to establish two classes of stock is by dual-class recapitalizations. Years ago, firms that established dual classes of stock were delisted from the New York Stock Exchange for violating its rule of one-share-one-vote. But in June 1984, the Big Board put a moratorium on the delisting of dual-class equity firms. Studies both before and after the moratorium date indicate a small but insignificant effect on stocks with resulting inferior voting privileges.

Lehn, Netter, and Poulsen[9] compared dual-class recaps with LBOs. Firms with greater growth opportunities, lower agency costs, and lower tax liability, appeared more likely to consolidate control through dual-class recaps. Their study also found significant increases in industry-adjusted operating income for dual-class firms, but less than the increases found in a sample of LBOs. Dual-class firms allocated a higher percentage of subsequent cash flows to capital expenditures than LBO firms. A high proportion of dual-class firms subsequently issued equity securities. The evidence suggests that dual-class firms possessed more growth opportunities than the LBO firms.

A proxy contest represents another form of control struggle. Proxy contests are attempts by dissident groups of shareholders to obtain board representation or enough seats to control the board and the company. Various interpretations of the success of proxy contests have been offered. One is that the dissident group usually wins a majority of the board. Another view is that a proxy contest succeeds if at least two persons are elected directors—one to propose motions, and the other to second them, so they can get discussions into the minutes of the board meetings. Still a third view holds that the mere staging of a proxy contest is sufficient to indicate that changes will have to be made in the firm's management.

Studies of proxy contests indicate that they are associated with positive abnormal returns ranging on the order of magnitude of 6 to 10 percent. Even if there is conflict within the board as a result of a proxy contest, the results seem to indicate that the benefits of adversarial mutual monitoring between the two groups outweigh the costs. The positive shareholder gains indicate that there had been agency problems or potential for improved management performance prior to the proxy battle.

Proxy contests over the right to control the firm increase the likelihood that corporate assets will be transferred to higher-valued uses. They perform an important and effective disciplinary role in the managerial labor market. Finally, they provide yet another approach to takeover activity. Changes in laws and regulations to effect a reduction in the costs of a proxy fight would increase the use of proxy-contest mechanisms in the market for corporate control.

In a defensive context, the premium stock buy-back is actually a euphemism for "greenmail." The company repurchases the shares that have been acquired by outsiders as the opening wedge to mounting a hostile takeover, and the "raider" group drops its bid. The proceeds usually include a premium over the market price of the stock and the deals often are replete with standstill agreements that bar the raider from launching a new bid for a specified period of time, such as 5 to 10 years.

Some authorities believe that greenmail and standstill agreements are harmful to shareholders because the raider may have been able to provide more short-term value for them. The counter-argument is that existing management may see greater value potential in the future, which justifies paying greenmail. Additionally, management may feel that given sufficient time it can develop multiple offers, initiate a bidding contest for the firm, and obtain higher value for shareholders than if the raider's efforts succeeded. In many cases, targeted companies indeed have generated large increases in shareholder values after raiders had been bought out. However, the initial impact of greenmail and standstill agreements may be small negative changes in the value of the firm's shares.

Along with the financial innovations that stimulated mergers and restructurings, takeover defenses have proliferated. The four principal categories of defenses include:

Defensive Restructurings: These techniques shake up the target company to a great degree. They include the scorched earth policy in which target sells much of its operations and channels the proceeds into a special dividend to shareholders, and the crown jewel approach in which the segments most attractive to a raider are sold off. Other responses include issuing new equity to dilute the bidder's interest, a self-tender share repurchase, and enlisting a friendly, or "white squire," investor.

Capital Structure Changes: Dual classes of common stock fall into this category but the most common technique is the "poison pill," a right giving shareholders an opportunity to buy stock at reduced prices should the firm be attacked. The debt side variant is the "poison put option," an attachment to bonds that make them immediately callable if control of the company changes.

Charter and By-Law Amendments: This covers a wide variety of defensive weapons, such as staggered boards, fair-price provisions, supermajority votes for mergers and divestitures, and blank-check securities. While the enactment of antitakeover amendments typically is associated with negative effects on stock prices, shareholders historically have approved 90 percent of the proposals. Approval of the barriers actually may have positive effects on stock prices if they are regarded as signals that a takeover offer is likely.

Golden Parachutes: Severance payments to executives who lose jobs when control of their companies change.

The issue of whether takeover defenses benefit shareholders is largely unresolved. Defenses may entrench incompetent managers, yet foil unscrupulous raiders while maximizing the prices target shareholders eventually receive. Apologists for defensive actions suggest that such actions will promote an auction for the target firm by providing time for bidders to enter the takeover contest. They argue further that defenses strengthen management's bargaining position for a better deal or eliminate the pressure for shareholders to tender their shares into coercive tender offers.

Opponents of defenses argue that defenses increase the cost of takeovers, thereby reducing the incentive for potential bidders to search for profitable targets or causing an outstanding bid to be withdrawn. For opponents, defensive actions largely constitute a manifestation of a conflict of interest between management and the shareholders. In general, they propose a rule of strict managerial passivity.

Finally, there is the view that measures are needed to reduce the conflict of interest in situations involving a change of control. A case in point is the golden parachute contract that provides compensation to managers for the loss of their jobs under a change of control. In this view, shark repellents and other defenses prevent disruption of the contractual relationship between managers and shareholders by, in effect, putting restrictions on hostile tender offers.

Evaluation

Some generalizations from the restructuring movement of the 1980s are possible. It should be recognized that M&A activity should be a part of a long-run planning strategy. The strategy comes first, and the takeover activity should be placed in that appropriate strategic long-range planning framework. The touchstone should be that the acquired firm should be of greater value as a part of the combined company than either standing alone or purchased by another concern. This is an important way acquirers avoid paying too much.

Changes in the environment plus corporate governance tensions produced the restructuring movement of the 1980s. The restructuring movement itself created new turbulence, stresses, and tensions. These represent broad adjustment processes in an enterprise system. While the pressures have caused the managements of many firms to be uncomfortable, strong competitive pressures harness energies for creative responses, and the restructuring movement has made contributions in that direction.

THEORIES OF ASSET REDEPLOYMENT

Many of the restructuring forms have stirred controversy and debate. Are they good for the economic health of the nation, or are they bad? Do they divert the energies of managers from bona fide economic activity to financial manipulation? Do they use up financial resources that otherwise would be employed in "real" investment activities? Why has heightened merger activity been a phenomenon of the last 20 years?

In attempting to provide further understanding of these many activities, it will be useful to treat the expansion group of activities separately because it alone involves combining and recombining real assets. The remaining groups involve rearranging ownership and control structures in firms without necessarily altering asset positions.

Theories that underlie the efficacy of mergers, tender offers, and joint ventures can be grouped under five major headings:

- Efficiency
- Information
- Agency problems
- Market power
- Taxes

Efficiency Theory

The efficiency theory hypothesizes that a merger can either improve the performance of incumbent management or produce a more efficient company by achieving some form of synergy. During the heyday of the conglomerate merger movement in the late 1960s, exaggerated claims for synergy were made under what came to be known as the "2 + 2 = 7" effect. The theory was that a merged firm would produce far better results than its constituent parts would if they remained independent entities. While the projected results from asset deployment were exaggerated, there is a solid basis for achieving positive net present value investments by recombining the activities of business operations. The synergies that produce these benefits generally fall into three classifications: operating synergy, financial synergy, and strategic realignment.

Operating Synergy.   Operating synergy, or operating economies, may result from both horizontal and vertical mergers. For horizontal mergers, operating economies must stem from some form of economies of scale. These economies, in turn, may reflect indivisibilities and better utilization of capacity after the merger. Or important complementaries in organizational capabilities may be present to produce gains not attainable in the short run from internal investments.

In vertical integration, combining firms at different stages of an industry may achieve more efficient coordination of the different levels. The argument here is that costs of communication and various forms of bargaining, and opportunistic behavior can be avoided by vertical integration.

Financial Synergy.   Possible financial synergies involve some unsettled issues of finance theory. Nevertheless, empirical analysis of mergers may shed some light on the fundamental issues. Financial synergy proponents argue that the cost of capital function may be lowered for a number of reasons as a result of merger. If the cash flow streams of the two companies are not perfectly correlated, bankruptcy prob-abilities may be lowered. The prevailing view in finance theory is that if firms could fail and new ones be formed to take their place without costs, bankruptcy would not matter. But the losses or costs from the failures of firms may be substantial. These losses include not only the direct costs of legal and other administrative fees but also the indirect costs of losing key managers and employees, as well as the loss of customers (especially for makers of durable equipment, who may not be around to supply parts for maintenance in the future). Perhaps the largest indirect cost of bankruptcy is the loss of an effective, functioning organization that took years to de-velop. These direct and indirect losses can wipe out the value of shareholders' equity and reduce the value of creditors' claims as well. Thus, to the extent that bankruptcy and its attendant costs can be reduced by mergers that reduce the instability of com-pany revenue streams, stockholders, creditors, and society as a whole benefit.

This debt-coinsurance effect benefits debtholders at the expense of sharehold-ers. However, this effect can be offset by increasing leverage after the merger, and the result will be increased tax savings on interest payments. Indeed, Stapleton,[10] in the context of the option pricing theory, demonstrates that the increase in debt capacity does not require the existence of bankruptcy costs.

Another dimension, emphasized by Levy and Sarnat,[11] is economies of scale in flotation and transactions costs that may be realized by conglomerate firms. Argu-ments may be raised about the potential magnitude of these financial factors. Fur-ther questions could be raised as to why joint activities might not be taken by unmerged firms to achieve the same economies of scale in flotation and transaction costs. However, the heterogeneity of firms and the costs of contracting would seem to make such activities prohibitive, because such joint activities seldom take place in the real world.

Strategic Realignment to Changing Environments.   The literature on long-range strategic planning has proliferated in recent years, specifically in the area of diversification through mergers. The emphasis of strategic planning research is on matters related to firms' environments and constituencies, as well as their operating decisions. The strategic planning approach to mergers appears to imply either the possibilities of economies of scale or utilization of some unused capacity in the firm's present managerial capabilities. Another rationale is that by external diversi-fication, the firm acquires management skills for needed augmentation of its pre-sent capabilities. This approach still leaves some questions unanswered. New capabilities and new markets could be developed internally. The less risky strategy may be to buy established organizations, but a competitive market for acquisitions implies that the net present value to acquirers from such investments is likely to be small. Nevertheless, if the changes in the environment call for a rapid adjustment, the combinations of existing firms may have significant positive benefits. Further-more, if these investments can be used as a base for still additional investments with positive net present values, the strategy may succeed.

Information Theory

A second possible reason for mergers, tender offers, and joint ventures is the "infor-mation hypothesis." This refers to the revaluation of the ownership shares of firms because of new information that is generated during the merger negotiations, the tender offer process, or the joint venture planning. Alternative forms of the information hypothesis have been distinguished.

One is the "kick-in-the-pants" explanation. Management is stimulated to implement a higher-valued operating strategy. A second is the "sitting-on-a-gold-mine" hypothesis. The negotiations or tendering activity may result in dissemination of new information or lead the stock market to judge that the bidders have superior information. The market then may revalue previously "undervalued" shares.

A third aspect of information effects is a variant of the undervaluation hypothesis, which suggests that firms have stepped up diversification efforts in recent years by expanding, or by entering new product or market areas on a bargain basis. The inflation of the 1970s had a double-barreled impact. Stock prices were depressed during the 1970s and did not recover until the latter part of 1982, after the rate of inflation declined and business prospects improved. The second impact of inflation was to raise current replacement costs of assets substantially above their recorded historical book values. These twin effects resulted in a decline of the q-ratio, defined as the ratio of the market value of a company's shares to the replacement costs of the assets represented by those shares.

In the annual volumes of the *Economic Report of the President* (produced by the Council of Economic Advisers), the q-ratio was calculated for a period of years for all nonfinancial corporations as a group. The data were included in a table entitled "Determinants of Business Fixed Investment." From this and other sources, the q-ratio in the 1980s was running between 0.5 and 0.6. This means that the market values of firms' securities were little more than one-half the value of the brick and mortar behind them.

Thus, if a company seeks capacity to produce a particular product, it is cheaper to buy a firm that manufactures the product than to build brick-and-mortar from scratch. If Firm A seeks to add capacity, this activity implies that its marginal q-ratio is greater than 1. If other firms in its industry have average q-ratios of less than 1, it is efficient for Firm A to add capacity by purchase. For example, if the q-ratio is 0.6 and the premium paid over market value to make an acquisition is 50 percent, the resulting purchase price is 0.6 times 1.5, or 0.9. In that scenario, the average purchase price still would be 10 percent below the current replacement cost of the acquired assets. This potential advantage provided a broad basis for the implementation of the undervaluation theory in recent years, as q-ratios declined.

For companies in natural resource industries, q-ratios have been as low as 0.2 because of high estimated values of reserves in the ground that have been used in the denominator. Such a low q-ratio provided a basis for paying very large premiums when natural resource firms were acquired. For example, the cash and securities offered by U.S. Steel in November 1981 for Marathon Oil represented about $106 per share—about a 75 percent premium over the $60 price of Marathon in early September. However, some Marathon shareholders initiated lawsuits because they stated that earlier outside appraisals had estimated the value of Marathon's reserves in the ground and other assets at more than double the price paid by U.S. Steel. Of course, these appraisals were subject to considerable uncertainty. As it turned out, the sharp decline in oil prices that began in early 1983 impaired the values of oil and other natural resource reserves.

Agency Problems Theory

Jensen and Meckling[12] formulated the implications of agency problems. An agency problem arises when managers own only a fraction of a company's shares. Partial ownership may cause managers to work less vigorously than otherwise and/or consume more perquisites (such as luxurious offices, company cars, memberships in clubs), because the majority owners bear most of the cost. The argument can be made that in large corporations with widely dispersed ownership, individual owners do not have sufficient incentive to expend the substantial resources required to monitor the behavior of managers. A number of compensation arrangements and the market for managers may mitigate the agency problem.

Another market mechanism is the threat of takeover, which may substitute for individual shareholders' efforts to monitor the managers. The agency explanation of mergers extends the previous work by Manne.[13] Manne emphasized the market for corporate control and viewed a merger as a threat of takeover if a firm's management lagged in performance either because of inefficiency or agency problems.

A variant of the agency problem is the managerialism theory of conglomerate mergers that was developed by Mueller.[14] Mueller hypothesized that managers are motivated continually to increase the sizes of their firms. He assumed that the compensation to managers is a function of the size of the firm, and also argued that managers adopt an unduly low investment hurdle rate in their analyses of merger opportunities. But in a study critical of earlier evidence, Lewellen and Huntsman[15] presented findings that managers' compensation is significantly correlated with the firm's profit rate, not its level of sales. The basic premise of the managerialism theory, therefore, is doubtful.

Agency theory suggests that when the market for managers does not solve the agency problem, the market for firms, or merger activity, will come into play. This theory suggests, therefore, that merger activity is a method of dealing with the agency problem. The managerialism theory argues that the agency problem cannot be solved, and that merger activity manifests the agency problems of inefficient, external investments by managers. Empirical evidence presented later will enable us to test these competing theories.

Market Power Theory

An objection sometimes raised against permitting a firm to increase its market share by merger is that the result will be undue concentration in the industry. Indeed, traditional public policy in the United States held that when four or fewer firms accounted for 40 percent or more of the sales in a given market or line of business, an undesirable market structure, or "undue concentration," existed. The argument, in brief, was that if four or fewer firms account for a substantial percentage of an industry's sales, these firms recognize the impact of their actions and policies on one another. This recognized interdependence, the argument continued, leads to a consideration of actions, as well as reactions to changes in policy, that tend toward "tacit collusion." As a result, the prices and profits of the firms contain monopoly elements. Thus, if economies from mergers cannot be established, it was argued that the resulting increases in concentration were motivated by monopoly gains. If economies of scale can be demonstrated, then a comparison of efficiencies versus the effects of increased concentration must be made.

In 1982 and 1984, the Department of Justice announced new merger guidelines to supersede those issued in 1968. On April 2, 1992, the department and the Federal Trade Commission jointly issued restated guidelines that further confirmed the new approaches. The merger guidelines of the 1980s adopted the Herfindahl-Hirschman index (HHI), which takes into consideration the market shares of all of the firms in the industry. The theory behind the HHI is that if one or more firms have relatively high market shares, this is of greater concern than the combined share of the largest four firms. If, in market A, four firms each hold a 15 percent market share and the remaining 40 percent is held by 40 firms, each with a 1 percent market share, the HHI is

$$HHI = 4(15)^2 + 40(1)^2 = 940$$

In market B, however, one firm has a 57 percent market share and the remaining 43 percent is held by 43 firms, each with a 1 percent market share. As with market A, the four-firm concentration ratio is 60 percent. However, the HHI is

$$HHI = (57)^2 + 43(1)^2 = 3,292$$

Thus, market A would be considered unconcentrated while market B, with its very high HHI level, would be considered highly concentrated. However, the key difference from the old four-firm ratio is that HHI registers a concern about inequality as well as degree of concentration. Yet the economic basis for either concern has not been well established. Whereas some economists hold that high concentration, however measured, causes some degree of monopoly, other economists hold that increased concentration is generally the result of active and intense competition. They argue further that the intense competition continues among large firms in concentrated industries because the dimensions of decision making over prices, outputs, types of products, quality of products, service, and so on, are so numerous and of so many gradations that collusion simply is not feasible.

But there is a possibility that the value gains from restructuring result from increases in monopoly power rather than increases in efficiency. Several studies are relevant to this issue.

James Ellert examined the monopoly-efficiency conflict at great length.[16] He analyzed the data for 205 defendants in antimerger complaints from 1950 to 1972 and found that, for periods beginning four years before the complaints were brought, the residual performances were positive and statistically significant for the defendants. As expected, a residual became negative upon the filing of a complaint. However, the negative residuals were relatively small. Ellert observed that the record of effective management of assets by acquiring firms in the years preceding merger activity may be the real causes of complaints by their rivals to antitrust authorities. Ellert terms this a "harassment" hypothesis. He indicates that there are incentives for complaining rivals to follow this course. Government agencies bear the costs of prosecution and, if successful, their actions will handicap the defendants to the advantage of their rivals. The harassment hypothesis clearly is the opposite of a monopoly explanation of merger activity. If the monopoly theory is valid, both parties should gain from the merger.

The monopoly theory was weakened even further in studies by Robert Stillman and Epsen Eckbo, who looked at how mergers affected the rivals of acquiring firms.[17] Their studies appear to support the efficiency basis for mergers. Ellert emphasized that acquiring firms had positive residuals before their mergers and acquired firms had negative residuals before being taken over. Stillman's evidence was that rival firms did not benefit from the announcement of proposed mergers, which is inconsistent with the concentration-collusion hypothesis. Eckbo found positive residuals at the merger announcement, but no negative effects on rivals when it appeared that the merger would be blocked by the antitrust authorities. This pattern of relationships, he said, indicates that the main effect of a merger is to signal the possibility that the merging firms will achieve economies, thus providing information to rivals that such economies also may be available to them.

Tax Considerations Theory

A key tax benefit available in mergers can be the substitution of capital gains taxes for ordinary income taxes. A judicious acquirer can reap the advantage by purchasing a growth company that has paid little or no dividends, hanging on to it during its lushest expansion period, and selling it after the growth has peaked to realize capital gains. When growth of the property has slowed to the point that earnings retention cannot be justified to the Internal Revenue Service, the incentive for sale is created. Rather than pay out future earnings as dividends subject to ordinary personal income taxes, a seller can capitalize future earnings by divesting the business.

Another tax factor arises from the credits enjoyed by firms with accumulated tax losses. Although a business purpose other than the capture of tax credits must be demonstrated, a firm with tax losses can shelter the profits of another firm with which it merges. The Economic Recovery Tax Act of 1981 provided for the sale of tax credits from accelerated depreciation (without selling an entire business),and such transactions often were executed through sale-leaseback arrangements on physical properties. The popularity of this tactic suggested that tax inducements to mergers may lose appeal if there are alternative methods for securing equivalent tax benefits.

Tax considerations also are in play when the prospect of achieving stepped-up depreciable assets is a strong incentive to acquire. This motivation points up a way of trying to avoid the penalty of depreciation on lower historical costs during periods of high inflation.

Still other tax effects are associated with inheritance taxes. A closely held firm may be sold when the owners grow older, because they face uncertainty about the value placed on the firm for estate tax purposes. A sale also may provide greater liquidity for the payment of estate taxes.

A study of mergers in the newspaper industry illustrates the interlocked effects of stepped-up depreciation and inheritance tax influences.[18] The stepped-up basis for depreciable assets leads to competition among bidding firms, resulting in payment of substantial premiums to acquire newspaper properties. These high, demonstrated market values then are used by the IRS in setting values on newspaper companies for estate tax purposes. But the realization of the tax benefits of the higher depreciable values requires an actual transaction. This is a fact of life that has stimulated the purchase of individual newspaper companies by newspaper chains.

Whereas the expansion activities involve the combining of assets, the remaining groups of restructuring methods center on the uncombining of assets, or what some authorities have termed "reverse mergers." Even though shrinkage or contraction may characterize reverse mergers, a synergy argument also has been advanced on their behalf. Unlike expansions, in which proponents of synergy claim that the total is greater than the sum of its parts—the aforementioned $2 + 2 = 7$ effect—reverse mergers supposedly improve total results by subtraction, or an implied "$5 - 1 = 7$" effect. Obviously, there is no logical basis in mathematics for this approach, but some analysts believe that it works in the corporate context. For example, various forms of divestiture can be rationalized on the grounds that they transfer assets to a higher-valued use or to a more efficient user. Or a divestiture may enhance a firm's value by slicing off a business that was a poor fit with the remaining operations. If these theories are valid, good divestiture programs may increase market values of both the divesting and purchasing firms.

The basis for increases in value associated with restructuring relates largely to organizational aspects of running large business firms. These gains relate to identifying responsibility for the results and to more directly linking managerial rewards to stock price and performance. On average, various aspects of mergers, tender offers, and the rearranging of corporate ownership and control relationships seem to represent expected positive net present value activities. It would appear that they supplement other types of investment activity in improving business performance.

DRUCKER REVISED: RULES FOR SUCCESSFUL MERGERS

In his classic op-ed piece in *The Wall Street Journal* of October 15, 1981, Peter Drucker sets forth "five rules of successful acquisition." Noting that the current merger movement in the United States paralleled the tremendous wave of acquisitions in Germany in 1920–1922, a period of chronic inflation, Drucker saw a general principle at work: During severe inflation, fixed assets become available at prices below book value and even further below replacement costs. The low stock market valuations of companies, he noted, are due in substantial degree to sustained underdepreciation because of tax regulations. Thus, the basic cause of the increased merger activity under inflation represents a flight out of money and into assets.

Despite this financial rationale for M&A activity, Drucker said that for a merger to make business sense, it must follow five rules:

- Acquirer must contribute something to the acquired company.
- Acquirer and target must share a common core of unity.
- Acquirer must respect the business of the acquired company.

- Within a year or so, the acquiring company must be able to provide top management to the acquired company.

- Within the first years of merger, managements in both companies should receive promotions.

Drucker supports his prescriptions by selected examples of successes and failures. But does the mass of empirical research bear Drucker out? My survey of M&A studies since the mid-1970s would answer in the affirmative.

Buy and Build Correlations

The dollar value of merger and acquisition activity in the United States on average has been related to the dollar value of plant and equipment expenditures. Generally, when plant and equipment expenditures rise or fall, M&A activity similarly increases or decreases. When a statistical regression relationship is calculated, the dollar increase in M&A activity is about one-fifth the increase in P&E expenditures. Thus, in a year when P&E expenditures increase by $20 billion, M&A activity will rise on average by about $4 billion. While numerous factors affect M&A activity, the level of investment activity is a strong influence. This suggests that similar types of economic forces influence both types of investment activity and that there is a similar economic rationale for both.

Furthermore, the timing of annual merger activity is influenced empirically by the ratio of the market value of firms to their replacement costs. This q-ratio is a measure of investment opportunities in plant and equipment, either directly or through mergers. This factor can be split into two variables: the growth rate of GNP (positive), and the level of the realized real interest rates (negative). Statistically, these factors are related significantly to the level of merger activity. In addition, the studies indicate that financial variables are important particularly for pure conglomerate mergers.

Creation of Value

As detailed above, most studies of mergers in recent years have used residual analysis of stock performance. These studies compare the returns realized by investors in merger stocks when merger and tender offers are announced, to the returns realized in the general market. The difference represents abnormal returns on residuals from predicted market returns. The positive findings permit some generalizations.

The value of the merged firms appears to be greater than the sum of the components. This implies that value is created and increased by mergers, reflecting underlying economics and efficiencies of corporate fusion. Other findings include:

- Shareholders of acquired firms during the period just before the announcement date of a merger or tender offer gain by about 15 percent in mergers and about 30 percent in tender offers. However, in earlier periods, the abnormal returns of

acquired firms are negative, indicating that their managements were not performing up to their potentials.

- Shareholders of acquiring firms for the period before the announcement dates
realize modest positive returns, but these are not always statistically significant. In
earlier periods, however, their shareholders' abnormal returns are positive, indicating that acquiring firms previously had a record of successfully managing asset
growth.

- Target residuals do not decline after the merger. This further indicates that the
mergers, on average, are based on valid economic or business reasons.

The studies summarized above generally include all types of mergers—horizontal, vertical, and conglomerate. Studies of conglomerate mergers produced approximately the same pattern of results. Pure conglomerate mergers appear to
violate the Drucker imperative of relatedness. But because of antitrust constraints
against horizontal and vertical mergers, more than 75 percent of the mergers and
acquisitions since the early 1950s have been classified as "conglomerate" by the Federal Trade Commission. Furthermore, studies of conglomerate mergers have found
that their financial market performances for their shareholders have not been statistically different from the general market averages, or other broad composites
such as the returns from mutual funds.

Closer analysis suggests that the so-called conglomerate mergers that were studied did not violate the Drucker rules. In each case, acquiring and acquired firms
shared some relatedness. For some it was the ability to share sophisticated financial
planning and control systems or some generic managerial capabilities; for others it
was the ability to adjust effectively to changing economic environments. In most
cases, the acquiring firms had available managerial capabilities and cash flows, but
faced product markets whose growth prospects were below average.

Guidelines for the 1990s

Despite this analysis, examination of the systematic evidence suggests that the
Drucker rules may be unduly restrictive if interpreted too literally. A generalization
of the guidelines for management in restructuring activities would be the following
generalized ten "commandments."

- Incorporate the M&A program into long-range strategic planning.

- Involve top executives in the M&A process.

- Diversify by acquisition into related areas to augment core capabilities, but remember that "related" is a flexible term.

- Apply this critical test: The acquired firm should be of greater value to the combined company than it would be standing alone or as part of another business.
This is one way to avoid overpaying.

- Provide incentives for managements of both firms to stay. In future promotions,
distinctions between previous employment at the acquirer or the target must disappear.

- Invest top management with responsibility for postmerger coordination.

- Charge top management with actively working on postmerger integration, since it does not happen automatically.

- Communicate internally and externally as soon as possible after restructuring decisions are made.

- Separate excess managers and employees in an enlightened manner, because it is the proper behavior and impacts employee morale and firm culture.

- Remember that if the price isn't right, someone is going to get hurt even if the merger makes sense from a business perspective.

RATIONAL BEHAVIOR
AND MAXIMIZED VALUE

The preponderance of empirical evidence supports the judgment that corporate restructuring activity is rational, value-maximizing behavior. On average, the total gains measured as rates of return or in absolute amounts associated with restructuring events are positive. Thus, the evidence does not support the managerialism theory which holds that managements resort to restructuring simply to increase the size of firms, to increase their own compensation, or to achieve the prestige of controlling large corporate enterprises.

The major studies of the monopoly-versus-efficiency issue obtain somewhat complex empirical patterns. However, all interpret their results as supporting the efficiency theory. Thus, the wide range of corporate restructuring activities that we observe appears to represent a response to the characteristics of the economic environment, and facilitates resource reallocations within the economy.

To reiterate, changing environments, combined with weaknesses in corporate governance and control systems, produced the M&A activity of the 1980s. The restructuring movement in turn created new turbulence, stresses, and tensions—representing economic forces at work and producing broad adjustment processes. While excesses and mistakes occurred, on balance efficiency increased. Organization structures have been streamlined. Incentive systems have improved.

We are engaged in a competition between two types of economic systems. The weaknesses of centralized planning have become clear with the extraordinary upheavals in Eastern Europe: It is impossible to coordinate and administer thousands of input and output quantities and prices, tasks performed so well in an unregulated price system. Bureaucratic rigidities and lack of flexible feedback systems aggravate the deficiencies of centralized planning. A free market system solves many of these problems, but also has its own challenges, as illustrated by the M&A activities of the 1980s. High returns attract the flow of resources. Since the resource flow decisions are made independently by a large number of enterprise units, high returns can cause overshoots in both the quantity of investment flows and bidding prices.

The market system is now in competition for the minds and hearts of many peoples. Mergers and acquisitions were responses to some weaknesses in corporate governance and to changing environments, but restructuring carried its own excesses and mistakes. Our economic system should provide a model that will be attractive and useful for those nations and economies that are discarding centralized planning. This is a responsibility that cannot be legislated; it is something that responsible managerial leadership will have to produce.

NOTES

1. Katherine Schipper, and Abbie Smith, "Effects of Recontracting on Shareholder Wealth: The Case of Voluntary Spin-offs," *Journal of Financial Economics,* 12 (December 1983), pp. 437–467.

2. Gailen Hite, and James E. Owers, "Security Price Reactions around Corporate Spin-off Announcements," *Journal of Financial Economics,* 12 (December 1983), pp. 409–436.

3. T. E. Copeland, E. F. Lemgruber, and D. Mayers, "Corporate Spinoffs: Multiple Announcement and Ex-Date Abnormal Performance," in T. E. Copeland, ed., *Modern Finance and Industrial Economics,* Basil Blackwell, New York, 1987, chap. 7.

4. A. Klein, "The Timing and Substance of Divestiture Announcements: Individual, Simultaneous and Cumulative Effects," *Journal of Finance,* 41 (July 1986), pp. 685–697.

5. Bernard S. Black, and Joseph A. Grundfest, "Shareholder Gains from Takeovers and Restructurings Between 1981 and 1986: $162 Billion is a Lot of Money," *Journal of Applied Corporate Finance,* 1 (Spring 1988), pp. 5–15.

6. Chris J. Muscarella, and Michael R. Vetsuypens, "Efficiency and Organizational Structure: A Study of Reverse LBOs," *Journal of Finance,* 45 (December 1990), pp. 1389–1413.

7. United States General Accounting Office, "Employee Stock Ownership Plans: Benefits and Costs of ESOP Tax Incentives for Broadening Stock Ownership," December 1986, pp. 28–31.

8. Harry DeAngelo, and Linda DeAngelo, "Managerial Ownership of Voting Rights," *Journal of Financial Economics,* 14 (March 1985), pp. 33–69.

9. Kenneth Lehn, Jeffry Netter, and Annette Poulsen, "Consolidating Corporate Control: Dual-Class Recapitalizations versus Leveraged Buyouts," *Journal of Financial Economics,* 27 (October 1990), pp. 557–580.

10. R. C. Stapleton, "Mergers, Debt Capacity, and the Valuation of Corporate Loans," in M. Keenan and L. J. White, eds., *Mergers and Acquisitions,* D. C. Heath, Lexington, Mass., 1982, chap. 2.

11. H. Levy, and M. Sarnat, "Diversification, Portfolio Analysis and the Uneasy Case for Conglomerate Mergers," *Journal of Finance,* 25 (September 1970), pp. 795–802.

12. M. Jensen, and W. Meckling, "Theory of the Firm: Managerial Behavior, Agency Costs and Ownership Structure," *Journal of Financial Economics,* 3 (October 1976), pp. 305–360.

13. H. G. Manne, "Mergers and the Market for Corporate Control," *Journal of Political Economy,* 73 (April 1965), pp. 110–120.

14. D. C. Mueller, "A Theory of Conglomerate Mergers," *Quarterly Journal of Economics,* 83 (November 1969), pp. 643–659.

15. Wilbur G. Lewellen, and B. Huntsman, "Managerial Pay and Corporate Performance," *American Economic Review,* 60 (September 1970), pp. 710–722.

16. James C. Ellert, "Mergers, Antitrust Law Enforcement, and Stockholder Returns," *Journal of Finance,* 31 (May 1976), pp. 715–732.

17. Robert S. Stillman, "Examining Antitrust Policy towards Horizontal Mergers," *Journal of Financial Economics*, 11 (April 1983), pp. 225–240; B. E. Eckbo, "Horizontal Mergers, Collusion, and Stockholder Wealth," *Journal of Financial Economics*, 11 (April 1983), pp. 241–273.

18. James N. Dertouzos, and Kenneth E. Thorpe, "Newspaper Groups: Economies of Scale, Tax Laws, and Merger Incentives," Rand Corp. R-2878-SBA, Santa Monica, Calif., June 1982.

6

Gaining Competitive Position Through M&A

Keith Creehan

Principal, Mercer Management Consulting, Inc., New York, New York

Eleanor Leger

Principal, Mercer Management Consulting, Inc., New York, New York

Throughout the history of the industrialized economies, waves of merger and acquisition activity have been driven by changes in the finance and regulatory environments. The most recent example is the junk-bond-financed restructuring boom of the 1980s. History also has shown that many of the transactions undertaken solely for finance or legal benefits ultimately failed to produce increased value for shareholders. In a study of major corporate restructurings involving acquisitions, we found that less than half of the companies were successful in increasing their market value at a faster rate than competitors.

One of the most significant factors driving the success of corporate combinations has been the extent of the strategic fit that existed between the acquiring company

77

and its target. While financial combinations maintained the basic operating practices of both acquirer and target, strategic combinations involved major changes in the way the overall business was run. In these combinations, companies integrated activities, changed organizational structure, and implemented focused profit improvement programs. Our study found that the odds of success were dramatically higher for those companies that took a strategic approach.

The evidence thus clearly underlines what logic already suggests: for companies considering an acquisition, it is imperative to understand the impact of the proposed combination on the competitive position and operating effectiveness of the organizations involved.

For those companies grappling with the strategic challenge of achieving long-term profitable growth, acquisition can be a very successful option—provided there is a clear understanding of the strategic fit and risks involved. In this chapter we examine major sources of strategic value in acquisitions and discuss how they can be assessed realistically. We also address the broader issue of when acquisition should be used to accomplish strategic objectives as opposed to other types of growth initiatives. Finally, we include a brief summary of additional factors we have found to be critical in realizing the full potential of strategic acquisitions.

SOURCES OF
STRATEGIC VALUE

Generically, the strategic value of acquisitions derives from costs and competencies that can be shared between combining organizations and from sources of revenue that can be acquired more cheaply than they can be generated internally. The following four examples highlight the kinds of value enhancement opportunities we have found to be most successful.

Consolidation

Consolidation of Regional and Local Competitors to Rationalize Operations and Build National Brand Recognition.   In order to build a national network in fragmented industries such as food service distribution or the clinical testing business, significant value can be created by acquiring distributors or laboratories that have a good presence in their local markets. Sysco Corp., which has a P/E ratio significantly higher than those of its competitors, has successfully used this strategy to become the dominant player in its market. Corning, Inc.'s MetPath has employed this strategy to become one of the largest providers of medical testing services in the United States.

MetPath, for example, targets acquisitions in regions where it already has a presence or where the acquired laboratory has a strong operation. There are four elements in its integration strategy:

■ Raise service levels.
■ Increase test offerings.

■ Eliminate redundant activities.

■ Reinforce a bottom-line focus.

Customer service is a primary concern and a significant acquisition benefit. For example, its increased local scale of operations allows MetPath to offer its clients greater flexibility in report delivery and specimen collection. The acquired business also can benefit from MetPath's national scale, which has allowed the company to pioneer the development of new test offerings. There are many opportunities to reduce duplicated operating costs, ranging from consolidation of sales and distribution to integration of testing and administrative functions. Finally, MetPath brings management skills and techniques that help acquired businesses drive consistent margin growth.

The profit implications of this strategy are obvious. "With any acquisition opportunity we target a return on investment in the neighborhood of at least 20 percent. We are able to achieve these returns on a regular basis because of the efficiencies we obtain from our regional operational focus and the leveraging of 'best practices' across our national network of clinical laboratories," says Michael Bachich, CFO of MetPath. "Strategic acquisitions have been a primary factor in our 10-fold growth over the past decade."

Added Revenues

Acquisition of Revenue in Existing Market Segments to Lever Retail Outlet Infrastructure.   In businesses whose sales depend on a network of retail outlets, such as restaurants and consumer banking, acquisitions can be used very effectively to take advantage of the phenomenon known as "network scale." Simply put, network scale describes the effect that occurs when having the dominant outlet share in a given geographical market leads to a more than proportionate market share. The effect is subject to the law of diminishing returns, so that the resulting pattern of market share gain versus outlet share gain forms an S-shaped curve.

In attractive markets, competitors may achieve network scale benefits through the acquisition and rationalization of overlapping networks. This strategy was employed successfully in banking by Wells Fargo, & Co. Inc. in its acquisition of Crocker National in 1986. As shown in Figure 6.1, a net gain of 3 percent in outlet share after rationalization generated an 8 percent gain in market share.

Expansion

Expansion into New Segments or Geographic Areas to Lever Existing Expertise with Acquired Product or Market Knowledge.   In the increasingly integrated global economy, many businesses have seized opportunities to create value by acquiring local market knowledge that can be married to their existing technical or marketing expertise. The costs and risks of entering foreign markets without detailed understanding of local language and business customs have been documented in famous and infamous cases. The classic case was the introduction of the Chevy Nova in South America, where *no va* in Spanish means *doesn't go*. While this may be a

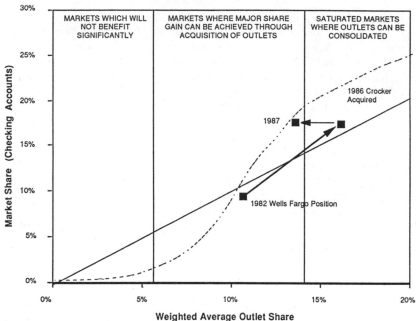

Figure 6.1. Network scale benefits can be a significant source of strategic value.

facetious example, U.S. companies often have found that acquiring local competitors overseas is an efficient way to gain the requisite knowledge quickly. At the same time, bringing technical and marketing expertise to bear on these foreign acquisitions can greatly increase existing revenues and profitability. This is particularly true if the acquiree already has a strong brand presence or customer franchise.

A splendid example of the marriage of local market presence with global expertise is Sara Lee Corp.'s European consumer apparel acquisitions. Beginning with the initial acquisition of a leading brand hosiery manufacturer in France, Sara Lee has leveraged its expertise in low-cost production, knit goods product extensions, and brand development to move geographically beyond France by acquiring local competitors in Italy, Spain, the United Kingdom, Germany, and Scandinavia. The category management skills that Sara Lee has used in North America to leverage the L'Eggs, Hanes, and Champion apparel brands have been cloned in Europe, on a more local basis, to extend the firm's dominance beyond hosiery to fuller lines in men's and women's underwear and active wear.

Rationalization

Rationalization of Manufacturing Operations in Mature Industries.   In highly competitive and mature industries the primary source of value in an acquisition often is a reduction in operating ratio, and more specifically in the number of manufacturing sites. This type of action has the potential to generate significant short- and long-term benefits. In the short term, a reduction in the combined firms' manufacturing sites probably will result in increased capacity utilization and lower overall costs. Over the long term, if the industry has overcapacity, reducing the number of manufacturing sites will result in reduced prices for the industry. This type of acquisition thus can provide both cost and revenue benefits to the acquiring firm.

In addition to financial benefits, an acquiring firm also can achieve long-term strategic benefits from understanding an "industry rationalization" acquisition. A strategic benefit can be obtained from an acquisition of this type by combining a series of low-cost manufacturing facilities with other higher-cost facilities. This combined firm then has the dual benefits of an overall low-cost position and the ability to balance industry supply and demand by closing an appropriate number of high-cost facilities. The strategic benefit is gained when the high-cost facilities are used as a threatened response to expansion or entry by any competitor. For example, if supply is tight and competitors plan to expand, the firm would reopen a closed facility to discourage entry by "crashing" prices. Using these facilities to maintain high prices and discourage competitor advances can provide a long-term competitive advantage to the combined firm.

This type of acquisition has been undertaken successfully by a major player in the building products industry. This company was the industry leader with the largest, lowest cost manufacturing facilities. When a marginal competitor was for sale, the market leader was able to outbid its other competitors for the company because of the "dual" synergies of cost reduction and pricing. This acquisition gave the market leader an even stronger position against its competitors and has resulted in significant growth and profitability.

ASSESSING STRATEGIC VALUE

The financial and operating impact of strategic acquisition opportunities can be quantified. A realistic, fact-based assessment of value potential requires detailed understanding of both the acquirer and target businesses along multiple dimensions:

- Business cost chain organized by function or activity rather than cost category
- Key cost drivers and their differences between the two companies
- Observed experience or scale "slope" of key functions or activities

A buyer cannot begin to identify synergies between combining organizations until it can compare their per-unit costs and revenues by activity. If an expected benefit of the combination is to centralize billing activities, the acquirer first must understand how much each firm was spending on billing on a per unit basis before the deal.

A fair assessment of relative performance requires understanding the key drivers of cost and their differences. For instance, in medical laboratory billing departments, data entry costs are driven by the type and number of bills flowing through the billing department. A physician's bill requires a fraction of the keystrokes necessary for a commercial insurance bill. Depending on the business mix of physician versus insurance bills, the efficiency of an acquisition target's billing operations may be significantly higher or lower than one would think, based on a simple total-cost-per-bill comparison.

Once true relative functional efficiency has been determined, it can be plotted against the observed functional scale "slope" to evaluate the potential value impact of combining operations. Figure 6.2 shows how combining the best practices of companies A and B should be expected to result in a combined productivity increase of 7 percent from greater scale effects and 15 percent from improved efficiency. This productivity increase can be translated directly into bottom line profit improvement and strategic value creation.

A similar detailed analysis should be used to evaluate the impact of the proposed combination on pricing and volume. The final objective of this analytical process is to determine and add up sources of value across all functional areas. Figure 6.3 demonstrates this for an acquisition in the medical products business. The results of the analysis also provide a clear set of operational objectives and performance targets for the integration process once the acquisition is completed.

ACQUISITION AS AN OPTION FOR ACHIEVING STRATEGIC GOALS

When an acquisition program is begun as part of a strategic plan, the techniques of strategic value assessment described above allow use of a fact-based, objective ap-

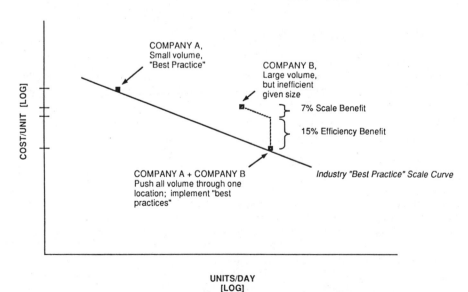

Figure 6.2. Valuing functional scale and efficiency gains from combining operations.

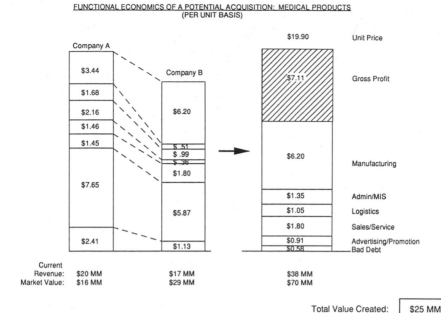

Figure 6.3. As a final step, sources of value are tallied up across functional areas.

proach to compare different acquisition candidates. Without such an approach, costly mistakes may be made. For instance, Figure 6.4 presents the results of the detailed medical products analysis described above for three potential candidates. While Candidate 3 initially looked like "the best" company, for the acquirer it actually represented an opportunity to destroy value. By comparison, both Candidates 1 and 2 offered significant value creation prospects for substantially lower purchase prices.

In the larger picture, acquisition is only one option for achieving strategic growth objectives. Others include sales investment, greenfield facilities investment, innovation, strategic alliances, and joint ventures. Determining the best option requires a thorough analysis of the potential value and risk characteristics of all alternatives. Strategic value analysis must be complemented by an assessment of the risks involved in achieving that value. The option with the most appropriate combination of value and risk then is easily identified.

There are four main sources of risk:

- Timing
- Degree of organizational change required
- Cultural fit
- Concurrence of long-term goals

The longer an option takes to achieve, the greater the risk that the environment will change or that competitors will move first. Risk will increase with the number of

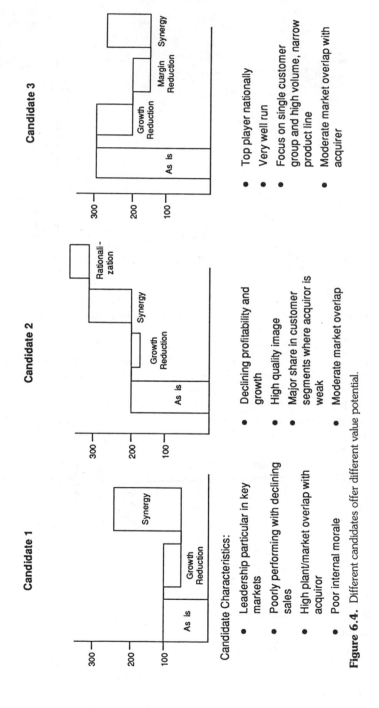

Figure 6.4. Different candidates offer different value potential.

functions impacted, the degree of impact, and the importance of those functions to the value of the business. For acquisitions, risk also will be affected by whether significant change is required in both the acquiring and acquired organizations. Internal growth options may be less risky than acquisitions where there may be significant differences in management approach, concern for employees, and other cultural factors between the acquiring and target organizations.

Finally, strategic alliances and joint ventures face additional risk when the long-term goals of the partners may be competing rather than complementary. One need look no further for an example than General Electric Co.'s disagreement with its 51 percent-owned subsidiary, Camco, Inc., Canada's largest appliance maker. General Electric's desire to rationalize production to its U.S. facilities was in direct conflict with the minority shareholders' ongoing efforts to continue Canadian manufacture and employment.

In any acquisition analysis, understanding the risks is critical. Such insight allows the buyer to get a reasonably complete measure of the strategic value it has identified and to expose the vulnerabilities of the combination that might lessen the chances of achieving that value. The risk analysis further impacts the decision on whether to acquire or pass up the acquisition opportunity and helps determine the price the acquirer is willing to pay for the target.

ADDITIONAL FACTORS THAT DRIVE SUCCESSFUL ACQUISITIONS

Two additional factors are critical to realizing the full potential of strategic acquisitions: effective negotiation and a detailed integration plan.

Successful negotiation depends upon a solid understanding of a business and its value under different ownership configurations. The techniques of strategic value assessment and risk analysis described above can be used to determine:

- The value to the potential acquirer
- The value to its current owner
- The cost for the potential acquirer to replicate the target business on its own

These values set the parameters of the negotiation and allow the acquirer to strike deals to its best advantage. On the other side, it is also true that divestors can maximize their sale prices by using strategic value analysis to identify the potential acquirers that will realize the most value from the divested operations. Kohlberg Kravis Roberts & Co.'s classic buy-out of Beatrice Cos. in 1986 illustrates the value of buying assets at open market prices and reselling them to strategic buyers who are willing to part with some of the value they would create with those assets in order to acquire them.

In deal after deal, experience has shown that the greatest potential value is realized only when the acquirer has a detailed integration plan that is focused specifically on achieving the strategic synergies identified during the value assessment process. To be effective, the integration plans should be developed with significant input from the acquisition value analysis, and must cover three key phases:

- Managing the transition
- Redefining the business
- Design and implementation of new programs

The acquirer must identify the specific steps required to accomplish the transition to new ownership. There may be key operational moves that can be accomplished shortly after closing. In addition, the tone of the new ownership should be set during the transition period. In one LBO, the first things the new CEO did when arriving at his new office were to lock the door to the executive men's bathroom, close the executive dining room, and ban all memo-writing for a month. This kind of signaling can be very effective in setting expectations about long-term changes to come.

Those long-term changes will flow directly from the strategic value analysis. The analysis should be used to define the "end-game"—what the organization and operations will have to look like in order to achieve the value identified. Once the business is redefined, programs must be designed and implemented to get there.

COMPETITIVE POSITIONING

M&A is a vehicle for competitive positioning and operational efficiency when it is driven as part of an overall strategic game plan and is grounded on a thorough understanding of the economic value and risks of acquisition candidates and alternative growth options. The approach we have described to identify and quantify strategic value provides our clients with a clear view of how strategic growth objectives can be achieved, and supports the effective implementation and realization of those objectives. By following a consistent value-based strategy, companies can reap returns from acquisitions over the long run.

7
Corporate Development Alternatives

Martin Sikora

Editor, Mergers & Acquisitions
Philadelphia, Pennsylvania

Mergers and acquisitions are but one weapon in a company's corporate development arsenal. The choices for executing business projects for generating value-creating growth are varied. It is likely that the well-managed firm will use all or most, depending on which format emerges from an analytical work-up as the most potent for a specific program.

In popular parlance, the options fall under the rubric of the "buy-versus-build" decisions. But that often overworked term touches only the extremes of the range—"buy" as the synonym for obtaining the resources needed to put a project across through acquisition, "build" as the emblem for doing all of the work in-house or through *de novo* expansion. Thus, the buzzword overlooks the myriad choices between the two flanks, such as:

- Joint ventures
- Strategic alliances
- Minority investments
- Venture capital
- Licensing
- Technology sharing

- Marketing and distribution agreements
- Franchising

Each choice has generic advantages and drawbacks, the proverbial trade-offs, and the pluses and minuses often become more complex and finite when applied to a specific business project. Key components of the checklist obviously are economic and financial—wringing the most out of the least investment in the fastest possible time. But tradition, culture, technological prowess, management competency, customer-supplier relationships, and other qualitative factors often figure strongly in the balancing act required to tap the best strategy.

THE BUY-VERSUS-BUILD DECISION

Although the corporate development commanders can push any number of buttons, their decisions often boil down to selecting "buy" or "build."

Acquisitions can be compelling because they are short-cuts to getting what is needed, but they are not for everybody; nor are they appropriate for every project or program launched by a business. Indeed, many highly successful firms eschew acquisitions entirely or rarely do them. Minnesota Mining & Manufacturing, with its diverse array of consumer and industrial products, Merck & Co. in pharmaceuticals, Texas Instruments in semiconductors, and Johnson & Johnson with its multiple lines of health care products are examples of companies that have bet successfully on internal development to sustain strong track records.

Nevertheless, even many of the most internally oriented firms usually don't overlook the potential of mergers and acquisitions in their screening processes. Acquisitions can add new products and technologies, widen customer bases, harvest critical skills, plant the company's flag in new geographic markets, and expand production capacity with almost lightninglike speed. Absorption of entire organizations can give the acquirer a leg up on competitors while generating immediate contributions (financial, technical, etc.) to the combined company. While purchases may involve large up-front outlays, acquisitions can be more cost-effective than the *de novo* route. Paybacks are faster and the learning curve for start-ups can be eliminated.

But these advantages disappear for many companies, especially deep-pocketed firms geared to heavy investment in R&D, new product development, and capital spending to enhance productivity—those typically on the cutting edge of technology, or those with such huge market shares that acquisition would be an overkill. External opportunities dry up because there seldom are businesses, people, plants, or processes outside the firm that are worth acquiring, or that even exist. These firms are far better off developing technologies, launching new products, or moving into new geographic territories on their own.

Yet, even when the choice is not so clear-cut, many companies prefer to do it themselves. For some, internal development is so embedded within their strategic game plans that they have learned to live with and manage the delayed paybacks and learning curves while producing very respectable returns. Frequently, these companies have developed unique skills in building new plants, shaking out new products, invading new territories, and recruiting critical personnel to cushion them from the most severe problems inherent in start-up projects. In a *de novo*-based strategic scenario, the acquisition may be viewed as a device for spreading the investment capital pool too thin.

But there are many other reasons for passing up acquisitions. Some companies simply have no stomach for buying. They may dislike shelling out large one-shot payments and favor staggering their outlays in smaller bites over the term of a start-up. The prospect of competing for target companies in the M&A market repels many managements, a large number of whom also are turned off by having to negotiate with people in another organization. And a number of companies admit they lack the skill or the will to integrate another business and its personnel into their organizations.

Timing also is important. When the M&A market is hotly competitive, many companies, including active acquirers, reject the high prices they might have to pay as uneconomical investments, and opt for internal development to achieve the same goals.

JOINT VENTURES (JV)

Corporate partnering has become increasingly fashionable in the 1980s and the 1990s. The most common form is the joint venture in which two or more firms join forces to create a new jointly owned business entity for a specific purpose. JV formations have been driven by financial, market, technological, and geographic forces, but, despite potentially great economic advantages, they are fraught with problems that invariably are cultural in nature. Indeed, many ventures don't pan out because of governance conflicts or culture clashes between the partners.

Generically, the joint venture format allows businesses to pool various types of resources for common gain. A major drawback from the start is that neither firm will get 100 percent of the rewards pie. Even though each partner might be better off than if it had not entered the alliance, the very idea of having to share the wealth rankles some businesses. This issue has to be addressed at the time the JV agreement is reached, or it can become an insurmountable hurdle to success.

The JV can be crafted at several strategic levels. A common type of venture is in essence a start-up business devised to develop a new technology, to commercialize products from newly developed technologies, or to set up in new markets. Each of the partners brings skills, knowledge, and resources to the venture that they would have had to acquire and develop had they chosen to go it alone. In addition, a joint project may be desirable to spread the escalating costs of technological advancement or acquiring complementary resources. IBM, Texas Instruments, Apple Computer, Du Pont Co., and Corning, Inc. are among the technology-centered companies that have formed alliances with both technology and nontechnology firms to push strategic development. Corning, for example, derives about half of its sales and earnings from technology-type joint ventures that leverage its skills in the glass and ceramic fields.

Another type of joint venture, sometimes referred to as a "near merger," combines existing subsidiary businesses of two or more companies. The aim is enhanced market clout. These types of partnerships frequently are forged in mature markets where the partners have relatively small shares but want to hang in as part owners of a larger enterprise. B.F. Goodrich and Uniroyal combined their tire businesses in efforts to create a stronger competitor to industry-leader Goodyear Tire & Rubber.

However, secondary players in growth markets have used the same tack. General Mills and Nestle joined forces to push worldwide expansion of their cereals businesses. General Mills also entered a JV with the Frito-Lay business of PepsiCo, Inc. to create a formidable player in the European snack food market. Eastman Kodak put its Sterling Drug subsidiary into a JV with Sanofi of France to create the research and marketing mass needed to compete in the globalizing and increasingly expensive pharmaceutical business. And Merck & Co. and Johnson & Johnson got together in a venture on over-the-counter pharmaceuticals, linking Merck's research prowess with J&J's marketing skills.

The JV log contains numerous cross-border combinations; that is, between companies situated in different countries. In entering a new country, a foreign firm frequently will take on a local partner that knows the territory and often is willing to chip in financially. The Toys "R" Us chain in Japan is a JV between Toys "R" Us of the United States, supplying the retailing skills and concepts, and McDonald's Japan, with its expertise in acquiring store sites in that land-scarce country.

There are numerous variations on the basic themes. JVs may be substitutes for acquisitions. When Philips NV of The Netherlands wanted to move its test and measurement instruments into the United States, it set up a reciprocal distribution venture with John Fluke Manufacturing, an American firm that makes similar products. Markets are widened for both firms as Fluke distributes the Philips lines through its established distribution system in the United States while Philips distributes Fluke products in Europe.

In a variation that combines elements of acquisitions and venturing, a JV can be created when a company sells part interest in a subsidiary to another business. Philips sold the Whirlpool Corp. of the United States a major stake in its home appliance business, which provided the American firm with entry into overseas markets. In some cases these deals may be preparatory to complete acquisition by the "investor," which is what happened when Whirlpool eventually bought out Philips's remaining interest.

There also has been considerable activity involving an operating company's sale of a part interest in a subsidiary to an LBO sponsor. Deals of this type often have occurred when the company regards its unit as being essentially in a different business, but cannot withdraw entirely from the scene. For example, manufacturing companies have sold partial interests in distribution subsidiaries to LBO investors, removed those assets from their books, and turned management over to the financial partner. The original parent decided that it must keep a hand in the distribution unit in order to keep its supply and distribution chain intact.

Finally, there is the joint venture acquisition in which two or more companies team up to buy an operating business, either to spread the cost or to carve up the jointly owned businesses at some future time and distribute specific assets to the partners that covet them most. When Loral Corp., the defense supplier, bought the Ford Aerospace unit of Ford Motor Co., it took in Lehman Brothers as a partner to help pay the purchase price of more than $1 billion.

A major trick in operating a JV is to ensure that the partners continue to like each other after the honeymoon, or at least as long as the perceived economic advantages can be realized. Obviously, many JVs collapse because the economics or technologies won't work. Indeed, many start-up type JVs are as big a gamble as speculative internal developments or acquisitions, and their casualty rate is high. But all too often, people clashes don't allow the venture even to reach that moment of truth.

As a result, it is imperative for joint venture partners to go beyond the numbers and the promises, and conduct due diligence probes as intensive as for any acquisition. Cultural hot spots must be identified and the partners must draft agreements—including mechanisms for exiting the investments on amicable terms— that deal with potential clashes. Up-front meetings of the minds on strategies, investment timetables, sharing of rewards, and the contribution of financial and other resources, as well as the proportionate distribution of ownership mirroring the contributions, are vital in preventing future sticking points.

While a sure-fire cure for cultural eruptions doesn't exist, experienced venturers say structure and governance systems are important. Ideally, the venture must be set up as an independent business, especially when there is 50-50 ownership, with the power and flexibility to make as many of its own decisions as possible without getting clearance from the parents. Personnel assigned to the venture should cut most of their ties with their old employers, even to the point of creating separate compensation and pension plans. A brand-new culture is desirable. The allocation of seats on the board and the board's powers should be spelled out.

Accounting, tax, financial, and legal issues also are prominent in JV formations. For example, owners of a 50-50 JV will use the equity method of accounting in plugging the venture's results into their own books, as will a partner with a minority interest. If one partner owns a majority, it can consolidate the JV's financials in its own. The JV may be structured as a corporation or a partnership, and the implications of each format must be studied before a choice is made.

STRATEGIC ALLIANCES

Except for the fact that they involve at least two companies, strategic alliances defy an exact definition. That is because they come in many formats and utilize many different approaches. However, it is generally agreed that a strategic alliance spreads an umbrella for longstanding business relationships between the allies. Under that rubric, the alliance may in fact lead to joint ventures on specific projects, technology sharing, marketing agreements, and other developmental approaches.

However, one feature that has been common to most arrangements is cross-shareholdings between the partners. Beverage producers Allied-Lyons of the United Kingdom and Suntory, Ltd., of Japan formed an alliance in which each bought small interests in the other and set the stage for a wide variety of allied projects such as distribution in each other's prime marketing territories. The strategic alliance between Renault of France and Volvo of Sweden included the purchase of interests in each other's truck units. And as illustrated by those examples, the strategic alliance invariably is a cross-border arrangement driven by the relentless globalization of key industries.

Since strategic alliances are relatively new and many of those formed are still being developed, their efficacy cannot yet be determined. However, the joint venture principles of establishing common goals and values and ameliorating culture clashes—especially critical in cross-border settings—are important.

MINORITY INVESTMENTS

Several large companies, especially in technology- or research-intensive fields, maintain active programs for taking minority positions in smaller businesses. Typically, the investee company is a smallish firm, public or private, that is working on a leading edge technology or product but needs a cash infusion to move forward. The big company provides the funds in return for positions on the board and other rewards.

The intent of the investment seldom is to eventually acquire the investee. Rather, many minority investments take on features of strategic alliances in which the investor company is interested mostly in manufacturing or marketing rights to the products or processes being developed. Why not acquire? The price of the investment usually is much cheaper, which mitigates risk, and if the investee is in a developmental stage, it is difficult to value. But perhaps most important, companies with active minority investment programs say they want the investee to maintain an entrepreneurial flavor that could be stifled if the small firm were incorporated within corporate bureaucracies.

As with all other corporate development initiatives, minority investments require considerable study before commitments are made.

Many investees remain stand-alone companies, and some have gone public with large returns for the investors. Eastman Kodak, IBM, Pfizer, Inc., AT&T, and SmithKline Beecham are among the companies with wide-ranging minority investment activities.

The minority investor also can be a "white squire" that insulates the investee company from being taken over unwillingly. For example, the voting power of AT&T's investment in Sun Microsystems expands sharply if Sun is attacked by a hostile suitor.

VENTURE CAPITAL

Venture capital investing by large companies is a first cousin to minority investments. The major difference is that investees are more like prototypical venture-capital-backed start-ups that have high promise but no track records. Easing the risk through relatively small commitments and the desire to let investees operate as entrepreneurial businesses also drive venture-capital investments.

The company with a venture-capital program typically sets it up as a separate unit staffed by experienced venture capitalists familiar with the risks and rewards and the analytical skills required to reach a decision.

Lubrizol Co., W.R. Grace, and the privately owned Hillman Co. are among the companies with venture-capital programs.

LICENSING

Licensing is a versatile corporate development device for adding value to an asset or increasing cash flow streams.

Licensing techniques are prominent in technology industries such as electronics, computers and computer peripherals, and pharmaceuticals. A company may license another business to use a patent or a proprietary product or process and receive royalties from the licensee. The technique can speed the payback from an expensive development and widen distribution in far-off markets with little or no investment. But the quid pro quo is that the licensing firm must surrender a part of the returns. Licensing also allows the developing firm to establish an especially strong process or technology breakthrough as the standard for its industry, thereby enhancing its position in its primary markets.

Licensing can also be used for names and trademarks. Rights to names can be licensed to firms in foreign countries; or they can be granted to firms outside the licensing firm's core business. Apparel manufacturers, for example, frequently license their brand names for clothing items they do not produce.

MARKETING AGREEMENTS

Companies reaching marketing agreements with other firms usually are trying to widen the distribution of their products at the lowest cost. In some cases, however, one of the parties to the agreement lacks marketing skills or a distribution network, and is joining with a firm that can do a better selling job. Additionally, marketing agreements may call for reciprocal distribution in which the partners have experience in different core markets. Marketing agreements often are made between companies based in different countries.

TECHNOLOGY SHARING

The escalating cost of developing technology has driven many research-intensive companies to share their know-how and their developments. For openers, the agreement usually covers a pooling of knowledge or joint efforts on a specific project. Marketing agreements, licenses, and royalties may follow.

FRANCHISING

Operating companies historically have suffered harsh experiences in franchising their names or operations. That is usually because franchising is a specific business involving a special mind-set and expertise in real estate, marketing, services, and often-fractious franchisee relations which most operating companies lack. Corporate development professionals seldom recommend franchising unless the company sets it up as a self-contained business staffed by franchising professionals, or farms the program out to a franchising specialty firm under very strict guidelines.

WHICH WAY TO GO

The choices are varied and none is perfect. But the options offer a business a menu of options that can be culled to determine which is best for reaching the perennial goal of generating value-creating growth. Since each is replete with numerous trade-offs, solid analysis is necessary to map out the optimal path.

8

A Game Plan for Development

Diane C. Harris

Vice President, Corporate Development,
Bausch & Lomb Incorporated,
Rochester, New York

Since the establishment of Bausch & Lomb's mergers and acquisitions program in the early 1980s, half of the company's growth has come from acquisitions, licensings, technology agreements, and, to a lesser extent, joint ventures and equity participations. Collectively, these external growth strategies are called "new ventures," and are distinguished from internal growth strategies such as research and development, market expansion, or new applications for current products. During the 1980s, there were 150 transactions completed, amounting to more than $500 million in market value. In addition, 20 operations were divested, many in the mid-1980s as part of a corporate restructuring, for a value of over $150 million. Acquisitions have been at the heart of Bausch & Lomb's 16 percent annual growth rate. Thirty of these acquisitions ranged in size from less than $1 million in purchase price, to $133 million for Dental Research Corporation in 1988. For 1990 through 1992, based only on acquisitions done during the prior five years, 15 to 20 percent of Bausch & Lomb's growth in any particular year came from acquisitions. Regardless of how the data are viewed, acquisitions and other new ventures have been, and continue to be, key strategies for Bausch & Lomb's growth.

As Bausch & Lomb changed, so too did Corporate Development, which supports the CEO in implementing the company's external growth strategies. Corporate Development at Bausch & Lomb has gone through four definable periods:

- Establishment
- Restructuring

- Central execution
- Decentralization

Corporate Development now is entering a period of balance between central execution and decentralization, flexibly providing both service and control. Each of these phases will be discussed.

PHASE 1 (1981–83): ESTABLISHING THE CORPORATE DEVELOPMENT FUNCTION

Although historically Bausch & Lomb had grown from both internal and external strategies, in 1981 we were not actively pursuing an organized new ventures program. In earlier years Bausch & Lomb had purchased a few companies and pursued several licenses, but by 1981 we were seeing very little deal flow and were executing, at most, only one or two small deals a year.

The establishment of Corporate Development followed a four-part strategy:

Strategic Planning.   A strategic planning process was developed to identify business strengths and weaknesses and focus on opportunities that could be captured through a new ventures program. A particular success was separation of strategic issues from financial plan development. Freeing strategic thought from the "numbers exercise" put more focus on opportunity and creativity. A management decision was made to capitalize on Bausch & Lomb's strengths. We used various outside consultants who were helpful in individual businesses, but not in the development of overall strategic vision. In the end, that had to be done internally.

Developing Deal Flow.   In 1981, Bausch & Lomb had contact with only a handful of banks and intermediaries for M&A purposes. We began to create a global network, which is still being expanded, to establish contact with more than 1,000 intermediaries worldwide and seek opportunities that meet Bausch & Lomb's acquisition criteria. The hardest part of developing deal flow was convincing intermediaries that Bausch & Lomb was going to become a true dealmaking company so that they could treat us like the "A team" and trust we would behave that way. Initially, we tried to use a third party to develop intermediary relationships. Although it gave us a model to follow, ultimately we had to develop our own relationships. The most important ingredient in turning around the intermediaries' mind-set was the way we actively began to do deals. Until then, it was only words and promises.

Some corporate development professionals do not believe in using banks, brokers, or intermediaries to find deals. In evolving a corporate development function, we took the opposite tack, deciding that not to use such help would be like climbing a rope with one hand tied behind our backs. The network we established continues to be helpful even many years later, and there certainly are deals we would not have been able to do without this kind of help. We see about 1000 deals per year, and consistently complete 2 to 3 percent.

Developing a Technical Base. Although we wanted to use outside help, we did not want to be dependent on outsiders. Therefore, we developed our own in-house valuation, deal searching, analysis, and due diligence capabilities. Besides adding those capabilities to Corporate Development, we found it necessary to work with many areas of the corporate staff to raise the corporation's overall dealmaking capability. Experience proved to be the test as well as the teacher.

Changing Internal Mind-Set. Just as it was necessary to change the attitudes of intermediaries toward Bausch & Lomb's M&A program, it was necessary to change our own internal mind-sets, to make our organization not just tolerant of but hungry for growth. It is easy for operating managers to be too busy to look at new ventures, for the "plate" to be "too full." The CEO's involvement in this process is critical. We had monthly operations committee meetings in which division presidents were expected to bring forth their growth opportunities. Lost opportunity has a real cost to the shareholder, too, and that needs to be recognized.

It is easy for Corporate Development inadvertently to become competitive with Research and Development in scrambling for funds. Often, millions of dollars are spent on a transaction, while R&D works under budgets constrained by current earnings-per-share considerations. We were committed to seeing that such competition did not evolve and were able to achieve harmony by involving R&D deeply in new business evaluation. Eventually, some of our acquisitions brought new R&D opportunities and cross-fertilization to the research and development process. We run corporate development as a 100% effort, as if R&D were never going to develop a new product, and we encourage R&D to run at a 100% effort as if the "new ventures" function would never find another "deal." Together, these complementary strategies give our management the best choices in "make versus buy" and our shareholders the best opportunity for returns.

Of the four elements of establishing a new ventures process, the most difficult was changing organizational mind-set. Changing mind-set is an effort that should never stop; a changed mind-set soon slips away, like a muscle unexercised. The biggest factor in changing mind-set was the CEO's involvement, followed by the success of a number of new ventures. Soon the excitement spreads and people, especially in middle management, want to work on deal teams.

During this early phase (1981 to mid-1984) we had some successes—notably the acquisition of Polymer Technology Corp., producer of gas permeable lenses, which grew from $6.8 million in sales in 1983 to the $85 million business it is today; and Charles River Laboratories, which broadened Bausch & Lomb's health care position in the new sector of biomedical supply.

All of our early deals were not successes, but we learned. From an early failure in the acquisition of a California-based laser company, we learned the importance of an "operating champion," a person who would personally be committed to the success of each new venture. We found out how necessary it is to be more comprehensive in our due diligence, especially regulatory due diligence which had failed to identify a major change in the regulatory environment of the Food and Drug Administration (FDA). We also learned how vital good management is to acquisition success. We continue to reject opportunities if the management doesn't plan to continue with the business.

During Phase 1 of Bausch & Lomb's new ventures program we began to clarify the kinds of companies we wanted—companies in a health care niche that enjoyed worldwide position, market leadership, profitability, good growth potential, and a committed management with whom we could share a common vision. Some people were surprised when we bought Charles River Laboratories, but it met all the requirements we had articulated for an addition to the Bausch & Lomb family, especially successful management that is willing to continue to do what they do best, unencumbered by interference from a new parent.

PHASE 2 (1984–85): RESTRUCTURING

After a few initial successful acquisitions, licensings, and other external transactions, it became clear that the other side of the strategic vision soon would need to be implemented. That was the divestiture of businesses that no longer strategically fit Bausch & Lomb's health care vision, diluted management attention and shareholder returns, and offered only low returns and inadequate opportunity for growth. In 1984 we announced a reserve of $9 million to divest the industrial instruments group. Being able to announce the divestitures publicly was of enormous benefit in having open employee communications that made our divestiture efforts even more effective. Managers and key staff people were given incentives for staying and assisting with the sale.

As a result of the openness, potential buyers had more open access to information, and a secretive, counterproductive environment was avoided. The "people" element was the key to divestiture success. The highest offer for one operation was turned down because the buyer would not guarantee to keep the operation where it was located and minimize the risk of terminating long-time employees. Minimum periods of employment and some continuation of Bausch & Lomb's severance plan were negotiated on behalf of the employees of the divested operations.

A number of industrial instruments businesses were sold off, including military optics, precision optics, spectrometers, analytical instruments, scanning electron microscopes, digital readouts for machine tools, recorders, plotters, digitizers, and CAD/CAM equipment. (The eyeglass frame and lens business, including ophthalmic laboratories, had been sold previously.) As of late 1987 we had also sold off the microscope, photogrammetry, and ophthalmic instrument operations.

Divestitures represent an intensive, all-consuming effort. A year in divestitures is worth about five years in acquisitions as a training ground for new M&A people and aspiring dealmakers. During this period, we met people who were as good as their word and those who weren't; those who "due diligenced" a deal to death, and those who were quick and efficient. We learned a lot from being on the selling side of the table, especially what kind of acquirer we wanted to be, how we wanted to be treated as buyers, and how we should treat sellers. On one transaction we contacted 480 prospective buyers; on another we negotiated for 28 hours straight. We learned that there are 100 reasons why any deal can't be done. The successful dealmaker finds the 101st reason to do it. When completed, the divestitures realized more than $100 million for redeployment, and the proceeds were within the reserves and time frame established.

PHASE 3 (1986–89): CENTRALIZED M&A

Following the completion of Bausch & Lomb's divestiture program, our deal skills were sufficiently honed to pursue further growth through acquisition. Management attention turned to implementing major growth strategies. In 1986, Bausch & Lomb acquired Berlin-based Dr. Mann Pharma, an ophthalmic pharmaceutical and over-the-counter health care products company, for nearly $100 million. Adding to this entry into a new sector was the 1987 acquisition of Pharmafair, a U.S. generic ophthalmic drug company. Then, in 1988, another new sector was entered with the $133 million acquisition of Dental Research Corp., implementing a long-targeted entry into the oral care business. Another worldwide sector, hearing aids, was entered on a small entrepreneurial basis in 1989.

The approach to new ventures at Bausch & Lomb has been flexible, utilizing whatever deal structure seemed most appropriate for the business needs of both buyer and seller. For that reason, licensing never has been separated from acquisition, as it has in some companies. Deal structure should not be driven by organizational structure. In some cases, a licensing agreement was a better alternative than full acquisition. In other cases, a technology agreement, minority investment, or joint venture was the most effective way to proceed.

By the end of the centralized period, Bausch & Lomb had completed 105 M&A transactions, accounting for more than $625 million in market value. Of these transactions, 26 were acquisitions, 13 were divestitures, and 47 were licensings. Of the remainder, 12 were technology agreements, five were joint ventures, and two were equity participations. Both the good news and bad news was that during this very active deal period, we bid in auctions but never won. This may be due in part to having control of our own valuation process and refusing to overpay.

A corporate strategic goal had been to reach $1 billion in sales by 1990 without significantly diluting our financial ratios. In 1989, a year ahead of schedule, the target was reached, and more than 50 percent of our growth came from the new ventures program. By the end of 1989, the four new sectors of biomedical research, ophthalmic pharmaceuticals, oral care, and hearing aids had been entered. New opportunities were being added in most sectors of Bausch & Lomb's business, creating synergies after the initial transactions. A new target was set—to reach $2.5 billion in sales by 1995, particularly by growing the oral care, over-the-counter health care, and international businesses.

The major acquisitions of 1986 to 1989 were accomplished mostly on a decentralized basis. Just two of us in Corporate Development negotiated most of the transactions, and centralized activity assured full coordination and control. But a reevaluation of the new ventures program was necessary if growth to the $2.5 billion level was to be reached without letting centralized control become a bottleneck. As a result of benchmarking the dealmaking process at some 20 other companies, we developed data that pointed to a correlation between centralization and lower deal intensity, so we systematically began to decentralize the new ventures process.

PHASE 4 (1990–   ): DECENTRALIZATION OF NEW VENTURES

Although divided into four phases for the purpose of this discussion, no phase was completely isolated from the others. In truth, a few aspects of new ventures were being decentralized to some degree as early as 1987, as operating units became capable of taking on various responsibilities.

We defined six aspects of dealmaking for decentralization purposes:

- The presentation/approval process
- Analysis and valuation
- Sourcing
- Due diligence
- "Running the deal"
- Negotiating and deal structuring

Approvals.   The first element to decentralize was presentation of deals for approval. The early advent of the operating champion concept, and the need for strong advocacy signaled the move of Corporate Development into more objective reviews of proposed operating unit transactions. Simultaneous with the increase in operating unit responsibility, a formal new ventures policy was put in place. One of the keys to effective decentralization is an adequate, but not overcontrolled approval policy. Still continuing today is a three-step approval policy:

- Approval to enter into final negotiation
- Approval of the proposed transaction
- Final contract approval, just prior to signing

It is also a corporate policy that letters of intent are subject to approval prior to being sent out and before vital resources are expended by both parties.

Analysis and Valuation.   The analysis of an opportunity, especially the valuation (usually based on deal-market multiples and discounted cash flow analysis) has been progressively decentralized to the operating units. It is a vital skill to have in place prior to beginning negotiations and deal structuring, and it gives an operating unit the opportunity to experiment with its own scenarios, sensitivities, strategies, and synergies. A corporate model and its attendant software were developed and made available to each operating unit. Any variation or exception in the use of the model is brought to our attention. It gives Corporate Development the opportunity to be more objective in the review process.

One element of valuation retained by Corporate Development involves the collection of multiples, especially deal multiples. To be sure the data base is up to date and that resources are not duplicated, we provide this service companywide.

Sourcing.   At one time, during centralized new ventures, if an opportunity were missed (i.e., a competing buyer bought a company or technology that would have been of interest to Bausch & Lomb without our having had an opportunity to bid), Corporate Development would have been almost entirely responsible. As decentralization proceeded, this responsibility began to be shared with the operating units. Their charters or missions are developed during the strategic planning process, and any opportunity that lies within a business unit's charter should now be pursued directly by the unit. This is in contrast to procedures at some companies where only Corporate Development makes these contacts. The control element that balances this degree of decentralization is that the units must keep Corporate Development posted on contacts being made and the progress of their deals. If a deal were missed today, the operating unit would have primary responsibility, because it should be pursuing opportunities of interest within its charter. Corporate Development, however, would also be responsible if the opportunity came through a banking, broker, or intermediary network.

Still reserved for Corporate Development, and likely to continue to be so in the foreseeable future, are the worldwide intermediary contacts. The global nature of banking today and the liability of fees or even double fees make this control reasonable. But the operating units make their needs known and Corporate Development maintains a regular program of updating intermediaries on what Bausch & Lomb wants. Operating units use all other methods for deal sourcing: consultants (on a fee-for-service rather than transaction basis), personal contacts, meetings, trade shows, and so on.

Due Diligence.   In order to truly have accountability for a transaction, it was obvious that an operating unit also would need due diligence responsibility. Bausch & Lomb divides due diligence into three areas: financial, legal, and business. Financial due diligence often requires the help of corporate finance, tax, treasury, and accounting as well as the outside auditors. Legal due diligence requires corporate counsel and sometimes outside counsel, especially in unfamiliar geographic areas. Outside counsel also may be involved in specialty matters such as patent, regulatory, and environmental issues. Although corporate resources may be used in both these instances, it is still an operating unit's responsibility to accept and endorse the due diligence done at its request and on its behalf. The business due diligence is even more clearly an operating unit responsibility. The further away the due diligence is from the current experience and expertise of the operating unit, the more likely that outside consultants will be used.

Running the Deal.   This element of dealmaking is as much a mind-set as an activity. It involves internal coordination of division resources as well as corporate resources needed for deal completion. It involves overseeing the contractualization effort, arranging timely meetings, assuring that all commitments are kept, elevating important issues, and, in short, doing whatever it takes to get the deal done. One characteristic of a successful new ventures person, whether at the corporate or operating unit level, is the ability to "multiplex," to juggle many different projects of varying priorities and yet move them all ahead. This is one of the more difficult skills to assess in potential M&A staff, and the inability of people to handle multiple projects is one of the most frequent reasons for failure.

Deal Structuring and Negotiation.   This has been the last of the six deal steps to decentralize. The risk is higher. It is important to have all of the other five steps in place before attempting to decentralize deal structuring and negotiating. We connect deal structuring and negotiating in the belief that dealmaking is an iterative process, as one moves from deal structuring to negotiating, then back again to deal structuring.

Corporate Development participates in the process of hiring divisional New Ventures personnel, and in their training. One of the more difficult aspects of training and teaching deal structuring and negotiating is how to give the potential dealmaker a sufficient repertoire of deal structuring skills to substitute for many years' experience at the negotiating table. Outside courses are used, as are co-negotiating, and a "buddy system" of contract review. New Ventures staff from the operating units are invited to gather once a month for deal-structure brainstorming, deal autopsies, and reviews of unusual structures for completed deals. Operating unit New Ventures staffs draw on each other, as well as on Corporate Development, as information resources. Equally important as basic skills training, is giving each negotiator a sufficient understanding of Bausch & Lomb's values and culture to enable him or her to represent the company credibly and fairly. A fundamental belief of our New Ventures training is that there is no substitute for individual and corporate credibility.

When a New Ventures person is ready, Corporate Development and the operating unit head jointly recommend to the CEO that he or she be named a "qualified negotiator." In 1992 we had four qualified negotiators at operating units, along with two in Corporate Development and three more in training.

Some operating units, usually because of insufficient deal flow or lack of dedicated New Ventures staff, do not have qualified negotiators and may not be decentralized in certain other aspects either. In these cases, Corporate Development provides needed services to the operating unit. If the transaction is large, the deal is outside of operating unit charters, or the project involves multiple divisions (such as Bausch & Lomb's worldwide sponsorship of the Olympic Games), all of the foregoing six steps are the responsibility of Corporate Development. Except for these cases, decentralization has cast Corporate Development as more of a coach and counselor, as well as wearer of the corporate governance hat of review and control. More importantly, decentralization has been effective in removing many barriers to further growth. In 1989, Corporate Development executed or played a major role in 16 of 21 deals. In 1992, 19 of 24 transactions were completed by operating units. Even more significantly, not being burdened with the execution of smaller transactions has enabled Corporate Development to play more of a coaching role, especially eliminating problems in deal structuring early in the process. We are expecting further benefits from being able to concentrate more on corporate strategic growth and do larger deals as decentralization solidifies.

PHASE 5 (1993–   ): FUTURE PLANS

We don't expect the current organizational structure to be static. There already are indications that in some years New Ventures personnel may transfer back to Corporate Development to serve multiple operating units, as a particular unit's deal needs change. Flexible resources, available when needed on a decentralized basis or provided when appropriate as a corporate service, will probably be the direction over the next few years. The emphasis on external strategies is being broadened to include new technology search beyond the normal planning horizon of the operating units. Bausch & Lomb also is moving to implement operating organization changes and to vest resources in fully regionalized headquarters in Tokyo for the Far East, Rochester for the Western Hemisphere, and London for Europe, Africa, and the Middle East. For the first time, a New Ventures person has been added outside the United States.

We believe that staying open and flexible is the key to making these structures work. Having been through the full centralization/decentralization cycle, we probably are better equipped than ever to deal with the appropriate future Corporate Development/Operating Unit New Ventures organizational structure and balance.

To better articulate such diverse roles, we've put forth a Corporate Development values statement, developed through consensus of the operating units' New Ventures staff (Table 8.1). Understanding "where we are coming from" contributes to

Table 8.1. Corporate Development Values

Maintain personal and departmental integrity and credibility, both inside and outside the company.

Inspire attitudes and activities that recognize and nurture new ventures as key to Bausch & Lomb's growth.

Capture the opportunity to look at any new ventures situation that fits corporate or operating unit charters.

Be responsive to and perceived as responsive to new ventures needs wherever they arise in the company, adding value without diminishing any operating unit's ownership of its own transactions.

Provide leadership to the new ventures process and quality monitoring and review of new ventures, advising as needed and being proactive in minimizing the risk of each transaction.

Provide quality mentoring and coaching to the new ventures team throughout the company.

Complete transactions that enhance shareholders' value and in which we all can be proud to have been involved, long after the transaction is completed.

the fine balance of teamwork and corporate governance and has gone a long way toward developing a positive working environment.

We've also clarified for the operating unit officers what it takes to effectively manage and evaluate New Ventures staff. A list of 17 elements of effectiveness for a New Ventures manager is in Table 8.2. Corporate Development encourages dialogue between a division president and New Ventures people to clarify expectations and focus on problems. The coaching role of Corporate Development continues to be important.

Finally, we're focusing more on the role of quality in Corporate Development and New Ventures departments. In 1991 we surveyed the internal customers to whom we provide service through both blind questionnaires and independent consultant interviews. The aspects of Corporate Development quality judged most important by internal customers were competence and creativity, with timeliness, relevance, and credibility also regarded as important. Overall ratings were excellent, but certain ideas that emerged are being implemented to create even more value, such as the formation of an internal venture program. Currently, we have an entrepreneurial task force addressing methods and processes for more effectively managing start-up and internal ventures.

Also on a blind basis, we surveyed banks and intermediaries with whom we've dealt for at least three years. Response to the mailing was 30 percent. We presented nine areas for the intermediaries to rate, and found that access to the CEO and responsiveness were most important to them in working with a corporate development department. Surprisingly, intermediary policy and regular communication were down on the list. We used a survey that rated Bausch & Lomb for each of the nine factors against each intermediary's perception of the very best company in that category, excluding Bausch & Lomb. Overall, our score was 8.2 percent compared to 8.4 percent for the "best companies."

Table 8.2. Division New Ventures Person (DNVP) Performance Appraisal

1. Has the DNVP understood and been responsive to the new ventures strategy set by the operating unit president, yet still evidenced independent thinking regarding potential deals, even to the point of internal advocacy? _____

2. Has the DNVP been responsive to all deal flow, whatever the source, and handled it in a timely manner, making sure none 'falls in the cracks,' that necessary decisions are requested and relationships maintained?_____

3. Has the DNVP been proactive in identifying companies which fit within the division's charter, in catalyzing appropriate contact with the companies of expected future importance, and in maintaining those relationships with a good sense of timing and follow-through?_____

4. Has the DNVP been proactive and aggressive in contacting the division president on a real-time basis regarding new ventures developments, and requesting decisions regarding projects for which the DNVP is not empowered to decide? _____

5. Does the DNVP request resource when needed, and effectively manage that resource during the dealmaking process (analysis, valuation, due diligence), involving that process neither too early (wasting resource) nor too late (putting the deal at risk)?_____

6. Does the DNVP efficiently and effectively bring in the appropriate people to each new ventures team, coordinate the due diligence effort to minimize disruption to the organization, and communicate important deal activity on a timely basis within the division?__

7. Does the DNVP understand the corporate new ventures policy and act in accordance with that policy, providing guidance to the division as needed, and maintaining the right balance between division and corporate needs? _____

8. Does the DNVP provide coaching, counseling and guidance to those other division personnel who participate in the new ventures process, and in general raise the level of functioning of new ventures within the operating unit?_____

9. Is the feedback received from outside the company with respect to the DNVP's representing Bausch & Lomb favorable to the company, credible, and consistent with the image and values the division president and Bausch & Lomb want to convey?_____

10. Does the DNVP effectively utilize corporate staff resources with respect to the new ventures process, stimulating a spirit of open communication and challenging others to reach a high quality of dealmaking? _____

11. Does the DNVP drive for 'truth' in the due diligence effort, elevating issues to division management on a timely and thorough basis, with recommendations for minimizing risk?_____

12. Does the DNVP identify and surface deal-killer issues early to protect resource utilization?

13. Is the DNVP technically competent in valuation, deal sourcing, initiation of contacts, confidentiality agreements, negotiating, deal structuring, due diligence and contractualization, and does the DNVP stay current in the field? _____

14. Does the DNVP pull together and make an appropriate presentation to the Management Executive Committee and/or the Board of Directors, assuring that all the relevant issues are addressed in a timely manner?_____

15. Is the DNVP creative in finding solutions to problems encountered in individual deals and in applying the strategic charter of the division to real-world opportunities? _____

16. Is the DNVP able to balance the larger aspect of strategic dealmaking with the detailed focus of negotiating and contractualization? _____

17. Does the DNVP's efforts result in meaningful transactions for the operating unit? _____

The third element of our quality program was to continue benchmarking "peer companies," a process begun in 1990 to validate our decentralization decision. Benchmarking will be an ongoing process as we work to stay on the leading edge.

Overall, the trend for the next three years should be a balance between centralization and decentralization, with flexibility in changing the degree of each, as needed. We see a finer balance between the collegial coaching/training/service aspects and corporate governance issues. We've matured enough to institutionalize the dealmaking mind-set and growth orientation, with values clarification, performance criteria, and a quality program. And we are working to attract new ventures staff who do well in both corporate and operating unit environments.

Our deal activity continues to grow. In 1992, we completed 24 transactions and added the largest dollar volume to our sales base through acquisition since we started the new ventures program. Our goal of $2.5 billion by 1995 continues to be on target. As we move toward that target, we must keep in mind that the portion of the company most completely dedicated to change, Corporate Development, always must be able to change.

9

Strategic Synergies: Fact or Fiction?

William F. Achtmeyer

Managing Director, Talisman, Inc.,
Boston, Massachusetts

How often in the acquisition business have you heard, "Of course this is a good deal! Look at all the synergies available"? That may well be true, but in reality, the hoped-for synergies often are far more elusive than most buyers understand or acknowledge in the heat of the battle.

What is synergy anyway? Literally, it is defined as "combined action," but specifically in the M&A world, it means the enhanced economic value created by the merger of buyer and seller. This is often translated into "2 + 2 = 5."

In a decade of helping corporations add value for shareholders through M&A transactions, I have developed these four rules:

- Paying more than 20 cents on the dollar for synergy is foolish.
- The best synergies are cost-related, not revenue-related.
- No synergy is realistically achieved after the first two years following the merger.
- There must be a clear-cut game plan to find the synergies *before* the merger and it must be understood by both parties.

SETTING UP THE GAME PLAN

Of these four rules, the last is arguably the most difficult, but in my opinion, the most critical to the success of a deal. To cite an oft-quoted financial spokesperson, the only way to create value is to "earn it." This means there's no silver bullet in finding the deal-saving synergies. What management needs throughout the merger and integration process is basic blocking and tackling. In forming your game plan, here are the key issues to keep in mind:

- Make sure you understand why you're buying the target instead of making its products in-house.
- Apply very strict guidelines to all acquisition candidates and be willing to wait to get them.
- Invest whatever it takes up front; your effort will pay rich dividends at the end.
- Decide what you're going to offer for the business and what your walk-away price is before you get involved in the deal. Otherwise, good luck!
- Communicate your plans to target company management as quickly as possible.
- Start the integration process immediately after the deal is closed.
- Ensure that you've got the best people working for you. With this plan in hand, management can do a better job of identifying the real synergies.

VALUE OF EARLY RETURNS

Since boards of directors and investors like to see a deal pay off in two to three years, look first for those synergies that yield a quick payback. While these fast returns are making you look good, you can begin to look for those that take a little longer.

Frequently the best synergies are cost synergies which offer the highest probability of being properly implemented if they are acted on quickly. Some of the most productive of these include distribution systems, sales force rationalization, and the consolidation and reduction of SG&A expenses.

Revenue synergies, on the other hand, are interesting and eventually profitable, but they are subject to time-consuming arguments about how they are going to be developed.

DUE DILIGENCE: BEYOND THE STANDARD PRACTICE

In the search of synergy, due diligence can be a most valuable tool. As traditionally understood, due diligence is an accounting, legal, and financial exercise that looks at the quantitative side of the valuation process but doesn't go very far in reviewing why the deal should be done in the first place, or how 2 and 2 will equal 5. This is because even the most proficient outside advisers—investment bankers, lawyers, accountants—who serve management in the due diligence process, don't have a clue about whether the new company is going to work. That's still up to management.

Unfortunately, senior management is usually the only group in the company that knows about the deal in advance, and the senior managers have their hands full. Yet, they must play a strategic role in an enhanced due diligence process, asking insightful questions and gathering information that is critical in planning for post-merger success.

To help management focus on its role, I suggest three steps:

Identify a transition team. The players on this team should be the stars of the business, not just the managers who have time on their hands. And the group should include the best people on both sides of the transaction—acquirer and target. They should begin by questioning the most fundamental assumptions of the business.

Identify the key profit and control levers. Organize the transition team's functions by profit levers, not by functions. This will require a reasonably detailed understanding of the action steps to find the desired synergies.

Set specific and realizable short-term goals. Everyone needs a win after a deal. But rather than simply setting goals for their own sake, set them in the context of the company's real long-term objectives.

INTEGRATION: THE FIRST SIX MONTHS

After the champagne and celebration, the buyer is faced with the reality of creating value and doing it fast. As the combined management team searches for synergies, two basic issues get in the way of the operation:

Merging is an unusual act! This is especially true for the acquired company! There are a large number of extraordinarily complex decisions (from who will be the surviving CEO, to how the benefits program should be merged) that must be made quickly. In fact, for the truly successful acquisition, the trajectory of the business must be changed within the first six months.

Merging isn't the only thing the companies are doing. In the euphoria of completing the deal it's tempting for the buyer to focus completely on integration. Unfortunately, there are still two businesses to be run—the acquirer's and the target's.

These two considerations hover in the background as the buyer ponders its approach to integration. On one hand, the buyer can keep hands-off and not rock the boat. After all, it paid a hefty premium for the new company as is and may not want the target management to do anything different. This inevitably will lead to confusion on the part of the acquired company, which recognized the premium paid for it and expects decisive leadership from its new parent.

On the other hand, the buyer may adopt the carpetbagger approach. Its people will go in with all guns blazing, making sure that all of them understand that they are going to be shot. That's a good strategy if everything is buttoned up before you start. It's particularly ineffective if your tactics are: ready, fire, aim! Either approach has the same effect—a downward spiraling situation.

It is difficult to get an in-between approach. But there are some things to think about in terms of shared commitment between the two companies, even if the merger was a hostile deal. The buying company should have a clear understanding of what it's doing in terms of management, values, and so on, and the ground rules should be well understood by the acquiree. New reporting relationships should be established quickly. When tough decisions are needed, they should be made in the first 90 days following the merger. People expect them, so they might as well be done as soon as possible. That brings a breath of fresh air and the honesty associated with it and puts the merged company on the path of realizing its full potential.

There are several elements required to do that well. One is an incredibly talented senior management team that's committed to the game plan. Second is a group of people under them that really helps them plan every step along the way. And finally, some outside facilitation. Acquirers should find someone with an independent view—be it a former employee or board member, an industry expert, or a consultant—to play the role of the facilitator. That person or group of people will learn a lot more than the insiders ever will learn as a transaction proceeds.

SUCCESS AND FAILURE

Finding success is difficult as the financial reporting becomes blurred post-merger. However, some of the more recent examples of success are:

- Baxter International's merger with American Hospital Supply Corp., in which distribution savings proved to be enormous.
- American Home Products Co.'s takeover of A.H. Robins, Inc., in which the combined force of the product lines in the consumer health care and pharmaceutical markets led to the elimination of significant costs in overhead, marketing, and operations.
- Dun & Bradstreet, Inc.'s merger with IMS International Inc., in which the financial and technological muscle of D&B permitted IMS to maintain its leadership position in the pharmaceutical market research industry.

Another case of a merger done beautifully was Allied Corp.'s purchase of the Bendix Corp. in 1983. Edward Hennessey, the Allied CEO, spent an inordinate amount of time on this transaction. He had other things he could have done, but he elected to speak to 500 Bendix managers and their spouses over an eight-week period. He made face-to-face presentations to 6,000 people, had them videotaped, and sent them to 105,000 additional people.

Hennessey spoke about specific items, such as why Allied paid as much as it did. He explained what was expected of the Bendix employees and noted exactly how the combined company was going to be reorganized. The stock went up 31 percent, profitability increased by 80 percent, and all the senior managers stayed.

Schlumberger, Ltd. had a different approach when it bought Fairchild Camera & Instrument Co., a technology company with a major position in semiconductors. Schlumberger managers walked in and said, "You're all frogs and we're going to turn you into princes." That went over so well with the Fairchild managers that they left in droves. Revenue dropped and Fairchild has never been the company it was when it was acquired.

PLANNING AND VISION

Determining whether there are strategic synergies in your deal calls for strong strategic vision. This comes from advanced planning. Involve yourself and get the top executives and most talented people from both firms to participate. Define the action plans specifically, along with the roles people will play. And apply strong merger principles throughout.

PART 2

Organizing to Merge and Acquire

10

The Internal Acquisition Team

Albert T. Olenzak
Strategic Planning Consultant,
Media, Pennsylvania

Malcolm I. Ruddock
Treasurer, Sun Co., Inc.,
Philadelphia, Pennsylvania

The acquisition of another company is an inherently risky proposition. The corporate landscape is littered with poorly conceived, planned, or implemented acquisitions that led directly to the acquirer's loss of shareholder value, and, in some cases, to corporate failure. However, there are also notable examples of corporations that have used acquisitions as a powerful long-term corporate development tool.

There is no absolute guarantee of success in the acquisition process, but the acquisition that is planned and implemented by a carefully chosen team of internal and external professional specialists, working with line management, has the best odds of improving shareholder value. The acquisition team consists of three distinct subgroups of individuals with overlapping responsibilities. They cover the following functional activities of the acquisition process:

- Planning
- Transaction analysis
- Implementation

115

The composition and size of the team are dependent on numerous factors, the most important of which are:

- Complexity of transaction
- Type of transaction: related business or diversification
- Size of acquisition versus size of acquirer
- Size and experience of acquirer's staff

The team always should be under the control of line management, and line management should participate actively in *all* stages of the process. Decision making for every stage should be controlled internally and not delegated to external professionals, such as investment bankers and lawyers. There can be a tendency to permit external professionals to make important decisions because of the complexities of transactions and difficulties with time constraints. At the same time, however, the team should heed the advice of those highly skilled professionals, who are retained at great cost.

If a proposed acquisition represents a diversification, the composition of the acquisition team should include outside expertise. This is especially important in the planning and evaluation stage. When Sun Co. diversified into wholesale distribution, for example, it retained as a member of the team a former chief executive officer of a large participant in the wholesale distribution industry. For planning and implementation of diversification into the general freight trucking industry, Sun retained one of the most experienced transportation consulting groups in the country to assist in planning, selection of criteria, and implementation. The consulting firm performed operating audits of acquisition candidates prior to closing that proved to be invaluable. In both of these major diversification moves, Sun was very successful. Without these outside groups, major mistakes could have been made by moves into unrelated businesses.

With these general comments on the overall process, the composition and activities of the subgroups involved in the acquisition process now can be explored in detail.

THE PLANNING PHASE

Successful mergers and acquisitions are the result of combining keen conceptual preparation with incisive and timely implementation. One without the other is an invitation to disaster. And there is a lot at stake: In few other activities can management significantly change the basic character of a company and affect the welfare of the shareholders in so short a time.

Academic analyses of case histories over many years confirm what most managers know intuitively. First, the target company's shareholders, who can pay taxes and reinvest immediately in a portfolio of similar companies, receive an instantaneous transfer of wealth. Second, although there may be big winners and big losers over time, the data show over and over again that, on *average,* the acquirer can expect to break even.

The general objective of all merger-acquisition activity is to increase shareholder value—a difficult task. Therefore, planners must be on the team and must be intimately involved—not only in the initial search phase, but in the final decision as well. The final purchase price not only must be a function of the heated give-and-take of negotiation, but must be constrained by estimates of true strategic value.

Selection for Strategic Fit

The initial selection of acquisition targets is a function of the strategic needs and preferences of the company and its management. Strategy should be stated explicitly. The most important consideration is whether the target is in a related or unrelated business.

The "related" merger is essentially a growth or expansion thrust aimed at increasing market share, expanding product lines, acquiring necessary resources, or fully utilizing an existing capability. It aims at synergy and is easily understood by management, but may trigger antitrust difficulties. Relatedness may vary from acquiring a company in the same business to building on a specific division's expertise—sometimes called "linked" relatedness.

Unrelated acquisitions are sought to diversify the ongoing earnings of the company; although antitrust problems are minimized, synergy is difficult to achieve, and companies run the risk of misunderstanding and mismanaging the new business. A number of theorists frown on conglomerate mergers because, critics claim, they accomplish little that shareholders cannot do for themselves.

Acquisitions also may be thought of as offensive or defensive. An offensive move is simply the best way among various alternatives to carry out a corporate strategy. Most related acquisitions and some diversifications fall in this class. Defensive acquisitions, on the other hand, are responses to the inability of management to create enough investment opportunities internally or to the threat of the firm itself being acquired. Defensive actions often are somewhat unfocused or opportunistic. However, most top managers feel a strong obligation to ensure the survival of the corporation and its employees by being certain that the firm has future investment opportunities. Often, this entails considerable risk and may take the form of venture or new technology company acquisitions.

In addition, managers will often set additional preferences or constraints such as size, geography, or financial parameters, the list being as long as the number of mergers done. Whatever the final selection screen, it is important to realize that consideration of strategic fit is but a rough measuring tool, and explicit valuation of those companies that pass muster will provide much finer ranking criteria.

Valuation Work by the Team

Having established a list of target candidates on the basis of strategy, management must consider if the acquiring company can win. In other words, will its shareholder value be increased? The best estimate of fair value for large public firms trading in efficient markets is the current stock price. But a premium must be paid to get the company. Thus, the basic question is: Can the company get its premium

back? This requires a trial-and-error solution, because the premium will be determined by subsequent negotiation. The planning team members can estimate the
potential added value of the combination by considering three components:

- *Static values.* The stock currently may be undervalued because of hidden assets,
  recent bad news, or a less-than-free information policy. If it is a private company,
  the owners may have a low estimate of its true value or be willing to accept a low
  value to achieve liquidity. Tax benefits and operating efficiencies achievable immediately after the combination also figure in the valuation process.
- *Dynamic values.* These may be passive or proactive. Passive values are present
  when an acquirer forecasts a more favorable future than that implied by the stock
  market valuation of the target. This is a future bet. Proactive values are achieved
  by all those changes the new management intends to effect to achieve synergy or
  financial efficiencies (discounted at the proper rate). Obviously, companies that
  are currently mismanaged or underleveraged may furnish large gains.
- *Costs.* All costs and expenses of combining the two companies must be
  subtracted.

The consideration of strategic fit is used mainly in the target selection phase.
Consideration of valuation, however, is a continuous process. It is used first to
sharpen the target selection process; its more important use, however, is to control
a fast-moving process involving many transaction variations and alternatives that are
suggested by people with different vested interests. It is not necessary for planners
to be part of the negotiating team, but constant communication is necessary between them and the negotiators.

Whether the deal turns out to be a good one in 5 to 10 years will depend on the
price paid, the structure of the transaction, and other specifics of the deal. But it is
the planner's job to argue value as the deal is being molded into final form.

THE TRANSACTION
ANALYSIS PHASE

The planning process has identified the acquisition candidate and the initial valuation of the target on the basis of an economic forecast. Transaction analysis takes
this information and uses it to evaluate legal, tax accounting, and financing considerations of alternative approaches to generate preferred acquisition structures, currency mode, and trade-off value. This analysis also provides information for
formulating the acquisition strategies to be pursued. The principal function disciplines to be included in this part of the team are legal, taxation, finance, accounting, and investment banking.

Legal Considerations

The degree of legal involvement at this stage depends on whether the target is a
public or private company. If the target is a public company, it may be advisable to

retain outside legal counsel, because most corporations do not have lawyers experienced in public takeovers, especially if hostile, or the necessary legal force to deal with the serious time constraints.

At this stage, the legal involvement will concentrate on the following areas:

- Review of appropriate federal securities law
- Review of applicable state takeover statutes
- Antitrust review and the necessity for a Hart-Scott-Rodino (HSR) filing
- Approval processes required for both companies depending on deal structure or currency utilized
- Legal ramifications of alternative acquisition strategies

If a company has a lawyer with experience in acquisitions, and the target is not a public company, there is no reason why the internal legal staff should not represent the company and save significant legal fees. If the transaction appears complicated or time will be extremely important, it may be advisable to retain outside counsel. The ability of a large law firm to provide, on short notice, the significant experienced staff required in complicated large transactions, including armies of secretaries who will work all night, can be more than worth the extra cost.

Sun very successfully has done most of its acquisition and divestment legal work inside and saved a considerable amount of money. However, an acquirer should recognize that it also makes good business sense to retain outside attorneys for the team when the job is just too big for inside counsel. The outside firms should not replace one's own lawyers; they should supplement staff counsel.

During this stage of the analysis, internal counsel should review the requirements for retaining local, state, or foreign counsel and/or special counsel (regulatory, labor, etc.) and then get outside counsel involved early in the planning process. This is especially true for foreign acquisitions or a domestic acquisition involving significant foreign assets. Many countries have laws restricting transfer of control of their domestic corporations. It is a mistake to wait until the implementation phase to attempt to retain foreign counsel, and to familiarize them with the transaction. There are many situations in which advice from special outside counsel can change the structure of the transaction or the overall strategy.

If the antitrust review indicates that there may be difficulty in avoiding a challenge during the HSR filing process, this is the time for lawyers to prepare the necessary documents, recommend changes in the transaction, or supervise the collection and assembly of operational data to support the HSR filing.

The lawyers' involvement in this stage also can prevent serious problems later in the HSR filing process by reviewing all presentation material that is prepared by the teams and given to lien decision makers. Any material of this nature relating to markets and competition must be submitted with the HSR filing.

Tax Ramifications

The involvement of tax specialists during the transaction analysis process is extremely important in effecting the most tax-efficient transaction. An in-house tax attorney and tax accountant experienced in mergers and acquisitions should be involved. If external counsel must be consulted, internal tax accountants should work closely with them.

The tax specialists will review the different tax structures available and have the economic analysts run case studies based on the tax considerations. With this exercise, a recommended tax strategy, and alternatives with trade-off values, can be calculated. Although it may not be possible to use the most tax-efficient structure, this analysis will suggest the costs of selecting the alternatives and the resulting reduction in purchase price that will be required to obtain a desired financial return.

A determination should be made as to the necessity of an IRS tax ruling. If the seller is expected to require a tax ruling, the timing and risk of the transaction will be affected. If the transaction is a public takeover, the tax impact on the various types of shareholders—individual, corporate, and trust—also should be thoroughly analyzed.

Bringing in the Finance People

Without an ample quantity of acquisition currency, whether cash, notes, or equity securities, most of the team's efforts are purely academic. If the proposed acquisition will require raising cash externally, the early involvement of financial people in assessing credit sources, terms, limitations, and the effect on the corporation's remaining financial capacity is imperative. The financing aspects of the team's activities could well be the critical path.

A member of the corporate finance department and/or an investment banker should participate in the financial planning of the transaction. If the acquirer is large and the acquisition a small cash purchase, the involvement of finance at this stage may not be needed except for the appropriate budgeting of required cash. If the transaction is large and taps significant financial resources of the company, the top financial officer of the company should participate directly.

When notes, preferred stock, a convertible security, or warrants are utilized, the finance members of the team should bring in an investment banker to assist in determining the satisfactory range of terms and conditions for the different currencies to obtain the required valuation, subsequent market acceptance, tax efficiency, income, and balance sheet impact.

Accounting Examinations

At Sun, a senior member of the accounting staff is on the acquisition team. For a larger transaction, the controller of the company actively participates. There are many occasions when representatives of Sun's public accounting firm are asked to participate indirectly and to comment on how they would treat certain aspects of a transaction. Pooling accounting is a good example, because it is difficult, at best, to accomplish and has a dramatic effect on the accounting characterization of the transaction.

At the stage where the transaction has been narrowed to several alternative structures, the accountant should calculate the effect of the transaction on the balance sheet and income statement. Through use of pooling or purchase accounting methodology, the new balance sheet should be approximated. The economic forecast should be recalculated by utilization of the accounting, financing, and tax input generated by other members of the team. The result should be a long-range forecast, five years or more, of the impact of the deal on the overall combined balance sheet and income statement. The effects on earnings per share, performance ratios, financial capacity, bond rating, and the probable impact on stock value should be estimated.

Investment Banker Relationships

Investment bankers are regular members of Sun's acquisition team for large transactions and for all transactions involving the acquisition of a public corporation, no matter how small. The banker brings to the corporate team professional expertise gained from assisting in hundreds of M&A transactions and financings, and should be brought into the process as early as possible.

An acquiring company that has never used an investment banker should have its people meet with the principal employees of the banker who are being assigned to the deal. The company insiders should assess the bankers' suitability for the specific type of corporate development activity being pursued and their familiarity with the appropriate industry. The key professionals of the investment banking firm selected for the team should be identified and acknowledged in an engagement letter.

The investment banker should be thoroughly involved in all aspects of the acquisition. Advice and service are expensive and should be used. Aside from advice on acquisition strategy selection and on tactics during implementation, the investment banker can provide a high-level approach to target management, fairness opinions, deal structuring, dealer/manager services in tender offers, and financial advice.

THE IMPLEMENTATION PHASE

Once the candidate has been selected and valued and the acquisition strategy has been determined, the action begins. The participants in this last phase include those in the transaction analysis phase plus some additional participants. There are two functional groups working closely together: those involved in negotiating, and those involved in due diligence.

Negotiating the Deal

Most transactions require negotiation of the final terms of the agreement between the parties. Even tender offers, except for the most hostile, involve negotiations. The person selected as lead negotiator should be an individual with good negotiating skills, an excellent familiarity with the subject matter, and experience in negotiating transactions. At Sun, all but the largest acquisitions are negotiated by individuals within the appropriate subsidiary and not by the parent company. Others involved are lawyers, tax counsel, accountants, investment bankers, and operational and financial experts.

Due Diligence

If the acquisition is friendly and not a tender offer, there will be ample time to complete a full due diligence review of the company to be acquired before the deal is consummated. This activity is extremely important, because it is designed to eliminate surprises after the purchase. A buyer cannot rely solely on representations and warranties by the target to protect against the unforeseen. Prior to making final commitment to purchase, the following should be considered:

Financial Audit.   Either an internal or public accounting group should perform an audit before closing on the purchase of any private corporation that does not have recent audited financials.

Risk Management Review.   An environmental review has become extremely important because of the rapidly rising cost of environmental remediation. Retention of an occupational health consultant to review the potential health risks of a target company's products or workplace also may be advisable.

Other Audits.   Depending on the nature of the business being acquired and judgment as to the likely areas of risk, an assortment of specialists can be fielded. When Sun made early investments in diverse industries, outside consultants familiar with an industry were retained to complete extensive operational audits as part of the due diligence procedures. These reviews were not only helpful in determining if the acquisition candidate was worth buying, but useful in determining operational problems and identifying weak management that should be replaced after the acquisition. Tax audits, legal audits, and human resource audits also should be considered.

In one acquisition, both the operational audit and the accounting audit uncovered a weakness in a target's new automated billing system that could have resulted in $1 million of lost receivables. The sellers did not agree with the findings and, therefore, were willing to set aside escrow funds from the sale proceeds. Within a year, Sun has collected a significant amount from the escrow for the receivables actually lost.

The largest due diligence team fielded by Sun had to validate real estate records for a multibillion-dollar asset purchase of oil and gas properties. Almost 400 professionals were involved.

Even tender offers, if friendly, can and should be subject to due diligence review. In one friendly takeover of a public company by Sun, the agreement was struck on a Friday night, after the close of the market. A preselected team of internal and external specialists came onto the premises within an hour of the agreement and worked around the clock until Sunday afternoon. There were no significant negative findings. The final commitments were made and the press release issued before the opening of the market on Monday. Although highly unlikely, financial statements filed with the SEC can be fraudulently prepared, and even a limited due diligence effort might avoid a potentially serious mistake in such cases.

For public takeovers, the acquirer in the implementation phase also must deal with printers, special legal counsel, public relations firms, proxy solicitors, information agents, and transfer agents.

From start to finish, acquisitions involve the active participation and coordination of numerous skilled professionals from inside and outside the company to complete successfully an acquisition that, in the final analysis, will increase shareholder value.

11

Pursuing Acquisition Candidates

Herald L. Ritch

Managing Director, Mergers & Acquisitions Department, Donaldson, Lufkin & Jenrette Securities Corp.

Notwithstanding a marked slowdown thus far in the 1990s, the overall U.S. merger and acquisition environment has been extremely competitive for most of the last 15 years. This competition makes it advantageous for would-be acquirers to be both well prepared and opportunistic if they are to make the most of attractive acquisition possibilities that come their way. My experience as a merger and acquisition professional suggests to me that would-be acquirers can dramatically enhance their abilities to identify and pursue acquisition candidates by, first, understanding key trends in the merger market and their causes, and, second, being well prepared in all major phases of the acquisition process in order to be able to move intelligently on short notice.

THE MODERN MERGER AND ACQUISITION MARKET

There are several historical developments leading up to today's merger environment that are worth describing and analyzing. In the late 1980s, competition was indeed frenzied, with multiple bidders frequently slugging it out for the same property. Prices, too, were very high in reference to many common pricing indices.

125

Quality companies entered the acquisition arena with a vengeance as both buyers and sellers. In contrast to the late 1960s and early 1970s, the sheer pace of transactions was blistering, with nearly 30,000 M&A transactions—including thousands of divestitures, hundreds of leveraged buy-outs, and hundreds of transactions in excess of $100 million in size—being consummated within the 1983–1989 period alone. As a result, the time frame in which acquirers' decisions were being made was greatly compressed via these competitive pressures. Thus far, the 1990s have been dramatically less active, but competition for targets particularly in sought-after sectors like certain branded consumer products continues to be ferocious and to feel like the competition of the 1980s.

The two basic causes of the energy-charged merger environment of the mid- to late-1980s were economic factors and the revolution over the decade from 1975 to 1985 in takeover techniques and tactics, or the "technology" of the merger business.

Economic Factors.   One of the important economic factors that sparked takeover fever was the much-discussed and well-documented idea that across a wide swath of American industries it was cheaper to buy existing companies than to attempt to replicate them *de novo*. Another key economic factor was the availability of enormous amounts of credit for acquisition financing from the commercial banking sector, insurance companies, and the bond market, with such credit available not only to blue chip borrowers, but to companies with lesser credit ratings and to leveraged buy-out groups. A final driving force behind the 1980s acquisition boom was the enormous liquidity in many sectors of the economy, caused in no small measure by corporate tax law changes in that decade.

Takeover Techniques and Tactics.   Many modern takeover techniques and tactics developed as the result of the influence of unnegotiated takeovers, particularly throughout the period beginning in the mid-1970s. Unnegotiated takeovers include any unilateral attempt by a would-be acquirer to gain control of a company without the approval of the company's management or board of directors. They may take the form of aggressive stock accumulation programs, tender offers, exchange offers, proxy contests, or a combination of them. Unnegotiated takeover attempts by corporations had their serious beginnings in the conglomerate acquisition wave of the 1960s, with companies such as LTV Corp. offering their securities as consideration, usually at modest premiums over the current trading prices of target company stocks.

STRATEGIES FOR UNNEGOTIATED MERGERS

Saturday Night Special

By the early mid-1970s, the "Saturday night special" had arrived with great force. The Saturday night special was a seven-day cash tender offer for all of the stock of a target, usually beginning on Saturday, both to gain a timing advantage and to prevent the defense from being able to easily round up key advisers during a weekend. In subsequent years, numerous other developments related to tender offers occurred, including new Securities and Exchange Commission (SEC) regulations that dramatically changed and lengthened the tender offer process, two-tier bids with multiple pro-ration pools, defensive self-tenders, and Pac-Man tenders (see Chapter 48).

Bear Hug

Another major development from the unnegotiated arena is the "bear hug." The bear hug is a unilateral offer to acquire a company made directly to its board of directors in letter form, and disclosing enough specifics regarding price and terms that an announcement of the offer must be made by the target, if it has not been made already by the offer. It may threaten a follow-up tender offer, or unstated other actions, if a favorable reply is not received in the allotted period of time.

Nibble Strategy

Perhaps the most common unnegotiated M&A technique is the "nibble strategy." This involves acquiring a minority stake of from just under 5 percent to, say, 30 percent of the stock of a public company in the open market. Legally, any purchaser of 5 percent of a company's stock must file a 13D form with the SEC indicating how much stock has been acquired, some background about the purchaser, and a statement of the purchaser's intentions regarding the target. In the classic case of the 1970s and 1980s, in which a nibbler took a position and then made a tender offer for the rest of the company's stock, the nibbler was in virtually a no-lose position. Either the nibbler took control of the company, having lowered its effective purchase price to the extent that no control premium was paid on the up-front stock it acquired, or the nibbler sold its stock position at a profit—to either the company in a "greenmail" buy-back or to a "white knight" bidder that offered a premium in a rescue bid for the target.

Swipe

A further unnegotiated technique is the "swipe." A swipe occurs when a company's board of directors signs an agreement to sell the firm, only to have an opportunistic bidder pounce on the seller with a higher offer. These are always powerful offers, because the target's board previously has indicated both a willingness to sell and to do so at a lower price. But swipes are especially powerful in thwarting management-led leveraged buy-outs, where independent directors are under greater than normal pressure, due to the compounding effect of the usual concerns about management's conflicts of interest and the sensitivity caused by having agreed to sell to insiders at a lower price.

All of these unnegotiated techniques, as well as numerous other tactical tricks of the trade emanating from the unnegotiated takeover area, have had a pronounced impact on negotiated transactions. This is true despite the fact that all forms of hostile takeover activity are much less prevalent today than a few years ago for several reasons, including:

- Heightened stock market volatility, as evidenced by two stock market crashes in the late 1980s
- Proliferation of "poison pill" defenses
- Emergence of increasingly tough state takeover statutes
- Greater difficulties in obtaining financing for raids from banks, insurance companies, and the junk bond market
- Enhanced credibility to the "just say no" defense in the wake of the Delaware Supreme Court's Time-Warner decision in 1990
- The stock market in the late 1980s and early 1990s frequently valued some companies more highly than the merger marketplace

In sharp contrast to the leisurely manner in which many companies approached acquisition transactions prior to the mid-1970s by drafting an agreement in principle and issuing a corresponding press release first, and getting down to brass tacks later, buyers of the 1990s typically run very scared, having learned many harsh lessons over the prior 15 years. If at all possible, no smart buyer should announce a transaction without a definitive agreement, all necessary financing, and tailor-made features to ensure the probability of ultimately consummating the transaction (so-called lock-ups) already in place.

PREPARING FOR A COMPETITIVE ENVIRONMENT

As the discussion of trends in the merger market and their cause demonstrates, would-be buyers of companies must be well prepared and ready to move in order to compete most effectively in the current acquisition environment. To be in the right place at the right time, many successful acquirers expend great management time and effort in most, if not all, of the following six phases of the acquisition process:

- Strategic planning
- Homework
- Opportunity identification
- Evaluation
- Approach
- Execution

By designing an acquisition program to direct sufficient attention to each of these phases, an acquirer can bring a great deal of discipline to bear on the acquisition process and, therefore, do a better job of completing those acquisitions that it should do on reasonable terms, while avoiding those transactions that do not make sense for it.

Strategic Planning Phase

Strategic planning is the first step in successfully implementing an acquisition program. Able acquirers know what their organizations are all about and why. Thus, before embarking on a corporate acquisition program and committing to the big stakes associated with it, most good acquirers spend considerable time going through a period of corporate introspection and self-analysis. Early in this process it is critical to determine whether growth via acquisition is desirable and, if so, why. If acquisitions are worth pursuing, what type of transaction is best? Should it be a related business, or is complete diversification the aim of the effort?

At the outset of the strategic planning phase, it is important to insert a consideration of the time commitment involved in an acquisition program. Even with fairly broad business objectives and acquisition criteria, the corporate acquisition process is very time-consuming, with no certainty of success in achieving stated objectives. Much time and money can be spent exploring situations that result in disappointment for any of a number of reasons. Therefore, a major acquisition program should not be started by a company that cannot devote sufficient top management time to the effort.

If it is clear early in the strategic planning review that acquisitions make strategic sense, it is a good idea to compile a list of desired acquisition objectives, whether they be of the financial, business, managerial, or other type. Moreover, it is usually enlightening to make an assessment of the strengths and weaknesses of both the would-be purchaser and one or two acquisition candidates. These exercises, taken together, help to develop a good understanding within an entity's top management as to what qualitative issues are critical to it as a buyer.

After those factors are considered, it is necessary to establish a framework for evaluating acquisition opportunities. Are the corporation's acquisition interests served only where a good business fit exists, or alternatively, does the corporation have a portfolio mentality? Is sheer opportunism the lifeblood and tradition of the enterprise? Will the corporation only do negotiated transactions? It is very important to answer these questions honestly so that much wheel-spinning and embarrassment are avoided. For example, if a company's board of directors is relatively indecisive and does not have the stomach for a fight, it should acknowledge that hostile takeovers are probably not its cup of tea.

Finally, after all of the above issues have been carefully and fully debated internally, it is important that a would-be acquirer's top management team establish fairly formal strategic acquisition criteria. The exercise requires great care to avoid manufacturing a "wish list" so stringent that no realistic acquisition could ever pass muster, or so general that the acquisition criteria provide no real guidance as to what is, or is not, a desirable acquisition candidate. Furthermore, top executives should be conscious of the trade-offs they are making as they set up these criteria. For example, executives should be aware that the more rigorous and selective the strategic criteria, the greater the odds of not consummating an acquisition in the desired time frame.

Homework Phase

The homework phase involves general preparatory work, including the organization of an entity's acquisition team and the education of that group about the basic mechanics of corporate acquisitions. The internal composition of an acquisition team varies significantly from one company to another. Indeed, internal acquisition team members can vary significantly within the same company from one transaction to the next, depending on the acquisition candidate's size, the key personalities involved, and myriad other factors. However, two worthwhile observations regarding the rational structuring of an internal acquisition team can be made. First, as transactions get larger, more public, and more complex, the greater the need for chief executive officer's involvement on the team. Second, able acquirers generally include on their team the senior line officer who will have direct profit-center responsibility for the business after it is acquired.

In addition to internal team members, external advisers, including legal and financial advisers, management consultants, and other appropriate advisers, usually are assembled when a major acquisition program is established. Interestingly, many accomplished acquirers espouse the view that it is useful for key internal and external team members to get to know each other in advance of an actual transaction. Intuitively, this makes sense because the people dynamics of a potential acquisition are so crucial to its ultimate outcome.

The second major aspect of the homework phase involves exposure to the basic mechanics of corporate acquisitions transactions. Frequently, informal primers are given by the external team members to internal team members on a variety of topics, including:

- Legal issues regarding acquisition, such as SEC matters and the rights and responsibilities of corporate directors in the acquisition area
- Accounting and tax matters
- Regulatory issues of likely interest
- Antitrust issues, including the practical implications of Hart-Scott-Rodino
- Stock market workings, such as those involving risk arbitrage

Being conversant in these areas is definitely desirable, but this knowledge should be tempered with the old adage that a little bit of knowledge is dangerous. For example, the rigid application of an acquisition approach that worked well in one context may prove a terrible technique in another, somewhat similar situation, because of a very slight difference in circumstance such as enactment of a new tax, a different regulatory context, or a different state of incorporation of the target company.

Opportunity Identification Phase

The first stage of the opportunity identification phase generally involves the top management of a company. After reflecting on its strategic acquisition criteria, management should determine whether it makes business sense to put industries that meet these criteria under the microscope and ascertain if these industries are really as attractive as they appear superficially and whether they are indeed congruent with the company's strategic interests. At this time, management consultants, research analysts, financial advisers, and other advisers may be called upon to provide perspective on the target industries from their respective disciplines. Ultimately, these inputs lead to the decision that a given industry is or is not strategically attractive to the corporation.

If it is determined that a particular industry is strategically attractive, the next step is to identify specific companies that make good acquisition candidates within the target industry. Sometimes this is a simple process, especially if the entire industry is composed of two or three public companies. However, an industry more often is fragmented and includes important private companies and divisions of public companies as competitors. Many industries have large numbers of players. Therefore, it is frequently very important to tap a variety of sources for ideas on specific companies. These sources generally include both internal and external team members, the business press, analysts, and investment bankers, as well as various business and personal acquaintances.

Two final, very important sources of specific-company ideas can be tapped by looking at targets in strategically attractive industries that are either current takeover targets or have announced transactions involving their sales in the last few years, only to have the deals fall through. These are two categories of acquisition candidates that have the single most important attribute—availability. As a result, it is especially important to focus on those companies in strategically attractive industries that recently have been, or currently are, the targets of unilateral takeover attempts, that are the subjects of takeover rumors, that have been parties to broken acquisition transactions, that have undergone recent substantial top management changes, or that might be in a transaction mode for other reasons.

As specific companies in target industries become more clearly identified, and more information about them is accumulated, it is important for the acquisition team members to create a list of prime acquisition candidates as well as a list of other companies of possible interest. All of these companies will be studied carefully in the evaluation phase of the process, which comes next.

A final key aspect of the opportunity identification phase involves a would-be acquirer's communication of its distilled acquisition interests to the business community. By identifying publicly those industries that it finds strategically attractive as targets of opportunity for acquisitions, an acquirer should experience an increase in the flow of acquisition ideas brought to it, as well as better overall quality in the ideas it receives. Moreover, this communication prepares the marketplace for any changes in the acquiring entity's strategic direction.

Evaluation Phase

In the evaluation phase, acquirers carefully review those companies on their list of prime acquisition candidates as well as other companies that are of secondary interest to them. In the first cut, the buyer compares each candidate with its strategic acquisition criteria. This has the effect of keeping the acquiring entity's eye on the ball.

The next portion of the evaluation phase includes a traditional business review of each company, including a risk analysis and a financial review. Understanding each target company's markets, market shares, competitors, customers, and market dy-

namics is critical. A qualitative feel for the target's management team and an assessment of any hidden assets and liabilities are also important at this stage of the process. Examples of hidden assets might include appreciated real estate or natural
resources with fair market values substantially in excess of their stated book value.
Hidden liabilities might include substantial litigation risks, an unfunded pension
liability, or an uneconomic contract with a supplier or customer. Not surprisingly it
is also necessary to make a practical assessment of the target's availability, not just in
a vacuum, but in light of the acquiring entity's world view. For example, if the target
company is available only via a hostile transaction and that is deemed to be too
difficult to accomplish or contrary to the would-be acquirer's policy, the candidate
should be regarded as not presently available.

In evaluating key acquisition candidates, it is important ultimately to make preliminary judgments about the economic values of these enterprises. Investment
bankers and consultants frequently can play a valuable role in providing independent assessments of the reasonableness of management's assumptions and conveying knowledge of specific industries and companies. These valuations should be
viewed as being subject to change when more information is gathered, particularly
if direct access to the target, its financial projections, and other confidential information become possible at a later time.

Another portion of the evaluation phase is a legal assessment of each key acquisition candidate. The paramount issue here is whether there are any show-stoppers
that would legally prevent the would-be acquirer from consummating an acquisition of a particular candidate. Specifically, are there any antitrust, regulatory, contractual, or other legal impediments that would present an obstacle to completion
of a transaction? If these barriers exist, this is the time to determine if there are
economical ways of overcoming them.

Approach Phase

If, after completing all of the analysis in the evaluation phase, a particular acquisition candidate continues to look attractive, the next step is to consider the approach strategy that makes sense. At this stage of the process, most able acquirers
consult with their internal and external acquisition team members, and review the
results of their evaluations of the candidate, together with an analysis of the motivations of the key players involved with the acquisition target. Do its owners want to
sell? Is there a management succession problem within the company? Have the directors of the company openly split with each other? How much stock do insiders
own? What is the cost basis of their stock? Have they been increasing or reducing
their positions recently?

This type of motivational assessment of the acquisition candidates has to be over-
laid on the financial structuring of a business combination. Tax, accounting, and
pricing issues have to be considered in designing an offer that will appeal to these
key individuals and yet remain attractive from the acquiring entity's viewpoint.
Other factors impinging on the financial engineering of a transaction include a
detailed analysis of the shareholder groups of both the acquirer and candidate, the
likely level of competition in the marketplace for the given company, and general
market considerations.

After a would-be buyer considers the motivations of the key people within an acquisition candidate and the financial engineering constraints and trade-offs present in a particular situation, it is time to develop customized approach tactics. Although each approach is unique, there are three general categories: the "friendly persuasion" approach, the opportunistic approach, and the completely unnegotiated approach described earlier. Most transactions begin with a "friendly persuasion" approach, in which the potential acquirer attempts to convince a target to negotiate its sale. The obvious advantages of a friendly transaction are that it is likely to be the least costly form of transaction, management of the desired company is more apt to remain, the acquirer will have more and better information for making a judgment as to the attractiveness of the target, the acquirer frequently has more time to evaluate the acquisition's merits, and lock-ups are more likely to be available.

The success of the "friendly persuasion" approach tends to be a function of three key factors. The first is the independence quotient of the target, that is, the degree to which the target's management and board of directors value their independence. The second is the ability of the acquirer's primary executive to relate well to his or her counterpart at the target. It is critically important in designing an approach to remember that most public company chief executives on the receiving end of a friendly approach initially are inclined to have two thoughts running through their minds. They are not interested in selling to anyone; and they are concerned about keeping the overture absolutely confidential to avoid leakage of information that could unleash market forces that eventually could force their companies to be sold. The third key factor in the success of a friendly approach is the price the acquirer is willing to pay.

Opportunistic approaches to acquisitions occupy the middle of the approach spectrum and may lead to negotiated or unnegotiated transactions. These approaches include overtures to a target company that has been hit with an unnegotiated takeover attempt, has telegraphed its salability through a broad solicitation being managed by an intermediary on its behalf, or already has agreed to sell itself to another potential buyer. (An approach in this latter case would use the previously described swipe technique.) If the target already is subject to a hostile takeover attempt, it is very important for a friendly would-be buyer to place an early call to the target to indicate any potential interest in acting as a white knight. This will maximize the probability of gaining direct access to the target's key people and advisers as the situation develops. If it is impossible to play the white knight role for reasons beyond the buyer's control, it may be possible for the acquirer to be a "gray knight," a bidder who enters the fray after the shooting has started but before it has reached an acquisition agreement with the target.

A buyer employing the opportunistic approach in response to a target's broad-buyer solicitation effort, even when the campaign involves an actual auction, can seek a competitive edge by trying to preempt the solicitation/auction process and transform it into a one-to-one negotiation. This sometimes can be done purely via conventional means—being very responsive to the seller's price and nonprice objectives, exhibiting a willingness to work virtually around the clock on the project, retaining able advisers for the project, and otherwise demonstrating a can-do mentality. If this "we try harder" approach does not work, consideration should be given to either making a preemptive bid with a short time fuse or attempting to split the target from its advisers, usually by convincing the selling principal that the potential acquirer qualitatively is the best buyer, and that it would be aggressive on price and other terms if the process were not akin to a big poker game.

Lastly, with respect to completely unnegotiated approaches, it is important to be alert to the fact that it is unwise to launch a hostile offer without first battening down the hatches. The fate of Bendix Corp. in its attempted 1982 takeover of Martin Marietta Corp. demonstrates the importance of having one's own defenses set before getting into a fight. Bendix exposed its flanks to a Pac-Man attack by Martin Marietta Corp. and ultimately extricated itself only by being acquired by Allied Corp. A final bit of advice in the case of unnegotiated offers is to set your maximum price in advance of launching a hostile bid and stick to that decision unless compelling new information surfaces to change your view.

Execution Phase

The execution stage is exactly what it sounds like: getting the job done. The roles of special legal and financial advisers are very important, because critical decisions frequently have to be made under fighter-pilot-like conditions and time constraints. In addition to being very knowledgeable about a host of acquisition-related subject areas and understanding idiomatic solutions to common issues that crop up in negotiations, these advisers frequently have special negotiating skills honed through sheer practice. This is clearly the area where the relative contributions of legal and financial advisers are greatest, and it is the area where most able acquirers will seek out and listen to advice.

Perhaps the most critical facet of the acquisition process for a would-be acquirer is the importance of its remaining focused on its strategic acquisition criteria in the exciting execution phase. In the heat of a hostile takeover or in the fervor of pursuing a friendly acquisition, acquirers have been known to make major mistakes, such as dramatically overpaying for target companies or effecting business combinations that do not achieve stated strategic objectives. However, the truly successful acquirer retains its concentration on desired objectives during this crucial phase, and goes through with the deal only if its strategic objectives can be achieved.

TIME IS COMPRESSED

The M&A arena has been extremely competitive for most of the last 15 years because of both economic reasons and the influence of increasingly sophisticated techniques and strategies that developed in the area of unnegotiated takeovers, but have heavily influenced market psychology and business practices in the area of negotiated transactions as well. The resultant compression in time available to would-be acquirers has forced successful buyers to undertake a substantial amount of advance preparation in various phases of the acquisition process in order to be ready to compete when they believe it is in their interests to do so. Corporations can enhance their ability to identify and pursue acquisitions successfully by understanding the dynamics at work in the current acquisition marketplace and preparing themselves accordingly to do business in this environment.

12

Broker
and Finder
Agreements

John W. Herz
Robert L. Davidson
Mark C. Silverstein
Partners, Wolf Haldenstein
Adler Freeman & Herz,
New York, New York

This chapter is directed primarily to the people who need it the most: the sellers of small and medium-sized businesses who need the services of an intermediary to find or deal with a potential buyer.

Early in the life of most acquisition plans, there is need to engage the services of a broker, finder, or other intermediary so the parties can obtain the best of all possible deals. The type of intermediary selected will vary according to the size of the prospective deal, the type of involvement desired from the intermediary, and the value of the business to be sold. For a large acquisition demanding heavy intermediary involvement and a high degree of sophistication, the services of an established investment banking firm are needed. At the other extreme, the seller and buyer may need only a finder's introduction.

For each of these intermediary types, and for all the shades in between, there are different standards and sources for selection.

BROKERS AND FINDERS

Distinctions Between Brokers and Finders

Brokers and finders are the two main types of intermediaries. A broker is involved in every stage of the transaction. For example, a broker may study the business, prepare a write-up of the business to distribute to prospective buyers or sellers, educate the seller in methods of finding a potential buyer, develop a list of likely candidates, and assist in negotiating the transaction and in designing it so that it will result in the optimum benefit to the client. A finder has the sole function of introducing the parties. Because there are many shades between true brokers and true finders, with the same people and firms filling all the possible roles, either in different transactions or throughout a single transaction, the terms are often used interchangeably to refer to any intermediary.[1]

Must Brokers or Finders Be Licensed?

Unlike real estate brokers, few states require business brokers or other intermediaries to be licensed. However, if a transaction involves a transfer of real estate, the laws requiring real estate broker licensing may apply. And if a transaction involves a sale of stock instead of assets, federal securities laws may require that an intermediary acting as a broker be a registered securities dealer.

Are Brokers or Finders Necessary?

Many people have begun to question the necessity for intermediaries, and they wonder whether they would be better off trying to arrange a sale or merger without an intermediary. The main complaint from the buyer's point of view is that the businesses listed with many intermediaries are not suitable, and time is wasted on these prospects. Of course, any complaints by buyers affect sellers, because the sellers rely on the intermediary to find prospective buyers. However, this complaint should be viewed more as a warning to choose the right intermediary than as a reason not to use one.

The proper intermediary will be of great assistance in many areas. An intermediary will be helpful in valuing a business for sale. A broker will aid in the negotiation of the deal. Using the broker as a buffer may encourage more open discussions than those possible between the buyer and seller alone. As a negotiator, a good broker can be invaluable. A broker will analyze the management structure of each party and establish a means of approach, while anticipating and adjusting for the reactions of the other side.

Overall, intermediaries serve many useful functions. However, be aware that an intermediary will not often do more than is asked. Business objectives should, therefore, be stated broadly in the first instance, so as not to foreclose any opportunities.

Types of Brokers and Finders in
Small Deals and Large Deals

The typical small or intermediate-sized business is interested in entering into a single purchase or sale transaction. The seller generally hires and arranges to pay the intermediary. The intermediary agrees to help the seller in the search for a suitable buyer by approaching potential acquirers unsolicited, or by working with buyers that are actively seeking acquisitions. However, even in those instances when the buyer approaches the intermediary, it is generally the seller who pays the intermediary's fee.

Large corporations looking for acquisitions may have their own specialized staffs or may continuously use the services of intermediaries, often keeping them on retainers. Corporations seeking to expand or diversify always are looking for acquisition prospects, while diversified corporations seeking to concentrate in a single industry may need to dispose of unwanted divisions or subsidiaries.

For small transactions, the names of brokers or finders active in sales of businesses in a particular trade are often known to people in that field. Many smaller broker or finder firms are listed in the Yellow Pages. Sellers also can speak to their bankers, accountants, or attorneys, who may either act as intermediaries or recommend intermediaries.

Deals involving hundreds of millions or billions of dollars utilize different types of intermediaries than do the smaller deals:

- Large investment banking firms will often act as intermediaries in addition to arranging financing.
- Large corporations hire their own staffs and bring their business acquisition work "in house."
- Large corporate buyers retain brokers and finders on a regular basis.

BROKERS' AND FINDERS' FEES

The Basic Types of Fee Arrangements

An intermediary's fee is often negotiable. The seller should know that though the intermediary may quote a fee as the standard rate, it "ain't necessarily so"—and may well be negotiable.

Generally, the intermediary's fee is contingent on the closing of the sale of the business and is based on some percentage of the sale price. The most usual fee scale, other than for a small deal, is what is known as the Lehman formula, or the 5-4-3-2-1 formula. Under that formula, 5 percent is paid on the first $1 million of sale price, 4 percent on the next $1 million, 3 percent on the next $1 million, 2 percent on the next $1 million, and 1 percent on the amount in excess of $4 million.

Several courts have accepted the Lehman formula as an appropriate method for determining damages in actions brought by intermediaries to recover the reasonable value of services rendered.[2] Of late, however, this formula has come under attack by smaller brokers, who find that inflation has rendered it penurious. In a small transaction, the intermediary's fee may range between 5 and 10 percent of the sale price. A fixed percentage, rather than a declining percentage, is frequently used in transactions of all sizes.

Appropriately, when the intermediary has special knowledge and expertise about the business involved, a premium above and beyond the formula compensation may be awarded.[3] On the other hand, the Lehman fee would be excessive in the case of a finder that merely introduces the parties and does not perform many of the functions ordinarily performed by a broker.[4] A formula should be, at most, a guideline. An intermediary's compensation should depend not only on the size of the deal but also on the nature and extent of the services rendered.

A purely contingent fee, though the general rule, may be inappropriate in some cases. A broker that performs services beyond finding the eventual buyer or seller may be unwilling to operate on a purely contingent basis. This is even more likely to be the case when the broker is retained by the buyer to find an appropriate business to acquire. Such a broker may want to be compensated, and the client may agree to compensate the broker, on a time basis with a contingent fee if a sale is consummated within a specified period. In other cases, the broker may be paid a fixed retainer in an agreed-upon amount, again with a contingent fee if a sale is consummated. The time charges or retainer would be credited against the amount payable under the contingent fee.

A broker and a seller also may agree to an incentive fee arrangement under which the broker is rewarded for helping to obtain a better deal. Under this fee schedule, the broker receives a fixed percentage of the sale price up to a certain benchmark and a larger percentage of the consideration above that threshold.

A broker retained on a contingent basis may be granted an "exclusive" for a fixed period of time. This means that the specified percentage commission will be paid if the client strikes a deal with anyone the client met during this period, even if the broker is not the introducing party and the sale is consummated after the period expires. The broker also may want to serve as a nonexclusive broker after the period of exclusivity expires.

While a contingent fee seemingly offers the advantage of not being payable if the deal falls through, that is also its disadvantage. If a broker is being relied upon to negotiate the transaction, consider whose interests will be of paramount concern. The broker cannot be relied upon to be totally objective as long as the fee is contingent on, or greatly increased by, the closing of the transaction. This does not mean that the client should not rely upon the broker or that the client should guarantee a fee to the broker; it means only that the client should view the recommendations of the broker more critically.

How the Structure of the Sale Affects the Fee

The intermediary's compensation normally is defined in terms of a percentage of the price of the sale. But in this context, sale price depends on what has been sold—stock or assets.

The sale price in an assets transaction is completely different from the sale price in a stock transaction, though the net economic effect to the buyer and the seller may be exactly the same in both cases. Assume that a corporation has $5 million in assets and $2 million in liabilities, and that the purchaser is to pay $4 million in cash for the business. If the transaction is a stock sale, the purchase price is $4 million. If the transaction is a sale of assets, with the usual assumption of liabilities, the purchase price consists of cash paid ($4 million), plus the liabilities assumed by the buyer ($2 million), for an aggregate of $6 million. Nonetheless, the intermediary's compensation should be the same in both cases: The services rendered are the same, and the resulting purchase price is the same to the parties. Thus, in the typical case, the fee should be measured by the cash price of $4 million.

Note that when a corporation has little net worth, and loans to the company were personally guaranteed by the stockholders, the assumption of those liabilities by the buyer and the release of the stockholders from those liabilities may be a key factor in the transaction. Provision for the intermediary's compensation should be made accordingly.

The problem of defining the purchase price is particularly difficult in the sale of a closely held corporation, because the true consideration paid by the buyer often takes some form other than direct payment of the purchase price. Thus, for tax or even business reasons, the buyer may pay the selling stockholders for their covenants not to compete. Similarly, a generous long-term employment contract may be a key part of the transaction. An intermediary might be justified in arguing that in such cases compensation should be measured by the payment for the covenant and in some part by the generous employment compensation.

When the sale is of a partial interest in a corporation, there may be benefits to the continuing stockholders apart from the payment of the purchase price. Thus, in addition to buying a portion of the stock, the buyer may agree to make a substantial loan to the corporation to provide it with necessary working capital. If a mortgage broker arranges for such a loan, there unquestionably would be a fee for placing the loan. So when a loan to the business is an integral part of a purchase transaction, the intermediary should receive compensation for helping arrange it.

It is impossible for the intermediary to anticipate all benefits to the seller at the time the initial agreement is made. Some forms of agreements have tried to cover such contingencies by providing that the intermediary's compensation be measured by the sale price and "any other economic benefits" inuring to the seller corporation or its shareholders. Within the confines of the usual one-page or two-page broker's or finder's agreement, only such a catchall phrase can seek to protect the intermediary from the myriad ingenious methods that have been devised for paying the seller for the business. As the deal takes shape, the parties should clarify in writing how the intermediary's fee is being measured if their original agreement has not clearly covered that phase of the transaction.

Fees in Stock Deals

The method of paying the intermediary becomes more difficult when the acquisition currency is stock. Frequently, the parties will expect the intermediary to accept the fee in the form of stock. This may create a tax problem for the intermediary, which must pay an income tax determined by the fair market value of the stock received, even though it is not a taxable transaction for the seller.

If the transaction is a stock-for-stock deal and the intermediary's fee is payable by the selling stockholders, they will not want to pay it in cash, particularly if the stock cannot be sold immediately, because the payment would have to come out of their own cash resources. In such a case, the intermediary might accede to the seller's request during the negotiations that the intermediary accept the fee in the form of stock, or at least mostly in stock. If the fee is paid in stock, the selling stockholders will have ample stock to make the payment.

Even in a stock-for-assets or a merger deal, the parties may want the intermediary to take the fee in the form of stock to preserve the cash in the business. When the intermediary receives the fee in the form of stock, the amount of stock that is received will be an agreed percentage of the number of shares transferred to the seller. If the sale price includes a contingent stock pay-out, the intermediary will receive the agreed percentages of shares out of each contingent stock payment when it is made.

If the seller receives stock and the intermediary is to be paid in cash, the shares must be valued in order the compute the fee. The same valuation question arises when the intermediary is paid in shares and the percentages of the value vary, such as under the Lehman formula. Generally, the traded price of the stock will be used for this purpose despite the fact that an appraisal of the value of the stock would show a lesser value. That is the case when the seller receives investment stock that may not be sold or transferred for some period of time.

WHO PAYS THE FEE?

Generally, it is the seller that retains the intermediary and is obligated to pay the fee. If the seller has the responsibility for the fee, it should not be assumed that this is fully allowed for by the parties in fixing the purchase price so that the final economic effect is that the fee is borne by the buyer. There are many factors that are involved in computing the sale price, and it is rare that a premium to cover the intermediary's fee would be included.

The seller's obligation to the intermediary does not, except in a merger, pass to the buyer unless expressly assumed. This is true not only in a stock purchase but also in an asset purchase. Though in the typical asset purchase the buyer assumes all disclosed obligations of the seller at closing, this provision usually excludes intermediary's fees payable by the seller.[5] Some buyers add a specific provision negating the assumption of any of the seller's expenses in connection with the sale.

There are instances, however, when the intermediary's fee is the obligation of the buyer. The buyer may be the party that retained the intermediary to find a business available for acquisition in a specific field. Or during the course of the negotiations, the buyer may assume the seller's obligation to pay the intermediary's fee. If the buyer has retained the intermediary, the agreement may provide that the intermediary will look to the seller for payment of the fee. In that case, the buyer generally will assure the intermediary's compensation if full payment cannot be obtained from the seller.

When the seller has the initial responsibility for the fee and the buyer is a large corporation, it is not unusual for the buyer to wind up paying the fee. The buyer also will bear the economic cost of the intermediary's fee in an asset purchase or merger if the fee is paid out of the assets being purchased following negotiation of a fixed sale price. To avoid this result, the sale agreement would have to provide for a reduction in the sale price equaling the fee or require that the seller pay the intermediary's fee out of the sale proceeds.

The Importance of a Written Agreement

In any event, the intermediary should not only have a written agreement with the party paying the fee, but obtain a specific paragraph in the contract of sale that specifies who pays the obligation. If a buyer and seller are to split the fee, there should be a disclosure of that fact to each of them by the intermediary and a written acknowledgment of the arrangement by both parties.

When the seller lists the business with an intermediary and agrees to pay the full commission, the seller may want written assurance that the intermediary will not seek any compensation from the buyer. The seller may want that prohibition not only to prevent a second fee from impacting the price the buyer is willing to pay, but also for the satisfaction of knowing that the intermediary will not be doubly compensated. This is particularly important when the intermediary is a finder, and can legally be paid by both parties.

When the transaction takes the form of a sale of stock, the seller's obligation to pay the intermediary rests with the selling stockholders. When the transaction takes the form of a sale of assets, the selling corporation is obligated to pay the intermediary. When the transaction takes the form of a merger, the obligation to the intermediary becomes, as a matter of statutory law, the obligation of the surviving corporation.[6] The form of the transaction and its impact on the obligation to pay the intermediary should be addressed in the written agreement between the parties.

Occasionally, an employee, officer, or director of a selling company may be offered a finder's fee. Be aware, however, that these insiders may be required to relinquish such fees because of their fiduciary duties to the selling company shareholders.[7] The recipients must receive the approval of either the selling company's board of directors or its shareholders to accept such finder's fees. The manner in which this approval must be granted varies from state to state based on statutory rules and common law.[8]

Must More Than One Fee Ever Be Paid?

The seller should make certain that more than one commission will not be owed. In the agreement with the intermediary, the sellers should require indemnification against the claims of any other person brought into the deal by the intermediary. This will make it clear that any commitment the intermediary makes to a cobroker cofinder, or any other party is not binding on the client.

Similarly, in the agreement with the acquirer, the seller should be indemnified against claims for compensation by anybody whose services were enlisted on the buy side. The buyer then may want a reciprocal covenant from the seller.

When and How Is the Fee Paid?

If the sale price is payable in a lump sum, the intermediary should be paid the commission in full at the time of the closing.

When the purchase price is payable in installments, the intermediary's commission usually comes out of the down payment. This may work a hardship on the seller, particularly when the down payment is small. If the seller anticipates an installment sale when the agreement with the intermediary is signed, provisions may be made to pay the intermediary out of each installment. Should the transaction take the form of an installment sale during the negotiations, the intermediary may agree at that time to accept the fee out of each installment rather than in full at the closing. On the other hand, if an installment plan is arranged primarily to benefit the seller's tax position, there is no reason why parts of the intermediary's fee should be deferred.

Escrows and Earn-outs

When a portion of the sale price is determined on an earn-out basis—that is, the amount of the payments are contingent upon operations after the closing—the intermediary must be paid out of those payments as they are made to the seller. That is because the parties have no way of knowing at the closing what the earn-out will be. The intermediary's compensation will be measured by the actual payments that are made by the buyer under the earn-out provision.

If part of the sale price is placed in escrow to assure fulfillment of the seller's warranties, the intermediary often will be paid in the same manner as if there had been no escrow, without deferral of a portion of the fee. However, if the escrow is a substantial portion of the sale price or covers more than the usual seller's warranties (for example, when the buyer and seller use an escrow as a device for handling an earn-out or other future contingency), the intermediary's fee on the escrowed portion is generally payable only when the funds are freed from escrow and delivered to the seller.

FEES IN TAX-FREE TRANSACTIONS

If the seller receives cash on the sale, the intermediary's fee can be paid out of the cash proceeds.

However, many sales of businesses are structured, primarily for tax reasons, so that the seller receives only shares of the buying corporation or its parent.

Despite the fact that the seller has not received cash, the intermediary usually will want the fee in cash. If the fee is paid in stock, the intermediary usually is subject to resale restrictions under securities laws. In addition, the intermediary has taxable income equal to the value of the shares received, notwithstanding the restrictions.[9] The issue, then, is how to pay the intermediary in cash without affecting the "tax free" aspect for the sale.

In a merger transaction, the obligation to pay the intermediary can be fulfilled by the surviving corporation without affecting the tax-free nature of the merger.

When the transaction is a stock-for-assets exchange and the seller must pay the intermediary, at least two methods can be used to pay the intermediary's fee in cash without affecting the tax-free nature of the exchange.

In one approach, the selling corporation can pay the fee prior to the exchange and then exchange only its remaining assets for the buyer's stock, or the seller can hold back sufficient cash to pay the fee after the exchange. If the seller's cash is insufficient, it can hold back enough accounts receivable or other liquid assets to realize cash for paying the intermediary. The holding back of assets is possible when the amount being retained is small relative to all assets so that the assets delivered will represent "substantially all" of the seller's assets.[10]

A second technique is to have the buyer assume the seller's obligation to pay the intermediary's fee.[11] The intermediary's fee in these cases must be paid directly by the buyer.

When the transaction is a stock-for-stock exchange, the sellers are the shareholders, and they are obligated to pay the intermediary's fee. In these transactions, there also are at least two methods for paying the intermediary in cash without affecting the tax-free nature of the exchange.

First, the buyer can assume the obligation of the selling shareholder.[12] Again, the buyer must pay the intermediary directly. Second, the selling shareholders can pay the intermediary's fee out of their own liquid assets, or they can sell some of their shares, subject to resale restrictions under the securities laws and the incurring of a tax on the sale, to pay the fee.

Must There Be a Written Agreement?

An intermediary's right to compensation depends on a written or oral contract. Many states have statute-of-frauds provisions which specify that an intermediary has a right to compensation only if there is a written agreement signed by the party from whom compensation is sought.[13] In the absence of such a statute, however, the contract can be express or implied in fact and, if express, it can be written or oral.[14] In those states that do not require an agreement in writing, a contract may be implied solely from the fact that the seller accepted an introduction to a prospective buyer knowing that the person who made the introduction expected to receive compensation for getting the parties together.[15]

In large public deals transacted by investment bankers, it is not unusual to proceed on faith alone. In smaller transactions, a written agreement is usual. But in all cases, an understanding should be reached at the start, and a written agreement is highly advisable to avoid future disagreements.

When the introducing party's usual business is not acting as an intermediary, the seller should ascertain whether compensation is expected before accepting the introduction. This applies when a banker, lawyer, accountant, or business acquaintance is the introducing party, as frequently happens.

The written contract gives all parties certain protections. It protects the seller by putting down in black and white the fact that the compensation is payable only if the deal closes, and that this provision applies even if failure to close is the fault of the seller. If an intermediary's sole function is to find a buyer or seller that fits the client's specifications, the seller will not want to pay any compensation unless the sale is consummated, regardless of how far the transaction progresses and which party caused the deal to fall through.

Without a written agreement, a client might be tempted to bypass an intermediary after learning of a prospective match. Therefore, an intermediary should try to withhold the names of prospective buyers until there is a written, signed contract. Sometimes, however, a client might insist on learning the identity of a proposed buyer or seller before signing an agreement. This creates a problem in a state that has a statute-of-frauds provision governing intermediaries. The intermediary may seek cooperation from the prospective buyer, though most buyers will be reluctant to become involved in disputes between sellers and intermediaries. A supportive buyer, however, may be willing to insist that the seller sign a written agreement with the intermediary before it will proceed with the deal. Even better, the buyer may agree to compensate the finder and allow for this payment in negotiating the purchase price. In the last analysis, the only real protection for the intermediary in a statute-of-frauds state is to obtain a written agreement before starting work.

What Is in the Agreement?

The initial agreement must set forth the contemplated transaction in the *broadest possible terms*. Often the final form of the deal is not known when the initial agreement with the intermediary is executed, or the format may change during negotiations. Thus, the agreement should state that the intermediary shall receive a commission when the selling company:

- Sells all or a substantial part of the assets
- Sells all shares or a controlling stock interest
- Merges with a party introduced by the intermediary

It is important to describe the exact parties to the transaction. Normally, a selling corporation executes the agreement with the broker or finder. But if the transaction is a sale of stock, the proper parties are the shareholders of the selling corporation rather than the corporation itself. If the agreement with the intermediary is executed by the selling corporation and the transaction takes the form of a stock sale, the courts may nevertheless impose responsibility for the fee on the stockholders. A court may be reluctant to do this, however, if the statute of frauds applies, and if the exact party being charged has not signed the agreement.

Sometimes an intermediary may assist the parties in a transaction that was not contemplated when the retainer agreement was signed and was not covered by its language. That may present problems in collecting the fee. If the statute of frauds applies, the intermediary's arguments that the contract was modified orally to cover the extraordinary deal may not overcome requirements that provisions for paying the fee be in writing.[16] Thus, if the deal process veers from the original path, the intermediary should obtain a new contract or a written amendment to the original agreement.

The contract also should set forth whether the intermediary is retained on an exclusive or nonexclusive basis. The normal arrangement will be nonexclusive, so that the seller is free to deal with any prospective purchaser not introduced by the intermediary. Conversely, the contract should specify a right to compensation if the eventual buyer is introduced by the intermediary even if the closing takes place after the termination of the agreement. A guaranteed fee eliminates any question of who initiated the deal. Disputes over whether a fee is due can arise, for example, when a purchaser or seller that is initially contacted shows no interest at first but returns later with a deal in mind. Or the fee can be disputed when negotiations are terminated, only to be resumed after the intermediary is out of the picture.[17]

If there is initially no sale and the client later hires another intermediary, the client should be wary of owing a double commission if the new intermediary presents the same prospective buyer and a sale is concluded. If that situation is likely to arise, the seller should include a clause in the agreement negating the fee of an intermediary if there has been a prior introduction to the same prospective buyer. It then becomes a question of fact as to who made the first introduction, but only one commission will be payable. Some finders, therefore, establish their positions by confirming each introduction by letter.

A broker's services normally consist of more than an introduction of the parties to each other, and thus, the definition of services to be rendered may include the intermediary's assistance in the negotiations. The agreement should, for the broker's protection, state that the intermediary will assist when requested by the seller. In this case, the seller cannot defeat the broker's rights to a full commission on the grounds that the broker performed no services in the negotiations when, in fact, the seller did not call upon the broker, or the broker was prevented from serving by the primary parties.[18]

The intermediary's right to compensation should apply to an introduction brought about directly or indirectly. This would help establish a claim should the intermediary introduce the seller to a prospective buyer which in turn introduces the seller to someone else that buys the business.

What Kinds of Special Agreements Can Be Reached?

There are several types of special intermediary agreements.

Sometimes an intermediary will advise the seller that he or she has a specific potential buyer in mind and wants to fix the terms of compensation before the introduction is made. As in any agreement, the intermediary should make sure the terms are sufficiently broad.

Sometimes a broker may insist on an exclusive agreement. There are, in general, two types of exclusive agreements. In one case, sometimes referred to as an exclusive sales agreement, the broker is entitled to a commission in the event of any sale of the business, no matter how it is brought about. In the other case, sometimes referred to as an exclusive agency agreement, the broker is entitled to a commission on any sale except one made directly by the seller without the intervention of an intermediary. But the agreement should not rely on such terminology. It should set forth whether the broker is entitled to a commission on all sales, and if not, classes of excluded sales should be specifically set forth. Finders generally do not receive exclusive agreements.

An exclusive agreement should have a fixed duration or be terminable by either party after a specific date or a specific notice period. The broker may expend substantial time and effort seeking to find a buyer and, therefore, the exclusive agreement should be long enough to give the broker a reasonable opportunity to earn a commission.

When Does the Agreement Terminate?

Normally, the agreement with an intermediary is terminable at will by either party, and there should be a provision for written notice of termination. Making the duration clear is only one of several important steps. The agreement should include a provision specifying that should a sale be consummated after the agreement expires to a party introduced to the seller by the intermediary (or if there is an exclusive, introduced by anyone during the terms of the exclusive), the intermediary is entitled to a commission. Because a broker may be required to assist in the negotiations, the proposed provision should state that the broker's obligation to assist will survive the termination of the agreement. The broker must, of course, be available to assist in any negotiations that take place after the agreement expires.

The seller and the intermediary may agree that after a sufficient period of time has elapsed following termination of the agreement, the intermediary no longer will be entitled to a commission even if a transaction is consummated with a party introduced by the intermediary.

HOW CAN CONFIDENTIAL INFORMATION BE PROTECTED?

The seller of a closely held corporation may not be eager to disclose basic financial information. Regardless of the reluctance, the seller must be prepared to give considerable detailed information during the negotiations. However, highly secret matters, such as customer lists and manufacturing processes, may be saved for the last.

The client must find an intermediary whose judgment can be trusted. Even so, the seller should consider stating in the agreement that no information about the business, or even the fact that it is available for sale, may be disclosed by the intermediary unless cleared by the seller. The seller then may take protective steps directly with the potential buyer.

If the buyer or seller is a publicly held company, the intermediary must treat the transaction as confidential and must neither trade in the company's stock before a public announcement nor tip off others who may trade in the stock.

NOTES

1. In this chapter the term "intermediary" will be used as the generic for all intermediaries, and the terms "broker" and "finder" will be used consistent with the definitions set forth.

2. *Ehrman v. Cooke Elec. Co.*, 630 F.2d 529 (7th Cir. 1980); *Havenfield Corp. v. H&R Block, Inc.*, 509 F.2d 1263 (8th Cir.), *cert. denied*, 421 U.S. 99 (1975); *Flammia v. Mite Corp.* 401 F.Supp. 1121 (E.D.N.Y. 1975), *affirmed* 553 F.2d 93 (2d Cir. 1977); *Schaller v. Litton Ind., Inc.*, 307 F.Supp. 126 (E.D. Wis. 1969).

3. *Flammia v. Mite Corp.*, supra, note 2.

4. *Havenfield Corp. v. H&R Block, Inc.*, supra, note 2.

5. It might be argued that if the seller fails to pay, and if the bulk sales law is applicable but has not been complied with, the intermediary may have the right to reach the assets sold in the hands of the buyer. Uniform Commercial Code (UCC) §6-104(1). Nonetheless, a question arises whether the intermediary is a creditor at the time notice is required under the code. See UCC §6-109(1).

6. See, e.g., N.Y. Bus. Corp. Law §906(b)(3); Del. Gen. Corp. Law §259(a).

7. See, e.g., *Delano v. Kitch,* 663 F.2d 990 (10th Cir. 1981).

8. See, e.g., N.Y. Bus. Corp. Law §713; Del. Gen. Corp. Law §144.

9. Internal Revenue Code of 1986 (Code) §83.

10. The statutory test is set forth in Code §368(a)(1)(C). The present ruling position of the Internal Revenue Service is that the "substantially all" requirement is complied with if the acquired corporation transfers assets constituting of at least 90 percent of the market value of its net assets and at least 70 percent of the market value of its gross assets. Rev. Proc. 77-37, 1977-2 C.B. 568.

11. Rev. Rul. 73-54, 1973-1 C.B. 187.

12. Ibid.

13. See, e.g., N.Y. Gen. Oblig. Law §5-701(10). The written obligation to pay an intermediary need not be in a contract between seller and broker, but may be set forth in the contract between buyer and seller and may arise even though the seller never expressly retained the broker. See *Morris Cohon & Co. V. Russell*, 23 N.Y.2d 569, 297 N.Y.S.2d 947, 245 N.E.2d 712 (1969); *Ficor, Inc. v. National Kinney Corp.*, 67 App. Div.2d 659, 412 N.Y.S.2d 621 (1979).

14. See, e.g., *John Fleming, Inc. v. Beutel,* 395 F.2d 21 (7th Cir. 1968).

15. *Consolidated Oil & Gas, Inc. v. Roberts,* 162 Color. 149, 425 P.2d 282 (1967).

16. *Intercontinental Planning, Ltd. v. Daystrom, Inc.*, 24 N.Y.2d 372, 248 N.E.2d 576, 300 N.Y.S.2d 817 (1969); *Roberts v. Champion Int'l Inc.*, 52 App. Div. 2d 773, 382 N.Y.S.2d 790, *appeal dismissed*, 40 N.Y.2d 805, 389 N.Y.S.2d 1025 (1976). But see *Peters v. Sigma Data Computing Corp.*, 397 F.Supp. 1098 (E.D.N.Y. 1975).

17. See *Simon v. Electrospace Corp.*, 28 N.Y.2d 136, 269 N.E.2d 21, 320 N.Y.S.2d 225 (1971).

18. Ibid.

APPENDIX. BROKERAGE AGREEMENT FORM*

Comments.   This was a brokerage agreement for the sale of the assets or shares of a financially successful, closely held corporation with two stockholders. Because it was not anticipated that any part of the sale price would be paid in the form of a covenant not to compete or other indirect method, as might otherwise be the case in the sale of a close corporation, the broker required no protective clauses for such possibilities.

The seller had confidence in the brokerage firm and thus did not require the broker to submit to the seller in advance the names of prospective purchasers. But the seller did retain the right to control the information to be submitted to prospective purchasers and the people to whom it would be submitted.

In this case, the broker was to be paid in cash regardless of the form of the consideration received by seller.

The form does not provide for a merger or consolidation of the selling corporation (or the reverse merger of another company into it), because the possibility of such a transaction was remote.

---

*This form is a modified version of that appearing in J. Herz, C. Baller, and P. Gaynor, *Business Acquisitions,* 2d ed., Practicing Law Institute, New York, 1981, Vol. III, Part III.

June ___, 199___

Mr. John Doe
XYZ Corporation
Number and Street
City, State   Zip Code

Dear Mr. Doe:

This letter confirms the terms upon which you have retained us to serve as brokers in the sale of XYZ CORPORATION (the Company) or its shares:

(1) If and when a sale of the Company or its shares to a party introduced to the Company or its shareholders, directly or indirectly, by us has been consummated, we shall be paid a commission by the Company or its shareholders, computed on the basis of the following percentages of the consideration, or the value thereof if not paid in cash, received by the Company or its shareholders:

Five percent (5%) of the consideration up to $1 million, plus

Four percent (4%) of the consideration from $1 to $2 million, plus

Three percent (3%) of the consideration from $2 to $3 million, plus

Two percent (2%) of the consideration from $3 to $4 million, plus

One percent (1%) of the consideration in excess of $4 million

The commission shall be payable in cash.

No commission shall be payable if a sale is not consummated, regardless of whether or not the failure to consummate is due to the fault of the Company or its shareholders.

A sale of the Company or its shares shall be deemed to include a sale of all or part of the assets of the Company or a sale of all or a majority of the outstanding common shares of the Company.

In determining the consideration received by the Company or its shareholders:

(a) The consideration shall be deemed to include both cash and any securities or other property received by the Company or its shareholders in the transaction. Assumption of the Company's debts in the transaction shall not be deemed consideration.

(b) Securities that are listed on a national exchange shall be valued at the average closing price on the twenty (20) trading days before the date the sale is closed.

(c) Securities that are traded over the counter shall be valued at the average closing bid price on the twenty (20) trading days before the date the sale is closed.

(2) If any part of the consideration shall be payable in installments or shall be contingent upon future earnings, our commission shall be payable in the same

proportionate amounts and at the same times as such installments or contingent payments are made. In all other cases, payment shall be made at the closing of the sale.

(3) We shall assist the Company or its shareholders in its or their negotiations with any party introduced, directly or indirectly, by us to the extent that the Company or its shareholders request us to do so.

We shall not disclose any information regarding the Company, including financial information, that the Company or its shareholders direct us not to disclose or to anyone to whom the Company or its shareholders directs us not to disclose.

(4) We may, in our sole discretion, engage the services of any persons (including other brokers) without additional cost to you. In such event, all the commissions payable pursuant to paragraph (1) shall be paid to us and, upon such payment, we shall indemnify the Company and its shareholders against any liability for brokerage fees or other compensation claimed by such other persons. We shall not seek to accept a commission from any party to the sale other than the Company or its shareholders.

(5) This agreement may be terminated by the Company and its shareholders or by us at any time on thirty (30) days' notice, provided that such termination shall not affect our right to commissions on the consummation of a sale subsequent to such termination to a party introduced to the Company or its shareholders, directly or indirectly, by us prior to such termination, and our obligation to assist in the negotiations with such a party on the request of the Company or its shareholders shall survive such termination.

If the foregoing correctly reflects our understanding, please so indicate on the duplicate copy of this letter, whereupon this letter shall constitute a binding Brokerage Agreement between us.

Very truly yours,

_____

AGREED AND ACCEPTED:

XYZ CORPORATION

By: _____
        John Doe, President

_____
        John Doe

_____
        John Doe

13

Confidentiality Agreements That Work

Henry Lesser

Partner, Irell & Manella,
Los Angeles, California

Ann Lederer

General Counsel, First Federal Bank of
California, Santa Monica, California

Charles Steinberg

Associate, Fried, Frank, Harris, Shriver &
Jacobson, Los Angeles, California

With deals taking longer to complete and increasingly involving negotiations among competitors in the same industry, the confidentiality agreement has assumed greater importance in mergers and acquisitions of the 1990s.

The basic function of the agreement—protecting sellers against misuse of confidential information they provide to potential buyers—is more critical than ever. But the new M&A environment also demands special attention to other goals of the versatile agreement. A sampling includes complying with securities laws, when applicable; preventing bidders from forcing unfair offers on the target; governing an auction process; blocking the raiding of target personnel; and timing the announcement of negotiations or acquisition agreements.

In this analysis, we will discuss the confidentiality agreement as the first step in the process that can lead to a possible corporate combination and address how it can be negotiated and structured given current M&A market conditions. Although we will focus on the type of agreement often used in deals involving public companies, many of the same principles and practices are equally applicable to private company transactions.

It is important to stress that the confidentiality agreement is a method of reconciling the conflicting objectives of a target company that is negotiating a change-of-control transaction or a significant minority investment by an outsider. Once the target has decided to entertain acquisition or investment offers, it will be requested to provide sufficient information to enable bidders to make their best offers. However, the release of confidential information to interested buyers, many of whom might be direct competitors, poses obvious dangers that the target will want to minimize.

Indeed, the risks have been exacerbated during the early 1990s. Protracted negotiations leave the seller's confidential information exposed for longer periods and increase the likelihood that it can be misused or misappropriated. Sellers sometimes fear that a potential bidder may be more interested in accessing the target's closely guarded information than seriously negotiating a transaction. And if a deal can't be struck—an increasing possibility at a time when financing is hard to get—there is danger that a potential buyer may leave with precious business secrets.

Besides dealing with these acute worries, the confidentiality agreement for a public company also must provide comfort that a bidder armed with confidential information won't be tempted to end-run the seller's board. Unless restrained, the bidder can publicly issue an unsolicited proposal in an attempt to have stockholders pressure the board or make an unsolicited tender offer directly to shareholders. The bidder's aim would be to consummate the transaction at a lower price than the board would demand in direct negotiations.

The confidentiality agreement is a contractual device used to reconcile varying objectives and concerns by permitting the target company to provide confidential information to the bidder while protecting itself from the risks of misuse. The agreement typically contains:

- Confidentiality provisions to protect the company against the business risks of disclosure or misuse of information by competitors
- Standstill provisions to protect the company against unsolicited takeover attempts by bidders while providing for an orderly process for marketing the business

KEY ELEMENTS OF CONFIDENTIALITY PROVISIONS

Types of Information

The types of information of interest to a bidder include financial, technical, and human resource material. Each type of information has differing characteristics and the relative importance of each to the two sides will shape the context of the negotiations. For example, financial information, such as projections, typically has a short "shelf life" of usefulness. On the other hand, technical information, such as manufacturing techniques, may have an indefinite shelf life and may be easily exploitable by competitors.

Financial Information

The bidder and its representatives generally need confidential financial information regarding the target, including both historical data, particularly for nonpublic companies, and projections. In addition, the bidder may want detailed business information, including pricing details and data on individual business units (such as stores, factories, divisions, profit centers, and other strategic business units). The seller and its advisers must be sensitive to antitrust concerns if they intend to provide pricing and market information to competitors.

Technical Information

In the category of technical information, serious and complex issues may arise with regard to the scope of detailed information to be provided to competitors. The tensions, moreover, have increased given the higher incidence of mergers and acquisitions in technology-driven industries.

This is an area where the buyer can be as anxious to protect the legal position as the seller. A competitor may request that confidential technical information be excluded from the material that is provided, and seek only information deemed "nonconfidential" in order to avoid any possible future claim that it misused the target's proprietary information. While that theoretically solves the problem of giving a competitor access to sensitive information, in reality it is difficult to implement, particularly if the bidder is permitted to conduct interviews with the target's employees. Similarly, the bidder will sometimes request that the company identify the written documents it seeks to protect by marking them as "confidential."

The bidder also may request that oral discussions be reduced to writing in order to be protectable. This obviously shifts the burden to the target. The seller could fairly point out that a requirement for complete documentation would inhibit full and frank discussions between the bidder and the company's employees.

Another problem is that the company may be prohibited from disclosing confidential technical information under terms of contracts covering classified government work or joint research and development ventures or other collaborative efforts. The target's investment advisers should be sensitive to the existence of those restrictions in preparing "selling books" or other documents containing company information.

Access to Employees

It is good practice to require that all contacts be made through one source (usually, the target's investment banker) to control the number and identity of the employees being interviewed and to assure that they are properly briefed. The seller also may fear that the bidder will raid its important employees, particularly at a time when they are likely to be concerned about corporate stability and their own future. The concern is addressed by inclusion of a nonsolicitation clause in the confidentiality agreement that bars employment offers to executives or other key employees of the target.

Disclosure of Negotiations

The agreement may prohibit a bidder from disclosing, unless the seller consents in writing, that it has obtained confidential information or that merger negotiations have begun. The bidder in turn may ask for a reciprocal provision that prohibits the target from announcing the negotiations.

Discussions among Bidders

The target also will try to control a bidder's ability to discuss the possible transaction with other potential acquirers. Without a prohibition on such talks, a bidder could reach a secret agreement with another party to submit a joint bid. Or the bidder may agree to the postacquisition sale of target assets to a third party that otherwise might have bid for the company.

If such scenarios develop, the target may be precluded from getting the best possible price, since the company has lost much of the benefits of competitive bidding. Aside from the pricing considerations, the target's negotiating leverage may be weakened if there are parties privy to the confidential information that it doesn't know about. Explicit knowledge of exactly which parties are sharing the information will influence the choice of the appropriate information to deliver. From the bidders' viewpoint, the requested information may differ, depending on their chief business perspectives. While one bidder may be primarily interested in technical information, another may emphasize financing information. In addition, one bidder's market share may raise antitrust concerns not applicable to other bidders.

Standstill Provisions in the Confidentiality Agreement

If the target is a public company, the confidentiality agreement typically contains "standstill" provisions setting forth the terms under which the bidder may acquire, vote, or dispose of stock of the target. The variety and combination of standstill provisions are infinite, depending upon the special circumstances of the parties and their relative bargaining strengths.

Stock Acquisitions and Dispositions

When negotiations start, the target's opening position is usually to try to prohibit all acquisitions of the company's securities by the bidder. Sometimes the bidder may request a "basket" that would permit it to acquire up to a specified percentage of the company's stock. The appropriateness of this request depends upon the facts of each case.

A bidder with separate trading and investment functions may request that some of its units be allowed to continue trading in company stock without violating the standstill. An example would be a broker-dealer, mutual fund, pension fund, or other concern with ongoing market trading activities that may have an investment division separated by a so-called Chinese Wall to prevent leaks of confidential information. Such Chinese Wall exceptions are not unusual, provided the seller can be assured that the bidder has an effective means to police and enforce the barriers.

In any event, the target usually will not want the bidder to acquire more than 5 percent of its stock, since that normally would trigger the filing of a Schedule 13D with the Securities and Exchange Commission. The notification in turn would require disclosure of the bidder's plans and purposes with respect to the seller and the bidder's contracts with respect to the target's shares (including the confidentiality agreement). This disclosure may put the company "in play"—that is, create public anticipation of a pending transaction and cause a run-up in the company's stock.

Note that the bidder, in any event, will need to be sensitive to the requirements of federal securities laws restricting trading while in the possession of material inside information. Broker-dealers use "restricted lists" so trading personnel will not solicit orders in the target's stock while their investment banking executives are in possession of inside information.

If the bidder already owns a substantial block of the target's securities, the company may wish to restrict the disposition of those shares. If the stock is sold to a party not covered by the standstill agreement, that could destabilize the competitive bidding process.

Proxy Solicitations

The target typically will try to prevent bidders from attempting to acquire control of the company through a proxy contest. Since the law concerning proxy solicitation is extremely fact-specific, the confidentiality agreement may approach the subject by prohibiting:

- Outright solicitations of "proxies" by the buyer
- Buyer participation in a "group" seeking proxies
- Any other effort to control or influence the target's management

Timing of Proposals

The target usually wants to restrict the ability of the bidder to offer proposals concerning the types of transactions cited above, as well as any transactions that can be effected only with the seller's cooperation, such as mergers, recapitalizations, and asset sales. Although the bidder may question how the target's interests are advanced by such prohibitions, this is, in fact, one of the most critical aspects of a standstill in the context of an auction process for a public company.

A variety of factors could force the target to publicly disclose any proposal it receives concerning a change-in-control transaction. The target could determine that its previous disclosures may become misleading without a follow-up statement, if it has not followed a strict "no comment" policy in the past. Or the target may feel obligated to make an announcement if there is a sudden increase in stock market activity based on rumors. Any public disclosure could put the company "in play" and reduce the chances of completing a negotiated transaction.

Moreover, control over proposals gives the target control over the auction process itself. The company, through its financial advisers, often will circulate bidding guidelines governing the substance, timing, and manner of submission of acquisition offers. These guidelines enable the company to maximize the competition among bidders and stimulate the best available prices. For example, setting a fixed deadline for submission of offers may help neutralize any timing advantage enjoyed by one bidder over another.

The guidelines also can help ensure that the seller receives sufficient information with the bids so that they can be evaluated as to the seriousness or viability of the bidders. Additionally, uniform guidelines help draw bids that are more easily comparable with each other.

The confidentiality agreement can give authority to the company's bidding guidelines by restricting the ability of bidders to make proposals without the seller's consent. The bidding guidelines then can provide that only bids submitted in accordance with those ground rules are in compliance with the confidentiality agreement.

Restrictions on Requests for Waivers

The restrictions on proposals are most effective when coupled with a provision in which the bidder agrees not to request any waivers or amendments of the standstill. Since the principal harm to the target by an unsolicited proposal results from its public disclosure, the sales process can be impeded if the bidder publicly requests a change in the confidentiality agreement. As noted above, even nonpublic proposals hold dangers for the selling company, since neither the bidder nor the target may have perfect control over when disclosure of acquisition proposals is actually required.

Enforceability of Standstill Provisions

Despite the prevalence of confidentiality agreements, there are relatively few court cases that offer guidance on their enforceability.

In one case, the Delaware Chancery Court condoned the use of confidentiality agreements with standstill provisions when the target conducted an auction after receiving an unsolicited bid.

In another case, a federal district court held that a standstill provision provided the basis for issuing a preliminary injunction against an unsolicited tender offer. The court noted that:

- The bidder had received confidential information from the target pursuant to a confidentiality agreement.
- The information was material and would have to be disclosed in the tender offer.

- The information was "competitively sensitive" and the target would be irreparably harmed by its disclosure.

- The confidentiality agreement prohibited disclosure of the information and the making of a tender offer for as long as the information remained confidential.

Additional guidance as to the enforceability of standstill provisions can be found in a line of cases dealing with the furnishing of confidential information of bidders by former employees of the target. In these cases, the fiduciary duty of the employees replaces the confidentiality agreement as the source of the obligation not to disclose the confidential information. If the misappropriated information obtained by the bidder is competitively sensitive to the target, courts have been willing to enjoin a tender offer rather than force disclosure of the material. When the bidder's unlawful behavior is less egregious, and the harm to the target as a result of curative disclosure is less than clear, courts have been reluctant to enjoin a tender offer indefinitely.

Survival of the Confidentiality Agreement

There are a variety of approaches to specifying time limits on a confidentiality agreement. The options include setting a specific term of duration, making no reference to a term, or specifying that some provisions survive termination while others do not.

The standstill and nonsolicitation provisions typically will specify a term during which the bidder will be subject to restrictions. Other provisions, such as the obligation to keep records of confidential information, may be perpetual or may expire after a stated number of years or upon a stated event.

The target may be able to make a persuasive argument that certain proprietary information, such as technical "know-how," has an indefinite life. Such information would remain proprietary until it is disclosed. If the information indeed is proprietary, the seller may argue that the bidder should be prevented from disclosing or misusing it until it becomes publicly available from some other source.

"Most-Favored Nation Clauses"

A bidder sometimes may request "most favored nation" status—that is, the right to get the same preferential concessions granted to any other potential buyer. The target, on the other hand, can assert its need to respond with flexibility to bidders, depending upon their individual circumstances.

For example, if a bidder already has begun a tender offer, or already has a significant block of shares, the suitor may argue that it is entitled to special considerations in the negotiation of the standstill provisions.

It sounds simple, but the implications can be messy. Let us assume that one bidder already has launched a tender and because that offer is under way, it has obtained a confidentiality agreement that does not contain a standstill provision. An agreement with a competing bidder contains a standstill agreement as well as a "most favored nation" clause. Arguably, the target should not have to waive the standstill with the competing bidder because the tender offerer has preferential treatment.

The target may have trouble justifying its refusal to grant a concession to future bidders that demand it, after it already has agreed to the concession for an early entrant in the contest. However, if the target can cite special facts or circumstances that made the concession appropriate, it should be entitled to discriminate.

As a negotiating tactic, the target's counsel may resist the concession until the bidder refuses to sign the confidentiality agreement without it. However, if the negotiations reach that point, the target's board must be able to justify to shareholders why one potential bidder was denied a concession that the directors were willing to make to a competing bidder.

Pointers for Drafting Solid Agreements

It is helpful for the seller's counsel to establish ground rules at the outset, and to make sure that the target and its financial advisers agree with these rules.

If a company ultimately reaches an acquisition agreement, the board's actions face scrutiny by a court to determine whether the directors acted in good faith to maximize shareholder value through the sale. This has been interpreted to include an obligation that the board maintain a "level playing field" when entertaining offers from multiple bidders. Although some departures from the concept of "level playing field" may be supportable by the board, such as withholding pricing information from a competitor because of antitrust concerns, the deviations should be avoided whenever possible.

Because a multitude of specific facts and circumstances makes each negotiation unique, the specific points discussed in this article will vary in importance. Most important is that the target's legal and financial representatives work closely together. Then the confidentiality agreement can be an important tool in maximizing value in an acquisition or sale.

PART 3

Pricing, Valuation, Negotiating, and Deal Structuring

14

Discounted Cash Flow Valuation

Alfred Rappaport

*Adjunct Professor, J. L. Kellogg Graduate
School of Management,
Northwestern University, Evanston, Illinois,
and Principal, The LEK/Alcar
Consulting Group, L.P.,
Skokie, Illinois*

Mergers and acquisitions have become an increasingly important part of corporate growth strategy. Nevertheless, most acquisitions will fail to create value for the acquirer's shareholders.

Only a limited supply of acquisition candidates is available at the price that enables the acquirer to earn an acceptable return on investment. A well-conceived financial evaluation program that minimizes the risk of buying an economically unattractive company or paying too much for an attractive one is particularly important in the modern M&A market. The premium that must be paid by a successful bidder calls for more careful analysis by buyers than ever before.

Because of the competitive nature of the acquisition market, companies not only need to respond wisely but often must respond quickly as well. The growing independence of corporate boards and their demand for better information to support strategic decisions such as acquisitions have raised the general standard for acquisition analysis. Finally, sound analysis, convincingly communicated, can yield substantial benefits in negotiating with the target company's management or, in the case of tender offers, its stockholders.

This chapter shows how management can estimate how much value a prospective acquisition will, in fact, create. In brief, we present a comprehensive framework for acquisition analysis based on contemporary financial theory—an approach that has been profitably employed in practice. The analysis provides management and the board of the acquiring company with information both for making a decision on the candidate and for formulating an effective negotiating strategy for the acquisition.

STEPS IN THE ACQUISITION ANALYSIS

The process of analyzing acquisitions falls broadly into three stages: planning, search and screen, and financial evaluation.

The acquisition planning process begins with a review of corporate objectives and product-market strategies for various strategic business units. The acquiring company should define its potential directions for corporate growth and diversification in terms of corporate strengths and weaknesses and an assessment of the company's social, economic, political, and technological environment. This analysis produces a set of acquisition objectives and criteria.

Specified criteria often include statements about industry parameters, such as projected market growth rate, degree of regulation, ease of entry, and capital-versus-labor intensity. Company criteria for quality of management, share of market, profitability, size, and capital structure also commonly appear on acquisition criteria lists.

The search-and-screen process is a systematic approach to compiling a list of good acquisition prospects. The search focuses on how and where to look for candidates, and the screening process selects a few of the best candidates from literally thousands of possibilities, according to objectives and criteria developed in the planning phase.

Finally comes the financial evaluation process, which is the focus of this chapter. A good analysis should enable management to answer such questions as:

- What is the maximum price that should be paid for the target company?
- What are the principal areas of risk?
- What are the earnings, cash flow, and balance sheet implications of the acquisition?
- What is the best way to finance the acquisition?

Corporate Self-Evaluation

The financial evaluation process involves both a self-evaluation by the acquiring company and the evaluation of the candidate for acquisition. The scope and detail of corporate self-evaluation will necessarily vary according to the needs of each company.

The fundamental questions posed by a self-evaluation are: (1) How much is my company worth? (2) How would its value be affected by each of several scenarios? The first question involves generation of a "most likely" estimate of the company's value based on management's detailed assessment of its objectives, strategies, and plans. The second question calls for an assessment of value based on a range of plausible scenarios that enable management to test the joint effect of hypothesized combinations of product-market strategies and environmental forces.

Corporate self-evaluation, when conducted as an economic assessment of the value created for shareholders by various strategic planning options, promises potential benefits for all companies. In the context of the acquisition market, self-evaluation takes on special significance.

First, while a company might view itself as an acquirer, few companies are totally exempt from a possible takeover. Second, the self-evaluation process might well call attention to strategic divestment opportunities. Finally, self-evaluation offers acquisition-minded companies a basis for assessing the comparative advantages of a debt versus equity-financed offer.

Acquiring companies commonly value the purchase price for an acquisition at the market value of the shares exchanged. This practice is not economically sound and could be misleading and costly to the acquiring company. A well-conceived analysis for an exchange-of-shares acquisition requires sound valuations of both buying and selling companies. If the acquirer's management believes the market is undervaluing its shares, then valuing the purchase price at market might well induce the company to overpay for the acquisition or to earn less than the minimum acceptable rate of return. Conversely, if management believes the market is overvaluing its shares, then valuing the purchase price at market obscures the opportunity to offer the seller's shareholders additional shares while still achieving the minimum acceptable return.

Valuation of Acquisitions

Most major acquisition-minded companies rely extensively on the discounted cash flow (DCF) technique to analyze acquisitions. While mergers and acquisitions involve a considerably more complex set of managerial problems than the purchase of an ordinary asset such as a machine or a plant, the economic substance of these transactions is the same. In each case, there is a current outlay made in anticipation of a stream of future cash flows.

Thus the DCF criterion applies not only to internal growth investments, such as additions to existing capacity, but equally to external growth investments, such as acquisitions. An essential feature of the DCF technique is that it explicitly takes into account that a dollar of cash received today is worth more than a dollar received a year from now, because today's dollar can be invested to earn a return during the intervening time.

To establish the maximum acceptable acquisition price under the DCF approach, estimates are needed for (1) the incremental cash flows expected to be generated because of the acquisition and (2) the "discount rate" or "cost of capital," that is, the minimum acceptable rate of return required by the market for new investments by the company.

In projecting the cash flow stream of a prospective acquisition, what should be taken into account is the cash flow contribution the candidate is expected to make to the acquiring company. The results of this projection may well differ from a projection of the candidate's cash flow as an independent company. This is because the acquirer may be able to achieve operating economies not available to the selling company alone. Furthermore, acquisitions generally provide new postacquisition investment opportunities whose initial outlays and subsequent benefits also need to be incorporated in the cash flow schedule. Cash flow is defined as:

Cash flow = (operating profit) (1 − income tax rate) + depreciation and other noncash charges − (incremental working capital investments + capital expenditures)

The Forecast Period. In developing the cash flow schedule, two additional issues need to be considered:

- What is the basis for setting the length of the forecast period—that is, the period beyond which the cash flows associated with the acquisition are not specifically projected?
- How is the residual value of the acquisition established at the end of the forecast period?

A common practice is to forecast cash flows period by period until the level of uncertainty makes management too "uncomfortable" to go any further. Although practice varies with industry setting, management policy, and the special circumstances of the acquisition, 5 to 10 years appears to be an arbitrarily set forecast duration that is used in many situations. A better approach suggests that the forecast duration for cash flows should continue only as long as the expected rate of return on incremental investment required to support forecasted sales growth exceeds the cost-of-capital rate.

If for subsequent periods one assumes that the company's return on incremental investment equals the cost-of-capital rate, then the market would be indifferent to whether management invests in expansion projects or pays cash dividends that shareholders can in turn invest in identically risky opportunities yielding an identical rate of return. In other words, the value of the company is unaffected by growth when the company is investing in projects earning at the cost of capital, or at the minimum acceptable risk-adjusted rate of return required by the market.

Thus, for purposes of simplification, we can assume a 100 percent payout of "cash" earnings after the end of the forecast period or, equivalently, a zero growth rate without affecting the valuation of the company. The residual value is then the present value of the resulting cash flow perpetuity beginning one year after the horizon date. Of course, if after the end of the forecast period the return on investment is expected to decline below the cost-of-capital rate, this factor can be incorporated in the calculation.

The Cost of Capital. When the acquisition candidate's risk is judged to be the same as the acquirer's overall risk, the appropriate rate for discounting the candidate's cash flow stream is the acquirer's cost of capital. The cost of capital or the

Table 14.1. One Company's Weighted-Average Cost of Capital

	Weight	Cost	Weighted cost
Debt	0.20	0.05	0.01
Equity	0.80	0.15	0.12
Weighted-average cost of capital			<u>0.13</u>

minimum acceptable rate of return on new investments is based on the rate investors can expect to earn by investing in alternative, identically risky securities.

The cost of capital is calculated as the weighted average of the costs of debt and
equity capital. For example, suppose that a company's aftertax cost of debt is 5 percent and it estimates its cost of equity to be 15 percent. Further, it plans to raise
future capital in the following proportions: 20 percent by way of debt and 80 percent by equity. Table 14.1 shows how to compute the company's cost of capital (the
risk-adjusted, weighted-average cost of debt and equity).

It is important to emphasize that the acquiring company's use of its own cost of
capital to discount the target's projected cash flows is appropriate only when it can
be safely assumed that the acquisition will not affect the riskiness of the acquirer.
The specific riskiness of each prospective candidate should be taken into account
in setting the discount rate, with higher rates used for more risky investments.

If a single discount rate is used for all acquisitions, then those with the highest
risk will seem most attractive. Because the weighted-average risk of its component
segments determines the company's cost of capital, these high-risk acquisitions will
increase a company's cost of capital and thereby decrease the value of its stock.

MITNOR CORP.:
HYPOTHETICAL
RUNTHROUGH

As an illustration of the recommended approach to acquisition analysis, consider
the hypothetical case of Mitnor Corp.'s interest in acquiring Rano Products. Mitnor
is a leading manufacturer and distributor in the industrial packaging and materials
handling market. Sales for the most recent year totaled $600 million. Mitnor's ac-
quisition strategy is geared toward buying companies with similar marketing and
distribution characteristics, similar production technologies, or a similar research
and development orientation. Rano Products, a $50 million sales organization with
an impressive new-product development record in industrial packaging, fits Mitnor's general acquisition criteria particularly well. Premerger financial statements
for Mitnor and Rano are shown in Table 14.2.

Acquisition for Cash

The Value Planner and The Merger Planner microcomputer models developed by
The Alcar Group, Inc., generate a comprehensive analysis for acquisitions financed

Table 14.2. Premerger Financial Statements for Mitnor and Rano (in millions of dollars)

	Mitnor	Rano
Statement of Income (year ended December 31)		
Sales	$600.00	$50.00
Operating expenses	522.00	42.50
Operating profit	$ 78.00	$ 7.50
Interest on debt	4.50	.40
Earnings before taxes	$ 73.50	$ 7.10
Provision for income taxes	36.00	3.55
Net income	$ 37.50	$ 3.55
Number of common shares outstanding (in millions)	$ 10.00	$ 1.11
Earnings per share	3.75	3.20
Dividends per share	1.30	.64
Statement of Financial Position (at year-end)		
Net working capital	$180.00	$ 7.50
Marketable securities	25.00	1.00
Other assets	2.00	1.60
Gross property, plant, and equipment	216.00	20.00
Less accumulated depreciation	(95.00)	(8.00)
	$328.00	$22.10
Interest-bearing debt	$ 56.00	$ 5.10
Shareholders' equity	272.00	17.00
	$328.00	$22.10

by cash, stock, or any combination of cash, debt, preferred stock, and common stock. The analysis to follow will concern only the cash and exchange-of-shares cases. In the cash acquisition case, the analysis follows six essential steps:

- Develop estimates needed to project Rano's cash flow contribution for various growth and profitability scenarios.
- Estimate the minimum acceptable rate of return for acquisition of Rano.
- Compute the maximum acceptable cash price to be paid for Rano under various scenarios and minimum acceptable rates of return.
- Compute the rate of return that Mitnor will earn for a range of price offers and for various growth and profitability scenarios.
- Analyze the feasibility of a cash purchase in light of Mitnor's current liquidity and target debt/equity ratio.
- Evaluate the impact of the acquisition on the earnings per share and capital structure of Mitnor.

Step 1: Develop Cash Flow Projections. The cash flow formula presented earlier may be restated in equivalent form as

$$\mathrm{CF}_t = S_{t-1}(1 + g_t)(p_t)(1 - T_t) - (S_t - S_{t-1})(f_t + w_t)$$

where CF = cash flow

S = sales

g = annual growth rate in sales

p = operating profit margin as a percentage of sales

T = income tax rate

f = incremental fixed capital investment required (i.e., total capital investment net of replacement of existing capacity estimated by depreciation) per dollar of sales increase

w = incremental working capital investment required per dollar of sales increase

Once estimates are provided for five variables, g, p, T, f, and w, it is possible to project cash flow.

Table 14.3 shows Mitnor management's "most likely" estimates for Rano's operations, assuming Mitnor control; Table 14.4 shows a complete projected 10-year cash flow statement for Rano.

Before additional scenarios for Rano are developed, some brief comments should be made on how to estimate some of the cash flow variables. First, the income tax rate is the cash rate rather than a book rate based on the accountant's income tax expense, which often includes a portion that is deferred.

Second, for some companies, a direct projection of capital investment requirements per dollar of sales increase will prove a difficult task. To gain an estimate of the recent value of this coefficient, simply take the sum of all capital investments less depreciation over the past 5 or 10 years and divide this total by the increase in sales from the beginning to the end of the period. With this approach, the resulting coefficient not only represents the capital investment historically required per dollar of sales increase, but also impounds any cost increases for replacement of existing capacity.

One should estimate changes in incremental working capital investment with care. Actual year-to-year balance sheet changes in working capital investment required for operations may not provide a good measure of the rise or decline in funds required. There are two main reasons for this: (1) The year-end balance sheet figures may not reflect the average or normal needs of the business during the year;

Table 14.3. Most Likely Estimates for Rano's Operations under Mitnor Control

	Years		
	1–5	6–7	8–10
Sales growth rate (g)	0.15	0.12	0.12
Operations profit margin as a percentage of sale (p)	0.18	0.15	0.12
Income tax rate (T)	0.46	0.46	0.46
Incremental fixed capital investment (f)	0.20	0.20	0.20
Incremental working capital investment (w)	0.15	0.15	0.15
Employing the cash flow formula for year 1:			

$$CF_1 = 50(1 + 0.15)(0.18)(1 - 0.46) - (57.5 - 50)(0.20 + 0.15) = 2.96$$

Table 14.4. Projected 10-Year Cash Flow Statement for Rano (in millions of dollars)

	Year									
	1	2	3	4	5	6	7	8	9	10
Sales	$57.50	$66.12	$76.04	$87.45	$100.57	$112.64	$126.15	$141.29	$158.25	$177.23
Operating expenses	47.15	54.22	62.34	71.71	82.47	95.74	107.23	124.34	139.26	155.96
Operating profit	$10.35	$11.90	$13.70	$15.74	$18.10	$16.90	$18.92	$16.95	$18.99	$21.27
Cash income taxes	4.76	5.48	6.30	7.24	8.33	7.78	8.70	7.79	8.74	9.78
Operating profit after taxes	$5.59	$6.42	$7.40	$8.50	$9.78	$9.12	$10.22	$9.16	$10.25	$11.49
Depreciation	1.60	1.85	2.13	2.46	2.84	3.28	3.74	4.25	4.83	5.49
Less incremental fixed capital investment	(3.10)	(3.57)	(4.12)	(4.74)	(5.47)	(5.69)	(6.44)	(7.28)	(8.22)	(9.29)
Less incremental working capital investment	(1.13)	(1.29)	(1.49)	(1.71)	(1.97)	(1.81)	(2.03)	(2.27)	(2.54)	(2.85)
Cash flow from operations	$2.96	$3.41	$3.92	$4.51	$5.18	$4.90	$5.49	$3.86	$4.32	$4.84

and (2) the inventory accounts may overstate the magnitude of the funds committed by the company.

To estimate the additional cash requirements, the increased inventory investment should be measured by the variable costs for any additional units of inventory required.

In addition to its most likely estimate for Rano, Mitnor's management developed two additional (conservative and optimistic) scenarios for sales growth and operating profit margins. Table 14.5 gives a summary of all three scenarios. Mitnor's management also may wish to examine additional cases to test the effect of alternative assumptions about the cash income tax rate and both the fixed capital investment and working capital investment per dollar of sales increase.

Recall that cash flows should be forecast only for the period when the expected rate of return on incremental investment exceeds the minimum acceptable rate of return for the acquisition. It is possible to determine this in a simple yet analytical, nonarbitrary fashion. To do so, we compute the minimum incremental pretax return on sales or incremental threshold margin (ITM) needed to earn the minimum acceptable rate of return on the acquisition (k). Necessary components include the investment requirements for working capital (w) and fixed assets (f) for each additional dollar of sales and a given projected tax rate (T). The formula for ITM is:

$$\text{Incremental threshold margin} = \frac{(f+w)k}{(1-T)(1+K)}$$

Mitnor's management believes that when Rano's growth begins to slow down, its working capital requirements per dollar of additional sales will increase from 15 cents to about 20 cents and its tax rate will increase from 46 percent to 50 percent. As will be shown in the next section, the minimum acceptable rate of return on the Rano acquisition is 13 percent. Thus:

$$\text{Incremental threshold margin} = \frac{(0.20+0.20)(0.13)}{(1-0.50)(1+0.13)}$$

$$\text{ITM} = \underline{0.092}$$

Mitnor's management has enough confidence to forecast pretax sales returns above 9.2 percent for only the next 10 years, and thus the forecast duration for the Rano acquisition is limited to that period.

Table 14.5. Additional Scenarios for Sales Growth and Operating Profit Margins

| Scenario | Sales growth (g) | | | Operating profit margins (p) | | |
| | Years | | | Years | | |
	1–5	6–7	8–10	1–5	6–7	8–10
1. Conservative	0.14	0.12	0.10	0.17	0.14	0.11
2. Most likely	0.15	0.12	0.12	0.18	0.15	0.12
3. Optimistic	0.18	0.15	0.12	0.20	0.16	0.12

Step 2: Estimate Minimum Acceptable Rate of Return for Acquisition.

In developing a company's cost of capital, measuring the aftertax cost of debt is relatively straightforward. The cost of equity capital, however, is more difficult to estimate.

Rational, risk-averse investors expect to earn a rate of return that will compensate them for accepting greater investment risk. Thus, in assessing the company's cost of equity capital, or the minimum expected return that will induce investors to buy the company's shares, it is reasonable to assume that they will demand the risk-free rate as reflected in the current yields available in government bonds, plus a premium for accepting equity risk.

Assume that the risk-free rate on government bonds has been in the neighborhood of 8.8 percent. By investing in a portfolio broadly representative of the overall equity market, it is possible to diversify away substantially all of the unsystematic risk—that is, risk specific to individual companies. Therefore, securities are likely to be priced at levels that reward investors only for the nondiversifiable market risk—that is, the systematic risk in movements in the overall market.

The risk premium for the overall market is the excess of the expected return on a representative market index such as the Standard & Poor's 500 stock index over the risk-free return. Empirical studies have estimated this market risk premium (representative market index minus risk-free rate) to average historically about 5 to 5.5 percent. We will use a 5.2 percent premium in subsequent calculations.

Investing in an individual security generally involves more or less risk than investing in a broad market portfolio. Thus one must adjust the market risk premium appropriately in estimating the cost of equity for an individual security. The risk premium for a security is the product of the market risk premium times the individual security's systematic risk, as measured by its beta coefficient.

The rate of return from dividends and capital appreciation on a market portfolio will, by definition, fluctuate identically with the market, and, therefore, its beta is equal to 1.0. A beta for an individual security is an index of its risk expressed as its volatility of return in relation to that of a market portfolio. Securities with betas greater than 1.0 are more volatile than the market, and thus would be expected to have a risk premium greater than the overall market risk premium, or the average-risk stock with a beta of 1.0.

For example, if a stock moves 1.5 percent when the market moves 1 percent, the stock would have a beta of 1.5. Securities with betas of less than 1.0 are less volatile than the market and thus would command risk premiums that are less than the market risk premium. In summary, the cost of equity capital may be calculated by the following equation:

$$k_e = Rf + B_j (R_M - R_F)$$

where k_e = cost of equity capital
R_F = risk-free rate
B_j = beta coefficient
R_M = representative market index

Table 14.6. Mitnor's Cost of Capital

	Weight	Cost	Weighted cost
Debt	0.23	0.051	0.012
Equity	0.77	0.140	0.108
Cost of capital			0.120

The acquiring company, Mitnor, with a beta of 1.0, estimated its cost of equity as 14 percent with the foregoing equation:

$$k_e = 0.088+1.0(0.052)$$

$$= 0.140$$

Since interest on debt is tax-deductible, the rate of return that must be earned on the debt portion of the company's capital structure to maintain the earnings available to common shareholders is the aftertax cost of debt. The aftertax cost of borrowed capital is Mitnor's current before-tax interest rate (9.5 percent) times 1 minus its tax rate of 46 percent, which is equal to 5.1 percent. Mitnor's target debt/equity ratio is 0.30; or, equivalently, debt is targeted at 23 percent and equity at 77 percent of its overall capitalization, as Table 14.6 shows in estimating Mitnor's weighted average cost of capital. The appropriate rate for discounting Mitnor cash flows to establish its estimated value then is 12 percent.

For new capital projects, including acquisitions, that are deemed to have about the same risk as the overall company, Mitnor can use its 12 percent cost-of-capital rate as the appropriate discount rate. Because the company's cost of capital is determined by the weighted-average risk of its component segments, the specific risk of each prospective acquisition should be estimated in order to arrive at the discount rate to apply to the candidate's cash flows.

Rano, with a beta coefficient of 1.25, is more risky than Mitnor. The formula for cost of equity capital for Rano is:

$$k_e = 0.088+1.25(0.052)$$

$$= 0.153$$

On this basis, the risk-adjusted cost of capital for the Rano acquisition is as shown in Table 14.7.

Table 14.7. Cost of Capital for Rano Acquisition

	Weight	Cost	Weighted cost
Debt	0.23	0.054*	0.012
Common equity	0.77	0.153	0.118
Cost of capital			0.130

*Before-tax debt rate of 10 percent times 1 minus the estimated tax rate of 46 percent.

Step 3: Compute Maximum Acceptable Cash Price. This step involves taking the cash flow projections developed in step 1 and discounting them at the rate developed in step 2. Table 14.8 shows the computation of the maximum acceptable cash price for the most likely scenario. The maximum price of $44.51 million, or $40.10 per share, for Rano compares with a $25 current market price for Rano shares. Thus, for the most likely case, Mitnor can pay up to $15 per share over current market or a 60 percent premium, and still achieve its minimum acceptable 13 percent return on the acquisition.

Table 14.9 shows the maximum acceptable cash price for each of the three scenarios for a range of discount rates. To earn a 13 percent rate of return, Mitnor can pay at maximum $38 million ($34.25 per share) assuming the conservative scenario, and up to $53 million ($47.80 per share) assuming the optimistic scenario. Note that as Mitnor demands a greater return on its investment, there is a drop in the maximum price it can pay. For example, in the most likely scenario, the maximum price falls from $44.52 million to $39.67 million as the return requirement goes from 13 to 14 percent.

Step 4: Compute Rate of Return for Various Offering Prices and Scenarios. Mitnor management believes that the absolute minimum successful bid for Rano would be $35 million, or $31.50 per share. Mitnor's investment bankers estimated that it may take a bid of as high as $45 million, or $40.50 per share, to gain control of Rano shares. Table 14.10 presents the rates of return that will be earned for four different offering prices, ranging from $35 million to $45 million for each of the three scenarios.

Table 14.8. Maximum Acceptable Cash Price for Rano—Most Likely Scenario, with a Discount Rate of 13 Percent (in millions of dollars)

Year	Cash flow from operations	Present value	Cumulative present value
1	$ 2.96	$ 2.62	$ 2.62
2	3.41	2.67	5.29
3	3.92	2.72	8.01
4	4.51	2.76	10.77
5	5.13	2.81	13.59
6	4.90	2.35	15.94
7	5.49	2.33	18.27
8	3.86	1.45	19.72
9	4.32	1.44	21.16
10	4.84	1.43	22.59
Residual value	11.48	26.02*	48.61
Plus marketable securities not required for current operations			1.00
Corporate value			49.61
Less debt assumed			5.10
Maximum acceptable cash price (shareholder value)			$44.51
Maximum acceptable cash price per share (shareholder value per share)			$40.10

$$*\frac{\text{Year 10 operating profit after taxes}}{\text{Discount rate}} \times \text{year 10 discount factor} = \frac{11.48}{0.13} \times 0.2946 = 26.02$$

Table 14.9. Maximum Acceptable Cash Price for Three Scenarios and a Range of Discount Rates

	Discount rate				
Scenario	0.11	0.12	0.13	0.14	0.15
1. Conservative:					
Total price ($ millions)	$48.84	$42.91	$38.02	$33.93	$30.47
Per-share price	44.00	38.66	34.25	30.57	27.45
2. Most likely:					
Total price ($ millions)	57.35	50.31	44.51	39.67	35.58
Per-share price	51.67	45.33	40.10	35.74	32.05
3. Optimistic:					
Total price ($ millions)	68.37	59.97	53.05	47.28	42.41
Per-share price	61.59	54.03	47.80	42.59	38.21

Under the optimistic scenario, Mitnor could expect a return of 14.4 percent if it were to pay $45 million. For the most likely case, an offer of $45 million would yield a 12.9 percent return, or just under the minimum acceptable rate of 13 percent. This is as expected, because the maximum acceptable cash price as calculated in Table 14.8 is $44.51 million, or just under the $45 million offer. If Mitnor attaches a relatively high probability to the conservative scenario, the risk associated with offers exceeding $38 million becomes apparent.

Step 5: Analyze Feasibility of Cash Purchase. While Mitnor management views the relevant purchase price range for Rano as somewhere between $35 million and $45 million, it also must establish whether an all-cash deal is feasible in light of Mitnor's current liquidity and target debt/equity ratio. The maximum funds available for the purchase of Rano equal the postmerger debt capacity of the combined company less the combined premerger debt of the two companies plus the combined premerger marketable securities of the two companies. (Funds beyond the minimum cash required for everyday operations of the business are excluded from working capital and classified as "marketable securities.")

In an all-cash transaction governed by purchase accounting, the shareholders equity of the acquirer is unchanged. The postmerger debt capacity then is Mitnor's shareholders equity of $272 million times the targeted debt/equity ratio of 0.30, or $81.6 million. Mitnor and Rano have premerger debt balances of $56 million and $5.1 million, respectively, for a total of $61.1 million.

The unused debt capacity is thus $81.6 million minus $61.1 million, or $20.5 mil-

Table 14.10. Rate of Return for Various Offering Prices and Scenarios

		Offering price			
Scenario	Total ($ millions) Per share	$35.00 $31.53	$38.00 $34.23	$40.00 $36.04	$45.00 $40.54
1. Conservative		0.137	0.130	0.126	0.116
2. Most likely		0.152	0.144	0.139	0.129
3. Optimistic		0.169	0.161	0.156	0.144

lion. Add to this the combined marketable securities of Mitnor and Rano of $26 million, and the maximum funds available for the cash purchase of Rano will be $46.5 million. A cash purchase is therefore feasible within the tentative price range of $35 to $45 million.

Step 6: Evaluate Impact of Acquisition on Mitnor's EPS and Capital Structure. Because reported earnings per share (EPS) continue to be of great interest to the financial community, a complete acquisition analysis should include a comparison of projected EPS both with and without the acquisition. Table 14.11 contains this comparative projection. The EPS stream with the acquisition of Rano is systematically greater than the stream without acquisition. The EPS standard, and particularly a short-term EPS standard, is not, however, a reliable basis for assessing whether the acquisition will in fact create value for shareholders.[1]

Several problems arise when EPS is used as a standard for evaluating acquisitions. First, because of accounting measurement problems, the EPS figure can be determined by alternative, equally acceptable methods—for example, LIFO versus FIFO. Second, the EPS standard ignores the time value of money. Third, it does not take risk into account. Risk is conditioned not only by the nature of the investment projects a company undertakes, but by the relative proportions of debt and equity used to finance those investments.

A company can increase EPS by increasing leverage as long as the marginal return on investment is greater than the interest rate on the new debt. However, if the marginal return on investment is less than the risk-adjusted cost of capital or if the increased leverage leads to an increased cost of capital, then the value of the company could decline despite increasing earnings per share.

Primarily because the acquisition of Rano requires that Mitnor partially finance the purchase price with bank borrowing, the debt/equity ratios with the acquisition are greater than those without the acquisition (see Table 14.11). Note that even

Table 14.11. Mitnor's Projected EPS, Debt/Equity Ratio, and Unused Debt Capacity—without and with Rano Acquisition

Year	EPS		Debt/equity		Unused debt capacity ($ millions)	
	Without	With	Without	With	Without	With
0	$ 3.75	$ 4.10	$0.21	0.26	$25.60	$20.50
1	4.53	4.89	0.19	0.27	34.44	9.42
2	5.09	5.51	0.17	0.28	44.22	7.00
3	5.71	6.20	0.19	0.29	40.26	4.20
4	6.38	6.99	0.21	0.30	35.45	.98
5	7.14	7.87	0.24	0.31	29.67	−2.71
6	7.62	8.29	0.26	0.31	22.69	−7.77
7	8.49	9.27	0.27	0.32	14.49	−13.64
8	9.46	10.14	0.29	0.33	4.91	−22.34
9	10.55	11.33	0.31	0.34	−6.23	−32.36
10	11.76	12.66	0.32	0.35	−19.16	−43.88

NOTE: Assumed cash purchase price for Rano is $35 million.

without the Rano acquisition, Mitnor is in danger of violating its target debt/equity ratio of 0.30 by the ninth year. The acquisition of Rano accelerates the problem to the fifth year. Whether Mitnor purchases Rano or not, management now must be alert to the financing problem, which may force it to issue additional shares or re-evaluate its present capital structure policy.

Acquisition for Stock

The first two steps in the acquisition-for-stock analysis, projecting Rano operating cash flows and setting the discount rate, already have been completed in connection with the acquisition-for-cash analysis developed in the previous section. The remaining steps of the acquisition-for-stock analysis are:

- Estimate the value of Mitnor shares.
- Compute the maximum number of shares that Mitnor can exchange to acquire Rano under various scenarios and minimum acceptable rates of return.
- Evaluate the impact of the acquisition on the earnings per share and capital structure of Mitnor.

Step 1: Estimate Value of Mitnor Shares. Mitnor conducted a comprehensive corporate self-evaluation that included an assessment of its estimated present value based on a range of scenarios. In the interest of brevity, only its most likely scenario is considered here.

Management made most likely projections for its operations, as shown in Table 14.12. Again using the equation for the cost of equity capital, the incremental threshold margin (the minimum profit margin as a percentage of sales increase needed to earn Mitnor's 12 percent cost of capital) is 10.9 percent.

$$\text{Incremental threshold margin} = \frac{(f + w)(k)}{(1 - T)(1 + k)}$$

$$= \frac{(0.25 + 0.30)(0.12)}{(1 - 0.46)(1.12)}$$

$$= 10.9 \text{ percent}$$

Table 14.12. Most Likely Estimates for Mitnor Operations without Acquisition

	Years		
	1–5	6–7	8–10
Sales growth rate (g)	0.125	0.120	0.120
Operating profit margin as a percentage of sales (p)	0.130	0.125	0.125
Income tax rate (T)	0.460	0.460	0.460
Incremental fixed capital investment (f)	0.250	0.250	0.250
Incremental working capital investment (w)	0.300	0.300	0.300

Since management can confidently forecast pretax return on sales returns above 10.9 percent for only the next 10 years, the cash flow projections will be limited to that period.

Table 14.13 presents the computation of the value of Mitnor's equity. Its estimated value of $36.80 per share contrasts with its current market value of $22 per share. Because Mitnor management believes its shares to be undervalued by the market, in the absence of other compelling factors it will be reluctant to acquire Rano by means of an exchange of shares.

To illustrate, suppose that Mitnor were to offer $35 million in cash for Rano. Assume the most likely case, that the maximum acceptable cash price is $44.51 million (see Table 14.8); thus the acquisition would create about $9.5 million in value for Mitnor shareholders. Now assume that, instead, Mitnor agrees to exchange $35 million in market value of its shares in order to acquire Rano. In contrast with the cash transaction, in the exchange-of-share case, Mitnor shareholders can expect to be worse off by $12.1 million.

With Mitnor shares selling at $22, the company must exchange 1.59 million shares to meet the $35 million offer for Rano. There are currently 10 million Mitnor shares outstanding. After the merger, the combined company will be owned 86.27 percent by current Mitnor shareholders and 13.73 percent by Rano shareholders. The $12.1 million loss by Mitnor shareholders can then be calculated as shown in Table 14.14.

Table 14.13. Estimated Present Value of Mitnor Equity—Most Likely Scenario, with a Discount Rate of 12 Percent (in millions of dollars)

Year	Cash flow from operations	Present value	Cumulative present value
1	$ 6.13	$ 5.48	$ 5.48
2	6.90	5.50	10.98
3	7.76	5.53	16.51
4	8.74	5.55	22.06
5	9.83	5.58	27.63
6	10.38	5.26	38.15
7	11.63	5.26	32.89
8	13.02	5.26	43.41
9	14.58	5.26	48.67
10	16.33	5.26	53.93
Residual value	128.62	345.10*	399.03
Plus marketable securities not required for current operations			25.00
Mitnor's corporate value			$424.03
Less debt outstanding			56.00
Mitnor's shareholder value			$368.03
Mitnor's shareholder per share			$ 36.80

*$\dfrac{\text{Year 10 operating profit after taxes}}{\text{Discount rate}} \times \text{year 10 discount factor} = \dfrac{128.62}{0.12} \times 0.32197 = 345.10$

Table 14.14. Calculation of Loss by Mitnor Shareholders (in millions of dollars)

Mitnor receives 86.27% of Rano's present value of $44.51 million (see Table 15.8)	$38.4
Mitnor gives up 13.73% of its present value of $368.03 million (see Table 15.13)	(50.5)
Dilution of Mitnor's shareholder value	$12.1

Step 2: Compute Maximum Number of Shares Mitnor Can Exchange.

The maximum acceptable number of shares to exchange for each of the three scenarios and for a range of discount rates appears in Table 14.15. To earn a 13 percent rate of return, Mitnor can exchange no more than 1.033, 1.210, and 1.442 million shares, assuming the conservative, most likely, and optimistic scenarios, respectively. Consider, for a moment, the most likely case. At a market value per share of $22, the 1.21 million Mitnor shares exchanged would have a total value of $26.62 million, which is less than Rano's current market value of $27.75 million—that is, 1.11 million shares at $25 per share. Because of the market's apparent undervaluation of Mitnor's shares, an exchange ratio likely to be acceptable to Rano clearly will be unattractive to Mitnor.

Step 3: Evaluate Impact of Acquisition on Mitnor's EPS and Capital Structure.

The $35 million purchase price is just under 10 times Rano's most recent year's earnings of $3.55 million. At its current market price per share of $22, Mitnor is selling at about six times its most recent earnings. The acquiring company always will suffer immediate EPS dilution whenever the price/earnings ratio paid for the selling company is greater than its own. Mitnor would suffer immediate dilution from $3.75 a share to $3.54 a share in the current year. A comparison of EPS for cash versus an exchange-of-shares transaction appears as part of Table 14.16. As expected, the EPS projections for a cash deal are consistently higher than those for an exchange of shares.

However, the acquisition of Rano for shares rather than cash would remove, at least for now, Mitnor's projected financing problem. In contrast to cash acquisition, an exchange of shares enables Mitnor to have unused debt capacity at its disposal throughout the 10-year forecast period. Despite the relative attractiveness of this financing flexibility, Mitnor management recognized that it could not expect a reasonable rate of return by offering an exchange of shares to Rano.

Table 14.15. Maximum Acceptable Shares to Exchange for Three Scenarios and a Range of Discount Rates (in millions of dollars)

	Discount rate				
Scenario	0.11	0.12	0.13	0.14	0.15
1. Conservative	$1.327	$1.166	$1.033	$0.922	$0.828
2. Most likely	1.558	1.367	1.210	1.078	0.967
3. Optimistic	1.858	1.630	1.442	1.285	1.152

Table 14.16. Mitnor's Projected EPS, Debt/Equity Ratio, and Unused Debt Capacity—Cash versus Exchange of Shares

Year	EPS Cash	EPS Stock	Debt/equity Cash	Debt/equity Stock	Unused debt capacity ($ millions) Cash	Unused debt capacity ($ millions) Stock
0	$ 4.10	$ 3.54	0.26	0.21	$20.50	$25.60
1	4.89	4.37	0.27	0.19	9.42	35.46
2	5.51	4.93	0.28	0.17	7.00	46.62
3	6.20	5.55	0.29	0.18	4.20	48.04
4	6.99	6.23	0.30	0.20	0.98	46.37
5	7.87	7.00	0.31	0.21	−2.71	44.29
6	8.29	7.37	0.31	0.23	−7.77	40.90
7	9.27	8.22	0.32	0.24	−13.64	36.78
8	10.14	8.98	0.33	0.26	−22.34	29.90
9	11.33	10.01	0.34	0.27	−32.36	−21.79
10	12.66	11.17	0.35	0.29	−43.88	−12.29

NOTE: Assumed purchase price for Rano is $35 million.

TWOFOLD RESULTS

The experience of companies that have implemented the foregoing approach to acquisition analysis indicates that it is not only an effective way of evaluating a prospective acquisition candidate, but serves as a catalyst for reevaluating a company's overall strategic plans. The results also enable management to justify acquisition recommendations to the board of directors in an economically sound, convincing fashion.

Various companies have used this shareholder value approach for evaluation of serious candidates as well as for initial screening of potential candidates. In the latter case, initial input estimates are quickly generated to establish whether the range of maximum acceptable prices is greater than the current value of the target companies. With the aid of a recently developed microcomputer model, this can be accomplished quickly and at relatively low cost.

Whether companies are seeking acquisitions or are acquisition targets, it is increasingly clear that they must provide better information to enable top managements and boards to make well-conceived, timely decisions. Use of the approach outlined here should improve the prospects of creating value for shareholders by acquisitions.

NOTES

1. For a more detailed discussion of the shortcomings of earnings as a financial standard for corporate performance, see Alfred Rappaport, *Creating Shareholder Value: The New Standard for Business Performance* (New York: The Free Press, 1986).

15

The Fine Art of Valuation

Judson P. Reis

Managing General Partner, Sire Partners, L.P.,
New York, New York

Charles R. Cory

Managing Director,
Morgan Stanley & Co., Incorporated
New York, New York

In the end, the M&A business is always a debate about value. Accordingly, the process of determining, in a rational way, what a certain asset, group of assets, or company is worth is the foundation of the investment banker's role in any merger or acquisition assignment.

A well-executed valuation of a company under study as an acquisition candidate enables an investment banker to:

- Determine the appropriate range of acquisition values for the company, and advise the company as a seller or a buyer
- Advise the client regarding the feasibility of a proposed transaction (either acquisition or divestiture) using the valuation as a frame of reference and the client's own views about value as guidelines
- Prepare for negotiation with the principals and the advisers on the other side of a transaction
- Opine on the fairness of the transaction to the shareholders of the client

The advice that stems from a thorough valuation, in short, is precisely the advice for which a client turns to a banker.

APPROACHES TO ACQUISITION ANALYSIS

Because valuation is the foundation for so many facets of advice, it is not surprising that "valuation" may encompass several distinct but closely interrelated concepts. None of these valuation tools is inherently better than the others, and each method is used in different circumstances. The two primary valuation concepts used by investment bankers are intrinsic financial value and acquisition value.

Intrinsic Value

Intrinsic financial value captures the discounted present value of the free cash flows generated by the assets of a business as a going concern plus a terminal value of the business, also discounted to the present at an appropriate discount rate. Thus, intrinsic valuation looks at a time series of financial flows over a certain period and attempts to estimate what a purchaser would pay for these cash flows from a purely financial point of view. The discounted cash flow (DCF) methodology used to arrive at this value is necessarily predicated on a series of assumptions about the nature of the cash flows and a judgment as to the appropriate rate at which to discount these flows. The calculated intrinsic value of the company, therefore, *changes* as the assumptions from which the forecasts are generated or discounted are changed. As is true in most analyses, then, a DCF valuation is only as good as the assumptions or projections on which it is based.

The investment banker will assume a leading role in testing the credibility of any forecasts used for the DCF analysis and even may be called upon to develop a forecast in consultation with the client. Whether supplied by the seller or the buyer, or developed by the banker, the projections always must be subjected to a test of reasonableness. One of the most exacting tests of reasonableness is to compare the historical performance of the company on certain key financial measures (e.g., rate of sales growth, profit margins, capital intensity) to the forecasted performance. A forecast that, for example, projects dramatic improvements in margins (as is often the case in the classic sellers' "hockey stick," or overly optimistic, projections) must be investigated further before it is accepted at face value. As a cross-check, the investment banker often will prepare an analysis that compares the historical and projected financial performance of the specific company being valued to the performance of comparable companies. Moreover, by analyzing the forecast and using his or her knowledge of industry economics, the banker can give closer scrutiny to the line items that are most crucial to the free cash flow generation of the target.

Acquisition Value

The acquisition value of a company, which may differ significantly from its intrinsic financial value, seeks to estimate the price at which the company would "trade" in the "market for corporate control." Acquisition value thus is the price an acquirer would pay to control the target's assets and the free cash flows (FCFs) they generate. Two other observations about acquisition value are appropriate. First, a market for corporate control undoubtedly exists. Transactions occur almost daily at prices significantly above current secondary trading levels. Investment bankers continually are conducting public and private auctions which attract a number of bidders. Experience shows that these contests in the market for corporate control can be very competitive and therefore should accurately reflect value.

The second observation about acquisition value is that the value of a company as an independent entity often will be different than the value of the company when it is combined with another firm. The acquisition value will reflect the incremental cash flows generated by consolidated tax savings, cost savings due to the elimination of redundant operations, distribution economies, or other such synergies. Synergy is a controversial topic, and the actual realization of synergies is infinitely more difficult to achieve than the recognition that they should exist in certain situations. But if synergy is reduced to this limited definition—incremental increases in free cash flow that come about *because* of the combination—it is clear that valuation should take into account the synergistic elements of any proposed business combination.

Liquidation and Replacement Value

There are other valuation concepts that an investment banker may consider. In transactions in which assets are important factors, both liquidation value and replacement value can be quite useful. Liquidation value is an estimate of the net proceeds (after expenses) of selling the assets of the company at their fair market values and satisfying all liabilities, including taxes that might arise due to the liquidation. Some estimate of the time horizon over which the liquidation will take place must be developed also, so that the present value of the liquidation can be estimated. Liquidation value will often represent a floor or minimum value for a transaction. An estimate of the replacement value of the company—duplicating at current costs all of a company's assets—also may be a relevant measure, especially if a potential buyer is viewing an acquisition as an alternative to entering the business *de novo* or by internal expansion.

In addition to intrinsic and acquisition value, investment bankers typically attempt to estimate, on a pro forma basis, the market valuation of a publicly traded acquirer after a contemplated acquisition transaction is completed. To perform this task, the pro forma financial and business effects of the merger on the acquirer are calculated (especially the pro forma earnings pickup or dilution and key credit statistics), and a judgment is made as to how the combined entity will trade in the marketplace, both in the near term and over time. Pro forma financial analysis can be especially critical when the contemplated transaction is large in relation to the size of the acquirer. It is usually desirable to evaluate the pro forma impact *prior* to initiating a transaction, because it helps to clarify the relative attractiveness of the transaction over a range of values and because it may help to set limits on the value the buyer will (or should) pay.

PRACTICAL VALUATION CONCEPTS

Having laid out various types of valuation analyses that investment bankers perform and some of the rationale for their use, we can present a more detailed discussion of these concepts and the attendent methodologies. One should realize that in many real-world situations all of these valuation processes will proceed simultaneously, waxing and waning in importance according to the client's state of mind and the competitive dynamics of the transaction. Most important, valuation analysis often must be performed in a compressed time period and based on remarkably incomplete information.

Intrinsic Financial or DCF Valuation

To state the premise again, DCF valuation posits that the buyer purchase a time series (into infinity) of free cash flows that are generated by the assets purchased. DCF does not value the *total* cash flow of the business. Rather, it values only the *free* cash flow. In so doing, this analysis separates and ascribes value only to the cash flows that can be taken out of the business. Cash that is generated but used to sustain the business (such as increases in working capital and capital expenditures) does not count in the DCF value. Cash flow that must be retained in the business creates no incremental value for the buyer.

Another methodological nuance should be noted before free cash flow can be fully defined. As explained in detail below, DCF valuation uses a discount rate that reflects the firm's weighted-average cost of capital or the price it must pay to suppliers of both debt and equity. Accordingly, the free cash flows to be discounted should be developed independent of financing costs. In valuing a going concern with existing liabilities, therefore, the aftertax cost of interest is added back to the cash flow to create an unlevered free cash flow. It is this series of free cash flows that, when discounted to the present and combined with a terminal value (also discounted to the present), represents the economic value of the firm on a standalone basis. Thus, free cash flow in any given year of operation is defined as:

	Net income (after taxes)
plus:	noncash charges
plus:	aftertax interest cost (interest expense) $(1 - \text{tax rate})$
less:	capital expenditures
less:	net investment in working capital
equals:	free cash flow (unlevered)

Terminal Value

As noted earlier, DCF valuation seeks to value the company as a going concern into infinity. As practical matter, however, no banker or businessperson is comfortable with projections going out 20 years, let alone 100 years or infinitely. So DCF valuation is separated into two components: a forecast of FCFs for some term of years, and a terminal value that is a surrogate for the present value of the FCFs that occur in the years after the end of the forecast period. Typically, one constructs 5 to 10 years of pro forma financial statements, derives the FCFs for the forecasted years, and then estimates a terminal value for the company.

Terminal value at the end of the period of cash flow forecasts may be arrived at in different ways, such as estimating book value, applying a price/earnings multiple to forecasted earnings—either net income or earnings before interest and taxes (EBIT)—or employing a method to estimate a terminal cash flow multiple. Terminal book value is estimated by projecting the balance sheet forward to the last year of the forecast horizon and arriving at the book value of the common equity account at that time. It is assumed, under this scenario, that the interim free cash flow has been paid out. A terminal price/earnings or EBIT multiple essentially values the firm at the end of the horizon in the same way that the stock market would value it—by capitalizing the then-current earnings. The choice of the proper multiple will, obviously, have a large effect on the terminal value, and care therefore should be taken to choose a multiple consistent with the characteristics of both the industry and company at that time. It would be nonsensical, for example, to use a very high P/E at the end of the horizon for a company that was forecasted to have stable margins and relatively low growth rates.

The third means to estimate a terminal value, deriving a multiple of FCF at the terminals, is slightly more complicated but methodologically more consistent with the premises of DCF valuation. In essence, this technique multiplies the FCF in the last forecast year (or a "normalized" FCF if there is something unusual about that year's FCF) by a multiplier that attempts to estimate the value of the cash flows in perpetuity. The multiplier is derived by the formula

$$\frac{(1+g)}{(k-g)}$$

where g is the assumed rate of growth of the cash flow stream into the future and k is the weighted-average cost of capital. This formula capitalizes a stream that is growing at g percent into the future being discounted to the present at k percent. In practice, the banker may use all three of these terminal value estimation techniques in an attempt to cross-check each method and instill greater confidence in the terminal value estimate.

Present Value Calculations

Once the series of free cash flows and terminal value are estimated, the present value of these two components must be calculated. An acquirer is paying today for access to the cash flows generated by the assets in the future; therefore, these flows must be discounted to the present. The proper discount rate can be estimated by calculating the marginal weighted-average cost of capital (k):

$$k = k_e(\% \text{ equity}) + k_d(1-t)(\% \text{ debt})$$

where k_e = cost of equity
     k_d = pretax cost of debt
      t = marginal tax rate
% debt = percentage of debt/total capitalization
% equity = percentage of equity/total capitalization

The cost of debt can be calculated fairly easily by looking at new-issue, medium-term debt rates for similar credits. The cost of equity, however, is calculated using the capital asset pricing model; that is,

$$k_e = r_f + B\,(r_m - r_f)$$

This equation shows that the return to equity holders, and so its cost to the issuer, depends on the level of return of a riskless investment (r_f) plus an additional return determined by taking on the level of risk associated with this company (B or Beta) and the long-term market return in excess of the risk-free rate ($r_m - r_f$). Investment bankers hew pretty closely to modern financial theory here, going so far as to un-lever the beta (a measure of the risk of shares of publicly held companies) and releveraging it to the targeted or optimum balance of debt and equity. Bankers also will construct "surrogate" betas for calculating the cost of equity for nontraded sub-sidiaries or private companies. As a practical matter, however, the weighted-average cost of capital never is used as a point estimate of the "right" discount rate. Instead, this calculation defines the center of a range of discount rates (usually one to two percentage points on either side of the estimate) that will be used to discount the cash flows.

Cost of Capital

Another DCF methodological point needs to be made. The proper weighted-average cost of capital to be estimated is that of the *acquiree*, not that of the acquirer. This strikes some clients as counterintuitive: Why not use the *buyer's* weighted-average cost of capital? The acquiree's cost of capital, to give the shortest answer, captures the inherent risk associated with its assets and, thus, the uncertainty regarding the timing and the magnitude of the cash flows generated by those assets. (Stated another way: The target's cost of capital is the price it must pay to the suppliers of capital to motivate them to invest in that company.) When this approach is utilized, it becomes clear that use of the acquirer's cost of capital focuses on the wrong bundle of risks in constructing a discount rate.

Investment bankers spend a goodly portion of their time performing sensitivity analysis on a DCF valuation. A DCF is only as accurate as the assumptions underlying it, and the most direct way to delineate the margin of error is by varying the assumptions—in effect, designing different operating or financial scenarios for the company—and noting the results. Sensitivity analysis always focuses on the key line items that most affect the valuation. Throughout these financial gymnastics, the range of discount rates is held constant. (Remember that the discount rate captures the risk associated with these assets; that is, it accounts for the variability in the timing and magnitude of the cash flows.) The result of the sensitivity phase of analysis is a range of values for the company or assets in question at a given discount rate.

Acquisition Valuation Methods

Acquisition valuation is perhaps less theoretical and more concerned with the real world than DCF valuation. It is an attempt to estimate where a company will "trade" in the market for corporate control. An obvious starting point in determining acquisition value is current stock market trading levels, or for a private company, an estimate of where it would trade in the public market if it were publicly traded. Such estimates usually can be made easily, and within reasonably tight parameters, by comparison with similar public companies and by analyzing the financial and business characteristics of the property in question. The value of a company in the market for corporate control usually is higher (and often very much higher) than its value in the secondary trading market. This result is news to some financial reporters and baffles some academics, but in the end redounds to the benefit of the shareholders.

Why is this? Part of the answer is found in the word "control." If nothing else, control of assets and the ability to direct all of the free cash flow generated by assets are worth more to a business manager than participation in a small percentage of a business, without control, is worth to the individual stockholder.

Although in some instances acquisition values will be very similar to DCF values, in other instances they may be quite different. In arriving at acquisition values, an investment banker must go beyond DCF analyses and use accumulated knowledge and judgment. A thorough knowledge of comparable precedent transactions, and an up-to-date and accurate assessment of the wishes, corporate strategies, business economics, peculiarities, and points of view of the known and potential participants in any given merger or acquisition transaction, are all essential to this valuation.

One final word on "market premium," a concept that commands much attention in the press and in certain scholarly journals. It has been our experience in practically all major control transactions that the premium paid over the market trading level of the target company's stock is a derived figure rather than an analytical tool or concept in its own right. When the various types of analyses outlined in this chapter justify values over current secondary trading levels, an acquirer may execute a transaction at a premium over those share prices. But the decision to pay a premium to current market value rests on the conclusion of the analysis and is not a valuation exercise in its own right. DCF values and comparable transaction multiples, adjusted for specific transaction or environmental factors, offer a much more consistent explanation of values paid in control transactions than a history of premiums paid over stock-price levels.

However, market premium is a useful concept in assessing how a seller or its shareholders may react to a specific proposal. There are examples of control transactions being completed at very low or negative levels (i.e., discounts) to market. But as a practical matter, if no premium is offered, many transactions have little likelihood of success, regardless of the validity of the valuation analysis supporting the buyer's proposition. The major exception is in the "merger of equals" share-exchange deal, which involves little or no premium to either side.

Multiples in Acquisition Prices

Analysis of acquisition precedents—or the record of comparable transactions—is a fairly straightforward means to begin to establish acquisition value. The investment banker is looking at price as a multiple of _____, and the "blank" can be filled in with any number of financial measures. The most commonly used measures are earnings, book value, and cash flow.

These multiples will vary in the acquisition market for the same reason they will vary in the secondary trading markets made on the floor of the New York Stock Exchange. Companies with characteristics such as superior sales and earnings growth records, better financial returns and prospects, sustained consistent performance, and strong brand franchises will be *acquired* for higher multiples—just as companies with these characteristics will *trade* at higher multiples on the Exchange. A fundamental assumption of this analysis is that companies in the same industry share common characteristics that should be reflected in their acquisition valuation. In fact, the evidence shows that multiples paid in acquisitions in a given industry will cluster around a certain norm. The variations around these benchmarks can be significant, however, and it is the investment banker's job to understand thoroughly the reasons for the variability.

The investment banker also must be wary of any distortion in the financial statistics used in such calculations. These figures always should be calculated on a consistent basis—free from distortion because of accounting conventions, for example. Two very common sources of distortion are cyclicality and leverage. For a company whose margins and earnings fluctuate markedly throughout the business cycle, the point in the cycle at which the business was sold will affect the P/E paid. Cyclicality can be corrected for quickly, however, by using an average operating margin over a full business cycle and restating the target's income statement in the period prior to acquisition, thus using a "normalized" margin rather than the actual or reported margin. Normalization—and this point should not be lost in the elegance of the solution—necessarily assumes that the margin pressure is cyclical and not due to some long-term, secular alteration in the margin structure of the industry. Additionally, an investment banker may find that normalization is not an adequate solution because a buyer always will ascribe less value to the company when the target is on the downward leg of the cycle (where the cash flow picture is weakening and improvement is well in the future) than on the upward leg (where cash flows are improving over the near term). A second major area for scrutiny is the effect of interest expense on earnings. The solution to this problem is to restate the P/E paid on a gross unlevered basis—that is, total price paid (the purchase price of equity and the market value of the debt on the acquiree's books) divided by earnings before interest and taxes. This adjustment may be particularly important when dealing with a subsidiary of a company that carries debt only at the parent level.

The multiple of book value paid is, for certain types of companies, also a useful pricing mechanism in the market for corporate control. Again, one must ensure that different accounting conventions are adequately taken into account. A book value multiple is a better predictor in industries that employ stable technology and are relatively capital-intensive. Book value multiples also are used widely in the financial services industry, where they function partially as surrogates for net liquidation value because the assets and liabilities are carried at values (theoretically at least) close to market. The multiple of cash flow, intuitively attractive because of the potential relationship to DCF valuation, also can be very useful.

Many other specialized multiples are employed in the valuation process in situations where the denominator of the fraction bears particular business significance for the industry. Oil companies, for example, can be valued on the basis of dollars paid per net equivalent barrel of reserves to recognize the underlying asset value of the hydrocarbon assets. Cable TV operations, to cite another example, often are valued by looking at multiples associated with their subscriber base. Acute care hospitals are analyzed on a per-bed basis, cellular telephone companies on a per-POP (potential operating property) basis. Examination of comparable transactions, using either traditional or industry-specific multiples, is not a mechanical process but an exercise of judgment. As with DCF valuation, the process does not produce one "correct" value but a range of defensible values. In examining this range of values, assuming they are based on comparable statistics, an investment banker also must be aware of environmental factors such as the level of interest rates, or the general expectation of the direction of certain commodity prices, such as the price of oil, at the time specific transactions were negotiated.

The Art and the Judgment

In the end, even when armed with the results of various analyses such as DCF values, secondary market trading levels, a history of comparable transactions, and estimates of liquidation or replacement values, the evaluator moves from the arena of seeming precision and science to the realm of judgment and art. What seems dear to one professional may be cheap to another. Factors such as market knowledge, negotiating ability, and even good luck all can cause changes in the perception of value. A company with tax loss carryforwards, excess distribution capacity, a strong business imperative to round out or add a specific product line, and an unhappy history of building new businesses from scratch can look at exactly the same analyses as a similar company without these characteristics and find much more value in a specific acquisition candidate. Likewise, a company with a certain culture or way of doing business may find more value in a company whose culture is similar than will another would-be acquirer whose approach to managing its business is very different. The knowledge of these intangible factors, the ability to use this knowledge, imagination, and creativity enable a good investment banker to elevate valuation from a science to an art.

Fairness Opinions

Performing the analysis and arriving at a value view puts the investment banker in a position to play many roles for the client. Bankers often are engaged primarily to form objective, third-party views on the value of the business to be bought or sold. The valuation exercise also can be a part of a more comprehensive involvement, in which the banker comes to a value judgment and articulates and defends that position in a negotiating context.

If negotiations lead to a transaction, the banker also may be asked to render a "fairness opinion" on the deal. A fairness opinion, which is addressed to a board of directors, expresses the investment banker's opinion that the price paid in the transaction is "fair from a financial point of view" to the shareholders of the company. The import of the opinion varies depending on the context in which it is rendered. When the banker represents the seller, the opinion gives comfort to the seller's board that the target's shareholders are receiving a fair price for their shares. When the banker represents the buyer, on the other hand, the opinion gives the board comfort that the price to be paid for the target is not so unreasonable that it is unfair to the shareholders of the acquiring company.

16

Pricing Your Deal for Optimum Value

Stephen M. Waters

Managing Director,
Morgan Stanley & Co., London

Joel T. Schwartz

Former Financial Analyst,
Morgan Stanley & Co., New York, New York

The *price* an acquirer must pay for a business does not necessarily reflect the *value* that is realizable from that business. The distinction made by many professionals is that price represents the amount that must be paid for a business in the situational context at the time of the deal, while value, which represents the ultimate worth of the business to a specific buyer, is only proven over time.

There are a number of guidelines that help an acquirer arrive at a bid price. A careful consideration of changing M&A market trends, historical trading and pricing multiples, industry rules of thumb, and competing third-party bidders are among the factors that can shape a buyer's pricing decisions. Motivations and objectives of both buyers and sellers vary from case to case and also affect pricing. Intelligent assessment of the full range of these forces enables a buyer to price a deal effectively.

However, determining whether this price will provide optimal value for an acquirer requires a different, forward-looking approach. Realized value can be assessed only in the future when an acquirer can judge with certainty the cost of buying the business compared to the contribution of its actual performance. Estimating this future value today requires:

- Forecasting tools such as discontinued cash flow analysis
- Synergy estimates
- An understanding of the opportunity cost of the buyer's capital
- An analysis of the potential value of internal alternatives such as a restructuring or recapitalization

An acquirer should use its available current information to bridge the gap to future value by paying the lowest workable price. This will allow a buyer to realize the largest increment between purchase price and ultimate value.

This chapter will examine major pricing influences that acquirers in the United States should consider to price a deal for optimum value. They include:

- The states of the M&A and capital markets
- Pricing benchmarks
- The competitive landscape
- Transaction-specific parameters

THE STATE OF THE M&A AND CAPITAL MARKETS

The M&A Marketplace

Overall activity levels in the M&A marketplace directly affect how buyers and sellers price transactions, as do the particular aspects of a given market.

Levels of merger activity have been closely related to the health of the economy. For example, in 1988, real gross domestic product (GDP) increased approximately 4 percent and there were more than 700 announced M&A transactions in the United States valued at more than $35 million. In 1991, real GDP declined by almost 1 percent and there were approximately 350 announced M&A transactions. The strength of the U.S. economy in the late 1980s fed the dramatic increase in merger and takeover activity as well as the increase in prices paid in M&A transactions during that period. Similarly, the recession of late 1990 and 1991 coincided with a sharp drop in M&A volume, with buyers less willing or able to pay the prices that were common in the late 1980s.

The supply/demand balance between buyers and sellers also influences pricing in the merger market, just as it does in other markets where prices are allowed to reach levels at which buyers and sellers are willing to transact. This balance reflects several issues.

Access to Capital. Financing is often the primary consideration in determining the feasibility of paying a certain acquisition price. Relatively cheap bank funds, active junk bond markets, and large foreign investment capital fueled high levels of M&A activity during the late 1980s and raised the absolute prices of deals themselves. Interest rates clearly define access, availability, and cost of capital for acquirers. High interest rates in the early 1980s paralleled a level of activity that was approximately one-third to one-half the volume of the late 1980s, when interest rates were several hundred basis points lower. Governmental regulation also affects the availability and cost of capital for businesses. For example, federal banking regulators' defined rules for highly leveraged transactions (HLTs) and federal government jawboning severely restricted the availability of bank loans for use in acquisitions in the early 1990s, even as interest rates dropped.

Corporate Strategic Planning. Disappointing operating performance and heightened focus on shareholder value caused many U.S. companies in the early 1990s to curtail external growth or diversification efforts and to focus instead on base markets, internal restructurings, and downsizing. Poor economic conditions and stock market fads also led to divestitures of noncore businesses. At the same time, planning efforts caused some companies, particularly European companies, to pursue aggressive cross-border objectives, resulting in a number of large acquisitions and strategic alliances around the world.

Antitrust Policy. Industry consolidation often tests the will of politically appointed regulators. Risk of regulatory interference can meaningfully affect attitudes of buyers and sellers in any given M&A situation. This is true both in the United States and in Europe, where the problem is compounded by conflicting European Economic Community and local country jurisdictions.

Creative Structures. The willingness of M&A market participants to pursue transactions using innovative approaches led to a number of significant transactions in the 1980s. Creative tactics, such as two-step tender offers, spin-offs, joint ventures, and contingent value rights also have expanded the universe of qualified buyers.

Finally, industry-specific considerations such as consolidation pressures and deregulation can significantly affect merger activity and pricing. Industries such as insurance and metals and mining recently have seen little merger activity while others such as commercial banking and consumer products have been quite active. Increased merger activity in a particular industry can drive pricing multiples far above normal market levels. Pricing decisions must reflect the competitive situation of a specific industry. In commercial banking, for example, once a company is recognized as a takeover target, there are often a number of other banks that can make the same acquisition, but only a few that can realize significant synergies from the transaction.

Equity Capital Markets

The equity capital markets sometimes play a major role in M&A pricing decisions. The equity market historically has served as a valuation base for pricing publicly traded companies, with premiums for change-of-control transactions set about that base level to generate actual selling prices. In addition, the gap between public and private market valuations—which changes as equity market conditions change—is an important pricing tool. In a weak equity market, sellers typically achieve a higher value by selling in a private market transaction, while in a strong equity market, selling a company in the public markets via an initial public offering (IPO) may be a better financial alternative. In the 1980s, premiums averaging 50 percent and ranging in specific deals from 10 percent to 100 percent had to be applied to public trading valuations to put them on par with private valuations. These premiums declined dramatically in the early 1990s as the stock market surged and the relative dearth of buyers in the M&A market weakened private sale values.

The strength of the stock market in 1991 and the beginning of 1992 led to a wave of IPOs; taking a company public became equally, if not more, attractive than selling a company in the private market. In 1988, the dollar volume of announced M&A transactions was almost 25 times that of public stock offerings, while in 1991, M&A volume was only about 1.5 times greater. It is interesting to note that the timing of the 1991–1992 upswing in the stock market spawned the trend of reversed leveraged buy-outs (LBOs)—that is, companies taken private in LBOs of the 1980s were resold in IPOs during the strong equity markets of the early 1990s. Given the finely tuned return requirements of financial buyers (which will be discussed below), an end to the IPO boom would be unlikely to stem their desire to exist from investments made three to five years before. One can, in fact, envision a return to high-yield bond financings and creative private market alternatives if and when the public equity markets recede.

Debt Capital Markets

Access to borrowed funds is, to reiterate, critical to M&A activity. Debt capital has been available from traditional sources such as banks and from "mezzanine" (non-bank) sources, the most notorious being junk bonds. The ability of a buyer to arrange sufficient debt financing on a timely basis can determine the outcome of a competitive M&A situation, especially when financial buyers are involved. This is why many financial buyers created their own subordinated debt funds and why Drexel Burnham Lambert, the investment banking house that led the junk bond market briefly, did so well in the 1980s.

Junk bonds provide the promise of high yields to investors and unsecured financing for issuers. The development of this financing alternative in the mid- to late-1980s spawned a wave of financial buyers. Their liquidity fueled the merger boom in the late 1980s and "bid up" prices in many transactions. The near elimination of junk financings, due to rising defaults and restrictions on lenders, correspondingly contributed to a severe drop-off in purchasing power for financial buyers in the early 1990s. By then, Drexel Burnham's era had passed—the firm crashed in bankruptcy—and its employees had moved to other would-be powers.

PRICING BENCHMARKS

General Criteria

To determine whether a potential acquisition price is reasonable, buyers often consider statistics from "similar" past transactions. While no single yardstick is used exclusively by any particular industry, common benchmarks include multiples of sales, earnings before depreciation, interest and taxes (EBIT-D), earnings before interest and taxes (EBIT), net income, cash flow, and book value.

It is important to recognize that the levels of common pricing benchmarks change, as does the relative importance of the benchmarks themselves. For example, the median cash flow multiple paid for acquisitions rose steadily from 1982 until 1987; but then remained relatively flat from 1988 to 1991. Similarly, in 1987, the median net earnings multiple for acquisitions was approximately 21 times, whereas in 1990 the median multiple was only 16 times earnings. Which benchmarks are considered relevant also change. In the 1970s, the premium over stock prices, price-to-earnings ratios, and price-to-book-value multiples were widely considered the most important pricing tools. By the late 1980s, pricing decisions relied more heavily on cash flow-based multiples such as EBIT and EBIT-D. These changes reflect acquisition financing considerations, industry conditions, and fluctuations in the public equity markets.

Industry-Specific Criteria

It is often worthwhile to consider industry-specific acquisition benchmarks, particularly since some industries place more emphasis on special rules of thumb. These industry-specific benchmarks reflect different underlying operating economies of industries. Competitive environments, industry cyclicality and seasonality, market concentration, and growth traits help determine which are chosen. For example, some industries are characterized by high growth after break-in periods marked by heavy losses for leading companies. It would clearly be inappropriate to focus on trailing price-earnings multiples for such emerging growth industries. Conversely, for mature manufacturing businesses, buyers focus on multiples of EBIT-D or cash flow.

Specific industries where benchmarks apply include:

- *Cellular telephones.* Prices are paid per POP, a specifically defined index based on population density. Cellular companies are typically characterized by high growth, high depreciation, and low net earnings, and are measured by EBIT-D and not net earnings multiples.

- *Oil and gas.* Assets often are analyzed by using multiples of proven reserves, based on uniform industrywide definitions set by the Securities and Exchange Commission. The benchmarks are unique to this industry.

- *Health care services.* Health maintenance organizations (HMO) transactions often are priced on multiples of dollars per member under managed care. Alternative site care transactions consider multiples of revenue per center. Hospital and nursing homes are priced on a per-bed basis.

THE COMPETITIVE LANDSCAPE: THE UNIVERSE OF BUYERS

Most U.S. M&A activity is driven by four types of buyers: U.S. strategic, foreign strategic, financial, and distressed property. Each type of buyer has its own perspectives on pricing. The relative volume of activity for each of these types of buyers changes. For example, foreign acquirers accounted for approximately 3 percent of announced acquisitions in the United States in 1985 and 32 percent of announced acquisitions in the United States in 1990. When an acquisition is priced, especially in competitive situations, it is critical to know the types of competing buyers and how these competitors might make their pricing decisions. It is also important to try to know the identities of the specific competitors in any situation.

U.S. Strategic Buyers

A typical U.S. strategic buyer—that is, an American-based operating company—is interested in acquisitions that improve financial returns by strengthening its competitive position, while expanding its operations. Acquisitions often can provide a means for growth and expansion, and most importantly, increased market share. These goals can be achieved, for example, by acquiring a distribution channel, customer base, or new technology, or by realizing increased goodwill from a combined trade name. An acquisition also can be defensive—by preventing a competitor from acquiring the same target and gaining its advantages. Some strategic acquisitions are undertaken to meet corporate portfolio diversification objectives. Companies whose profitability depends on a single business segment or product line often seek to reduce their risk exposure by entering other markets. It was this diversification mentality that, through mergers and acquisitions, led to the formation of numerous multi-industry conglomerates in the 1960s and 1970s. Far-reaching diversification strategies are not popular in the 1990s because many of the conglomerates put together three decades earlier were not successful.

A key factor in many strategic acquisitions is an acquirer's synergy expectations. Synergies come in the form of cost reductions, increased sales, strategic position improvements, or financial benefits. Cost reductions arise from staff rationalizations, removing redundant nonpersonnel overhead, and utilizing excess capacity. Strategic improvements can include realizing economies of scale, achieving critical mass in a particular market, or improving leverage with customers and suppliers. Financial synergies include tax benefits such as utilization of net operating losses, asset step-ups, and possible enhancements that reduce the cost of borrowing.

Strategic buyers usually have long-term investment return criteria and may be willing to wait as long as 10 years to realize the benefits from an acquisition. However, for strategic buyers with public stockholders, such long-term objectives often are overridden by concerns over short-term earnings dilution. This makes amortization of goodwill unattractive. Strategic buyers want to protect credit ratings, and are wary of capital expenditure and other cash flow effects that could reduce a company's stock price. Strategic buyers also face concerns regarding the meshing of "corporate cultures" of existing and acquired businesses. The 1980s proved that extremely different corporate cultures can seriously damage or delay the realization of synergies.

Foreign Strategic Buyers

Foreign strategic buyers (i.e., overseas-based operating companies) have objectives similar to those of U.S. strategic buyers, including expansion or enhancement of existing operations. Similarly, if they already have U.S. businesses, foreign companies can look to potential synergies. Usually, the overseas-based strategic buyer has a long-term focus as it grows businesses outside its home market. Some seek a strategic foothold in the United States to achieve global expansion plans and consider acquisitions to be quicker and more economical than developing U.S. operations from scratch.

Non-U.S. buyers with public stockholders have shareholder and stock price concerns similar to their U.S. counterparts, but they often are perceived as having less concern over short-term earnings dilution. Furthermore, accounting rules in many countries, particularly with regard to nonamortization of goodwill and the treatment of reserves, can provide a competitive advantage over U.S. counterparts.

A foreign buyer also may benefit from different financing considerations, such as government support and lower required rate of return criteria, that can enable it to pay more for an acquisition than a U.S. competitor could afford. Capital market influences in the foreign company's home country, such as the cost of availability of debt or equity financing, significantly differentiate the attractiveness of an acquisition to a non-U.S. entity. At the same time, non-U.S. buyers face complicating foreign exchange and tax issues in making U.S. acquisitions, including the optimal timing of a purchase and the repatriation of earnings. Finally, a prospect of regulatory interference or negative publicity sometimes can cause non-U.S. buyers to abandon aggressive acquisitions programs, especially in sectors such as the defense industry.

Financial Buyers

The typical financial buyer consists of a group of individuals organized to invest a pool of institutional funds in the purchase of businesses, while financing these transactions on a leveraged basis through nonrecourse borrowing. These buyers repay debt from the operating cash flows of the acquired businesses. Once debt has been substantially reduced, they sell the business either privately or to the public through an IPO. Financial buyers do not face the same shareholder concerns that typically confront strategic buyers such as earnings dilution, but they are responsible to their investors who expect high returns.

Since financial buyers are principally in the business of buying and selling companies to generate investment returns, their investment objectives and expectations differ from those of strategic buyers. Financial buyers typically have annual return of 30 percent to 40 percent and exit horizons of three to seven years. Return and exit objectives are constrained by the terms that must be negotiated with lenders. Lender-imposed constraints include required debt-to-cash-flow coverage ratios and specified periods over which debt must be paid down before dividends can be declared.

Financial buyers typically invest in mature businesses because such companies generate the steady cash flow necessary to ensure debt repayment and have minimal capital expenditure and working capital requirements. Financial buyers also look for companies in which there is a potential for rationalization and cost eliminations to improve cash flow. These opportunities could include reductions in overhead or divestiture of noncore assets.

Distressed-Property Buyers

Distressed-property buyers comprise a small group of acquirers who share traits of both strategic and financial buyers. The distinguishing feature of these buyers is that the businesses they seek are typically in trouble, ideally allowing an acquirer to pay bargain prices and gain value by effecting a turnaround. They are willing to confront the complexities of consensual workouts and the Bankruptcy Code—such as debtors' exclusivity rights, varied interests of trade creditors and secured and unsecured lenders, idiosyncrasies of bankruptcy courts, and an evolving legal framework for bankruptcy cases with issues ranging from fraudulent conveyance statutes to the complex set of tax rules that apply.

It is worth noting that distressed-property buyers can include strategic acquirers seeking inexpensive properties, although most are financial buyers who need very little equity capital. The proliferation of distressed-property buyers reflects a dramatic increase in companies facing bankruptcy in the late 1980s and early 1990s. In 1980, there were approximately 60 bankruptcies of good-sized businesses with total related assets of approximately $10 billion, while in 1991 there were over 125 major company bankruptcies with assets in excess of $60 billion.

TRANSACTION-SPECIFIC PARAMETERS

Seller's Objectives

In any M&A transaction, the objectives, and the motivations, of the seller must be carefully examined. A thorough understanding of the seller can be critical in bridging the often contradictory objectives of winning a competitive bidding process and pricing a transaction to realize optimum value. In some cases, motivations are made by the seller to all interested parties; in others, they can be learned only by tapping market sources and exercising diligent pursuit.

Aside from particular sensitivities of senior management and board members that can be explained only by the unique character of a seller, some of the more common concerns include:

- Value maximization (the most logical from a textbook perspective)
- Heightened sensitivity toward one or more stakeholder groups, usually shareholders, but also management, employees, suppliers, customers, or affected communities
- Optimization of tax, legal, and accounting objectives
- Minimization of disruption to ongoing operations
- Maintaining confidentiality of the sale process or of trade secrets
- Alleviating regulatory pressures such as antitrust, environmental, or labor relations
- Timing considerations

The Sale Process

Another major factor affecting an acquirer's pricing decisions is the nature of the competitive bidding process for the target company. Typically, a company is sold through either an auction or a negotiated sale. Auctions can arise from a seller-designed process in which the selling company contacts a number of parties privately or from a public bidding competition. Negotiated sales typically result from an approach by either the buyer or the seller to the opposite party with a transaction proposal.

In a privately managed competitive auction, a buyer's pricing decisions are dictated by a process and timetable determined by the seller. These situations are likely to maximize the selling price. Typically, such auctions have two to three bidding rounds during which the seller attempts to reduce the pool of buyers, based on price indications and ability to complete and finance the transaction. An assessment of competing bidders therefore is critical to a potential acquirer. An acquirer needs to price its bids in each round high enough to survive to the next round (and to be the ultimate winning bidder), but low enough to prevent overpaying, losing negotiating advantage, or being used as a stalking horse for others. To make optimal bids throughout the process, a buyer needs to analyze a seller's objectives and, if possible, to gauge the financial capacity and objectives of competing bidders, as well as the depth of the "field" of buyers. Often market knowledge and industry rumors are the only sources of such elusive information.

In situations in which an acquirer is seeking a controlling block (usually more than 50 percent voting control) and a friendly merger is not an option, the bidding process may take the form of a tender offer. In a tender offer, the acquirer unilaterally proposes to buy shares directly from target stockholders at a specified price for a specified period of time. A significant premium over the current stock price is usually necessary to receive shareholder support. The most important factor to consider in pricing such a tender offer is the potential for competing bids from others free to mount a tender offer. A buyer needs to assess the potential for interlopers carefully and to price its offer high enough to discourage these parties from bidding. In uncontested control situations during the 1987–1991 period, premiums averaged 40 to 50 percent above unaffected market prices, while in contested control battles for the same period, they were 10 to 20 percentage points higher.

In negotiated sale situations, absence of overt competition relieves some of the price pressure that a buyer faces in an auction process. Therefore, negotiated sales do not necessarily maximize the price a seller could achieve for its business, but they can often provide smooth, easier business combinations due to the "friendly" nature of the discussions. The price range often is established at the outset of discussions. Buyers in negotiated deals need not focus on competing bids and therefore can spend more time and effort examining the seller's motivations and objectives. The initial bid range needs to be high enough to get the parties to the negotiating table and not so low that the seller walks away. In our experience, the ultimate price usually is not maximized when a buyer perceives it doesn't face bidding competition.

Payment Consideration

Varying the form of payment consideration is one way an acquirer can affect the actual price it needs to pay. Buyers typically use some combination of cash, equity securities, and debt securities as consideration for the acquisition. In many cases, differences in perceived value and noneconomic considerations can be addressed by designing a package that meets opposing objectives of both buyer and seller.

In the 1980s, all-cash transactions were the most common form of acquisition payment, but transactions involving securities have been more frequent in the 1990s. In 1986, approximately 63 percent of announced transactions involved all-cash consideration, 26 percent had some combination of cash and securities, and 11 percent involved payment with only securities. In contrast, by 1991 approximately 44 percent of announced transactions involved all-cash consideration, 17 percent had some combination of cash and securities, and 39 percent were paid with all securities.

An acquirer also can reduce the price through alternative payment structures, such as earn-outs. In an earn-out, the buyer typically pays an up-front purchase price and an additional amount after the deal, contingent on whether earnings, or some other agreed benchmarks, are reached. These structures often require the buyer to pay a higher amount in the future if projected results are exceeded, and a correspondingly lower amount if the goals are not met. Pricing an acquisition with an earn-out allows the buyer to limit the initial pay-out, and to pay a full price only if the target business experiences the growth performance that was represented at the time of the purchase. It should be noted, however, that earn-outs are often difficult to negotiate and administer.

DETERMINING THE OPTIMAL PRICE

A buyer's task is to distill the "analysis" of standard valuation techniques and the "art" of assessing intangible situational factors into an intelligent decision. The extent to which this price will translate into value for an acquirer can be determined only over time. A synergy estimate used in pricing an acquisition is merely that, an estimate; it is the realization of the estimate that translates into value for an acquirer. Furthermore, attempting to measure value at the time of an acquisition involves measures or benchmarks that may become less relevant in the future, when the true value of the business will be judged.

Nevertheless, realizing value from an acquisition requires careful analysis of a broad range of pricing influences on a case-by-case basis. The important factors to review include:

- The dynamics that influence pricing trends in the M&A market
- Financing sources and equity market alternatives
- The use of common and industry-specific historical pricing benchmarks
- The objectives, motivations, and concerns of competing buyers

- Considerations that influence selling shareholder perspectives
- The nature of the sale process and its impact on pricing
- Variations in payment considerations

These considerations, most of which require judgment and experience to assess properly, are critical elements of pricing a transaction for optimum value—an assessment that ultimately will be made in the future by those having perfect hindsight.

17
Merger Negotiations

James C. Freund

Partner, Skadden, Arps, Slate,
Meagher & Flom, New York, New York

When you cut through all the financial and legal hocus-pocus—the accounting treatment, the tax aspects, the corporate and securities considerations—an acquisition is basically a deal between two parties. If they can't agree, the deal doesn't get done. The way they reach agreement is by negotiating.

FRAME OF REFERENCE

Talking about merger negotiations requires a frame of reference—a sense of where you are. Otherwise, it's like blind people feeling parts of an elephant.

There are three principal elements of the framework:

- The characteristics of the deal (including the nature of the companies, the form of purchase price, and the kind of transaction)
- The point you're at in the acquisition chronology
- Whether you're the seller or the purchaser

Seller or Purchaser

Take the last point. It's not just the purchaser wanting to buy cheap and the seller wanting to sell dear. It's two totally different points of view. The seller knows what's being sold, but the buyer isn't quite sure what's being bought. So the buyer's efforts

201

are directed at finding out as much as possible about the seller, both to judge whether the deal makes sense and to create protections in case the seller proves to possess less than meets the eye.

By contrast, the seller is ducking and weaving—walking a thin line between disclosing enough of the bad stuff so that the buyer won't have future recourse, but not so much as to cause the buyer to walk away from the deal.

Characteristics of the Deal

Public or Private Seller. The first significant characteristic of the deal is whether the seller is publicly or privately owned. With a private seller, the purchaser works hard at unearthing the basic facts about the acquired company and seeks two types of contractual protection: the ability to walk away prior to closing if important aspects of the company turn out to be mirages (what lawyers call "conditions"), and the opportunity to be made whole if negative facts turn up after the closing (what lawyers call "indemnification"). With a public seller, the purchaser is buying less of a pig in a poke (since the seller has been subjected to the rigors of public reporting and Securities and Exchange Commission scrutiny), so less digging may be needed. On the other hand, indemnification is usually not available—so the moment of truth arrives at the closing. Obviously, this can affect the negotiating.

Form of Purchase Price. Next is the type of consideration being offered, which bears on what offensive negotiations the seller has to initiate. Cash is the cleanest; all the seller has to worry about is whether it will be there at the closing. If the purchaser is issuing notes or debentures, then the seller has to be concerned with the purchaser's credit down the road. And if the price is paid in the purchaser's common stock, then the seller isn't just selling a company, but also making a significant equity investment in the purchaser, which calls for a lot more knowledge and a judgment on the paper being received. (Today, of course, many deals—particularly those in the public area—involve part cash and part paper.)

Type of Deal. The third characteristic is the type of acquisition. For example, when a private company is being acquired, the issue may be whether the purchaser is acquiring the seller's assets (subject to certain agreed-upon disclosed liabilities) or the seller's stock. In buying stock, the purchaser will be stuck with all the seller's liabilities, known or unknown. This requires the buyer to ferret out the seller's contingent liabilities, tax exposures, and other possible problems, and to negotiate for provisions under which the seller's stockholders will indemnify and hold the buyer harmless from any losses or expenses incurred through contractual misrepresentations. The buyer of assets has fewer concerns along these lines.

If the seller is public, the difference is often between whether the acquisition is done in one piece, as with a merger-type transaction, or in several steps—combining, for example, block purchases of shares, a tender offer to all shareholders, and a back-end merger. The complexities here can be elegant—particularly when the multistep deal also involves part cash and part stock. Such intricacies obviously have an impact on the negotiating.

Chronology of the Deal

Finally, the point that's been reached in the chronology of the deal can affect many of the strategic and tactical decisions the buyer and seller are called upon to make.

In most acquisitions, there's an initial period of preliminary negotiations prior to any meeting of the minds. If these negotiations are successful, the parties agree in principle on the basic points (such as price); this is often memorialized in a letter of intent. A press release may be issued concurrently. While not a binding contractual obligation, the letter of intent evidences a serious mutual intent to go forward, and—as a brief, straightforward document—is particularly useful in getting a private seller over the hump of parting with the business. This method may be preferable to risking a potential negative reaction by presenting the seller initially with an 80-page "insurance policy" (the acquisition agreement), with him or her as the "insurer."

The parties then enter into detailed negotiations that cluster around a formal, legally binding acquisition agreement that contains all the terms and conditions of the deal. Typically, most significant acquisition transactions are closed not simultaneously with the signing of the agreement, but rather several weeks or months down the road. The extra time provides for actions that can occur only subsequent to signing or that take time to accomplish, such as soliciting the approval of public stockholders.

So, for purposes of evaluating various issues that may arise, or deciding whether to introduce other issues that haven't yet been on the table, the negotiator must ask what point has been reached in the acquisition process: Have the parties' minds met? Are they legally bound? Is this the best time, from your perspective as buyer or seller, to negotiate particular issues?

For example, as a general rule, it's in the best interests of a seller of substance (who isn't teetering on the verge of bankruptcy and seeking any port in the storm) to negotiate as many significant points as possible before agreement in principle is reached and the transaction announced. In this preliminary stage—when the purchaser is smacking lips over the prospects of bringing the seller into the fold, but the seller hasn't agreed to the price—the seller possesses the maximum leverage to extract real concessions from the purchaser. The seller's edge lies in such areas as the terms of employment with the purchaser, seats on the buyer's board of directors, registration rights for stock issued in the deal, the terms of any notes to be received, and permitted dividends prior to closing.

Conversely, announcement of the proposed deal usually constitutes a big change in position for a seller. Once suppliers, customers, employees, and competitors know about the acquisition, the seller's business is viewed in quite a different light. If, for any reason, the deal does not go through—no matter what the ostensible reason disclosed to the public—everyone will assume that the purchaser discovered some serious negatives about the seller's business that can have obvious ill effects on the seller's future prospects. The seller's strong interest in seeing that nothing goes wrong, once the transaction has been announced, weakens the seller's bargaining position in the later rounds. The purchaser, realizing what the seller now has at stake, often takes the tack that the parties should just agree on the price and leave everything else for a later date. ("We'll let the lawyers worry about that other stuff" is a typical remark at this point.)

That, at least, is the conventional wisdom. On the other hand, many purchasers prefer not to announce an agreement in principle without having the seller locked up—the fear being that other bidders will promptly get on the telephone and try to snatch the prize away.

Another issue underscoring the negotiating significance of the time frame is the valuation of the purchaser's stock that will be issued to the seller. The agreement on the purchase price may call for $10 million worth of the purchaser's shares, but what value should be assigned? Presumably, it will relate to the market price of the purchaser's stock, but as of when? Should the value be premised on the time the agreement in principle is reached; or when a binding agreement is signed; or at the closing, when the seller actually gets the shares; or on an average price over a specific period? This can be important, because prices can change dramatically over the course of a long-winded acquisition transaction. This same negotiating issue also can arise in the much more complex context of a part-cash, part-stock, tender offer/merger combined transaction, involving such esoteric items as "collars" (placing limits on the number of shares issuable should the stock price change dramatically in the course of a deal) and "cramdowns" (requiring someone who opts for cash to take stock, or vice versa, in order to ensure the required relative percentage selection of cash and stock).

NEGOTIATING THE PURCHASE PRICE

Let's talk about purchase price. As a lawyer, I'd never presume to advise a buyer how much to pay for an acquisition or counsel a seller on how much to accept for a company. But if I know what they really have in mind—which isn't always the case, because many clients (in effect) negotiate with their lawyers—I can offer some helpful advice on how to get there. Here are my personal 10 guidelines in this area:

So Long, Buddy.   At the point in the deal when you're negotiating price, neither party is committed. So, if you take an unreasonable position—which might have some appeal under the rubric of playing hardball—you have to realize that the negotiators on the other side may just get up and walk away. It's not like a labor negotiation, for instance, where the two sides ultimately have to do business. Nor is it like settling litigation, where you're paying a price to remove uncertainty. There's usually somebody else waiting in the wings to buy the seller, and another target of opportunity for the buyer.

Don't Win Big.   Moreover, I've always felt that, at least from a psychological point of view, if you *really* win, you lose. For example, a purchaser offers $6 million; the seller asks $10 million; the purchaser sticks at $6 million. The seller says "it's a deal." Now, the purchaser whirls around to his or her advisers and cries: "Hey, wait a minute—what's going on here? What does this seller know about the business that I don't know?" The purchaser would be much happier paying something more than

$6 million and feeling that some hard-fought negotiations had been endured. Tight is better.

Don't Let It All Hang Out.   In this day and age, it's simply foolish to start out with your best offer as a purchaser, or express your minimum acceptable price as a seller—even if you label it as such, and ooze sincerity. The other side just won't believe you. In addition, they want to have the satisfaction of seeing you move in their direction.

No Unilateral Bidding.   Try not to get in the position of bidding against yourself. For example, a purchaser offers $6 million; the seller says, "That's way too low; I won't even consider it; you'll have to do better." The purchaser bids $6.5 million. Not wise. Why go up in price without knowing what the seller is looking for? The buyer is better off holding fire and trying to persuade the seller to name a price. An exception is where you have reason to believe that the seller will put forth an absurdly high price—much above the actual goal—and thereby dig a hole from which it will be difficult to escape. You should use other means to ascertain the seller's level of interest and keep the bidding unilateral for the moment.

A Pox on Small Gradations.   If the bid is $6 million and the asking price is $10 million, and the buyer inches up to $6.1 million, $6.15 million, and so forth, it's possible that a deal may be reached in a few years. But in the real world, the likelihood that negotiations will be aborted along the way is just too great. Also, constant changing of the price proposal—even with small changes—encourages the other side to wait for next week's version; there's no credibility, no finality, to any particular offer. I recommend a limited number of bolder moves.

The Real Key.   Stated affirmatively, the most important ingredient for successful acquisition negotiations is taking responsible positions and making meaningful concessions at appropriate junctures.

Here's Why.   Always develop and express to the other side a rationale for your initial price proposal and any subsequent moves. It helps, of course, if the rationale makes good sense. But even if it doesn't make sense—even if it's something as subjective as a seller saying, "I just want to walk away from this deal netting $5 million for myself after taxes; that's been my long-term personal goal"—the other side has to give it some credibility. A reasoned approach puts some backbone into your position. By contrast, numbers that appear to have been plucked out of the air carry little weight in your adversary's assessment.

Stick for a Day.   If you come into a meeting and offer a price, together with good rationale to back it up, then no matter what cries of inadequacy it provokes from the other side, you shouldn't retreat from it at that session. If you do, it will undermine the force of your proposal. By all means, keep talking. Find out as much as you can about the other party's needs, discuss other issues, even suggest (if necessary) that you ultimately might have some price flexibility. But don't waffle that day.

No Bluffs. Never state definitively that a certain price is as far as you're willing to go if that's not your actual walkaway price. You run too great a risk that the other side will either believe you, find the price unacceptable, and terminate the negotiations; or will not believe you, call your bluff, and place you in the embarrassing position of having to back down. There are other ways to get across the relative solidity of your position without getting yourself in this uncomfortable position.

Slow Down on Splitting. When the bidding starts to get close—let's say the range has been narrowed to $7.6 million and $8 million—don't rush prematurely into the middle, offering to split the difference. Assume the purchaser does offer to split at $7.8 million. That becomes the purchaser's new position, while the seller is still at $8 million. The deal probably will end up closer to $7.9 million. There are more subtle means of ensuring that both sides move toward the midpoint.

ISSUES BEYOND PRICE

Once beyond price, most of the issues to be negotiated involve the acquisition agreement. The representations and warranties, the covenants, the conditions to closing, and the indemnification provisions generate quite a bit of heat (and not just among lawyers, although they tend to lead the charge). Pitched battles are fought over such seemingly innocuous concepts as materiality and such reasonable-sounding phrases as "to the best of seller's knowledge."

I suggest the negotiators keep these important ABCs in mind:

A—for gaining Advantages, where appropriate

B—for never forgetting there are Businesspeople involved

C—for solving problems and achieving Compromises

The key for any negotiator is achieving a functional balance between getting a leg up on the adversary and working out satisfactory compromises, while not losing sight of the human elements involved. You win some, you lose some (not the really crucial ones, however), you compromise some, and, above all, you keep communicating.

Gaining Advantages

Let's start out on the offensive. After all, there are gamelike aspects to the acquisition business, and attaining your goals not only makes good business sense but induces a heady sense of satisfaction.

The biggest advantage in negotiating most agreements, including those in an acquisition, is drafting the document. The other side can kick and scream over the contents, but in my experience, it never gets all the way back to an even-handed contract. Typically, drafting the document is the purchaser's prerogative, which definitely should be asserted; but if you're a seller, at least you can volunteer to draft those portions inserted into the agreement at your insistence. But remember, the most egregious provisions rarely go unnoticed. They're inevitably contravened, which leads to hard negotiations and often unsatisfactory compromises. The real value lies in subtlety—the ability to inflict legal results on your adversaries without their knowing they've been had.

You need persistence to prevail in this trade. Never show up for an out-of-town bargaining session with your suitcases packed, having checked out of the hotel. Instead, convey the impression that you have all the time in the world to hold fast on basic points. But remember, you also need perspective. You must know when to press and when to yield—and you can't hang tough on all the little issues.

Labeling your position on each issue as nonnegotiable is not calculated to make a deal; and banging your fist on the table, whether out of frustration or to show toughness, is out of place in these sorts of transactions. But remember, there are times when it's important to take a stand on a real deal breaker (not a sideshow). Sometimes a momentary flare-up of emotion is needed—for example, when your adversary tries to retract what has already been conceded—as a warning of a dangerous road ahead.

The gut issue is whether to give up points that you can afford to cede, or hold them back as trading bait for other matters that may arise later. This is part of the broader issue of timing, which comes up at so many points in the acquisition context. If there's little ostensible justification for your position, it's probably better to yield on the spot, because you'll undoubtedly need your adversary's cooperation on different issues later on. If your position has merit, the key aspect to weigh is what's still ahead. If you suspect there's much yet to come, there's probably no rush to reach an accommodation.

When you have negotiated more than one acquisition, you'll find yourself picking up some of the tricks of the trade. One is to use a really absurd example to illustrate the crazy result your adversary's overbroad draftmanship could produce. Another is to listen carefully to what your adversary says in one context, and then throw these words back in another. Don't be ashamed to indulge in such tactics. They work, and you need all the help you can get.

The People Involved

It's easy to lose sight of the people involved in one of these deals, but a good negotiator never does. I've seen acquisitions negotiated over a period of several months, to the point where all problems appear to have been solved and both sides are on the verge of signing an agreement. Suddenly, the seller walks away. The seller hasn't been properly stroked, or fears unwelcome changes will occur as part of the purchaser's corporate bureaucracy.

When negotiating, make sure to determine who the real decision maker is on the other side. It may not be the person who's doing all the talking. But the decision maker is the one to make your pitch to—and if that person is not in the room, then save your breath. Above all, don't get caught in a situation where you are authorized to make concessions, but the person sitting on the other side of the table lacks the same discretion.

I find that I need to spend more time in an acquisition discussing matters—negotiating, if you will—with my clients than with the adversaries. Energizing a corporate team to move in a constructive direction is not an easy task for businesspeople or lawyers because there are lots of bases to touch. Those furthest from the negotiations tend to take the toughest line. And whoever plays the role of the moving force (since most movement is toward the center) has to risk being perceived as "giving away the store." But I'm convinced that this is the only way deals get done, and you must allow time for the process.

A word about lawyers. Many businesspeople subscribe to the view that lawyers not only don't make deals, they break them. Much of this attitude stems from the timing of the situation. Often, after the parties' minds have met on the subject of price, the lawyers are called in and they proceed to ask hard questions on which the negotiators have neglected to focus. These questions involve such touchy matters as escrows and noncompetition covenants. As disagreements inevitably surface, the attorneys shape up as the handiest scapegoats. Nevertheless, there is some truth to the observation, because many lawyers—trained to view propositions with a cynical eye, searching for what could go wrong, ferreting out the problems ignored by others—have a tendency to overdo this negativism, often at the expense of the deal. You should be able to distinguish between a lawyer who acts constructively, pointing out a problem and suggesting possible alternative solutions, and one who simply nitpicks. It takes large doses of flexibility and improvisation to see an acquisition through to fruition, and you ought to feel comfortable that your lawyer is working effectively toward achieving your goals.

Compromise

I start with the proposition that almost all situations of seeming impasse are ultimately soluble. It may, however, take a little imagination. So many issues that masquerade under other colors really just involve money. By moving that commodity around a little—sometimes dressed up in acceptable costumes to save face—buyer and seller can work most things out.

It often takes some real creativity to discover the common ground on which both sides can agree. They have to distinguish between the positions that each is taking, and their respective real interests, which may be considerably narrower. The key often lies in splitting into segments what had appeared to be an indivisible issue.

Finally, as you get down to the short strokes at the end of a deal, little issues tend to become magnified out of all proportion to their actual importance. Try to put things in perspective. Keep cool, keep communicating, and keep your eye on the ball, which—when it gets down to the wire—is getting the deal done.

18

Payment Modes and Acquisition Currencies

W. Peter Slusser

President, Slusser Associates,
New York, New York

Rory Riggs

President, Providence Capital
Partners, Inc., New York, New York

The means of payment used to effect a merger or acquisition is a critical element of the transaction. It may well determine both the ability to complete the acquisition and the success of the business after the transaction has been accomplished.

In the following discussion, we will describe the advantages and disadvantages of different forms of payment from the perspective of both the buyer and seller, and demonstrate how transactions may be structured to the benefit of both parties. The value that can be gained by structuring a transaction that is mutually beneficial to both parties is a primary reason why friendly, negotiated transactions generally are favored over hostile means of gaining control. It is through friendly negotiations and mutual determination of payment structure that many transactions are made workable and practical financial arrangements can be reached.

THE NEED FOR FLEXIBILITY

The flexibility available through different means of payment and the ability to balance the requirements of both buyer and seller typically are the key ingredients of negotiated settlements. Both elements can be brought into play with significant value for both buyer and seller when the transaction matches cash requirements of both sides. If the payment terms are stretched over a considerable length of time, for example, the seller's desire to reduce current tax exposure can be matched with the buyer's desire to minimize current cash costs.

Similarly, flexibility can help if there is a large gap between bid and asked prices. One solution is to structure the transaction by paying a portion of the purchase price up front and making the rest contingent on the target's future earnings performance. Through this technique, commonly known as an earn-out, the owners of the acquired company get a chance to prove their assertions about the value of the business. At the same time, the buyer is afforded a framework for justifying a premium price and protecting itself against potential downside risks.

In late 1984, First Interstate Bancorp acquired Commercial Alliance Corp., a leading equipment leasing company with an outstanding record. A substantial premium was justified—provided that Commercial Alliance could maintain its record. First Interstate initially paid $18 a share, or a total of $184.3 million, and earmarked another $4 a share for disbursement if Commercial Alliance met specific earnings targets through 1986. In a similar situation, General Motors Corp. paid a full price for Electronic Data Systems Corp. (EDS)—a 1984 transaction valued at $2.5 billion—but tailored the terms to let EDS shareholders take part of their payment in a special class of common stock whose value was tied entirely to the performance of EDS. This contingent value was estimated at approximately 20 percent of the total transaction price, based on the value differential offered EDS stockholders.

While both First Interstate and General Motors structured offers with contingent payments based on continued earnings of the acquired companies, the acquisition of Seafirst Corp., Seattle, by BankAmerica Corp. in 1983 offered a converse situation. BankAmerica acquired an ailing institution that was near bankruptcy. It structured the offer with a preferred stock that based the final principal payment on the future performance of Seafirst's loan portfolio. In this case, BankAmerica used the contingent payment technique both to protect itself from continued losses on Seafirst's portfolio and to reward Seafirst's shareholders if conditions improved.

In essence, these cases outline the reasons contingent payments can be effective. If there is a significant difference between the best case and the worst case that a reasonable businessperson can expect, the fairest solution is often a contingent payment based on actual results. The flexibility provided through techniques such as earn-outs demonstrates why the means of payment are vital to a transaction.

SPECIFIC SECURITIES IN ACQUISITIONS

The forms of payments in mergers and acquisitions run the gamut from cash to stock to debt to mixtures of securities that combine many features. The issuance of securities to target shareholders in public transactions is very common. In all cases, the basis for evaluating specific M&A currencies is the value received by the sellers. In many transactions, securities issued in a merger may sell for less than their stated value in public markets. For example, when Occidental Petroleum acquired Cities Service for $4.2 billion in 1982, it issued five series of notes with an aggregate principal equal to a value of $25.32 per share, which sold for approximately 50 percent of the stated value after the securities were issued. Occidental also issued preferred stock with a stated value of $100 per share, which later traded at approximately 60 percent of the stated value. There are many reasons why the public market values the securities below the so-called merger price. But the fact that the market value of securities issued in a merger may not equal their stated value typically is not the critical issue in the transaction. Generally, both the buyer and the seller know the value of securities issued, and that value is fully considered in the offer. The important considerations from the seller's point of view are that it (1) receives a value greater than that offered by any other bidder and (2) receives the compensation more quickly than if it waited for another acquirer to raise the money. From the buyer's viewpoint, the most important consideration is that it was able to issue securities cost-effectively and in the denomination necessary to close the transaction.

Although selected securities require a great deal of study, the most common medium of exchange in mergers and acquisitions during the 1980s was cash. It is the quickest and easiest payment form to evaluate, and it provides both parties with maximum flexibility after the closing.

The value offered in a transaction also may depend on the type of currency used. For example, if more than 50 percent of the transaction value is in the form of equity securities, the transaction usually is structured as a tax-free exchange insofar as the equity portion is concerned. The equity securities received by the target shareholders would not be taxable until the securities are sold. This structure, although advantageous to target shareholders, may not be to the acquirer's advantage, because it prevents the buyer from realizing certain postacquisition tax benefits.

In considering the attributes of taxable versus tax-free transactions, it is not uncommon for an acquirer to place one price on a tax-free transaction and another price on a transaction that is fully taxable to target shareholders.

Seller Financing

It is important to consider the value of securities issued in acquisitions in general, and, more specifically, the matter of seller financing. A transaction in which the target receives considerable amounts of debt securities is effectively seller-financed. Seller financing thus becomes important because the selling shareholders, in essence, are financing the acquisition by taking fixed obligations of the surviving company. Conceptually, seller financing is similar to a contingent payout, except that in seller financing, the payment is a binding, fixed obligation of the surviving company that is not tied to future performance. Like contingent payments, seller financing is used as a means by which the seller ultimately can receive the price it was asking. But the selling shareholder needs to be thoroughly apprised as to the real value of the paper he or she is getting.

There are several areas in which seller financing may be used. For example, in the sale of a division, seller financing may allow the selling corporation to receive the book value of the assets being sold. An extreme example is the sale of Atari by Warner Communications to Jack Tramiel in 1984. Tramiel, former president of Commodore International, acquired a money-losing computer business, which, given both its recent performance and its projected capital expenditures, would have been extremely difficult to finance for cash or ordinary securities. But by providing Warner with debt securities and warrants to purchase Atari stock, Tramiel effectively was able to finance the acquisition entirely through the future earnings of the operations under his management. Several leveraged buy-outs (LBOs) of public companies provide other examples. Seller financing in the form of subordinated securities sometimes provided the layer of equity financing that allowed the buyer group to finance the purchase. This is different from asking shareholders to take securities of an acquiring company. In the LBO case, the securities offered to the sellers are backed only by the operations of the business being sold. Contrast that with having sellers take securities from Mobil or General Motors.

With that background, we can describe the principal forms of payments as well as their strategic aspects, financial considerations, and accounting issues.

PAYING WITH CASH

Strategic Issues

Full-cash transactions were the most common in the 1980s. Cash is clean. All parties know the value. A cash deal generally can be transacted faster than deals with any other currency, and if the transaction takes the form of a cash tender offer, it does not require extensive proxy registration with the Securities and Exchange Commission. Noncash payment modes typically require some form of registration, which can complicate and lengthen the timing of the transaction. In addition, securities that otherwise might be issued in an acquisition often can be issued after the deal is closed to refinance the cash paid out in the transaction.

Financial Considerations

There are a number of important considerations in paying cash for an acquisition. A primary reason that cash is most frequently used and generates the highest premiums is that the all-cash transaction allows the purchaser the greatest flexibility from a tax standpoint, although the transaction is clearly a taxable event to selling shareholders. The purchaser has certain posttransaction tax elections that may produce significantly greater cash flow than the target enjoyed before the acquisition. Much of the tax benefit comes from writing up the tax basis of the assets in order to create larger noncash depreciation or amortization expenses that reduce taxable earnings and increase cash flow through resultant tax savings.

But on the pure economics of the deal, the advantages or the disadvantages of using cash versus securities are less clear-cut, and the buyer virtually must determine the appropriate payment mode via a case-by-case analysis. The issue to be determined is which structure will provide the best postacquisition returns.

Accounting Issues

The acquisition of a company for cash also is clean from an accounting standpoint. Whether cash is used to purchase stock or to purchase assets, purchase accounting methods are required under generally accepted accounting principles (GAAP), and all acquired assets and liabilities must be carried at their market values. Because the purchase price may reflect that the target valued its assets below the market, the buyer may be required to write up the assets to comply with GAAP. Thus, GAAP also recognizes that when assets are written up for tax purposes, they indeed have greater value because of the increase in cash flow.

It should be noted that in order to increase the tax basis for the assets, the government may require the repayment of certain tax credits or deductions taken since the original purchase of the assets. Unless the benefits gained from writing up the assets are greater than the "recapture" tax expense, a buyer typically will not write up the assets. This choice, however, is not available according to GAAP purchase accounting rules, which require a buyer to write up the book value of an acquired company's assets to at least the purchase price.

COMMON STOCK TRANSACTIONS

Strategic Issues

On the surface, the issuance of common stock as payment in an acquisition may seem to be as simple and as straightforward as paying in cash. From a strategic viewpoint, however, an exchange-of-shares deal has diverse implications, perhaps the most diverse of any form of payment. Beyond the payment stage, the framers of the deal must consider such elements as the shareholder base and stock market performance of the acquiring company, the buyer's future financial performance, and various long-range tax consequences. Thus, many aspects of a common stock transaction that may appear to be tactical considerations in the execution of the deal may well turn out to be strategic.

Perhaps the most common appeal of paying in common stock is that it substitutes paper—albeit paper that presumably can be easily converted to cash by recipients—for a large outlay of cash or a heavy accumulation of debt. It might be advantageous for both parties—especially if the seller intends to remain a stockholder for a considerable length of time into the future—to produce a combined company that is not encumbered by heavy debt or a liquidity squeeze.

Second, the exchange of shares is tax-free under federal laws. The recipients pay no tax on the stock received but do have to pay taxes when and if they sell the stock. Moreover, in a stock transaction, many of the complicated purchase accounting requirements of a cash deal can be avoided if the transaction can be accounted for on a pooling-of-interest basis—or combining the earnings and other financial data of the two firms—which is permitted under an exchange of shares.

Despite these advantages, there are several potentially negative consequences. A paramount concern is that the issuance of additional shares could threaten to dilute the buyer's earnings per share, a key element that is factored into the stock price.

The entire matter of stock market performance and the seller's relationship to the combined company as a shareholder offers a host of ramifications. In a straight-cash deal, it is axiomatic that the seller simply can walk away and not worry about future performance. Not so with a stock deal. While the seller may benefit if the shares of the combined company rise, its compensation always is at risk and constantly threatened by loss of value should the shares decline. The seller's stock-holder relationship also can have varied consequences. Substantial stock ownership in the acquirer could induce the seller's executives to remain with the company, work hard to increase the value of their investment, and even serve as a defensive strong point should the acquiring company itself become a takeover target. The trade-off is the continual threat that the stock may be sold after the completion of the acquisition. If the block received by the selling company is large relative to the total outstanding shares of the acquirer, sale of these shares can create considerable pressure on the postacquisition price of the buyer. In the long run, the economics of the transaction will outweigh specific technical factors. But investment bankers and other intermediaries who help structure transactions will try to avoid any major overhangs on the buyer's stock price.

Financial Considerations

In making the decision on whether to use common stock or an alternate currency, the two parties must determine:

- The perceived value of the buyer's stock from the viewpoint of both the acquirer and the target
- Whether the fixed charges involved in the financing of the acquisition with debt or securities are so great that common stock is desirable

Value depends on the specifics of each transaction. As market prices fluctuate up and down, so do buyers' and sellers' perceived value of the securities. The most important issues are that the acquirer, who best knows the prospects of its business, believes that its stock is fairly priced and that the seller is secure in the belief that the securities received will not deteriorate in value after completion of the acquisition.

The matter of whether the fixed charges incurred in an acquisition are too great is a risk/return determination. In reality, management of public companies generally must approach any acquisition with the risk/return profile of its common shareholder firmly in mind.

Accounting Issues

The key accounting consideration is the trade-off between pooling-of-interest and purchasing accounting. Pooling, to reiterate, is available when an acquisition is financed primarily with common stock and both the acquirer and seller must meet specific guidelines. When the consideration paid in an acquisition is significantly greater than the target's net asset value, the acquisition may work better from an accounting standpoint under a pooling of interests, because the fixed charges to income associated with purchase accounting adjustments can be avoided. This is the singular case where value given and value received may be identical but where the choice of accounting methods may yield materially different results. Thus, this is the key type of transaction in which accounting procedure well may be a strategic issue.

ACQUIRING FOR DEBT OR PREFERRED STOCK

Strategic Issues

The issuance of debt or preferred stock in a merger or acquisition is generally a financing decision. It becomes a strategic decision when the acquisition is difficult to finance without issuing securities, or the securities can be structured to provide target shareholders with certain tax benefits.

Acquisitions that are difficult to finance without debt or preferred securities typically fall into two categories:

- Transactions that are so large that the size of the required financing is hard to get in timely or cost-effective fashion
- Acquisitions of businesses whose earning power precludes sufficient financing by alternative modes

There are two important implications for this type of financing. If the target is a sound business, the relative size of the transaction should not be an obstacle. Further, because debt or preferred instruments generally are issued in friendly, negotiated transactions, the structure can be arranged to match the objectives of the shareholders and the merging companies.

The previously cited acquisition of Cities Service by Occidental Petroleum is a good example of a transaction that allowed an acquirer to issue denominations of securities that it would not have been able to issue cost-effectively prior to the acquisition. The Atari sale is a classic example of an acquisition that could not have been financed without acquisition paper. However, because Warner Communications, Atari's parent, believed that there was a sound business reason behind Tramiel's plan, it was willing to take notes of the acquired company. Specifically, they were notes that did not require principal payments for several years, so the pressures on Atari's cash would be relieved in the early years of the new ownership. Many leveraged buy-outs of corporate subsidiaries have resulted in the issuance of acquisition securities to the selling parent in order to complete the transaction. If there is a sound business plan behind an acquisition and it will justify the proposed price, it often is possible to have the seller accept acquisition securities.

The tax position of the target shareholders also may be cause for paying debt or preferred securities. A common method of deferring the tax liability of the selling shareholders is the installment note. Under the tax code it is possible to structure a note so that the sellers will not be taxed until the principal payments are made. Through this method, people who sell a business can defer their tax liability over several years while earning interest on the pretax amount of the note until the principal is paid. Installment notes are difficult to structure in transactions with public companies that have large, diverse shareholder groups. However, they are frequently used in the sales of closely held companies.

Financial Considerations

The issuance of debt or preferred stock in a merger or acquisition is generally a financing decision. Certain questions should be examined, such as:

- What would it cost to issue the security in the acquisition versus raising the money through other means?
- Are there ways of structuring the instrument so that the target shareholders may get certain tax benefits and, in return, accept a lower coupon rate?
- Is it better for the buyer, from a cost or a balance sheet standpoint, to issue debt or preferred stock than another type of acquisition currency?

Accounting Issues

With the issuance of debt or preferred stock, an acquisition will be treated as a purchase. The balance sheet for book purposes will reflect the value paid, according to purchase accounting. The value of the securities issues is booked in the same manner as if they had been issued prior to the acquisition, except that they become a cost of the acquisition. The only possible exception is the case where the principal payment is based contingently on the future earnings of the company. In this case, only that value of the initial payment typically is accounted for. The remaining value is booked when the payment of the balance is considered likely.

CONVERTIBLE SECURITIES AS COMPENSATION

Strategic Issues

Securities convertible into common stock offer an excellent means of issuing common stock in an acquisition without immediate share dilution. A company issues either debt or preferred stock with the stated value equal to the purchase price, but specifies that the security is convertible into its common stock at some future point at a price greater than its current market value. This effectively allows the acquirer to issue fewer shares than if the acquisition had been financed entirely with common stock. It requires payment of fixed interest yields or preferred dividends for a period of time.

In practice, the use of convertible securities focuses almost entirely on convertible preferred stock. Because of tax laws related to acquisition indebtedness, it sometimes is very difficult to deduct for tax purposes the interest payments on convertible debt utilized in consummating a deal. But if a preferred equity security is issued, it is possible to structure the transaction so that target shareholders receive the new securities tax-free, until the securities are sold.

Financial Considerations

The principal financial considerations in issuing convertible securities are the value of the acquirer's underlying common stock, and the current dividend yield of both the target's stock and the stock of the acquirer.

It is not uncommon for target shareholders to be receptive to convertible securities because they provide a dividend stream superior to the yields the target paid. At the same time, if stock makes sense, convertible securities represent a way for the acquirer to lessen the dilution.

Accounting Issues

Convertible securities have implications for both the balance sheet and earnings per share.

As long as any security other than common stock is used in a transaction, the acquisition is accounted for as a purchase for book purposes. The treatment for tax purposes will depend on many factors.

The effect on earnings per share depends on the relative amount of securities issued and on the terms. Generally, convertible securities are treated in the calculation of primary earnings per share as if they were a straight debt or preferred instrument. The only exception is when the interest rate on the security is less than three-quarters of the rate on bonds of AA caliber. In this instance, for book accounting purposes, primary earnings per share is calculated on the assumption that the security had been converted. As a normal procedure, however, most companies calculate a fully diluted earnings per share, which treats all convertible securities as if they were converted into common. It is important to note that if there is a material conversion premium, fully diluted earnings per share always will be greater if, for the same dollar amount of acquisition value transacted, convertible securities are used rather than underlying common stock.

CONTINGENT PAYMENTS

Strategic Issues

Contingent payments usually are structured so that part of a purchase price is contingent on the target's postacquisition achievement of certain performance goals. For example, the buyer may agree to pay the seller a prearranged amount if the seller achieves 10 percent earnings growth for each of the two years after the acquisition. The use of the contingent payment has two important strategic considerations. It helps bridge the gap when there is a large difference between the bid price and the asking price for a business, and contingent payments provide an excellent means to keep and motivate former owners of a business during the years immediately following an acquisition.

Financial Considerations

The most important financial consideration in a contingent payment is the fair evaluation of the cost and benefits of the structure. Because contingent payments are structured to bridge a gap between bid and ask prices, the buyer should consider the overall cost relative to what might be paid up front.

Accounting Issues

Accounting for contingent payments has two levels. The first is the treatment of the payments as they are made. The second involves the accounting rules followed in determining the formula.

From an accounting viewpoint, one of the most difficult aspects of contingent payments is that all payments generally accrue to goodwill. Because this results in an aftertax payment for which there is no tax benefit, a cost/benefit analysis is necessary. Another important aspect of accounting for contingent payments is that their existence eliminates the use of pooling-of-interest accounting.

The most important accounting issues in arriving at a contingent formula are:

- Basing the earnings on the same operating standards used to develop the buyer's historic earnings
- Setting guidelines to minimize possibilities of one-time aberrations that may unduly inflate or reduce the contingent payments

Two common methods used in contingency arrangements are utilization of pretax earnings as a base to eliminate inconsistencies in accounting, and paying the earn-out either on a cumulative earnings basis or on a basis that generates pro rata payments stemming from a consistent earnings record.

Hybrid Currencies

Although we have addressed the major issues in structuring acquisition currency, some topics, such as warrants, have not been discussed because, in essence, they fall into other categories. In the case of warrants, it is very difficult to separate them from convertible securities as far as implications and strategies are concerned. However, it should be noted that in certain specific cases, there may well be accounting or tax considerations that make hybrid currencies advantageous. A key role of the acquisition professional is understanding the interplay among different forms of payment and structuring the payment form that is acceptable to all parties. It is through careful analysis of the needs of the parties and the matching of these needs with appropriate acquisition currencies that value can be created.

19

Tax Planning for Mergers and Acquisitions

Edward J. Abahoonie
*Partner, Coopers & Lybrand,
New York, New York*

Jonathan S. Brenner
*Manager, Coopers & Lybrand,
New York, New York*

Although most mergers and acquisitions are driven by economic factors, proper tax planning maximizes the value of the transaction for both buyers and sellers. Tax planning primarily is concerned with the structural aspects of the transaction. Differences in the form of the consideration, the legal form of the transaction, and the sequence and timing of events can yield very different tax results to both sides.

The starting point for structuring any transaction is identifying the objectives of the parties. Successful tax planning will attempt to strike a balance between the competing interests when developing an optimal structure.

There are four basic types of M&A transactions:

- A tax-free acquisition of the target's stock
- A tax-free acquisition of the target's assets
- A taxable purchase of the target's stock
- A taxable purchase of the target's assets

A tax-free transaction is generally more advantageous to the seller, who is able to defer tax on its gain. However, the purchaser cannot increase the basis (or value) of the assets to reflect its acquisition cost. Alternatively, a taxable purchase is often more advantageous to the buyer, who will obtain a cost basis in the acquired assets, while the seller must recognize immediate gain on the sale of the target's stock or assets.

In certain circumstances, it is also possible to structure a "hybrid" acquisition— part taxable, part tax-free—in order to accommodate the tax objectives of selected target shareholders.

TAX-FREE TRANSACTIONS

Section 368 of the Internal Revenue Code defines a tax-free corporate reorganization. In transactions that fall within this definition, the transferor of stock or property does not recognize either gain or loss on the transaction if stock in another corporation is received in return. The rationale behind this rule is that the stock represents a continuation of the old investment and, therefore, any gain or loss on the investment should be deferred until the investment is sold. With this in mind, the general tax consequences to the seller and the purchaser in a Section 368 tax-free reorganization are as follows.

On the sell side:

- The target corporation recognizes no gain or loss if it transfers its assets (as well as liabilities) to the acquirer.
- The target corporation's shareholders recognize no gain or loss on the exchange of their stock for stock of the acquirer.
- A form of payment other than stock, such as cash or debt instruments (known as "boot"), is taxable to the extent of gain.
- The basis of the stock received by the target's shareholders is the same as the tax basis of the shares surrendered, less the amount of boot received, plus the taxable gain.
- The holding period of the stock received by the target's shareholders includes the holding period of the stock that was surrendered.

On the buy side:

- The acquirer recognizes no gain or loss when it issues its stock in exchange for the target's property.
- The acquirer assumes the seller's tax basis and holding period in the acquired stock or assets.
- In a forward or reverse triangular merger (to be discussed later), the parent's basis in the merged subsidiary generally is the total basis (or value) of the target's net assets.

■ The acquirer inherits the tax attributes of the target (e.g., net operating loss carryovers), but may be subject to limitation on their use.

General Requirements

A transaction will qualify as a tax-free reorganization only if it meets the specific technical requirements of one of the provisions in Section 368. In addition, every reorganization must be done for a genuine business purpose and also meet several other requirements in order to qualify as a tax-free reorganization.

Continuity of Shareholder Interest. The shareholders of the target corporation must have a continuing interest in the acquired or surviving corporation. The continuity-of-interest requirement is met when the target's shareholders receive equity, as opposed to cash or debt, in the acquiring or surviving corporation. For this purpose, both common stock and preferred stock, whether voting or nonvoting, are considered to be equity. The Internal Revenue Service requires that the target's shareholders receive stock for at least half of the value of the target in order for the IRS to issue an advance ruling that the transaction is tax-free. Courts, however, have ruled that the continuity-of-interest requirement was met when the stock received by the target shareholders represented a lesser percentage (approximately 40 percent) of the total consideration paid. The continuity-of-interest requirement must be met on an aggregate, and not an individual, shareholder basis. Thus, if two shareholders each own half of the target corporation, the continuity-of-interest requirement is met even if one shareholder receives only cash, as long as the second shareholder receives stock of the acquiring corporation.

Continuity of Business Enterprise. In order to preserve the status of a tax-free reorganization, the acquiring corporation must either continue the target's historic business or use a significant portion of the target's historic business assets in its continued operations.

Specific Requirements

"A" Reorganization. The most common type of reorganization is a statutory merger, or "A" reorganization. In order to qualify as an "A" reorganization, the merger must meet the requirements of domestic corporate law. The appeal of an "A" reorganization is that it offers a great deal of flexibility in structuring the transaction.

In an "A" reorganization, the target's shareholders exchange their stock for stock of the acquiring corporation. There is no requirement that the stock vote or participate in earnings. Thus, nonvoting preferred stock qualifies. Additionally, the target's shareholders also may receive cash or other property in the exchange, subject to the continuity-of-interest limitations discussed above. Therefore, target shareholders can have the option of receiving cash or stock and the transaction still will qualify as an "A" reorganization as long as approximately 50 percent of the total consideration is stock of the surviving corporation.

"B" Reorganization. In a "B" reorganization, the buying corporation acquires the stock of the target *solely* in exchange for the acquirer's voting stock. Voting preferred stock will qualify. After the exchange, the acquiring corporation must own a controlling interest in the target. Control, for this purpose, is at least 80 percent of the voting power plus at least 80 percent of the total number of shares of all nonvoting classes of stock. Control of the target corporation does not have to be obtained in a single transaction, but can be accomplished in several related transactions pursuant to a plan of reorganization. The principal danger in structuring a "B" reorganization is that any consideration other than voting stock will disqualify the transaction.

"C" Reorganization. In a "C" reorganization, the acquiring corporation acquires substantially all of the assets of the target corporation, solely in exchange for the acquirer's voting stock. After the exchange, the target generally must liquidate and distribute the acquirer's stock and any remaining assets to its shareholders.

Taxable boot is permitted in a "C" reorganization for up to 20 percent of the value of the target's total assets. Generally, the assumption of liabilities is not treated as the receipt of additional consideration. However, such liabilities are applied against the 20 percent limitation on the receipt of boot. As a result, it is not possible to use any consideration other than the acquirer's stock in most "C" reorganizations.

A major difficulty in structuring a "C" reorganization is the requirement that "substantially all" of the assets of the target must be acquired. The IRS views this test as having been met, for advance ruling purposes, by the transfer of at least 90 percent of the fair market value of the target's net assets and 70 percent of the fair market value of the target's gross assets. The advance ruling requirement is merely a safe harbor, however, and courts have held that a transfer of all necessary business assets satisfies the "substantially all" test.

Forward Triangular Merger. A forward triangular merger is a statutory merger of the target into a first-tier subsidiary of the acquiring corporation in exchange for stock of the acquiring parent corporation. No stock of the acquiring subsidiary can be used in the transaction. The amount of boot that can be used is limited, as in an "A" reorganization, to approximately 50 percent of the value of the target corporation on an aggregate basis. As in a "C" reorganization, the acquiring subsidiary must acquire "substantially all" of the target's assets.

Reverse Triangular Merger. In a reverse triangular merger, the first-tier subsidiary of the acquiring corporation is merged into the target and the target becomes the surviving entity. The target must retain substantially all of the subsidiary's assets (if any) and substantially all of its own assets. The target's shareholders receive voting stock of the acquiring parent corporation in exchange for the parent's assumption of a controlling interest in the target. As in a "B" reorganization, control is defined as ownership of at least 80 percent of the voting power plus at least 80 percent of the total number of shares of all nonvoting classes of stock. Thus, boot in a reverse triangular merger is limited to 20 percent of the value of the target's stock.

TAXABLE TRANSACTIONS

Taxable transactions include both cash transactions and transactions using stock or securities that do not qualify for tax-free reorganizations.

In general, the sale of the stock of a corporation will give the seller a capital gain or loss and the purchaser a cost basis in the stock. The target's basis in its assets, however, will remain unchanged.

The sale of assets by a target corporation will produce taxable gain or loss for the seller. The purchaser of the assets will have an aggregate basis in the assets equal to the amount paid plus any liabilities that are assumed.

Asset Transactions

Treatment of the Seller. In a taxable asset transaction, the seller will recognize gain or loss on each asset separately by allocating the purchase price among the assets sold and subtracting its basis in each asset. For this purpose, liabilities assumed by the purchaser constitute part of the purchase price.

Some of the seller's gain may be ordinary income. Since capital gains of a corporation are taxed at the same rate as ordinary income, the character of the gain or loss is relevant only if the corporation has otherwise unusable capital losses.

If the target liquidates after selling its assets, the target's shareholders will be taxed on the distribution of the proceeds from the asset sale. If the target is an 80-percent-owned (or more) subsidiary of another corporation, however, there is no further tax.

Treatment of the Purchaser. The purchaser obtains an aggregate basis in the assets purchased that equals the amount paid plus the liabilities assumed.

Purchase Price Allocation

The purchase price of the acquired assets is allocated by the buyer to specific assets, which are divided into four classes. Class I assets are cash, demand deposits, and similar assets. Class II assets are so-called near-cash items such as certificates of deposit, government securities, readily marketable stock, or other securities and foreign currency. Class III assets are all other assets, both tangible and intangible, other than "goodwill" and "going concern" value. Both physical assets and identifiable intangible assets are amortizable for tax purposes. Class IV assets are goodwill and going-concern value, as distinct from other identifiable intangible assets.

During the allocation process, the purchase price first is allocated dollar-for-dollar to the Class I (cash) assets. What is left then is allocated to each Class II (near-cash) asset until each asset in the category has been allocated its full fair market value. The remainder of the purchase price then is allocated to each Class III asset until each also has been allocated its full fair market value. If there is any remaining portion of the purchase price that cannot be allocated to these three classes, it is allocated to Class IV.

When there is not enough basis to cover an entire asset class, the purchase price is allocated to each asset within a class in proportion to the asset's fair market value.

The allocation is a critical process in securing maximum tax benefits available to an acquirer. There are some key points to note. One is that Class III assets usually comprise the bulk of the target's assets. Secondly, fair market value—generally the price a Class III asset can command if sold into the marketplace—typically exceeds the book or carrying value that the target has recorded for it. The concept under which acquired assets can be revalued, usually upward, from book to fair market value is called the "step-up." Finally, to reiterate, goodwill (or going-concern value) in the acquisition context is any gap that remains between the purchase price and the allocated assets as revalued.

Thus, the buyer can benefit by properly revaluing the Class III assets and executing a sensible allocation that will reduce the level of goodwill and generate tax benefits from subsequent write-downs of amortizable assets. (This also has positive implications for postacquisition cash flow.) In the case of "hard" assets, step-ups are relatively easy, since there are established valuation mechanisms for buildings, machinery, inventories, and so on. Intangibles present problems and their allocations frequently have been subject to attack by the IRS, which has challenged their valuations or whether they should be regarded as amortizable.

Intangible Assets. Class III intangible assets are those that are separable from goodwill or going-concern value. They have some value in operating the business and have limited useful lives. The group includes patents, trademarks, copyrights, trade names, beneficial leaseholds or contracts, customer lists, and covenants not to compete. If the buyer can prove a limited useful life, the value of the intangible asset can be amortized over that period.

Class IV intangible assets—notably acquisition goodwill—are not amortizable. A key IRS strategy has been to try to move many intangible assets claimed by the buyer into Class IV to minimize revenue losses. Therefore, it is in the purchaser's best interest to identify and value all intangible assets and prove a limited useful life to maximize tax deductions.

Legislation pending in Congress in 1993 would, if passed, clear up many of the controversies surrounding allocation of purchase prices to assets. The bill would allow straight-line amortization for all intangibles, including goodwill, over periods of 14 years.

Bargain Purchase. A bargain purchase occurs in an asset purchase when the fair market value of all the acquired tangible and intangible assets, other than goodwill or going-concern value, exceeds the purchase price. In a bargain purchase, the amount of purchase price allocable to Class III assets is less than their fair market value. Thus, each asset, including accounts receivable and inventory, will have a basis less than its value. Consequently, taxable income will be recognized when the receivables are collected at face value and as inventory is sold. This exposure can be mitigated by selling receivables to a third party prior to the acquisition and electing the last-in, first-out (LIFO) inventory method after the acquisition.

Stock Acquisitions

Treatment of the Seller.   The seller generally will have a capital gain or loss on the sale of stock. If the target is an 80-percent-owned (or more) subsidiary of a selling parent corporation, however, the seller is generally prohibited from recognizing a tax benefit for any loss realized on the sale.

Treatment of the Purchaser.   The purchaser will have a cost basis in the acquired stock. The basis and tax attributes of the target corporation are unaffected.

Section 338(h)(10) Election.   If a corporation purchases at least 80 percent of a target's stock from a selling parent corporation in a taxable transaction and the purchaser and seller make an election under Section 338(h)(10) of the Code, the purchase of the target's stock will be treated for tax purposes as the purchase of the target's assets.

A Section 338(h)(10) election substitutes gain on the sale of assets for the gain that the seller's consolidated group would have recognized on the sale of the target's stock. Thus, unless the seller has a substantially higher basis in the target's stock than the target has in its net assets, it will frequently be economic to make this election.

HYBRID ACQUISITIONS

A hybrid structure, utilizing Section 351 of the Code, can provide certain shareholders with stock on a tax-free basis in an acquisition that would not meet the continuity-of-interest requirements for a tax-free reorganization. The hybrid structure requires that the participating shareholders of the target exchange their shares for stock in a newly formed company that subsequently acquires the remaining target shares for cash or debt securities. The shares received by the target shareholders do not have to participate in earnings or vote, and, thus, nonvoting preferred stock qualifies.

A hybrid acquisition can be useful in providing target managers with a tax-free rollover of their shares in a deal that is principally a cash buy-out. Similarly, it can be used as an estate-planning technique for shareholders who want to postpone recognition of gain until the basis of their stock is stepped up (tax-free) upon death.

ADDITIONAL TAX CONCERNS

Utilization of Net Operating Losses

Normally, a company can carry its net operating losses (NOLs) back 3 years and forward 15 years. If the acquirer has an NOL, future operating income of the target can be offset by loss carryovers. Under Section 384 of the Code, losses of the acquiring company may not be used to offset the realization of preacquisition "built-in gains" of a target company within 5 years of the acquisition. The built-in gain prohibition applies if, on the acquisition date, the aggregate basis of the target's assets is at least 15 percent of the excess of their fair market value over the aggregate adjusted loss of the assets or $10 million.

Section 382 of the Code may eliminate or limit the ability to utilize the target's NOLs in order to prevent the "trafficking" or sale of NOLs. Section 382 applies if there is a greater than 50 percent change in ownership of the loss target corporation within three years. An ownership change occurs if one or more "5 percent shareholders" of the loss corporation have increased their ownership by more than 50 percentage points during a testing period, which is generally three years. Shareholders owning less than 5 percent of the corporation's stock are usually treated as a single 5 percent shareholder. In general, the annual Section 382 limitation is the product of a prescribed interest rate set monthly by the IRS (currently about 7 percent) and the value of the loss corporation's stock immediately before the ownership change. The recognition of "built-in" gains or losses can, respectively, increase or decrease the Section 382 limitation for a given postacquisition taxable period.

Transaction Costs

Seller Transaction Costs. Expenses of the selling shareholder are an addition to their stock basis, reducing their deferred gain in tax-free acquisitions and their recognized gain in taxable transactions. In general, however, the IRS takes a fairly limited view of the deductibility of any target expenses. Expenses of the target company in a stock transaction (whether taxable or tax-free) are a nondeductible capital cost. A selling company's expenses in an asset transaction increase the seller's basis in the assets sold and, thus, reduce deferred gain in tax-free acquisitions and recognized gain in taxable transactions. Expenses incurred by a target company in defending against a hostile takeover are deductible. However, expenses incurred in a friendly takeover or in securing a "white knight" to defeat a hostile takeover bid are generally capitalized.

Purchaser Transaction Costs. Expenses of the purchaser are added to the cost of the stock or assets purchased. Expenses incurred in obtaining debt financing are generally capitalized and amortized over the term of the loan. Expenses incurred in raising equity, however, reduce the proceeds and, thus, are neither deductible nor amortizable.

20

Golden Rules of M&A Financing

David B. Still

*Senior Vice President, Core States
Investment Banking,
Philadelphia, Pennsylvania*

One of the principal reasons that mergers and acquisitions activity enjoyed a boom in the 1980s was the availability of large amounts of credit to finance dealmaking. In general, commercial banks, insurance companies, and other credit sources found both leveraged and nonleveraged M&A lending to be highly profitable and acceptable from a credit standpoint. Many developed specialized skills and innovative financing products to meet the demands of a clientele that ranged from operating businesses seeking strategic acquisitions to financial buyers executing leveraged buy-outs.

The supply of credit tightened in the late 1980s and early 1990s, largely because of financial and operating pressures on banks and other financial institutions. Government regulation also is a driving force that places heavy pressure on banks and insurers. Together, they have restricted the availability of funds for M&A and resulted in tougher standards for lending into M&A transactions. However, the expertise and creative techniques developed during the 1980s have survived and will be applied to the right deals. New techniques and ways of handling M&A transactions also have evolved.

This chapter reviews the types of credit that borrowers may tap to finance their acquisitions in the private debt markets as well as the ancillary financing techniques that can be used with primary M&A financing to structure an acceptable package.

In addition, the chapter explores some of the qualitative considerations that bankers and other financiers rely on to reach lending decisions, including examination of the borrower's creditworthiness and the due diligence exercises to determine if the deal should be financed.

REVOLVING CREDITS AND TERM LOANS

Revolving credits and term loans are the most widely used credit products for financing acquisitions and capital expansion programs.

A revolver is a formal commitment by a lender (a bank or a commercial finance company) to make a loan up to a specified dollar amount for an established term, generally one to eight years. The borrower has the ability to draw on the funds and to prepay the loan at any time without penalty. Consequently, the borrower may prepay and reborrow during the "life" of the revolver, as long as it is in compliance with the covenants in the "credit agreement."

With a term loan, the borrower also is granted a specified amount of credit for a specified period of time. However, the funds may not be reborrowed after payments are made in accordance with a payment schedule for retiring the loan.

Revolvers frequently are used by borrowers as debt "insurance" for unspecified major events that are anticipated to occur in the future—that is, the credit is available to finance the project when it is needed. In the M&A context, the credit may be available so it can be drawn upon when needed to complete a deal. Term loans normally are used to finance a specific expenditure, such as the acquisition, and usually will be specially arranged around the time of the deal to provide necessary funds. The caveat is that there be identifiable cash flows and/or asset sales for serving a repayment or "debt amortization" schedule.

Revolving credits and term loans often are structured by a lead lender (known as the agent) that may distribute portions of the loan to other banks (known as participants). The agent receives an up-front structuring or syndication fee normally ranging from 10 to 300 basis points of the committed amount of the credit plus an annual fee for administering the credit facility. If one bank commits to the entire amount of the credit facility, it is paid an underwriting fee that normally ranges from 50 to 500 basis points of the committed amount of the credit. The actual payment depends on the creditworthiness of the loan and financial market conditions.

All lenders, including the agent, also are paid a closing fee, which is a percentage of the revolver or term loan amount. The range is 0.125 to 2 percent, payable to each participating lender at the closing and based on its pro rata share of the total credit facility. The actual payment amount depends on the creditworthiness of the loan and financial market conditions. The borrower also is required to pay the legal fees of the lender and the lender's customary out-of-pocket expenses in the process of closing the facility.

Interest rates on revolving credits and term loans normally are set on a "floating rate" basis. The key components are the agent's prime rate or the London Interbank Offered Rate (LIBOR), whichever is lower, plus the applicable risk spreads.

An example is an interest rate option that equals a lender's base rate (prime) plus 150 basis points or LIBOR plus 300 basis points. The risk spreads differ, according to the actual or implied credit rating of the credit facility.

The rates charged by commercial finance companies generally are higher than those charged by banks, and even though nonbank credit sources tend to accept higher risks, they also demand higher rewards in return. An advantage to using commercial finance companies is that they are not highly regulated unless they are bank subsidiaries.

Revolving credits may have a portion of the credit facility that is unborrowed or unused. Lenders require payment of a commitment fee equal to the average unused portion of the credit facility times a percentage which ranges from 0.125 to 0.75 percent. Occasionally, the borrower also may be required to keep compensating balances at the lead and participating banks. Compensating balances normally are kept in noninterest-bearing checking accounts and must be maintained at specified levels throughout the life of the credit facility.

Revolving credits and term loans are binding legal commitments by both the borrower and the lender and must be documented by a formal credit agreement. The document covers all important components of the "bargain," including the amount and term of the credit, the amortization schedule, the borrower's status with other lenders, security and collateral for the loan, the names of guarantors, the use of proceeds, interest rates and fees, financial and nonfinancial covenants, representations and warranties, and events of default and indemnification.

BRIDGE LOANS

A bridge loan can be advanced through a variety of structures such as a term loan or revolving credit. However, it is of relatively short duration, compared with other types of loans and often is considered temporary financing from the viewpoint of the borrower. The bridge loan depends on subsequent refinancing, such as through issuance of either debt or equity to obtain funds for repayment. The distinguishing feature of a bridge loan is that a lender's risk varies with the borrower's financial strength and with changes in financial market conditions that may impact the primary source of repayment.

Bridge loans were common elements in M&A during the 1980s, when the acquisition market was highly charged and transactions had to be expedited. Borrowers generally use bridge loans so they can secure acquisition financing quickly in accordance with an accelerated timetable for closing a deal. The plan is to retire the bridge loan by selling debt or equity securities or obtaining more permanent credit facilities from financial institutions. Junk bond issues during the 1980s were commonly used to pay off bridge loans in highly leveraged transactions.

However, bridge loans are rarely used in M&A transactions of the 1990s because of the loss experience of lenders and heightened regulatory scrutiny. In their place, borrowers use a boutique of different products structured to satisfy lenders. It has become inadvisable to approach lenders for pure "bridge loans" unless the transaction can stand on its own merits as term financing.

Bridge loans are more expensive than normal credit products because the lender generally extends credit quickly and takes an additional risk that the refinancing won't occur if there is a change at the borrower or in the financial markets. Structuring and/or underwriting fees can range from 1 to 5 percent, and closing fees and interest rates usually are higher than the borrower would normally incur. As with all committed credit facilities, the lender's legal and direct costs are paid by the borrower.

Interest costs for bridge loans bear a premium over normal borrowing costs that can range as high as 2 to 5 percent over prime and may involve escalating interest costs or equity kickers for the lender. Equity kickers, such elements as warrants or rights to purchase stock in the borrower, provide additional compensation for lenders in order to bring their overall return on the loan to between 15 and 30 percent, depending on market conditions. Most bridge loans include a penalty fee if the loan is not refinanced by a set date.

PRIVATE PLACEMENTS

A private placement is a sale of corporate securities to a limited number of sophisticated investors. Companies obtaining funds through private placement channels may sell senior secured and unsecured debt, medium-term notes, subordinated debt, convertible debt, and preferred and common stock. Principal purchasers are large investors such as insurance companies and pension funds, although mutual funds are becoming a significant market force.

Private placements have grown significantly as sources of funds to refinance initial acquisition financing. Because they take a considerable amount of time to arrange in an environment where speed often is required, they generally replace bank debt. However, the private placement has been used with somewhat more frequency by deal makers in recent years. For example, the private placement market was used to obtain part of the financing for Crown Cork & Seal Inc.'s $336 million acquisition of the food and beverage can business of the former Continental Can Co. in 1990. Crown sold $100 million in three-year senior notes, earmarking the proceeds to help pay for the deal.

A factor that may promote wider use of private placements for acquisition financing is Rule 144A issued by the Securities and Exchange Commission in 1990 to provide more liquidity for privately placed securities. The rule allows buyers to resell the notes shortly after purchase.

In most cases, privately placed securities are long-term senior debt issues. The issuer can use them to reduce floating rate short-term debt, extend the maturity of existing debt obligations, and finance projects, such as acquisitions, that have long-term cash flow paybacks. Among the advantages of the private placement are generally confidential treatment of financial information, lower costs of issuing securities, a wide range of issue sizes, structural flexibility for complicated transactions, the ease in obtaining amendments or waivers in original agreements, and the securing of institutional support for future capital needs.

Most private placements are marketed by a placement agent that is paid a success fee ranging from 20 to 100 basis points for a senior note issue. The agent's fee is also a function of the amount of the issue. Buyers generally don't charge up-front fees for investment-grade private placements, but for noninvestment-grade placements, up-front fees can range up to 200 basis points of the private placements.

The fixed interest rate on private placements is based on a spread over prevailing U.S. Treasury securities rates for the average life of the issue.

EMPLOYEE STOCK OWNERSHIP PLANS

An employee stock ownership plan (ESOP) or employee stock ownership trust (ESOT) is a qualified worker retirement plan that also provides expansive financing and tax-saving opportunities for companies using them. The most prominent public perception is that the ESOP is a way to give employees a vehicle for owning all or part of the company they work for. However, the well-crafted ESOP, because of tax and other advantages, can be a source of fresh, low-cost, tax-advantaged permanent capital for the company.

In the most publicized cases, the ESOP has been a "change of control" vehicle through which the owners of the company sell it to the employees. In other cases, ESOPs have been set up, partially as an alternative to other compensation and benefit programs, to own a portion of the employer's stock. Private companies also use ESOPs as alternatives to IPOs in facilitating estate planning for the owners.

For compensation and benefit purposes, ESOPs are classified as defined contribution plans. A worker/participant's retirement benefit is based mainly on the amount of employer contributions made to the plan on his or her behalf. As a qualified plan, the employer's contributions to the ESOP are deductible from federal income taxes. In addition, an ESOP is not subject to taxation and participants are not taxed until they receive stock or other consideration from the ESOP.

The two basic types of plans are leveraged and nonleveraged ESOPs.

Leveraged ESOPs

A leveraged ESOP is most commonly used to acquire a company that becomes employee-owned. The plan borrows money, generally with a guarantee from the employer corporation, and utilizes the cash to buy the company's stock. The employer contributes cash annually to the ESOP to amortize the principal and interest due the lender. Contributions to the ESOP generally are tax-advantaged in that they may be deducted from federal taxes. The employer is not taxed until the shares distributed to his or her account are distributed on retirement. In the case of a private company, the employer usually sells the shares back to the firm for cash.

Nonleveraged ESOPs

Nonleveraged ESOPs, by contrast, don't borrow to acquire the employer's stock. Rather, the employer company periodically contributes stock or channels cash to the plan so it can buy company stock. The employer gets a tax deduction for either the cash contribution or the fair market value of the contributed stock, subject to a specified limit.

The nonleveraged ESOPs often are part of a company's retirement benefit program—the employee can take out his or her stock upon leaving the company—but are quite versatile. They have been used as employee incentive programs. And a number of public companies have created them as antitakeover devices in the belief that employees will use their shares to oppose hostile offers that they perceive as threats to their jobs.

ESOPs are highly structured financings and employee benefit plans that have multiple fees and costs which go beyond most financing transactions. There are up-front fees for establishing the employee benefit plan, valuing the securities in the plan, establishing a corporate or noncorporate trustee for the plan, documenting the loan and guarantees, reporting on considerations under the Employees' Retirement Income Security Act (ERISA), and paying for legal work.

Financing costs and prices are the same as they would be for revolving credit and term loans with one exception. If the ESOP owns more than half the company's equity, and therefore has control, the lender may exempt some of the interest payments for tax purposes. The savings are passed on to the borrowing plan and effectively result in its paying a lower interest rate than is charged on other types of financings. The rate reduction often has made the ESOP transaction feasible.

When the ESOP owns more than 30 percent of the stock, the selling owner may indefinitely defer, and in some cases avoid, paying income taxes on gains from the sale.

Leveraged Buy-outs

In a leveraged buy-out, an investment group purchases an operating business with mostly borrowed funds and uses the assets and cash flow of the acquired company to support and service the debt incurred in acquiring the company. An objective of the buy-out group is to contribute the minimum amount of equity necessary to complete the transaction.

Leveraged buy-outs were easily financed transactions during much of the 1980s. Financing came from banks, insurance companies, commercial finance lenders and the public debt markets. However, LBOs were essentially regulated out of the financing markets in the early 1990s by the highly leveraged transaction (HLT) definition promulgated by federal bank regulators (which was dropped in mid-1992) and a new rating model by the National Association of Insurance Commissioners. New LBOs still are being financed in the 1990s if they include larger equity contributions, and with a change in market conditions they are once again a viable financing vehicle.

LBO debt may come in several forms and involve a number of sources. Commercial banks and commercial finance companies are the principal suppliers of senior debt, usually through revolving credits and term loans. Insurance companies and pension funds are the buyers of securities used in the senior layer and the mezzanine layer of the capital structure which often is required to close the gap between senior debt and equity. Major sources of equity are funds that are assembled and managed by firms that specialize in being LBO sponsors, while some venture capital firms also have invested in leveraged transactions. High-yield debt securities also have been sold publicly or in private placements to retire senior debt, create a subordinated debt strip, or become part of the mezzanine tranche.

Because of the admitted risk involved in creating highly leveraged business entities, lenders and investors commit to them cautiously. Interest rates on loans and revolving credit are usually higher than for standard acquisition loans and often carry equity kickers. Mezzanine securities, which may include such instruments as convertible preferred stock and convertible debt, are expensive because the buyers demand high returns. And all players put the leveraged deal through an intense screen to assure that it is viable.

The senior lender looks carefully at market and regulatory conditions, the value of the target's assets, the quality of management, and both the magnitude and sustainability of cash flows on both a historical and projected basis. A key aim is to structure a deal that assures that the cash flow adequately covers both interest and principal payments, regardless of conditions in the economy. The borrower must produce a comprehensive business plan that emphasizes the company's strengths, identifies asset sales, and includes contingencies for overcoming any perceived weaknesses.

In addition to dealing with the basic risk of lending to a highly leveraged company, the senior lender's intensive due diligence also is driven by the specter of fraudulent conveyance should the business go sour. It has long been recognized in the courts that the transfer of property for less than its realizable value or for less than reasonably equivalent value may be attacked as a fraudulent conveyance. This is a legal concept which turns on whether the debtor was insolvent, rendered insolvent, or left with inadequate working capital at the time of the asset transfer. It usually arises if the leveraged company goes into bankruptcy proceedings.

If such insolvency can be proved, it suggests that the company would not have survived. There are three key measures or tests utilized to prove or disprove that concept—the strength and structure of the company's balance sheet, the value of its assets, and whether the cash flows are sufficient to pay down the debt. Lenders will check these measures out carefully to guard against being accused of knowingly providing funds for a deal that could not succeed.

One of the principal penalties against a lender is the loss of its status as a senior or secured creditor in bankruptcy proceedings and its demotion to that of equity participant—basically a stockholder. If that occurs, the lender's claims may be deeply subordinated to those of other creditors.

Although the law on fraudulent conveyance is unsettled and constantly evolving as a result of judicial decisions, recent trends have intensified the pressure for intense preacquisition due diligence. For example, in a case involving the buy-out of O'Day Corp., a boat builder, the federal bankruptcy court in Boston subordinated the claims of the chief lender, Meritor Financial, on the grounds it should have known that the deal was ill-fated. O'Day suffered a decline in sales after the acquisition that has been attributed to the federal luxury tax on boats. But in a case with a similar fact pattern, federal courts have ruled that the buy-out of Jeanette Corp., a manufacturer of china and glassware, was not a fraudulent conveyance. Jeanette went into bankruptcy when it lost business to low-priced imports.

OPERATING AND CAPITAL LEASES

Sale/leaseback programs can be important techniques for financing acquisitions. Leasing also can be a good tool for maximizing postacquisition cash flow, such as for highly leveraged companies. The most frequently employed formats are the sale/leaseback, service or operating leases, and financial or capital leases.

Under a sale/leaseback, the company sells such physical property as land, buildings, and equipment and simultaneously executes an agreement to lease the property back for a specified time period and according to certain terms and conditions.

An operating lease generally includes both the financing and maintenance service of the leased property. Generally, operating leases do not fully amortize the cost of the property. Therefore, the lessor assumes the "residual risk." Operating lease payments are accounted for as rent expenses on the lessee's financial statements and are not shown as a liability on its balance sheet.

A capital lease is primarily a financing vehicle. It does not provide for lessor services and the property cost is fully amortized to zero residual value. Capital lease obligations are accounted for as a liability on the lessee's balance sheet.

SECURITIZED CREDIT

Securitized credit is a form of financing that combines established concepts of securities issuance and asset-backed lending. It is handled by issuing an asset-backed security or selling assets to a special-purpose conduit and can be an effective tool for financing leveraged M&A transactions.

The securitized credit process basically starts when a borrower packages like-kind assets that are on its financial statement. The assets could be residential mortgages, commercial mortgages, installment loans, or other trade receivables. Working with a "structurer," the borrower then aggregates the assets and structures a security or sells the assets to the special-purpose conduit. The borrower and structurer obtain credit insurance in the form of a letter of credit for a portion of the new security or over collaterilization. Finally, another institution places and/or invests in the security and frequently trades it in the open market.

The borrower benefits from securitized credit because the overall cost of raising funds usually is less expensive than in traditional financing approaches, since the security is backed by high-quality assets and external credit enhancement. In addition, sale of the asset-backed security moves the issuer's debt off the balance sheet, thereby reducing its leverage. Generally, there is limited recourse to the borrower.

Buyers needing borrowed money to finance an M&A transaction should review securitized credit options to partially finance the acquisition.

INTEREST RATE MANAGEMENT

Interest rate management techniques are used to alter the nature of the pricing in credit agreements. They can be essential adjuncts to the primary financing vehicle in an M&A transaction because they offer the opportunity to hedge financial market and interest rate risks in the deal.

The most prevalent techniques are:

- *Interest rate swaps*—switching from fixed to floating rate instruments, or vice versa
- *Interest rate caps*—purchasing an instrument that fixes a ceiling rate on floating rate debt
- *Interest rate collars*—purchasing an instrument that sets both a ceiling and a floor rate for floating rate debt

SYNDICATION OF CREDIT

Many acquisitions, especially the larger deals, are financed through credit supplied by a group of banks that are assembled on a best-efforts basis as a syndicate. The "lead bank," which takes the initiative in forming the syndicate, is usually the institution that is closest to the acquirer and provides the largest dollar share of the credit. Syndicating the loan allows for a relatively quick development of the necessary credit at reasonable prices. By supplying only a portion of the total credit, each participating bank reduces its risk, and syndication also permits some smaller and middle-sized institutions to participate in deals that would be beyond their means on an individual basis.

Closing fees are payable at the closing of a credit to all participants to cover set-up and analysis costs, in proportion to each bank's commitments. These fees are deferred under Financial Accounting Standards Board (FASB) Statement 91 on amounts retained. Additional up-front fees normally are paid to the syndication or lead manager to cover costs of organizing the lending group. The lead agent usually gets an annual fee for the administration of the credit. A commitment fee is charged on the unused portion of the credit until it is either drawn or the facility expires or is canceled. A facility fee is similar except that it is based on the entire amount of the credit, whether used or not.

The interest spread on a syndicated loan is the interest rate premium or discount charged on a loan over a reference rate, usually the base rate (prime), LIBOR, the certificate of deposit rate, or the Federal Funds rate.

RATING DEBT

Almost every credit facility is rated by prospective lenders according to some internal or external risk scale. The scale may be widely publicized, such as those used by Standard & Poor's, Moody's, Duff & Phelps, Fitch, and other rating agencies that determine debt quality. But it is more likely to be an internal scale that is unique to the lender weighing the deal. In some cases the in-house test may simply mirror the relevant regulatory rules or the internal loan review ratings of the lender, while in others the screen may tie into a more public rating system.

The rating of a credit, whether "actual" or "implied," is the main determinant of deal structure, syndication strategy, up-front fees, ongoing fees, interest indices and spread, credit structure, and documentation. Under certain market conditions, the rating of the debt facility will determine whether credit is available under any pricing or structural conditions.

DUE DILIGENCE

The rating process, in fact, is part of an extensive due diligence effort that lenders undertake to assess the viability of the borrowing company and provide it with as much protection as possible. This examination leads to assessment of straightforward financial criteria, as well as more qualitative subjective concerns. Legal pressures, such as the aforementioned threat of fraudulent conveyance, are raising the stakes and mandating the most intensive of investigations prior to parting with funds.

The predominant debt philosophy focuses on the lender's "way out" of a loan—that is, how it will be repaid. Cash flow is the primary form of repayment and asset liquidation is the second major source. If lenders can get comfortable with cash flow coverage and leverage (as a proxy for asset coverage), a loan generally will be approved.

Whether the deal is highly leveraged and axiomatically demands regulatory scrutiny and the three tests for fraudulent conveyance or it is a more orthodox acquisition, the lender will check through:

Cash Flow Coverage.   Is there sufficient and reliable cash flow to finance business investments and service fixed charges with ample coverage?

Value and Quality of Assets.   Are there sufficient good assets to support the business and the cash flow stream? If the company gets into trouble, are there enough assets to sell so the lender may be repaid?

Business Plan.   Is the program for managing the company's future and expanding the business realistic and achievable? Does it include a "worst case" scenario that allows for continued generation of cash flow during an economic downturn? Are there enough financial resources to repay the loan while investing for growth or improved productivity?

Quality of Management.   Does the incumbent management have the skills to execute the business plan? Or will a new executive team have to be enlisted?

Environmental Concerns.   If the target company operates an environmentally sensitive business, the lender is certain to demand an investigation to determine whether the firm is in compliance with environmental and safety laws or if there are any hidden problems that could cause trouble later. But even in less obvious cases, most lenders will demand environmental audits for businesses changing hands.

The lender has many concerns in the environmental area. One is a fear that if the business incurs large liabilities, they may impair the value of the assets or generate costs that divert money from repayment of the loan. A second is the lender's position should it have to take over a business that has gone bad and is in default on the loan.

A major worry for lenders that assumed control of sick businesses has been that they might have to make good on the environmental liabilities. The Environmental Protection Agency, however, issued a rule in 1992 that can ease that problem. The rule exempts a lender from the liability if it takes normal steps to monitor and protect its interest in a troubled borrower. But to get the exemption, the lender must conduct environmental due diligence up front to obtain reasonable assurances that problems did not exist, or were on the road to being corrected, at the time the loan was made.

PANOPLY OF CHOICES

Today's acquirers enjoy a vast array of credit products, sources, and intermediaries from which they can select and obtain the "best financing" for financing an acquisition and arranging for credit on an ongoing basis after the deal. The "golden rule" is to utilize these resources to structure the "best financing" that will optimize corporate objectives.

21

Asset-Based Financing

David N. Deutsch

Managing Director, Investment Banking,
Congress Financial Corp.,
New York, New York

Asset-based lending long has been applicable to highly leveraged and troubled-company finance and remains the central discipline in the structuring and financing of leveraged buy-outs. While the original leveraged buy-out "formula" has been modified somewhat over time, the largest component of the LBO capital structure, senior debt, always has been shaped by collateral considerations.

The concept of a leveraged buy-out is relatively simple. Acquire a cash-flow-producing asset with a relatively modest amount of equity capital and mostly debt secured by the acquired asset. Over time, free cash flow amortizes the debt, and the investor's rate of return on equity is superior to that of an identical, all-equity-financed transaction.

In this chapter, we will study the genesis, structuring, and financing of the leveraged buy-out and survey the relative considerations of each of the primary financing constituents in the LBO capital structure: senior debt, subordinated debt, and equity. In particular, we will examine asset-based lending and its importance in shaping the leveraged transactions of the 1990s.

GENESIS OF AN LBO TRANSACTION

A leveraged buy-out typically arises as the result of one of three scenarios:

■ A going-private transaction

- A corporate divestiture
- A sale of a private company

While each of these scenarios is characterized by a different set of strategic and financing considerations, all are predicated on the theory that return on equity may be enhanced through the optimal use of financial leverage. In each case, cash flow characteristics and asset values are relatively more important than earnings or growth potential in the rationale for the transaction.

Here are common characteristics of each of these three LBO scenarios:

Going Private Transaction (Stock Transaction)

- Book value of assets is at historical levels versus replacement cost.
- Market value of equity is attractive vis-à-vis prevailing market multiples of comparable public companies.
- Acquirer has the ability to accumulate or tender for shares at a reasonable premium to market price.
- Opportunity to deconglomerate at attractive business-unit sale values.
- Company is managed by corporate stewards rather than owner-entrepreneurs.
- Alternative to leveraged recapitalization.

Corporate Divestiture (Stock or Asset Transaction)

- Book value of assets is at historical levels versus replacement cost.
- Not "core" business of parent company.
- Opportunity for negotiated purchase price and ability to acquire selected assets.
- Corporate overmanagement, bureaucracy, and excessive corporate overhead allocations or corporate neglect and inadequate funding.
- Alternative to spin-off, IPO, leveraged recapitalization, or liquidation.
- Opportunity for seller financing, reinvestment, or earn-out.

Private Sale (Stock or Asset Transaction)

- Book value of assets is at historical levels versus replacement cost.
- Inflated owner-expenses represent cost-cutting opportunity.
- Lack of access to adequate financing in the past.
- Opportunity for negotiated purchase price and ability to acquire selected assets.
- Company management retiring or lacking depth, new owner can take to "next level."

■ Alternative to IPO, leveraged recapitalization, or liquidation.

■ Opportunity for seller financing, reinvestment, or earn-out.

The classic leveraged buy-out candidate is an asset-rich manufacturing or whole-sale distribution company with leading market share, relatively stable operating cash flow, and modest capital requirements in a relatively slow-growth industry. Such companies are better able to bear the additional fixed cost of debt and the burden of amortization of debt principal than faster growing companies with more volatile cash flows. Rapid growth generally requires above-average investment in plant and equipment and requires additional working capital to finance increasing levels of accounts receivable and inventory. As a result, faster growing companies are generally too cash-consumptive to bear much additional debt. Slow-growth, cash flow generators, on the other hand, generally are able to lower their weighted average costs of capital and increase returns on equity by replacing equity with debt.

In the 1980s, as a result of relatively undervalued market prices for assets (vis-à-vis book value, replacement cost, and "break-up" value), increased availability of debt and equity capital for leveraged transactions, and a generally speculative environ-ment, companies in virtually every industry, with varying levels of underlying asset values and cash flow stability, were acquired in leveraged buy-outs. Many large public companies were taken private on the theory that business-unit values (not underlying asset values) would provide adequate "collateral" to senior lenders. Sub-ordinated lenders, including investors in the increasingly liquid public high-yield debt market, accepted the risk of unsecured lending into these highly leveraged transactions primarily on the basis of cash flow projections. In the late 1980s and early 1990s, many of these transactions resulted in financial distress, and many sen-ior and subordinated lenders were forced to write down large amounts of loans related to highly leveraged-transactions.

Because of these events and resulting changes in availability of financing, the lev-eraged buy-outs of the 1990s will more closely resemble those of the 1970s and early 1980s, featuring more stable, asset-rich companies and less leveraged capital struc-tures.

TRANSACTION STRUCTURE

Calculating Transaction Value

The *total transaction value* of a leveraged acquisition is composed of several items in addition to the cash purchase price of the stock or assets acquired. Any assumption or refinancing of debt, noncompetition agreements, earn-outs, liabilities for taxes, unfunded pension or other employee benefit plans, environmental clean-up costs, and other contingent liabilities should be included in any calculation of total pur-chase price, as well as transaction costs.

Transaction costs typically include expenses relating to due diligence, audit, ap-praisals, accountants' fees, attorneys' fees, opinion letters, and financing fees and expenses. While not necessarily included in the calculation of purchase price, any accounting of financing requirements for the transaction also should include any payments necessary to satisfy past-due accounts payable.

Transaction values typically are quoted as a multiple of operating earnings or operating cash flow. As with other investments, the "value" of a leveraged acquisition is considered within the context of comparable situations. Leveraged buy-out multiples typically are considered in terms of both premiums to comparable publicly traded companies and value relative to recent comparable acquisitions.

Capital Structuring

LBO capital structures must not only satisfy the immediate "uses of financing" at closing, but must contemplate the nature of the business acquired. If the borrower's business is cyclical, more equity is required to finance the downturns. If, on the other hand, the borrower generates stable and predictable cash flow, little equity may be required for a prudent capital structure. The object is to maximize the rate of return on equity by financing the transaction with as little equity as is prudent and that financing markets will allow.

LBO capital structures are composed of two primary tranches of capital:

- Equity, which constitutes the "down payment"
- Debt, including senior and subordinated debt, which constitutes the "mortgage"

Depending on the transaction and financing sources, the entire amount of debt capital, as well as a part of the equity capital, may be provided in "strips" by a single lender or in layers by individual providers of senior and subordinated debt.

Table 21.1 shows a generic capital structure for the financing of a leveraged buy-out and the uses of the proceeds.

The relative risk tolerances and reward expectations of various financing markets change over time and, consequently, so do the availability and cost of each tranche of financing. In the 1980s, when bank and subordinated debt financing for leveraged transactions was more readily available, transactions were structured with relatively large amounts of senior and subordinated debt financing and relatively little equity. The financing markets of the 1990s, characterized by a relative scarcity of

Table 21.1. Financing a Leveraged Buy-Out

Sources of financing	Uses of financing
Revolving credit	Cash purchase price
Senior term debt	Assumption/refinancing of debt
Subordinated debt	Noncompete agreements
Equity	Taxes
	Earn-outs*
	Unfunded pension liabilities, etc.*
	Environmental clean-up costs*
	Other contingent liabilities*
	Transaction costs

*May not require funding at time of closing.

senior debt for leveraged transactions and increasing requirements for equity, are structured with less senior debt, more equity, and generally less mezzanine financing. Equity has replaced subordinated debt and purchase prices have declined from lofty 1980s multiples. (See Table 21.2.)

FINANCING SOURCES

The difference between the LBO transactions of the 1980s and the 1990s relates not only to a change in capital structure, but to a fundamental shift in the sources for, and limitations imposed by, each tranche of financing in the LBO capital structure.

Senior debt, typically composed of a revolving line of credit and senior term debt, is the largest and most defining tranche in the entire capital structure. Senior debt is the least costly element of financing because of its priority in liquidation, and its portion of the total capital structure always has been determined at least partially on the basis of collateral values. Today, every lender that considers providing financing for highly leveraged transactions considers collateral values to a great degree in making lending decisions.

The most fundamental shift in the financing of LBO transactions is the resurgence of asset-based lending. While "cash flow" senior lenders continue to exist, their lack of complete collateral protection and control—and their harsh experiences of the late 1980s and early 1990s—has prompted their systematic withdrawal from the leveraged financing marketplace. By contrast, asset-based lenders whose loans are well secured and assiduously monitored have continued to fund highly leveraged transactions.

Because of their reliance on cash flow as well as collateral, commercial bank senior lenders typically require a panoply of financial covenants, including limitations on incurrence of additional indebtedness, maintenance of certain fixed charge and cash interest coverage ratios, limitations on capital expenditures and other uses of funds, as well as limitations on the sale of assets, negative pledges, and other balance-sheet-oriented tests. Asset-based lenders, alternatively, often require only those covenants that relate directly to the protection of collateral. Such covenants consist principally of restrictions on sale of assets, maintenance of net worth and working capital, and, as required by all lenders, restrictions on the borrower's ability to pay

Table 21.2. LBO Capital Structures

	1980s		1990s			
55%	▦	45%	▦	▦	Senior debt
		30%	▩	▩	Mezzanine financing
40%	▩	25%	▦	▦	Equity
5%	▦				

cash dividends, repurchase common stock, and make certain other "restricted" payments.

The senior lender—whether cash flow or asset-based—is most concerned with stability (versus growth) and repayment of principal. For this reason, subordination issues and principal amortization schedules also are very important to this only true "debt" layer in the LBO capital structure.

Subordinated debt, along with any other "mezzanine financing," typically comprises the second largest portion of the LBO capital structure. This unsecured layer of debt may be considered "risk capital," as distinguished from "secured debt," and typically includes some form of participation in equity of the borrower. In certain cases, mezzanine financing may be found in the form of unsecured debt without equity participation. However, mezzanine financing almost always is more costly than senior secured debt.

Because of their reliance on cash flow to service and amortize their loans, subordinated lenders typically require maintenance of fixed charge coverage and cash interest coverage ratios as well as certain other financial covenants for protection. However, subordinated lenders must concede priority in amortization of principal and in liquidation to senior lenders. Because of this acceptance of "downside risk," the subordinated lender is especially concerned with limitations on additional indebtedness and restricted payments issues and generally requires some participation in the "upside" of the transaction.

Equity capital is the riskiest, yet the most freely available, tranche of financing in the LBO capital structure. This layer of pure "risk capital" is the speculative down payment which, while last in line in a liquidation, is the primary beneficiary of growth in the equity value of the LBO. The provider of equity is typically the "sponsor" of the transaction and generally must agree to limitations on its ability to liquidate its interest in the company before lenders are satisfied.

The sources of each tranche of financing (senior, mezzanine, and equity) have changed markedly from the 1980s to the 1990s. Table 21.3 summarizes LBO financing sources by category, then and now.

Because financing markets are in constant flux, the supply and demand for each tranche of debt and equity financing will, undoubtedly, continue to change. Among the various credit markets, the availability of bank debt, the tenor of the private placement and public debt markets, and the evolution of the covenant "market" will continue to drive LBO capital structures. In equity markets, the value of publicly traded equities vis-à-vis underlying asset values and private market values will continue to affect the availability of equity for LBO transactions.

COMMERCIAL FINANCE COMPANIES

Given the importance of senior debt in the overall LBO capital structure and the resurgent role of the asset-based lender in providing senior financing, an understanding of commercial finance companies and their credit methodologies is essential to leveraged buy-out finance.

Table 21.3. LBO Financing Sources

1980s	1990s
Senior debt	
Commercial banks	Commercial finance companies
Commercial finance companies	Commercial banks
Senior notes/Mezzanine financing	
Insurance companies	Funds/entrepreneurial lenders
Savings and loan associations	Seller
Public high-yield debt	Acquirer
Funds/entrepreneurial lenders	Public high-yield debt
Commercial finance companies	Commercial finance companies
Seller	Additional equity
Equity	
LBO sponsors	Strategic acquirers
Strategic acquirers	LBO sponsors

Debt financing provided by asset-based lenders exceeded $100 billion in the early 1990s and commercial finance companies steadily gained senior financing market share as commercial banks withdrew from the financing of highly leveraged transactions. While commercial banks and other nonasset-based lenders may return to the leveraged financing marketplace at some time in the future, recent bank write-offs, increased public scrutiny, and government regulation of bank investment practices and capital requirements suggest that commercial banks will, once again, focus on lending to less leveraged corporate credits. Thus, commercial finance companies will remain a most relevant and reliable source of senior financing for leveraged buy-outs.

The hierarchy of various categories of commercial finance companies from "business value lenders" to "small independents" includes:

Business Value Lenders. Larger commercial finance companies that extend secured and unsecured loans on the basis of cash flow and going-concern values as well as collateral values.

Bank Direct Marketers. Bank-owned asset-based lenders that generally extend only secured loans to better corporate credits. These lenders market directly to potential borrowers.

Bank-Owned Independents. Bank-owned asset-based lenders that generally adhere more closely to traditional asset-based lending practices and preference and extend credit to more highly leveraged transactions on the basis of collateral coverage.

Bank System Networkers. Bank-owned asset-based units or divisions that cater primarily to their parents' own troubled or highly leveraged borrowers.

Factors. Traditional collateral lenders that provide only working capital financing against accounts receivable and inventory.

Small Independents. Traditional collateral lenders that provide primarily working capital financing for smaller transactions.

While each category of commercial finance company has a slightly different orientation (size parameters, degree of emphasis on various types of collateral, willingness to extend unsecured financing, etc.), each extends credit primarily on the basis of collateral values and, secondarily, on the basis of earnings and cash flow. Business value lenders emphasize cash flow. However, even these lenders are returning to asset-based lending techniques in their LBO credit approval and monitoring procedures.

The Asset-Based Lending Thought Process

The asset-based lending credit review process involves three sets of interrelated considerations:

- Business issues
- Collateral issues
- Structural and legal issues

The asset-based lender, like any other lender, is concerned primarily with the ability of the borrower to make timely payments of interest and principal from earnings and cash flow in the ordinary course of its business. While the asset-based lender has greater protection in the form of collateral if earnings and cash flow are not sufficient to service and amortize debt, it will not extend credit unless it believes in the viability of the enterprise. This judgment is based on numerous subjective considerations, including an assessment of the dynamics of competition in the prospective borrower's industry and its market position. In addition, many leveraged acquisitions are predicated on significant operational and management changes, as well as an increase in leverage, which must be assessed.

The essence of asset-based lending is an understanding of the interrelationship between working capital flows and "availability" from collateral. The asset-based lender must understand the nature and seasonality of its prospective borrower's business, including the timing of shipments, billings and collections, and other activities that result in cash inflows and outflows (e.g., other financing activities, asset dispositions, capital expenditures, amortization of debt, extraordinary items) and ongoing *eligible* amounts of various categories of collateral.

"Eligibility" of collateral and "advance rates" are central issues to the asset-based lender. While an asset-based lender may require first and only liens on *all* of the assets of the acquired company, the lender may not allow all collateral to be "eligible" for borrowing purposes. In fact, asset-based lenders typically advance against only eligible amounts of each of four categories of "hard" assets: accounts receivable, inventory, machinery and equipment, and real estate. Other categories of assets, including most intangibles, are generally not eligible for borrowing purposes and are often viewed as "side collateral." In certain transactions, additional collateral may be identified in the form of valuable patents, trade names, customer lists, and the like, as well as personal assets and/or guarantees of the acquirer.

Advance rates are a function of many variables, including accounts receivable "dilution" and concentration, inventory type and location, and fixed asset category and salability. The ranges of percentages that generally apply are shown in Table 21.4.

Structural issues include determination of additional reserves, side collateral, excess availability requirements, inventory and other sublimits, overadvance allowances, balance of reliance on various forms of collateral, "clean-up" and amortization requirements, provisions for letters of credit, inter creditor issues, cross-collateralization and guarantee issues, and syndication structure. Legal issues relate to perfection of security interests, subordination issues, and myriad lender liability issues such as bulk sales, fraudulent conveyance, and environmental matters.

PUTTING THE PIECES TOGETHER

O.K., you've identified an LBO candidate, negotiated the purchase price, determined all costs, and have come to the "party" with an adequate amount of equity capital. Your first stop is for senior financing, probably to a commercial finance company or commercial bank. Based on the amount of financing, largely dictated by collateral, that the senior lender can provide, the financing markets reveal how much mezzanine financing is required. If mezzanine financing can be raised at reasonable cost and on terms acceptable to the senior lender, you determine whether the aftertax free cash flow (net earnings, plus noncash charges, less capital expenditures, less changes in working capital) is sufficient to amortize debt, increase equity value, and provide a satisfactory return on equity to compensate for the risk of investing in such a highly leveraged and illiquid transaction.

Final Thoughts

Remember that a leveraged buy-out is still, essentially, an equity investment, albeit a highly leveraged one. The LBO investor must believe that it is investing in a fundamentally good company with good management and that, even in a cyclical downturn, the newly capitalized entity can service its obligations and have enough excess cash flow for capital spending and debt amortization. Generally, the confidence of the sponsor and management in the transaction is reflected by the degree of their respective investments in the equity of the transaction.

The transaction must be more than financeable; it must be rational.

Table 21.4. Advance Rate Ranges

Assets	Advance rates
Accounts receivable	70–90% of eligible receivables
Inventory	25–75% of eligible inventory
Machinery and equipment	70–90% of acceptable appraisal
Real estate	Varying percentages

22

Financing in an Illiquid Market

Steven J. Sherman
Partner, KPMG Peat Marwick,
Chicago, Illinois

A hectic environment existed throughout the 1980s for most M&A professionals. Buyers, sellers, and intermediaries actively pursued deals that often were completed with cheap and easy money. High-yield or "junk" bonds became available for larger deals, while banks offered cash flow financing on middle market transactions.

Beyond junk bonds, M&A activity was encouraged by the government. When Ronald Reagan was elected president, he dramatically reduced the amount of antitrust enforcement. At the same time, the government continued to encourage debt. For many years, borrowers have been able to deduct interest payments for tax purposes, but they have not been able to deduct dividend payments, making debt much less expensive than equity.

Pricing of transactions in the marketplace created an unhealthy trend. The multiples of four to six times earnings before interest and taxes (EBIT) in the early 1980s became six to eight times EBIT or higher as the decade progressed. Of course, by the early 1990s much lower multiples had returned.

Other factors characterized M&A activity in the 1980s. Strategic buyers often were pushed out of the marketplace by the multiples required to win deals. Similarly, start-up businesses were not given the attention that they had been accorded earlier. This resulted because venture capital firms shifted their focus away from start-ups or even second-round financings to pursue leveraged buy-outs. Capital for small start-up companies in Silicon Valley, the Midwest, and the East Coast was hard to find. And, of course, foreign buyers became major acquisition players.

In early 1990, several events transpired concurrently to change the M&A environment. The insider trading scandals came to a head. Drexel Burnham Lambert encountered significant problems, and, overnight, the junk bond market crashed. Savings and loan institutions were major holders of junk bonds and suffered significant losses. As taxpayers, we are continuing to subsidize these losses through Resolution Trust Corp. (RTC), and we will be doing so for many years to come.

When the junk bond market crashed, financing immediately dried up for larger deals. At the same time, the Federal Reserve began to require that banks report the percentages of their loan portfolios that were invested in highly leveraged transactions (HLTs). Banks that had high percentages of investments in HLTs saw the value of their stocks discounted in the marketplace. This resulted in few new loans and a greater focus on reducing the percentage of bank portfolios invested in HLTs.

The above factors have influenced the current environment, including the recession, which began in 1990. Many of the bankruptcy situations of the 1990s resulted from companies that were overleveraged during the 1980s. The recession and increased bankruptcies have contributed, along with other factors, to a significant downturn in dealmaking.

Lenders went from one extreme to the other. In the 1990s, they are requiring that real equity in the 20 to 30 percent range be invested in deals. This is in contrast to the 1980s when banks were very flexible regarding the amount of equity generally required to complete transactions. In extreme situations, investors would put, perhaps, 10 percent in a deal, but would take $1 million or $2 million out in fees at the closing. So, if the net investment in a deal was truly analyzed, it was sometimes negative. This type of structure was shocking and often made no economic sense.

TIGHTENING THE RULES

The current environment has changed dramatically. Cash flow financing has become limited and due diligence, especially on environmental factors, has become more extensive.

How has the current environment changed the terms of typical deal structures? In the late 1980s, a company with an EBIT of $100,000 might sell at seven times that figure, all in cash, resulting in a purchase price of $700,000. The capital structure might consist of four elements: a revolving credit line, a term loan, subordinated debt, and equity. Loans drawn using typical advance rates on the revolver would likely be collateralized by the underlying assets. It would not be unusual to have an advance rate of 80 percent on receivables and an advance rate of 50 percent on inventory. The revolver would be used to provide working capital funds.

The term loan might be advanced at 70 percent of the orderly liquidation value of the fixed assets. In the 1980s, there was a lot of creativity regarding how appraisals were done to support term loans. Whether it was orderly liquidation value, value of machinery and equipment in place, auction value, or another basis, some bankers focused on more aggressive versus more conservative definitions of appraised value.

Subordinated debt was utilized to complete the debt structure. On larger deals, this would consist of junk bonds. On a smaller deal, a cash flow "overadvance" was a common structure.

Equity is the last element of the capital structure. It was not uncommon in the

1980s for the debt-to-equity ratio to be eight to one. This, of course, has changed dramatically.

In a deal more typical of the 1990s, the EBIT multiple might only be five. The advance rates for revolving credit lines are more conservative, such as 70 percent on receivables and 45 percent on inventory. Appraisals for fixed assets are carefully scrutinized, especially for real estate and the related environmental factors. It is not unusual in today's environment for there to be no subordinated debt provided by lenders.

In the above example—regarding a typical deal in the 1990s—the company may be sold at five times EBIT, but most likely not all in cash. The capital structure may require that the seller take back a note to meet the financing needs. Current debt-to-equity ratios are more likely to be four to one rather than eight to one.

WHERE ARE WE HEADED?

There has been renewed interest in start-ups. Venture capital firms that have capital realize that they are not going to generate the returns on investment that were expected in the 1980s. Therefore, many of these firms are returning to their roots.

As for bank lending, 20 to 30 percent real equity will continue to be required in deals. Asset-based lending will predominate, although there may be modest amounts of overadvances on high-quality, well-capitalized transactions.

Seller financing will be common for a long time to come. Besides taking back notes or accepting earn-outs, sellers also have agreed to partial buy-outs, in which a company's entire asset base is leveraged to buy 50 to 70 percent of the business. That puts the buyer and the seller in more of a partnership, since the company must perform well for the seller to be fully bought out in the future.

The 1990s will represent a two-tiered environment. Strategic buyers that have capital will drive the process by dictating the terms of many deals. By contrast, middle market sellers and buyers that are dependent on leverage are going to struggle for a number of years.

So where is the money? Beyond strategic buyers with capital, several sources exist for equity and subordinated debt. Investment pools and leveraged buy-out funds represent one source. Also, a number of venture capital firms have equity and mezzanine pools available.

With regard to senior debt, lenders regularly enter and exit the marketplace. Buyers and sellers must therefore closely track the risk appetite of lenders. The credit committees in financial institutions change, the mindsets change, and there continually are new lenders pursuing deal activity.

The auction process can be a useful tool for arranging financing. It is similar to playing one buyer off against the other, as was common in the 1980s. A buyer with a solid financing plan can play lenders off against one another in an auction-type process to determine the most attractive lending structure.

Strategic partnering and relationships with foreign companies are going to be a major area of opportunity in the 1990s for M&A activity. Synergy may be an overused term, but there are many reasons for companies to capitalize on relationships with customers, suppliers, and firms in complementary geographic areas of the country or even other parts of the world. Synergistic opportunities do not necessarily require an acquisition. It therefore may make more sense for some companies to set up joint ventures or partnerships which limit the need for financing.

European and Japanese companies, some fairly small in size, are anxious to develop relationships with American concerns. At the same time, many American firms believe they are too small to go overseas on their own, but could benefit from partnerships with foreign companies to accelerate their pursuit of business opportunities. Foreign companies are especially appealing as partners and providers of financing if their countries enjoy strong currencies.

PART 4

Subsets of the M&A Market

23

Leveraged and Management Buy-outs

Carl Ferenbach

*General Partner, Berkshire Partners,
Boston, Massachusetts*

The objective of a leveraged acquisition is to combine a capital structure that incorporates a disproportionate amount of debt with a substantial and predictable cash flow, to provide higher than normal returns to investors. This chapter will discuss how this can be accomplished by describing the assumptions inherent in a leveraged transaction and by analyzing the companies that seem to best fit the model. It also will cover the nature and composition of the investor groups in leveraged buy-outs and the form of governance and controls they employ.

STRUCTURE OF THE LBO

Because leveraged acquisitions increase financial risk by allocating a large portion of corporate cash flow to interest and principal payments that are fixed by contract, the creditors and investors demand higher returns than they would from a business that has similar operating characteristics but is capitalized substantially with equity. These higher returns result from changing the financial risk of the business by adding debt in place of equity. How much the equity can be levered is determined by

Table 23.1. Widget Corp. of America (in thousands of dollars)

	Year 1	Year 2	Year 3	Year 4	Year 5
Revenues	$50,000	$53,000	$56,180	$59,550	$63,124
Operating Income	5,000	5,300	5,618	5,955	6,312
Taxes	2,000	2,120	2,247	2,382	2,504
Net Income	3,000	3,180	3,371	3,573	3,788
Depreciation	450	477	506	536	568
Investment	450	477	506	536	568
Net Cash Flow	3,000	3,180	3,371	3,573	3,788

matching the cash flows from a five-year operating plan to a capital structure that is divided into several layers of risk. That risk is based on the company's expected generation of cash after its own capital spending commitments and the availability of its assets to collateralize loans.

To understand how this works, it helps to look at a hypothetical case. Assume that Widget Corp. of America has had a sound history of profits with modest growth. Widget's product is well-positioned in its markets and has little risk of technological obsolescence. Widget invests continually in improving its product and in customer service, but is able to generate more cash each year than is needed to maintain market leadership. Widget has no debt. Expectations for revenues and operating income for the current fiscal year and for the next four fiscal years are in Table 23.1.

Widget has experienced relatively little cyclicality and needs to invest only about 15 percent of its free cash flow to keep up with its business growth. (To keep things simple, depreciation is assumed to match investment.) With so predictable a business, Widget has a straightforward and debt-free balance sheet, as shown in Table 23.2.

Widget Corp. is an attractive business. It turns its inventory eight times, collects its receivables in 45 days, and doesn't require much new investment. It is growing and will earn about 16.2 percent on its equity.

However, it's 82-year-old owner has decided to sell the business to put his affairs in order. The very capable, in-place management team would like to buy it. Accordingly, they open discussions with lenders and investment groups, and they learn that Widget is worth $25 million to $35 million in the acquisition market. Based on the company's assets and cash flow, a bank would be willing to lend $12 million to $16

Table 23.2. Widget Corp. of America Statement of Financial Condition

Assets ($ thousands)		Liabilities ($ thousands)	
Cash	$ 1,000	Accounts Payable	$ 5,000
Accounts Receivable	6,250	Other current liabilities	1,000
Inventory	6,250		
Current Assets	13,500	Current liabilities	6,000
Property, Plant & Equipment		Long-term debt	0
(gross)	5,000	Stockholders Equity	12,500
		Total liabilities and stockholders	
Total Assets	18,500	equity	18,500

million to a new company organized to do a leveraged buy-out. The bank will require investors to commit $6 million to $8 million in equity to the transaction. Professional equity investors who are able to provide this capital will require annual internal rates of return of 25 to 35 percent, roughly twice what the company earns on its present equity. To make these high equity returns possible and to fill out the missing $8 million to $12 million, an institutional investor willing to buy a subordinated note must be found. The noteholder will require both a high rate of interest and an equity participation, either purchased directly or in the form of a warrant, for taking this risk.

To analyze whether it is possible to meet the needs of these parties, return to Widget's forecast of income and cash flow and assume that:

- The seller will accept $29 million and that $1 million in fees and expenses will be incurred in completing the transaction (for an aggregate purchase price of six times operating cash flow)
- The senior lender will require an adjustable rate of 1.5 percent over its base rate
- The subordinated noteholder will require an interest rate of 13 percent

Given these assumptions, which approximate the market for these accommodations, Widget might have a postacquisition capital structure that looks like this:

Senior debt	$16,000,000
Subordinated debt	8,000,000
Equity	6,000,000
Total	$30,000,000

Assume that the senior debt, with an interest rate of 8 percent throughout the term of the loan (generally five to seven years in LBO transactions) can be retired by the available cash flow. Also assume that the subordinated debt is retired only after the senior lender is paid in full. Under those conditions, Widget Corp.'s income statement and cash flow in a leveraged environment would be changed as shown in Table 23.3.

Its opening balance sheet would be as reflected in Table 23.4.

Before an explanation of the consequences of the proposed transaction, let's look at what happens to Widget as a result of the acquisition.

Table 23.3. Widget Corp. of America Projected Statements of Income and Cash Flow (in thousands of dollars)

	Year 1	Year 2	Year 3	Year 4	Year 5
Revenues	$50,000	$53,000	$56,180	$59,550	$63,124
Operating Income	4,640	4,919	5,214	5,526	5,858
Interest	2,320	2,179	2,017	1,832	1,620
Taxes	928	1,091	1,278	1,477	1,695
Depreciation	810	858	910	965	1,022
Investment	450	477	506	536	568
Net Cash Flow	1,752	2,025	2,323	2,646	2,997
Remaining Debt	22,248	20,223	17,900	15,254	12,257

Table 23.4. Widget Corp. of America Statement of Financial Condition

Assets ($ thousands)		Liabilities ($ thousands)	
Cash	$ 1,000	Accounts payable	$ 5,000
Accounts receivable	6,250	Other current liabilities	1,000
Inventory	6,250		
Current assets	13,500	Current liabilities	6,000
Property, plant equipment	9,000	Long-term debt	24,000
Goodwill	13,500	Stockholders' equity	6,000
		Total liabilities and stockholders'	
Total assets	$36,000	equity	$36,000

The purchase price of $30 million is $17.5 million more than Widget's net asset value before the acquisition. The allocation of this excess is an important part of any acquisition, and there will be differences in the treatment of certain assets for taxes and for book accounting purposes. In most acquisitions some of the purchase price can be allocated to receivables and inventory, and accelerated depreciation can be used for tax purposes. These adjustments often result in a first-year tax loss.

For our purposes, Widget has allocated $4 million of the purchase price to fixed assets, depreciating them as before, and the balance to goodwill. A more aggressive allocation, which would likely be permitted, would result in cash savings from taxes that were not incurred; this money would be applied to debt payment, thereby enhancing the ending equity value.

The capital structure for Widget would be driven to a considerable degree by a senior lender. It would examine Widget's assets and determine its interest in providing a revolving credit, advancing its customary 80 percent against receivables ($5 million) and 50 percent against inventory ($3,175,000). In addition, the bank would be asked to provide a $9 million term loan based upon both the available fixed assets and the company's unusually stable cash flow.

In our model, Widget never uses more than $16 million of these credit facilities; but by structuring the loans this way, the organizers provide the company with some excess credit for working capital. The bank is being asked to stretch its normal standards to extend this much credit, since the assets do not fully cover its loan. If the lender agrees, it will do so based on Widget's strong cash flow, its ability to retire the entire facility in slightly more than six years, and the general strength and predictability of Widget's business.

It also is important to the senior lender that the management be willing to invest its own cash in Widget's equity (assumed in this case as 10 percent of the dollars) and that a respected private equity firm agree to organize the transaction, commit to investing the required balance of $5.4 million, and arrange any additional financing. The subordinated noteholder would base its decision on many of the same considerations. The organizers will need to provide it with a total annual internal rate of return on its investment of approximately 20 percent, assuming that Widget is resold after the fifth year at the same multiple of cash flow.

The basic pieces of this structure can be said to apply fairly consistently to leveraged acquisitions, whether the amount of financing required for the acquisition is $30 million, $300 million, or $3 billion. The proportions, however, have varied somewhat during the modern LBO period (roughly 1975 to the present) depending on economic conditions, acquisition and stock market valuations, and the availability of credit. For instance, when inflation was high, stock prices were depressed and credit was accessed inefficiently, transactions such as WesRay's famous 1982 acquisition of Gibson Greetings were accomplished with little equity. In the later 1980s, when equity and acquisition values were full, inflation was moderate, credit was readily available, and the high-yield bond market was open for newly issued debt of freshly minted LBOs, 10 percent of the purchase price was all that was required of deal sponsors. That often was because it was believed that values available in the then highly liquid acquisition marketplace made the operating components of any given company worth more than the whole. In the no-nonsense 1990s, with very low inflation, high common equity values, low acquisition values, and illiquid credit markets, sponsors must contribute as much as one-third of the purchase price in equity. These changes in proportions, of course, affect the returns and risks of the various parties in predictable ways.

In the case of Widget, the organizer has arranged the acquisition with a 20 percent equity component. If management receives an additional 5 percent in stock for free (for a total ownership of 15 percent) and the subordinated debt holders receive a warrant for 20 percent of the company, each of the investors earns its targeted returns if Widget performs according to plan and is sold again in year five at six times earnings before interest and taxes (EBIT).

CHARACTERISTICS OF A SUCCESSFUL LBO

As the description of Widget Corp. of America suggests, words like stability and predictability apply to leveraged acquisitions. To be a financial success, a leveraged buy-out must accomplish several very straightforward objectives. It must retire its debt on time and, hopefully, faster than the agreed schedule. It also must reward the equity investors who took the financial risk with commensurate returns. Annual internal rates of return of 25 to 35 percent over an assumed five-year holding period have been considered appropriate.

While meeting the needs of its investors in both debt and equity, the business also must invest in itself to prolong or improve the value of its products to its customers. Therefore, it must have generated sufficient cash over and above its debt obligations to invest in retaining or enhancing its competitive position. If this is not done, the company will not command an attractive price in the acquisition or equity markets that represent its investors best options for liquidity.

Businesses whose stars are hitched to variable prices, that are highly cyclical or dependent upon technologies, and that change frequently are generally poor candidates for highly leveraged capital structures. Others that are dependent on a small number of customers or on regulations that might change are at risk of having their cash flows interrupted. On the other hand, businesses with well-established franchises such as leading distributors, producers of leading brand products, or communications franchises have been successfully leveraged repeatedly, as have the leading producers of certain industrial products.

The leveraged model also has been successfully applied to underperforming businesses, particularly ones with large asset pools that represent attractive collateral to lenders. In these transactions, the rewards are gained from improving the company's operating performance. During the LBO boom of the 1980s, many such opportunities were found within the highly diversified conglomerates that had grown up in the 1960s and 1970s. The aforementioned Gibson Greetings, purchased from the former RCA Corp., is a case in point. U.S. Can Company, the big success story in general packaging, was a captive can maker for Sherwin-Williams Co. before it was bought out and refocused as an independent company.

Finally, the leveraged model has been successfully applied to the purchase of diversified businesses that were subsequently broken up through sales of their component units. This can be a relatively high-risk and sophisticated game of arbitrage and, generally speaking, credit has not been available for this type of transaction since the collapse of Campeau Corp. empire in 1989 following its leveraged acquisition of Federated Department Stores, Inc. Reduced pricing in the M&A market also has hampered the execution of breakup deals.

But the most common LBOs are those like Widget Corp. in that they enjoy the characteristics of stability and predictability, with reasonable barriers to entry and balanced relationships with customers and suppliers.

A leveraged buy-out also must be financed in a manner that simultaneously will meet lenders' requirements and will produce the desired valuation for the prospective equity holders. While senior lenders are able to look to both collateral and available cash flow to retire their loans, subordinated noteholders, although interested in the asset pool, are, by virtue of their junior position, typically at risk. Hence, like the equity holders, they are focused on the cash flows and future values of the business.

Businesses with large asset pools often are believed to be attractive LBO candidates because of the availability of collateral and their ability to shelter income from taxes through depreciation and amortization. If, however, they are capital intensive and operate in a competitive environment, the lender's first claim on their cash flow can leave them at a competitive disadvantage in a weak operating environment if they cannot invest in internal operations and their competitors can. Nonetheless, such capital-intensive businesses as textile producers and railroads have been successful leveraged buyouts.

Non-asset-intensive businesses also can be successful LBO candidates. If margins are attractive and can be protected, lenders often will rely primarily on cash flows backed by the available assets and by pledges of stock. Many light manufacturers, particularly those that mainly design and assemble products from purchased components, are excellent LBO candidates. In a world of just-in-time inventory and rigid receivables collections, such companies may have relatively few assets but large cash flows. Certain specialty retailers fall into this category, as does Widget Corp.

As in any successful business, management is an essential ingredient of the leveraged acquisition. The common wisdom, which is also good wisdom, is that an incumbent management that knows the business probably is the best management. To focus the organization on retiring debt, management will need to implement policies that emphasize cash generation for debt retirement without compromising long-term investment. The team will need strong leadership to implement these policies and will need depth and capability in operations and finance. The chief financial officer will need to think about the business strategically, not merely as an exercise in keeping score. The rules of the road are that management invest its own savings in equity along with the organizers'. If they are unwilling to do so, it's a signal not to acquire the business.

EQUITY INVESTORS

The private equity investors that organize leveraged acquisitions include:

- Firms that specialize in these investments and which manage investment funds organized specifically to make them
- Institutional investors in the private equity markets that organize some of their own acquisitions
- Individuals or significant private corporations controlled by individuals
- Management teams able to mount some personal capital for the required equity

I will focus on the firms that specialize in organizing and investing in LBOs because financing markets of the 1990s require a substantial equity component in each transaction.

The tasks of the LBO firms are to identify attractive candidates, negotiate and finance their purchase, oversee each acquisition, and, eventually, realize returns on the capital invested, a process referred to as exiting.

There are numerous approaches to identifying acquisitions. It is believed, for instance, that there are as many as 100,000 U.S.-based companies that have revenues of more than $10 million. Most are privately or closely held, meaning liquidity is an issue for their owners; and for many others that are publicly owned but have limited followings, being public offers limited liquidity at best. In a typical year, between 2,000 and 3,000 of these companies are sold to new owners.

Prospective acquirers can focus their efforts by industry, by the size of business and its stage of development, or by its operating characteristics, such as capital intensity, competitiveness, or a weak financial condition that offers turnaround potential.

Companies that are actively for sale often are represented by intermediaries. An intermediary may be an investment bank, a commercial bank, an accounting firm, an attorney, or a small firm specializing in M&A advice. It is not unusual for a business broker to intercede with the parties to provide an introduction for a fee. All of these and others are, therefore, sources of information that a business is for sale. Because sponsors of leveraged buyouts are acquiring businesses primarily to earn a return on their invested capital, their interests are likely to be based on size—how large or small a company can be and fit within a goal of acquiring a diversified portfolio of businesses—as well as operating characteristics and assessment of management.

The target company, once identified, may be open to a negotiation; that is, those who control it may have a price in mind. Or the intermediary may be offering the business for bid under a tight set of rules designed to obtain the best available price and terms for the selling shareholders. Financing is among the primary issues the seller wants addressed. In particular, how does the buyer, a new company organized by the LBO firm with no meaningful assets and no prior business history, intend to pay for the purchase? Since the investment group will commit to a price before it has been able to obtain financing, its judgment about what price to pay is critical to success. If the price is too high, it may burden the company with too much debt or dilute equity returns.

Most investment groups prefer negotiated acquisitions because the process of give and take permits both parties to evaluate the availability of financing. The financing project runs concurrently with the buyer's due diligence investigation. The investment group tries to have the seller accept its offer on the condition that it obtain the financing. But the only condition most sellers will accept is that the business investigation is satisfactory to the buyer. While this may leave the buyer room to wiggle out if it cannot arrange financing, such an outcome could damage its reputation among deal sources. Its judgment whether the transaction can be financed is, therefore, critical.

Another reason buyers prefer a negotiated process to an auction is it affords an opportunity to evaluate management. Among the important considerations are management's history and track record, the depth of the system of internal controls, the nature of the dialogue between the CEO and CFO, and the quality and depth of people in the key functions. For most investment groups, and for most management groups, a meaningful ownership interest for the managers is a key to achieving common interests. Most investor groups ask the key managers to make a meaningful personal investment as the best means of securing common financial interests. In return for this investment, the group offers a disproportionate interest in the equity, and often an incentive interest tied to achieving financial results that exceed the forecasts on which the acquisition is based.

Early LBOs were organized around existing managements. Low prices and high leverage ratios allowed management, in effect, to lead the process, and these deals often were called MBOs or management buy-outs. Until well into the 1980s, most LBOs were announced in the name of management to provide assurances of continuity to suppliers and customers. However, as prices increased, as more equity was required, and as investor groups developed their own reputations, management became less important to the deal. In most auction processes, in fact, management is not allowed to compete and is forced to sit by until a winner is anointed.

Managers and investors are parties to a shareholders' agreement that establishes:

- The circumstances under which shares can be transferred, and to whom
- What happens to stock if a manager leaves
- Who participates in sales of stock, whether partial or complete, and whether public or private
- Who has the right to initiate such transactions

If issues of control emerge, this agreement is an essential document.

The investor group also must organize the governance of the newly acquired company. Usually it depends on some combination of formal board of directors meetings and informal exchanges of information and discussion. Reserved for the board are such customary issues as compensation, capital investment, financing, refinancing, and changes in ownership. Issues of strategy and tactics at the operating level and how they are discussed depend on the style and type of relationships that evolve between the investor group and management.

Most lenders, senior or subordinated, do not join boards, preferring to rely on observation rights and the provisions of their formal agreements. In forming a board, then, the investor group typically will include two members of management, representatives from its own staff, and one or more outsiders who, it is believed, can help management with important operating issues.

The important facts of this form of organization and governance, those which differentiate it from its public and private cousins, are that the company is controlled by investors who have performed an extensive, on-sight investigation, talked with customers, and negotiated with management. They know the company well and are familiar with the critical decisions it faces. They have analyzed or developed a model for the future of the company and have a plan in mind for executing it. The investor group and the management invest in the ownership, and in the company's future, on the basis of the same business plan, and they have the same financial incentives. Finally, they have capitalized the company with a substantial amount of debt which must be retired by contract. This means, in effect, that all strategic efforts will be focused on generating cash from the existing portfolio of products and/or businesses.

To understand how an investor group looks at exiting its investments, one must know how the investor groups are organized. While there is no single model, investor groups dependent upon institutional capital have found themselves working under an increasingly common set of terms.

Most investor groups start by organizing investment funds. The fund is composed of commitments by institutional investors to provide their pro rata shares of capital to each acquisition organized by the sponsor group. The fund participants include such large institutional investors as insurance companies, state and local retirement systems, corporate pension funds, endowments, and others interested in the private equity market. They commit to the fund with the understanding that they will pay its manager, the sponsor, a fee to seek out and organize acquisitions and that the sponsor also will receive a share of the profits, which is generally called the override. The override traditionally has been up to 20 percent after providing the institution with a preferred return. The sponsor or general partner of the fund is required to invest at least 1 percent of the capital committed to the fund, although many invest much more.

The structure matches the sponsor's incentives to those of management. The sponsor has committed personal capital and has a success incentive structured similarly to the managers. The investment of the sponsor's own money also insures that the sponsor risks a loss. The fund typically has five years in which to invest its capital (the investment period) and another five to seven in which to return it. Capital not put to work during the investment period is returned.

The investor group's performance is measured by return on investment, calculated as the internal rate of return to investors on capital actually employed after fees, expenses, and override. Because investor groups must compete for funds in the risk-capital segment of the financial markets, they must provide investors with returns well above the averages for other investment categories. If they do not, they will have difficulty raising additional funds at the end of each investment period.

The typical leveraged buy-out approaches its maturity as an investment in four to five years. If it is performing according to plan, it has retired sufficient debt and accumulated sufficient equity to slow the rate of appreciation in its equity value. As this point approaches, the investor group is motivated to liquefy its investment.

While there may be a number of alternatives for gaining liquidity, essentially, they boil down to:

- Selling the company
- Recapitalizing through another leveraged transaction
- Taking the company public

For the investor group, selling and recapitalizing are quite straightforward. Going public, however, is a much slower form of exit. To avoid the appearance of a "bailout," the investors normally will be restrained by the underwriters of the public offering from selling stock in the company's initial offering. After the company is public, U.S. securities laws limit the amount of stock that can be sold in the open market by insiders. Hence, the investor group either can await the opportunity to sell under a subsequent public offering or, if they have owned their stock for more than the three-year holding period required by securities laws, distribute the stock to the fund investors and permit them to make their own decisions.

The public offering therefore is a far slower form of exit than a sale or recapitalization. It is employed, nonetheless, as a means to reduce debt, and therefore risk, when the values available in the public market will result in denominating a significant gain for the investor group.

DRIVEN BY HIGHER
INVESTMENT RETURNS

The modern leveraged buy-out has its roots in the owners of private companies, need for liquidity, and the inefficiency of fixing underperforming business units owned by diversified corporations. While its application was expanded to restructurings of large public companies during the 1980s, the LBO has moved back to its roots in the tighter, more disciplined capital markets of the 1990s. Its professionalization during the 1980s, however, has carried over.

The large pools of institutional investment capital that predominate today are happy with the disciplines imposed by the organizational form described in this chapter. They also like the consonance of interests that is required by the various structures and is not available to them in public companies. For these reasons, private equity investing in the form of leveraged acquisitions appears to be assured an important place in the asset mix of our financial institutions in the foreseeable future.

24

Strategic Divestitures

Carroll R. Wetzel, Jr.,

Managing Director, Chemical Bank
Investment Banking, New York, New York

A colleague of mine once said that heaven would be a place where one could have a career buying small businesses from large companies.

In this chapter, I will discuss a number of topics that might help those charged with divesting relatively small, and frequently noncore, businesses from large companies. These topics include working with an adviser, handling management of the business being sold, using valuation techniques, planning the form of the transaction, and making public disclosure. I will highlight key decision areas of the divestiture process and present potential solutions to several obstacles often encountered by a seller.

Briefly, I will cover the execution of the divestiture from the time the management of the parent company has reached the decision to sell. Although an outside adviser may help the top executives arrive at the decision to sell, this article does not discuss whether or not a unit should be kept or sold. Divisions, subsidiaries, product lines, and so on, are sold today for all sorts of reasons. They may be outside the parent's mainstream strategy or core competency, too small to warrant attention and resources, or situated in a market, a mature one for example, that lacks appeal. On the flip side, the business may be too good and require a disproportionate amount of time and money to nurture growth when a finite supply of capital is available. The many reasons for selling a business are not the subject of this article.

Regardless of the rationale for selling a business, the adviser-led divestiture process is to gain maximum value for the seller for assets that presumably will be put to better use by the purchaser. The mechanics of the divestiture process effectively connect the seller's strategic goals with the workings of the mergers and acquisitions market where the property will be sold. During the 1980s, divestitures represented a major prop of the marketplace, accounting for about a third of all M&A transactions logged during the decade.

THE ROLE OF THE ADVISER

Frequently, corporations hire an adviser only to write an information memorandum describing the business for sale and to find a buyer. These can be valuable services for a seller and, in themselves, can justify hiring an adviser. Many corporations, including large ones, do not have staffs experienced in, and dedicated to, writing information memoranda and do not maintain up-to-date files of potential buyers. However, the real value of an adviser goes far beyond writing a memorandum and finding a buyer.

The adviser's roles can include orchestrating the marketing of the business, setting the schedule, contacting buyers, overseeing due diligence visits, and getting lawyers and accountants involved at the right time, among other duties. However, managing the process means more than overseeing this kind of external event for the seller. Two of the greatest services an adviser can provide also include helping to manage the process inside the seller and performing "buyer's due diligence."

Since divestitures are not everyday events for most companies, they usually involve delegating special authority to that person responsible for carrying out the divestiture. For example, it is common in large corporations to delegate the responsibility of divesting a small unit to a staff person (e.g., the corporate development officer) and give that person special authority for the transaction. Clearly, that should not include the ability to commit the corporation in matters as significant as setting an acceptable price, which might be the province of the board of directors. It should, however, include the authority to ask line managers to attend meetings on the sale when they would rather be attending to other problems, or to ask the legal department to give priority to reviewing an information memorandum.

Because not every issue can be foreseen, the staff person at times has to run back up the chain of command to get authority. What happens, for example, when an important employee, who might even outrank the corporate development officer, attempts to improve his personal prospects with potential buyers? In that case a major decision needs to be made quickly. Perhaps the employee needs to be dismissed. At times the adviser helps manage the process internally by letting the seller know when, for example, its own decision-making process is not working well, or when the internal staff is having a hard time getting the job done.

Another role of the adviser is to perform "buyer's due diligence," or, in other words, review the business through the eyes of a potential buyer. Almost by definition, a buyer will look at a business differently from the seller; indeed, that is what the seller should hope. Frequently, an adviser can highlight and emphasize those elements of a business that might appeal to buyers and discover value in areas where the seller saw little or none.

More importantly, the adviser's role in performing "buyers due diligence" is to unearth problems before a buyer can discover them. A good buyer of businesses eventually will understand the business better than the seller, certainly better than management at corporate headquarters, and frequently better than management of the entity being sold. Generally, the less important a business is to the parent company, the sooner the buyer's knowledge will surpass that of selling management.

In performing "buyer's due diligence," the adviser must have not only the experience and the time to do investigative work but the skills, both technical and interpersonal, to help solve any problems that are discovered. For example, it is not uncommon to discover financials that are not prepared in accordance with generally accepted accounting principles (GAAP). Often, both the parent and local management were unaware of that deficiency. In addition to being able to discover the problem, the adviser must have the ability to help solve it. Sometimes this is not an easy task if the solution requires that the parent recognize past mismanagement.

In rare instances, it becomes apparent during "buyer's due diligence" that a clandestine management buyout effort is under way. In such a case the adviser needs to proceed very carefully. But there will be more later on dealing with management.

The role of the adviser can be quite narrow or quite broad, depending on the needs of the specific deal. And it is not always apparent at the outset what the needs will be. The message to readers is that in selecting an adviser, the seller must be aware of the importance of having an adviser consultant with a broad range of skills and experience.

HANDLING MANAGEMENT

No issue is more important than how the parent corporation treats the management of the business to be divested and in no other area can mistakes have more dire consequences. A seller should make the assumption that at some point during the divestiture process management's loyalty will switch from the seller to the buyer. At a minimum, management will be interviewing with prospective buyers for jobs. At the extreme, the managers will be trying to help the buyer purchase the business on favorable terms, especially if they have become part of the buying group, a situation quite common in the leveraged buy-outs of divested businesses during the 1980s.

One of the most common solutions to the problem of shifting loyalties is to pay a bonus to management if the members stay during the divestiture period and help facilitate the sale. Not only can a "stay bonus" help keep a manager focused on selling the business, but preserving the management team can even add substantial value to the business. One of the most important elements of value to a buyer can be an enthusiastic management team that is willing to work as hard for the new owners as it had for the former employer. The questions are how big the bonus should be and on what conditions should it be paid?

The first recommendation is not to be penny-wise and pound-foolish. The amount of money at risk in a divestiture generally far surpasses the amount required to motivate management. For the manager of a modest subsidiary, stay bonuses typically range from 50 to 150 percent of base salary. The amount needs to be large enough to motivate the manager to help sell the business, but it should not be tantamount to winning the lottery. Obviously, the proper amount depends upon the individual manager's economic and other circumstances. In some cases, the bonus can be assumed by the new owner and paid out over time, giving the new owner some control over the behavior of the acquired group of managers.

Conditions of bonus payments vary greatly. The simplest condition is only that managers remain employed at the company until the closing of the deal. Such a condition does not, however, assure that the manager will represent the owners diligently in the selling process. To assure that, the bonus should be tied to the results of the divestiture, such as the manager's level of cooperation throughout the sale process or the price ultimately attained. If management trusts the parent leadership, the bonus can be left to the subjective judgment of the seller. If there is a lack of trust between them, performance may be determined by the selling price, i.e., the higher the price the greater the bonus.

The major difficulty with keying the bonus to purchase price is that to do so requires revealing the price objective of the seller to the managers whose loyalties will shift. Second, keying the bonus to purchase price does not motivate the manager to aid the seller on matters other than price; for example, on improving representations and warranties. One solution to this dilemma is the "Emperor's Letter," named after a Chinese emperor who, upon recognition that there would be a succession struggle between his two sons, designated his successor in a document to be opened at his death. Applying this principle, a seller would draw up a contract stipulating the bonus range for a corresponding range of prices, leaving some flexibility for subjectivity. The bonus range would be revealed to the manager but the price level would not. The letter would be opened at the closing. This technique has worked in certain divestitures. Parenthetically, the actual emperor's letter was blank, but peace prevailed during his reign.

Problems with management also can be avoided by excluding management from any discussions on value. The management of a business being sold should not be party to or have any role in initial valuation discussions, preliminary price discussions, solicitation of bids, review of bids, or final price negotiations. Should potential buyers, employees, competitors, and other unit managers ask about price, the manager of the divested business should be coached to respond truthfully that he or she has not been privy to any discussions of value.

Finally, what is the best way to handle management that wishes to buy the business by executing its own leveraged buy-out, namely a management buy-out (MBO)? From the perspective of senior management of the parent company, an MBO of a subsidiary can seem to be an easy way to repay employees for years of good service by giving them the opportunity to become business owners. An MBO also may appear to be a convenient way to complete a transaction, because the employees do much of the work related to the sale. However, perhaps the most difficult situation for a seller to manage well is an MBO. All to often one sees an MBO that sputters, that drags on and on, often because the managers have trouble arranging the financing. There are some simple rules to help avoid that state.

The selling parent never should indicate to the management of a subsidiary that they will be given the opportunity to put together an MBO until the parent has decided, without help from management, that a leveraged transaction is easily achievable at a price that meets the parent's objectives. In other words, the parent needs to complete a thorough valuation that incorporates up-to-date terms for debt and equity financing. Frequently, the parent will rely upon outside expertise to handle the calculations.

If an MBO group can, in fact, meet the parent's price, and the parent wants to give management a shot, the management-led team should not be simply told to proceed with a deal. The parent should give the MBO group written instructions on exactly how to proceed. Those instructions should include, among other matters, a schedule specifying the deadlines for obtaining financing and crossing other hurdles; an outline of the information to be used in speaking with investors and lenders; and an indication of the terms of confidentiality. The parent ideally should introduce the MBO team to one or more equity sponsors with a reputation for getting transactions done and for simple, straightforward dealing. The parent should keep a record of all outside investors and lenders that review the transaction in case the parent must get involved with the transaction. Finally, if the MBO does not work—which should not happen because the parent should give subsidiary management the green light only when there is a very high probability of success—management should be told that they have lost their opportunity forever. It is essential to stop the sputtering.

When the parent does not want to give management the opportunity to buy the business, the best way to handle management's natural desire to become proprietors is to convince them that their best strategy is to help sell the business. While the potential rewards of sponsoring their own transaction might seem great, they could become aligned with a weak equity partner and, in fact, lose the bid. Then they would have to scramble at the last minute to save their jobs. On the other hand, if they help sell the business and the winner is a buyout firm that lacks operating capabilities, management most likely will receive an equity interest. Moreover, the selling parent should be aware that many buyers simply will not compete if management is a potential bidder.

In conclusion, many potential problems associated with an MBO can be avoided by following the aforementioned principles. To indicate how bad things can get if these principles are not adhered to, I recall one *Fortune* 100 company, which, after deciding to divest a noncore subsidiary, instructed the manager to find a buyer and negotiate a transaction—in essence to do the deal himself. The manager, whose loyalty probably shifted immediately upon receiving the instructions, generated two offers: one was from a buyer who wanted him to stay with the business; the other from a buyer who did not want him. Not surprisingly, the value of the first bid was substantially higher than the second. Also not surprisingly, the manager asked for a substantial portion of the difference to be paid to him personally as a bonus. Blackmail? Perhaps! But the manager had put himself in a position to create substantial value for the seller, and he wanted a piece of it to close the higher bid.

VALUATION

The principal techniques for valuing a business are generally well understood and well practiced by both good advisers and corporations, and their use has become almost routine. Some combination of a discounted cash-flow analysis, a review of public market values, a review of comparable acquisition transactions, a leveraged acquisition model, and a merger pro forma or dilution analysis, along with a little judgment, can produce a reliable range of value. What varies among sellers, and produces some interesting lessons, is the way in which the range of value is used, once it is derived.

A range of value indicates what a buyer will theoretically pay, and therefore builds the expectations of the seller as to price. Every seller focuses on the high end of the range with wishful expectations. However, every seller does not focus on the low end, as has been painfully evident in recent years, when financial buyers frequently had difficulty completing transactions because of financing constraints. One frequent result was that disappointed sellers chose to keep the business rather than accept what they considered fire-sale prices.

Because of the typically rosy-colored focus on the high end of the range, sellers of noncore businesses often do not commit themselves to keeping the unit if the price is lower than expected, or worse, less than what the boss expected. If buyers have their walkaway prices to avoid overpaying for acquisitions, sellers should have walkaway prices to avoid getting too little for divestitures. But few sellers use the valuation range actually to determine before commencing the divestiture process what an adequate price would be and thereby force a decision as to the price below which they would be unwilling to sell the business. The decision involves development of a fallback plan for retaining the business before the subsidiary or division goes on the block.

The conclusion is that while much valuation work is reasonably accurate, frequently it is not pushed to its logical conclusion, which is determining the absolute floor price for a sale—coupled with a resolve to keep a business drawing lower price—as well as the implications of a failed deal.

TRANSACTION FORMAT

The nature of the business and the concurrent state of the financial markets will determine the method of marketing and selling the business and the format of the transaction. The methods vary from an announced auction to draw many bidders, to a quiet auction among a few selected bidders, to negotiations with a single buyer, among various other approaches. Among the popular formats are straightforward asset or stock sales for cash or stock, asset swaps between two companies, and initial public stock offerings. In the heady days of the mid-1980s, when bank credit was abundant and equity capital readily available, the leveraged buy-out firm frequently could pay top dollar. In those years, the most common strategy for carrying out divestitures was an announced auction. The early 1990s are thus far quite different and so a comment on the method of marketing and form of transaction is in order.

The announced auction is alive and well, although not as common as in the 1980s. For businesses that will appeal to several buyers and have a virtual certainty of being sold, the publicly announced sale still is highly recommended. There is little doubt that all potential buyers will hear of the opportunity and, if properly handled, the process will maximize the price. Some buyers claim that as a matter of principle they will not play in auctions. However, a serious buyer will play, especially if the target business is desirable, and those who say they will not participate in auctions are really saying that they do not like the prices.

The businesses that tend to sell better through announced auctions deal in non-differentiated products, including natural resource assets, such as oil, gas, and coal properties; distribution companies; and financial services companies whose assets are in paper, such as mortgage servicing and credit card portfolios. Businesses that do not fit the auction mold require a high level of subjective judgment to confirm value, on either the positive or negative side. For example, the values of many high technology businesses depend on the buyers understanding their unique technologies and business plans. On the negative side, a business with a potential environmental problem does not lend itself well to a rigorous auction. Businesses with a great number of people issues—i.e., service businesses dependent on human talent, and firms with management succession problems—also are not good candidates for an open auction.

Most divestitures in the 1990s are handled in "modified auctions," which generally means approaching a small number of potential buyers and attempting to create the same kind of bidding competition that can be achieved in an announced auction. Targeting the appropriate buyers clearly requires a good understanding of who they are, their corporate strategies, their financial wherewithal, and their decision-making processes. For the strategic buyers, these factors can be determined in relatively straightforward ways. For the financial buyers who are generally more opportunistic and not looking for an investment to fit an existing corporate strategy, the key question to the seller is whether they can close. Frequently, the financial buyer who at the outset indicates a willingness to pay the highest price is not the best buyer with whom to enter negotiations. Since the debt capacity of a given business does not vary from one financial buyer to the next, the auction need not involve many in the process. A few with reputations for closing transactions is sufficient.

Announced auctions and modified auctions are only two of the most common ways in which businesses are taken to market. With the difficulty financial buyers have had raising funds in recent years, there has been a proliferation of more complex forms of divestiture. One is selling to a joint bidder, a combination of an industry buyer and a financial buyer that capitalizes on the strategic synergies or management expertise of one partner and the financial wherewithal and skills of the other. Examples of such transactions are the purchase of the Six Flags amusement parks by The Blackstone Group and Time Warner, Inc., and the purchase of Ambase Corp.'s Home Insurance business by Donaldson, Lufkin & Jenrette and a group of three insurance companies, both in 1991.

Another form of divestiture is the asset swap in which two companies trade businesses. The rationale is that each business has more strategic value to the receiving partner than to the entity letting it go. The swap can eliminate or limit cash payments by either side and provides the potential for reducing taxes which might otherwise have been triggered by a cash transaction.

In 1992 Du Pont Co. and Imperial Chemical Industries PLC engineered a swap of assets in two mature segments of the synthetic fibers industry, which strengthened their respective worldwide positions. Du Pont received ICI's nylon business in return for its acrylics operations. The exchange enabled Du Pont to expand its nylon share in Europe while ICI widened its acrylics business in the United States. Earlier, Borden Co. and Thomas J. Lipton Co. carried out a swap that played to each other's strengths. Borden got the Pennsylvania Dutch business to increase its leadership position in the U.S. pasta market and ceded its Crystal Time powdered drinks unit to Lipton whose primary business is beverages.

Finally, a business may be divested by selling the stock to the public in an initial public offering (IPO) or by dividending the shares to the public in a tax-free transaction. An initial public offering (IPO) is naturally dependent on the proper stock environment. However, the strong equity market of 1991 and 1992 generated a number of IPO divestitures including Du Pont's sale of its controlling interest in Haemonetics Corp., Henley Group, Inc.'s disposition of Fisher Scientific International, Inc., and the General Host Corp. sell-off of Calloways Nursery, Inc.

In the spin-off, a separate company is formed from a subsidiary, and the shares are distributed to stockholders of the parent tax-free. In 1991, Quaker Oats Co. shed its Fisher-Price, Inc. toy and game unit through a spin-off and in 1992 Union Carbide Corp. spun-off its industrial gases business as PRAXAIR, Inc.

PUBLIC ANNOUNCEMENT

One question that will inevitably come up is, "Should there be a public announcement regarding the prospective divestiture?" There are advantages and disadvantages to a public announcement. While many sellers have a predisposition to keep things quiet, our bias is in favor of an announcement, primarily to assist in managing the process to the seller and secondarily in marketing the business.

(Sometimes the decision is academic. If a public company decides irrevocably to sell a business, accounting conventions require that the businesses marked for divestiture be treated as discontinued operations. Thus, the sell decision can be disclosed in the company's financial statements.)

Indeed, I believe a public announcement is of marginal benefit in marketing a business. A rare buyer might come forth spontaneously, and an announcement makes the initial discussions with potential buyers easier. However, most businesses are sold to parties that already are known to the seller or its adviser, and the lack of an announcement certainly does not impede discussions with those parties.

The answer to the question of whether to make an announcement hinges upon weighing, on the one hand, the damage that the business might suffer as a result of an announcement (i.e., the loss of customers or key employees) against, on the other hand, the damage to the business as a result of having some employees in the know and others not and the damage from a surprise leak. The conservative position is to make the assumption that sometime before closing the word will get out anyway. An early announcement lets both the buyer and the seller proceed without having to worry that, as the layers of the business are peeled away in due diligence, a mistake will be made, the wrong person will be spoken to, management will be embarrassed, and the sale process will be delayed needlessly.

A MANAGEMENT PROCESS

The goal of the divestiture process generally is to sell a business for an optimal price. Involvement by top management is critical to achieving the goal, and that means that management must participate in the process and work to identify potential problems before they arise.

The parent company's management must focus on motives of the managers and the relationships among the management and employees of the business to be sold. That will help the parent select an adviser who can work well with a sale candidate's management and ensure better communication and information flow between the subsidiary, the parent, and the buyer, and ultimately, produce a higher sale price.

This chapter has presented problems that frequently occur in the divestiture process and some solutions top management can use to avoid those problems and keep a divestiture on track. However, all businesses and all divestitures are unique and there is no guaranteed formula for success. If a parent company's management focuses on the issues I have highlighted as a starting point for managing the divestiture process, many potential problems will be avoided and the likelihood of a successful transaction can be enhanced.

25

Corporate Restructuring

Barbara Moakler Byrne,
Managing Director, Lehman Brothers,
New York, New York

Robert Willens,
Senior Vice President, Lehman Brothers,
New York New York

The 1980s witnessed a wave of corporate restructurings that substantially changed the structure and dynamics of Corporate America. The restructurings primarily were efforts to increase shareholder value by one of two methods: maximizing asset value or creating more effective or efficient capital structures. Such restructuring assumed new importance in the 1980s—which we like to call "the decade of hidden assets"—for many reasons:

- The growing importance of institutional investors, who focused on shareholder value as a measure of security performance and who were willing to accept a greater degree of financial risk through leverage
- The recognition of hidden asset values, which were carried at historical book value after the inflationary period of the 1970s and which were not adequately reflected in equity market values
- The renewed focus on core businesses
- The emergence of a substantial, and until recently liquid, junk bond market
- Low nominal interest rates, coupled with a generally strong equity market

- The emergence of the financial buyer
- Changes in tax law that accelerated depreciation (which in turn increased emphasis on cash flow), equalized treatment of income and capital gains, and raised corporate tax rates above individual tax rates

Clearly, the restructuring of the 1980s addressed the financial and structural factors that caused corporate undervaluation. The financial factors essentially were excess cash and underutilized debt capacity. Obviously, how one characterizes "underutilized" is changing. The conventional wisdom of the 1980s was that replacing equity with debt increases value. Today's conventional wisdom, which is really a return to the original conventional wisdom, is that there is a risk reward ratio; or, put another way, some companies should not be leveraged. Each decade tends to reverse the excesses of the previous one.

The structural factors that made restructuring attractive were essentially underperforming subsidiaries, overhead bonus, and corporate buyer synergies. Underperforming subsidiaries pulled down the overall value of the parent. An overhead bonus is simply the fat in the organization. Corporate buyer synergies are the increased value found in linkage with a perfect partner.

Within the parent company, assets, operations, subsidiaries, divisions, or whatever might be undervalued because of:

Small size. A high-growth entity could have a high P/E ratio buried in a parent company where it can't really be seen.

Hidden strengths. These generate little income but have substantial value, typically real estate or off-balance-sheet assets.

Inappropriate valuation. Usually companies with disparate operations, some of which would be valued on a price-earnings ratio, others on a cash flow basis.

Inappropriate ownership structure. A situation in which a subsidiary might better be owned in a partnership as opposed to a corporate structure, such as a master limited partnership in the case of real estate or natural resource assets.

Inappropriate management incentives. The inability to create value in a very entrepreneurial subsidiary, which can be set up away from the parent company and properly incented by entrepreneurial compensation schemes.

Potential synergies. Subsidiaries whose operations might benefit from being associated with another entity with better operating, financial, or tax synergies.

These factors are very basic, and intentionally so. The tuning fork illustrated in Figure 25.1 can provide a framework for understanding the various restructuring tools. Asset restructuring and financial restructuring are not mutually exclusive. The tools can be combined, and usually are. We've arranged them along the "Y" from what we think is the least radical to the most radical.

The tools can be highly customized to meet the business objectives and characteristics of an individual company. And they are customized for tax and accounting purposes. We can't emphasize this enough. Tax and accounting issues frequently drive the rather peculiar and arcane structures one reads about in the press.

Let's look first at asset restructuring options. Clearly, fundamental decisions have

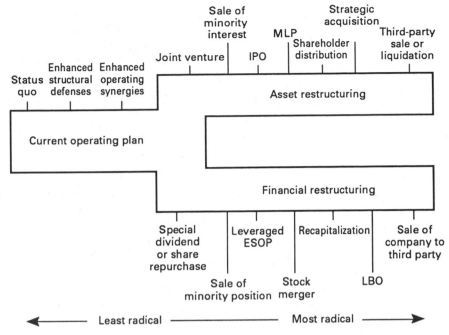

Figure 25.1. Restructuring options.

to be made here. Are you going to unbundle assets? Should you retain an interest in them? How should you actually divest them?

If a parent decides to retain an interest in a subsidiary, there are several options. One is a *joint venture,* which we think is going to become increasingly popular in the next year or two. Generally, in a joint venture the subsidiary can be used as currency to deconsolidate itself or to create a strategic alliance to tap into new markets, technology, or distribution channels. A good example of a joint venture is the one involving Philips NV and Whirlpool Corp., whereby Whirlpool was able to tap into the European market through established distribution channels.

A company can also sell a minority interest in a subsidiary to a corporate buyer, which is not all that uncommon. It can be done very effectively with a foreign partner. Generally speaking, the company sells less than a 20 percent interest to maintain tax consolidation.

The *spin-off* options include an initial public offering (IPO), a master limited partnership (MLP), and a shareholder distribution. An *IPO* is very flexible if there is a good equity market. There are a variety of different structures—primary and secondary offerings, or a leveraging-up of the company so the parent can take a pre-offering dividend. Typically, in an IPO some 13 to 18 percent of the stock is sold so the parent can continue to tax consolidate. The IPO has been used as an alternative to a third-party sale.

The *MLP* is now fairly limited to real estate and natural resource assets. There are ways you can pull in additional assets, but they must be principally natural resources. An MLP allows you to value a company as a multiple of distributable cash flow, as opposed to net income. It avoids the corporate layer of tax and it gets the asset off the balance sheet of the parent company. Yet the parent can continue to control it. An example is the Plum Creek MLP, a spin-off by Burlington Resources, Inc. of its timber operations.

There have been a number of *shareholder distributions,* and we think we're going to see quite a few more. Shareholder distribution actually is the technical definition of a spin-off. They are usually structured to qualify as a tax-free distribution. Of all of the spin-offs done since 1975, approximately 95 percent have been tax-free. There are three types: a spin-off, a split-off, and a split-up. In order to be tax-free, five criteria must be met:

- You have to own at least 80 percent of the subsidiary that you want to spin off.

- You have to spin off at least 80 percent of it.

- You must have a valid business reason for wanting to spin off the subsidiary.

- It has to have been a controlled subsidiary for five years and engaged in an active business for five years, and the parent has to be an active business as well.

- The spin-off cannot be considered to have been a device to distribute capital gains income as opposed to ordinary income.

The reason we think there may be more spin-offs and split-offs is because they are really the only way to do a tax-free reorganization since the repeal of *General Utilities.*

Let's turn now to the unbundling options in which the parent divests itself of all interest in the subsidiary.

In an IPO you can sell the whole subsidiary in a public offering if you choose. In a very good equity market it can yield the greatest value, provide management with incentives, and position the company competitively in the market. Aristech Chemical Corp. is an excellent example. USX Corp. sold it to the public in a 100 percent IPO.

A shareholder distribution also can be used to spin off 100 percent of a company to the parent company's shareholders, or a shareholder distribution of a subsidiary can be used as a consideration in a stock swap. An example of the latter is the Mobil-Esmark-Vickers transaction. Mobil wanted to acquire Vickers, an Esmark subsidiary. Mobil bought a block of Esmark stock in the public market and swapped it for the Vickers subsidiary stock. This type of transaction has had some limitations imposed on it. However, a tax-free split-off is a way of accomplishing a tax-free share exchange by using subsidiary stock to repurchase parent company stock.

An MLP also can be used to sell 100 percent of a company. Or a company can be divested through a *third-party sale.* When there are synergies, this is the option that generally creates the greatest value.

Besides all the unbundling options just discussed, you can look at restructuring through *strategic acquisitions,* which is the flip side of restructuring that most people don't think of. Obviously, you could reposition your company that way. *Liquidation* of the entire company is another option. It's usually the least tax-efficient way of trying to do something, but for the sake of completeness we include it.

Now to financial restructuring options. The key questions here, of course, have to do with your vulnerability to a takeover. To the extent that you feel that you are on somebody's screen, you almost definitely will want to take steps to concentrate and solidify insider control of ownership. And these financial restructuring options (see Fig. 25.1) lend themselves to accomplishing that objective. Obviously, the particular technique or techniques you select depend to a great extent on whether management has decided to grow through acquisition or, alternatively, to consolidate what has been built already and accept a smaller level of growth with a more rational business profile.

Obviously, there is a degree of prudence involved here. To the extent that you undertake a financial restructuring, you will be increasing your financial risk through increased leverage. In certain industries, and at certain points in the business cycle, that may not make a lot of sense. For example, in the commodity chemical industry, Quantum Chemical is being adversely affected by what might, in retrospect, be viewed as a very substantial $50 special dividend which the company paid in late 1988. Quantum discovered it wasn't able to maintain its regular dividend while continuing its planned capital expenditures. The company suspended its dividend because of covenant violations on its debt, a move which disappointed the market to a great degree. You really need to understand the business you're in, and you have to anticipate whether high levels of debt can be serviced when the business cycle troughs.

With those generalities as a back-drop, let's get back to the tuning fork and begin looking at financial restructuring techniques, starting with the least radical and working our way up.

SPECIAL DIVIDEND OR SHARE REPURCHASE

Special dividends are relatively flexible and obviously quite popular. They're nonrecurring, one-time events as opposed to a dividend increase, which investors expect will be permanent. A share repurchase can increase earnings per share in cases in which the earnings yield—the inverse of the price-earnings ratio—exceeds the net aftertax returns to be earned on the redemption proceeds.

From a tax point of view, a special dividend generally is taxed as ordinary income to the extent of the company's current and accumulated earnings and profits, which is a tax term that is pretty much the equivalent of cash flow. To the extent that the distribution exceeds the earnings and profits, it's a return of capital; and to the extent that it exceeds your basis in the stock, it's a capital gain.

A share repurchase, on the other hand, is simpler. It's taxed almost always as a capital gain to the extent that the buy-back proceeds exceed the shareholder's basis in the stock. Obviously, with the elimination of the capital gains differential, the tax consequences at the shareholder level are a little less important than they were in the past. However, if a capital gains break is restored in any new tax legislation, that would tip the scales in favor of a share repurchase, all other things being equal.

SALE OF MINORITY POSITION

This is an interesting technique that has become a bit of a cottage industry. Warren Buffett is good at buying minority positions at what to him are attractive prices. This is typically a defensive strategy known sometimes as a white-squire or blocking position. We're going to be seeing this more as a growth strategy. Company X will take a minority position in Company Y for the purpose of eventually exchanging the Y stock for a Y subsidiary that X would like to own for strategic reasons. This is more or less the Mobil-Esmark-Vickers deal. The tax law has changed since then. One can no longer do that kind of transaction back-to-back. In Mobil-Esmark-Vickers, the stock was acquired in the morning and surrendered after lunch for the desired subsidiary. This kind of transaction has to be done today as a tax-free split-off. The shareholder must be established as a historic shareholder, which means owning the stock with more permanence than was the case in Mobil-Esmark-Vickers. Nevertheless, you will see this minority sale strategy with increasing frequency, both for defensive and growth purposes.

LEVERAGED ESOPs

All of us have read, probably more than we want to, about leveraged ESOPs. The most recent tax bill dealt with two familiar benefits—the tax advantaged loan and the dividends-paid deduction. The tax-advantaged loan essentially is a thing of the past except where the ESOP owns more than 50 percent of the stock of the company, a situation we're not going to see very often. On the other hand, the more important benefit, the dividends-paid deduction—the ability of the company to deduct dividends paid on stock held by the ESOP—pretty much survived intact. And in response to that survival, Chevron Corp. announced—literally the day after the bill passed—a billion-dollar ESOP for tax reasons and probably for the traditional defensive purposes. The ability to deduct dividends is a powerful incentive to create a leveraged ESOP. They are going to be with us for a while.

STOCK MERGERS

These are what in the tax world are called tax-free reorganizations. These are invariably strategic transactions typically done by companies whose stock is relatively fully valued. It is a powerful form of acquisition currency. Taxes are not due at any level on the exchange itself. There can also be accounting benefits if the transaction qualifies as a pooling of interests under APB 16. This is very difficult to do—almost impossible, as a matter of fact—although the Bristol-Myers-Squibb transaction qualified as a pooling. A new basis of accounting for the assets cannot be established for the transaction to qualify. The assets are carried over at their historic value. Most importantly, goodwill is not created on the surviving company's books. There is no periodic amortization of that intangible asset against earnings. So, this is a powerful incentive for companies that are sensitive to the effect of goodwill on earnings.

RECAPITALIZATION

Recaps combine many of the attributes of other financial restructuring techniques. They leave the public shareholders with a stake in the equity and they invariably enhance management's stake in the company. And in light of the fact that an equity stake is retained in the company, the returns need not be as high as they might have to be in an LBO or other total cash-out.

LBOs AND SALES OF COMPANIES TO THIRD PARTIES

These are the most radical options about which very little needs to be said. The labels are self-explanatory.

In restructuring, timing is everything. The key thing to focus on is not what happened in the 1980s but what it means for the 1990s. If you're going to restructure and restructure well, you have to be concerned about what's going to happen tomorrow. We have characterized the decade of the eighties as the decade of the hidden asset. We think the nineties might be the decade of the hidden liability. Here are some trends you may want to look out for:

Foregone Capital Expenditures. Managements have not just cut out the fat in terms of capital expenditures, they've gone to the bone in many, many companies. Turnarounds have been delayed. Maintenance has been reduced. We think it's going to come home to roost. If we're going to stay competitive, we have to fully fund capital expenditures.

Post-retirement Benefits. This is a major issue. Most managements are focusing on it now, with the Financial Accounting Standards Board (FASB) proposing a change from cash to accrual accounting. You might say, "Big deal . . . Doesn't the market know we have this $500 billion to $2 trillion liability sitting there? It's always been there." While you can argue about ways in which the accounting should be changed, the fact is that it exists. Recognition of post-retirement health care and life insurance liabilities presents a substantial challenge in the 1990s. They will cause a number of companies to change their benefits to reduce future liabilities.

Environment Costs. This trend represents the privatization of environmental costs. While up to now we've mostly been paying for them with our lungs, as opposed to our cash, these costs will come home to roost for a number of companies.

Increased Earnings Volatility. If you have cut to the bone, if you have cut through all your variable costs due to market cycles (which some managements have forgotten actually do exist), you're going to have increased earnings volatility. There isn't any fat left to protect you in a down market.

Changing Restructuring Environment.   What are the implications of all these trends? The restructuring market is evolving. It's changing. Some of the changes we may like, some we may not. But if you analyze carefully all the aspects of corporate legal developments, tax legislation, public policy questions, and market trends, we think you can come up with some new and creative restructuring approaches. We think the pressures to increase shareholder value will continue. There will be a new emphasis on strategic business combinations to emphasize long-term positioning in core businesses, including cross-border transactions. We think you'll see some restructuring to address financial and international accounting inefficiencies as well.

Newly Attractive Restructuring Techniques.   We think changes in the market environment will make certain restructuring techniques very applicable. The common emphasis of these techniques will be the sharing of risk between buyers, sellers, and partners. Joint ventures will increase in popularity for a number of reasons, but especially to achieve deconsolidation or obtain a partner with cash to grow a core business. You will see greater use of parent or subsidiary stock as currency in exchange offers, new forms of equity consideration—such as the contingent value rights in the Dow-Marion transaction—as contingent compensation, and the use of noncash currency in such ways as to mitigate the negative financial and tax impact of a transaction.

   In summing up, we think the days of the easy financial engineering type of restructuring transaction are pretty much over. We see continued emphasis on employees as owners, core business growth, and strategic restructuring to increase international competitiveness.

26
M&A in the Middle Market

Joel S. Lawson III

Managing Partner, Howard, Lawson & Co.,
Philadelphia, Pennsylvania

T. Patrick Hurley, Jr.

Partner, Howard Lawson & Co.,
Philadelphia, Pennsylvania

Every year, some 10,000 middle-market businesses change hands. The dynamics of the marketplace change from year to year, but the same basic factors always are at work. Founders want liquidity, families disagree about the future, rapidly growing companies need resources, industries consolidate, and corporate divisions or subsidiaries are divested. The middle-market transaction, especially when a privately owned business is sold, has some special characteristics and can require a somewhat different approach from the merger of two larger, publicly owned enterprises.

WHERE IS THE MIDDLE MARKET?

First, a definition of "middle market" is needed. We consider the middle market to be businesses which have grown beyond single manager entities to significant regional, or even national, stature. Usually this implies revenues between $10 million and $200 million. Most of the middle market, however, is made up of businesses built around a single product area and its natural extensions, so they normally are not multimarket corporations with a group of divisions. This characteristic means the enterprise is an integral unit that does not lend itself to being sold in pieces.

WHO ARE THE SELLERS?

Owners of middle-market companies come in a variety of types. Generally the businesses can be categorized as closely held by a family or small group, or as an independent subsidiary or division of a larger enterprise. Owner/managers of the closely held middle-market companies usually have invested so completely in the business, financially and emotionally, that the sale of their company is a very significant event in their lives. This is distinct from the situations in which the corporate development officer of a *Fortune* 500 company dispassionately executes a strategic shift by a redeployment of global resources. It is important to note that both of these types are participants in middle-market transactions and, as a result, the sensitivities required vary dramatically from transaction to transaction.

GETTING READY TO GET
THE BEST PRICE

Price is important to everyone. Dedicated corporate sellers who are determined to complete a transaction within predetermined time frames, at almost whatever price the market will pay to get the business sold, are rare in the middle market. More often, the sellers have not experienced the process and complexities involved in a sale. Many will soon retire, and they view the prospect of getting top dollar for the sale of their interest in the business as a vitally important financial consideration and a one-time opportunity.

A business is most valuable to a new owner if it is highly profitable, has attractive prospects, and is the missing piece for someone else's strategic jigsaw puzzle. Getting the highest price is a function of offering the business to the prospective buyer audience that can profit most from the acquisition opportunity, presenting the business with an organized and realistic description of the benefits and value for the buyer, and carefully cultivating competition among buyers so that the seller has alternatives and is well informed about the market for the transaction.

The combination of a clear and convincing financial presentation and an attractive business fit with the buyer will win the brass ring for the seller. The worth of the business is what an informed and motivated buyer is willing to pay for it. Owners of middle-market businesses can work with their advisers to "reverse engineer" what a public company or other buyer is likely to be able to pay or want to pay.

Corporate housecleaning is an early priority and will benefit the seller even if a sale transaction is not consummated. Agreements between the seller's company and others should be reviewed with a focus on strengthening the company's position on existing and new arrangements, providing flexibility, and identifying problematic areas that require creative solutions that can be implemented in a reasonable time frame. Sellers also must at least be aware of the buyer's approach to measuring return on investment, discounted cash flows, and the target's potential strategic contribution to the buyer's overall plan.

Add-Backs and Adjustments

Clear and reliable financial information is an absolute requirement for maximizing price. Pro forma adjustments to financial statements (called add-backs) are the norm for illustrating how the target company performed in the configuration the seller anticipates for the new owner. Expenses usually are reduced to eliminate obviously unnecessary items. Good historical financial data represents the best starting point. Audited financial statements are strongly preferred. Buyers are much more comfortable discussing add-backs when they have comfort that the actual reported results have been determined with audit scrutiny. The investment in having audited financial statements reduces clutter later in the negotiations and in the preparation of definitive agreements.

Add-backs and adjustments should be reasonable and consistent with the overall expectations of the seller. Buyers, for instance, do not appreciate being asked to value a business for which the seller has added back $500,000 of the CEO's compensation if the CEO expects to continue to be paid at the unadjusted level. The important guidelines for add-backs are to have as few as possible and for those few to be logical and easily identifiable.

STRATEGIC AND FINANCIAL FIT

Two examples from our experience illustrate how value differs for alternative buyers and how flexibility on structure can produce successful sale programs. We represented a manufacturer of proprietary packaging products that was acquired by a large public company whose subsidiary manufactures the application equipment for our client's products. The buyer had decided to sell to its markets on a "systems approach," whereby they would provide the machinery (the razor) and the packaging (the blades) to strengthen the commitment to and from their customers.

The seller was one of the three main players in its segment of the packaging products product market but it was the *only* independent manufacturer of these particular products. The other two competitors were divisions of larger companies that had adopted the systems approach much earlier and had established a competitive advantage over the equipment company that bought our client. For the buyer, there was no viable alternative to acquiring our client if it needed to adopt the systems approach. The buyer eventually paid our client nearly double the price other prospective buyers had offered. The reason was that there was no other way to get what the buyer wanted.

In another example, our client was willing to sell on a pooling of interests basis to a larger company which recently had gone public. The accounting treatment for the business combination allowed the buyer to report a full year of very strong earnings, relative to its current results in a transaction that closed on the last day of its fiscal year. Equally important was that the research analysts following the acquirer in the public market had keen interest in current operating results, which in turn were attractive because of the inclusion of the target's full-year operating results.

The structure for the sale provided enough cash, through a distribution of already-taxed Subchapter S corporation retained earnings, so that our client was comfortable with a large holding of the buyer's stock. (It proceeded to increase in value as an active trading market developed and provided liquidity for the seller.) The fortunate outcome for both parties was based on the willingness to value the company highly because of the pooling-of-interest structure and the timing of the transaction relative to the buyer's newly public status.

OVERALL VALUE

It is essential for sellers to define exactly what is being sold, to determine how the seller prefers to price and structure the transaction, to understand how the buyer analyzes the acquisition opportunity, and to plan a win-win tone for discussions with prospective buyers. The overall value to the seller in a transaction is the combination of the price and the factors. The form of the consideration received at closing (stock, cash, combination, etc.), tax treatment, release from personal guarantees, earn-out payments related to the achievement of operating forecasts, and successful integration of the business with the buyer's others activities all are integral parts of the overall value of the transaction.

Continuity of leadership and management may be less a requirement imposed on the sellers of subsidiaries or divisions of large companies than the intensive transition effort that accompanies the sale of an owner-managed business. In most closely held businesses, customer and supplier relationships are longstanding and personal to the seller, who also may not have nurtured a strong supporting team with clear succession plans.

BEGINNING THE PROCESS

The decision to pursue a sale should be based on an awareness of the general level of interest that prospective buyers are expected to have for the company, a realistic valuation range, and the ability to deliver the goods. Prudent sellers anticipate hurdles to completing a transaction. We urge our seller clients to confirm that good title and all the essential elements of their business can be transferred to a new owner. Thoughtful and thorough advisers work closely with sellers to identify and resolve issues that could prevent the seller from completing a transaction and can provide a realistic and practical framework for what to expect throughout the sale process.

Accounting issues are becoming increasingly complicated. Benefit programs and pension liabilities for current and former employees, the adequacy of warranty reserves and product liability, and the whole area of environmental responsibility usually are handled quite differently by the larger company selling a middle-market business and the privately held company. The buyer will require the seller to conform to its level of disclosure and accounting standards.

Owners usually know their businesses well and have a general awareness of the desirability of the companies. This applies to both the closely held private business and the corporate divestiture candidate. The key managers of these companies also know the problems and challenges associated with these businesses. Sellers are well advised to identify, review, and investigate potential sale issues with financial, legal, accounting, and tax advisers to avoid surprises. It is best to take a hard look before leaping into the market.

Seller's Marketing Plan

The seller's financial adviser should absorb information about the company and the acquisition market conditions in order to recommend a marketing plan. Considerations for developing a marketing plan include the complexity of the seller's business, the number of likely prospects, the degree of screening to qualify interest, timing, the level of confidentiality required, and other items specific to the personalities and pressures of the situation.

The result should be a clear strategy for how the acquisition opportunity should be positioned, who the prospective buyers should be, who should initiate contact, how prospects will be qualified, the anticipated process of exchanging information and ideas, site visits, and the coordination of negotiations with alternative prospective buyers.

Offering Memorandum

Opinions vary about what information prospective buyers "need" or "should have." An offering document that feels like it's been widely distributed is not in the best interests of the seller. Each situation is different, but buyers expect owners who genuinely want to sell to be willing to provide the information buyers believe that they need to analyze the business and reach some conclusions on price and deal structure.

The form of the information document should be tailored for its audience. It generally is accepted that a "book" is prepared for corporate divestitures and most closely held businesses which are for sale. We have worked in several situations in which the marketing plan called for variations from the customary presentation materials. These usually were transactions involving buyers that were interested in technology, consolidation within a market segment or region, or other circumstances in which the required information differed from a straightforward overview of a niche company in a mature market for domestic companies that may not know the markets and industry well, or foreign buyers that need even more background and explanation.

Cover Story and Confidentiality Agreements

Sellers must assume that at some point in the sale program, someone inside or outside the organization will ask questions about the owner's intentions and whether the business is for sale. Disclosure of appropriate information must be made to prospective buyers if serious discussions are to be developed. Some commotion inside the seller's company is likely to be created by unusual activity and visitors.

We recommend that sellers manage the disclosure inside their companies. In some instances, public announcement of intentions is customary, as when a corporation decides to divest a group of businesses that no longer fit its overall strategic objectives. Usually, the owners are not committed to a particular course of action and they do not want others in their organization to become distracted by the possible implications of a change of control. Our advice to owners of closely held middle-market companies is to prepare a response to the general topic which is consistent with growth and expansion of the business and the strengthening of its competitive position.

The response, however, is not a solution. It is merely a holding action until key members of management are apprised of developments that may lead to the owner's decision that a sale is the best alternative. By confiding in a small group, which can in turn be sensitive to employee concerns, the seller can be aware of concerns as they arise, and then manage disclosure within the organization.

Counsel to the seller will prepare a confidentiality agreement for the prospective buyer to sign before receiving information about the seller's company. Most prospective buyers are willing to enter into confidentiality agreements.

GOING TO MARKET

Initial screening should be conducted by the seller's financial adviser without disclosing the target's identity. The way in which the contact with prospective buyers is initiated sets a tone for the process and the way the seller manages the sale program. Direct calls from a seller to prospective buyers are inappropriate in most cases. Not only should the preliminary interest of a prospective buyer be screened, but other issues should be addressed before the seller becomes known. Some logical prospective buyers may not be able to conform to the seller's schedule or preferred form of transaction, or may have priorities that keep them from being in a position to pursue the proffered acquisition.

The most valuable use of the CEO's time throughout the sale process is to run the business and concentrate on producing attractive results. Management operating efforts will be diluted enough by participating in meetings with prospective buyers and negotiations with the most interested parties. It is important for the seller to remain "above the fray" during the meetings and negotiations. In nearly all sale transactions, the seller has an incentive to preserve the basis for a good working relationship with the buyer. There also are a series of representations and warranties, and indemnification provisions which sellers can delegate to advisers to establish some insulation from the demands of buyers.

When to Talk Price and How

Sellers never should permit themselves to be rushed on price and always should consider buyers to be within reason for asking about price at any point in the discussion. Buyers want to know that sellers are rational on the topic of price. Sellers should be realistic if they expect to complete transactions.

Price can be addressed as an overall value and then assigned to various forms of consideration such as initial purchase price, installment payments, contingent payments, noncompetitive agreements and personal services agreements. Another approach is to determine the form and mix of the consideration components, and then define an overall package as having a particular value or price.

Sellers know what they want by the time they meet with prospective buyers. An asking price always should be accompanied by a term sheet and analytical support. Price should not be discussed before the seller and its advisers agree that the value of the company, to the buyer, and the business fit of the two firms have been illustrated and confirmed. Preventing selective memory and clearly defining the proposed transaction are good examples.

LETTER OF INTENT THROUGH CLOSING

A written understanding of what the seller and buyer think that they have preliminarily agreed to becomes the point of reference for due diligence and the preparation of definitive agreements. Many buyers are not interested in letters of intent because they may trigger a requirement for public news releases. Sellers often are more reluctant than buyers to announce a transaction that could be derailed.

We recommend the use of terms sheets and letters of intent, because the parties should be able to reduce to writing the basis on which due diligence can be launched. In some situations, although they are rare in the 1990s, sellers are able to negotiate the definitive agreement in advance of due diligence by the buyer. In most cases, the seller must decide whether to authorize the buyer to conduct due diligence. At that point, the buyer asks the target owner to discontinue discussions with other interested parties.

Our experience has been that owners of middle-market businesses are in a better position if they require letters of intent from the buyers. It doesn't matter that the letter of intent is usually a nonbinding understanding with sometimes vague language about the terms of the proposed transaction. Those documents are not issued lightly, and they force both parties to clarify their intentions.

The due diligence and preparation of definitive agreements can proceed in tandem. Sellers should focus first on the business terms of the transaction and then focus on the representations, warranties, and indemnification expectations of the buyer. Owners of middle-market companies often are unpleasantly surprised by provisions that even their own counsel might consider reasonable. We have found that corporate divestitures generally involve very limited provisions of this type, because the seller wants no continuing potential liability; or they are relatively loose, because the seller wants to achieve a high price even if offsets occur later because of the indemnification obligations associated with the agreement.

Sellers must take the time to thoroughly understand the intricacies of all material documents associated with the sale. Subtle changes can result in costly consequences. Sellers must issue clear guidelines to counsel on the level of discretion in lawyer-to-lawyer discussions. The devil often does reside in the details.

Momentum must be established and sustained. It is most efficient to have an aggressive timetable for completing due diligence and deal documentation. Unanticipated developments can be disastrous on the downside, and pleasant surprises always can be factored in for upside reward. In general, the amount of work and expense in closing transaction will expand to fill the time available.

ODDS AND ENDS

Closing actually is only the beginning for the buyer. Sellers, for example, should be aware that the buyer's success has everything to do with whether clauses in the sale agreement about claims and arbitrating disputes will be activated.

Communications between the seller and the troops at the company should begin immediately after the definitive agreement has been signed and closing occurs, if not sooner. The first year after closing is critical for executing the operating transition. Private company sellers cannot afford for the changeover not to go smoothly. Corporate sellers almost never concern themselves with the topic unless it affects some other part of the parent company's business.

Forget auctions for the middle-market companies. Sellers whose accountability to shareholders is limited to themselves or small private groups (as opposed to public shareholders) tend to place value on items not directly associated with price. In those discussions, the personal chemistry and perception of the buyer's future handling of the company cannot be nurtured in a process intended to remove the human element of negotiated transactions.

TACKLING UNIQUE ISSUES

Middle-market transactions represent the bulk of M&A activity in the United States and for foreign in-bound acquisitions by foreign acquirers. These transactions require extra effort to complete because of the characteristics of the sellers. Corporate divestitures are much more straightforward and businesslike than the disposition of closely held businesses where founders or owners march to the beat of their own drum.

The transactions are complex and the pitfalls are many. Specialists who serve the middle market are valuable to sellers. Owners should not become embroiled in negotiations that limit their overall flexibility. CEOs of sellers should focus on delivering a healthy and strong business at the closing table. Sellers should carefully plan before going to market with a sale program.

Once the process is started, it should maintain momentum and intensity through completion. Sellers should make every effort to help the new owner get off to a strong start and execute a smooth transition. A sale program in many ways is the most important financial transaction in an entrepreneur's career, so it should not be taken lightly. But it should be very rewarding.

27

Acquiring Troubled Companies

Thomas J. Barry
Norman H. Brown, Jr.
Mark D. Gerstein
C. Kenneth White

PART I. FINDING THE RIGHT COMPANY

C. Kenneth White
Partner, Ernst & Young, Chicago, Illinois

How does a buyer identify an acquisition candidate that is in a troubled situation?

One route is work through the network that has developed around troubled companies. It includes turnaround artists who are very skilled at going in and dealing with a company's problem. Often they take equity positions. There also are firms that stand behind management teams by putting money into a troubled company. And there are workout bankers that are trying to enhance the positions of their institutions. They can offer indications of what public companies are having problems and what public data are available.

This network is becoming very formal and it can be accessed by talking to the workout bankers, attorneys that specialize in the restructurings, and others that may have properties for sale.

In the public company arena, tips come from public disclosures, including the required 10K and 10Q documents as well as the 8Ks when there are bond or debt defaults. Press releases announce troubled situations. And when the audited financials come out, the troubled company may present explanatory language regarding its ability to continue as a going concern that suggests an opportunity to move in on a distressed situation.

There also are troubled industries to explore. Real estate, as an industry, was moving into a distressed situation by the late 1980s. Earlier, it was energy and steel, and the steel industry is still having problems. So a buyer can track the industry with problems and identify the specific companies that are most troubled because of such difficulties as loss of market share or attacks on markets by foreign competitors. The machine tool industry is one such example. And, of course, there are the distressed situations caused by excess leverage. LBO companies as a group may be considered a troubled industry.

DISTRESS SIGNALS

What are the early warning signals? Where are the red flags? Extended poor performance is one sign. The number of companies that can sustain continued losses for five, six, or seven years is amazing. They survive by divesting valuable assets such as divisions or product lines in order to meet their obligations as they come due, particularly the institutional debt. This is a way for them to cure loan defaults, although they get a little weaker each time.

These are the most obvious signs of trouble, because they recur year after year. Other signals develop in conjunction—management turnover, director turnover, and a very unstable environment generally. If the company is in a troubled industry, a buyer should look for external factors, such as increased market share for foreign competition, major technological changes, or the onetime glamour industry that is moving out of the product growth cycle into a mature cycle. The companies hurt by these forces require change, particularly management that can assess the changes that need to be made.

Often, such as in the case of the troubled LBO, the business is strong. But there were hockey stick projections of great growth and improvement in market share that didn't develop to support the highly leveraged structure. A strong management team may be in place, but the capital structure is out of sync. So a financial fix is required, as opposed to an operational fix.

However, there are a lot of companies in mature industries or industries moving into the declining life cycle that really require an operational fix. Some may be characterized by management ineptitude and management's inability to deal with the changing environment.

GETTING A FIX ON RISKS

Well, how does a buyer evaluate the risk before jumping into a troubled situation?

For starters, whether the company is in Chapter 11 or in an out-of-court workout, we calculate what the bondholder group and the creditor group would get if the company were liquidated. We start drawing the baseline from there and then negotiate with the creditors and others in terms of trying to spread the pain of the economic hit or the restructuring hit.

In addition to understanding the economics and the strengths and weaknesses in the balance sheet, the buyer also must assess management. Maybe management has to change after acquisition.

Next it's necessary to identify and examine off-balance sheet issues. Until the accounting profession required companies to record retiree medical liabilities as they are accrued, these were generally off-balance-sheet matters.

A large restructuring that I worked on included the sale of some divisions to satisfy part of the company's obligations. But the investment bankers and the company's other financial advisors missed the very critical issue of retiree medical claims in trying to put the plan together. They were hidden, and disclosed only in the footnotes. That makes it tough to get a handle on the problem because the footnotes only describe cash outflow and not the gross liability. My actuaries told me that when gross liabilities were included, the annual P&L statement hit was a multiple of six to eight times the cash outflow.

In another distressed situation, the company was trying to sell a division that hadn't earned money in four years. The division had an annual cash payment in retiree benefits of about $1 million on an incurred basis. The total liability was estimated to be $42 million on the low side to $56 million on the high side. But it was not on the balance sheet. This was a $160 million business with a fair market value of around $50 million or $60 million. But the buyer was not going to assume that liability unless he believed he could work down that claim $42 million to $56 million by reducing benefits, by putting in higher deductibles, by coming up with a way to annuitize the liability to reduce it, or by making changes in some other way.

Beyond that, the buyer must look at various competitive advantages that the business might have, as well the disadvantages, such as whether it's vulnerable to foreign competition or to competitors with better technology.

SIFTING THE FACTS

The real key to playing in the tough arena of acquiring a distressed or troubled company is that information is very critical, whether it's in court or out of court. Knowledge is power. In acquiring a distressed company, the buyer wants to know as much as possible, and often more than the other parties. This brings strength to the negotiating table. So due diligence is very important.

Timing is everything. In both in-court and out-of-court workouts, the debtor gains by very quick action and by acting preemptively. If the process begins to drag out, then the creditors begin to get a leg up. They are gathering information that helps them understand the value of the business. The longer the case works its way through the process, the more the debtor company begins to lose some of its value and some of its negotiating edge. And the creditors begin to take control.

What are the leading indicators as far as assessing the opportunities to jump in and identify a troubled situation?

The chief indicators are management's capability and credibility. Are they capable of dealing with the turnaround? What is their track record? Has there been any self-dealing? What is the integrity of the management team? Have they cashed out of their stock option positions or their stock positions? Do they know something that the public does not? What is the quality of the earnings within this organization?

Based on the quality of the earnings—and discounting any hockey stick projections—what is the status of the company? What is its product life cycle? Is it in the growth stage where it needs more capital to continue to grow the business? Or is it in the maturation stage where there is an opportunity to harvest cash out of the business? Or has the company and the industry actually moved into such a decline that there is going to be a serious loss of market share? And what must be done after the deal is completed? Does the company need a strategic realignment of the business to move it into another mode, such as a niche strategy or a role as a low-cost producer?

The quality of earnings analysis requires a determination of how much of the earnings are attributable to creative accounting.

For instance, one company that I worked with was a foreign-language learning center that sold foreign-language encyclopedias. A large accounting firm was the auditor. But when we got behind the numbers, we found that the company was recognizing earnings on a 12-volume set of encyclopedias that had not been fully produced. It booked the entire amount for the sale of 12 volumes, but had produced only two of them.

In another situation, we encountered a very large communications company with a management of questionable integrity. They did sale/lease-back arrangements on equipment that they didn't even own. They sold this equipment to a customer through subscription, yet they didn't have title to it.

So, what is the quality of the earnings? The integrity of management? The integrity of the balance sheet? A buyer really has to get behind the earnings numbers to find out.

The process really requires a diagnostic assessment to understand the numbers and analyze the company's strategic position. In particular, answer these questions: What went wrong in the last four or five years? And why can't this management group deal with the problems and get the business turned around? Often it takes unique individuals to do the turnaround. The incumbents may not be accustomed to crisis management and in making the deal work, a new owner may really have to go in there and cut to the bone.

CONTROL BY THE COURT

If the company is not in bankruptcy but is part of a court proceeding, by submitting a bid to the court, a buyer can gain control through a direct purchase. These situations result when there is a debt default and a class-action lawsuit. What are some of the more favorable attributes? Well the purchase, which may involve an exchange of securities to satisfy creditors, is exempt from registration with the SEC. The court confirms the class and brings everybody together. So the buyer is really working hand-in-hand with the class-action claimants and the debtor to make this work.

Another beauty of the process is that the court determines the fairness of the transaction. That gives the management some protection, particularly if the purchase doesn't work and the company has to flip into a bankruptcy in one or two years, because the court stood behind the valuation and there was a court order and court-approved exchange. In addition, all bondholders are bound by the terms of the exchange.

Finally, the buyer must deal with issues on a personal level in acquiring a troubled company that is not in bankruptcy. A problem with out-of-court workouts is that there is no effective sharing of the pain. The buyer has to go to a large, concentrated creditor group which may contain the secured banks, the unsecured banks, and the subordinated debtholders. The message to them is that if they want to realize more through an acquisition than they would get through liquidation, everybody has to share in the pain. It's very difficult to get all of these constituencies plus the trade creditors to share the pain.

Secured creditors are very reluctant to budge. They are confident that they have valid liens and that they basically have perfected their positions. So they are always going to be in a holdout mode unless there is some issue, such as fraudulent conveyance, to soften them up. Working with the secured creditors may involve a long fight that may not be worth the buyer's time because the company is going to lose value until there is a resolution. So the time involved and the outcome of the negotiations are key factors that are going to impact the basic strategy of the acquisition.

PART II. BUYING THE COMPANY IN BANKRUPTCY

Norman H. Brown, Jr.

Managing Director, Donaldson, Lufkin
& Jenrette, New York, New York

Some of the problems involved in acquiring a company that is involved in an out-of-court workout are mitigated if the company is in Chapter 11. However, buying assets of a company in bankruptcy or the entire company itself has still other difficulties that are hard to resolve.

To understand the transaction opportunities presented by a company in bankruptcy, it is helpful to know how the Chapter 11 process works.

In very simple terms, a company that files Chapter 11 gets the benefit of the automatic stay which holds up all of its debts and typically stops all litigation. The company has a period of time, called the "exclusive period," during which the debtor in possession, i.e., the management of the company, is afforded an opportunity to come up with a plan of reorganization. The longer this period is extended, the more information the creditors groups develop, and, generally speaking, the better organized they become.

At some point, a plan is put forth. It may be the debtor's plan, it may be a consensual plan agreed to by all of the constituents, or it may be a creditors' plan. A disclosure statement is prepared, circulated just like a proxy, and voted on by all of the constituent groups. The plan is approved if it secures favorable votes from creditors who represent two-thirds of the dollar amount of all the impaired creditor classes, as well as 50 percent of the creditors by number. It then must be confirmed by the bankruptcy court judge before the company emerges from Chapter 11.

That process takes between 20 and 24 months on average, although there are ways to shorten it.

CHOICES FOR THE BUYER

An investor can make acquisitions before or after a bankruptcy filing. If there is an all-equity plan, in which stock is exchanged for claims and a massive equity distribution to creditors is made, there is an opportunity to buy the company after consummation of the plan.

An acquirer considering companies or assets that are in Chapter 11 has three different ways to do a deal. The first way is simply passive investing. Vulture funds, high yield mutual funds, and individual investors have become quite skilled at this technique, basically buying and trading claims. They see fundamental value in the claims that they will be able to capitalize on when the reorganization plan is completed, or they believe they can profit by just participating in market arbitrage.

There also are proactive investors, including those that will aggressively try to establish a blocking position. These blocking positions often are interesting tactics for acquirers. For example, the buyer of one-third of the dollar amount of an impaired class of claims will be in a blocking position to stop anyone else from completing a plan of reorganization. That, in effect, is what Japonica Partners did in gaining control of Allegheny International in 1991. In essence, the road to a reorganization of Allegheny, which was renamed Sunbeam-Oster, had to go right through the offices of Japonica Partners.

Blocking Positions

Blocking positions usually are used by securities investors as opposed to companies or individuals trying to acquire the entire company. But an observation that may be of interest to strategic buyers is that generally speaking, with the notable exception of convertible securities, acquirers of creditor claims don't have to file 13-D statements with the SEC. So a company can acquire 5, 10, or 50 percent of the claims associated with a bankrupt company and not have to file disclosure documents. That often is helpful in forming alliances within groups of creditors, to be stronger and more assertive than a single party.

One warning on the blocking position is that the claims holder is not going to make many friends in the bondholding community. What goes around comes around, and these people have very long memories.

The final technique is acquisition of control of the company that is in Chapter 11. There are essentially three ways to do it.

One is an equity infusion, in which the investor essentially becomes a partner with the debtor in possession. The investor becomes a co-sponsor of the plan of reorganization and works with the debtor to negotiate with the creditors on a successful plan. That approach is time consuming. It's cheapest at the beginning and most expensive at the end, because the investor gets sucked into the mud that has swallowed the debtor and becomes a partner in the struggle with the various creditors.

The second approach is the conversion approach, or buying debt securities with the expectation that after the bankruptcy they will become the equity of the reorganized company. A classic example of how it can work is the Public Service Co. of New Hampshire reorganization, which culminated in 1992 with an acquisition by Northeast Utilities. But well before the plan was completed, investor Martin Whitman believed that the utility's third mortgage bonds, which were trading in the 1970s, were, in fact, going to become equity in the reorganized company. So he, Shearson Lehman, and two or three other investors bought about 75 to 80 percent of that particular class. The bottom line is that they were wrong. There was more value in the company than they thought. The claims that they bought at 72 cents were worth 140 cents or 150 cents on the dollar when the company emerged from Chapter 11 by being acquired.

In another case involving a company called LaSalle Energy, the bondholders did not trade the debt securities and ended up owning 85 percent of the equity in the reorganized company.

The negative to buying claims, and to some degree the negative in the equity infusion approach, is that the investor's equity ownership of the company is subject to dilution. The investor is going to be a participant in the bankruptcy or a participant in a class of creditors. As a result, it is only going to get a pro rata share of whatever equity becomes available.

The last way to buy equity essentially is to be a standby purchaser and acquire the equity from former creditors upon the consummation of the plan.

Japonica used both techniques two and three in getting control of Allegheny. First, they tried to be the standby purchaser of equity, but after they were turned down by the secured creditors, they decided to become more assertive. So they bought enough claims to effectively block the company's consensual plan with those creditors. Then they stepped up again and offered to buy all the remaining claims on essentially the same basis as that with which they bought the initial claims. That provided cash liquidity for the creditor group that was getting equity as the result of the plan of reorganization.

The standby purchaser faces a high probability of not completing the acquisition. But the approach features generally lower costs and lower risks going into the transaction. And at the end of the case the buyer has a better handle on what the company is likely to be worth than it might have had at the beginning of the case.

PART III. VALUING THE TROUBLED COMPANY

Thomas J. Barry

Senior Vice President, Donaldson,
Lufkin & Jenrette, New York, New York

Valuing a troubled company isn't much different from valuing a nontroubled company, except for the quality of the information the buyer has to deal with. The values still are based on multiples to book, multiples to cash flow, and discounted cash flows.

The key problem is that these numbers may have been produced by the management that got the firm into trouble in the first place. So they must be questioned vigorously as to their accuracy.

I had an experience working with a troubled company in the Midwest, and the first question I asked was, "Exactly what does your cost structure look like?" The chief financial officer shot back, "Well if I knew what my costs were, would I be selling for less than cost?" I then asked for the following year's projections. I got a similar answer. So part of the problem with the valuation exercise is finding reliable parameters against which to measure.

Therein is both a problem and an opportunity, because there is a premium for really understanding the business. There is a premium for getting inside, and there is a premium for knowing the company better than its management does.

ENTERPRISE VALUE

There is a two-step process for determining the "enterprise value" of a company in bankruptcy. The first step is an orderly analysis of the company to value the left side of the balance sheet and find out what the assets are worth. The second step comes in valuing the liabilities. Here, the bankruptcy process helps the buyer a great deal in some ways and hinders the buyer in others.

Through the claims process, presumably everyone with a claim against the company has mailed in a piece of paper. So the due diligence universe has been at least partially created in advance. At this point, the potential buyer must be careful to consult with its lawyers to make sure of the bar date, the date beyond which nobody can make a claim. But even that is not a foolproof guarantee of the exact parameters of the liabilities, because sometimes there is a group of creditors that has escaped notice. They still may have claims. So the potential buyer really needs to do extensive due diligence on the process of how the claims were established.

There are two kinds of main claims for financial analysis purposes: liquidated and unliquidated. With a liquidated claim, the creditor seeks a specific amount for services rendered, merchandise sold, a judgment in a lawsuit, and so on. An unliquidated claimant does specify the amount.

The problem is that the so-called total claims that are used in the proceedings often don't include the unliquidated claims because they are not easily quantifiable. So a potential acquirer needs to be careful to go through all the claims and get a handle on true total, and not just the commonly used aggregate numbers.

Another issue in dealing with the claims is reinstatement. Claims can be reinstated after initially being dismissed. It's difficult for the people on the deal side to understand the process which is designed to protect people against having their legal rights impaired. And it's a slow process for the typical buyer. People that a buyer may view as unimportant in the dealmaking sense may have a disproportionate ability to slow down the process.

The buyer can try to accelerate the proceedings by agreeing to settle various types of difficult claims. But this represents an economic trade-off, because it can raise the effective purchase price. And any of the options involves a considerable amount of time. Time is not the acquirer's friend in the bankruptcy process.

IMPORTANCE OF TIMING

The time issue is critical. Let us say the buyer is able to go through the analysis, understand the business, get comfortable with all the numbers, and develop the "right" value. Well, will it be the right value a year from now? If the bidding process gets held up, will the value still be there? If the buyer is not able to get control of the company before the next selling season and is not able to supply customers, is the valuation technique correct? That's why time is such an important weapon for the people involved in the case and a great problem for the people valuing the company. Even if the business is valued correctly today, it may take a year to get the company. Thus the buyer needs to be fairly ruthless in evaluating whether it is worth continuing with the process and determining what the real values are over a considerable period of time.

The key is to become sensitive to the values in the company that are not going to be eroded by time. It helps to identify the hidden values that aren't going to show up in the financial statements, such as distribution systems, customers, and brand names. Those are assets that, even as the company is being mismanaged or is taking write-offs, sometimes have surprisingly resilient characteristics and retain value throughout the entire process. So the buyer needs to be driven not just by the financial numbers. Some of the best elements' value may not show up in the financial statements.

A full valuation also should consider the need to raise additional capital after the transaction. That requires sensitivity to the fact that there is still some negative perception to bankruptcy, although probably not as much as in the past. Nevertheless, that financing may not be easy to obtain.

PART IV. THE BANKRUPTCY AUCTION

Mark D. Gerstein

Partner, Katten Muchin & Zavis,
Chicago, Illinois

To prevent dispositions of valued assets from dragging on until a plan of reorganization is adopted, creditors and other parties increasingly are using a procedure authorized by Section 363 of the Bankruptcy Code, what I would refer to as a bankruptcy auction.

This is a quick, cost-effective manner in which to handle the principal assets in a case. Early in the proceedings, the judge allows selected assets, or even an entire company, to be sold quickly at auction. The creditors then fight over the proceeds; this prevents the company's value from deteriorating while the claims are thrashed out.

STARTING THE AUCTION

The bankruptcy auction can be initiated by three different categories of people. The first is a buyer who approaches the debtor or the trustee and negotiates a purchase agreement. The court then is asked to initiate a Section 363 sale. If it agrees, the business goes out for a public auction.

The second group that might initiate a Section 363 sale consists of the debtor company's creditors. They may recognize one of two things. The company is never going to be reorganized, and assets will deteriorate substantially in value during the pendency of the bankruptcy proceeding. Alternatively, if the company eventually is going to be reorganized, the process will be lengthy, and the short-term cash-flow needs of the debtor may be met by selling selected assets quickly to meet its financial requirements. In either case, the creditors will ask the court and the debtor to initiate the sale of assets or operations. The creditors alone cannot initiate a Section 363 sale.

The third route is a prearranged bankruptcy auction. Typically, this starts when the debtor, facing an inevitable bankruptcy filing, will find a purchaser for the company before it actually enters bankruptcy, so that it can move quickly through the bankruptcy process and maximize the value of its assets. The company involved in this process often has some type of special financial problem—such as huge product liability claims or large retiree medical liabilities—and may be effectively worthless because of them.

The parties will negotiate an acquisition agreement with full-blown due diligence, and when it is executed, they will file a bankruptcy petition and immediately move for a Section 363 sale. With the right company in the right circumstances, this technique enables the purchaser to obtain a financially clean operation and minimizes the deterioration of value that otherwise takes place during a bankruptcy proceeding.

If the court is inclined to allow the sale, regardless of who initiates it, there will be a notice to participants in a bankruptcy and public notice, such as a newspaper advertisement. Once the notice is provided, there is a 30-to-60 day period for other bidders to offer competing bids and for creditors to object. The court will hold a hearing at the end of this period. If the court approves the sale, the closing usually occurs on the tenth day after the approval.

COURT APPROVALS

In determining whether to approve the sale, the court looks at five factors.

The first is the proportionate value of the assets being sold in relation to the whole estate. If it is a small asset or a small operation, the courts generally will allow the sale if fair value is being paid for the asset.

However, if the assets constitute a large part of the operation or the entire company, the process gets a little more difficult. Then the court is going to look at the other four factors very carefully.

One is the likelihood that a plan of reorganization will be proposed and confirmed in the near future. Usually this is not the case, but courts like to consider the proceeds received for assets in the context of an entire plan. The courts want to know what will be done with the money from a quick sale; if a plan is likely to be proposed soon, the court will be inclined to sell the assets in the context of the plan.

Another factor involves the proceeds of the sale versus the appraised value of the assets. Everyone wants to "steal" an asset in bankruptcy; however, the courts are not in the business of making bargains. There has to be some reasonable relationship between what is being paid and what the asset is worth, even discounting for the fact that the company is "heading south."

The court also will consider the effect of a proposed sale on future plans of reorganization. Historically, courts have been in the business of rehabilitating debtors, not liquidating them. A court will seek a compelling reason why it should send the company, or assets that the company needs for reorganization, out the door and preclude the debtor's reorganization.

Finally, and perhaps most important, the court will want to know whether the asset is increasing or decreasing in value. If the asset is going to decrease in value over time, the court is more likely to be convinced that the time to sell that asset is now.

THE PURCHASER'S PERSPECTIVE

What kind of factors should the buyer consider in deciding whether to participate in a Section 363 sale?

First, the dominant creditors should be in agreement that it is time to sell the asset that the purchaser seeks. That establishes credibility with the court for the offer and increases the probability that the buyer's efforts will be rewarded.

Second, the purchaser must be able to demonstrate that no future improvement in the value of the assets is realizable by the debtor. If the creditors think the value could be increased or held even, they probably will want time to explore alternatives.

Third, are there limited financing alternatives for the debtor? That is what very often drives the sale. The debtor cannot get a working capital line and it's going to strangle in a few weeks without selling some pieces for cash.

That happened frequently in the bankruptcy of the Revco DS, Inc. drug store chain. Selected segments of the chain were sold off during the bankruptcy to generate cash for operations while the reorganization plan was worked out.

Fourth, fair value must be provable. A professional likely is going to have to testify that full value is being paid. It is possible to reconcile this requirement with the purchaser's desire to get a bargain, because experts are willing to recognize that assets in bankruptcy should be accorded a substantial discount in value.

BENEFITS OF THE SECTION 363 SALE

One of the benefits of going through this process is the cleansing effect of a bankruptcy order. A purchaser at a bankruptcy auction obtains the same benefits the debtor company would get in discharging claims through a plan of reorganization. Unfunded pension plan liabilities, retiree medical claims, burdensome long-term contracts, and known product liabilities remain with the estate.

The accelerated sale also minimizes the deterioration of customer and supplier goodwill that invariably takes place during a long bankruptcy proceeding.

Finally, this is a very quick-decision process. It takes only a few months, so the commitment of time and money to an unsuccessful acquisition is very limited. In addition, in most bankruptcy auctions, the initiating bidder will get price and bid protection from the court. For example, the court may declare that the initial bid cannot be topped unless a competing offer exceeds it by some specified factor— such as 5 or 10 percent. And if the initiator does lose, the court often will reimburse it for due diligence and financing expenses.

RISKS IN THE BIDDING

Of course, there are risks. If a sale is blocked by creditors, the company's assets may never leave the bankruptcy estate and the time and effort spent will be lost.

There is also the auction risk. The first bid could be topped, although with price and bid protection, that risk can be mitigated.

Third, not all liabilities are discharged by a bankruptcy court order. Trade creditors' claims ostensibly could be left behind. But if the acquirer needs to have an ongoing relationship with trade creditors, such as suppliers, they will have a stranglehold on the purchaser. These creditors need to be repaid or they will never again do business with the buyer.

Environmental liabilities in most cases follow the buyer. However, if the business includes an environmentally contaminated facility that the purchaser does not need, it can be excluded from the sale and the environmental claims left with the debtor in possession. Unknown liabilities also can be a problem. An example is the defective product that has not yet injured anybody but may cause injuries in the future. These claims may follow the purchaser.

Unpaid taxes also may be a problem. Several states have statutes that take state tax liability and transfer it to the successor, regardless of the bankruptcy court order.

Finally, it is important to remember that these are not pleasant circumstances. In one bankruptcy I know of, hundreds, if not thousands, of former employees with pension plans and retiree medical benefits had all of those obligations canceled by the debtor. Even though the purchaser is not the source of these problems, it will become associated with them. Buyers should consider potential public relations risks before becoming associated with the debtor.

MITIGATING RISKS

How does a buyer mitigate these risks?

The first and most important question to ask the financial and legal advisers is whether the debtor's business can survive the uncertainty created by the bankruptcy. What is the value going to be in six months or a year? Is it going to be substantially lower at the end of that period? Can it survive at all? Will the purchaser end up with only a shell of the company it thought it was going to acquire?

Second, conduct full and customary due diligence. The bankruptcy court order does not discharge every claim, and the purchaser should identify every material risk. In particular, there often is a deterioration in risk management activities at the troubled company. For example, when cash flow gets tight, the company may stop managing its environmental problems. It does not pull its underground storage tanks and may not be careful as to who handles its off-site disposal.

Finally, there should be a standard acquisition agreement with indemnities. Some claims are not going to be discharged and if they are not disclosed, the buyer should have recourse against the seller. Obviously, it is difficult to sue a bankrupt company. But there are two alternatives that can be written into the agreement:

- A hold-back on a portion of the purchase price
- Contingent payments beyond the initial price that can be set off against potential liabilities in order to fund indemnity obligations

Bankruptcy auctions offer great opportunities, but a buyer needs to look at all the benefits and risks in each situation. As more and more companies get dragged into bankruptcy, there will be frequent acquisition opportunities through that vehicle. However, by taking the right approach, the buyer does not get involved in the bankruptcy reorganization itself and has the chance to obtain an operation quickly and cleanly.

28

Merger Arbitrage*

Guy P. Wyser-Pratte

President, Wyser-Pratte & Co., Inc.,
New York, New York

Arbitrageurs are not investors in the formal sense of the word; that is, they are not normally buying or selling securities because of their investment value. Arbitrageurs do, however, commit capital to the "deal"—the merger, tender offer, recapitalization, and so on—rather than to the particular security. They must take positions in the deal in such a way that they are at the risk of the deal, and not at the risk of the market. They accomplish this by taking a short position in the securities being offered, as part of the deal, in exchange for the securities they purchase. So, in a merger of Company X into Company Y, the arbitrageur's investment is one of X long and Y short, or the merger of X into Y. Once they have taken this hedged position, arbitrageurs no longer are concerned with the vagaries of the marketplace—so long as the deal goes through.

There is a definite and fairly common sequence to arbitrageurs' financial analysis that allows them to arrive at investment decisions. They (1) gather information about the particular deal, (2) calculate the value of the securities offered, (3) determine the length of the time that capital should be tied up in the deal, (4) calculate the expected per-annum return on invested capital, (5) determine and weigh all the possible risks and problem areas that might preclude consummation of the transaction, (6) assess the various tax implications and establish a tax strategy, (7)

---

*This chapter is excerpted from Guy P. Wyser-Pratte's monograph, "Risk Arbitrage II," published by the Salomon Brothers Center for the Study of Financial Institutions at the Graduate School of Business Administration, New York University.

determine the amount of stock available for borrowing in order to be able to sell short, and (8) determine the amount of capital to be committed to the deal based on a careful balancing of (1) through (7) above.

GATHERING INFORMATION

The arbitrageur's task begins with the announcement of a proposed merger, which will appear in the financial press, usually *The Wall Street Journal,* or perhaps the Dow Jones or Western Union *Newswire.* The arbitrageur's first question will be: "Is this a good deal?" The question pertains not so much to the potential profitability for the arbitrageur's firm, but rather to the business logic of the merger, the quality of the two partners proposing the marriage, their record of successful marriages, the fairness of the financial terms of the merger to the shareholders of the "bride," and a postmerger pro forma evaluation of the "groom." The essential question here is: "Will the deal go through?"

The answers to many of the above questions may be obtained by an analysis of the annual reports of the companies, plus the write-ups in either Moody's or Standard & Poor's Stock Records. The business logic of the merger may require deeper analysis, particularly an assessment of industry trends together with an evaluation of the financial and competitive postures of both companies within their respective industries. It is often best to hear from the companies themselves the purported reasons for their proposed merger. It is at this point that the curtain rises on one of the great comic operas of Wall Street: obtaining information from the involved companies about their proposed merger. It is indeed comic because the companies will always present a rosy prognosis for the successful consummation of their proposed marriage, while the arbitrage community, always suspicious, will, in their conversations with the companies, try to draw out the hard and cold facts about the real state of affairs: the actual stage of the negotiations as well as the matter of business logic. Because of Securities and Exchange Commission (SEC) police actions in the securities industry during the 1970s, getting answers from the companies, much less straight ones, is becoming extremely difficult. Yet, even when companies do answer, the arbitrageur must carefully read between the lines, as the companies are aware that their answers may influence an arbitrageur to buy or sell their respective securities, and managements are extremely sensitive to market price fluctuations.

Approaching companies to gather information is thus ticklish for the arbitrageurs. They must tailor their approach depending on whether they are interrogating the bride or the groom. The bride normally is totally cooperative, realizing that the arbitrageur can, by purchasing her stock, accumulate votes which will naturally be cast in favor of the merger. So, to the bride, the arbitrageur can candidly state his or her business. The groom is an entirely different matter. He will not be pleased that his stock may become the subject of constant short selling by arbitrageurs; he is thus often elusive in his responses. To counteract this, the arbitrageur often must become the "wolf in sheep's clothing" by assuming the role of the investment banker who seems to be desirous of assisting the groom with his acquisition program—both the present proposed merger and future plans. In this manner arbitrageurs ingratiate themselves with the host in order to ask those delicate questions about the pending merger negotiations. The arbitrageur may also don the garb of the institutional salesperson who is attempting to place with institutional investors the new securities that may be offered to the bride. If the salesperson is to sell those securities effectively, he or she must know the details of the merger, particularly the date when these securities will be issued, which will coincide roughly with the closing of the merger transaction. Not surprisingly, most grooms with active acquisition programs are well aware of the guises of the arbitrageur. Some cooperate, others don't. Those whose stocks will least be affected by short selling seem to cooperate most.

The information that is sought from the companies is hardly of an "inside" nature—a fact most companies do not realize—but rather has to do with the information set and related decisions that will have to be made to consummate the merger, and the current status of the information. The arbitrageur's questions, therefore, deal basically with the following:

1. The accounting treatment (purchase versus pooling)
2. The type of reorganization under the Internal Revenue Code: statutory merger, sale of assets, etc.
3. Whether a preliminary agreement has been reached, or whether the negotiations consist only of a handshake
4. If a definitive agreement has been reached, and if not, when it will be
5. Conditions under which the definitive agreement may be terminated by either party
6. Whether a formal tax ruling will be required from the IRS, or whether parties will proceed on advice of counsel
7. The approximate date the application will be made for the tax ruling
8. The approximate date that the proxy material will be filed with the SEC
9. The date the proxy material is expected to clear the SEC and be mailed to the shareholders
10. The dates for the respective shareholder meetings
11. Where the major blocks of the companies' stock are held
12. The other rulings that may be required—FCC, CAB, Maritime Board, Federal Reserve Board, ICC, Justice Department, Federal Trade Commission
13. The probable closing date

Once the arbitrageur has established the answers to some or all of the above, he or she will continuously check to verify what the companies are selling. The arbitrageur will, for example, check with the SEC to determine that the proxy material has really been filed, with the IRS to ascertain that the tax ruling application has been filed, and so forth. As the seriousness of the companies' intent to merger is corroborated by activities meeting the various requirements, the arbitrageur will become increasingly interested in either taking a position or adding to it. That the companies are serious is evidenced by the extent of the paperwork carried out.

But further evidence of the merits of the merger proposal is required. It is necessary to analyze the financial terms from both parties' points of view, to see, first, if the terms are likely to be favorably voted upon. For the bride, this entails among other things a comparison of its market price with the market value of the securities to be received; the current dividend rate with the rate to be received on the package of the groom's securities; the current earnings with the earnings represented by the securities offered by the groom; and a comparison of the growth of those earnings. Brides often find these days that they are giving up future earnings for current market value.

The groom requires a pro forma evaluation. Whether or not the groom will experience dilution now or in the future depends on the respective earnings growth rates translated through the proposed payment to be made for the bride. Too much initial dilution is something that would cause immediate concern to the arbitrageur, as would the danger of this in the future. For example, the proposed merger of C.I.T. Financial Corporation and Xerox never reached the altar due to the drag that C.I.T. was expected to cause on Xerox's future earnings.

FIGURING OF PARITIES

Hardly a day passes without the announcement of at least one or two new merger or exchange offers. As each particular deal is promulgated, an arbitrageur may or may not immediately decide to take a position. In any case, the arbitrageur must be able, with relative agility, to figure out what each package of securities is worth, for he or she is in the precarious position of having to commit the firm's capital to a high-risk situation. The total, or "work-out," value of a particular package is commonly referred to as the parity.

Packages of securities offered in all types of reorganizations are becoming increasingly difficult to calculate because of the use of warrants, debentures, sliding ratios, and so on. The moral of the story is that a deal, more often than not, is worth neither what the newspapers nor what the merger parties say it is worth. It is generally worth less. So investor beware!

DETERMINATION OF THE TIME ELEMENT

An accurate determination of how long it will take to consummate a particular arbitrage transaction is of the utmost importance to the arbitrageur, for it represents one of the key elements determining the potential return on invested capital. Determination of the probable period of time the funds will be tied up is by no means an easy task, for there are many variables involved in each of the requisite steps to complete a merger, any one of which may involve incalculable delays postponing the legal closing of the deal.

RETURN ON INVESTMENT

With the calculation of the expected dollar profit, plus an estimate of the amount of time that capital will be employed in the particular transaction, an arbitrageur can estimate the (annualized) return on investment.

THE RISKS

Prior to establishing a position in an arbitrage situation, the arbitrageur must carefully weigh the various potential risks involved. Any one of a number of elements can result in an enormous loss if the deal is not consummated, or may sharply reduce the return on investment if it is not completed according to schedule. The following are considered to be the normal risks involved during the course of merger negotiations.

Double Price Risk

Premiums ranging generally from 10 percent to even 50 percent—exceptionally even 100 percent—may be offered for acquisition targets. An arbitrageur, when taking a long position, is thereby assuming a great part of this premium in the price he or she pays. Should the deal be sabotaged for some reason, the downside price slide can be rather large. So one must carefully calculate the downside risk.[1] In addition, there is a price risk in the stock of the groom, which has been sold short. If there is a lack of liquidity in this stock there may be an equally large loss on covering the short sale. When a merger proposal is terminated, all arbitrageurs try to cover their short sales at the same time, causing an artificially higher price for the groom.[2] (If the short sales had artificially depressed the price of the groom during the period the groom was subject to arbitraging, one can assume that upon the short covering the groom will return whence it came, pari passu.) In any case, the arbitrage position is a double-edged sword if the merger breaks.

Alteration of the Terms

If the exchange ratio is changed after a position has been taken, the change is likely to alter the projected profit. For example, if there was an exchange of Y common for X common, and more Y common was subsequently offered for X, it would mean greater profit. However, if in place of Y common it was decided to give Y debentures plus Y warrants, then the arbitrageur would be short Y common, which would have to be covered, possibly eliminating the profit. Naturally, less Y common for X would also result in the arbitrageur being short Y common (or short X), with an accompanying reduction in projected profit.

A Sharp Increase in the Market Price of the Groom

This will often cause the groom to feel he is perhaps paying too much for the bride, and if he tries to renegotiate a cheaper price for her, she may decide not to accept the lower offer. In any case, a sharp run-up in the groom's price causes great discomfiture to the arbitrageur, who is forced to pay a greater premium for the bride—over her investment value—as the parity, which corresponds to the price of the groom, increases. If the arbitrageur has taken a full hedge position before this run-up, then the threat of a broken deal looms ever more ominous.

A Sharp Decrease in the Groom's Market Price

The reverse situation has the bride becoming disenchanted over the diminishing value (parity) of the offer, with an eventual attempt at renegotiation.

Competing Bids

It is a nice feeling to be long on a stock that is the subject of a bidding contest. However, when one has taken the full arbitrage position, long and short, the necessity to cover the short in the face of another's bid may prove disastrous.

Shareholder Dissent

Certain shareholders of the bride may feel they are selling out too cheaply, or those of the groom may feel that they are paying too much. These feelings may lead to what are termed "nuisance suits," usually resulting in delays in the timetable.

Shareholder dissent may present a real threat when, by state law, shareholders are accorded appraisal rights on their securities. Managements of both companies will normally have set a limit on the number of shareholders who can request appraisal and payment of cash for their shares in lieu of the securities of the groom. If the limit is substantially surpassed, there is a high probability of termination of the merger agreement. This sometimes stems from the fact that the tax-free status of the merger may be endangered by the payment of too much cash.

Substantiation of Financial Warranties

The financial warranties promulgated in the definitive agreement are subject to auditing reviews. One of the usual termination clauses stipulates that there will have been no material changes in the business or financial status of Company X between the date of the execution of the contract and the date of the legal closing. There is thus the need for the accountant's "cold comfort letter" to cover this interim period. A deterioration in earnings picture of the bride may sufficiently discomfort the groom so that negotiations are terminated.

Tax Problems

There is always a chance—albeit a small one—that the IRS will render an unfavorable ruling as to the tax-free status of the merger. In addition, there are often insider tax problems, which may not be obvious but which may nevertheless sufficiently dishearten an insider about the deal so that a vote is cast against it.

Governmental Intervention

If applicable, the strongest threat is that of the Department of Justice. When the latter decides to prevent a merger, it usually gets its way. The risk is especially great because, as standard practice, the Department of Justice must request a temporary injunction to prevent the legal closing; and unfortunately for arbitrageurs, it usually chooses to do so at the "eleventh hour." The granting of the injunction is the death knell for the deal, as both parties normally are unwilling to fight lengthy and expensive court battles. The arbitrageur is indifferent to the fact that a merger may be attacked after its legal consummation. In fact, the eventuality of a court decision against a completed merger may provide additional business in the form of a divestiture, which may then become a spin-off.

The Federal Trade Commission (FTC) is another intervenor that has become more aggressive by virtue of being authorized on January 4, 1975, to represent itself in court. In addition, FTC complaints often result in consent decrees, which essentially are out-of-court settlements.

Unusual Delays

There is always the chance that negotiations may become hopelessly bogged down, or that inexperienced officials may be handling the enormous quantities of paperwork involved, resulting in errors, legal tie-ups, and extended periods of SEC scrutiny.

Personalities

Personality clashes are always a possibility when two sets of officers, each accustomed to its own modus operandi, begin to realize that things may be done differently after the merger. Officers of the bride in particular have to be treated with just the right amount of respect, in order that they are not left with the feeling that they "had" to merge. Such respect is represented by proper jobs, appropriate titles, financial compensation, options, and so on.

AVERAGE EXPECTED RETURNS

Both a subjective and an objective element combine to formulate what to the arbitrageur is a satisfactory return, or an average expected or required return, in any given arbitrage situation.

The subjective element involves discounting the specific risks inherent in the deal. Those risks to which the arbitrageur ascribes the greatest importance are the price risk—both long and short—and the antitrust risk. The arbitrageur's discount for these two risks—and thus the required return—will be directly proportioned to his or her evaluation of the seriousness of said risks.

The objective element is the aggregate of the alternative risk arbitrage situations. Experience has shown that at a time when there is a great variety of situations in which to commit their risk capital, arbitrageurs are afforded the luxury of choosing among the available spreads, as there is less competition in the arbitrage community for a specific spread. Also, the amount of capital available to arbitrageurs as a group is fairly fixed in size over a given time span. Thus, when there are fewer attractive arbitrage deals, the same fixed capital is chasing the fewer spreads, often leading to a phenomenon referred to as "spread squeezing." This is an important factor to keep in mind, as popular brokerage clichés such as "the normal discount"—that is, spread, considered to be roughly 10 percent—will not be appropriate when referring to merger spreads in a risk arbitrage market characterized by a supply curve that has shifted upward.

Combining both the subjective and the objective elements, then, what is a normal or average required rate of return?

In establishing their requirements, arbitrageurs will calculate, for a quick point of reference, the return on investment rather than on capital. The latter normally is determined only after the transaction has been consummated. Assuming then that we have a typical merger arbitrage transaction involving a standard set of risks, and furthermore that there is an ample number of attractive spreads available, arbitrageurs will require and will aim to take the long and short positions at prices that will yield a return on investment of 40 percent per annum. In the final analysis, however, they usually are willing to settle for 30 percent, as they will inevitably encounter unexpected delays in either the consummation of the merger or in the physical exchange of securities. Therefore, as a rule of thumb one aims at 40 percent but settles for 30 percent per annum. This does not necessarily imply that arbitrageurs will forgo a return of 20 percent. The 40 percent rate is after all only an average, and if they can obtain a rate of return of 20 percent in a transaction in which they visualize very little risk, then they will take a position so long as their financing cost is exceeded. It is, in fact, safe to say that, when a spread is well below the normal rate of return for a "risk" arbitrage situation, that the arbitrageurs, by collectively taking their positions, view it closer to the "riskless" variety. On the other hand, a return of 60 percent per annum may not warrant a position if it is thought that the Justice Department is lurking around the corner with an injunction request in hand, or if a stock selling at $40 is worth only $10 per share without the deal.

TAKING A POSITION

Having (1) studied the merger, (2) calculated the profit potential, (3) weighed the possible risks, and (4) compared these calculations with other arbitrage situations, an arbitrageur may decide to take a position in the subject deal. Let us assume that X is merging into Y, and that each X will get one Y in the exchange of securities, with X selling at $35 and Y at $40, and neither company will pay dividends prior to consummation. It is estimated that the merger will close four months hence, yielding a potential gross return on investment of 42.9 percent per annum before taxes, at the current prices.

$$\frac{\$40 - \$35}{\$35} \times 3 \text{ (four-month periods per year)} = \frac{\$5}{\$35} \times 3 = 42.9\% \text{ per annum}$$

The size of the position which may now be taken will depend on (1) availability of capital, (2) degree of risk, (3) supply of X, (4) demand for Y, and (5) the availability of Y to be borrowed for delivery against the short sales of Y. With the Stock Exchange attentive to the "fail-to-deliver" problem, the ability to borrow stock has attained unparalleled importance, and often restricts the size of the position that may be taken when the Street supply is thin, or when Y has a small capitalization.

Selling Y short in merger arbitrage is an integral part of the position. In buying X at $35, one is also creating Y at $35, assuming that the merger is consummated. So, for all intents and purposes, one is long Y at $35 by virtue of the purchase of X. The actual price of Y—$40—is the price that must prevail at the closing of the transaction if the arbitrageur is to realize the projected profit. The only way to assure this profit is to sell Y short, thereby removing exposure to the vagaries of the marketplace. As a result of this short sale, the arbitrageur is strictly at risk of the deal, and not at the risk of the market.

A further reason for selling Y short is to realize potential tax benefits, which result in the creation of long-term capital gains, and also possibly short-term capital losses, which can offset short-term gains. This matter will be considered later in the chapter.

In actually taking a position in X long and Y short, one must carefully gauge the general market atmosphere as well as the liquidity of both X and Y. For example, if X is thin and there is a good demand for Y, it would be unwise to short Y prior to establishing the long position in X, particularly in a strong market. Similarly, in a weak market one would presumably have difficulty in shorting Y due to a need of an uptick, so that it probably would be better to short Y prior to going long X. As a general rule of thumb, it is better to short Y before buying X in a falling market, and better to buy X before shorting Y in a rising one. In a static market, the short sale should also precede the purchase.

Positioning small lots—300 to 500 shares at a time—is also a wiser course than attempting 3,000 to 5,000. The latter involves substantial market rise, unless the corresponding blocks of the "mate" are immediately available for positioning. To short 5,000 Y with only 300 X available at the desired spread would be sheer folly. And vice versa.

TURNING A POSITION

Let us again assume a share-for-share exchange of X for Y, with X at $30 and Y at $40. The merger is scheduled to be closed four months hence. An arbitrageur decides to take a position with this roughly 10-point spread, and let us say that one month later the spread has narrowed to four points. Having an unrealized profit of six points or 20 percent in one month, an arbitrageur will often turn the position; that is, close it out, rather than maintain it in order to make the remaining 13 percent, which would necessitate holding it for an additional three months.

A more delicate and precarious impetus for turning a position may develop when an arbitrageur has reason to believe that a deal will not be consummated, or that it may be delayed for a considerable period of time due to legal or antitrust complications. Arbitrageurs, if they wish to obtain the optimum prices for their long and short positions, must try to liquidate them unobtrusively. This often involves the use of "stooges," for were the arbitrage firm's name revealed on the floor of the Stock Exchange, it could well cause panic, price deterioration on the long position that is to be liquidated, and the disappearance of sellers in the case of the short position that must be covered. Bailing out of a listed stock simply involves utilizing a friendly "two-dollar broker" to execute the order. The latter is not obliged to give up the name of his or her sponsor until after the expiration of the day's trading, which is normally sufficient time to liquidate a major portion of the position. In a nonlisted stock, one must try to find a friendly over-the-counter firm that, for a commission, will try to liquidate a sponsor's position among the brethren of the arbitrage community. Every arbitrage firm has its established "stooge" to whom it can turn in such an emergency. This points out the very dangerous nature of risk arbitrage, for bad positions are often graciously turned over to one's competitors, who presumably are not aware of the problems in the deal until it is too late to do anything about it. Arbitrageurs cheerfully contend that this is all part of their role; that all is fair in love, war—and arbitrage.

CONSUMMATION

In the normal course of events, after shareholder approval has been obtained, the only remaining requirement for the legal closing to occur is the receipt of a favorable tax ruling from the Internal Revenue Service. Once this has been received, the New York Stock Exchange usually will declare a "short exempt ruling" on the security, which has previously been the object of short sales.[3] This indicates that the Stock Exchange itself is satisfied that all conditions for merger between X and Y have been met and that there is practically no chance that any further complications will arise to prevent the merger. This short exempt ruling allows those investors who are long X and who wish to dispose of the shares to do so either as X, or if they prefer, in the form of Y, even though in the strict legal sense X is not yet equal to Y. This ruling also permits the sale to be effected without the normally required uptick, and for private investors without a 50 percent "good faith" margin deposit. Those individual investors who henceforth buy X and simultaneously sell Y can hold both positions on a margin of only 10 percent of the long position. Thus, from the time the ruling is rendered, the simultaneous purchase of X and sale of Y is recognized by the Stock Exchange as a bona fide arbitrage situation. For a member firm of the Exchange, long and short positions taken henceforth can be held in a "special arbitrage account" with a zero charge to the firm's capital.[4] In addition, the long X and short Y positions in the investment accounts no longer require a 30 percent capital charge once the short exempt ruling is delivered.

The short exempt ruling is a key factor of which few investors are aware. For if they wish to sell their X, they would often fare far better if they sell it as Y, as the X can only be sold to the discount (from parity) bid of the arbitrageur. The interesting fact is that the discount is somewhat greater than the normal commission that would be charged plus the carrying costs to be incurred pending exchange of securities. In fact, arbitrageurs do a huge volume of business after the closing of a merger by bidding over-the-counter for a newly delisted stock of the "just married" bride. The arbitrageur, by purchasing the public's X and immediately selling it as Y, cashes in on the public's indolence or ignorance.

The short exempt ruling has the additional effect of causing sudden pressure to be brought to bear on Y, as all sales of Y by arbitrageurs no longer require the uptick. Thus, often just as a merger is completed, there is an appreciable price erosion in Y. This pressure is strictly technical and usually abates once all the floating X is taken out of circulation. This artificial pressure is something that predictably coincides with merger closings, and may provide excellent buying opportunities for the shrewd investor.

TAX STRATEGY

An important reason for selling Y short is to derive certain tax benefits. The short sale gives the arbitrageur some strategic options in the qualitative, that is, after-tax returns of not only the department but of the firm as well. This potential benefit arises from the fact that the shares of two companies—X and Y—planning to merge are, as a rule of thumb, considered to be not substantially identical for tax purposes until the shareholders actually vote favorably on the merger proposal. Thus, if X and Y are respectively bought and sold in separate investment accounts prior to shareholder approvals, they are considered to be not substantially identical.

Between the date of the shareholders' meeting and the day when the New York Stock Exchange will declare Y "short exempt" (which signifies that there is no longer any risk involved and that holders of X may, if they wish, sell X in the form of Y without the uptick and related margin requirements), there may exist a gray area as to whether or not securities are substantially identical. The Treasury Regulations say that this is to be judged on the basis of "the facts and circumstances in each case" and suggest as guidelines "the relative values, price changes and other circumstances." Even though shareholders have approved a merger, such approval does not necessarily render the securities substantially identical especially where there is still opposition to the merger by dissenting shareholders or government authority. Thus, if one wishes to continue building the position in X long and Y short, it should be done in a separate, or "number 2" investment account. Then, should the IRS take the position that X and Y were substantially identical during the latter period, it could be argued that the "number 2" account functioned as an "arbitrage account."

In the normal course of events, when there is little likelihood of further problems after shareholder approval has been obtained, so that X and Y are most assuredly substantially identical, any further positions should be placed in a "special arbitrage account" so as not to endanger the positions in the investment accounts of X and Y. Any gains or losses resulting from the special arbitrage accounts are naturally short-term. There exists the danger, however, that purchases in the special arbitrage account may contaminate short sales of Y in the investment account. This danger can be minimized by closing the positions in the special arbitrage accounts prior to closing those in the investment accounts. Also, care should be taken to leave no net short position in the arbitrage account at the close of any business day.

A long-term capital gain can be created in the X and Y investment accounts simply by establishing the requisite one-year holding period. When the merger is consummated, X is exchanged for securities of Y, so that the resulting positions in the two investment accounts are Y long and Y short. When the requisite holding period is attained, the arbitrageur is in the highly desirous position of having two alternatives. First, if Y is higher than $40 (recalling that we sold Y at that price)—let us say $45—then he or she can, on succeeding days, buy Y and sell Y until the Y long and Y short positions are completely closed out. In this manner, the Y long (formerly X) is sold for a long-term capital gain greater than the initial five-point spread. The covering of the Y short position results in the recognition of a short-term capital loss, which can be utilized to offset short-term capital gains of the arbitrage department and also for the firm. The net economic gain is still the initial five-point spread per share, but the character of the gain and loss is significantly different.

Second, if after the requisite holding period, Y is below $40, so that it would not be advantageous to reverse the positions as above (indeed, reversing would produce a long-term capital loss and a short-term capital gain), then the arbitrageur can record a long-term capital gain simply by pairing off the Y long and Y short positions with a journal entry.

The same general procedure as outlined above would be employed if, let us say, instead of an exchange of Y for X there would be a new issue of Y convertible preferred offered in exchange for X. In this case, the arbitrageur would, before the shareholders' meetings, go long X and short the amount of Y common represented by Y convertible preferred, so as to hedge the market risk in the new issue. After consummation and the exchange of securities, the accounts would show Y convertible preferred long and Y common short. The position is then held open for the requisite period, after which the arbitrageur simply converts and pairs off the positions or reverses them, depending on market price relationships.

The closing out of positions in the marketplace for tax purposes thus produces increased activity in the securities for the former groom. Many arbitrage firms may be doing this during approximately the same time span as their respective positions attain long-term maturity. Their aggregate interaction in such cases will lend additional liquidity to the marketplace, particularly in a taxable year in which there are large arbitrage short-term gains to offset.

NOTES

1. Reference to technical charts and knowledge of the probable size of the arbitrage community's positions are helpful indicators in determining the downside risk.

2. A clue to the magnitude of this potential danger may be found in the monthly "short interest" figures published by both the New York and the American Stock Exchanges.

3. New York Stock Exchange rules.

4. Ibid.

PART 5

Finishing Touches

29
Closing Services

Robert E. Shields
Partner, Drinker Biddle & Reath,
Philadelphia, Pennsylvania

The negotiations have been long and patience sometimes short. But, finally, the acquisition agreement is signed. Corks pop, bubbles flow, and off the parties go: the investment bankers to arrange another deal; the executives to explain the transaction to their key people; the managers to begin planning in earnest.

But some important tasks must be accomplished before the merger can close. The deal must be announced and reported to various agencies. The warranties in the merger agreement must be tested. Consents and approvals must be obtained. Shareholder meetings must be held. Various other conditions to closing the transaction must be satisfied.

REPORTING THE NEWS

Because of the possibility that another potential acquirer will appear once it becomes known that the target is for sale, the negotiated acquisition normally proceeds to the executed agreement stage in complete secrecy. In some cases, however, disclosure requirements of securities law may, depending on the circumstances, have prompted an earlier announcement that negotiations were under way. But when the definitive agreement has been signed, the time for a public announcement clearly has arrived.

Good business practice, stock exchange requirements, and risks of legal liability all prompt timely and controlled dissemination of the news of the impending acquisition. There are frequently good business reasons for delaying a public announcement until key managers, union officials, customers, suppliers, and others can be informed. But once the news gets beyond the small group involved in the negotiations, it spreads like wildfire. The largely uncontrollable factor is the public equities securities markets, which currently operates from 9:30 a.m. to at least 4:00 p.m. Eastern time. Securities exchanges do not look favorably upon requests for trading on the day the agreement is signed and before the market opens the next morning, when the press release will be issued.

A carefully worded press release will explain the rationale for the transaction to securities analysts and reduce the risk of interference from outside interests. Thus, drafting the announcement should not be left to the very last minute. Key executives, financial relations, and legal representatives of the buyer and the seller should turn to the press release when the definitive agreement approaches the final stages. Although the rationale for the transaction can be explained to some extent in the press release, securities laws constraints on premature proxy solicitation and "gun jumping" (if securities are to be issued in the acquisition) will prevent the parties from going too far.

DEALING WITH THE REGULATORS

The circumstances of each acquisition determine the reports that must be filed with various governmental agencies. Most sizable acquisitions must be reported to the Federal Trade Commission (FTC) and the Department of Justice under the Hart-Scott-Rodino Antitrust Improvements Act. The Hart-Scott-Rodino report requires extensive information on both the acquirer and the target. This report gives the FTC or the Justice Department—depending on which agency assumes primary responsibility for assessing the combination—an opportunity to review antitrust aspects. The acquisition may not proceed for 30 days following submission of the report unless the time period is accelerated by the FTC or the Justice Department. A request for accelerated treatments must be printed in the Federal Register, which forces public disclosure of the deal. Moreover, a new 30-day period begins if the information is not complete or the agency requests additional data.

An option on a significant block of stock of a public company obtained in connection with the definitive agreement normally will necessitate the acquirer promptly filing a Schedule 13D with the Securities and Exchange Commission (SEC). The target also will be required to file a report with the SEC if the grant of the option constitutes a change in control.

In regulated industries, governmental approvals of the acquisition may be required. Bank acquisitions normally must be approved by the Federal Reserve Board under the Bank Holding Company Act or the Change in Bank Control Act. Approval of the Comptroller of the Currency in the case of a national bank, or an appropriate state banking official in the case of a state-chartered bank, also is required. Following those approvals, the parties must wait for at least another 30 days for the transaction to be reviewed by the Justice Department under the Bank Merger Act. Acquisitions of other regulated businesses such as insurance companies will involve similar application and approval processes. If either part is an insurance holding company with significant operations in several states, it may be necessary to get approval from officials in each state. Also, if the buyer is not a U.S. person, the Exon-Florio Amendment to the 1988 Omnibus Trade and Competitiveness Act (adding a new section to the 1950 Defense Production Act) may make advisable a filing with the federal interexecutive department group called the Committee on Foreign Investment in the United States.

Planning is the key, particularly when regulatory approvals are required. Attention to the relevant regulatory requirements in the early stages of the transaction can pay handsome rewards. Background briefings of key regulators promptly after the transaction is announced may uncover concern about a relatively minor aspect of the deal. Armed with insight into the thinking of regulators, the parties may well be able to make relatively modest changes in the structure of the transaction and thereby garner prompt regulatory approval that will expedite consummation.

TESTING THE WARRANTIES

The typical acquisition agreement contains a number of representations and warranties whose functions are twofold. First, a material breach of a warranty by one party will give the other party a justification not to proceed with closing the deal. Second, a breach by the seller that the buyer discovers after the closing may give the buyer a right to financial recompense.

Between the signing of the agreement and the closing, the major focus is on the first function of the warranties, namely, whether there is a material undisclosed problem that causes the buyer to change its mind about the acquisition. Once the transaction is closed, realistically it cannot be undone. Thus, the last chance to avoid a terrible mistake may be the due diligence investigation between the signing and the closing. The usual emphasis is on the buyer's testing of the seller's warranties. When the seller's shareholders are receiving the acquirer's securities, testing of the buyer's warranties also can be important.

The extent of the investigation between signing and closing will depend on the amount of work done before the agreement is signed. If a privately held company is being acquired, the parties may have enjoyed the luxury of extensive investigation of the seller by the buyer before the agreement is signed. At the other extreme, the buyer may be a "white knight" brought in at the last moment to rescue the seller from an undesired takeover. The white knight's investigation may not begin until after the agreement is signed. Many transactions fall in between. What is important, however, is that the important information be verified prior to the closing.

Financial and Business Investigations.   The representations and warranties that a buyer usually exacts from the seller about its business can be divided into financial, business, and legal segments. Investigation of the financial areas may be limited to testing warranties concerning previously reported operating results and statements of financial condition, a review of the prior audit work papers, and discussions with present (and former) outside auditors. Even if the financial and business investigations have been substantially completed before the agreement is signed, the figures can be updated and the buyer can obtain a more comprehensive understanding of the seller's business between signing and closing.

Legal Investigations.   The appropriate legal investigation of the business will vary from transaction to transaction. In most cases, however, the investigation will begin with the organization of the corporation and its subsidiaries. Were the legal formalities observed when the corporations were organized? Was the stock properly issued? Were any preemptive rights honored in connection with using additional shares? Does the seller own all of the stock of each of its subsidiaries, and can it find the needed stock certificates? Investigation of these matters will include a review of the documents on file with the secretary of state in the various jurisdictions in which the target and its subsidiaries are incorporated, and an examination of their minute books and stock books. Review of the minute books may reveal references to other material matters that were not previously known to the buyer, thus necessitating further investigation.

The legal review also will cover material papers relating to pending litigation against the target company, and it will include review of any consent order or decrees by which prior litigation or governmental investigations were resolved. Agreements to adopt, or to refrain from, certain business practices that resolved prior litigation may have a disastrous impact if they restrict the acquiring company. The investigation of any pending or threatened litigation against the company being acquired will extend into a review of law compliance programs. If the target company's attitude toward regulatory matters, such as environmental OSHA requirements, is only to attempt to control fires when they flare, significant further investigation may be warranted. But if the target company has an active legal compliance program, the buyer may feel less need to conduct a detailed investigation.

The legal investigation should extend to the target company's various benefit plans. Failure to update benefit plans promptly so that they comply with the frequent changes in applicable laws may have a significant financial impact on the company and its employees.

The various instruments governing the indebtedness of the acquired company should be reviewed, particularly if the indebtedness is to be kept in place after the acquisition to determine whether consent of the lender will be necessary to close the transaction. Important contracts also must be reviewed to determine that the transaction will not adversely affect contractual relationships. (This review is in addition to, and not a substitute for, review of customer relationship issues.) In most cases, investigation of these subjects will be made before signing the agreement as a part of the process for deciding on the structure of the transaction.

Careful review must be given—particularly in acquisitions of privately owned companies—to relationships between the target company and interested managers or shareholders. Typical "boilerplate" warranties that there are no self-dealing transactions may have been given unthinkingly by the company being acquired. In a related area, it is extremely important for the acquirer to be certain that it is acquiring the totality of the business. If, for example, there is an important contract between the target and one of its shareholders that is terminable upon short notice, the situation will have to be resolved to the satisfaction of the acquiring company.

Depending on the circumstances, there are several other legal aspects that might be investigated, including title to properties, liens on real and personal property, the nature and extent of insurance coverage, and exposure to the burgeoning environmental laws, to name a few.

Finding Surprises. The testing of the warranties frequently uncovers minor surprises. Fringe benefit programs may not have been amended to reflect the latest legislative changes. The lien structure on the target's assets may not be precisely as warranted. What the seller perceived as labor peace may be seen by the acquirer as serious rumblings. In rare circumstances, the surprise is major. The result is either abandonment of the acquisition or renegotiation of the financial terms.

Another major task is satisfaction of various conditions that must occur before the closing can take place. Generally the conditions that must be satisfied are that:

- The warranties be correct when made and continue to be correct at the closing
- The target company has refrained from engaging in certain actions pending the closing
- Various other specified events have occurred as prescribed in the agreement, such as obtaining consents of lenders and others whose interests are affected

MONITORING THE COVENANTS

Many acquisitions involve a substantial delay between signing the agreement and closing. The principal reasons for the delay normally are the need for stockholder, and perhaps regulatory, approval. The acquiring company usually wants to preserve the status quo during this interim period. Accordingly, the acquisition agreement normally restrains the ability of the target company to make changes in its capitalization or business between the signing and the closing.

Frequently, the target company agrees to operate only in the ordinary course of business and in accordance with past practice. This commitment often is amplified by prohibitions against: issuing additional equity securities unless they are required by existing commitments; departures from current dividend policy; significant business or asset acquisitions or dispositions; charter amendments; changes in compensation or fringe benefits for key personnel; and significant capital expenditures or commitments. The company to be acquired frequently agrees to continue its current insurance coverage. Many agreements prohibit the target from creating additional liens on assets.

Managers are not accustomed to operating under those types of restrictions; accordingly, it is important that new procedures be implemented to ensure that the restrictions will be honored. Many of the prohibited transactions are so extraordinary that board approval would be required under normal circumstances. Restrictions on these activities easily can be implemented at the board level. Other restrictions—for example, a general prohibition against engaging in transactions outside the ordinary course of business—require implementation at lower levels in the organization. Because a prohibition on transactions not in the ordinary course of business can become a subjective issue, interpretation and explanation of the restrictions are necessary. Responsibility in instituting these control procedures falls on the official of the target company.

The restrictions normally are subject to the proviso that any of the otherwise prohibited transactions may be permitted with the consent of the acquiring company. Therefore, it is important to designate an appropriate executive in the acquiring company to monitor the target's operations and deal with requests for approvals of restricted transactions.

OBTAINING CONSENTS

Besides regulatory approval, many transactions also require consents of private third parties. To a large extent, the structure of the transaction will determine the number of third-party consents required. If the transaction involves a sale of assets and assumption of liabilities, it is possible that many third-party consents will be required. The need for such consents results largely from "boiler plate" contractual provisions preventing assignment without the consent of the other party to the contract.

Many real estate and equipment leases normally require the lessor's consent for assignment. Bank loan and other financing agreements require the lender's consent for substituting the acquiring company as the obligor on the indebtedness. Supply and sales contracts may require consents for assignments. Agreements for sales of assets frequently contain a provision that if a third-party consent is required but not obtained, the selling company will retain the asset and endeavor to make its benefits available to the acquiring firm. Nevertheless, the need for so many consents to assignment—and the possibility that important consents may not be given or that they may be given only if a price is paid—is a factor that causes many transactions to be structured as mergers rather than asset sales.

Merger transactions frequently require fewer consents than sales-of-assets transactions. Although many contracts require the consent of another party for assignment of the contract, most do not require such consents in changes of ownership. In a merger, the contract remains in place. All that has changed is ownership of the stock of one contracting party. Some contracts, however, are written to require consent of the other party even in the case of a change in ownership accomplished by merger. Thus, it is important that contracts be reviewed and that appropriate consents be obtained.

The structuring of the transaction will be determined only after a review of all material factors: tax ramifications, protection of the acquiring company against liabilities, regulatory approval, and the need for third-party consents are all important. The merger structure frequently is chosen, however, principally because it minimizes the need for third-party consents.

Although state laws usually require shareholders of both companies to approve a merger, approval by shareholders of the acquirer (if not required by controlling law or stock exchange policy) easily can be eliminated by the use of the subsidiary merger. In this structure, the acquiring company forms a subsidiary which is then merged with the company to be acquired. Approval of the shareholders of the target company still is required. But shareholder approval on the buyer's side will be sufficient if the parent corporation of the acquiring subsidiary delivers its endorsement. In any event, the target's "poison pill" or shareholder rights plan often must be amended, redeemed, or neutralized in some other fashion.

COMPLETING FINANCING ARRANGEMENTS

If the purchase price is payable entirely or partially in cash, the acquiring company may borrow the money. A loan commitment obtained when the agreement was signed must blossom into a formal loan agreement by closing. Necessary consents or approvals for the borrowing must be obtained, and preparations must be made for closing the loan transaction concurrently with the closing of the acquisition.

If the stock of the target company is selling at a substantial discount from the merger price, or if the acquiring company wishes to reduce the dilution that will result from issuing its securities in the merger, it is economically advantageous for the buyer to acquire target company stock in the open market. Care must be taken to give full consideration to the accounting, tax, and securities regulation aspects of such purchases. For example, pooling-of-interests accounting (which avoids the creation of nonamortizable goodwill in the transaction) may be adversely affected by open-market purchases of target company stock. The partially tax-free nature of a combined stock and cash acquisition may be destroyed if too much target company common stock is purchased in the open market. Depending on the timing of the purchases and the formula (if any) in the merger agreement for pricing the transaction, open-market purchases of the target company stock by the acquiring company may violate the SEC's Rule 10b-6. (That rule is designed to prevent issuers from supporting the price of their stock when a stock issuance is imminent.)

The target company may have outstanding publicly held preferred stock or debt securities. If the merger agreement contemplates that these securities will remain outstanding, no action is required. On the other hand, particularly if the securities are convertible into the target's common stock, the parties may agree that they be called for redemption. If so, appropriate arrangements must be made for giving the requisite advance notice of the call and paying the redemption price of any unconverted securities. If the conversion provisions in the securities provide that after a merger the convertible securities will be exchanged for acquiring company stock based on the merger ratio, a call may not be required. Financial covenants or change of control or other provisions in a loan agreement may require consent of the lenders in the target's sale. A simple written consent by lenders may suffice, but it may be necessary to make extensive revisions on the loan agreement. The documentation must be in place by the time of the closing.

THE PROXY STATEMENT

If the securities of the company being acquired are relatively widely held, it is almost always necessary to prepare a proxy statement describing the proposed acquisition. When the target company's stock is registered under the Securities Exchange Act, proxy materials must be filed with the SEC or, in the case of a bank, the appropriate banking regulator.

In an acquisition not requiring regulatory approval, the preparation of the proxy statement and the obtaining of shareholder approval are frequently the principal factors responsible for the delay between the signing of the agreement and the closing. If the parties wish to reduce the interim period, preparation of the proxy statement should commence at the earliest possible date.

The proxy statement normally must contain extensive information about the proposed acquisition transaction and about the company being acquired. If securities are being issued by the acquirer, the proxy statement also will contain a description of the securities and of the acquiring company. If both the acquiring and acquired company file annual and other periodic reports with the SEC, much of the proxy statement may consist of material already contained in the most recent annual reports, although it must be updated in some respects to the date of the proxy statement. The principal additional information will be the description of the proposed merger and its background and, in many cases, pro forma financial statements reflecting the acquisition.

Unless the securities being issued in the merger are exempt from registration under the Securities Act of 1933 (for example, because they are being issued by a bank or issued after a hearing on the fairness of the transaction by a state regulator), the acquiring company is required to file a registration statement registering the securities under the Securities Act. The proxy statement generally is the major part of any such registration statement.

Because preliminary proxy material for a merger is not publicly available if confidentiality is requested, it is customary to file the documents with the SEC in the form of preliminary proxy material and to obtain the SEC staff's initial comments. The document then is revised and filed as a publicly available registration statement under the Securities Act. If the SEC staff comments have been responded to adequately, the registration statement will be declared effective shortly after it is filed. The proxy statement, which comprises the bulk of the registration statement, then is mailed to the shareholders.

Approval by the acquirer's shareholders also may be required if mandated by state law or by the policies of the securities exchange on which the acquiring company's securities are listed. However, directors of the acquiring company may wish to obtain shareholder approval even though it is not legally necessary. When approval by both shareholder groups is sought, the custom is to prepare a joint proxy statement that will be used by both companies.

As noted earlier, if the acquiring company is issuing securities in connection with the acquisition, the proxy statement also must be filed with the SEC as a part of registration statement covering the securities to be issued. Normally, the issuance of securities by the acquiring company—particularly if it is not listed on a national securities exchange—will require filings with various regulators under state securities or "blue sky" laws. These filings must be closely coordinated to ensure that the proxy materials can be mailed to all shareholders promptly upon the effectiveness of the SEC registration statement.

ARRANGING THE
SHAREHOLDER MEETING

When the schedule for receiving SEC staff comments on the proxy material becomes clear, shareholder meeting and record dates can be finalized. Normally, the proxy statement will be mailed at least 30 days in advance of the meeting, to permit as many shareholders as possible to vote by returning their proxy cards.

Because of increasing institutionalization of the securities markets and the use of securities depositories in recent years, large percentages of the shares of many companies are held for customers of banks and brokers in nominee names. Although under state laws nominees are entitled to vote shares held in their names, members of national securities exchanges are prohibited by exchange rules from voting on merger transactions without instructions from the beneficial owners. Thus, it is necessary for corporations to send proxy statements to the brokerage firms and for those firms to redistribute the materials to the beneficial owners and solicit their instructions.

SMOOTHING THE EDGES

If the target company has a stock option plan, appropriate arrangements must be made to terminate the options or to convert them into options to purchase the acquiree's securities, based on the merger ratio. Many option plans permit such substitutions or allow directors of the target to terminate the options if they are not exercised by the merger date.

When the acquisition involves the issuance of securities that are to be listed on a securities exchange, appropriate listing applications must be filed by the acquirer. Normally, the listing application will consist essentially of the proxy statement for the merger. It is important, however, that the listing application be filed early to obtain exchange comments and allow sufficient time for formal exchange approval before closing.

If the parties wish a tax ruling from the Internal Revenue Service, it must be sought well in advance. As the time for the closing approaches, they should contact the IRS for a formal ruling before the closing date.

Trading in the stock of the company being acquired usually continues until the time of closing. It is important that the appropriate securities exchanges, or the National Association of Securities Dealers (NASD) in the case of over-the-counter securities, be notified of the contemplated timetable for closing the transaction, particularly as the time for closing approaches. The exchange or the NASD will arrange for the necessary termination of trading in the target company securities.

Whether securities or cash is being issued, the target's shareholders will be required to surrender their share certificates before receiving payment. A form of transmittal letter and accompanying instructions usually are mailed to shareholders of the acquired company immediately after closing. They must be prepared in advance and be ready for printing and mailing upon closing.

CLOSING ARRANGEMENTS

If no further regulatory approvals are required, the acquisition is accomplished by the delivery and filing of documents at a closing meeting held soon after the shareholder approvals. Often the closing is held on the same day as the shareholders' meeting. In many cases, all of the documents have been signed and packaged the day before the formal closing. This procedure is adopted to ensure that all goes smoothly at the closing and that it is over quickly.

The preclosing is the name given to the meeting—normally the day before closing—at which the closing documents are reviewed and signed, but not delivered. Typically, documents will have been agreed to by exchanges of drafts between representatives of the merger partners over an extended period before the preclosing.

Merger and Transfer Documents.   The closing documents will, of course, include the operative acquisition instruments. In the case of a merger, the key instrument is the articles or certificate of merger, which will be filed with the secretaries of state in the states where the merging companies are incorporated. Executed copies of the articles or certificates of merger frequently are signed at the preclosing and delivered to agents of the acquiring and acquired companies in the appropriate state capitals. They are filed upon receipt of telephone instructions after the closing has been completed.

In a sale-of-assets transaction, the operative documents are the instruments under which the assets are transferred and the liabilities are assumed. Generally, these instruments include a bill of sale, an assumption-of-liabilities agreement, and various collateral documents assigning other assets not included within the bill of sale. Such collateral documents could include deeds of real estate; assignments of leases; assignments of patents, trademarks, and copyrights; assignments of titles to motor vehicles; assignments of unemployment compensation and similar accounts; and transfers of deposits from the target's bank account to the buyer's.

Counsel's Opinions.   Formal written legal opinions of counsel for both companies always are among the collateral documents. Normally, the contents of the opinions are specified in the acquisition agreement. Often the agreement calls for opinions from attorneys in several geographic areas on questions of local law. Timely delivery of these opinions is important to a smooth closing.

Comfort Letters.   Many acquisition agreements call for the delivery of so-called comfort letters by the independent accountants for the company being acquired. Comfort letters usually state in substance that the accountants, based on a recent review that does not rise to the level of a formal audit:

- Have no reason to believe that the financial statements of the acquired company are not presented in accordance with generally accepted accounting principles consistently applied
- Have no reason to believe that specified financial or statistical information concerning the acquired company in the proxy statement is not in accordance with the company's books and records
- Have no reason to believe that there has been a decline in the earnings of the target (compared with the corresponding period in the prior year) or a decline in specified balance sheet items from those shown in the proxy statement

If securities of the acquiring company are being issued, the acquisition agreement normally will provide for the issuance of a similar comfort letter by its independent accountants.

Collateral Documents. Other collateral documents typically include certificates of:

- Appropriate state officials, as to the good standing of the acquired company and its subsidiaries in their states of incorporation and states in which they do business
- Corporate secretaries, as to the adoption of resolutions by their directors and shareholders approving the deal
- Principal officers, that the representations and warranties continue to be true and correct and that all covenants have been complied with
- Corporate secretaries, concerning the incumbency, signatures, and authority of the officers executing the operative and collateral documents

The closing documents also may include escrow agreements, employment contracts, noncompete agreements, resignations of directors and officers, and, in asset sales, an amendment of the seller's certificate of incorporation to change its name.

When securities are involved, individuals who may be deemed to be controlling persons of the target usually are required to deliver letters acknowledging that resale of the securities is subject to the limitations imposed by Rule 145 under the Securities Act of 1933—principally that stock sales not exceed approximately one percent of the total stock outstanding in any three-month period. If pooling-of-interest accounting is involved, the letters also contain a barrier (required by SEC interpretation of the accounting rules) to resale of the securities until publication of an interim earnings statement of the acquiring company that includes at least one month's operating results of the acquired company.

AT THE FINISH LINE

If all goes well at the preclosing, the documents are executed and packaged. This permits the closing to consist of simply a handshake and acknowledgment by both sides that the deal is done. In securities transactions, even arrangements for the issuance of the securities will be made at the preclosing. If the purchase price is payable in cash, however, the cash will not be delivered (typically by wire transfer) until the day of closing. Unfortunately, wire transfers of funds often do not arrive as rapidly as desired. Corporate treasurers should plan ahead for and then monitor the transfer process to avoid situations in which frustrated senior executives and professionals sit at a conference table awaiting confirmation of the receipt of wired funds.

With good planning and hard work, all necessary matters will be accomplished by the time of preclosing. All of the documents have been signed and packaged. The next morning the shareholders meet and approve the acquisition. Blessedly, the funds arrive on time. The parties shake hands. The deal is closed. Corks pop, bubbles flow, and off they go.

30
Forms and Paperwork

Alan H. Molod

Partner, Wolf, Block, Schorr & Solis-Cohen,
Philadelphia, Pennsylvania

When negotiations on a proposed acquisition reach the point of agreement, the lawyer faces an elaborate process of document drafting to reflect the terms of the transaction. Whether the acquisition takes the form of a merger, stock purchase, asset purchase, or some complex combination or variation, the fundamental document is the acquisition agreement itself, setting forth the terms and conditions of the agreement between the parties. Sometimes it is preceded by a brief and often rather general document known as a letter of intent, which describes the basic intention of the parties to accomplish an acquisition. The acquisition agreement often is accompanied or followed by a variety of documents required by federal and state laws regulating acquisitions, as well as a variety of documents pertaining to the acquisition agreement itself.

THE LETTER OF INTENT

The use of a letter of intent in an acquisition is optional. The typical letter of intent expresses the intention of the parties to accomplish the transaction. It states the agreed-upon or approximate purchase price, the nature of the consideration to be paid (cash, property, debt securities, or equity securities), employment arrangements, noncompetition covenants, the obligation of the potential buyer to hold in confidence certain matters learned during its investigation, and the various conditions to consummation of the transaction. Usually, the letter of intent will state that it is not a binding document. Typical language may state, "This letter is a letter of intent only and is not binding upon the parties. A purchase and sale of the business shall become binding only upon the execution and delivery by the parties of a formal acquisition agreement satisfactory in content and form to the parties." A general letter of intent might merely acknowledge the intent to enter into an acquisition transaction and state that the precise price, structure, and mode of payment are among the matters to be agreed to, after the buyer's further investigation of the business to be purchased.

Conversely, a letter of intent can be quite specific as to price, payment terms, and other important matters. A highly detailed letter may provide that the only condition to the transaction's becoming binding is the preparation of formal documents setting forth the terms in the letter of intent. These documents would contain the warranties, representations, and agreements customarily contained in such acquisition agreements. Indeed, a letter of intent may go as far as to provide that the transaction is binding, committing both parties to proceed in good faith (often with a specific timetable) to create and execute formal acquisition documents containing customary representations, warranties, and agreements, and committing the seller not to negotiate with any other parties for the sale of the business. Letters of intent are often binding in certain limited respects only, such as commitments to maintain certain matters in confidence, to consult before issuing press releases, to refrain from negotiating with others, and so on.

Why a Letter of Intent Is Needed

Why have a letter of intent? For the party most anxious to have the transaction consummated, the letter of intent creates a certain moral obligation that many business people will respect. It also provides a sound basis for setting fundamental terms, thus acting to minimize friction and disagreement about such terms during negotiation of the formal acquisition documents. For the party that is least anxious for the transaction and is being "courted" by the other side, the letter offers an opportunity to gain concessions in writing that might be harder to get when the finer details are being worked out. The letter of intent also is a signal that an appropriate point has been reached for disclosing an agreement in principle to people beyond the direct negotiators. If a publicly held company is involved, the signing of the letter generally permits announcement of the news to the public to avoid problems of insider trading. Timing is an important matter in a public disclosure. Premature announcement of a proposed acquisition, especially if the transaction falls through, might be considered manipulative of a company's securities. But undue delay can result in improper insider trading and rumor-based trading of the securities. Thus, a written letter of intent is a convenient and appropriate device for triggering a public announcement. Even companies without publicly traded securities must be concerned with the impact on business of rumors that reach its employees, customers, suppliers, financing sources, and others.

However, if formal acquisition agreements can be prepared and entered into promptly after the agreement in principle, it often is desirable to forgo a letter of intent. Transactions still can be abandoned following execution of a letter of intent, and a deal that is aborted after public disclosure can be embarrassing and even harmful to one or both parties. Such embarrassment usually can be avoided if the parties make their announcement after entering into a formal acquisition agreement, as the likelihood that the transaction will be consummated is substantially higher than at the letter-of-intent stage. From a buyer's standpoint, although a public announcement creates pressure on a seller to consummate, it also announces to the world the availability of the seller and thus can trigger competitive offers.

THE ACQUISITION AGREEMENT

The acquisition agreement, to reiterate, is the basic document with respect to an acquisition. Generally, closing takes place days or months after execution of the acquisition agreement. This document spells out all of the conditions that must be met before a closing can take place, although some acquisitions close simultaneously with the signing of the agreement.

Acquisition agreements customarily are drafted by counsel for the buyer. From a seller's standpoint, an acquisition agreement can be very simple, ideally a one-page bill of sale conveying the assets or corporate shares on an "as is" basis in return for a bank check representing the entire purchase price. The buyer, on the other hand, is not fully familiar with what it will receive in the form of assets, business relationships, personnel capabilities, and other facets of the acquired business. Consequently, when drafted by counsel for the buyer, an acquisition agreement often is quite extensive. The largest part of the agreement deals with various representations and warranties of the seller about the nature and condition of the business and assets being sold. The counsel doing the first draft of an acquisition agreement or any collateral document (such as an employment contract, lease of real estate not being acquired, etc.) has a strong psychological advantage over opposing counsel. Many changes that the opposing counsel might wish to make, and they often are numerous, might be dismissed by the drafting attorney as nitpicking even when they are justified. Thus, the side that is not doing the actual drafting may have to overcome considerable resistance in trying to insert legitimate terms favorable to its position.

Contents of the Agreement

The acquisition agreement generally contains:

- A statement of the purpose of the transaction
- A list of definitions of terms in the agreement
- A description of the assets or shares to be sold and the selling price
- Representations, warranties, and agreements of both the buyer and the seller
- Provisions on the conduct of the target business between the agreement and closing dates
- Conditions precedent to the obligation of each party to close

- Identification of the time and place of closing, along with an itemization of the documents and other material to be delivered by the parties at closing
- An indemnification provision often specifying procedures for resolving disputes, particularly breaches of seller's representations and warranties
- Covenants restricting postacquisition competition by the sellers or controlling stockholders of a corporate seller
- Miscellaneous matters such as escrow provisions, provision for payment of brokerage commissions, and conventional "boiler-plate" provisions dealing with choice of law, notices, and other matters

Representations and Warranties

In negotiating the terms of an acquisition agreement, the buyer must be concerned with the nature of the seller's representations and warranties. They generally are very broad and comprehensive. Warranties with respect to environmental matters have become increasingly important in recent years. Even a seller that is very familiar with its own business inadvertently can overlook certain conditions and circumstances that actually exist but, on the basis of the warranties, are claimed to be nonexistent. If disclosed at the time of the signing, many of these matters might be accepted by the buyer without any effect on the purchase price. But if they are discovered after closing, they can constitute a breach of warranty and lead the buyer to demand a reduction in the price. Often, the seller may not be aware of any problems, such as a claim that was asserted only after the business changed hands. But the seller still is at risk if its representations and warranties are not limited strictly to circumstances within its knowledge. In an asset acquisition, the buyer may want the parties to comply with bulk sales laws, if applicable. More often than not, there is no such compliance and the seller indemnifies the buyer against any liability by reason of noncompliance.

Two matters almost always are subject to negotiation in the area of the seller's representations and warranties. They concern whether various representations are limited to the "knowledge of the seller" and whether the representations are limited to those that are "material." The honest seller that discloses everything it knows, except perhaps nonmaterial matters, wants to have no postclosing liability. Moreover, a seller can seek to minimize postclosing liability by negotiating a damages "basket" arrangement, under which the buyer agrees to absorb a certain amount of damages from breach of warranty before asserting claims against the seller. But, typically, a buyer will want to have the purchase price reduced if the business is not exactly as represented, regardless of whether the seller knew of any problems or whether such problems are material.

A buyer's draft acquisition agreement usually provides that all representations and warranties of the seller must be true at closing, or the buyer is not obligated to close. Taken literally, such an instrument can be little more than a buyer's option to purchase the business. For example, a multimillion-dollar acquisition may contain a seller's representation that the business being sold is not a defendant in any litigation. If, on the morning scheduled for closing, a $1,000 nuisance suit is instituted, the acquisition agreement, if read literally, can permit the buyer to avoid closing.

Sophisticated sellers therefore negotiate for materiality qualifications, for variations from the warranties and representations because of events that occur in the ordinary course of business, and, often, for a provision that closing must take place even in the case of certain material breaches, with a part of the price to be set aside pending resolution of the amount of damage created by such breaches.

The Disclosure Schedule

Practitioners often abandon conventional representations and warranties in favor of a separate disclosure schedule that is warranted by the seller for accuracy. Rather than build 20 to 30 pages of warranties and representations into the acquisition agreement and attach 15 to 20 supporting exhibits, the negotiators will settle on a warranty that the disclosure schedule initialed by the parties is true and correct. This disclosure schedule often is many pages longer than the acquisition agreement itself. It sets forth all of the representations and warranties desired by the buyer of the seller, and often provides for attachment of material documents such as leases, major contracts, and so on.

There are advantages to using a disclosure schedule. If the parties wish to move quickly, the purchaser's counsel can generate a discussion draft acquisition agreement much more promptly if the representations and warranties are omitted (although a first draft of an acquisition agreement can, of course, make provision for subsequent insertion of representations and warranties). And when public filing of an acquisition agreement is required, the voluminous materials that can be relegated to a disclosure schedule often can be excluded from the filing. This generally is desirable not only because it simplifies matters, but because the disclosure schedule has a great deal of information abut the business being sold, and it often is not desirable to make all of that information public knowledge. Such a disclosure schedule might, for example, contain information about the status of certain litigation matters that the company would not like the other parties to the litigation to see.

Breach of Warranties

In most acquisition transactions the representations and warranties of the seller survive closing and, if breaches occur, give rise to a claim by the buyer for damages. Thus, a mechanism for the establishment of damages often is provided in the acquisition agreement. The buyer generally is required to give prompt notice to the seller of circumstances or third-party claims that might give rise to a claim against the seller. The seller often negotiates for the right to participate with its own counsel in the defense of any claims by third parties. Additionally, the seller frequently negotiates a damages "basket" to eliminate the nuisance of minor claims and seeks a cutoff date after which the buyer may not assert additional claims. The typical deadline is fixed at a point before the statute of limitations on the seller's liability expires. Often, there is a provision for arbitration of disputes.

The measure of damages for breach of warranty frequently is subject to difficult negotiation. If a buyer has calculated its purchase price as a multiple of the seller's earnings, a breach of warranty that can have a permanent, or even short-term, effect on earnings should reduce the purchase price by the same multiple, although as a practical matter sellers virtually never agree to such a formula. In situations where impact on earnings is not the issue, a breach in the nature of an undisclosed liability generally is accounted for in damages on a dollar-for-dollar basis. However, sellers often negotiate for an aftertax calculation of damages, as a breach can result in a deductible expense.

DEBT AND EQUITY INSTRUMENTS

The purchase price in an acquisition transaction often consists of debt and/or equity securities in addition to, or in lieu of, cash. In the case of equity securities that are not the fundamental common shares of the acquiring company, such as preferred stock, creation of the new security by amending the buyer's certificate of incorporation often involves a very elaborate and detailed description of the security being created. This description covers voting rights, dividends, redemption and liquidation features, call provisions, convertibility features, and complex antidilution provisions, among other characteristics.

When debt instruments are used, they often have many of the same complex features as equity securities, particularly if debenture holders are to have any voting rights, if the debenture is to be callable, or if it has any convertibility features or income rights other than a flat interest rate. In addition, the creation of a series of debentures often is accompanied by an indenture of trust, which contains a variety of provisions designed to protect the debenture holders.

SECURITIES AND EXCHANGE COMMISSION FILINGS

When the acquiring company is issuing securities, their issuance constitutes a "sale" under the Securities Act of 1933. A registration statement must be filed with the Securities and Exchange Commission (SEC) unless an exemption, typically the "private placement" or intrastate offering exemption, is available. The registration statement is designed to provide the shareholders of the target company with sufficient information about the acquiring company to make an informed judgment on the proposed transaction. Often it is a lengthy and elaborate document, although in certain instances much of the information can be incorporated by reference to previously filed documents.

If the target company has securities that are registered under the Securities Exchange Act of 1934, it must use a proxy statement or information statement that complies with the SEC's Regulation 14A governing the shareholders' meeting called to approve the acquisition. An exception is when the acquisition is being accomplished by an exchange of securities directly with the target's shareholders. If a target company proxy statement is used, a Form S4 registration statement, essentially a wraparound of the Exchange Act proxy statement, generally is used.

The principal exemption from registration, the private placement exemption, is available when the number and nature of the target company's shareholders render a registration statement unnecessary. To obtain a private placement exemption, counsel for the acquirer must prepare all documents necessary to establish it. The exemption can be requested under the self-implementing provisions of the 1933 statute or under one of the "safe harbors" of the SEC's Regulation D, which offers greater certainty of getting the exemption and requires modest filings with the agency. The intrastate exemption is available when the acquirer is incorporated in, and does its principal business in, the state in which all of the target's shareholders reside.

STATE SECURITIES
LAWS FILINGS

When an acquisition transaction involves the "sale" of the acquiring company's securities, the buyer must comply with state securities laws ("blue sky" laws) in all states where its securities are being offered (namely, each state where the target company's shareholders reside). Although registration requirements are generally similar from state to state, each state statute has its own peculiarities. If a registration statement is being filed for the securities under the Securities Act of 1933, then in almost all states the securities can be registered by coordination, essentially by filing with the appropriate state agency a copy of the registration statement filed with the SEC. When a state does not allow coordination, the securities must be registered by qualification. This is a more complex process that is similar to registering under the federal Securities Act. Most states offer exemptions from registration for securities already listed on a national securities exchange or its equivalent. Exemptions frequently are allowed for limited offerings, such as offers to no more than 25 nonexcluded persons (generally financial institutions and other institutional buyers can be excluded in counting the number of offerees) in the state during any period of 12 consecutive months. But even offerings exempt from registration often require some type of filing with the state regulatory agency, and such a filing can be lengthy and complicated.

THE HART-SCOTT-
RODINO ACT

The Hart-Scott-Rodino (HSR) Antitrust Improvements Act requires the parties to certain acquisition transactions to provide the Federal Trade Commission and the Antitrust Division of the Department of Justice with information about the businesses of the companies involved and the proposed deal. The law stays the consummation of covered acquisition transactions for at least 30 days. The purpose of this legislation is to help the government enforce antitrust laws relating to acquisitions, particularly Section 7 of the Clayton Act, by giving regulators time to evaluate a proposed acquisition and to determine if it should be challenged. The law is extremely complicated, and the filing is complex. In very general terms, an HSR filing is required when:

- The seller has annual sales or assets of at least $10 million and the buyer has sales or assets of at least $100 million, or vice versa
- After the acquisition the buyer holds 15 percent of the outstanding securities or assets of the seller or the buyer's interest in the seller's securities or assets is valued at $15 million or more

RULING REQUEST TO THE INTERNAL REVENUE SERVICE

A frequent condition to consummating an acquisition is the securing of a favorable ruling from the Internal Revenue Service (IRS) on tax treatment of the deal. The most typical request is that the IRS rule the transaction a tax-free reorganization. The ruling request is an extensive document that describes the acquisition in detail, formally asks for the ruling, and sets forth the applicant's supporting legal grounds. The service's response often takes several months.

ERISA FILINGS

The Employee Retirement Income Security Act of 1974 (ERISA) was enacted primarily to protect the interest of employee benefit plan participants and their beneficiaries. The law creates a number of "reportable events" related to acquisitions and requires the filing of reports with the Pension Benefit Guaranty Corp. in such cases. Reports must be filed when the acquisition changes the plan employer, leads to a complete or partial termination of a plan, or results in the merger of two or more plans. In certain circumstances, filings also must be made with the Internal Revenue Service.

LEGAL OPINIONS

Legal opinions, which are standard features of acquisition agreements, typically are rendered by counsel for both the buyer and seller on behalf of their respective clients. Besides stating that the parties are duly incorporated and in good standing, they affirm that the acquisition agreement:

- Has been duly authorized, executed, and delivered;
- Constitutes a binding obligation on the parties; and

- Does not violate the corporate client's charter, by-laws, or agreements of which the counsel has knowledge.

In addition to these typical opinions, there are a host of other matters on which the seller's counsel is asked to opine. These include the existence and status of litigation matters, the quality of title to securities being delivered, the quality of title to real and personal property of the business being sold, the validity and enforceability of various agreements to which the selling business is party, and qualification to do business in various jurisdictions.

Buyers often request from the seller's counsel extensive and unqualified opinions that may parallel many of the seller's representations and warranties. From the buyer's standpoint, such opinions provide two principal benefits. First, if the seller's counsel is responsible, it will not render opinions without being satisfied that such opinions are correct. Thus, the buyer is provided with the results of an independent investigation, and confirmation of the seller's representations and warranties. Second, responsible counsel provides an available deep pocket (from its own resources and/or malpractice insurance) in the event a representation of warranty that also is covered in the legal opinion is false.

Many opinions requested of the seller's counsel involve questions of fact or a mixture of fact and law, and are not strictly legal opinions (i.e., an opinion that the seller is not in default under any material contracts, or an opinion that the seller is not a defendant in any material litigation). Therefore, in its opinion the seller's counsel must take care to state the extent of the investigations on which the opinion is based, and the extent to which the factual portion of the opinion is limited to the counsel's knowledge.

MISCELLANEOUS REGULATORY FILINGS

When an acquisition takes the form of a statutory merger, documents (generally the plan or agreement of merger) must be filed in each state in which a corporate party to the transaction is incorporated. The merger documents must comply in form and content with the requirements of the business corporation law of each state in which they are filed. In many states the merger documents to be filed include state tax clearances, which can be time-consuming to obtain. When a corporation will, as a result of merger or acquisition, do business in a state where it had not previously operated, the company usually must obtain a certificate of authority to do business in the newly entered state before the effective date of the acquisition. When an acquisition is in a regulated business such as banking, transportation, or communications, filing with regulatory agencies such as the Federal Reserve Board, Interstate Commerce Commission, or Federal Communications Commission often is required.

In a recent trend, several states, notably New Jersey, require their environmental authorities to be notified of a company's change in ownership and to conduct environmental audits when those events occur.

31

Effective Due Diligence

H. Richard Grafer
Partner, Arthur Andersen & Co.,
New York, New York

P. Michael Baldasaro
Partner, Arthur Andersen & Co.,
New York, New York

Many acquirers operate under the theory that once the handshake has taken place, the deal is done. On the contrary, the work has just begun. It's time to determine whether the deal is as good as it looks on the surface. This requires further investigation, "due diligence" review, and verification of the seller's representations. A canny buyer should be conducting this "purchase investigation" even before the handshake.

Although a thorough investigation sounds like motherhood, it's amazing how often this basic principle is violated and buyers risk severe financial losses by proceeding on the basis of inadequate information and half-truths. When they are performed, purchase investigations frequently are handled ineffectively and don't obtain enough of the right information to evaluate the target and make a sound decision. This may stem from poor communication, misunderstandings, lack of careful planning, failure to fix responsibilities and coordinate the inquiry, and, perhaps most important, because the investigation often focuses on the quantity rather than quality of the information. For example, with respect to marketing informa-

341

tion, an acquirer should focus on how the target is different from others in the marketplace and whether its competitive strategy is working, not on how it resembles competitors. With respect to financial information, the acquirer should probe major exposure areas, trends, and unusual financial characteristics rather than every item in the financial statements.

NATURE AND SCOPE OF THE INVESTIGATION

A purchase investigation may be performed by company personnel, with or without help of outside consultants (e.g., accountants, investment bankers, lawyers, special industry consultants, actuaries, appraisers). The decision depends on the experience and availability of in-house personnel. We recommend that management play a major role in the investigation, because it will learn first-hand information that is important both to the decision to proceed with the deal and to successful operation of the target after the acquisition. Management, in fact, should be the prime mover, setting the scope and taking the lead. By delegating the entire investigation to subordinates or consultants, management frequently overlooks a lot of hard information and misses the opportunity to get a "feel" for the target management and other qualitative concerns that are critical in the purchase decision.

The scope of an investigation may range from a minimum effort (reviewing available financial information, visiting the target's facilities, and talking to selling management) to a maximum effort that involves a comprehensive investigation and audit. Depth depends on the size and relative significance of the acquisition candidate, price, availability of audited financial information, degree of inherent risk, time allowed, and so on. In the case of an unfriendly tender offer, the ability to analyze internal information on the target company may be limited. Consequently, the acquirer and its professional advisers may not be able to do much more than gather, compile, and analyze available public information. But if the seller is a private company, the need for a full-scale investigation is much greater. Divestitures also require intense buyer scrutiny.

Frequently, it is advisable to perform more than one type of investigation on a candidate. A preliminary investigation may be conducted before the handshake or the signing of a letter of intent or preliminary agreement. A complete or partial purchase audit would follow to verify the candidate's representations and help establish a price before final agreement is executed.

The Businessman's Review

The businessman's review is a comprehensive review and analysis, usually without independent verification, of a target company's financial and accounting records and related information. The initial stage comes after preliminary interest is expressed, when the buyer needs to obtain additional information regarding the seller's operations to reach the handshake stage. It is designed to provide a broad understanding of all aspects of the company's business, including industry information; marketing, manufacturing, and distribution methods; financial reporting systems and controls; and industrial relations; as well as in-depth comprehension of the target's financial statements, accounting data, and tax position. At this stage, questions should be raised about research and development programs, regulatory reporting requirements, international factors, and legal matters.

Management is advised to prepare a checklist of questions it wants to raise with the target during a preliminary review so that it gets the information it needs. Because this stage of the review usually does not involve verification procedures or detailed analysis of accounts, it easily can be performed by the buyer itself in cooperation with the target's personnel.

The second stage of the businessman's review typically begins after the handshake. It is a more detailed review of tax, financial, and accounting records with or without verification, and often is performed with the help of the acquirer's independent accountants. Usually, the accounting and tax principles and practices of the target are reviewed in depth, with special emphasis placed on whether they pose any problems to the specific transaction. It is important that the buyer and its accountants agree on the scope of this review and that the acquirer understands its objectives and limitations.

Purchase Audit and Other Verification Procedures

Independent verification or audit of the seller's financial statements and representations made by its management may be required, depending on the degree of assurance the buyer wants, the seller's past audit history, and the time permitted for premerger investigation. Verification procedures may involve a full-blown purchase audit or specially designed auditing procedures applied to specific accounts or exposure areas. For example, inventory is such a significant item to manufacturing and distribution enterprises that accountants frequently are asked to observe and test the physical inventories, audit their valuation, and determine any excess and obsolete inventory and valuation practices.

Verification procedures often disclose problems not previously known, and are especially valuable in the current environment when integrity is not always considered a virtue. Although management frequently shuns the cost of an audit, the expense can buy an additional level of assurance that is hard to come by any other way.

When the target has a good audit history (i.e., a reputable accounting firm has examined the historical financial statements and prepared the tax returns), comprehensive verification procedures may not be necessary except in areas not normally covered by the annual audit and not previously verified. Quality of the target's products, its reputation with customers, and similar nonfinancial areas may be appropriate subjects for verification. However, as a minimum, workpapers of the target's auditors should be reviewed in detail to identify exposure areas, problems, and issues not fully disclosed in the financial statements.

Note that the businessman's review and purchase audit primarily are concerned with financial and accounting matters. Obviously, the buyer should investigate operating matters just as thoroughly. If the buyer does not have the in-house capability to do this, outside consultants should be retained to evaluate marketing, manufacturing, technology, competitive position, product capability, and so on.

AREAS OF INVESTIGATION

The businessman's review, with or without verification, should focus on a variety of matters.

Company Background and History

The general nature of the business, principal locations and facilities, history, and similar information should be collected in the early phase of this investigation. In addition, information should be obtained on the management, directors, and outside advisers. Whenever possible, information on the company's recent developments, plans for the future, and major problems—including lawsuits, government restrictions, environmental considerations, and sensitive transactions—should be covered. This information offers initial understanding of the prospective acquisition and identifies areas for further investigation.

Industry Information

When the target operates in an industry that is unfamiliar to the buyer, a detailed industry review, often with help from expert consultants, is prudent. It should precede the investigation of a specific candidate and include:

- Competition and competitive strategies, both within the industry and from other industries
- Industry growth rates in sales and profits (past and projected) and external factors affecting industry growth and profitability
- Mergers and acquisitions in the industry, to determine if a business combination is crucial for survival or growth in the industry
- Government regulations, decrees, and trends
- Patents, trademarks, copyrights, and so on, and their importance to competitors in the industry
- Essential elements of success and barriers to entry

Financial and Accounting Information

It is useful to compare financial ratios by major business segments for a period of years to determine important trends. These ratios usually include returns on assets and stockholders' investment, gross profits, profit margins, fixed charge coverage, current ratios, net quick ratios, and debt/equity ratios. Information concerning the impact of inflation or recession on operations, the company's ability to operate in the environment, current value and replacement cost data, and future capital requirements also should be obtained.

The buyer's sources can be balance sheets of prior fiscal years, statements of income, statements of changes in financial position, budgets, and forecasts for the future. In addition, it is important to understand any differences between buyer and seller in accounting principles and practices. Occasionally, such differences disclose questionable accounting practices.

A review of a manufacturer of electronic parts that was up for sale disclosed that its returned goods were accounted for differently than the buyer's returned goods. Further investigation determined that the seller's inventories were substantially overvalued. The prospective buyer called off the deal.

An investigation of a dealer in fertilizers revealed that, in accordance with industry practice, a dealer's purchase is binding, but customers can back out because there is no legal requirement that they fulfill their side of the transaction. Because fertilizer prices were declining rapidly at the time of the proposed acquisition, this was important to the buyer because of the likelihood that fertilizer customers would refuse to take delivery. Because these "open" transactions should have been valued at current market values, instead of the higher contract prices, an inherent loss existed, and the deal was aborted.

Taxes

A review of the target's tax status serves a dual purpose. It satisfies the buyer that the tax liabilities of the target, as reflected in the purchase price, are properly stated on the target's books. It also focuses on the ability of the buyer to monetize a portion of the purchase price through proper tax planning strategies and tax attributes of the target.

The tax review essentially asks: "Has the target paid all of its tax liabilities on a current basis, and has a reasonable reserve been accrued for known and anticipated adjustments likely to arise on in-progress and future audits by various taxing authorities?" Generally this involves a review and analysis of the tax returns filed for a minimum of three prior years. Special emphasis should be placed on the reconciliation between financial statements and taxable incomes, on the most recent report of adjustments made by the various taxing authorities, and on adjustments in years still open for examination. The results of this review, when compared with the reserve for taxes, the so-called cushion, determine whether the target has provided adequately for past tax exposures.

Timing Items

Aside from absolute dollar liabilities, the audit should review so-called timing items, such as capitalization of repairs and other costs spread over a span of years. Any changes won't increase total taxes over time, but the IRS could dispute the capitalization schedule and claim that larger tax payments should have been made in prior years. The key expense here is interest costs, because interest assessments on past taxes have escalated in recent years and have been applied on a compound basis. Sometimes, the ultimate interest cost could exceed the tax deficiency.

State Taxes

State taxes are a very important item for examination. Many states have become extremely aggressive in imposing and collecting taxes from multistate enterprises. And with the federal government adopting an accelerated depreciation schedule in 1980, state taxes are becoming an increasing share of the overall corporate tax bite. In the case of multinational corporations, country-by-country tax reviews may be warranted.

Gaining Tax Attributes

Because potential tax benefits and opportunities to recoup purchase prices through postacquisition assets sales are key elements in setting the price tag on a deal, the audit should determine which of the seller's tax attributes succeed to the buyer and any limitations that will be imposed under the tax law on the utilization of such attributes after the acquisition. Net operating loss carryforwards, unutilized investment tax credits, and other available credits should be identified and quantified. Quantification goes beyond merely pulling numbers off a tax return. It is necessary to get behind the target's numbers and adjust the attributes for any potential softness that may result from such things as an aggressive tax policy that is open to successful challenge by taxing authorities or to future limitations.

A buyer purchasing stock from an existing consolidated group should seek safeguards to protect against loss of tax benefits from postacquisition operating losses or from excess credits that can be carried back for tax purposes to the preacquisition period. This requires a tax-sharing agreement between the two parties that is tailored to the specific peculiarities of the transaction.

When a substantial premium is being paid over the target's asset tax basis or the buyer plans to sell off some of the target's assets after the acquisition, the audit should consider the opportunities for "step-up" or writing up the value of the acquired assets, and the tax consequences of this procedure. This should focus on the tax incurred to step up the assets and potential taxes due on the sale of the assets; the current tax basis for the assets, which often is lower than the book carrying value, and any other costs associated with the target's ability to step up asset values. Note, however, that the Tax Reform Act of 1986 significantly reduced the ability of buyers to step up without incurring a prohibitive tax cost. In addition, the postacquisition alternative minimum tax consequences of the transaction should be evaluated.

Essentially, the step-up analysis begins by allocating the purchase price to the target's various assets. Recapture costs associated with the allocation then are quantified and compared with the tax savings derived from stepping up the tax basis of the target's assets. Recapture taxes must be paid within a short period of time after the acquisition, but the step-up typically is realized over several years. Thus, a true comparison will discount future tax savings by using a reasonable interest rate.

Management, Organization, and Industrial Relations

The buyer must appraise the capabilities of the seller's management, particularly when buying in an unrelated industry. The buyer should interview the senior officers and managers, review their prior business experience, investigate their backgrounds, and compare compensation benefit levels and plans, because changes often will result from the transaction.

Union contracts, strike history, and related factors should be reviewed to determine any existing problems. Many planned personnel savings may not be possible because of labor agreements. Pension, profit-sharing, and other employee benefit plans must be studied to determine their effect on the future operations of the combined business. One target company had many valued, long-term employees, all in their late fifties, who would have caused a drain on the buyer's cash flow when the unfunded pension benefits had to be paid at their retirement. Consequently, the terms of the transaction were substantially lowered. On the other side of the equation, many pension funds have surpluses that serve to make the acquisition less expensive, although recent changes in the tax law have made it difficult to use these surpluses.

Marketing

Product and marketing factors to be analyzed include:

- Sales, profit, and backlog by product line
- Major products, new product developments, and obsolescence
- Annual and monthly sales histories (long-term trends and seasonal or cyclical fluctuations)
- Government sales
- Marketing and sales organization, including special compensation arrangements
- Sales planning and forecasting methods
- Advertising and promotion expenditures and methods
- Market shares of key competitors
- Product life cycles and technologies
- Competitive strategies
- Key factors for success, including threats and barriers to entry
- Customer attitudes and buying power

The target's trends should be compared to industry averages to determine the company's relative performance. An example of how product obsolescence affects the transaction concerns the target company that manufactured a leading, long-established angina medication and demanded a high premium for its reputation. The acquirer discovered that, although the target's trend had been good, a new product, encompassing new technology and application, had just come on the market and ultimately would make the target's product obsolete. The buyer substantially reduced its offer. The marketing intelligence also should be compared to an analysis (aging and usage by item) of inventory to detect slow-moving, excess, and obsolete inventory. Some buyers who don't perform this inventory analysis frequently are forced into the costly scrapping of inventory after acquisition because they later find items that are components of discontinued or declining lines.

Manufacturing and Distribution

A review should include:

- Each production facility (name, location, owned or leased, book value, fair market value, capacity, employees, present condition, alternative uses)
- Manufacturing processes and efficiency
- Suppliers of major raw materials
- Physical distribution methods (purchase, intracompany transfers, final sales to customers)

Acquirers should also examine the following other areas:

Research and Development. The buyer should analyze costs and benefits of the past, current, and planned R&D programs, personnel and facilities used in them, and methods of accounting for R&D.

Reporting Controls. Understanding a seller's internal reporting and control systems is particularly important when the target is in a different industry than the buyer or has weak controls that can affect the business. Often, it is not possible to install identical systems in both companies because of operating or philosophical differences such as the degree of autonomy for subsidiaries. When such differences arise, any required changes should be made at reasonable cost after the acquisition.

Regulatory Reporting Requirements. Reporting requirements promulgated by regulatory authorities should be given special attention. They can have a profound effect on the future of the combined business and lead to substantial fines and embarrassment if ignored. The buyer should satisfy itself that the target company's facilities are in compliance with requirements of the Environmental Protection Agency and the Occupational Safety and Health Administration.

International Factors. Foreign operations of a target should be studied as to how they affect overall operation. Questions concerning the foreign country's investment climate, trade and investment restrictions, exchange controls, inflation rates, and reporting requirements should be addressed.

Discretionary Expenses. Certain expenses, such as research and development costs and repair and maintenance costs, can be deferred for the short term by the seller with adverse long-term consequences to a potential buyer. A careful review will help avoid unanticipated future outlays of capital that effectively increase the cost of the acquisition.

COMMON PROBLEMS OR EXPOSURE AREAS

It is helpful to know some of the more common financial and accounting problems uncovered in purchase investigations.

Inventory Distortions.   Undervaluation of inventory by private companies minimizes taxes but can lead to distorted earnings trends and potential.

Overvaluation of Inventory.   A key source of overvalued inventory is unrecorded inventory obsolescence caused by product overruns, changing technology, new product development, and maturing or discontinued products. The undervaluation usually results from excessive obsolescence, write-downs, or failure to count inventory on hand accurately.

Litigation.   Few firms are free of litigation, the most common resulting from product liability. This type of liability often surfaces well after the acquisition.

"Dressing up" of Financial Statements before Sale.   "Dressing up" tactics can include deferral of R&D expenses and repairs and maintenance, "release" of inventory reserves, unduly low reserves or estimates for such things as bad debts, pension accounting, sales returns and allowances, warranties, slow-moving and excess inventories, and undisclosed changes in accounting principles or methods.

Receivables Not Collectible at Recorded Amounts.   Doubtful accounts, cash and trade discounts, dated receivables, and sales returns and allowances may not be adequately reserved for.

Unrealizability of Certain Investments.   Investments accounted for by the equity method and nonmarketable investments are required to be written down only for "permanent impairments" of value, not for temporary declines. Liberal judgments may have been applied to eliminate recognition of permanent impairment.

Credibility and Integrity of Management.   A private investigation may be needed to obtain sufficient information and background on target management to determine if it is right for the job and trustworthy.

Personal Expenses in the Financial Statements of a Private Company.
Personal expenses usually reduce reported net income. But such costs also can be

used to affect trends and produce a favorable appearance that is misleading. Pro forma adjustments by the seller to eliminate such expenses often are overstated.

Tax Contingencies.   Tax contingencies represent one of the biggest problem areas in an acquisition, because most companies tend to be very aggressive when preparing their tax returns.

Unrecorded Liabilities.   Unrecorded liabilities may include vacation pay, sales returns, allowances and discounts (volume and cash), pension and postretirement health and insurance liabilities, claims items resulting from poor cutoffs, loss contracts, and warranties, among others.

Related-Party Transactions.   Most often found in private companies, related party deals can have a material effect on the company under new ownership, or on the historical trends presented during negotiations.

Poor Financial Controls.   Included in poor financial controls are poor pricing and costing policies, and deficient budgeting systems and controls.

Regulatory Problems.   Lack of compliance with environmental laws has become a significant problem. Outside experts should be retained in most cases to evaluate compliance. Other regulatory problems may exist in the areas of safety, taxes (including state, local, sales, and customs duties), labor, and so on.

Reliance on a Few Major Customers or Contracts.   Loss of a major customer can have a material effect on operations.

Need for Significant Future Expenditures.   Significant future expenditures needed might include plant relocation or expansion, replacement of aging property, plant, and equipment, or new product development requirements.

Foreign Operations.   Overseas units not only pose labor, management, and operating difficulties, but also may have poor quality accounting information and differences in accounting principles and practices.

Unusual Transactions.   Extraordinary actions such as sales of assets often improve the trend presented by the target.

THE SELLER'S ACTIONS

The seller, of course, must respond to the many requests for information made by the buyer. If proper planning has gone into the sale process, the effort involved should be routine, thereby allowing the seller to concentrate on fine tuning the sale agreement and working out final details. Unfortunately, sale planning is frequently inadequate, making this period traumatic.

The seller also should consider making an investigation of the buyer to determine if that buyer is best able to capitalize on the seller's strengths, is compatible with the seller, and has no skeletons of its own. This is particularly important if the seller is continuing in management. The seller's investigation should focus on basically the same elements as the buyer's investigation. However, it need not be as comprehensive, unless the paper being accepted is subject to considerable risk.

32

Risk Management: Environmental Liabilities

Halley I. Moriyama

*Vice President, ENSR Consulting &
Engineering, Acton, Massachusetts*

Prepurchase environmental due diligence investigations now are routine for most nonresidential property transactions, including the sales of operating businesses. Buyers are concerned about unknowingly assuming hidden environmental liabilities that could turn an investment opportunity into a financial disaster. Lenders fear the possibility of a loan default by the borrower, or, worse yet, a total loss of the value of the loan collateral, or even assumption of a major Superfund liability. Investment bankers and underwriters have a potential interest in environmental liabilities, for they often are required to render "fairness opinions" on the adequacy of price and other deal elements. Failure to disclose a major environmental liability could result in shareholder litigation should an unrevealed liability materially impact the financial condition of the acquiring company and adversely affect its stockholders as a result.

REGULATORY DRIVING FORCES

How various federal and state regulations can impact upon the purchase and sale of businesses and real property, as well as upon financial institutions who are involved in the funding of these transactions, is important to understand.

The Superfund Pressures

The Comprehensive Environmental Response, Liability and Cleanup Act (CER-CLA, or Superfund), with its provisions for joint, several, strict, and retroactive liability, has proven to be the cornerstone of federal regulation that has exposed buyers and lenders to extensive financial liabilities. Enacted in 1980, CERCLA essentially deals with the "sins of the past," and is intended to promote the cleanup of abandoned hazardous waste sites. Because of its onerous provisions, companies can be held liable for all or part of the cleanup costs, regardless of fault and regardless of whether the waste disposal activity was conducted legally prior to the enactment of the law. Because of the retroactive liability, the responsible party may not even have caused the situation, but merely inherited a past problem through acquisition. Lenders also can be affected, particularly in those situations where they take title to contaminated property through foreclosure.

Prior to the implementation of the Superfund Reauthorization Act (SARA) in 1986, few defenses were available to the "innocent purchaser" who unknowingly bought a contaminated site. Under SARA, however, a highly conditional innocent purchasers' defense was developed and is premised on the execution of appropriate inquiry prior to the purchase. While this defense is available under CERCLA, no such "safe harbor" typically is available in terms of comparable state regulations. In almost every state, the liability remains strict, regardless of fault.

Liability under CERCLA is not limited to those commonly referred to as property owners or facility operators. Lenders can become responsible parties under certain circumstances. The statutory definition of "owner or operator" specifically exempts a person who holds only a security interest in the facility or property. However, lender liability has been receiving an increasing degree of attention, particularly since the *Fleet Factors* case (*U.S. v. Fleet Factors Corp.*, 901 F2d 1550, CA 11, 31 ERC 1465) in which a federal court said that a secured lender may be liable, without being an operator, if it simply had the capacity to influence a company's waste management decisions.

However, in response to the unsettling effect that the decision of the U.S. Court of Appeals for the Second Circuit had on the lending community, the U.S. Environmental Protection Agency issued final regulations in April 1992 (57 Fed. Reg. 18344) to provide lenders with some cushion. These regulations allow secured creditors to engage in a broad range of activities intended to properly manage their loans without running afoul of the secured creditor exemption.

State Environmental Laws

In addition to federal environmental regulations, each state has implemented its own set of laws, which are at least as restrictive as those found at the federal level. Additionally, a number of states have devised unique ways to force the discovery and cleanup of hazardous waste contamination, the common approach being to directly or indirectly tie these regulations to property and business transactions.

New Jersey's Environmental Cleanup Responsibility Act (ECRA) is viewed as the toughest anticontamination law in the country. It requires that prior to completing certain types of transactions, an environmental assessment must be conducted. Any serious contamination problem that is identified must be remediated to the satisfaction of the state before the deal closes. Alternatively, the responsible party may enter into an administrative consent order with the state and post appropriate financial assurance that guarantees that the cleanup will be conducted within a predefined, postclosing schedule. Finally, the state has the ability to nullify the transaction if these procedures are not followed.

At least five states (New Jersey, Connecticut, Maine, Massachusetts, and New Hampshire) have implemented so-called "super-lien" laws, which enable the state government to place a priority lien on any property on which it has had to spend its own money for decontamination work. The lien takes priority over all other encumbrances, including first mortgages. The threat of the super-lien strongly encourages commercial lenders to require prospective borrowers to investigate a property in detail before the loan is approved.

A large number of states also have implemented disclosure-type laws regarding environmental problems. These laws require sellers to affirmatively disclose the environmental conditions of their properties to prospective buyers; in some cases, disclosure statements must be submitted to the state as well, or be registered in the deed. Failure to abide by the disclosure requirements normally carries both civil and criminal penalties.

THE TRADITIONAL APPROACH TO RISK REDUCTION

The traditional approach to covering business risks, whether they involve company finances, product liability, or environmental concerns, has been to rely upon insurance and/or indemnifications and warranties such as those in acquisition agreements. With respect to environmental liabilities, these traditional tools have proven to be inadequate as the sole basis for shifting risk.

The insurance industry has been badly damaged by pollution-related claims. As a result, environmental impairment liability insurance is becoming more difficult and more expensive to obtain. Although insurance is available, most providers have drastically capped the coverage. Most insurers also require an environmental audit before even offering coverage.

Indemnifications and warranties have their practical limitations as well. Aside from the question of whether the indemnifying party has the financial resources to support a future claim, there also is the paramount issue of being able to discern, with a reasonable degree of confidence, that the offending problem took place prior to the transaction as opposed to after the acquisition. This is particularly difficult to determine where site contamination is concerned, and when the indemnified buyer continues to operate the plant in the same manner as before, using the same chemicals, and producing the same types of wastes.

The prepurchase environmental due diligence investigation, on the other hand, often provides the necessary information to support a later claim that a representation or warranty has been breached. If developed early enough in the transaction, the results of the investigation also may assist the buyer or lender in negotiating contract provisions that either cover or shift the environmental risk, or perhaps obtain a more important business concession from the seller.

ENVIRONMENTAL DUE DILIGENCE INVESTIGATIONS

Although there is no universal agreement on what constitutes environmental due diligence, such studies do tend to focus on one or more of the following broad topics:

- On-site hazardous waste liabilities resulting from past or current practices associated with the use, storage, treatment, or disposal of hazardous materials or substances on or near the subject site
- Hazardous waste liabilities associated with past or current off-site disposal practices
- Regulatory compliance and permit status of the site and its developed activities

On-Site Hazardous Waste Contamination

The evaluation of potential on-site hazardous waste contamination most often is conducted through a phased approach. The initial activity, often referred to as Phase I, typically focuses on identifying whether there is reason to suspect that a problem exists. The Phase I investigation normally does not include any analytical testing, but is based upon "desk top" research coupled with a walkover of a site. Based on the results of the Phase I investigation, a follow-up set of activities involving testing of soils or groundwater may be undertaken during a Phase II program. Should this analytical program identify significant problems, a third phase of activity might be performed. This would involve more extensive field studies, ultimately leading to the preparation of a site cleanup plan.

Probably the most important initial activity in the Phase I investigation involves establishing the history of the use of the subject property. While the title search will provide some clues, it is important to understand that "use," not "ownership," is the key consideration. Knowledge of the past uses of a property provides the basis for identifying the range of hazardous materials and wastes that may be present, including their possible locations on the site. In our experience, nearly half of all site contamination problems are related to past uses of the land rather than current activities and practices (those existing at the time of the sale).

Various forms of testing often are performed to verify the results of the initial Phase I investigation. Entering into a Phase II investigation can be costly and time consuming; but no single criterion can be applied universally in making the decision to pursue a more intensive investigation. The implementation of a testing program can be triggered by various factors:

- The Phase I study identified a potential problem of significance that can be verified through testing.

- The lender or buyer desires an additional level of comfort, given the size of the transaction or the initial findings of the Phase I investigation.

A well-prepared Phase I investigation, combined with a well-planned analytical testing program, can provide useful and accurate information. Ill-conceived investigative programs can provide useless analytical testing data. For example, without knowing in advance that the site's groundwater is controlled by bedrock conditions, it is quite possible to conduct a groundwater sampling program that totally misses the problem.

Although it may be desirable to conduct an analytical testing program, there are certain associated risks. If a minor or major contamination problem is found as a result of analytical testing, the property owner or operator may be subject to various reporting requirements at the federal and/or state levels, a situation that could trigger a time-consuming and expensive governmental investigation. As a result, all parties to the transaction should be aware of this potential beforehand and reporting responsibilities should be worked out in advance when possible.

Off-Site Disposal Practices

Most of the federal Superfund sites involve abandoned, off-site disposal locations. Identifying potential or future involvement of a manufacturing facility may be difficult, because many disposal sites have yet to be identified and company files may be incomplete with regard to identifying prior disposal sites used by both current and past owners. Because of the joint and several liability provisions of CERCLA, a new owner or operator of a facility or site may assume liabilities originating from the on- and off-site disposal practices of predecessor owners or operators, even if the alleged disposal activities took place many years before in a manner consistent with all regulations in place at the time. It is important to note that while a buyer may be protected against CERCLA claims under the innocent landowner provisions of SARA, this "safe harbor" applies only to purchased properties and does not extend to claims related to off-site disposal activities.

The difficulties in securing reasonably accurate information on current and past disposal facilities are compounded by the fact that the principal federal regulation covering these activities, the Resource Conservation and Recovery Act (RCRA) became effective only in November 1980. Therefore, mandatory record-keeping provisions, including those covering transportation of hazardous wastes, have been in place for only a relatively short period of time.

On-Site Regulatory Compliance

Environmental liabilities go beyond hazardous waste problems. Many nonhazardous waste regulations allow for the imposition of substantial monetary penalties of $25,000 or more per day for noncompliance. Some violations can result in an immediate plant shutdown. In still other cases, there may be significant environmental regulatory constraints to future plant expansions. With the increasingly stringent enforcement of Occupational Health and Safety Administration (OSHA) regulations, health and safety evaluations affecting workers are becoming a necessary part of compliance investigations, particularly when industrial transactions are involved.

In some cases it may be important to also evaluate the general physical condition of pollution abatement equipment. If the equipment is old, outdated, or in poor repair, a substantial future cost may be incurred, a condition that could represent a significant monetary liability to the buyer. In addition, it often is necessary to look at expected near-term, future regulatory requirements, particularly those that may impose a substantial financial burden on the operating company. For example, the buyer of facilities that emit hazardous chemicals into the air should pay particular attention to the financial implications of the federal Clean Air Act Amendments of 1990 whose expensive control requirements are being phased in over a ten-year period.

ENVIRONMENTAL LIABILITY COSTS

Many transactions require that liability cost estimates be developed once the initial due diligence is completed. Placing monetary values on identified liabilities is both difficult and tricky, even under the best of circumstances.

While estimating costs of pollution control equipment is relatively straightforward, developing monetary cost estimates for contamination-related liabilities is far more difficult and requires much more information. Site cleanup cost estimates require detailed knowledge of such factors as:

- Identification of the full scope of the identified contaminants
- Spatial extent of the contamination in both a horizontal and vertical direction
- Information on subsurface conditions surrounding the contamination (i.e., permeability of the soils, rate of groundwater flow, bedrock conditions, etc.)
- Assessment of the health and safety risks associated with the known contaminant levels, including synergistic effects associated with combinations of contaminants
- Evaluation of alternative treatment and disposal option(s) and selection of the most appropriate techniques

Moreover, the cost to remediate soil and/or groundwater contamination is highly dependent on negotiations with government agencies and the sometimes arbitrary and unpredictable nature of agency officials charged with handling the discussions. Even with the implementation of a Phase II analytical testing program, a substantial degree of uncertainty still will exist with respect to many of the variables described above.

Estimation of site remediation costs is far from an exact science. With only a very limited time period normally available to evaluate a property during the due diligence period, the *potential* uncertainties inherent in cleanup cost estimates are exacerbated, although it is impossible to determine by how much.

If the development of environmental liability cost estimates involve publicly held companies, certain problems may emerge relative to whether these estimates may provide additional exposure to Securities and Exchange Commission reporting requirements. The answer is unclear and must be handled case by case.

Over the past several years, there has been increasing debate over these disclosure requirements, particularly as they relate to possible environmental liabilities. In part, the debate focuses on the vagaries of the current guidelines in effect, embodied in Financial Accounting Standard 5 (FAS 5), which were developed in the 1970s when environmental issues probably were not even considered. Under FAS 5, reporting liability is required when it is reasonably probable that a loss has been incurred and the amount of the loss can be reasonably estimated. Given the complexity of environmental issues, what constitutes "reasonably probable" and "reasonably estimated" is subject to a broad range of interpretations. These matters are further complicated in contamination cases by the uncertainty as to whether the acquiring company may be reimbursed through old insurance policies or through successful private party suits against prior site owners or other potential contributors.

RESOLVING TRANSACTIONAL PROBLEMS

Experience has shown that most properties, particularly older ones in industrial use, have actual or suspected environmental problems in one form or another. Some of these problems may be significant; others may be minor. Although the environmental due diligence study may identify these problems as representing potential issues, the proposed transaction does not necessarily have to terminate as a result.

Clearly, buyers and lenders would like the seller to "cure" the problem prior to the closing. However, in the real world of transactions where time is of the essence, this is not always possible, nor are all sellers willing to expend the time or money to take the necessary steps without receiving an offsetting concession on the part of the buyer; and there are other situations where the seller may not even have the ability to cure the problem. For instance, the seller may have sent wastes to an off-site landfill that has been identified by the due diligence study as being under active governmental investigation. The seller has no control over such an external investigation, including the timing or the likely response action in the event that a cleanup is mandated. In other cases, the identified issue may be only a suspicion, with no follow-up verification activities having been performed. A suspected on-site contamination problem is a good example of such a situation. There are many instances where neither the buyer nor the seller wishes to open up "Pandora's box" by implementing an analytical testing program, though both parties may recognize that a contamination problem, if present, could require expending considerable resources to remedy.

These are all typical situations that arise during the course of a transaction. There is no single method for dealing with an identified environmental problem. Usually it becomes part of a negotiated process whereby each party to the transaction individually assesses its respective business needs and attempts to gain the best deal possible. In many cases, environmental considerations are traded off against other business issues. In other situations, the lender may dictate the requirements.

Absent the desire to kill the transaction, buyers and sellers have three broad options when dealing with environmental liabilities: The buyer can accept them, the seller can retain them, or an agreement can be reached to allocate the liabilities between both sides.

Most of the strategies for dealing with identified or suspected problems involve the use of what may be referred to as "paper" protections in the acquisition agreement. For example, the seller may indemnify the buyer for all liabilities arising from the seller's involvement in a particular contaminated disposal site. Another example of a paper protection involves a warranty. A seller may warrant that it has all necessary governmental environmental permits required for the continued operation of the plant.

While these and other forms of paper protections can reduce the risks to an acceptable level and thus allow the transaction to proceed, several important issues should be considered in crafting such protections and evaluating their true effectiveness in shifting risk.

Financial Guarantees

Paper protections can be meaningless if the provider does not have the financial resources to guaranty that it will make good on any promise. When the seller is a "deep pocket," the ability to pay may not be a concern. On the other hand, if the seller is a "lesser pocket," there may be significant concerns over the issue of financial resources. In such cases, buyers typically attempt to have the seller provide some form of financial guarantee. This could involve the seller's setting aside or escrowing money with a third party to cover the anticipated costs, obtaining a surety bond, or securing a letter of credit. All of these financial guaranty mechanisms have monetary implications for the seller. Obtaining a bond or letter of credit requires paying the issuer anywhere from one-half percent to three percent of the face value amount. Additionally, these guaranties tie up the seller's capital and make it unavailable for other uses. Hence, an opportunity cost also is involved. For these reasons, the size of the financial guaranty and the time period over which it is to remain in effect become major issues that often require considerable negotiation between the buyer and seller.

Triggering and Capping the Claim

The point at which a buyer can make a claim against the seller for costs incurred is another important issue that should be addressed. If the closing document is silent on the subject, substantial problems and sources of disagreement can emerge.

From the buyer's perspective, it would be preferable that the "trigger" be defined as the point in time when a problem is discovered and not when an actual claim is made by a governmental agency or a loss is incurred as a result of an enforcement action. That is because there may be substantial legal and consultant fees to be paid during the intervening period. This approach can financially benefit the seller as well, for it may allow either party to undertake a private, voluntary action, such as a cleanup, that normally would be less costly than a project developed and implemented by the government and its contractors. It also may help avoid a monetary fine or penalty that is commonly associated with enforcement actions.

Conversely, the seller may be reluctant to accept such broad language. It could enable the buyer to force the seller to rectify myriad environmental problems, many of which may be relatively innocuous or petty. Moreover, such an open-ended provision may provide an incentive for the buyer to aggressively seek out problems.

To overcome these potential issues, the seller will want to limit its obligations in several respects. First and foremost, the seller will want to establish a monetary cap above which it will have no further responsibility. Second, the seller will want to limit its obligations to correcting only those matters that were defined and agreed to prior to the close of the transaction, or to those problems that the buyer finds within a fixed period of time, typically one to two years after the acquisition. Finally, the seller may want to have the buyer take responsibility for covering a fixed-dollar portion of the initial costs in order to provide a disincentive for the buyer to aggressively seek out each and every conceivable problem, regardless of its significance.

Who Controls Corrective Actions?

Defining who will be responsible for planning and implementing corrective measures is another important consideration. Again, buyers and sellers have conflicting interests.

If the problem's resolution is left to the control of the seller, the buyer may want assurances that the seller does not attempt to employ "cheap fixes" that only solve the identified problem temporarily. Moreover, the buyer wants to be assured that the seller's activities do not interfere with the facility's ongoing operations, and that identified problems are expeditiously corrected so that the new owner is not exposed to potential government enforcement actions.

On the other hand, if the problem is left to the control of the buyer, the seller will be concerned about the potential for excessive expenditures aimed at achieving a solution well beyond what any government agency would require.

One common method used to resolve these conflicts is to allow the seller to control the corrective activity with the stipulation that the method chosen must be consistent with prevailing governmental standards or guidelines. In those cases, the seller assumes responsibility for any government enforcement action that may result from either delays in implementation or a failure to get results. Often there is a further stipulation that the buyer may retain a consultant to provide oversight of the seller's activities.

Defining Covered Costs

Identifying and satisfactorily resolving environmental problems can be a long and expensive process involving substantial consultant and legal fees, not to mention diverted management time. On top of these expenses can be the actual capital costs and operating and maintenance expenses to implement the agreed-upon corrective measures. Other costs may be related to actual fines or monetary penalties that may be imposed by a government agency, including damages, government response costs, and in some cases oversight expenses when private parties assume responsibility for conducting all necessary studies and corrective actions.

In short, the direct cost of a site cleanup, for instance, may be only a portion of the total expenses associated with rectifying a particular environmental problem. Therefore it is important that the parties to the transaction clearly define up front what they consider acceptable costs in order to avoid disputes after the deal closes.

NO ESCAPE

Consideration of environmental liabilities in M&A transactions has become increasingly important. If buyers or sellers are unwilling to deal with such issues, they may be forced to by lender requirements when conventional financing is necessary to support the transaction.

Understanding environmental liabilities, including the inherent uncertainties involved in both their identification and estimation of financial impact, has become increasingly critical to the success of a typical deal. Environmental risks do not have to kill a transaction. There are creative ways to cope with them in a transaction and to deal effectively with the inherent risks that they present.

33

Risk Management: Products Liability

Charles J. Israel
Attorney, New York, New York

Control of product liability issues that arise from a company's existing operations is a complex challenge to every corporate risk manager and in-house attorney. Dealing with current damage claims and engineering safeguards to prevent known problems represents just one dimension of difficulty. Even more vexsome is projecting whether the use of the products or materials will cause future injuries or illnesses that could expose the company to liability. Imagine, then, how the issues compound in an acquisition when the time to intelligently assess a target's product liability potential is short, its business may be somewhat different from the acquirer's, and a large up-front investment is on the line.

But *any* buyer that closes a deal without trying to evaluate a target's product liabilities may be blindsiding itself. Future claims from problems that are known or have yet to surface may be so enormous that they can destroy the economic value of the acquisition.

And the stakes for acquirers have risen. Product-related litigation is increasing, and recent court decisions have saddled acquirers with liabilities for products made by targets or their predecessors many years earlier. New types of injuries and illnesses constantly are being discovered, and hazards as yet unknown can haunt acquirers that buy targets on the leading edge of advanced technology. Moreover, many of the most active M&A industries—such as drugs and other health care products, chemicals, metals, machinery, and electronics—are highly prone to product-liability exposures. How, then, does a wise buyer protect itself from the shocks of product liabilities?

UP-FRONT INVESTIGATION

The answer lies in a relatively straightforward three-step analysis that should be undertaken in connection with virtually every transaction that involves some measure of actual or potential product liability exposure. First, the nature of the actual and potential liabilities must be defined. Second, the potential liabilities must be evaluated to determine the true extent of the problems that may exist. Third, the risks must be assessed in terms of their potential impact on the transaction itself or on the future of the business.

Contract Protections

As the first step in defining the risks, the buyer should be satisfied that the purchase agreement itself contains adequate protections in the product liability area. The provision in the purchase agreement that defines the nature of the pertinent risks and liabilities is the "representation and warranty." That section should include within its scope matters relating to product liability. A litigation representation, for example, generally will state, among other things, that there are no lawsuits pending against the target company beyond those specifically articulated in the purchase agreement.

However, more may be needed than general assertions. A pure litigation representation that does not specifically address product liability concerns may not always provide adequate assurances to the buyer, because it may not cover pertinent details that fall short of actual litigation. Among other things, these issues would include product recalls and retrofits. The particular circumstances of a target, therefore, may require explicit recitations with respect to product liability matters.

A representation by the seller serves to provide the purchaser with a degree of certainty as to what it is buying. It places the onus on the seller to disclose all pertinent information. The ball is, therefore, in the seller's court to ensure disclosure. Otherwise the seller is susceptible to a claim for breach of the representation or, even worse, for fraud. Representations, together with other provisions of the contract, also may provide the buyer with some measure of recourse in the event that the representations prove to be inaccurate.

Targeting Problem Areas

Beyond the basic agreement, there still is a need for the purchaser to investigate the risks the seller discloses. The representation really is no more than a safety net in this regard, and cannot provide complete solace to the purchaser. There can be no truly effective substitute for actively investigating product liability matters, which can be as important to a transaction as other general business or environmental issues.

Unfortunately, product liability concerns all too often are overlooked, not given the credence and attention they rightfully deserve, wholly ignored, or, as often as not, forgotten until the last minute. Given the aforementioned perils, those are foolish courses. Nor should a buyer delude itself that the size of the deal is so great that no product liability matter could have a material impact on the target or the transaction itself. There has been a major increase in the incidence of large companies with colossal product liability problems that threaten the continued viability of the business. To see the actual and potential magnitude of the problem, one need only look as far as the Chapter 11 proceedings arising from Dalkon Shield litigation against A.H. Robins Co. and the bankruptcy cases involving at least five asbestos product manufacturers, including Manville Corp. And even if corporate existence is not threatened, these problems divert management's attention from running the company and ultimately have an adverse impact on the bottom line.

Product Analysis

What areas, then, are properly the subjects of the pre-acquisition "due diligence" investigation into product liabilities? And how should such investigations be conducted? Although not intended as an exhaustive list, the following is offered by way of example, to demonstrate the variety of subjects that should be addressed. (Although outside the scope of this article, matters pertaining to insurance coverage for the target company frequently are of equal importance in evaluating product liability concerns, and therefore should not be overlooked.)

The first logical question is: What type of product or products are manufactured by the target? Naturally, some types of products tend to create greater risks of harm than others. Carcinogenic chemicals and industrial machinery are obvious examples. The likelihood that harm will result from the product, and the severity of the injury, largely will determine the depth and scope of the subsequent investigation.

It should be kept in mind, however, that a substantial number of relatively minor injuries also can create large problems, from the standpoint of litigation management and defense costs, as well as from a liability perspective. Cosmetics manufacturers and food companies seem to experience a large volume of claims involving minor injuries and a large volume of nuisance claims. While the number of claims may amount to only a small percentage of unit volume of sales, managing these claims can be a burden to a company.

A profitable source of information concerning the product and any litigation involving the product is publicly available information obtained from searching legal data bases and topical litigation reports. Inquiries along these lines should focus not only on the specific company and its products but also on other companies in the same or a similar business.

Loss Runs

Company loss runs always should be reviewed to the extent that they are available. A review of loss runs covering several years of claims history sheds important light on the number of claims experienced, the costs incurred in defending lawsuits, and the amounts paid to settle or otherwise dispose of them. This provides the acquiring entity with some indication of what its costs in this area are likely to be in the future. The review also provides a useful check on the seller's completeness in disclosing pending lawsuits. For example, the seller may list ten pending lawsuits against the target, but the loss run may reveal a greater number. While the discrepancy may not always be of great significance, it provides an indication of the seller's thoroughness and may, in fact, reveal telling omissions.

Loss runs that reveal the product involved and the type of injury also may provide insight into whether a product is involved in an inordinate number of incidents. Such experiences may indicate, for example, a design flaw in need of correction and/or that a product recall is warranted. Particular attention should be paid to any case in which punitive damages were assessed against the company.

Loss runs are listings of claims pending against a company, typically prepared by an insurer, showing certain details of the claims including the type of product and injury involved, how much was paid to defend the claim, and amounts paid in settlement or in satisfaction of judgments.

Unfortunately, a review of loss runs may not be enough. One specific instance that showed the inadequacy of relying solely on loss runs involved a selling entity that disclosed two product recalls to the buyer. Recalls are not listed on loss runs. In reviewing actual litigation files, it became apparent that the seller had considered conducting a recall of another product but had rejected the idea because of the "adverse publicity" attendant to the recall. When this discovery was brought to the attention of the seller by the buyer, the seller suddenly revealed the existence of several other proposed or actual recalls that had not been disclosed previously.

Recalls and Retrofits

Careful scrutiny must be given to the subject of product recall, retrofit, or post-sale warning campaigns. An investigator also should determine whether the company is considering a recall or similar program or whether the company previously has considered and rejected the idea of conducting a recall.

A retrofit can be part of a recall. A recall involves actually seeking the return of the product to the manufacturer for repair or for repair or replacement of part of it. A retrofit is the repair of the product or replacement of parts, and does not necessarily involve a recall. It could be a field retrofit, in which the manufacturer sends representatives into the field to perform repair or replacement work.

To be sure, even the tightest due diligence provides no guarantee that a buyer will uncover all of the skeletons lurking in the corporate closet. Generally, available time is short, and that tends to impede the thoroughness of the task. A more difficult problem may be the reluctance of the target's employees to be totally candid in responding to inquiries for fear of reprisal in the event the deal does not go through. Nevertheless, an acquiring company, armed with the right approach, generally will succeed in ferreting out the major problems.

ISSUES OF ATTITUDE

A series of questions then must be drafted in order to properly evaluate the risks revealed by the due diligence investigation. These questions relate to many aspects of product liability concerns, and the answers will tend to shed useful light on the subject of the investigation. Among these questions are:

1. *Does the company evidence a sufficient degree of concern about product liabilities and is it properly organized to deal with product liability issues?*

Many companies devote little time and effort to minimizing product liability risks and exposures. They also may have little in the way of any organizational structure that is properly geared toward evaluating risks posed by products and effectively managing product-liability-related litigation. The acquiring company can be well served by evaluating these aspects of the target's business.

An adequate concern for product liability matters may be seen in the existence of written company policies pertaining to such issues. This would include a written recall policy that sets forth the methods for conducting a recall and delegating responsibility for seeing that the recall is properly conducted; claims/litigation management policy procedures; and quality assurance and quality control policies and procedures. This adequate concern also would be evidenced by an organizational structure that could include one or more committees responsible for various aspects of product liability matters, including committees to evaluate the safety of new products before they are placed into production.

2. *Are there product liability risks that have yet to surface or become fully apparent because of the nature of a particular product or because the product is relatively new?*

Many products have the potential for causing harm that may not manifest itself for some time after exposure to them. Similarly, the company's experience in manufacturing the product may have been for too short a period to fully appreciate the potential for harm. Conversely, a product that has been manufactured for many years and possesses a fairly long useful life may begin to experience a higher failure rate the longer it remains in use.

Products that may cause future harm would include substances such as chemicals, drugs, and other materials, such as asbestos. Injury may become apparent only after many years of exposure to the substance and, in the case of at least one drug, DES, injury may manifest itself only in later generations. Products that may experience a higher failure rate as time progresses would include machinery that becomes less reliable with age and consequent deterioration, and machinery with safety devices that may be removed over time.

3. *If a recall or retrofit program has been conducted in the past or is currently under way, has the program been adequately conducted?*

The results of the investigation may indicate that a recall should have been conducted in the past and was not, or that one should now be conducted. Recalls, if not properly conducted, can expose a company to serious liability problems. Likewise, the failure to conduct such a program also can lead to monumental problems in the future.

The adequacy of a recall is judged by reference to the severity (degree) of harm that the defective product is likely to cause and the likelihood (risk) that the harm will, in fact, occur. The greater the degree and risk of harm, the greater the burden on the manufacturer in conducting the recall. A thorough recall must involve determining how many units are involved and where they are located; appropriate efforts must be made to identify and locate the products and impress upon the public the importance of returning the product. An accurate accounting must be kept of all products that have been successfully recalled, repaired, or replaced.

IMPACTING THE PURCHASE DECISION

Knowing what the current product liability situation is for a target company and what is likely to be in store quite obviously may affect the ultimate decision to purchase, the price to pay, and the negotiating stance to take with respect to representations and warranties. The less known, the more important the representations become. But even ironclad, exhaustive representations can be illusory if the proceeds of the sale are not traceable by the time a breach becomes apparent. If a buyer is looking for recovery from the seller, the seller may no longer exist and the proceeds of the sale may have been passed on to stockholders.

Warranty Worries

In actual practice, representations may not always survive beyond the closing date or survive sufficiently beyond the closing date to provide much protection. For example, the buyer may find it useful to have the seller indemnify it for future liabilities. But if the buyer purchases the stock of the seller or the target is liquidated following an asset sale, there may be no surviving entity to provide the indemnification should it come due. In any case, indemnifications invariably are difficult to negotiate and can become deal killers. And in a corollary to the often slipshod investigations into product liabilities, the buyer may pass up indemnifications altogether because none appear to be necessary when the deal is consummated.

In one instance, a buyer temporarily put off signing the purchase agreement because it could not satisfy itself that a pending recall was being adequately conducted. In discussions with various engineers of the seller, the buyer could not get a consistent response to inquiries about the nature of the problem that had brought about the decision for a recall, how many units were involved, or how many products actually had been recalled. Because of the potential severity of injury involved, the buyer deemed it prudent to postpone signing until the matter was clarified to its satisfaction.

Successor Liabilities

The precise nature of the transaction contemplated and details of the purchase contract provisions naturally will impact the extent of due diligence that is required. The nature of the information gleaned from the investigation also may have an impact on the structure of the deal or provisions of the purchase agreement. Thus, for example, while it may be the purchaser's original intention to assume all of the target's past and future liabilities, the information acquired during due diligence may convince the buyer that no liabilities should be assumed at all or that some allocation of liabilities between buyer and seller is appropriate.

Even when the buyer does not intend to assume any liabilities, it may be important to consider the possible applicability and implications of successor liability principles. Under successor liability principles, an acquiring company may be liable to third persons for the acts of the acquired company or its previous owners, even though the buyer had no intention of assuming such liabilities.

To reiterate, the foregoing is not intended as a thorough explanation of the analysis required in a product liability due diligence investigation. Rather, it is meant to demonstrate the variety of matters that need to be considered. The main point to remember is that virtually every buyer should have at least some product liability analysis performed, even if only to confirm that no problems exist or are likely to surface down the road.

34

Safeguarding Intellectual Property

Craig S. Medwick

Partner, Rogers & Wells,
New York, New York

Kathleen L. Werner

Associate, Rogers & Wells,
New York, New York

Intellectual property no longer is just for the high tech. From a financial services firm with its own on-line market index to an international wallpaper manufacturer with original product designs and sales data bases, a company's investment in intellectual property is more than ever vital to its operations and its competitive position in the marketplace. As the law continues to develop regarding the commercial protection of intellectual property, businesses must take proactive steps to evaluate and safeguard intellectual property assets, especially in the context of acquisitions.

Parties to an acquisition must not ignore crucial due diligence in a transaction involving intellectual property assets. In many cases, the target's intellectual property rights are its most valuable assets. A buyer cannot assume that the mere existence of a patent, trademark, or copyright provides adequate protection for these assets. The buyer must be certain that:

- The protections are in good order.
- The assets are not the subject of an existing or threatened infringement claim.

- The target has the right to transfer the property free and clear of claims and restrictions.

In addition, the buyer should carefully scrutinize the activities of the target's main competitors. A buyer needs to know whether a competitor already has obtained patent, copyright, trademark, or other protection for technology similar to the target's, thereby effectively preventing the target from marketing its technology without risking an infringement claim.

WHY BOTHER? FROM THE BUYER'S PERSPECTIVE

A thorough due diligence investigation into the intellectual property rights of the target and its competitors may "crater" a few deals, but in most cases the parties can design solutions to their problems. If the buyer discovers that the target's assets are vulnerable because of weak intellectual property protections, the buyer can try to negotiate a reduction in the purchase price of the assets. In addition, the parties can craft insurance and indemnification provisions to give the buyer long-term comfort. If the buyer discovers that third parties have rights restricting the transfer of the target's assets, it can negotiate with the outside interests to remove the restrictions altogether or enter into royalty or other profit-sharing arrangements. It is imperative, however, that the buyer have advance warning of these problems. A failure to obtain and maintain adequate intellectual property protections can have dire results—ranging from contentious and expensive infringement litigation to the loss of a market to a competitor that had the foresight to obtain and maintain these protections.

The due diligence investigation also will give the buyer insights into the target's operations by revealing problems that may not otherwise be apparent. Due diligence may reveal collaterally that key personnel are integral to the future value of the target's assets. In response, the buyer may decide to negotiate incentives to encourage personnel to remain with the company after the transaction. The buyer also can include appropriate confidentiality provisions, work-made-for-hire clauses, and covenants not to compete in its employment contracts.

The due diligence investigation should confirm, among other matters, the typical representations and warranties to be made by the target in the acquisition agreement, including the following:

- The licensed technology does not infringe on any copyrights, trade secrets, or patents of which the target should have reasonable knowledge.
- The buyer shall receive free, good, and clear title in the licensed property.
- The target has the right to furnish the property to the buyer free of all liens, claims, and encumbrances, and the buyer may quietly and peacefully possess the property.
- All federal and state filings necessary to maintain the patents, copyrights, and trademarks have been made.

WHY BOTHER? FROM THE
TARGET'S PERSPECTIVE

From the target's perspective, a due diligence investigation may uncover weaknesses in its intellectual property program and result in a less advantageous deal than was originally contemplated. Conversely, if the target is able to demonstrate well-protected assets and an unfettered right to use, exploit, and transfer its assets, then the selling business has a very important bargaining chip that might translate into a higher purchase price. Companies should, as a matter of course, institute programs for maintaining intellectual property protections so that the firm and its assets will command the highest price possible in M&A transactions.

THE DUE DILIGENCE
INVESTIGATION

The two main goals of the buyer's due diligence investigation are to detect any defects in the target's intellectual property rights and to institute a program to correct those defects before they destroy the value of the seller's assets.

The first step in the investigation is to identify the target's intellectual property assets. The assets will include not only patents, copyrights, and trademarks or servicemarks, but also any proprietary trade secrets, designs, processes, software, names, abbreviations, symbols, product designation numbers, or other proprietary marks that may not be used or treated as trademarks. Often, the list of proprietary information and techniques entitled to legal protection is much longer than the target believed, leading to the potential forfeiture of the competitive advantages such proprietary items could enhance. Once the buyer has identified the assets, it must determine which are most valuable to the target's operations and decide whether the target's current methods of protecting those assets are sufficient, or whether they will need to be improved.

In deciding whether the current protective methods are adequate, the buyer will have to investigate the target's competitors. If the buyer discovers that the target's competition is developing a product similar to one of the target's, the buyer may want to strengthen the protection of that product. The buyer also may discover that a competitor is infringing on a property right of the target. If this is the case, the acquirer will want to make sure that target's property right is in good order before proceeding with an infringement action.

The buyer also will need to review a great deal of documentation on the assets, including all license and maintenance agreements, employment agreements, personnel manuals, consulting agreements, federal, state, and international filings and applications, Uniform Commercial Code (UCC) filings and results of lien searches, contracts, technical notes and papers, and marketing and correspondence files. In the United States, federal copyright filings are made with the U.S. Copyright Office and filings for patents and trademarks are made with the U.S. Patent and Trademark Office. The buyer will have to be very familiar and comfortable with the context in which the target first came into possession of its assets, as explained below.

Acquisition Issues to Consider

In the acquisition context, the two most important areas of inquiry in a due diligence investigation of the target's intellectual property assets are the circumstances
surrounding the target's claims of ownership in a particular piece of intellectual
property and the methods chosen to protect that property.

Ownership Rights

The concept of origin is basic to determining the scope of ownership rights in intellectual property assets. The person who creates a work is its originator or "author"
and has full ownership rights.[1] The buyer must carefully examine works created by
an employee of, or an independent consultant to, the target. Under the "work
made for hire" doctrine, an employer will be deemed the author and owner of an
employee's works created within the scope of his employment. However, in 1989
the Supreme Court narrowed the definition of "employee" so that most independent consultants fall outside the scope of "employee" and, therefore, retain
ownership rights in a work until those rights are transferred by specific agreement.[2]
Therefore, the buyer should ascertain whether any of the target's intellectual property assets was created for the target by independent consultants, and, if so, whether
the target required the consultants to sign over all rights in the work pursuant to an
appropriate agreement. If there are no waivers, the buyer may need to approach
each consultant to obtain a waiver, and may have to agree to a profit-sharing arrangement with the consultants.

The U.S. Court of Appeals for the Third Circuit, in a 1991 decision, held that, in
determining whether a person was an employee when he created a work, the focus
of the inquiry must be the actual relationship of the person to the alleged employer,
and not the appearance of the relationship to third parties.[3] In that case, MacLean,
a former employee of the consulting firm of Wm. M. Mercer-Merdinger-Hansen,
Inc., founded a competing software business after leaving Mercer. However,
MacLean continued to service a Mercer customer, with Mercer's full knowledge and
authorization. A U.S. District Court found that MacLean's use of Mercer stationery
for his correspondence and his failure to inform the customer that he was no
longer an employee of Mercer created an apparent agency relationship; therefore,
MacLean was an employee of Mercer when he created a software program for the
customer and Mercer owned that program under the work-made-for-hire doctrine.

The Court of Appeals reversed the lower court, holding that an apparent agency
relationship does not create an actual employment relationship. The pertinent inquiry is whether MacLean actually was an employee of Mercer when he created the
software program. In this case, both MacLean and Mercer knew that MacLean was
no longer an employee of Mercer; therefore, a jury could reasonably have found
that MacLean was acting as a paid consultant when he created the software program. If MacLean was an outside consultant, then the work-made-for-hire doctrine
would not apply, and absent a specific agreement transferring ownership rights to
Mercer, MacLean would be the sole owner of the program.

Experience indicates that, in addition to the threat to a company's proprietary
information that arises when an employee leaves the company and establishes a

competing business or goes to work for a competitor, a company's proprietary information is at great risk if proper protections were not in place when the company acquired intellectual property assets from third parties. A buyer must review all of the target's license agreements with third parties and pay particular attention to whether the target's rights include the exclusive, perpetual right to make and market derivative works incorporating elements of the work owned by the third party. Was the third party precluded by contract from further marketing the proprietary product or the underlying know-how, for example, to the target's competitors? The buyer also will need to know whether the target obtained the rights to any improvements and enhancements of the third party's work, and, if so, at what price. The buyer may discover that it needs to expand the target's licensing rights. These and related issues are particularly sensitive in areas involving customized development of proprietary products that work with existing third-party products.

Third-Party Rights

The buyer must investigate other third-party rights in the target's intellectual property, such as security interests and liens. Often in financing agreements, a lender will accept an interest in the debtor's property, including intellectual property, as collateral against repayment of a loan. The buyer must be aware of any such liens or other encumbrances and obtain the appropriate releases. The buyer also should do a UCC lien search to determine whether all security interests in the property were properly perfected. A purchasing company must be certain that any party selling an intellectual property asset is able to transfer that asset free and clear of claims by any other party.

Furthermore, the buyer should be on the lookout for works created by two or more authors. These may be considered joint works.[4] Anyone who makes an independently copyrightable contribution to a work is an author and owner of that joint work, and thus may exploit that work.[5]

Therefore, in determining the target's ownership rights in its intellectual property assets, the buyer must resolve the following questions:

- When was the work first created?
- Who were the creators or authors?
- What were the relationships of the authors to the target? Were they employees or independent consultants?
- Was the work part of the target's regular business?
- Did the work incorporate any confidential information or the target's trade secrets?
- Was the work performed within the scope of the employee's regular employment responsibilities?
- Did the target initiate the project or did the creator make initial contact with the target?
- If the creator was an independent consultant, did the consultant sign an agreement transferring all ownership rights in the work to target?

- When did the consultant sign such an agreement? (The Federal copyright statute provides that an author of a work other than a work-made-for-hire may terminate a license or grant of rights in a copyright within five years after the thirty-fifth anniversary of such transfer of rights or publication of the work.)

- If the target purchased the work from a third party, did the third party demonstrate that it had full ownership rights in the work? Or, is there an author of the work who still may have a claim in the work?

- Has anyone ever made a claim of ownership to the property? Is the company involved in any pending or threatened proceeding relating to the work?

- Has a security interest ever been granted in the property as collateral for a debt?

- If one or more persons created the work, what was the involvement of each party? Did anyone make an independently copyrightable contribution that enabled him or her to exploit the work?

PROTECTING YOUR RIGHTS

In order to retain the full benefits of ownership rights in a piece of intellectual property, the target should have protected its property with federal, state and international filings for patent, copyright, trademark, or servicemark protection. It is important that these filings were done correctly. In 1990, a California court invalidated copyrights in several computer programs because of inaccurate disclosure in the copyright registrations.[6]

The buyer also must review whether the target complied with all maintenance fee and filing requirements so that the property has continuous protection. In particular, any copyrights obtained for works created before January 1, 1978, when the new copyright law came into effect, must be renewed.

In addition to formal filing protections, the buyer must be concerned with protecting the secrecy of the target's assets. For example, in the context of software, the buyer needs to know how the target has handled source codes when it licensed its property to third parties. Were these codes held in escrow? Does the licensee have the right to all updated versions of the source codes? The buyer needs to be generally comfortable with the steps the target has taken to protect the confidentiality of its assets. If those steps are inadequate, the buyer must improve on them.

Therefore, the buyer's inquiry into protection should include answers to the following questions:

- Is the asset protected?
- What is the form of protection?
- Were all necessary state and federal filings made?
- Were the registrations correctly done?
- Have the registrations been properly maintained? If annual maintenance fees are required, have they been paid? If an agency requires intermittent filings of affidavits of use, were these affidavits filed?

- Has the copyright on a work created before January 1, 1978 been renewed?

- Were all transfers of rights and license agreements filed with the proper state and federal authorities? Have any termination events occurred under the license agreement?

- Have all security interests in the property been properly perfected? In a 1990 case, a federal court in California held that a security interest in a copyrighted work must be perfected by filing with the U.S. Copyright Office rather than according to the rules of the Uniform Commercial Code.[7]

- Would another form of protection be better for the property? That is, would another form provide stronger protection?

- What steps has the target firm taken to preserve the confidentiality of its assets? Are those steps adequate?

- Who is responsible for maintaining the condition of the work? Have the maintenance fees been paid to date?

PREPARING FOR THE FUTURE

Any company that relies on intellectual property assets should have in place institutionalized mechanisms for creating and maintaining rights on its assets so that they will have the strongest protection possible. Toward that end, the following are some general recommendations:

- The company should have in place a system for making sure that all federal, state, and international registrations for patents, copyrights, and trade and service marks are done properly and that these protections are continued by filing the necessary maintenance fees and affidavits of continued use.

- The company should have a mechanism for policing infringement of its patents, copyrights, and trade and service marks by third parties, as well as for its own infringement of others' rights.

- All company employment contracts should include covenants prohibiting its employees from competing and confidentiality agreements acknowledging the employee's obligation to treat the company's proprietary information as secret.

- Employment contracts should include, as a matter of course, covenants requiring employees to relinquish all rights to works created within the scope of employment.

- Before the work is begun, all independent consultants hired to create or assist in creating a work must agree that all rights to the work will belong to the company. Covenants for the protection of confidential and proprietary information, and negative "anti-raiding" covenants should be included in the agreements.

- The company should regularly review the activities of its competitors.

- If the company licenses intellectual property from third parties, it should be sure that it has the right to make and market derivative works and enjoy the benefit of all improvements and enhancements of the property.

WORTH THE EFFORT

The ever-increasing use of technology in business demands that the buyer thoroughly investigate the target's intellectual property assets before acquiring them. Only through a sound due diligence investigation can the buyer accurately value the target's assets and gain protection against contingencies that may seriously damage their value in the future. The buyer needs to ask the right questions—and probe into the circumstances under which the target deems an intellectual property asset "protected," rather than simply accepting the existence of a patent, copyright, trademark, or servicemark as sufficient. The buyer must also do UCC and lien searches and review all of the target's license agreements to be certain that the target can freely transfer its assets. The target, meanwhile, will want to make sure that its intellectual property protections are in good order so that it will be in the strongest possible negotiating position.

Although the due diligence investigation may seem time consuming and costly at the outset, the price of the buyer's awareness is a solid investment in the future.

NOTES

1. "Author" is a term of art in intellectual property law. See, e.g., 17 U.S.C.A. § 201 (West 1992). The Supreme Court has stated that "[a]s a general rule, the author is the party who actually creates the work, that is, the person who translates an idea into a fixed, tangible expression is entitled to copyright protection." *Community for Creative Non-Violence v. Reid,* 490 U.S. 730, 737 (1989). 17 U.S.C.A. § 201(b) (West 1992).

2. *Community for Creative Non-Violence v. Reid,* 490 U.S. 730 (1989). The Supreme Court set forth a number of factors to be considered in determining whether the creator of a work is an employee: the skill required; the source of the instrumentalities and tools; the location of the work; the duration of the relationship between the parties; whether the hiring party has the right to assign additional projects to the hired party; the extent of the hired party's discretion over when and how long to work; the method of payment; the hired party's role in hiring and paying assistants; whether the work is part of the regular business of the hiring party; whether the hiring party is in business; the provision of employee benefits; and the tax treatment of the hired party. *Id.* at 751–52 (footnotes omitted).

3. *MacLean Assoc. Inc. v. Wm. M. Mercer-Meidinger-Hansen, Inc.,* 952 F.2d 769 (3d Cir. 1991).

4. 17 U.S.C.A. § 101 (West 1992). A joint work is a "work prepared by two or more authors with the intention that their contributions be merged into inseparable or interdependent parts of a unitary whole."

5. See *Childress v. Taylor,* 945 F.2d 500 (2d Cir. 1991) and *Ashton-Tate Corp v. Ross,* 916 F.2d 516 (9th Cir. 1990).

6. *Ashton-Tate Corp. v. Fox Software, Inc.,* 760 F.Supp. 831 (C.D. Cal. 1990).

7. *In re Peregrine Entertainment Ltd.,* 116 B.R. 194 (C.D. Cal. 1990). This decision has not been extended to trademark law. See *In re 199Z, Inc.,* 137 B.R. 778 (C.D. Cal. 1992).

35

Noncompetition Agreements that Keep the Peace

Mark H. Budoff

Partner, Camhy, Karlinsky & Stein,
New York, New York

When a business is sold, prohibitions against the seller's future competitive activities obviously are important to both the buyer, who wants protection, and the seller, who wants to avoid undue restraints on its ability to continue to pursue a livelihood. The large number and the frequency of litigations relating to the post-sale activities of sellers, as well as the intensity with which such litigations usually are conducted, demonstrate the need for careful consideration of the legal issues by the parties and their attorneys.

The courts in New York and other states generally have recognized two bases for imposing prohibitions or restrictions on the activities of the seller. These are:

- Express provisions in the contract of sale
- Common-law principles established by the courts over the years

A significant common-law principle recognized by the New York courts is that the seller of a business is prohibited after the sale from diminishing the value of what is sold by soliciting the customers of the business. This prohibition lasts for an unlimited time and covers an unlimited area.

The common-law bar against solicitation arises only if the acquirer is buying the goodwill of the seller's company. Goodwill, in its most basic form, is the customer relations that the company has built up and maintained. Therefore, it is just common sense that a seller should not be allowed to take back the goodwill it sold by going after the company's customers. If the company's goodwill is not part of the sale, then the seller would be free to solicit the company's customers and otherwise compete with it unless the contract of sale includes provisions expressly restricting such activities.

It is important to note that the common-law rule only applies to solicitation of customers by the seller. It does not prohibit the seller from competing with the business it sold.

A FINE LINE

Distinguishing between permissible competition and improper solicitation is often difficult. Generally speaking, "competition" means engaging in the same business. "Solicitation," on the other hand, refers to actively seeking to do business with particular customers. Thus, under the common-law rule, a seller may never contact a customer of its former company to solicit that customer's business. However, if the customer comes to the seller unsolicited, the seller is permitted to compete with its former company by accepting the customer's business.

Since the common-law rule applies only to solicitation, restraints on the seller's post-sale competition can be achieved only by including express, restrictive language in the contract of sale. Such provisions, however, will not be accorded the same broad scope as the common-law bar against solicitation. Rather, contractual provisions limiting or prohibiting competition will be enforceable only for a "reasonable time" and in a "reasonable geographic area," with "reasonableness" being determined by the facts in a given case.

Indeed, while New York's courts will "blue-line" the contractual provision—i.e., enforce it only for the time and area the court deems reasonable—the courts in a number of other states simply will throw out a provision in its entirety if the courts find the stated time and area to be "unreasonable." Indeed, in at least one state, California, such contractual restraints are void by statute, although its courts have created some limited exceptions.

CONTRACT RESTRAINTS

Express provisions in the contract also can be used to limit the common-law rule barring solicitation. This point was mired in considerable confusion for a number of years. In an early case, the buyer of a business sought to restrain the seller from competing by soliciting its customers even though the time period fixed in the contract had expired. The restraint was granted by the court and upheld by New York's highest court, suggesting that a contractual provision barring competition for a specified time did not limit the common-law prohibition against solicitation. This decision was viewed by many as rendering meaningless most, if not all, contractual provisions restricting the seller's postsale activities.

In a case decided in 1989, New York's highest court revisited the issue and clarified the interplay between the common-law rule and contractual prohibitions. In that case, the contract expressly barred the seller from performing services for three specified customers for a five-year period after the sale. During the five-year period, the buyer sued the seller, seeking to prohibit the seller from soliciting other customers.

The court held that by contractually agreeing to prohibit the seller from doing business with specific customers for a stated period of time, the buyer had, in effect, overridden the broader protection it would have had under the common-law rules, which would have prohibited solicitation of all customers forever. Accordingly, the court said that the seller was free to solicit any of its former company's other customers and after the five-year term expired would be free to solicit the three that were specifically identified in the contract.

AFTER THE HONEYMOON

In negotiating the sale of a business, both the buyer and seller need to consider not only the terms of the sale but what happens afterward. The buyer should think about the ways in which the seller could hurt the business in the future, and how best to protect itself against the potential harm. Should express restrictions and prohibitions be included in the contract, and, if so, under what terms?

The seller likewise should consider what activities it wants to be free to engage in, and how to avoid or limit being prohibited from doing so. In some instances, that may mean that the seller should itself suggest that the contract include a provision barring its solicitation of customers for a stated period of time. While the seller would appear to be creating a self-imposed restriction on its postsale activities, it also would be freeing itself of the common-law bar against solicitation for an unlimited time and area.

36

The Value of a Happy Customer

Steven Keith Platt

Managing Director, AM&G Capital Corp.,
Chicago, Illinois

The failure to properly manage customer relationships before, during, and after the sale of a business can have a devastating impact on a company's value. It is incumbent on both acquirer and seller to recognize the customer base as a preeminent contributor to value and, accordingly, to develop a customer management strategy that sustains critical patronage. Individual strategies may be tailored to specific facts and circumstances, but an essential element in each is appropriate communication with key customers throughout the process to ensure that they will be retained after the transaction closes.

In general, we have found that if accorded the proper degree of deference, customers are not particularly concerned with who owns the business. Rather, they want to be assured that, if the target is a manufacturer, it will continue to ship merchandise of consistent quality on time, and if it is a service firm, it will continue to provide its services in a professional manner. In either case, customers will be concerned that the new owners will not leverage the company to such an extent that its survival or competitiveness will be threatened. They may want special assurances when a significant change in management accompanies the sale and they will have to deal directly with new people.

A PLAN IS CRITICAL

Customer management strategy involves a well-devised plan to retain customers, and, therefore, a company's value, during a period of uncertainty in the life of a company. While not all customers need to be addressed, certainly those that account for a significant portion of revenue require special attention.

Both sides have a huge stake in preventing customer erosion during a change of ownership. This acquirer's due diligence process should, among other things, try to ascertain the strength of the relationship between key customers and the target, and whether those customers will continue the relationship after the deal closes. The seller initially has to worry that if there are major customer desertions at the time the deal is announced, the sale may fall through. And over the long run, customer relationships could be important if the seller's proceeds include contingent payments dependent on the company's continued success.

The concerns of both are critical because the value of a company is significantly affected by the quality of its customer base. Yet the value of this intangible, off-balance-sheet asset is not ascertainable separate from the company itself, as a building or piece of equipment might be. Rather, the value of a customer base, like the value of a management team, directly impacts a company's revenue stream and, therefore, its value.

However, absent a contractual relationship, critical material, or special know-how, customers have total discretion as to with whom they do business. It is this risk (i.e., the inability to calculate the value of a customer and determine whether that customer will remain with the company) and its effect on the company's value that makes customer retention and, therefore, customer management so critical in the acquisition process.

Cases in Point

To best illustrate the points to be discussed, assume that we are working with the three hypothetical, although not atypical, selling companies:

Ad, Ltd. is a medium-sized advertising firm. Since the firm's founding 12 years ago, its three partners have drifted apart, and problems exist in their relationship. Because of these problems, they have decided to sell. Most of Ad, Ltd.'s accounts are small, such as automobile dealerships and community banks. However, Ad, Ltd. has two large clients, a regional chain of fast-food restaurants and a national lumber retailer, accounting for 8 and 25 percent of revenue, respectively.

Crumble Co. is a private-label cookie manufacturer. The company's sole owner wants to sell and retire. Crumble Co.'s sales are divided among supermarkets, hospitals, and schools. Of these customers, two large supermarkets each account for 15 and 20 percent of sales.

Motown Manufacturing is a manufacturer of stampings for the automotive industry. The company's two owners are concerned about its future, because as it continues to grow, more and more capital is required to invest in equipment to keep the company competitive. To meet these needs, the owners have decided to sell their company or merge it with a deep-pocketed partner. Motown Manufacturing sells its products to Detroit automobile companies and other original equipment manufacturers. One customer, including its separate operating divisions and subsidiaries, accounts for 40 percent of revenue.

Nature of Relationships

Prior to announcing that a company is for sale and before potential acquirers are contacted, the target company should address the following issues:

- Which customers need to know that the company is for sale?
- What strategy should be devised to deal with these key customers?
- How to plan for management changes.

It is evident that the degree to which a particular customer needs to know that a company is for sale is directly related to how much sales volume it generates. This is because the loss of a critical customer would adversely affect the value of a company and could derail the sale process. Thus, if one customer accounts for a significant portion of a company's sales, the company is said to have a high customer concentration. In such cases, the customer is a critical asset of the company and must be dealt with accordingly.

Ad, Ltd., for example, has two significant customers that may require attention prior to initiating the sale process: the fast-food chain and the lumber retailer.

The fast food chain, which accounts for eight percent of Ad, Ltd.'s revenue, may or may not need to be contacted. The benefit of contact is to secure the relationship after the transaction closes. The major deterrent in contacting this or any significant customer is the risk that vital information may be leaked to the public.

The lumber retailer, accounting for 25 percent of Ad, Ltd.'s revenue, should be contacted regarding the proposed sale because its business clearly is an important asset of Ad, Ltd. Because of this customer risk, an acquirer will want to contact the lumber retailer during due diligence and may structure a portion of the purchase price on the retention of this customer over a certain period of time. It can safely be assumed that the many smaller accounts that were probably serviced by nonpartner employees do not need to be notified at this stage of an impending sale of Ad, Ltd.

Constructive Strategies

Prior to the meetings with such key customers, a constructive strategy should be developed. The central concerns of these customers will be the reasons for the sale and its ramifications to them. Side issues that the seller should address include who delivers the message, and the timing of the meetings.

Important customers will want to know—in fact, are entitled to know—why an owner wants to sell; e.g., the owner is reaching retirement age, the business unit no longer fits within the company's strategy, and so on.

In Motown Manufacturing's case, the need for capital to allow the company to remain competitive and, ultimately, to better serve the needs of its major customer should be favorably received by the key customer. Thus, the sale of Motown Manufacturing should have positive ramifications. At Crumble Co., the owner's desire to retire likewise should not be adversely received by its two large supermarket accounts. Depending on the identity of the ultimate acquirer, the sellers of Ad, Ltd., Crumble Co., and Motown Manufacturing should be prepared to stay around long enough to assist in a smooth transition of customer relations, if necessary.

As noted earlier, generally we have found that customers are not concerned with who owns a company, provided that their needs continue to be served. In addition, it is important that they learn of a proposed sale directly from the company, rather than through the rumor mill. In practice, we have found that such key customers will adopt a "wait-and-see" attitude. Thus, customer service during this tenuous time is more important than ever.

THE MESSAGE AND THE MESSENGER

The side issues of who delivers this message and when it should be delivered must be examined carefully. Either a company's president or the head of sales should visit with such critical customers. This could be tricky when, for example, a company has two or more key customers and there is risk that word of the company's sale will reach customers before the firm can inform them. The timing for meeting with customers will depend on how the deal is being marketed and whether the acquirer is in the same industry.

If there is not a high customer concentration, a negotiated sale will not require customer notification until negotiations are far advanced. If the business has a high customer concentration and there is a negotiated sale, the timing of customer meetings will be influenced greatly by the identity of the potential buyer. If the buyer is not in the same industry, e.g., a financial buyer, this meeting can be delayed. If the buyer is in the same industry, e.g., a competitor, supplier, and so on, early contact is advisable. In either case, if an auction is employed, consider advising key customers of the intention to sell before contacting potential buyers.

As noted earlier, when a significant change in management accompanies a divestiture, customer retention becomes even more problematic. Short of purchase price adjustments, the best strategy is a slow transition of management. Thus, assume that the owner of Crumble Co. has a strong personal relationship with the owner of one of its large supermarket accounts. In such a case, the acquirer should retain the services of the selling owner for a sufficient period of time to ensure a smooth transition.

The Limbo Period

During the time between the sale announcement and the transaction's close, several communications needs will arise. They include:

- The acquirer's need to satisfy itself that key customers will remain with the company
- The key customers' need to be kept apprised of the transaction's status

A diligent acquirer will request detailed information regarding the relationship between the selling company and its key accounts. The target company will be extremely sensitive to such disclosure, regardless of a nondisclosure agreement, especially if the acquirer is a competitor. The best balance between these two competing needs is to slowly release bits of key customer information to the acquirer as the transaction progresses. Thus, as the process continues, the seller can release more and more necessary information.

When a competitor is the acquirer, extreme care must be exercised. Critical customer information such as pricing, margins on products sold, and so forth, should be delayed until all other due diligence items are resolved and the attorneys have completed their negotiations. Further, contact with customers should be delayed until immediately prior to closing.

If a meeting between a key customer and an acquirer is to take place, the seller should be included to prevent the acquirer from potentially damaging the relationship. For example, assume that in Motown Manufacturing's case the need for capital is critical to survival. If the potential acquirer determines this and discusses it with Motown's key customer, the traditional relationship could be damaged.

As a further illustration, assume that a direct competitor of Crumble Co. seeks to acquire its business. If critical information is released to the acquirer and the transaction does not close, Crumble Co. is at risk with regard to its key supermarket accounts. This risk exists even if a nondisclosure agreement was executed. This is because in all likelihood the competitor already has been calling on the customers, and it will be difficult to prove that it relied on Crumble's information to conduct business. At best, Crumble Co. buys itself an expensive lawsuit and no one wins.

Critical Communications

Throughout the transaction process, communication with key customers is critical. Expediting the transaction is the best way to keep them calm. But frequent meetings between senior managements are helpful, as is advising the key customer on the transaction's progress and anticipated closing time.

If possible, avoid specifically identifying the potential acquirer, because if the key customer has preconceived ideas about the buyer, or discussions with one potential acquirer break down and resume with another, the key customer may become rattled needlessly. Delay disclosure of the buyer's identity for as long as possible.

After a transaction is closed, meetings between the new owners and key customers may be necessary. If management of the target company is retained, the new owners may not need to be involved. But if the sale is accompanied by a significant change in management, the new owners and new management should meet with such key accounts frequently. This is because these customers will be insecure regarding the acquired company's financial and operating stability.

In Motown Manufacturing's case, for example, if the acquirer is a financial buyer, its major customer would want assurances that the company is not so highly leveraged that the new ownership can't invest the capital necessary to keep the company competitive. Assume, conversely, that the acquirer is a financially strong, noncompetitive industry supplier. Key customers would want to be assured about the new owner's operational plans for the company so that they can maintain a level of comfort about supply and service.

THE RULES CHANGE

The key to the customer management strategy is the realization by both buyer and seller that major customers, regardless of how loyal or well-served they were in past, cannot be counted as "sure things" when a business changes hands. From a pure business perspective, significant customers will want to know that their interests are being served by the new ownership. There is no substitute for face-to-face contact to provide these assurances.

Moreover, both sides must be aware of how vulnerable they are during the sale of the company. Competitors often seize on the sale announcement as an opportunity to pitch for business, playing on customer fears that a new ownership will radically change existing relationships and jeopardize their businesses.

Continuity in the form of continued patronage from longtime key customers is most essential at a time when the company itself is undergoing the strains of transition. The M&A parties that neglect the customer relations issue are risking a major source of present and continued value. This chapter has presented some general methods for properly managing customer relationships. But in the final analysis, each transaction requires its own specific planning, based on the unique characteristics of the business, its markets, and its traditional customer relationships.

37
Fairness Opinions

Chester A. Gougis
*President, Duff & Phelps Financial
Consulting Co., Chicago, Illinois*

In the aftermath of the "deal mania" that characterized the 1980s, corporate boards of directors are giving more careful consideration to proposed corporate restructurings. Even in the present tight credit environment, which makes acquisitions and management buy-outs difficult, there is a higher standard of care to ensure that those transactions that can be completed, including subsidiary spin-offs, squeeze-out mergers, and joint ventures, make economic sense and are fair to shareholders. Directors increasingly turn to financial advisers who have developed the specialized expertise in addressing these issues. As a result, greater attention is being paid to fairness opinions.

Fairness opinions are used to aid fiduciaries in making decisions that affect the people whose financial interests are at stake. Fiduciaries include boards of directors, corporate debt trustees, bankruptcy trustees, ESOP trustees, and personal trustees.

ON THE SHAREHOLDERS' BEHALF

Fairness opinions provided to a company's board of directors typically do not address the interests of employees or creditors. They are directed toward one group—the shareholders of the company. As a result, the fairness opinion conclusion is based primarily on the valuation of the stock held by (or issued to) the shareholders. If an acquirer has proposed the acquisition of all of the company's existing stock, the analysis supporting the fairness opinion would compare the offer price to the estimated true economic value of the company. If a stock merger has been proposed, the valuation of the acquirer's stock also must be completed.

The question of whether the transaction is equitable is a separate issue. In some transactions, particularly LBOs, the shareholders can receive a considerable premium over the trading price—in some cases as much as a 100 percent premium. However, key managers may receive much more through equity granted in the new company. This type of deal may not be equitable, but it may be fair, which is what the fairness opinion is designed to measure.

Integrity under Attack

In recent years, the integrity of the fairness opinion has come into question. In the past, most acquisitions involved one company buying another company, and the buyer and seller were clearly defined. Each side was represented by its own investment banker. In most cases, the investment banker had a longstanding relationship with the company and felt that one of its responsibilities was to advise the company and its board of directors about these types of transactions.

Today, a company's investment banker also may be an equity participant in the proposed transaction—which creates a conflict of interest. The completion fees to be paid to the investment banking firm may create another area of a conflict of interests. In many cases, the size of the fee depends on whether or not the offer is accepted. This creates a conflict of interests in terms of the pure advisory role these firms play.

It is not only the external players who have conflicting roles but also the internal players. In a takeover situation, management sometimes may be influenced by the desire to preserve the status quo—i.e., their own jobs. In other cases, they may have lucrative golden parachute or incentive schemes that may bias them in favor of a buy-out. Management also may play a key role as one of the bidders in a transaction.

This is a cause for concern in transactions, because management may be able to gain unfair advantage by using information about the company to which they have exclusive access. As a result, a fairness opinion from an independent source often is requested by the board of directors of a company to ensure that an objective, unbiased assessment of the fairness of the transaction price can be made.

Fiduciary Responsibilities

Fairness opinions also are used by other fiduciaries who have the responsibility to protect their group's interests. Because of the nature of a fiduciary's responsibilities, as well as exposure to potential liabilities, a fiduciary will want an outside expert to confirm his or her own judgment. For example, fairness opinions are used to advise ESOP trustees on their responsibility in voting ESOP shares for or against transactions that affect the ESOP, which may have different interests than the shareholder group as a whole.

Similarly, in situations of bankruptcy or restructuring, in which covenants have been violated and corporate debt trustees are asked to waive them, those trustees have a fiduciary responsibility to the bondholders to make sure that whatever action the company takes is for the benefit of their particular constituency. Fairness opinions also are provided in some cases to personal trustees, who have a fiduciary responsibility to make sure their actions are in the best interest of trust beneficiaries.

SPREAD TO PRIVATE COMPANIES

Historically, fairness opinions have been used primarily by public companies. Because public companies have a diverse group of owners with different interests, there is the possibility of class-action suits. Also, because public companies are bigger—and the stakes are higher—it makes more economic sense to get a fairness opinion.

Increasingly, fairness opinions are being used in private companies, as their similarities with their public counterparts become more obvious. Private companies are getting larger. In the past, when a company reached a certain size, it was almost inevitable that it went public. Now, there are numerous large private companies with no intention of going public.

Often, as these companies grow and mature, the number of shareholders increase and their interests become more diverse. The boards of these larger private companies often include outside members who recognize that they have a fiduciary responsibility to make sure their actions benefit all shareholders rather than simply the members of a controlling family group.

There also has been an increasing tendency for private company situations to get "messy." That is, as the stakes get larger, cohesive family groups often break apart, accompanied by acrimonious litigation. As a result, there has been a trend for private companies to obtain fairness opinions to validate some of their most critical corporate decisions.

WIDE LATITUDE

Fairness opinions must comply with legal and regulatory requirements. With all the attention being paid to issues of fairness, it is surprising that there are no formal requirements for a company to obtain a fairness opinion. The means of determining whether an offer is fair is solely at the discretion of the company's board of directors.

The SEC requirements regarding fairness opinions deal mostly with disclosure. According to Rule 13e-3, directors must disclose the following factors:

- Current market price of the stock
- Historical prices of the stock
- Net book value of the stock
- Going concern value

- Liquidation value
- Prices paid in company repurchases
- Outside fairness opinions or valuations
- Other offers.

Although the SEC does not require that a board get a fairness opinion, if one is received it must be disclosed.

Third-Party Objectivity

A few years ago, U.S. Representative Edward Markey (D., Mass.) introduced legislation requiring that a fairness opinion be obtained from an outside source—i.e., not the company's investment bank—on any management buy-out or similar transaction. The legislation was written to prevent sweetheart LBO deals, in which management came in with a quick offer to buy the company, without entertaining other offers, and as a result bought the company for a very favorable price.

It was argued that several deals in the early years of LBOs fell into this category. In recent years, as the visibility of these transactions to both regulators and alternative buyers increased, the ability of management to do this lessened. However, many legislators still feel that there is a need for regulations to ensure the fairness to shareholders of the price paid by management in a buy-out.

Legal Drivers

Developments on the legal front have been the biggest impetus for directors to get fairness opinions. Several court decisions have held directors liable in takeover transactions in which it was determined that the directors did not act in the shareholders' best interest. These cases are somewhat extreme in the sense that the boards of directors apparently ignored the normal standard of care in representing shareholders. Nonetheless, such cases emphasize that directors have a fiduciary responsibility to shareholders that must be taken very seriously.

The case law suggests that directors facing a takeover or buy-out bid need to:

- Establish a clear record of consideration of fairness
- Obtain a fairness opinion
- Ensure that the opinion is sufficiently thorough and extensive
- Negotiate terms and price, and, in certain circumstances, seek other bidders

Two cases establish the responsibility of independent directors in this area. One, *Weinberger v. UOP Inc.,* decided by the Delaware Supreme Court in 1983, dealt with a "squeeze-out merger," a transaction that resulted in the forced termination of equity ownership for many minority shareholders. Interestingly, the directors had obtained a fairness opinion, but it was discovered to be a cursory opinion provided over the weekend by the company's investment bank (which was also receiving significant fees in the transaction).

In the other case, *Smith* v. *Van Gorkem,* decided by the Delaware court in 1985, the board did not get a formal fairness opinion, yet approved a fairly sizable acquisition only a few hours after hearing about it.

Directors can be held personally liable in some cases. This has been the principal motivation behind the increased focus on fairness opinions in takeover battles. Several court rulings in corporate takeover battles—for example, Revlon, Inc., SCM Corp., and Freuhauf Corp.—suggest that at some point in a takeover transaction, directors may be required to conduct an auction, or at least act in a neutral manner, to encourage the highest possible price for shareholders. Fairness opinions may need to address the fairness and adequacy of the auction process.

MINORITY PROTECTION

The board of directors of a private company particularly must be concerned with protecting the interests of minority shareholders, a group that generally has little influence or control over corporate policy and is subject to decisions made by the majority shareholder. For most public corporations, there rarely is a majority shareholder who exercises control over the direction of the firm; thus, the board of directors must be responsible to, and protective of, all of the shareholders' interests. Although the fairness issue must address minority interest concerns, the basis of valuation used to assess proposed transaction's fairness is often at a "control value" level.

For illustrative purposes, if a public company's stock was selling for $60 a share (representing a minority share price) and an offer was made for 100 percent of the stock at $80 a share, how can the board of directors turn down an offer that represents an easy $20 per share profit?

That offer may be inadequate, since it is for a controlling interest in the company. Perhaps the company would be worth $90 to $100 per share to a buyer who would dispose of undervalued assets, consolidate administrative functions, reduce personnel costs, and improve working capital management, as well as make numerous policy changes involving production, pricing, distribution, and marketing of the company's products.

The basis for determining a fair acquisition price should consider that there are several buyers who typically are willing to pay a price significantly higher than the aggregate minority interest value for 100 percent of a company.

Sometimes, however, there is a unique buyer who can afford to pay even more than the general universe of control buyers because of special benefits that only this particular buyer can realize from the transaction (i.e., unique synergies, special cost savings opportunities, etc.). In such cases, a fair acquisition price need not fully reflect these unique benefits. Instead, the financial adviser should assess the probability of a higher price being offered by competitive market bidders within a reasonable time period. Often, this is difficult to assess, and misjudgment could result in a fair offer being refused and no higher offer forthcoming. Nevertheless, an informed financial adviser should be able to assess the relative likelihood of such additional offers.

TESTING THE MARKET

Much of the past criticism of fairness opinions has focused on the lack of due diligence that accompanied many opinions. Directors and the company's legal advisers should anticipate the need for a fairness opinion so that a thorough analysis can be completed. If time permits, the shareholders may be well served if the directors allow for a "testing of the market" to see if other bidders would likely be forthcoming.

In summary, as corporate financial transactions receive increasing scrutiny from shareholders and regulators, the role of the fairness opinion has become more important. If care is taken to ensure objectivity, independence, and thoroughness by the fairness opinion provider, these opinions can be effective tools in protecting corporate boards and shareholders.

PART 6

After
the
Merger

38

First Stage Review: Cold Light of Day

James M. Needham
*President, Fieldston Investors L.P.,
New York, New York*

Did I get what I planned for? Did I get what I paid for? For many acquirers the answers to these questions are in the negative as the euphoria of the honeymoon evaporates while unforeseen developments arise after the acquisition is completed. The seeds of these unforeseen developments may have predated the acquisition or the developments may have occurred subsequent to the acquisition as a result of the acquirer's actions or circumstances that the buyer could not control. How the acquirer can increase its chances of getting favorable responses to the opening questions will be addressed in this discussion.

The question "Did I get what I planned for?" assumes that the acquirer had realistic expectations against which it could measure postacquisition results, and that the plan and the results were measurable in a meaningful time period by objective criteria.

The acquirer's expectations may be based on preexisting beliefs about the target company and its industry, or derived from an acquisition staff's interpretation of its investigative results. An acquisition investigation will provide a basis for assessing the acquired company's resources (financial, tangible, and intangible), markets (for both its raw materials and end products), and personnel (operational and administrative), as well as the impact of the acquisition structure and any acquisition contingencies on the target's ability to perform.

Assumptions serve as putty in the piecing together of an analysis by the potential acquirer. Because both industry and market knowledge and the results of an investigation of the acquisition candidate are limited, assumptions must be used to fill in the gaps. Unfortunately, putty is easily molded to almost any shape, and is only a temporary measure at best. Too often, the expectations of the acquirer result from an analysis heavy with putty and molded to fit the expectations. This highlights the importance of a thorough investigation prior to the acquisition. The performance of a quality acquisition review anticipates and identifies many of the problems that arise after an acquisition. Accordingly, these postmerger piper problems can be anticipated, foreseen, and provided for in the development of the purchase price, transaction structure, and contract terms.

Acquirers make a "buy" decision on the presumption that the sellers will provide certain attributes. Unless those desired attributes are clearly stated, it will be difficult for the acquirer's review team to address them, much less validate their existence or even recognize the need for validation. Similarly, downside risk often may be ignored as a result of the acquirer's enthusiasm for the perceived upside potential of the acquisition. Basic strategic questions tend to go unanswered in the plethora of detail that is gathered—such questions as: What are the key operating factors necessary for success in this business? Who in the organization is responsible for achieving these success factors? Have we missed a changing competitive position? Is there a product substitution threat? Have we organized ourselves to find strategic and business deal breakers? This is the time when deal breakers external to the basic business must be identified, such as regulatory and tax compliance and product liability exposure.

Currently the biggest potential deal breaker or source of significant potential liability in making an acquisition is the hazardous environmental mine field. Liability for potential environmental liability most often is not ascertainable until at least a month or two into the acquisition process. Determining the extent of any environmental liability and providing for it in the acquisition contract is, in my opinion, the single most important liability overlooked in the initial stages of the acquisition process.

The seller has no interest in determining its environmental liability prior to sale because it is then obligated to report any violations to the government and then incur the expense of remediation. This costs *cash*. If the sale is not consummated, the seller is left with an immediate cleanup liability that could have been postponed if no sale process had occurred. Therefore, the buyer can assume, contrary to reassurances from the seller, that neither the seller nor buyer will know the full extent of any environmental liability until the acquirer's engineers and investigators, which will have to be approved by its lenders, have made an inspection of the seller's property and off-site dumping exposure. The postmerger piper loves environmental and regulatory liability because of the constant changes in regulations and the constant uncertainty of seller or buyer compliance with the maze of regulations in multiple governmental jurisdictions.

To avoid paying the postmerger piper, a buyer should understand that the purpose of the acquisition investigation is both to validate assumptions on which the buy and price decisions will be made and to provide an assessment of the risk and potential downside exposure. In addition, a postacquisition plan should be in place prior to consummation of an acquisition so as to ensure that the assets the buyer purchased—whether they be people, physical, or intangible—remain after the acquisition.

DEFINING ACQUISITION OBJECTIVES

Acquisition objectives often are regarded as either strategy- or finance-driven. What often is lost sight of is that acquisitions are, first of all, business-driven. Businesses are more than just amalgamations of assets and liabilities. They include people and know-how, reputation and market position, product quality and technology, which, in combination, produce more than the sum of the parts that may be easily measured and quantified. Some concepts that help explain a business are culture, people, style, values, and strategy—none of which can be easily transplanted from seller to buyer. These intangible and hard-to-measure characteristics may not guarantee the success of the business. But if they are lost, an ongoing business can be destroyed.

In setting both the acquisition objectives and acquisition criteria, it is important for the acquirer to state explicitly just what the acquisition is expected to provide, and what the buyer is expected to supply or is capable of supplying to the seller's business. Is the buyer seeking only an expanded product line? Production facilities? Technology? Market access? A proven management team? Or is the buyer seeking the synthesis of all these factors—a profitable ongoing business?

If the buyer is seeking only limited assets from an acquisition, such as a new product line to distribute through the buyer's distribution system, the chances of paying the piper after the acquisition are lessened. A review can be tailored to the explicit characteristics of the new product line and its anticipated benefits to the buyer. Some may argue that such an acquisition is really not an acquisition of a business, but an acquisition of a specific asset.

If the buyer is seeking an entity with all the intangible assets that make a business attractive, those elements must be identified and ranked in some order of priority. Candidates then can be screened not just on financial considerations and other quantifiable criteria, but on those substantial intangibles of business that indeed provide a competitive edge. Accordingly, a well-thought-out listing of needs that an acquisition candidate should supply, including those intangibles that make a business, is the first step on a hazardous journey toward a successful acquisition.

In my experience, acquisition searches often are limited and produce poor results because they rely exclusively on financial and product screens. Substantial data on industries and companies within those industries are publicly available. What is missing from all these data bases is a guide to the substance of the business. That search for substance forms the core of the acquisition search and review. Substance is a qualitative characteristic that can be found only through a synthesis of experience and judgment. This synthesis is often found in industry and functional peers.

DEFINING THE SCOPE OF THE ACQUISITION REVIEW

With a clear set of acquisition objectives and criteria, the buyer has standards for measuring an acquisition candidate. In addition, a purchaser will have identified those assumptions on which a buy decision will be made and a price and structure determined.

But selection of the best target company to approach still is a most difficult decision. Unfortunately, no foolproof method of candidate selection exists. Certain steps taken at this stage can save much time, expense, and potential disaster. Depending on the nature of the acquisition and the closeness of its strategic fit with existing businesses, the selection process will vary from company to company and industry to industry.

A buyer that acquires a company in its own industry will have a greater chance of success because it already has a sense of those intangibles, such as management, culture, and values, that the seller may possess. Similarly, the buyer's organization will have a peer appraisal of counterparts in the target company. Much less quantification is required for such an acquisition, and the scope of the review can be directed at areas of potential downside risk, which prior knowledge of both the seller's industry and seller itself will help to identify. As the buyer moves away from its area of detailed knowledge of specific businesses and markets, it will have to rely on greater quantification of information, and the experiences and insight of industry experts who have direct knowledge of the candidates under review.

Companies often perform financial screens and limit their acquisition reviews to superficial financial analyses. It is in these cases that the greatest risk of postacquisition failure exists. For example, an understanding of the current and potential sources, uses, and timing of the acquisition candidate's cash flow is essential to valuing and structuring a transaction. How else can the buyer make an informed decision regarding an appropriate debt/equity structure and financial terms?

Superficial financial analysis will not provide the insight into a business or provide a prudent buyer with comfort concerning the reliability of internal financial statements and analyses. Internal financial information should provide the basis for a trend analysis of what products have produced the most profits over the last 5 to 10 years and point out the changes in product line mix, seasonality, geographic and customer concentration, and intercompany or affiliated company sales.

The tax area is another part of an acquisition that may be strewn with pitfalls for the haphazard investigator. For example, it is not uncommon for buyer and seller to reach an agreement and then find out that they ignored the matter of significant amounts of recapture taxes and just which side had the responsibility of paying for them. Indeed, the tax sector is so far-reaching that it requires a point-by-point examination of as many as three dozen different aspects of the deal, both before and after it is completed. Understanding the seller's tax position in assessing different transaction structures often is not addressed until much time is wasted by the buyer in concentrating only on its own objectives.

Gauging the Qualities of the Target

Corporate growth and management performance cannot be measured or reflected merely in terms of accounting measurements. The financial statements of a company for a given year may have little to do with the major decisions the company management took during that year. Actions by management to achieve corporate growth often take years to add value to the company. Management and personnel development, the building of a distribution system, research and development expenses, investments to expand market share, and customer relations programs are only some examples of areas where payoffs may be long in coming. It is the quality of these management decisions that one must assess in making judgments about a company's performance and growth prospects. This approach will help avoid the common trap of accepting the short-term hype in performance or cyclical bounce in earnings as having a residual benefit to the buyer.

While the decisions of management ultimately are reflected at the bottom line, it is difficult to capture the true state of health of a corporation solely from its year-end financial statements. Often, financial statements don't provide investors and acquirers with much more than an indication of how the target performed in relation to a trend—such as a specific development that affected demand for its products or services—or within the context of the health of the general economy and its own industry. In fact, overreliance on "snapshots" of corporate performance may have provided public companies with disincentives for true overall growth by focusing too much attention on earnings per share growth as a way of rewarding both management and shareholders. Because corporate growth might be defined as adding value to the corporation, an acquisition analysis should pay more attention to the quality of the growth rather than to arbitrary financial measurements. In fact, financial statements alone will not provide insight into many identified assets that a company or business may have, particularly if those assets are underutilized; it is basically those assets that may be the real prizes to be acquired. Identifying those elusive and underutilized assets requires disciplines other than straight financial analysis. It is for this reason that I often consult with industry specialists, and people who have spent substantial parts of their lives in a particular industry, to gain insight into the target industry and its competitive dynamics. These industry insiders should be able to provide in-depth knowledge of the businesses and the corporate intangibles that exist within the seller, and pinpoint those attributes not defined in financial statements.

Accordingly, in determining the scope of a candidate review prior to the initial contract, one can make judgments about the intangible qualities of a business through personal experience, or through the retention of seasoned insiders who can provide information the acquirer may lack.

Not all acquisition review procedures can be easily segregated into prior-contact and postcontact procedures. In fact, they may overlap and will overlap.

CONDUCTING THE FINANCIAL REVIEW

In a financial review, the objective is to determine significant financial and accounting policies of the acquisition candidate and to compare them with the buyer's own policies for the purpose of putting together a pro forma consolidated set of financial statements. Adjustments generally are made to the seller's financial statements to bring them into conformity with the buyer's accounting policies. The impact of these changes and the cash impact of any tax effects from the acquisition should be well thought through prior to structuring the acquisition agreement. Other areas of investigation will be determined by the results of the nonfinancial review process. For example, the buyer, through its own experience or knowledge of the seller's industry, should be able to identify business areas that face the greatest tax exposure. And in reviewing the seller's projections of future performance, the buyer should determine whether forecasts made in previous years were achieved, in order to determine the reliability of the most recent projections.

Opinions of Outsiders

On the basis of my experience, an acquisition review always should include an assessment of the candidate by its industry peers. It is unlikely that negative aspects of a company will be highlighted by the seller during the selling process. But those negatives often are well known to competitors. Industry insiders, suppliers, and customers are the best sources of information on the competitive dynamics facing the acquisition candidate. The postmerger piper surely will be paid if industry insiders, suppliers, and customers are not interviewed early in the acquisition process. This process should point out areas of acquisition risk and opportunity. One can, prior to an acquisition, and even prior to contact, interview a number of competitors, customers, and suppliers, synthesize their comments about various companies within that industry, and put together a matrix that will provide sufficient insight into not only the target company but its competitors as well. My experience is that while competitors may not be anxious to talk about themselves, the various people in their organizations may be more than happy to give you opinions about other companies. Although these opinions might have to be treated with some degree of skepticism, they will form the closest thing to a peer review of the intangible aspects of the acquisition candidate that an acquirer will be able to obtain. Similarly, the buyer's own managers can identify their functional counterparts at the selling company and render a similar peer review. Such a review is not unlike the evaluation an executive search firm would perform when seeking qualified candidates for a management post. All of these reviews can be conducted by professionals who are retained by the buyer on a "no-name" basis.

Sources of Excessive Costs

The postmerger costs that exceed planned expenditures are the "piper's" payments. These costs can be divided into those that result from factors that are either internal or external to the combined organization. In both instances, the factors fall into controllable, impactible, and uncontrollable factors. Though the level of control in each factor may vary from one business to another, examples of typical factors that fit each category include the following.

Controllable Factors

Internal—Line of authority, compensation levels, staffing levels

External—Service to customers, payments to suppliers

Impactible Factors

Internal—Employee perception of the acquisition, the amount of time it takes to return to normality after the acquisition, the sense of common goals and shared values within the organization

External—Customer perception, service and product quality, fixed versus variable interest rates to finance the acquisition

Uncontrollable Factors

Internal—Death or disability of key employees, regulatory changes affecting the company

External—Financial health of customers, interest rates, reaction of suppliers

The goal of the postmerger plan is to establish an orderly methodology for minimizing the payment to the postacquisition piper and maximizing the expected benefits. Specifically, this entails minimizing the costs of changing various aspects of the acquirer's organization and the costs of taking the steps necessary to meet the acquirer's expectations. The thorough investigation that took place in the acquisition review should have identified the factors important to achieving expectations as controllable, impactible, or uncontrollable. As with any business plan, a series of alternative scenarios should be examined to determine how sensitive operations are to each factor, or to a combination of factors. Once the effects are identified, contingency measures can be planned to minimize the impact of various downside scenarios.

A critical factor at this phase of the planning process involves the acquirer's identification of where it must act to maximize benefits or cushion the blow from a reversal, and the determination of what actions must be taken in such circumstances. If this is not done, the buyer will deprive itself of a critical early warning signal that tips it to the best time for implementing a contingency plan. Precious time may be lost by waiting for financial information to pinpoint a problem, and corrective action may be applied too late. Above all, acquiring management must agree that all proposed actions are sound and can achieve desired results.

DEVELOPING THE POSTMERGER PLAN

The final stage in any acquisition is the implementation of the postmerger plan to integrate the acquired company into the acquirer. The primary elements of this plan should revolve around what changes are necessary, how to implement those changes, and how to manage the fear of change. Many postmerger plans fail to recognize the basic problems of organizational changes—that the required changes rarely are perceived as beneficial by those people who are required to change. The absence of incentives to alter employee behavior may result in a number of adverse outcomes, ranging from a snail-paced integration process to outright sabotage of the integration effort.

The postmerger plan needs to address the fear of change—regardless of whether actual changes are planned—in each component of the business, including:

- Customers' fears of product or service changes
- Suppliers' fears of detrimental changes in the acquiree's financial strength or buying habits
- Labor's fears of major layoffs
- Managers' fears of staff redundancy, concern over career paths, and compensation levels for key executives
- Some executives' fears of additional administrative burdens
- Target management's fears of loss of resources, especially financial, as a subsidiary company
- The acquiree's fears of becoming a "stepchild" (the "we–they" syndrome) in the combined company

In many cases, operational integration will be avoided, in line with the axiom "If it ain't broke, don't fix it." If so, only financial and operational monitoring will be required.

The postmerger plan should draw heavily on the information gained during the acquisition review, and focus especially on the particular attributes that comprise the substance of the business. The key managers—organizationally, operationally, and politically—need to be identified, addressed as to their futures, and provided with incentives to promote the desired changes. The overall level of operational autonomy needs to be decided with an eye to the perceptions of customers, suppliers, and employees, as well as the level of autonomy (or dependence) with which the buyer feels comfortable. Decisions regarding qualitative aspects of the business must be reached on such questions as:

- How does the proposed level of autonomy fit with the acquiree's corporate style and culture?
- How much internal competition is desirable?
- What steps will be taken to foster the level of cooperation and/or competition desired between the employees of the acquirer and target?
- What changes in accounting and clerical procedures should be made to provide better administrative contacts to the acquiree as well as the requisite information to the acquirer?

And, of course, difficult questions regarding the adjustment of compensation and benefits must be addressed.

In short, the postmerger plan for integration seeks to mold the working of the acquiree and acquirer to minimize the potential detriment to the substance of the acquiree's business. Central to this process is for the buyer to make it known to the seller's management that it is "they" who are the business, that both parties are buying into the future business together, and that both will reap appropriate rewards. When this message is conveyed to the seller's management prior to the signing of the acquisition agreement, the chances of shortchanging the postmerger piper increase.

39

The Stakes in Combining Companies

Alok K. Chakrabarti

Dean and Distinguished Professor,
School of Industrial Management,
New Jersey Institute of Technology,
Newark, New Jersey

Mergers and acquisitions have remained a favorite game for corporations to play. But do they work? There are many celebrated cases where corporations have lost billions of dollars and hundreds of jobs when highly touted "synergies" failed to materialize.

Two factors are generally needed to predict acquisitions success: strategic fit in terms of product market and technology, and organizational fit. Our research shows that fit is far more important and requires commitment from the top.

There are so many dimensions along which two merger candidates can be examined for synergistic similarities or complementary attributes that no merger can achieve a smooth match-up on all dimensions. There will always be rough spots to manage. Exchange of help in terms of technology sharing, capital availability, marketing, and manufacturing expertise are the means to achieve synergy. This is when the organizational factors come into play. Many of these problems can be anticipated with careful analysis, but they seldom are in the heat of the premerger courtship.

In a study of 31 acquisitions, we found that most of the stated management motives for making an acquisition were not related to actual performance. Achieving acquisition objectives seems to be a very difficult task; the lure of quick, profitable growth through acquisition does not often materialize regardless of the motive. Our overall finding was that there was no important association between postacquisition performance and strategic fit in terms of either motives or product line synergy. Given our sample size, we cannot say that strategic fit is of no importance but our study joins others in supporting such a conclusion.

The key to the success of an acquisition seems to be in the level of integration between the division and the corporation. Integration is defined as the quality of the state of collaboration between the organizational units. More specifically, we found that the level of integration between the division and its parent was related to all of the performance dimensions such as sales growth, profit growth, return on investment, market share growth, technological innovation, and a broadened customer base.

TANGIBLE HELP IS A PLUS

We learned that in the successful mergers there was an exchange of tangible help between the parent and the acquired unit. Our study clearly shows that postacquisition performance is dependent on a variety of factors and assistance accorded to the division by the corporate organization. Based on the responses from the divisional management, we found that sharing of technology, access to corporate market, capital availability, and help from the corporate channels of distribution all were correlated with performance improvement in the postacquisition period.

The exchange of help between the acquired division and corporate organization did not occur in a vacuum. Intensive communication between the acquired division and the other organizational units on technology, joint projects, and the like were key elements in the sharing process. In addition, some companies used job rotation and joint projects to improve linkage between the acquired division and the corporation. Both the quality and quantity of information transferred between the division and other parts of the corporation seemed to be positively related to performance of the division. Absent steady, efficient information flows, the managers in various acquired division felt a great deal of anxiety owing to a lack of information on the goals and objectives of the corporation. Moreover, they anticipated a forced, unwelcome change in culture and operating procedures.

FORMALITY IS A DEBIT

Corporations in the sample generally imposed formal planning and management control systems on the acquired division to evaluate and control its operations after an acquisition. The level of formality differed for various functions, such as planning, resource allocation, research and development, project selection, and other miscellaneous management activities. Increased level of formalization in resource allocation and other management decision areas was generally negatively related to performance, and was especially negative in regard to market share growth.

According to the R&D managers we surveyed, increased levels of formality in planning, resource allocation, and R&D project selection were negatively correlated with performance. The increased levels of red tape and bureaucracy hindered the divisional management's ability to act promptly following the acquisition.

The dominant competitive issues frequently changed from the time the merger was planned to the time it was implemented. These unexpected competitive changes could be coped with only through close working linkages between the merger partners.

Rapid turnover of senior technical and management personnel was adversely related to performance of the acquired divisions. When a large company buys a relatively small entrepreneurial firm, it is important that the founder-manager and the key technical personnel be retained for a smooth transition. The technical information about the product and the production processes often lies with key personnel. Transfer of this organizational knowledge is a slow process and seldom can be affected by formal mechanisms such as reports and memoranda. Small entrepreneurial companies depend heavily on their key people for their personal knowledge of the markets and the needs of specific customers. Acquirers need to keep key personnel to maintain the customer base after the acquisition. Employees in small organizations often are loyal to the key managers, because these organizations are run in a family-type environment.

ACTIVE MANAGEMENT IS VITAL

Regardless of the premerger possibilities for successful synergy and problem areas, both synergies and problems must be actively managed before, during, and, most important, after the merger. Effective lines of communication and mutual problem solving need to be established back and forth at several levels of the two businesses. This takes management and board time and attention; only after these channels are established can the exchange of help begin to deliver the integration essential to high performance.

Firms that look forward to acquisition as a quick way to improve their financial performance generally do not invest the amount of time, attention, and money necessary to establish an effective exchange of help. In some of the more obvious cases, we have seen R&D and other functions cut out as a cost-saving measure to boost short-term profits at great expense of the long-term development of products and processes.

As the old saying goes, there is many a slip between the cup and the lip. The motives behind mergers and the potential from product synergies are by no means consistently achieved. Organizational factors intervene and essentially determine which of the premerger potentials actually are achieved and which are not.

40

Postmerger Integration

Mark L. Feldman

Managing Director, Rubicon Group
International, Orinda, California

Michael F. Spratt

Managing Director, Rubicon Group
International, Saratoga, California

Corporate acquisitions are not just announced. They are trumpeted with great fanfare, optimism, and hype. Competitive advantage and new business opportunity are confidently declared, as if just doing the deal is evidence of its merit. Increased shareholder value is promised and the expectation of accelerated growth is proclaimed.

Unfortunately, failure to achieve business expectations from the merger is common. Disappointing operating results and returns below the cost of capital frequently undermine shareholder value. Even well-managed growth companies have sustained setbacks, despite expanding markets. These shortfalls have been reflected in a divestiture rate (exclusive of shutdowns) that has averaged 30 percent or more in both industrial and service sectors.

WHEN MERGERS MISFIRE

It is not unusual for managers to attribute disappointing postdeal performance to high purchase premiums, excessive leverage, and the economy. However, a more sober look often reveals that deferred action, reduced productivity, lack of plan-

409

ning, low morale, loss of key personnel, mismatched cultures, inept downsizing, and slipshod integration are more common faults. All of this diverts attention from external markets to internal politics and hampers efforts to combine the organizations into a smoothly functioning whole.

An acquisition involves more than simply taking control of hard assets, a market base, technology, and intellectual property. And combining organizations involves more than consolidating and reallocating space, capital, and equipment to accommodate new strategies. The real challenges lie in merging organization structures, management styles, employee expectations, policies, and cultures. This is the human side of the postmerger equation. It drives performance, consumes most of the operating costs, and suffers the most severe and debilitating impact from a merger.

The Problem in a Nutshell

Change is the substance of a merger—not the gradual change that most people have grown to expect, but the rapid, traumatic change that accompanies a new order of things. With the close of the deal comes the need to integrate operations, consolidate functions, redeploy assets, and rethink product, market, and service strategies. In significant and subtle ways, operations are redefined.

The capture of postmerger opportunities always is slower than anticipated. Internal issues divert energy and attention, causing productivity to slide and service to deteriorate. The longer it takes to sort things out, the greater the likelihood that customers will go elsewhere, product development will suffer, key people will leave, and competitors will develop effective countermeasures. Managers often find themselves overwhelmed by damage control long before they can realize enhancement of shareholder value.

For example, a Rubicon Group survey of 76 acquisitions found that 81 percent of the companies cited access to new markets as the primary reason for doing the deal. But nearly all companies reported hampering their own efforts and losing potential opportunities because they waited too long and moved too slowly in taking action after the close. Forty percent of these companies also reported unfavorable changes in operating expense, profitability, and cash flow, while 30 percent reported reduced productivity and increased turnover.

The First Mistake: Not Having a Plan for Day 2

Most deals are driven by conceptual strategies, not operational realities. When the deal is done, there is no blueprint for implementation. Key decisions often take months and unanticipated hours of effort. In the meantime, the transition moves at a glacial pace. An extended transition erodes the strategic and economic value of an acquisition and delays and reduces shareholder returns.

To build focus and cohesion among the management team and to minimize deterioration in company performance, management must decide, as early as possible, which operating strategies represent the best balance of economic opportunity and near-term success. Tactical plans must be built around these strategies. This will establish key priorities and concentrate management time and energy on productive efforts. The result will be optimal allocation of resources on actions that will rapidly accelerate the transition and build early momentum.

THE PLANNING CIRCUS

To coordinate the scores of postmerger decisions and activities, many companies form transition teams composed of executives from both companies. The mandate is to plan the transition and integration process. That includes developing recommendations for combining a wide variety of functions—anything from manufacturing units to human resources policies—and proposing the configuration and cultural qualities of the new organization. Although it may be a well-meaning and early commitment to teamwork, the process often results in a planning circus that delays implementation and prolongs the transition because the team is asked to bite off more than it can chew.

One company, in a misguided attempt at postmerger democracy, established an executive transition team consisting of 17 members. This team oversaw 24 functional teams averaging 9 managers per team, 48 subfunctional teams averaging 6 managers per team and 8 cross-functional teams with twelve managers per team. After subtracting overlaps, nearly 500 managers were involved.

The teams met over a 10-month period after the deal. The opportunity costs, the loss of productivity, the delays, and the sheer expense of coordination escalated operating costs and stalled consolidation. Many group decisions were made under circumstances that required individual accountability.

The more people on a team, the more difficult it is to coordinate meeting schedules and arrive at decisions efficiently. This extends the time required for teams to complete tasks. As a simple matter of expediency, not everyone has to be involved in every decision. Size dilutes accountability.

Even the coordination of intergroup decisions can complicate matters. One team's failure to reach a timely conclusion can stall progress elsewhere and lead to irretrievable losses in markets and management.

Such extended and convoluted transitions occur repeatedly. A highly publicized example was the 1989 merger of SmithKline Beekman Inc. and Beecham PLC in which the company saw its operating costs, debt, and interest expenses rise and its R&D synergy falter while it stumbled through a byzantine hierarchy of 250 transition teams. The irony was that the $8.3 billion merger of the two pharmaceuticals had been designed to gain economies and combine R&D operations to generate quicker and more prolific delivery of new drug products.

In all fairness, however, it should be noted that the avoidance of transition teams can stall cooperative decision making and ultimately have the same effect. Tonka Corp.'s acquisition of the well-regarded Kenner toy and Parker game businesses fell victim to this phenomenon. Prolonged indecision on organization structure, management placement, and business strategy caused Tonka to flounder and left it frantically searching for a hit toy that would eclipse the company's lack of resolution on so many issues. Tonka later was acquired by Hasbro Inc. in a virtual rescue operation.

The primary purpose of a transition team is to focus key players on decisions that stabilize the organization and build early momentum. For this reason, it is best to organize small teams of results-oriented experts around postmerger projects that are likely to advance business opportunities, better utilize resources, produce near-term wins, and drive profitability.

THE AUTONOMY TRAP

As a practical matter mergers require early integration of policies and procedures—if only to facilitate coordination and consistency throughout the organization. Yet it is not unusual for an acquired company to be promised autonomy or, in a merger of two "equals," for each to agree that the other can maintain autonomy in defined markets.

Predeal promises of autonomy often become postdeal land mines. They slow integration and generate conflict. All mergers add unanticipated constraints on freedom to act, regardless of promises of autonomy.

The problem is that each company's policies and procedures reflect its own preferences and business practices. Repetition has reinforced these practices in the behavior of the managers and embedded the preference for these practices in their minds. Though a few changes always are welcome and one company always has a better pay or benefits policy, managers in each organization generally have vested interests in their own policies and procedures.

Autonomy in a merged organization cannot be absolute. It must be carefully defined or negotiated in the context of anticipated postmerger benefits. The effective integration of operations should not be held hostage to territorial politics. When the demands of autonomy interfere with the creation of shareholder value, it is time for the CEO to intervene.

Communicate, Communicate, Communicate

Mergers and acquisitions are case studies in uncertainty. Before the deal, employees, shareholders, and others understand, even if they do not accept, the need for confidentiality. After the deal, they expect answers. Pent-up demand for information is overwhelming. There are always more questions than answers and speculation runs high.

Unfortunately, the first response of management usually is to promote, rather than explain. Early announcements promise opportunity and advantage. Public commitments are made and expectations are raised. However, answers to significant implementation questions are postponed—sometimes for many months, sometimes indefinitely.

In the absence of significant answers, apprehension grips and distracts the workforce. Anger and indignation turn other stakeholders into pressure groups. Negative speculation and rumor grow. An information-starved and anxious constituency instills even trivial bits of information with distorted significance. Management efforts are misperceived and management image suffers.

These problems cannot be completely avoided. There always will be questions for which immediate answers cannot be provided. If a quick answer cannot be given, people usually will understand if they are told honestly and frankly that a decision has yet to be made. Nevertheless, if management is perceived as making a good-faith effort to communicate as much as it can, as soon as it can, employees and other stakeholders will be more patient—although not infinitely patient.

A well-planned and ongoing program of communications is necessary. This involves identifying all relevant internal and external audiences, anticipating the questions each group may have about business and organizational issues, scripting position statements, and determining what channels (newsletters, meetings, mailers, telephone hotlines, press releases, community speeches) should be used to communicate to each group. The communications plan should be reassessed weekly in light of feedback from the stakeholders.

TRIAL BY FIRE

Some organizations mistakenly believe that the postmerger transition period is useful for observing and comparing managers prior to placement. It is the acquirer's equivalent to Darwin's "survival of the fittest." Unfortunately, the dominant trait that persuades decision makers generally is political skill, as opposed to more constructive characteristics.

There is clearly a legitimate need to make early, thoughtful, and deliberate decisions about placement of managers, particularly when consolidation and reorganization is necessary. Early management placement is a critical factor in stabilizing the organization and positioning it for quick gains. Any delays in placing managers only lengthen and complicate the transition period by increasing uncertainty, diverting attention, and fostering internal competition.

To make things more difficult, the best and brightest managers immediately are targeted by recruiters who attempt to lure them to competing organizations. Senior managers clearly are working against time in choosing the winners. One executive, recounting a sobering postmerger experience, said, "It didn't take long to identify the winners. They were the ones who left us for other jobs while we sweated over smaller decisions."

The challenge for the acquirer is in deciding who to retain, who to redeploy, and who to dismiss in both the acquired company and its own. How can the acquirer select and combine the best managers from both organizations? A wide range of interviewing and testing techniques has been developed and used by hundreds of companies.

Some approaches rely on the judgments of senior managers individually or as a group. Other approaches utilize outside consultants and psychologists to objectively assess skill, capability, and potential. Typically, the use of outside parties sends a strong message that the acquirer intends to make decisions that are evenhanded and free of past bias. But, no matter what approach is used, managers still tend to feel insecure until the decision is made. This obstructs early progress and dampens morale.

The selection process should require neither months of observation nor the extreme of psychological testing. Third-party evaluators skilled in the behavior profiling techniques that are in common use can quickly evaluate not only what managers are capable of doing, but what their characteristic operating style is and how well it fits various jobs in the organization.

YOU CAN'T BUY COMMITMENT

Most experienced acquirers have learned that the acquired management team and technical staff do not always switch allegiances cheerfully and automatically align their interest with those of the new shareholders. Mergers and acquisitions inevitably encourage employees to reexamine their own situations—where they are going, what they want, and how strong their commitments to the company are. The longer the postdeal organization remains inert and uncertain, the more attractive alternative employment becomes.

Immediately after the deal, recruiters attempt to lure the best and brightest managers and technical personnel to competing organizations with attractive financial incentives. To counter this, the acquiring company frequently offers sign-up bonuses or other financial incentives—often called "stay bonuses"—to remain. Over time, some acquirers learn that it might have been best to let these employees go. Retention of talented people has its costs and you don't always get what you want—commitment.

In a survey of postmerger practices across industries, The Rubicon Group found that 50 percent of the companies implemented retention incentives. Of that group, only 48 percent were satisfied with the results. While the plans are effective in retaining key people, they typically fall short in returning real benefits to shareholders for risks incurred.

To retain key managers and technical contributors, companies have tried a dizzying array of sign-up bonuses, stock options, stock grants, and long- and short-term cash incentives. However, in the process of structuring these lures, the firms often lose track of the real objective. Retention may be the motivation, but the real objective is to drive sustained value creation by energizing and focusing the behavior of key people. You want not only good people, but to keep good people good.

Many golden handcuffs turn into golden anchors that induce inertia and obstruct progress. They capture only the body, not the heart and the mind. They reward willingness to stay, rather than results. They fail to link retention incentives to the creation of economic value.

The most effective retention incentives are high-stakes, attention-getting income *opportunities* called value-creation incentives. One popular technique creates a self-funding "pool" representing a percentage of new value created for shareholders over a three- to five-year period. This extended period allows the company to assess growth in value produced by the incentive plan participants. At the end of the period, payouts to managers are based on actual shareholder value that is created. Payouts may be in cash, stock, favorable options, or some combination of them.

Though the reward is at risk, managers stay with the company because the payout for performance is both significant in size and competitive with other potential opportunities.

Money Isn't Everything

Even when some turnover is desirable and encouraged (e.g., early retirement incentives), many of the first people to leave voluntarily are managers who are needed to direct operations in the challenging period ahead. They accept the separation incentives that are offered and move on to competitors or return as consultants and extract premium fees.

The people most likely to leave after an acquisition are career-oriented, high achievers. They are often formal and informal leaders in thought and action and they are sought by organizations competing in the same labor pool. When these people leave, they take with them established business relationships, spirit, momentum, and proprietary knowledge of the business and customers. They leave behind a leadership gap, unfinished projects, dispirited teams, and a learning curve for those who replace them.

Career-oriented achievers cannot be retained by money alone. They seek two other things as well. They want assurances that they will have opportunities to influence the direction, character, and shape of the company and they want clear indications that their career paths are reasonably secure. Their desires for influence can be indulged by allowing them to participate on key transition teams and by seeking their input on matters meaningful to their areas of expertise. Their desires for career opportunity can be accommodated by clarifying that the growth anticipated by the merger ultimately will create new and meaningful positions that will be filled by the best performers. In addition, they should be told they will get consideration in all succession planning, because vacated positions also will be filled by the best performers.

Hull Speed

In sailing, hull speed is the fastest that a ship can travel given a specific hull design. Once a ship reaches hull speed, even doubling the horsepower of the engines will not add much velocity. Going faster requires alternation of the hull design. But this will also influence stability, handling, and cargo capacity. Trade-offs have to be made based on the primary purpose for which the vessel will be used.

Organizations are like ships. Given a certain structure, they can accomplish only so much. To accomplish more or change some of the organization's functions, there must be an alteration of the structure. Whether structural adjustments are intended to reduce operating expense, increase process efficiency, facilitate resource sharing, advance technology transfer, or enhance employee productivity, each adjustment can influence the organization in many ways.

The implications of this concept extend well beyond organization charts, layers, and head counts. Change is disruptive at best. For this reason, structural adjustments should be executed only when necessary to capture the business opportunities that drove the deal.

Confusing Culture With Operating Style

When two organizations come together in a functional relationship, they tend to compete. Even under the friendliest of circumstances, each group will attempt to demonstrate that its way of conducting business—its operating style—is best.

Internal rivalry is especially evident in consolidations that require adjustment in organization structure, size, and staffing. These changes tend to break up or alter the composition of work groups, create new work groups, change work flow and decision flow, alter individual roles and accountabilities, and modify the real and perceived status of individuals. It should not be surprising that teamwork begins to suffer and gains come slowly.

The standard scapegoat for these difficulties is culture conflict—a clash of business values and beliefs. The conventional view is that a company's culture has developed over a period of years and cannot be expected to change in a shorter span of time. This point of view, however, overlooks a key factor.

Culture is a function of operating style. It is formed by the characteristic management practices in an organization. Early and firm decisions to selectively reinforce desired practices and terminate others will quickly bring about changes in behavior. This will accelerate change in corporate culture.

Kill Those Snakes

If you find a deadly snake threatening your home, you take immediate action to kill it. You certainly do not take the time to convene a task force to study it, determine its type, and assess the costs and benefits of alternative strategies for eliminating it. The same can be said for many of the hot emotional issues that surface in most mergers and acquisitions. They are snakes that must be dealt with as quickly as possible. Among the concerns that should be given priority are titles, salaries, positions, and contested policies and procedures. These are generally straightforward but nonetheless emotional issues that can and should be neutralized quickly before they silently slip by and poison postmerger progress. They tend to be issues of personal opportunity, security, and the quality of the working environment. We consistently have found that unless an acquirer quickly neutralizes these issues and simultaneously ensures the workforce that favorable policies will not be eliminated, progress on strategic objectives is set back.

THE BOTTOM LINE:
THE VISIBLE AND
DECISIVE LEADER

Ambiguity and uncertainty will undermine any postdeal transition effort. Under conditions of uncertainty, employees have elevated dependency needs. To allay their anxiety they require a visible and accessible leader—someone (or some group) who is present and to whom they can readily speak.

The greatest generals—from Sun Tzu 2000 years ago, to Napoleon, the Duke of Wellington, and George Patton—led from the front, not the rear. They were clear and articulate in their direction. They could communicate strategy in ways that were meaningful to the troops and they took early, firm stands on tough issues.

If postmerger managers, including the CEO, are to be regarded and respected as leaders, they must resist the urge to spend all of their time in closed-door meetings. They must spend time in contact with as many employees as possible, and be as visible as possible. They have to articulate the priorities and be decisive in the allocation of resources. Their positions on the issues must be clear, consistent, and rational. They are the role models that set the tone for the organizational climate and shape the culture. Ultimately, success or failure will be attributed to the quality of postdeal leadership.

41
Merging Benefit Plans

Kenneth P. Shapiro
President, Hay/Huggins Co., Inc.,
Philadelphia, Pennsylvania

Michael Carter
Senior Vice President and Manager,
Hay/Huggins Co., Inc.,
Washington, D.C.

Benefits continue to play an increasingly prominent role in assessing an organization's financial and competitive position—prominent enough, in fact, to cost benefits issues as potentially pivotal in merger situations. Benefit costs and terms are important in helping to determine the financial viability of a proposed combination, and then in determining the ultimate success of the mergers that are completed.

The nature of the benefits-related issues at stake in a merger scenario go beyond hard numbers to embrace important technical, administrative, and philosophical concerns that must be examined closely, and at an early stage, in studying a combination of separate business entities. This chapter will outline the steps that should be taken both during the assessment/negotiation process and after consummation of a merger. We will emphasize why benefits-related issues no longer can be treated as afterthoughts in a merger and must be integral and critical parts of the process.

PERIL FROM THE BENEFITS
COST SPIRAL

To underscore the magnified role of benefits issues in mergers, it should be noted first that from a current cost standpoint, benefits costs as a percentage of total operating expenditures continue to rise. The escalation is spurred primarily by steady boosts in average monthly health care premiums. Premiums have been climbing at a 15 percent annualized compounded rate over the past 10 years, according to the Hay/Huggins Benefits Database, despite coverage reductions and cost-shifting measures that have been instituted at many firms. The 15 percent growth rate has outpaced inflation, salary budget increases, and, in all but a few fortunate cases, growth in revenues at most firms, thus creating major strains on profitability.

Firms that have yet to get a firm handle on how to control the rising costs of health care and other benefits therefore may lose much of their luster as merger candidates, despite the other attractions they may offer. Analysis may show that there is upside potential for *improving* an organization's balance sheet performance by reducing premiums and cutting back on the benefits packages provided to employees. But companies that have not yet taken the sometimes harsh or bold steps needed to stem the benefits/cost spiral run the risk of major blows to employee morale, productivity, and recruiting/retention success rates as changes are instituted.

LONG-RANGE LIABILITIES

The hurdles related to daily benefits issues are minuscule, however, when compared with problems that a merged entity faces. The target may bring with it substantial liabilities in the form of unfunded long-term liabilities tied to pension funds and to plans that provide postretirement health care coverage to employees. Rule changes in recent years by the Financial Accounting Standards Board (FASB) in how these liabilities must be computed and expensed have highlighted the degree to which many companies are woefully unprepared to meet the full extent of obligations created by such plans.

Even in situations where accounting regulations have been liberalized, such as with FAS 106 rulings requiring annual recording of retiree medical costs, the numbers indicating corporate liability can be staggering. A $50,000 "pay-as-you-go" annual cost retiree health plan, for example, can represent an annual obligation of $500,000 under FASB standards. Companies that once showed no liability for retiree medical plans have now found they must add liabilities of many millions of dollars to their ledgers, as a result of formalization of the standards.

The extent of liabilities tied to pension funds can be even greater. Yet closer scrutiny of pension funding status under FAS 87 regulations often reveals that plans initially thought to be amply funded are, in fact, woefully underfunded. This, too, can have a major effect on the attractiveness of a proposed merger, even to the point of becoming the determining factor of a deal's viability. Adding $2 million, $5 million, or more to an organization's liabilities because of underfunded pension obligations may by itself be enough to transform a seemingly attractive financial posture into an unattractive position.

Even if the effect is not so straightforward, the added liability may be enough to hamper the merged company's effort to implement planned strategies, because of restrictions on the new organization's ability to reduce its pension fund exposure. Organizations adopting the attitude that "if there's a problem with the pension plan, we'll just close it down" are bound to be unpleasantly surprised by the financial, legal, or philosophical roadblocks that will surface as they attempt to terminate a plan.

The "Double Whammy"

Steps one and two of any study into the benefit implications of a proposed merger must assess the potential effect of the "double whammy" that can be imposed by liabilities for pension funds and retiree medical coverage.

With respect to pension funding as determined through FAS 87 regulations, these key questions must be asked:

- What is the funded status of the pension plans offered by each organization that will be combined into the merged entity? Are any of the plans severely or fully underfunded? If so, how can proper funding be achieved, and how will it affect that organization's balance sheet?

- If an organization appears to have a properly funded pension plan, have sound actuarial assumptions been made to justify this conclusion? Or have "games" been played with the numbers to merely create the appearance of proper funding?

- If a company's pension plan can be shown to be legitimately overfunded, can this truly be counted as an asset in the merged scenario? Or will it be difficult to recapture the assets represented by overfunding because of legal restrictions or tax penalties that will be tied to any efforts to terminate or reduce some or all of the pension exposure?

The key questions tied to assessment of retiree medical plan liabilities using FAS 106 methodology will be these:

- Have steps been taken to get a proper handle on the full extent of liabilities tied to retiree health coverage benefits offered at either or both of the merging companies? To what extent, if any, is this liability presently funded? Is the long-range exposure properly reflected on the organization's financial statements?

- To what extent will amendment or termination of existing retiree health plans be possible after the merger? If the plan must continue to exist, for legal or strategic reasons, after the merger, what powers will the new organization have to control future costs? Options may include changing carriers and shifting more costs to the covered retirees.

The importance of conducting thorough due diligence investigations of these two key benefits areas as early as possible cannot be overemphasized. "Horror stories" abound in the annals of merger situations that speak of the disastrous consequences of inadequate investigation of their full reach. Purchase prices sometimes have had to be adjusted significantly as a result of corrected calculations for funding liabilities. Lawsuits have stemmed from an organization's improper assessment of its ability to amend or terminate plans after a merger is completed. There even have been instances in which liabilities that were properly computed under FASB standards have proved to be larger than the net worth of a target company.

TEAM APPROACH TO BENEFITS INTEGRATION

Once it has been determined through careful, up-front study that pension fund and retiree medical liabilities will not be great enough to scotch a merger, other benefits-related issues can be addressed in a less urgent fashion as part of the negotiation and postmerger administrative processes. But here, too, it should be remembered that the manner in which benefits issues are handled can be pivotal to the ultimate success of the combined entity, in that benefits often reflect larger cultural or philosophical concerns that must be reconciled to successfully integrate two organizations.

To make sure these issues are given full and proper attention, a group of senior managers from both companies should be assigned to analyze benefits issues during premerger negotiations. Rather than leave this task solely to benefits specialists, it is advisable for the acquirer to use a committee approach with senior management direction and specialist support. In this way, the goals and strategies of the combined organizations are sure to be supported by an effective benefits program. Indeed, this may be the first time that either of the affected organizations ever addressed benefits issues through a top-down approach—a worthy objective in its own right, if benefits are to be given the attention demanded by their rising cost profile and importance in determining employee satisfaction.

Defined-benefit pension plans provide a determinable benefit, generally based on level of compensation and length of service with the company. If they pass the liability test, five alternatives are available for managing them after the merger. The options include:

- Terminating the plan(s)
- Freezing benefit accruals
- Merging the plan(s)
- Maintaining separate plans
- Converting to an alternative vehicle

Terminating the Plan.   Terminating a pension plan may not be a clear-cut alternative. A termination may run afoul of the Employee Retirement Income Security Act (ERISA) and the rules of the Pension Benefit Guaranty Corp. (PBGC), which was created by the law to assure that retired workers receive pensions due them. Under the law, companies must pay for any unfunded, vested liabilities in a benefit plan that is terminated. Currently, this reimbursement can be as high as 30 percent of a corporation's net worth.

When the options for terminating a plan are considered, the liability must be measured against three factors:

- The accelerated cash flow requirements, including recognition that the PBGC liability is an immediate claim
- The cost of continued fundings
- The increase in the PBGC liability if the plan continues

Nonfinancial factors such as the existence of a plan at the acquiring company and the levels of benefits paid by that plan also are relevant factors.

Freezing Benefits.   An alternative to terminating a pension plan is freezing the benefits accrued up to the acquisition date. Although no additional benefits accrue under this option, employee service after the acquisition date must be counted toward vesting of the benefits already accrued.

This alternative serves two purposes. It honors the commitment made before the takeover, and it avoids the psychological trauma that can be experienced by employees when a plan is terminated. In addition, because a freeze allows for the future funding of liabilities, there is a potential cash flow advantage.

However, it must be recognized that PBGC liabilities will continue to grow, albeit slowly, as more participants approach the vesting threshold. When weighing a freeze, therefore, the cost of maintaining the frozen plan should be measured against the current and protected PBGC liability. Any funds produced from the overfunding of a frozen plan will not be returned to the employees; instead, they remain plan assets that can be used to honor future liabilities.

Merging Plans.   Merging the pension plans of the two companies is an especially attractive option if one firm's employees clearly enjoy superior benefits. Even if the benefits for future service with the combined company are reduced, a plan merger still represents a better deal for employees than freezing or terminating their plans. When one company's plan clearly is better funded, as illustrated by the target company in Table 41.1, merging the assets and liabilities of the two plans will reduce the overall PBGC liability and may trim the total pension expense as a percentage of payroll. The pension expense of the combined plan is less than the sum of the two unmerged plans, because the combination reduces future service benefits for the target company's plan.

Maintaining Separate Plans.   By selecting the option of maintaining separate pension plans after the merger, new management adopts a "wait and see" approach that allows it to keep its options open for the future.

Converting to Another Vehicle.   Under the conversion option, a pension plan is converted into a defined-contribution vehicle such as thrift savings, profit sharing, or a 401(k) plan that accepts employee contributions from earnings in pretax

Table 41.1. Example of Pension Fund Comparisons: Premerger and Postmerger

	Before the merger		After the merger
	Acquiring company	Target company	Combined company
Covered payroll	$10,000,000	$4,000,000	$14,000,000
Pension expense:			
Dollar amount	700,000	250,000	870,000
Percent of payroll	7.00%	6.25%	6.21%
Present value of			
vested benefits	10,000,000	4,000,000	14,000,000
Assets	8,000,000	4,600,000	12,600,000
Funding ratio	80%	115%	90%
PBGC liability	2,000,000	–0–	1,400,000

dollars and provides for matching contributions from the employer. As in plan termination, conversion triggers PGBC liability. But the conversion approach still maintains a plan for covering the employees of the acquired company.

Multiemployer Pension Plans

If either of the companies participates in a multiemployer pension plan, some unique considerations arise.

The Taft-Hartley Act set up provisions for participation in a multiemployer plan so that several companies in one industry could negotiate unified benefits. Until passage of the Multiemployer Pension Plan Amendment Act (MPPAA) in 1980, employers participating in such a plan were liable only for a "cents-per-hour" negotiated contribution and a potential liability if the plan was terminated. A single employer could leave the plan without being liable for any unfunded liability, as long as the plan survived for another five years.

Under MPPAA, however, employers that withdraw from a multiemployer plan are liable for any unfunded liability that they leave behind, and withdrawal liability payments can last as long as 20 years. Potential withdrawal liabilities should be accounted for, and purchase prices adjusted accordingly, if a multiemployer plan is part of the picture.

Retiree Medical Plans

The alternatives that can be weighed when looking at integration of retiree medical plans will be similar to those associated with pension plans. Because there are no PBGC-type requirements for payment of liabilities incurred through health plans providing benefits for retired workers, it may seem that a stronger case can be made for using a merger as a good reason to terminate these plans, particularly in the face of continually soaring health care costs.

However, management should carefully study issues of employee goodwill and obligation to existing retirees before making a decision. A more palatable and more publicly acceptable course of action might be to grandfather those currently drawing benefits under the plan, while eliminating the plan for all future retirees. The savings from this measure may not be realized for many years, but costly negative publicity and poor employee morale can be avoided.

When weighing the options for terminating, freezing, or amending pension and retiree medical plans, decision makers should bear in mind the risk of litigation. The action may spur lawsuits on behalf of employees claiming that the benefits were outlined in company literature before the merger and therefore amount to entitlements for those employed by the two companies prior to the deal. Courts have been mixed in their interpretation of just how "contractual" these obligations have become. But the possibility of lawsuits and the costs of defending them should be weighed against the potential savings that will be realized through any action that is taken.

Tax Implications

After any action, the combined company should make sure that the resulting defined-benefit/contribution plan remains in compliance with sections of the Internal Revenue Code (IRC) that seek to protect against discriminatory benefits practices. These sections establish minimum participation levels as well as procedures for regular testing of the plans to demonstrate their nondiscriminatory nature. The merger benefits team should not put the "cart before the horse" by allowing discrimination concerns to affect the way in which it wants to redesign a plan. But it should be prepared to make adjustments that are necessary to ensure that what remains of the plan is in compliance with code requirements and tests.

ADJUSTMENTS OF
OTHER BENEFITS

Clearly, the issues tied to defined-benefit pensions and retiree medical coverage are the thorniest that a merger team will have to confront when blending the benefits packages of two companies and determining what sort of coverage will be provided to the employees of the new entity.

But even benefits issues that are seemingly more clear-cut, such as vacation allowances or profit-sharing percentages, should not be treated lightly. Increasingly, these elements of an employee's total compensation package are being viewed as every bit as pivotal as salary or bonus provisions in determining levels of employee satisfaction in the workplace, degrees of employee motivation and productivity, and the ability of an organization to recruit and retain quality personnel. All of these factors can have a direct bearing on an organization's competitiveness, and, thus, should not be viewed as "minor" or "incidental" details in a merger.

The first key decision is whether the nonretirement elements of the benefits packages previously offered at the two separate organizations should be merged at all. The degree of integration that is desired or effected should be a direct representation of the strategy, operating style, and organizational structure of the combined businesses. In a holding company environment, for example, it may make sense for a newly acquired business that will be run with great operating autonomy and little or no interaction with other units to retain entirely separate benefits plans. A horizontal merger of two companies in the same industry, on the other hand, probably would call for development of a common benefits philosophy and program.

Figure 41.1 depicts the relationships of operating style and business diversity to the benefits integration decision. The need for integration intensifies as businesses become more centralized and related. Any degree of integration, however, no matter how slight, should center around striking the proper balance between the benefits philosophies and costs that are involved. The greater the differences in benefits philosophy between the merging organizations, the greater the risk and difficulty that will be incurred in merging their plans.

Comparing Benefits Philosophies

How should benefits philosophies be compared? Benefits should be viewed in a total compensation context, as a contributor to the overall risk-to-reward ratio, or leverage, that is built into both an organization's pay and benefits plans. At one

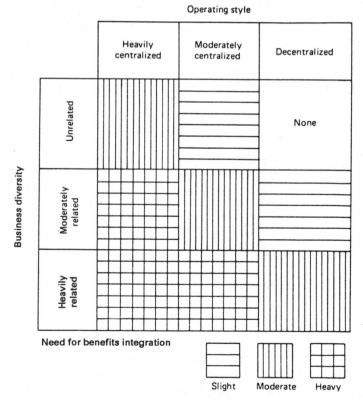

Figure 41.1. Model of integration needs for benefits. (*Note:* This model can also be applied to compensation in general per Figure 42.1.)

extreme on the scale are the security-oriented organizations that pay only fixed base salaries and offer only defined benefits. At the other end are highly leveraged organizations that put significant amounts of compensation at risk through incentives. These firms typically ask employees to bear more of the cost of benefits or limit their use of benefits to a customized set that is selected from a menu of available options.

Figure 41.2 provides a model for analyzing the "integration gaps" that will exist after the complete nature of the benefits programs offered by the two organizations has been determined. The degree of horizontal difference between two organizations plotted on the matrix indicates the relative cost of integration—small in this example for companies B and D, but greater for companies A and C. The degree of vertical difference represents the difficulty in integrating differing benefits philosophies—small for companies B and C, but great for companies D and A.

Careful analysis of these factors can provide important input during the merger negotiation phase, and also help eliminate "honeymoon period" surprises once the marriage has been brought about and the process of combining benefits packages has begun.

As the integration process begins, this checklist of specific factors should be used to make sure the benefits offered by the merged organization will fit well with the overall business strategy that has driven the deal:

- *Competitive position*—How should the benefits package stack up in terms of value and attractiveness vis-à-vis the external marketplace (peer or comparable companies, competitors, etc.) with which it should be compared?

- *Cost containment*—How much of the costs can be shifted to the employee base without jeopardizing levels of satisfaction with the benefits program? Where should the line be drawn between maximizing cost savings and maintaining a competitive program? What are the trade-offs involved, for example, between

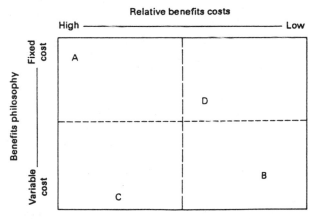

Figure 41.2. Integration analysis model for benefits. (*Note:* This model can also be applied to compensation in general per Figure 42.2.)

placing all insurance coverage with one carrier and distributing the coverage among several carriers? Giving all of the business to one insurer offers administrative efficiencies and convenience but splitting the business may allow the firm to take advantage of the best possible rates.

- *Plan design*—Should early retirement be encouraged or discouraged? Should HMOs be given equal status with traditional health insurance coverage? Should the same plans be in effect for both union and nonunion employees?

Employees in the Loop

Taking the pulse of workplace sentiment through an employee survey mechanism can be one way to help find the appropriate answers to these questions. In this approach, a tailored questionnaire measures the perceived value of compensation and benefits and quantifies the perceptions of employees against a normative data base (Figure 41.3). These perceived values, when related to actual costs of benefits that have been computed using actuarial models of salary equivalent values, then can be used to show where company expenditures will produce maximum and minimum "returns" in the form of employee satisfaction.

FLEXIBLE PROGRAMS

Mergers of benefits programs have to be performed carefully to avoid higher costs. Generally, the approach of providing the higher level of benefits of the two firms is

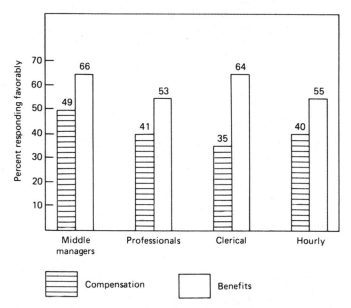

Figure 41.3. Measuring the perceived value of compensation and benefits.

not a viable option because it does raise expenses. "Averaging out" the benefits sometimes is workable, but it frequently is not a practical approach and it typically serves to make employees at both firms dissatisfied. A solution to this problem that also maximizes value to employees is a flexible benefits program that allows employees to choose between various plan options.

A new flexible benefits program could be designed to enable employees in both of the merged organizations to replace their previous plans. Moreover, if the two merged companies had very different levels of benefits, a flexible benefits program could be drawn up to offer both companies the same plan designs and options, but different levels of company contributions (credits to purchase benefits). Over time, the contribution levels could be brought into line by holding constant or gradually reducing the higher level, while increasing the lower level contributions.

Because employees can replace their former plan, the new program should not create discontent if employees don't pay more or minimum discontent if they have a higher cost. In addition, the company will maximize the return on its benefit expenditures since employees will be receiving value from a plan that they designed to best meet their needs.

Going to a "flex" approach also may provide a relatively seamless opportunity to establish the newly merged culture as one in which individual choice and direction will be emphasized.

The major potential drawback to instituting flexible benefits in a merged setting is that it creates administrative challenges that could be greater than what existed when the partners were stand-alone firms. But because the merger already has created a "clean administrative slate," it may present the optimum time to launch a full-scale change such as the overhaul represented by a flexible benefits program.

42

Combining Compensation Programs

Walter I. Jacobs

*Managing Director, Rubicon Group
International, Philadelphia, Pennsylvania*

On D-Day minus one Gen. Dwight D. Eisenhower addressed the 101st Airborne Division as they prepared to enplane to make night drops in Normandy. Ike began with a rhetorical question, "Is this trip necessary?" He was obviously successful in persuading his audience that the trip certainly was necessary. If one were to paraphrase that famous line and ask, "Is this chapter necessary?" too many would answer in the negative. They are, of course, incorrect.

This chapter will review the historical relationship of compensation issues to merger and acquisition activity, explain the critical role of compensation in the M&A environment, provide guidance on methodology to integrate compensation plans in merging organizations, and discuss how specially designed incentives can be utilized as the catalytic agent to drive postdeal initiatives.

Deals are done to create shareholder value. How compensation is managed can play a large part in influencing the degree to which planned values are realized.

THE REAL ROLE OF COMPENSATION

The management of compensation during and after the deal can greatly influence the degree to which postdeal goals and results are achieved. There is considerable

431

research and a great deal of empirical observation that show a dip in performance measures after a merger or acquisition. This manifests itself in losses in market share, reduced productivity, narrowed operating margins, slower than market growth, decreased cash flow, and the like.

Thus, the real role of compensation must be viewed against the backdrop of these disappointing results. The unpleasant surprises usually are attributable to a common and predictable trait of human nature—stress reaction to a change situation. In a merger, which axiomatically signals great change, employees typically experience great stress from the time the deal is reported until all their uncertainties are adequately cleared up.

The main source of the stress, moreover, is the fear of the unknown in relation to the individual's career. Will I still be employed? What type of place will this be to work? Under stress, most people become risk averse. They are not willing to show initiative and begin new projects. They become inert and unproductive at the very time that the need for organizational change and increased productivity is most pressing. Until employees have enough answers to relieve stress, organizational float continues and operating results suffer. Compensation programs can help clear up much of the uncertainty.

Sound compensation planning can be the catalyst to break postdeal inertia and allow organizations to capture the values that drove and justified the deal. Well-planned, well-designed, well-implemented, and well-communicated compensation programs not only address the most important tie between employee and employer but are important symbols and communication tools. When these issues are addressed quickly and effectively, they help jump-start employees and minimize the negative impact of a prolonged transition. Quality and speed are both required to facilitate the transition.

ASSESSING INTEGRATION NEEDS

Even before the deal closes, a general assessment can be made that will determine whether difficult and costly actions will be required to integrate the existing compensation plans of the merging businesses.

The first variable in this analysis is the necessity for integrating plans. The degree of integration needed in compensation programs will be a direct function of the strategy, operating style, and organizational structure of the combined businesses. For instance, in a holding company environment, a newly acquired business that will be run with great operating autonomy and little or no interaction with other businesses may very well retain entirely separate compensation plans. On the other hand, a horizontal merger of two companies in the same industry probably would require common compensation philosophy and programs. Figure 42.1 is a schematic representation of the relationships of operating style and business diversity with the need to have integrated compensation programs. The need for integrating programs intensifies as businesses become more centralized and more related.

A slight need generally would indicate that plans for most employees should be designed independently and adjusted to fit the needs of the business units, the industry, and the overall economic conditions. In almost all mergers, some executive

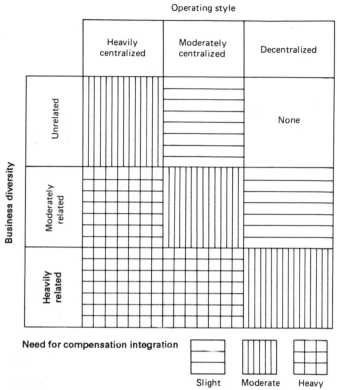

Figure 42.1. Model of integration needs for compensation. (*Note:* This model can also be applied to benefits per Figure 41.1.)

compensation plans would be integrated, especially long-term incentives, but often short-term incentives and perquisites as well. Because the cost and difficulty of the integration process would be moderate, no further consideration usually needs to be given until after the close of the deal.

A moderate need calls for a well-articulated compensation philosophy and policy. All compensation programs should be tested within this paradigm for two purposes: to determine proper fit, and to see if separateness or commonality between the business units best meets business goals. Although this process may be appropriate after closing a deal, management should at least consider it as early as possible in the negotiating process.

A heavy integration need points toward a combined compensation program for the merging entities. At the very least, it indicates the necessity of further study to estimate feasibility and cost.

When the combining of programs is required, any evaluation should focus on two general indicators:

- Compensation philosophy
- Compensation cost

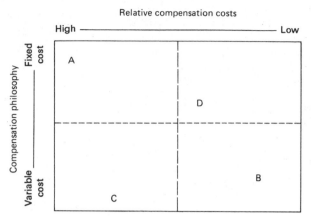

Figure 42.2. Integration analysis model for compensation. (*Note:* This model may also be applied to benefits per Figure 41.2.)

The greater the differences in compensation philosophy, the greater the risk and difficulty in merging plans. How does one compare philosophies of pay and benefits? Perhaps the most revealing element is the risk-to-reward ratio or the leverage built into compensation plans. At one extreme is the security-oriented organization that generally pays only fixed base salaries and offers defined benefits. At the other end are the highly leveraged companies, with significant amounts of compensation at risk through various incentive plans.

Cost is an obvious factor. With rare exceptions, any joining of plans between merged companies often tends to raise compensation to the highest program level offered by either company. Almost every company has internal data and external survey data available for a general analysis of pay levels and a quick estimate of the cost implications of moving to the higher level.

Figure 42.2 presents a matrix that is helpful in analyzing the difficulty and cost of integrating compensation plans. Each organization can take a place on the two-dimensional matrix based on its pay philosophy and cost. The degree of horizontal difference indicates the relative cost of integration (small for companies B and D, but great for companies A and C). The degree of vertical separation represents the difficulty in integrating differing pay philosophies (small for companies B and C, but great for companies A and D).

When done in a timely and thoughtful manner, analysis of these factors lends important input to merger and acquisition negotiations. The data are important in pricing and can help eliminate honeymoon period surprises that may sour organizations at the critical point in their marriage.

INTEGRATION WORK AFTER CLOSING THE DEAL

Once a merger is finalized, the actual integration process begins. If the parties have done their preclosing homework, they already have a good feel for the difficulty of the task ahead. Fortunate are those who require little or no integration of their respective compensation programs. The challenge is far greater in those situations where heavy integration is required.

Setting the Objectives

First, to support the business strategies of the organizations, specific program objectives must be established. The architecture of the compensation programs not only must support business goals, but must foster the type of employee behavior necessary to reach those goals. Compensation plans can be designed to create individualistic, entrepreneurial, and high-risk behavior. Conversely, they can be designed to create team-oriented, low-risk behavior—or almost any combination desired. Business plans and strategy will dictate the appropriate employee behavior; the design of the compensation plans will either support or hinder achievement of those goals.

Testing the Concepts

After the specific objectives have been set, the compensation programs of the merging organizations should be reviewed according to those objectives. Measurement of the competitiveness of the compensation packages of the merged companies against each other and the chosen external marketplace is a primary step. A by-product of this analysis is the measurement of both the adequacy and the internal equity of the compensation programs of the merging companies.

With this overall set of objectives established and approved by management, the compensation professionals then can begin adding, deleting, and modifying programs to provide the integrated compensation package.

Obviously, when a large change in either philosophy or cost is required in the plans of one or both parties, design of the combined plan becomes more difficult. When changes in cash compensation programs also require alterations in philosophy, a multiyear phasing of the new compensation schedule often is helpful. Behavioral change in an organization can be managed, but not overnight.

Through this careful process, the salary, short-term incentive, long-term incentive, and perquisites programs of the combining organizations can be integrated. The company can begin quickly to communicate new initiatives to all employees. Rapid and thoughtful action will start the process of focusing employee attention and effort toward the challenge ahead, and away from nonproductive rumination about the past or about an uncertain future.

VALUE CREATION INCENTIVES

In many cases simply integrating the compensation plans of merging units is not sufficient to assure achievement of planned merger benefits. For example, a mature company may purchase, for a premium over current results, a smaller company that is nearing market introduction of a high-potential new product. Unless product development is finalized and a successful product launch achieved, the deal will have negative results. In such a case, it is critical to retain and focus the acquired management team toward achieving the results that will create value for the parent company. Specially designed value creation incentive plans are ideal in such situations.

A value creation incentive plan is a self-funding, multiyear incentive providing participants with a "high stakes" cash opportunity clearly linked to shareholder value creation. Executives earn "rights" to share a percentage of value created based on achievement of quantitative strategic objectives that position the business for sustained long-term value creation. These incentive plans are individually tailored programs, but they have common design characteristics.

First, they include only a limited number of executives who are central to the success of a defined and measurable business project or unit. Second, they incorporate a multiyear earn-out period, normally three to five years, to assure strategic as well as tactical focus. Third, they are self-funding in that the incentive pool is calculated as a percentage of created value above a threshold performance level. Discounted cash flow is a common measure of performance, but measures such as operating profit and revenue growth will be used in appropriate circumstances. Finally, they normally pay out in cash and are not subject to market fluctuations. Thus, while they drive actions designed to stimulate stock price, they do not dilute ownership.

PROGRAM IMPLEMENTATION

People in real estate are fond of saying that the most important factors in selling residential real estate are location, location, and location. In the context of following up the decisions to combine total compensation programs, the most important factors are communication, communication, and communication. Timely and informative communication is vital to address the concerns of employees during the merger process. Inevitably, many are skeptical, fearful, or angry. A strong message, delivered clearly and frequently, can help alleviate personnel unrest and maintain a productive environment.

Today, every company has professionals available to use a vast arsenal of media for communicating with its employees. Use them! But also make judicious use of the most effective employee communication system already intact at every company—the employees' managers and supervisors. Employee attitude studies consistently show that employees prefer to receive information from their supervisors, and that the information has higher credibility when it comes from the "boss."

Another adage of merit goes "If it ain't broke, don't fix it." This does not, however, rule out preventive maintenance. New or modified compensation programs should be audited regularly to determine if they are meeting stated objectives. Some will require change or fine tuning. Do the necessary preventive maintenance before replacing the entire piece of equipment.

A HUMAN FACTOR

Cash compensation is not a significant factor in the transaction phase of M&A activity. A few basic steps in the research, negotiating, and due diligence phases are mostly what is required. Once the deal is made, however, swift and proper handling of compensation issues is required to energize and focus the employees. If this is not done, employee unrest and uncertainty will result in a prolonged period of organizational float. Business operations will suffer during this period of inertia and, all too often, the advantages and goals envisioned during the deal will not be fully realized. Compensation issues after a transaction cannot be ignored or postponed. They must be addressed immediately and well.

43

M&A Payoffs for Executives and Managers

William L. White
National Director of Compensation Services,
Ernst & Young, Los Angeles, California

A combination of forces is exerting a reforming influence on executive compensation practices, and, by extension, on golden parachutes and other severance payments for terminated managers, principally those displaced by acquisitions

Golden parachutes represent a relatively small slice of a typical company's financial pie and are almost incidental expenses in an acquisition. Moreover, federal tax law enacted in 1984 blunted the excessive severance payouts that brought discredit to the practice in the early 1980s. Yet golden parachutes remain handy targets for the institutional investors and regulators that have waged an increasingly aggressive battle to shake up corporate compensation systems in the 1990s.

It is easy for compensation reformists to train their guns on parachutes because they appear to fly in the face of the goals being sought. Demands for changes in executive pay structures are buttressed on the premise that managers should be paid for creating shareholder value and that many of the most lucrative packages are going to people who have not produced. Golden parachutes, it is argued, often are paid to executives that have performed so poorly that acquisitions were needed to bail their companies out.

Regardless of the validity of the arguments, the reformists' sustained fervor has put all public companies in the goldfish bowl in the setting of executive compensation, including golden parachutes. This chapter will discuss the key elements of a golden parachute and suggest a reasoned approach to adopting parachute plans that will be acceptable to shareholders.

WIDENING COVERAGE

In practice, a golden parachute is a device that cushions an employee's fall from employment because of a change in company control. Quite simply, the employee is provided with special payments for exiting the company if his or her job is eliminated as a result of acquisition redundancies or other factors. Parachutes proliferated during the 1970s and 1980s as a result of increased merger and acquisition activity and were initially designed as shareholder protection mechanisms. The rationale was that if executives received a generous consideration—a "bridging payment" unless new jobs were secured—they would table their self-interests. Instead of fighting an acquisition offer, they would negotiate in the shareholders' interests for the best price.

Subsequently, parachute schemes became more expansive and took on new variations. In actuality, many companies have installed three levels of parachutes—"golden," for top executives; "silver," for middle managers and their peers; and "tin," for lower-level employees. Payment formulae differ commensurately. Golden parachutes typically generate severance payments pegged to 2.99 times a base amount, a derivative of federal law and regulation to be explained later. The multiple is smaller for silver parachutes and often is a fraction of the base amount for tin parachutes.

Parachutes also have been developed with single- and double-trigger mechanisms for payment. A single trigger releases severance funds on a change in control. However, this may be defined as occurring when another company buys as little as 20 percent of the target firm, thus allowing an executive to leave for the flimsiest of reasons. A double trigger applies when there is a change in control but no immediate decision on whether the employee will be retained or dismissed, pending a probationary period. The employee is compensated if dismissed after the trial period.

REGULATORY RESPONSES

Golden parachutes first came under regulation in the Deficit Reduction Act of 1984 in response to controversies over huge termination payments following acquisitions in the early 1980s. To discourage excessive payouts, Congress restricted capital gains tax treatment to severance packages that did not exceed three times an executive's average compensation for the five years prior to a change in control. Anything beyond that threshold triggered a loss of tax deduction for the company and a 20 percent excise tax on the departing executive. Implementing regulations adopted by the Internal Revenue Service set the permissible multiple at 2.99 times the five-year base.

Several amendments were passed in 1989 to sharpen various definitions, including the composition of the base amount and the types of employees that would be considered highly paid and eligible for golden parachutes. The changes also required that golden parachute programs be in effect at least a year before a change in control for them to be considered legal—thereby blocking target companies from instituting them while a takeover is under way.

Proposals by the Securities and Exchange Commission for greater disclosure of executive pay also would apply to golden parachutes. They would require companies to reveal the executives covered, the coverage provisions, and the payments made under a change in control after the fact.

CRITICAL UNREST

In the big picture of corporate finance and acquisition strategies, the premium paid for golden parachute coverage is small. It typically represents 2 to 4 percent of the acquisition price and 12 to 24 percent of the company's earnings before adoption of a parachute, according to Professor David Larker of the Wharton School. But other trends in parachutes, some of them conflicting, have been disturbing to critics and reformists. These trends include:

- The continually increasing number of companies that adopt parachute arrangements, which in many cases may signal that they are open to acquisition offers

- Expansion of parachute plans to middle and lower levels of the company, which (in contrast with the first point) many critics regard as an antitakeover defense

- Creative arrangements to get around the 2.99 times threshold by grossing up income and adding special perquisite and benefit coverage

- Installation of the single trigger which allows executives to walk when the first salvo in a change-of-control scenario is fired

After an analysis of trends for the years 1988 through 1991, based on a sample of 1,050 companies disclosing compensation arrangements with the SEC, *Executive Compensation Review* disclosed the following in its 1992 Golden Parachute Report:

- Seventy-one percent of public companies had at least one form of change-in-control provision in 1991, up from 69 percent in 1990.

- Those companies having individual executive arrangements for golden or silver parachutes stabilized at 52 percent of the total.

- The proportion of companies with tin parachutes climbed from 5 percent in 1990 to 6 percent in 1991.

- Thirty-four percent of golden parachute agreements include excise tax gross-ups, and 24 percent have single triggers.

- Plan-based change-in-control protection essentially has come to a halt, and change-in-control features in stock plans diminished between 1990 and 1991.

Toward Reasonableness in Golden Parachute Arrangements

Given the climate of reform, I expect compensation committees of boards of directors to become actively involved in determining the guidelines for golden, silver,

and tin parachute arrangements. The major considerations in determining reasonableness should include:

*Determine the Critical Core of Executives, Managers, and Employees to Be
Covered.*   Using the principle of criticality in continuing operations—in other
words, the *team* should be preserved to ensure the delivery of expected shareholder
value—determine the employee groups to be covered and the appropriate vehicles
(golden, silver, or tin parachutes). The addition of a substantial group beyond top
management may be viewed as an antitakeover defense. In certain industries with a
large number of advanced-degree professionals, however, it is difficult to exclude
these valued players from the team that contributes to shareholder value. However,
be leery of extending silver or tin parachutes companywide without calculating the
cost.

*Decide on the Specific Agreements to Be Made with Each Group Concerning
Termination Amounts in Relation to:*
- Base salary
- Short-term incentives
- Long-term incentives
- Nonqualified profit-sharing and deferred compensation plans
- Continuation of benefits, such as life insurance, pensions, and medical costs
- Continuation of certain perquisites, such as company cars, club dues, office ex-
  penses, and secretarial services

*When Parachute/Severance Agreements Are Fully Costed, Determine the
Acquisition Cost of These Arrangements as:*
- A percentage of equity
- A percentage of preacquisition profit

Consider the Use of Restraint When It Comes to:
- Exceeding the limit of 2.99 times the base amount, possibly by providing a "cap"
  before the limit is exceeded
- Providing an excise gross-up payment
- Installing a single trigger

Determine Payment Terms in the Event of New Employment:
- Will severance payments be mitigated if new employment is found before the
  severance period ends?
- Will incentive payments be offered for finding work early?

Decide How Valued Executives Will Be Retained

Devices for retaining executives until the change in control include loyalty bonuses,
double-trigger golden parachutes, and setting the severance pay multiple at the

2.99 limit. Mechanisms that can be used for keeping them after the deal include restricted stock, highest and best price options, and extended loyalty bonuses.

Resolve All SEC, IRS, Legal, and Accounting Issues:

- *SEC/IRS*—The parachute must be installed one year before change in control occurs. Provide appropriate proxy disclosure.
- *Legal*—Ensure plan definitions meet legal standards for IRS compliance.
- *Accounting*—Determine appropriate costing of "base amount" and "parachute" payments, including deferred, stock award, and stock option amounts contingent on change-in-control and vesting scenarios.

Reflect Impact of Golden Parachutes with Three-Year Evergreen Contracts if Necessary:

- Since golden parachutes imply three-year terms, limit contracts to three years and install on an evergreen basis. Avoid *all events* contracts as a solution to the golden parachute dilemma, since any change-in-control event will throw the payment into a golden parachute status.

Make Business Judgments in Certain Difficult Cases:

- Since the regulations are overly definitive, and certain cases require flexibility, the compensation committee must be prepared to address these issues with a good sense of business judgment. An issue is how punitive a committee will be when judging a lifelong employee, who has made a valuable contribution but due to restraint in his past pay package will be tossed out with a less-than-adequate parachute payment, versus a short-time employee whose performance is marginal, who has had excessive amounts of base pay over the last five years, and who stands to inherit an undeservedly large payment. Reasonable to generous parachute provisions may, in fact, be the only way to hold together the critical players who can ensure the accomplishment of desired shareholder value creation goals, especially during a difficult period.

Consider Golden Parachute Payments as Part of the Total Executive Pay Package:

- Develop a perspective about parachute and severance payments in light of the total compensation and benefit package. In the aggregate, consider their appropriateness, cost/benefit implications, and total acceptability by a shareholder activist group. Work with the compensation committee of the board to determine the appropriate positioning philosophy. Put together an appropriate communications package for both management and shareholders on all aspects of compensation, including golden parachute treatments.

PART 7
The Paper Chase: Regulation, Communication, and Defenses

44

Antitrust Guidelines

Douglas E. Rosenthal
Partner, Coudert Brothers, Washington, D.C.

William Blumenthal
Partner, Sutherland, Asbill & Brennan,
Washington, D.C.

In most proposed mergers, the antitrust laws present little more than petty annoyances. After cursory reviews, the bulk of transactions raise no serious competitive issues; and antitrust compliance consists essentially of filing premerger notification report forms for transactions above certain thresholds, paying a $20,000 filing fee, and sitting out any required statutory waiting period before closing the deal.

In a significant minority of mergers, however, the antitrust laws present serious obstacles. In those cases, the U.S. Department of Justice and the Federal Trade Commission (FTC), which share responsibility for antitrust enforcement, either may sue to block the deal or call for major revision or restructuring of the transaction (such as through selected divestitures). State attorneys general also may challenge mergers in the courts. Private parties also may mount challenges, although this rarely happens except in hostile tender offers.

LEGAL STANDARDS

The principal antitrust statute governing the legality of mergers is Section 7 of the Clayton Act, which prohibits any merger "where in any line of commerce in any section of the country, the effect of such acquisition may be substantially to lessen competition, or to tend to create a monopoly." The underlying goal of the statute is to prevent market power from developing. Other pertinent statutes include Section 1 of the Sherman Act, which prohibits contracts, combinations, and conspiracies that unreasonably restrain trade; and Section 2 of the Sherman Act, which prohibits monopolization, attempted monopolization, and conspiracies to monopolize.

Evaluation of a proposed merger under Section 7 is a two-stage process: defining the markets that the merger will affect and then assessing the competitive impact on these markets. If the parties compete in the same market, the merger will be regarded as "horizontal." If they operate in markets that have purchaser-supplier relationships, the merger is "vertical." If the parties operate in unrelated markets, the merger is "conglomerate." Each of the classes is assessed under separate legal tests, with horizontal mergers facing the strictest scrutiny.

Market Definition

Market definition is an important stage in the merger evaluation process. Market definition often will determine whether a specific merger is viewed as horizontal, vertical, or conglomerate. Thus, a merger between a can manufacturer and a bottle maker might be viewed as horizontal if "packaging materials" is regarded as a single product, but conglomerate if "cans" and "bottles" are regarded as distinct products. In addition, market definition generally will determine the market shares of the parties to the merger—an important factor in the second stage of the evaluation process. Thus, in a merger between two bottle makers, the parties' market shares might be small if "packaging materials" is considered the product, but substantial if "bottles" is considered the product.

A relevant market consists of product ("line of commerce") and geographic ("section of the country") dimensions. Basically, the product market is defined by examining the functional interchangeability of use among products. Substitutes are regarded as falling within a single market, and especially close substitutes may be deemed a submarket within the broader market. Similarly, the geographic market is defined by the locations where purchasers of the relevant product may turn for sources of supply.

In both the product and geographic dimensions, the aim is to identify an insular grouping, relatively segregated from external competitive pressures. Case law provides little systematic guidance as to the necessary degree of interchangeability among products deemed to constitute a single market. The Justice Department tried to remedy this shortcoming by incorporating in its 1982 Merger Guidelines the so-called 5 percent test for identifying the competitors in a market. Under this yardstick, a market was deemed to exist if a price increase of 5 percent or more did not drive customers to a substitute product. Revisions of the guidelines in 1984 and 1992 replaced the 5 percent threshold with the more general concept of a "small but significant and nontransitory" price increase in gauging customer reactions.

As a practical matter, however, market definition largely is determined by the facts surrounding a specific merger. This can cause uncertainty in assessing the antitrust risk of a specific deal, but it also provides considerable latitude for the merger partners to develop the strongest case they can. The aforementioned bottle maker, for example, might marshal facts that suggest a narrow product market when it seeks to merge with a can manufacturer, but argue for a broad market when it wants to merge with another bottle maker. However, the virtual case-by-case approach presents the danger that enforcement authorities will unduly emphasize facts that are of little competitive significance and that an improper market definition will result. In industries with government reporting requirements, for example, market boundaries sometimes have been set by reporting categories that may have little practical significance for actual competition in the marketplace.

Enforcement authorities also can seize erroneously on stray remarks contained in internal documents. The FTC nearly sued to block a chemical industry merger several years ago because it believed wrongly that the northeastern United States was a relevant geographic market. (This had the effect of inflating the parties' apparent market shares.) The agency jumped to this conclusion because one of the parties had arbitrarily created regional sales territories within its corporate organization and its employees kept referring to the "Northeast market," even though competition was on a nationwide basis.

Competitive Effects

Predicting a merger's competitive effects can be quite speculative. The courts historically have applied presumptive tests for analyzing horizontal mergers based on a market's structure and the merger parties' market shares. These tests have resulted in relatively strict enforcement. However, the courts, as well as the enforcement agencies, recently have shown greater willingness to look behind horizontal merger presumptions, resulting in some relaxation from the stringency of the past. Enforcement efforts against nonhorizontal mergers have been infrequent since the mid-1970s and remain so into the 1990s.

Horizontal Merger Standards

The legality of a horizontal merger historically has depended principally on the market's concentration level and the parties' market shares, but other considerations increasingly are being taken into account. The government's enforcement standards since the 1982 Merger Guidelines have been based on the Herfindahl-Hirschman Index (HHI). The HHI is calculated by determining the market share of each market participant, squaring the market shares, and adding up the resulting products. Thus, in a market where the participants have shares of 30 percent, 25 percent, 20 percent, 15 percent, 5 percent, 3 percent, and 2 percent, the HHI would be 2,188, or the sum of $900 + 625 + 400 + 225 + 25 + 9 + 4$.

An HHI increase is twice the product of the market shares of the merging parties. Thus, a merger between firms with market shares of 8 percent and 6 percent would result in an HHI increase of 96, or $2 \times 8 \times 6$. In markets with a postmerger HHI of less than 1000, or relatively unconcentrated markets, mergers generally will not be challenged. In markets with a postmerger HHI between 1000 and 1800, representing moderate concentration, the government is unlikely to challenge mergers that increase the index by less than 100 points. In markets with a postmerger HHI over 1800, or highly concentrated markets, the government is unlikely to challenge mergers unless they raise the HHI by more than 50 points.

Enforcement authorities have shown increased willingness in recent years to look beyond market shares. If past market shares do not accurately portray the future development of the market, it may be appropriate to adjust the shares for purposes of antitrust evaluation. Likewise, nonstatistical factors may be important, particularly if they indicate whether firms in the market could engage in tacit collusion or whether the merging parties could unilaterally raise prices. Such factors include ease of entry, product homogeneity, complexity of price structures, and frequency and size of orders.

Nonhorizontal Merger Standards

Concern over nonhorizontal mergers has waned in recent years, as the case law has discouraged challenges and as many economists have adopted the view that nonhorizontal mergers are unthreatening to competition. The case law does, however, articulate several theories as to how nonhorizontal mergers may reduce competition. A vertical merger, for example, may prevent a supplier from doing business with a customer that has acquired a competing supplier, and a conglomerate merger may eliminate either buyer or seller as a potential competitor in a market. Over time, the courts have erected many preconditions to application of such theories.

Defenses

Certain defenses may be available to legitimize a merger that otherwise would be unlawful. Most important is the failing company defense, a judicially created doctrine suggesting that an otherwise unlawful merger is permissible if one of the parties is in grave danger of business failure, the prospects of reorganization are dim, and a less anticompetitive purchaser is unavailable. Under the 1992 Merger Guidelines, the enforcement agencies also require a showing that the assets of the failing firm would exit the market unless the suspect merger is cleared. As a practical matter, the enforcement agencies have shown great reluctance to accept the failing company defense in recent years.

The so-called failing division defense may apply when an otherwise healthy company threatens to shut down an unprofitable division or plant if it cannot sell the operation to a competitor. The critical question usually is whether the threat of a shutdown is credible. Historically, if the threat has been credible, the government often would clear the transaction for both political and economic reasons—politically to prevent loss of jobs, economically to keep the productive capacity in operation, even if by a competitor. In recent years, however, the enforcement agencies seldom have been swayed by political considerations in failing division cases, and merger parties have had little success in satisfying the elements of the defense.

Under the 1992 revision of the Merger Guidelines, the enforcement agencies will listen to the merger partners' claims that an otherwise questionable transaction should be cleared if it creates significant net efficiencies that could not be realized through other means. Claims of this type historically have been rejected by the courts.

In recent years, the courts increasingly have recognized a defense based on the power of buyers of the relevant product. The Merger Guidelines do not expressly take account of this defense, but "power buyers" may be relevant to the guidelines' analysis of entry or competitive effects.

OBTAINING GOVERNMENT CLEARANCE

The formal process of obtaining government clearance for a merger begins with the filing of premerger notification report forms, when required, with the FTC and the Justice Department in compliance with the Hart-Scott-Rodino Act. The two agencies then decide which will review the proposed merger, based on their relative workloads and their expertise in a specific industry. The Justice Department tends to review mergers in steel, brewing, telecommunications, and financial services, for example, while the FTC usually handles the cement, food distribution, and chemicals industries. When both agencies are in conflict over a high-profile transaction that raises serious antitrust questions, bargaining usually determines which one gets the case. When Mobil Corp. launched a hostile tender offer for Conoco, Inc. in 1981, for example, both reviewing agencies asserted jurisdiction for several days, until the FTC yielded.

Under the Hart-Scott-Rodino Act, the transaction may not go forward for 30 calendar days (15 in the case of a cash tender offer) from the filing of premerger notification. If a merger presents no antitrust question, the parties may seek early termination of the waiting period. Otherwise, the reviewing agency will use the waiting period to conduct a preliminary investigation. If the agency concludes that the transaction is lawful, it will let the waiting period expire. But if the preliminary investigation has not satisfied the reviewing agency, it will ask for more information, a step that automatically extends the waiting period until 20 calendar days (10 in the case of a cash tender offer) after the parties have substantially complied with the request.

It generally is possible to negotiate with the agency to limit the scope of the request, but compliance with even a narrowed request may be disruptive and costly. Files must be reviewed and copied by attorneys, and executive time must be diverted to respond to interrogatory-style specifications. Besides answering specific questions, executives of the merger partners also may have to help prepare position papers supporting the merger and make themselves available for meetings with agency staff members to explain competitive practices in their industry.

As the extended waiting period expires, the regulatory agency may let the merger proceed or take these other steps:

- Propose that the transaction be restructured or otherwise revised to lessen competitive concerns.
- File suit seeking a court injunction halting the transaction.

- Allow the deal to go forward, but file suit later to break up the merger or obtain other relief.

- Request that the parties "voluntarily" extend the waiting period (usually under threat of seeking an injunction if they do not).

The merger is not necessarily doomed if the partners cannot work out an accord with the government. Except in cases when the buyer previously has agreed to get government clearance before making an acquisition (such as in consent agreements or litigation settlements involving prior mergers) or when a deal needs clearance from an industry regulatory authority, explicit federal approval is not required. If the government chooses to fight the merger in the courts, it has the burden of proving that the transaction violates the antitrust laws. In recent years, the government has lost more than half the merger cases it has initiated.

This suggests that merger parties that are threatened with suit and that have some legal support for the transaction may wish to consider litigation. As a practical matter, however, the timing and risk of litigation depend on whether the reviewing agency is the Justice Department or the FTC. Litigation against the Justice Department normally proceeds through a preliminary injunction hearing and sometimes an expedited appeal. It usually is completed within six to eight months; and if the department loses, it normally drops the case. By contrast, litigation against the FTC can drag on for years, since the agency normally pursues a full administrative trial before its own administrative law judges even if it loses an effort to obtain a preliminary injunction in the courts.

The Hart-Scott-Rodino Act cites quantitative thresholds for deals that must be filed with federal authorities. Filing is required if the deal is between two companies that have gross assets valued at a minimum of $100 million and $10 million respectively, and in the case of manufacturing companies those figures apply to their respective sales. Deals also must be listed with the government if the buyer will obtain more than $15 million of the target's voting securities or 50 percent or more of the voting securities of a company with annual sales or gross assets of $25 million or greater. In practice, these minimum requirements mean that few mergers between two operating companies—only the very smallest with the least market impact—can legally avoid government notice in the M&A environment of the 1990s.

Strategic Considerations

Because of the variety of options available to antitrust authorities, the merger partners should devise a strategy for obtaining government clearance, balancing what they really want out of the deal with what they might have to accept. Between allowing the deal to go forward and suing to block it, the spectrum of possible government decisions includes:

- Allowing the merger to proceed but continuing the investigation with an eye toward having the merger partners divest some businesses that may have anticompetitive trappings

- Filing suit after the deal has been completed to have it rescinded or reduced in scope

- Permitting the deal to be closed, but requiring the buyer to hold the acquired business separate and unintegrated for a specified period of time

- Requiring the buyer to agree to certain nonstructural conditions in return for having the deal cleared. Examples include adopting certain price policies or agreeing to supply smaller customers equally with larger customers in times of shortages

- Requiring the buyer to divest certain assets after the deal goes through

- Demanding a restructuring of the transaction so that fewer assets are acquired than originally proposed

Many large mergers go forward only after strings are attached. The two giant oil mergers of 1984—Gulf Corp. into Chevron Corp. and Getty Oil Co. into Texaco Inc.—were cleared by the FTC only after the buyers agreed to sell off several refining, marketing, and pipeline properties and to meet several nonstructural conditions. The Justice Department, before giving the green light to the massive 1992 banking consolidation of BankAmerica Corp. and Security Pacific Corp., prodded divestiture of operations holding more than $7 billion in deposits to prevent concentration in specific markets in Western states. And antitrust implications even have been raised in a leveraged buy-out (LBO). When Kohlberg Kravis Roberts & Co. executed the RJR Nabisco Inc. LBO, the deal drew FTC scrutiny because KKR controlled another food concern, Beatrice Cos., that had competing lines. The agency ordered the sale of one ketchup, one Oriental frozen foods, and one packaged nut business from either firm.

The strategic interests of buyers and sellers may be quite different. In general, the seller, anxious to close the deal and pocket the proceeds, cares little about postacquisition investigations, decrees, or encumbrances. In contrast, the buyer's interests may fall anywhere along the spectrum, depending on its business objectives in undertaking the merger.

A second strategic decision facing merger parties concerns their degree of cooperation with the reviewing agency. The approach may range from effusively assisting the agency to acting belligerently and complying only with the bare letter of the Hart-Scott-Rodino Act so that the agency is signaled that litigation would be trench warfare. The chosen strategy should turn on an array of factors, including the antitrust merits of the transaction, the reputation of the reviewing agency staff, the personal style of the parties' lawyers and executives, and the willingness of the parties to suffer disruption in their regular operations. If a merger appears to be a close call, a strategy of cooperation generally will require senior executives to devote substantial time and effort to working with enforcement authorities.

The form and the timing of the advocacy campaign are also important strategic elements. Although a thorough presentation can be convincing, it also tips the advocate's hand and binds the parties, both at higher levels within the agency and before the courts. The parties also must decide whether to direct their primary efforts at the agency's investigating staff, its professional managers, or its political leadership. In most instances it is best to begin by focusing on the staff, which is usually the most enforcement-minded. If the staff can be convinced that the merger is lawful, its view seldom will be overruled by superiors in the agency.

Factors Other Than Antitrust Merits

Government clearance for a merger may depend on factors not related directly to the antitrust merits. Enforcement agencies have limited resources that must be allocated through prosecutorial discretion, and the resulting enforcement pattern sometimes seems arbitrary. The vigor and depth of an investigation may depend on the staff's workload and on the publicity surrounding the transaction. Some industries are more interesting than others and tend to attract greater attention; industries and companies with histories of antitrust problems often are monitored most closely. Among the industries that historically have attracted the government's attention are oil, chemicals, steel, automobiles, paper, cement, soft drinks, and electrical equipment.

Antitrust enforcement also has a political side. This is not to say that the enforcement agencies are commonly susceptible to direct political pressure. Quite the contrary, such pressure often has a counterproductive result. But a touch of politics always seems to be present, both because the antitrust laws have deep populist roots and because political considerations often are related to competitive effect. A merger is more likely to be cleared if it is necessary to prevent a plant shutdown or to allow an industry to cope more effectively with foreign competition. In contrast, a merger is more likely to draw a challenge if it strikes a populist nerve, especially by threatening to raise prices to consumers. Until the early 1980s, mergers in the relatively unconcentrated oil industry were vulnerable to challenge because of such concerns.

Perceptions, often unsupported, also can influence enforcement authorities. Documents submitted to the government may reflect typical management tendencies toward exuberant optimism and may distort the power and size of the merged company. This would work against a merger, as would negative concerns among customers. In contrast, protests by competitors suggest to the government that the deal is procompetitive, since they are viewed as unlikely to voice concern over a transaction that will enhance collusion, but likely to oppose a deal creating an aggressive rival.

Nonfederal Threats

Even if the federal government clears the merger, state attorneys general or private plaintiffs may sue to enjoin the transaction or to recover damages. The state attorneys general were largely dormant in antitrust matters until the mid-1980s, when they stepped in to fill the enforcement vacuum left by the federal government's reduced level of activity under the Reagan administration. The state attorneys general largely have grown quiet again in the merger field as federal enforcement has picked up during the 1990s and as state enforcement budgets have been reduced.

Some pillars of the former state activism remain in place. In 1987, the National Association of Attorneys General issued its Horizontal Mergers Guidelines, which set tougher criteria for clearing deals than the current federal standards. But a more important development was a U.S. Supreme Court decision in 1990 that allowed states and others to sue in efforts to break up mergers that already had been consummated and had passed a federal screen. That decision was rooted in a state of California attack on the merger of American Stores Co. and Lucky Stores Co. in the supermarket industry. The case eventually was settled when American agreed to sell a large number of stores in California.

Historically, private plaintiffs rarely have brought antimerger suits except in fighting hostile tender offers. A private plaintiff usually has standing—a sufficient interest to entitle it to assert legal rights—if it is a customer of the merger partners or a target of a hostile tender offer. In many instances, however, competitors will be deemed to lack standing.

STRUCTURING THE TRANSACTION

Merger partners often can structure the transaction both to reduce the likelihood of antitrust challenge and to protect against certain business risks if a challenge does materialize.

Transactions of Narrower Scope

If antitrust considerations preclude a merger (or a similarly broad transaction such as the sale of an entire division), there are several vehicles available for structuring a narrower transaction. The simplest is to sell selected assets and retain a competitive presence in the market. Thus, a producer with a large number of facilities might sell several plants, portions of product lines, trademarks, and pieces of equipment. The crucial antitrust issue is whether the seller remains a viable competitive entity in the market after the transaction has been consummated. If the transaction sharply diminishes the seller's market share and either renders the seller noncompetitive or induces the seller ultimately to liquidate the assets it retains, the partial sale might well be viewed as if it were a complete sale.

An alternative approach is to divest selected assets of the target. This may be preferable if the likelihood of antitrust challenge appears slight or if the scope of divestiture is small relative to the entire deal. However, the approach carries at least three risks. First, it may delay the closing of the initial deal. Second, the divestitures often must be made at fire-sale prices. Third, the divestitures often will be difficult to accomplish, especially when parts of product lines sold to consumers are involved. For the divested portion to be viable, it may be necessary to devise some means of sharing goodwill, such as trademark licensing.

Another approach is for the parties to pool selected assets in a joint venture that could compete with the two parents. Although this is becoming increasingly fashionable, it too carries risks. First, joint ventures are notoriously difficult to control, and partners seldom are willing to have just one of them in control. Consequently, control is often split 50-50 (or 33-33-33 in a three-way venture), and the venture in effect answers to no one. Second, joint ventures raise many ancillary antitrust problems. For example, the venture must be designed so that it does not become a conduit for an impermissible exchange of information between the parents. Likewise, the venture agreement must not contain provisions that unreasonably restrain competition.

An example of complex, creative structuring is provided by the brewing industry, which was characterized by attempts of several regional producers to go national through merger during the early 1980s. In 1982 Heileman Brewing Co. fought to acquire a majority interest in Pabst Brewing Co., a merger that had been rejected twice before by antitrust authorities. But a new structure was devised, the first step being a merger among Heileman, Pabst, and Olympia Brewing Co., 49 percent-owned by Pabst. Pabst then was resurrected as an independent company owning all of Olympia. Heileman kept some Pabst and Olympia breweries, trademarks, and other assets in return for supplying Pabst with cash. Thus, Heileman expanded its operations and Pabst/Olympia remained a brewing industry competitor.

In another deal that coincidentally touched on the Heileman-Pabst-Olympia arrangement, Stroh Brewery Co. bought Schlitz Brewing Co. after curing government objections that the deal would have lessened competition in the southeastern United States. Initially, Stroh promised to divest one of two Schlitz breweries in the Southeast. But after Pabst was recreated, Stroh worked out another arrangement. It traded a southeastern brewery for a Pabst brewery in the Great Lakes area. Pabst thereby shed excess capacity in the Great Lakes area and reentered the Southeast after it had ceded its former brewery there to Heileman.

Walkaway Point

In drafting the agreement embodying the terms of the transaction, the parties must decide how much heat they will take from the government or third parties before they will abandon their deal. The "walkaway point"—at which a party is entitled to withdraw from the deal without being in breach—normally is decided by careful bargaining.

The event triggering the right to withdraw can fall anywhere along a procedural spectrum. At one extreme, withdrawal would be permitted if the government issued a request for additional information. At the other extreme, withdrawal would be permitted only if a court issued an injunction against the transaction. Between these poles are various other possible triggering events—such as the passage of a fixed time period or a government announcement that it will challenge the merger.

In general, buyers seek the right to abandon the deal at the earliest possible stage because each successive step in the antitrust approval process imposes costs—in terms of out-of-pocket expenditures, executive time, organizational disruption, and diversion from pursuit of other opportunities. Sellers usually try to hold the buyer to the deal for as long as possible, preferring that the purchaser fight the government challenge and go forward with the deal unless enjoined.

Most transactions scrubbed because of antitrust problems in recent years were abandoned after the regulatory authorities formally signaled their intentions of opposing the deals. In 1988, McKesson Corp., a major national pharmaceuticals wholesaler, called off two acquisitions—Alco Health Services Corp. and Northwestern Drug Co.—after the FTC said it would oppose them. The year before, an FTC vote to oppose the transaction aborted Dun & Bradstreet Corp.'s bid for Information Resources Inc. And in 1991, Hershey Foods Corp. broke off negotiations to buy American Italian Pasta Co. rather than fight a looming challenge by the Justice Department, which had been concerned over merger-driven consolidation in the pasta business.

One seldom-publicized factor in aborting a deal is the reluctance of the merger partners to expose antitrust skeletons lurking in their closets. They may be called on to produce documents that suggest they have engaged in price fixing or other acts, sometimes unrelated to the merger at issue, and such evidence could lead to a broader inquiry. Reportedly, an FTC monopoly investigation involving the titanium dioxide industry was triggered by information discovered in a merger review. (The investigation resulted in a complaint, which was eventually dismissed.)

SPECIAL ISSUES IN THE HOSTILE TAKEOVER SETTING

Hostile takeovers present both problems and opportunities. The usual Hart-Scott-Rodino waiting periods are halved, the government usually is willing to permit the deal to go forward on the acquirer's promise that it will cure antitrust problems through future divestitures, and the buyer alone controls the terms on which it will abandon its tender offer.

But the target is certain to see that any antitrust problems are surfaced and usually will steer the government to facts that might not otherwise have been uncovered. This tactic may be risky, because it can limit the target's flexibility in finding a white knight or reaching acceptable terms with the would-be acquirer.

The target is also likely to begin private litigation. Under such circumstances, antitrust clearance must be obtained not only from the government, but also from a court, which may be less inclined to accept policy arguments and recent economic learning that favors mergers, and may rely instead on precedents that are less hospitable to mergers.

SPECIAL ISSUES AFFECTING INTERNATIONAL MERGERS

An increasing number of mergers are transnational. Among other things, that means that the mergers probably will be subject to antitrust review in one or more foreign jurisdictions. If the acquirer is foreign-based, the mergers also may be subject to the so-called Exon-Florio Amendment, which gives the President the power to block a merger that does not pose an antitrust violation, but could result in foreign control of a business in a manner adverse to a national security or defense interest of the United States.

45

Regulation of Mergers and Acquisitions

David B. H. Martin, Jr.
Partner, Hogan & Hartson, Washington, D.C.

The tattoo of hostile acquisitions subsided at the end of the 1980s and left in its aftermath an eerie silence. The armies of "deal" merchants and mechanics stood down, and battle-weary survivors emerged to treat casualties. The triage that followed involved further fortification of common and corporate law and a hesitant exploration of new governing alliances. Out of this still tentative lull, a seemingly more traditional handling of corporate control has emerged. There is little doubt, however, that the takeover contests of the 1980s have dramatically redesigned the legal structures governing the market for corporate control.

At the state level, transactions for control of public companies are governed essentially by two bodies of law—common law applicable to the conduct of corporations and their agents and corporate law governing specific transactions such as mergers. State corporate and antitakeover laws and their judicial interpretations cover such areas as corporate directors' fiduciary duties, the adequacy of purchase prices to shareholders, and requirements for shareholder approval. At the federal level, control transactions are governed principally by tender offer regulation—rules administered by the Securities and Exchange Commission that govern how acquirers can buy shares directly from shareholders to execute deals.

Substantial changes and refinements were made in key areas of state law in response to hostile takeover contests during the 1980s. Few changes have occurred in federal tender offer regulation.

COMMON LAW: THE BUSINESS JUDGMENT RULE

The major legal element that figures strongly in court decisions on mergers and acquisitions is the business judgment rule. Under the business judgment rule, a court will refuse to substitute its judgment for that of a corporate board. The rule, really more of an evidentiary principle than a written tenet, essentially presumes that directors have engaged in corporate decision making in good faith, on an informed basis, and with a rational business purpose. To think otherwise would lead courts to the slippery slope of second-guessing the risk assessments and instincts of businesspeople.

In 1985, the Delaware Supreme Court sent shock waves through the corporate community in the landmark case of *Smith* v. *Van Gorkom* by holding that directors of Trans Union Corp. were personally liable for failing to inform themselves and to understand a proposed transaction. (Delaware courts have delivered many key M&A decisions because of the large number of companies incorporated in that state.) The Trans Union case was triggered by the directors' acceptance of an offer by Marmon Group Inc. at a 50 percent premium over the stock price. In spite of that seemingly generous bid, the court held that the directors did not try hard enough to determine if the offer was fair or if a higher price could be obtained in the market. One fallout of the decision is that most companies involved in acquisitions almost automatically obtain a third-party opinion, from such consultants as investment bankers, accountants, and valuation specialists, on whether purchase prices are fair to shareholders.

Later in 1985, in *Unocal Corp.* v. *Mesa Petroleum Co.,* the same court shifted the burden of proving that a board acted in an informed and good-faith basis to the directors themselves before it would allow them the benefit of the business judgment rule.

A year later, in *Revlon Inc.* v. *MacAndrews & Forbes Holdings,* the court applied this enhanced duty requirement to transactions involving sale of a company. It found that if a company is for sale—that a definite decision to sell the business has been made—directors must function not as defenders but as auctioneers charged with "getting the best price" for the stockholders. In this case, Revlon directors attempting to fight off a hostile takeover by Ronald Perelman's MacAndrews & Forbes, agreed to an alternative transaction that provided lower returns to shareholders than Perelman's bid. The court decision cleared the way for Perelman to acquire the cosmetics giant.

More recently the business judgment rule has developed further and in a way that provides balance to the shifts in the rule under *Van Gorkom.* In *Mills Acquisition Co.* v. *McMillan* (1988), the Delaware Supreme Court refined the *Revlon* test in acknowledging that directors are not required to conduct an auction for the company or otherwise treat all potential acquirers uniformly if differing treatment can be justified as a means of advancing the interests of shareholders.

The Paramount-Time Impact

And in *Paramount Communications* v. *Time Inc.* (1989), *Cirton* v. *E. I. du Pont De Nemours & Co.* (1990), and *In Re MCA. Inc.* (1991), Delaware courts continued to shift the balancing that was signaled by the *Mills* decision. That shift was toward an intermediate application of the business judgment rule, one in which proper process and good faith are factors that mitigate judicial scrutiny of the substance of a board's decisions.

The *Paramount-Time* decision is considered especially noteworthy by M&A deal makers and their legal advisers. Time rejected a cash offer by Paramount in favor of pursuing a merger with Warner Communications Inc. that was aimed at advancing a specific strategy of becoming a worldwide giant in media and entertainment. Paramount sued and lost. Time argued that an expanded company would enhance shareholder value in a few years, while Paramount maintained that its offer would maximize value immediately.

Prior to the *Paramount-Time* decision, the prevailing view among corporate directors, based on prior trends in court decisions, was that publicly announced acquisition bids put their companies "in play" and automatically available for sale or auction. In that situation, the popular notion was that the board either had to accept the bid or generate an alternative that offered shareholders greater immediate value—such as a white knight buyer, a restructuring, a recapitalization, or a share repurchase.

In the view of many deal makers, the decision provided target boards with justification for rejecting acquisition offers—provided they were executing bona fide strategic plans designed to generate superior value over time. While not sanctioning outright rejection of acquisition offers under any circumstances—the so-called just-say-no defense—the decision appeared to provide directors with some breathing room for maximizing value.

These recent cases suggest that application of the business judgment rule, while not going entirely full circle, has been realigned around the basic proposition that decisions of corporate directors should be entitled to certain presumptions of propriety. In the rule's present form, directors who have not acted in bad faith and have adequately informed themselves through a reasonable process under the circumstances, are unlikely to be second-guessed by a court.

CORPORATE LAW

For at least 20 years, states have experimented with regulation of corporate control transactions—principally through "antitakeover" laws. Early attempts to provide substantive and procedural protection to shareholders of companies came to a resounding climax in 1982 when the U.S. Supreme Court in *Edgar* v. *MITE* ruled that the Illinois Business Takeover Act was unconstitutional under the Commerce Clause of the Constitution. The clause establishes federal supremacy over regulation of business conducted across state lines. The Illinois case essentially established the preeminence in M&A of federal tender offer regulation adopted under the Williams Act of 1968.

But in 1987, the Supreme Court provided new impetus to state antitakeover powers in *CTS Corp.* v. *Dynamics Corp. of America,* which upheld the Indiana Control Share Acquisition Statute. The rationale was that the act was a valid exercise of state corporate law authority to protect shareholders of companies incorporated in the relevant state. Since the *CTS* case, states have moved quickly to erect various forms of takeover protection.

Control Share Statutes. The most popular mechanism that states have adopted is the control share type of statute that was specifically upheld in the *CTS* case. Most of these statutes deny voting rights to "controlled shares" of a target company that has a particular connection with the state (such as incorporation, doing most of its business in the state, or having most of its shareholders or employees in the state). Typically, "controlled shares" are those acquired by outside interests in a series of related acquisitions that result in ownership above levels specified by the law. For example, in many states, controlled shares lose voting rights when the outsider's interest moves past $33\frac{1}{3}$ percent of outstanding stock.

These statutes usually restore voting rights if a required percentage of "disinterested" shares, those owned by persons affiliated with neither incumbent management nor the outside investor, approves. Most of these statutes provide a mechanism that triggers a special meeting of shareholders to consider restoration of voting rights to owners of controlled shares. Many control share statutes apply to target companies that are domestic corporations (incorporated in the applicable state) and meet other specified criteria relating to place of business, substantial assets, or number of shareholders. Some states require even less in the way of jurisdictional nexus, and many permit target companies to opt out of coverage of the control share statutes.

Moratoriums. Another variety of state antitakeover law is the business combination/merger moratorium statute. Basically, these statutes require the target board and shareholders to approve significant share purchases, mergers, or other "business combinations." If approval is withheld—such as in a hostile bid—the law imposes a moratorium on executing the second step of the transaction, which is actually completing the merger. Thus a hostile buyer can wind up buying a majority of the shares through a tender offer but be denied immediate control of the target company.

Freeze-outs. As with the control share statutes, so-called freeze-out laws vary as to the level of ownership that triggers the moratorium, the opt-out provision, and the jurisdictional connection with the state having the act. Delaware's statute, considered key because of the large number of incorporations there, imposes a three-year moratorium on the second-step merger unless a buyer purchases at least 85 percent of the target's shares in a tender offer. There is, of course, an exception for friendly deals that are characterized by approval of a majority of the board and two-thirds of disinterested shareholders.

Poison Pills. Still another type of state law provides specific enabling authority for boards to adopt poison pills. These statutes generally allow directors to issue rights that enable shareholders to buy stock at very attractive prices if the company is attacked by a hostile buyer. These statutes resolve any ambiguity that may have resulted from judicial pronouncements on the permissibility of poison pills.

Directors' Duties.   Finally, several states have adopted so-called directors' duties laws. They permit directors to consider expanded factors and constituencies, in addition to the then offering price, in reaching decisions on acquisition offers. Designed to protect directors who choose to oppose bids, these laws have come to be known as "stakeholder" or "nonshareholder" constituency statutes. Some require directors to consider long-term and short-term interests of the corporation, including the possibility that these interests may be best served by continued independence. More typically, these statutes expand the constituencies that directors may consider, in addition to shareholders, in determining the best interests of the company—such as employees, customers, communities, creditors, and even the national economy.

Proponents of these statutes argue that they do little more than codify common law, articulating the correct formulation of the fiduciary duties owed by directors to their corporations. Detractors, however, question how directors can serve the best interests of shareholders when they must take nonshareholder factors into account. These opponents even have suggested that the statutes could create additional duties for directors that may be in direct conflict with their duty to shareholders.

Many of the state antitakeover laws have been tested and successfully defended. Others have not been challenged. With the subsiding of hostile takeover activity, new state antitakeover laws may merely claim victory after most of the troops have left the field. On the other hand, there is still substantial belief that transactions involving the change of control of publicly held companies should be regulated (if at all) only on the federal level. The recent resurgence of state antitakeover law will stand in strong opposition to this principle. Given the sometimes almost impenetrable conditions of much recent antitakeover law, it remains to be seen how defensible that area will be if a more vibrant market for corporate control returns.

TENDER OFFERS

In a tender offer, an acquirer purchases shares—usually for cash—directly from stockholders of publicly held targets. The process was popularly associated with hostile bids during the 1980s because it provided a vehicle for skirting opposition of an unwilling target's board and management. In fact, most tender offers have been friendly and have gone forward with the approval of insiders. The tender is most useful in agreed bids because it allows the acquirer to proceed quickly, which is a major advantage when the mergers and acquisitions market is very competitive.

Tender offers are governed by the Williams Act of 1968, and rule making to implement the law is handled by the SEC. The basic requirement of the law is that tender offers remain open for at least 20 business days, although the offer may be extended beyond that span. The statutory minimum provides stockholders and directors with time to evaluate a bid, and, if it is deemed inadequate, to either reject the offer or develop a satisfactory alternative, such as seeking a white knight buyer who will pay more. Should an initial bidder change the price or the terms, the revised proposal must remain open for at least 10 more business days, regardless of how much time elapsed from the original offer.

Another basic element of tender offers is the pro rata requirement. It largely applies when an acquirer seeks less than 100 percent of the target's shares. If the magic percentage is 60 percent, for example, the acquirer is limited to purchasing 60 percent of the number of shares tendered by each tendering stockholder. Thus, the buyer will purchase 60,000 shares from a large shareholder that tenders 100,000 shares and 60 shares from a small shareholder that tenders 100 shares. The pro rata requirement is the opposite of first come, first served. It prevents discrimination against small shareholders and does not penalize those who tender their shares in the late stages of the 20-day offering period.

Besides allowing acquirers to wrap up their deals in as little as one calendar month, the tender offer faces fairly easy treatment from federal regulators, although state laws have created significant procedural hurdles for hostile tenders. Tender documents, divulging such key details as price, terms, and conditions, including the proportion of the target's outstanding shares that must be tendered for the offer to become effective, must be filed with the SEC, but only upon first use. Staff comments generally don't complicate scheduling of the bid, provided all key elements are disclosed.

CORPORATE GOVERNANCE REDUX

While antitakeover wounds have reconfigured state law and left it in shaky readiness for any resumption of hostilities, a new relief element is moving into place. Institutional investors, particularly in the form of public pension plans with huge equity investments, have come forward with authority to exercise voting rights and reinvigorate corporate governance. This class of investor, which grew dramatically in the 1980s, understands that its fiduciary obligations include the exercise of voting rights.

In part, this new institutional activism has been stimulated by pronouncements by the Department of Labor for private pension plans governed by the Employee Retirement Income Security Act of 1974. Institutional investors also are exercising their votes with more focus because their increased size has made the traditional "Wall Street walk," simply getting out of the stock, less attractive. Large investors now view the option of selling poor performers as less practical than in the past. They believe that their positions as large long-term shareholders arm them with the power to demand better performance.

Much of the intellectual consideration of this area finds its precedence in a corporate governance debate that was carried on in the 1970s. That debate, however, was sparked in the post-Watergate era in which the widespread corporate practice of paying for favors from overseas officials sparked great concern as to the need for governance that enforced higher standards of ethics. In the 1990s, corporate governance is the crucible not of the crusaders but of mainstream participants in the capital markets who view accountability of management to shareholders as the key to increased competitiveness in a global marketplace.

In seeking to revitalize the corporate governance system, institutional investors have brought pressures for change in the federal proxy system and in the principles by which directors of companies perform their tasks in such critical areas as executive compensation and selection of new board candidates. These institutions have sought to clear an area in the governance field that in their view is unduly and inappropriately cluttered with federal regulation. They also have sought to motivate and sustain greater involvement by both shareholders and directors. Their activities have ranged from increased levels of corporate governance proposals by shareholders to active negotiations with companies to aggressive lobbying in Washington.

For all of their activity, institutions may have their heaviest impact on specific mergers and acquisitions. On the buy side, institutions have not been hesitant to criticize acquisitions they consider unwise and have prompted directors of acquiring companies to proceed with care. On the sell side, they have required directors of target companies to consider attractive acquisition offers with even more care.

More generically, however, institutional investors have not conclusively demonstrated a clear and definitive link between governance issues and shareholder returns from an economic standpoint. This is a link that must be established if the governance movement is to sustain itself and if institutions and others interested in improved corporate performance through increased accountability to shareholders are to wield influence on ongoing governance as opposed to individual transactions.

46

Finding Your Way Around Washington

Alexandra LaJoux

President, Alexis & Co.,
Arlington, Virginia

Martin Sikora

Editor, Mergers & Acquisitions,
Philadelphia, Pennsylvania

The regulatory environment for mergers and acquisitions is continually changing, as minigenerations of lawmakers, regulators, and judges come and go.

During the 1980s, the trend was toward deregulation of the M&A process. In the late 1980s, the M&A pendulum began swinging back toward more regulation. Congress passed the Insider Trading Act of 1987 and the Financial Institutions Reform, Recovery, and Enforcement Act of 1989. Antitrust has also been an active regulatory area, with new merger guidelines for antitrust that became final in mid-1992.

Through all of these changes, the basic regulatory structure of M&A—as built, promulgated, and enforced by the three branches of government—has changed very little. Practically all M&A transactions must go through some type of federal government hurdles, and although people come and people go, the identity and mission of the hurdles stay about the same. The following "map" and primary regulatory players of M&A regulators should not go out of date any time soon.

THE EXECUTIVE BRANCH

The executive branch of the U.S. government has five main components, many of which have at least some say in merger policy.

The Executive Office of the President includes special offices for legislative affairs and for economic and domestic policy.

Affiliated agencies of relevance to merger policy are the Council of Economic Advisers, which advises the President on general economic matters, the National Security Council, which advises the President on security matters, and the Office of the United States Trade Representative, which represents U.S. interests in negotiations concerning U.S. investment abroad and foreign investment here.

Presidential advisory organizations come and go according to their sunset provisions. In 1992, there were approximately 45 such organizations.

The President's Cabinet is composed of 14 executive departments, including the Department of Commerce, the Department of Justice, the Department of Labor, and the Department of Treasury.

Departments

Commerce has a broad charter "to encourage, serve and promote the nations's international trade, economic growth, and technological advancement." It is a member of the Committee on Foreign Investment in the United States (CFIUS), created under the Omnibus Trade and Competitiveness Act of 1988.

Justice includes the Antitrust Division to "promote and maintain competitive markets by enforcing the federal antitrust laws." Chapter 44 outlines the antitrust guidelines in force since April 1992.

Labor has an important role in the merger process through its Pension and Welfare Benefits Administration, responsible for enforcing standards of the Employee Retirement Income Security Act (ERISA) as overseer of one million public and private pension plans.

Treasury includes the Internal Revenue Service (IRS), which is of obvious importance to all merger professionals because of its administration of taxes.

The IRS usually appears at two major points in the M&A process. Prior to the closing, one or both parties may ask the service to deliver an opinion on whether acquisition currencies paid to selling stockholders are subject to or exempt from federal taxes. Following the merger, the IRS requires the buying company to justify the price it paid by allocating the outlay among the assets it has acquired. If the IRS examination determines that there is a significant gap between the actual values of acquired assets and the purchase price, the difference is assigned to goodwill or going-concern value, two intangible assets that are not depreciable for tax purposes.

Departments overseeing particular industries also may have a say in merger policies. For example, the Defense Department may review acquisitions of defense contractors. And virtually any agency may get involved if the target company does business with it as a supplier or contractor. Federal procurement law requires that the acquirer be recertified by the appropriate agency as eligible to conduct business with the government.

Energy.   Within the Department of Energy there is the Federal Energy Regulatory Commission (FERC), which has jurisdiction over mergers, acquisitions, divestitures, and diversifications in all energy companies except for interstate utility holding companies, which are regulated by the Securities and Exchange Commission (SEC). In the natural gas area, FERC rules on transactions in which gas companies buy or sell physical facilities. The commission does not have jurisdiction in cases involving acquisition of gas company stock.

Financial Services. Treasury also oversees the Comptroller of the Currency, who is responsible for "consolidations or mergers of banks where the surviving institution is a national bank." (There are about 4,600 banks with national charters.) Treasury also includes the Office of Thrift Supervision (OTS), which oversees the work of the independent agency that sells government-seized thrift institutions, the Resolution Trust Corporation (RTC).

Other important authority over financial institutions mergers is exercised through independent agencies such as the Federal Reserve Board.

Independent Agencies

There are several independent agencies within the executive branch. While these often are considered as equivalents to executive departments, they in fact report not to the President, but to Congress.

Of greatest general importance for merger professionals are the Federal Trade Commission (FTC) and the SEC.

The FTC's charter grows out of its basic purpose, to "promote competition in or affecting commerce through the prevention of general trade restraints" such as price-fixing agreements, boycotts, illegal combination of competitors, and other unfair methods of competition. In that position, the FTC is one of the two federal agencies—the Justice Department is the other—that study the competitive aspects of mergers under the antitrust laws. This role is fully discussed in Chapter 44.

The SEC enforces the nation's securities laws, including the Securities Act of 1933, the Securities Exchange Act of 1934—after six decades still the core of U.S. securities regulation—and the Tender Offer Act of 1968, known as the Williams Act. It also has enforcement responsibilities under other laws regulating investment advisors and public utilities.

One of the chief functions of the SEC is to ensure full disclosure of material information in all significant transactions involving the issuance, purchase, and sale of securities. To this end, it requires and reviews various filings in accordance with the sections of the securities laws and the rules and regulations promulgated under these laws.

Common merger-related filings include those for the purchase of 5 percent or more of a company's shares (Schedule 13D per Section 12 of the Exchange Act), the mailing of proxy statements (Schedule 14A per Regulation 14A under the Exchange Act), the execution of "tender offers" to purchase a controlling share of a company's stock (Schedule 14D-1 per Rule 14d-3(a)), and trading in securities by corporate insiders (covered under Section 16(b) of the Exchange Act, more broadly, Rule 10-b-5 under the Securities Act).

These roles arm the SEC with considerable influence in the execution of mergers and acquisitions. SEC rules govern the making of tender offers—purchasing shares directly from target stockholders—under the Williams Act. The agency also figures in the most common alternative deal format, the statutory merger accomplished through an exchange of shares.

Statutory Merger. The more complex and time consuming of the two deal approaches, statutory mergers often require one or both companies to hold shareholder meetings to vote on the deals. The meetings may be required by individual firm charter or by-law provisions or by the New York Stock Exchange rule that listed companies get shareholder okay when expanding the number of outstanding common shares by 18 percent or more. In any event, the company holding the meeting must distribute proxy statements which first are examined in detail by the SEC to determine that elements of the deal have been fully disclosed to shareholders.

During heavily competitive periods in the M&A market—such as the 1980s—tender offers often are preferred to statutory mergers because they can be completed faster. The fear of partners in a statutory merger is that the target can be "swiped" by another bidder while they are awaiting SEC clearance and the holding of the stockholder meetings.

Two-Tier Tenders. Another deal format is the two-tier tender offer. At the "front end," the bidder typically buys a controlling or majority interest—around 51 percent, for example, for cash—and then exchanges securities for the remainder of the shares in the "back end." SEC rules require that the "back end" values be equivalent to the "front end" cash payments.

The SEC also has in force the "all holders" rule, which requires that all shareholders receive the same consideration in tenders, securities exchanges, and similar actions and bars the company from excluding certain holders from these transactions.

13D Filings. Under Rule 13D, any person, company, or group buying 5 percent or more of a public company's stock must report that interest to the SEC within 10 days. Subsequent increases or reductions also must be reported. Hostile offers often are preceded by purchases of 5 percent stakes to give potential acquirers footholds and shareholder status in the target companies.

Insider Trading. While its application is more pervasive than just mergers and acquisitions, Rule 10-b-5 has been a factor in M&A. Generally, the rule bars corporate insiders or their affiliates from buying or selling shares in public companies based on their knowledge of material information before it is made public. A number of prosecutions under Rule 10-b-5 stemmed from trading on pending mergers and acquisitions prior to public announcements.

Accounting. The SEC also has a voice in accounting treatment of mergers and acquisitions. Accounting standards are set by the accounting profession, which serves as a self-regulatory agency under the overall supervision of the SEC. Broadly speaking, there are two types of M&A accounting treatments. If the deal involves a cash purchase (such as in a cash tender offer), it receives purchase accounting treatment—the target's results and other financial characteristics are incorporated into the acquiring company from the day the deal is closed. With the statutory merger, pooling-of-interest accounting, which allows the surviving company to restate prior results as if the merger had taken place earlier, may be available. However, the partners must meet 12 rules to get pooling of interest, including a requirement that at least 90 percent of the purchase price be in stock. The SEC has overview authority on changes of standards within these broad parameters or may prod the accounting profession into initiating desired changes. In addition, the SEC may inspect the accounting treatments on specific deals and order changes.

Independent agencies also may oversee mergers in particular industries. In communications, there is the Federal Communications Commission; in energy, the Nuclear Regulatory Commission. Overseeing financial institutions are the Federal Deposit Insurance Corporation, the Federal Reserve System, and the Resolution Trust Corporation.

Communications. The Federal Communications Commission (FCC) is the principal independent agency regulating the communications field, with jurisdiction over broadcasters, telephone companies, and to some extent cable television operators. Strictly speaking, the FCC does not approve mergers and acquisitions directly, but rules on the transfers of licenses and certificates that go from seller to buyer and are required for operating authority.

In the radio and television area, the FCC acts on sales of all stations, and its inquiry emphasizes the buyer's fitness to hold a broadcasting license. In addition, the agency has a number of significant rules concerning mergers, acquisitions, and diversifications by companies owning radio and television properties.

Some of the more important include the following:

- A single company or interest may own no more than 12 VHF and 12 UHF television stations, 30 AM radio outlets, and 30 FM radio stations. Additionally, a single company's TV station may reach no more than 25 percent of the nation's TV households.

- Cross-media acquisitions in the same market are barred. Thus a newspaper is prohibited from buying another newspaper, a radio station, or a TV station in a market where it already operates. Cross-media ownerships that existed before the rule was promulgated generally have been allowed to continue under a grandfather clause.

- Broadcasting networks are barred from owning syndicators of television programs and are limited in the amount of television programming they can produce directly. Conversely, syndicators cannot own networks.

- Networks cannot acquire or own cable television properties.

- A foreign company or citizen is limited to a 25 percent interest in any U.S. broadcasting property.

- A TV station owner cannot acquire another TV outlet in a separate market when the two stations have overlapping signals that serve the same geographic territory.

Mergers and acquisitions in the telephone industry are regulated if either of the parties operates interstate or the combined company will serve an interstate public. The FCC's rulings in this field cover the transfer of public convenience and necessity certificates that interstate telephone companies must hold. In the cellular telephone area, the agency rules on transfers of licenses that enable holders to use radio frequencies in their operations.

Acquisitions in cable television come under FCC scrutiny if the deal involves a transfer of a microwave license—which allows the holder to use microwave equipment to boost signal power. In all other cable TV ownership changes, the FCC must be notified within 30 days of the sale, although the commission has no specific authority to rule on the transaction.

Energy.   While most M&A work in the energy sector falls to the Department of Energy, an independent agency monitors nuclear power matters.

The Nuclear Regulatory Commission (NRC) has limited jurisdiction in transactions involving nuclear energy facilities. Its authority principally covers situations in which partnerships or consortiums build and operate nuclear-generating plants. The NRC must act when a partial interest in such a facility is being sold, when a new partner is enrolled in the ownership group, or when an existing partner wants to withdraw from the consortium.

Financial Services.   The Federal Deposit Insurance Corporation insures the deposits of national banks and state banks that are members of the Federal Reserve System. It also "may make loans to or purchase assets from insured depository institutions in order to facilitate mergers or consolidations" among such banks. Finally, it reviews transactions that involve insured banks that are not members of the Federal Reserve System.

The Federal Reserve Board—the "Fed"—has primary authority when bank holding companies merge, when acquisitions involve holding companies as either acquirers or targets, and when a merger of banks creates a state-chartered institution that is a member of the Federal Reserve System. The Fed also has responsibility for holding company acquisitions of nonbank operations and regulatory say-so on certain acquisitions of bank stock or bank assets.

As a practical matter, the Fed handles directly only a handful of the M&A situations that fall under its jurisdiction. It has delegated authority to the 12 federal district banks to accept and review applications from banks in the geographic territories they serve and has established guidelines for rulings by the district banks.

Acting as the board's agents, the district banks may clear any deals covered by the guidelines, and typically approve more than 90 percent of the proposals put before them without involving the board. The district banks never reject a deal. But if they conclude that the merger proposals go beyond the guidelines or present special problems or issues, the applications are forwarded to the board for ultimate actions.

Diversification has been an important M&A issue for the Fed since the late 1960s. Through acquisitions, banking organizations have moved into a wide range of other financial services—such as mortgage banking, consumer finance, savings and loans, discount securities brokerage, and factoring—as well as nonfinancial services businesses.

As a result of banking deregulation, the only key financial service areas still generally off limits to banks as of the mid-1990s were securities underwriting and most types of insurance.

Transportation.   The Interstate Commerce Commission (ICC) reviews all mergers involving surface transportation "including trains, trucks, buses, water carriers, freight forwarders, transportation brokers, and a coal slurry pipeline." The Federal Maritime Commission has only an indirect M&A role, in that it grants licenses to freight forwarders. As mentioned above, airline mergers are regulated by the Department of Justice.

In the railroad industry, the ICC reviews mergers for competitive effects. Acquisitions of railroads by nonrailroad companies do not come under ICC jurisdiction.

A major policy change by the ICC during the 1980s permitted companies to build or buy companies in different modes of transportation, such as a railroad's purchase of a truck line. Prior to the shift, commission policy had barred a transportation company from owning more than one type of mode, unless an incidental unit was needed to service the core business. For example, a railroad could maintain a trucking operation only if that operation was tied directly to or serviced a rail unit. Now it may own an extensive and unrelated trucking business.

THE LEGISLATIVE BRANCH

The work of Congress, the legislative branch, is done through committees and subcommittees. While there is some parallel between House and Senate committees, the names of committees do not always reflect this. Also, efforts to streamline committee structure tend to be strongly opposed by vested interests, and appear far from being successful.

Congressional influence on M&A is wielded principally through legislative prerogatives in three areas: antitrust, securities regulation, and taxes. As a result, most important M&A legislation is handled by the three House committees and a like number in the Senate.

Antitrust—Responsibilities for antitrust legislation are held by the House and Senate judiciary committees. The Subcommittee on Monopolies and Commercial Law is the antitrust arm of the House committee.

Securities—Legislation affecting securities regulation is handled by the House Energy and Commerce Committee and the Senate Banking, Housing, and Urban Affairs Committee. The House committee assigns securities matters to its Subcommittee on Telecommunications and Finance, while the comparable Senate unit is the Banking Committee's Securities Subcommittee.

Taxes—The House Ways and Means Committee and the Senate Finance Committee deal with revenue-raising legislation. In the House, taxes related to mergers and acquisitions usually are handled by the Subcommittee on Select Revenue Measures.

In addition, the Senate Small Business and Budget Committees, the House Small Business Committee, the Joint Taxation Committee, and the Joint Economic Committee have some jurisdiction of general relevance.

Committees dealing with specific industries also may become involved in M&A-related legislation. These include the House Banking, Finance, and Urban Affairs Committee (financial services) and the Senate Commerce, Science, and Transportation Committee (transportation). The aforementioned House Energy and Senate Banking committees also cover specific industries.

THE JUDICIAL BRANCH

The federal courts get into the M&A process when cases are brought to them for decisions under applicable laws. Typical situations include:

- Requests by the SEC for decisions to support enforcement actions.
- Requests by the Justice Department or the FTC to block allegedly anticompetitive mergers and acquisitions.
- Appeals from decisions by federal agencies with primary powers to block or approve mergers and acquisitions in specific industries.
- Private complaints under antitrust laws.
- Appeals of U.S. Tax Court rulings. This Washington-based court considers taxpayer appeals from decisions by the IRS. In the M&A field, it frequently rules on disputes involving allocation of purchase price to assets and tax treatment of expenses incurred in completing merger transactions.
- Stockholder suits, including class actions, that attack the fairness of price and terms in an acquisition.

The ultimate judicial arbiter of M&A litigation, as in all legal issues, is the U.S. Supreme Court, which has handed down numerous major decisions affecting merger and acquisition activity, especially since the start of the twentieth century. At the lowest rung in the federal court system are the U.S. district courts, which basically function as trial courts in such areas as antitrust, securities regulation, and stockholder complaints. They also receive initial requests from federal agencies for injunctions and other enforcement actions. In between are 11 U.S. appeals courts, plus a Temporary Court of Emergency Appeals located in Washington.

- The First Circuit Court of Appeals covers Maine, Massachusetts, New Hampshire, Rhode Island, and Puerto Rico.
- The Second Circuit Court of Appeals covers Connecticut, New York, and Vermont. Because the nation's financial center, Wall Street, is located in New York, this is an active circuit in business and financial cases.
- The Third Circuit Court of Appeals has jurisdiction over Delaware, New Jersey, Pennsylvania, and the Virgin Islands. Because most major public companies are incorporated in Delaware, this is also an active circuit.
- The Fourth Circuit covers Maryland, North Carolina, South Carolina, Virginia, and West Virginia.
- The Fifth Circuit includes Louisiana, Mississippi, and Texas.
- The Sixth Circuit includes Kentucky, Michigan, Ohio, and Tennessee, and the Seventh Circuit covers Illinois, Indiana, and Wisconsin.

- The Eighth Circuit embraces a wide territory including Arkansas, Iowa, Minnesota, Missouri, Nebraska, North Dakota, and South Dakota.
- The Ninth Circuit territory is also broad, encompassing Alaska, Arizona, California, Hawaii, Idaho, Montana, Nevada, Oregon, and Washington, plus Guam and the North Mariana Islands.
- The Tenth Circuit territory includes Colorado, Kansas, New Mexico, Oklahoma, Utah, and Wyoming.
- The Eleventh Circuit covers Alabama, Florida, and Georgia.

U.S. bankruptcy courts located in each district have become more prominent in the M&A arena of the 1990s as reorganizations of troubled companies increasingly feature either complete sales of the firms or divestitures of selected assets to raise cash. Bankruptcy court judges must approve such transactions before they are completed.

FOREIGN INVESTMENT AND NATIONAL SECURITY

Acquisitions of American companies by foreign concerns—historically unregulated except for a few specific industries—took a major turn in 1988 with enactment of the Exon-Florio amendment to the Omnibus Trade and Competitiveness Act. This amendment, which added a new section to the 1950 Defense Production Act, originally required review of foreign acquisitions of U.S. firms with some ties to national security, but 1992 amendments elevated the screening process to a required formal investigation of each deal within the scope of the law. The President has final authority to approve or reject most in-bound deals with national security implications. But the 1992 amendments specifically banned companies owned by foreign governments from acquiring U.S. firms holding certain types of contracts with the Defense and Energy departments.

The investigatory work is spearheaded by the aforementioned CFIUS, which issues recommendations to the President. However, the 1992 amendments require that reports be obtained from the Central Intelligence Agency and the Federal Bureau of Investigation. The Office of Science and Technology Policy also may be included in the inquiry.

Outside the national security area, foreign investment may be limited by law or policy in specific industries. For example, Transportation Department policy limits foreign interests to a 49 percent equity position in U.S. airlines and puts a 25 percent cap on their voting powers. FCC rules prohibit foreign interests from owning more than 25 percent of radio and television stations and companies. Federal laws bar overseas companies and citizens from owning nuclear power facilities, as well as American-flag fishing boats and vessels operating along inland waterways. Finally, a reciprocity agreement is required for a foreign interest or government to buy an American concern with drilling and mineral rights on federally owned lands. The buyer's home country must allow American interests to have similar rights on government-owned lands.

47

Investor Relations: Protecting Stock Prices

Michael Seely

*President, Investor Access Corp.,
New York, New York*

Frank Jepson

*Vice President, Communications and
Investor Relations, Bausch & Lomb,
Incorporated, Rochester, New York*

In December 1988, Bausch & Lomb, the manufacturer of contact lenses, lens care solutions, and sunglasses, announced it would pay $133 million to acquire privately owned Dental Research Corp. DRC was a four-year-old company with only $40 million in sales the previous year. It served the dental market, a business in which Bausch & Lomb had no previous experience.

Bausch & Lomb officials asked their investment bankers how the acquisition would affect the company's stock price. They were told that the stock would probably decline by 10 percent.

Given the size of Bausch & Lomb's capitalization at the time, the company faced a projected loss in shareholder value of $100 million.

This presented a challenge to Bausch & Lomb and to Investor Access Corp., Bausch & Lomb's investor relations counsel. We had to find a way to minimize the anticipated loss in shareholder value associated with what was otherwise a highly attractive transaction.

To understand the approach we took to this crisis in investor relations, we first have to consider the reasons behind most stock price behavior. There can be only two explanations for an undervalued stock: either the market doesn't understand the company or management doesn't understand the market.

Stock prices are set by what the market knows. Any company's intrinsic value is determined by information available only to insiders (i.e., management, the board). The relationship of stock price to intrinsic value is shaped by the disparity or congruence of these two information sets. We view investor relations as a process by which companies manage the relationship between the two information sets so as to maximize shareholder value.

Typically, the stock of the acquirer declines on news of an acquisition. There is a good reason for this. The promise of acquisition seldom is fulfilled. It typically doesn't create value for the acquirer.

The first step Bausch & Lomb took in handling the DRC deal was to make a situational assessment, of an empathic kind. We sought to answer two simple questions: What do we know (i.e., what's the insider information set)? And what does the market know (i.e., what's the market set)?

Finally, we had to figure out how we could unify these two different information sets rapidly enough to minimize the loss in shareholder value predicted from the deal.

Clear disparities in the information sets obviously prevailed. (See Table 47.1.) The challenge was to manage, almost on a real-time basis, a massive transfer of information, so that the market and management both operated on equivalent information. This was made easier by the fact that 75 percent of Bausch & Lomb's outstanding shares lie in the hands of institutional investors. With a retail shareholder base, the transfer of information would have been much more difficult.

A key decision was to communicate quickly. Bausch & Lomb would not wait until closing the transaction to manage the projected value gap of $100 million. We would deploy our communications as soon as the agreement in principal was announced. This put pressure on Bausch & Lomb's corporate development team to achieve a definitive agreement in record time and also increased the risks if the deal failed to close. But it was the single most critical decision taken by Bausch & Lomb to seal the anticipated value gap.

Filling the communications vacuum to seal the gap involved four steps.

The Right Information Set. As Bausch & Lomb's corporate development team crafted the merger agreement, we worked through the weekend to create an information base on DRC and on the market that Bausch & Lomb was entering. This was important, since there were no public peers or Wall Street research on the dental industry.

Our information base included a detailed industry backgrounder in which Bausch & Lomb provided a detailed strategy statement for its new oral care division, pro forma financials, and a five-year outlook. Essentially, this was a niche strategy designed to exploit specific opportunities in the diagnosis, treatment, and prevention of peridontal disease. The backgrounder emphasized that Bausch & Lomb was targeting niche opportunities associated in part with an aging population and a

Table 47.1. Conflicts in Information

Capital market information set	Bausch & Lomb information set
Most deals don't make sense.	Company evaluates hundreds of deals a year; hence, a smarter buy.
Dilution usually.	No dilution; a key point. In fact, DRC contributed 17 cents to Bausch & Lomb's earnings per share in 1989.
It's another electric toothbrush.	Not a toothbrush; a plaque-removal instrument.
Electric toothbrushes lack health benefit.	Proven clinical efficacy.
More debt means more risk.	Bausch & Lomb is highly liquid; generates free cash flow.
Nonpublic peers describe potential or to facilitate comparison with DRC.	Dental market is huge, with excellent profit opportunities.
DRC is privately owned, so no knowledge. Wall Street not totally aware of Bausch & Lomb's success in global marketing.	Very rapid growth likely, including international.
No obvious fit to Bausch & Lomb's traditional competencies.	True synergy a major reason DRC approached Bausch & Lomb. DRC's product, like Bausch & Lomb's, is professionally promoted; Bausch & Lomb's R&D, manufacturing, and wet chemistry expertise provides DRC with a base to develop product extensions (rinse, toothpaste, etc.).
Make managers rich and they will leave.	Bausch & Lomb successful in retaining founder/entrepreneurs.
"They're competing with Proctor & Gamble."	A niche strategy envisioned for new oral-care business.
Instrument sales lead to continuing high-margin sales of replacement brushes.	Just like annuity nature of lenses and solutions.

well-established trend in dentistry away from "drill and fill" toward services and products geared to preventing tooth loss. In short, the DRC deal was not the first step toward a face-off with Procter & Gamble and other giants; it was a focused strategy.

Talking to Institutions. Because Bausch & Lomb is heavily owned by institutions and maintains close communications with sell-side security analysts, it was relatively easy to identify the audience—50 professional investors.

The Word to Analysts. On Monday, the deal was announced at the close of trading. At the same moment, messengers left Investor Access Corp.'s New York offices to deliver a complete information kit, including a sample of DRC's unique plaque removal device, endorsed by the American Dental Association, to 50 of the most knowledgeable professional analysts following Bausch & Lomb—"the lead steers." By phone and fax, they were invited to participate in a premarket opening telephone conference the next morning.

After the Tuesday morning telephone call, Frank Jepson initiated and fielded calls throughout the day, while crafting a formal presentation.

Face to Face.   On Wednesday morning, the entire Bausch & Lomb/DRC management teams, including the owner/founder of DRC, hosted a breakfast investor meeting in New York, then flew to Boston for a similar after-market meeting. (More than half the institutional capital in the U.S. is accounted for by these two cities.) Virtually all of Bausch & Lomb's analysts and more than half the shares were represented at the two meetings.

The result of this intensive effort was to seal the value gap predicted by Bausch & Lomb's investment bankers. The company's valuation was preserved.

In fact, over the next year, Bausch & Lomb outperformed two groups of similar companies. Part of the reason: DRC fulfilled or surpassed the expectations established at the time when the deal was announced.

Pursuing the strategy articulated then, Bausch & Lomb subsequently acquired a producer of peridontal probes and introduced a new interplak-compatible dentifrice, tangibly demonstrating the synergies sought by both managements when they merged.

48

Rigging Takeover Defenses

Martin Sikora
Editor, Mergers & Acquisitions,
Philadelphia, Pennsylvania

When the sharks are prowling, it's time to break out the shark repellent. That attitude has been adopted by hundreds of publicly held American companies and some in foreign lands over the last two decades as merger and acquisition activity intensified and hostile or unsolicited takeover offers became common. Responding to potential or actual takeover threats, these firms have adopted a bewilderingly wide assortment of antitakeover devices, collectively known as shark repellents. Specific techniques bear such colorful handles as poison pills, golden parachutes, staggered boards, and antigreenmail measures that have become fixtures in business argot.

Since they came into vogue, shark repellents have been among the most controversial storm centers in the business world. They have been reviled by institutional investors and advocates of a free market for corporate control as barriers to realization of full shareholder value through the sale of a company. Proponents, mainly from the corporate arena, support them as legitimate mechanisms to preserve shareholder value by preventing companies from being bought on the cheap. They have triggered reams of academic literature, clutches of legislative and regulatory initiatives, and bitter corporate governance battles. But do they work? Who knows.

The fact is that corporate defensive weaponry rarely has been tested directly in the courts or in the M&A marketplace. No poison pill has ever exploded in the face of an unwanted buyer. No staggered board has prevented an acquirer from taking control of an unwilling target. M&A professionals assert that no announced deal has ever been turned back because of the target's defensive strengths, although there is no count of the potential deals that fizzled at the idea stage because acquirers refrained from attacking armored companies.

Yet the debate continues to rage. In what has become an annual meeting ritual, institutional investors and dissident shareholders continue to press companies for repeal of existing takeover devices while refusing to vote for any new proposals that require shareholder approval. Court decisions not specifically centered on shark repellents sometimes have rendered them impotent, and even modern communications technology has negated them. Conversely, many companies that go public through IPOs or by being spun off by parents reach the markets with defenses already in place. But in perhaps the most ironic twist, several corporate defenses have been enshrined in state laws, which authorities claim actually have been effective checkmates to unwanted acquisitions. (See Chapter 45.)

Generally (and somewhat arbitrarily) shark repellents fall into three classifications:

Corporation Charter and By-Law Amendments.   These include such mechanisms as staggered boards, fair-price provisions, and supermajorities to approve mergers and acquisitions. They need shareholder approval to become effective. While these provisions dominated the defensive scene in the early and mid-1980s, they have been rarely tried in subsequent years as institutional investors mustered greater voting power and intensified their opposition to antitakeover devices.

Financial Techniques and Changes in Capital Structures.   The best known of these devices is the poison pill, which has become the most pervasive of all antitakeover weapons because it can be installed by directors without getting the go-ahead from stockholders. Other actions include increasing debt, changing pension provisions, and installing multiple classes of common stock, some of which require stockholder approval and some of which don't.

Structural and Strategic Actions.   These include a wide variety of techniques that change the looks or configuration of the company, the most extreme of which is the "scorched earth" dismemberment of the firm. Other initiatives to counter a hostile offer, such as finding a white knight buyer, also fall into this category.

POISON PILLS

Because of the realities posed by evolutions in corporate governance and in the M&A market, poison pills have become the defense of choice for American companies. They also have become the most pervasive antitakeover weapon—with an estimated 60 percent of major publicly held U.S. firms carrying them within their capital structures. Their adoptions continue because directors can install them on their own initiative and without risking rejection by shareholders.

What is a poison pill? Basically it is a right distributed to stockholders that allows them to buy additional shares under certain defined circumstances. In fact, most companies with pills polish their images by calling them shareholder rights plans or shareholder protection plans. There are several different types of pills, and the enumerated conditions and prospective outcomes vary from company to company. But the linkage is that they are activated by events that can lead to an unsolicited change in control of the company by a hostile acquirer. A hostile buyer, who typically is restrained from taking advantage of an activated pill, generally is defined as a bidder whose offer is not approved by the board. In many companies the bid must be blessed by two-thirds of the directors for it to become friendly. Conversely, a pill is redeemable in the event of a friendly acquisition.

There are several major variations.

Flip-in Pills

For openers, the flip-in right allows shareholders to buy additional stock in the company, but at an outrageous price far above prevailing market levels. However, the terms become far more attractive if the company is attacked and the pill comes alive. Most flip-in pills provide two major conditions for their being activated: a hostile bidder acquires a specified portion of the company's shares and/or launches a tender offer for a specified (and usually higher) percentage. For example, a pill may kick in if an unsanctioned bidder actually acquires, say, a 20 percent stake or if a tender offer is mounted for, say, at least 30 percent of the shares. These thresholds are called kick-in points.

If the pill kicks in (which has yet to happen), purchase of stock becomes more tempting. Some pills allow holders to purchase two shares at the originally excessive exercise price, while others may permit two shares to be bought at the prevailing market price for one share. The aim is to increase the number of outstanding shares that the acquirer must obtain and possibly raise the buyer's outlay.

Flip-over Pills

The flip-over pill in general has become a second line of defense. If the hostile buyer succeeds in getting control of the target, that company's shareholders have rights to buy stock in the acquirer at cut-rate prices. This too has never occurred. The purpose is to warn the buyer that it risks dilution of its own common share capitalization if the flip-over pill explodes.

The rights granted by most companies have both flip-in and flip-over provisions. If the flip-in doesn't work, the flip-over takes effect.

Flip-out Pills

The flip-out pill is largely a theoretical concept with no documented examples of actual adoption. When kicked in by a hostile offer, the right allows stockholders to buy shares in the target's subsidiaries and divisions. If the bidder obtains control of the target, it essentially owns an empty shell and not the firm's operations.

Back-End Pills

The back-end pill is one of several variations on the theme of loading up a company with debt to make it unattractive. If the back-end pill kicks in, debt securities are distributed to the shareholders. The buyer is supposed to be discouraged by the prospect of having to make good on the debts as the new owner.

Although among the most controversial defensive provisions, pills have been surprisingly resilient. Many companies have lowered the kick-in thresholds that were originally installed and have repeatedly renewed the purchase rights—which generally have life spans of 10 years—when they expire. While institutional investors constantly target them for rescission at annual meetings, their success rate is modest.

And the pills, while suffering some limited legal setbacks, generally have survived court battles. In what lawyers consider the most definitive ruling yet delivered, a flip-over pill was upheld—in a Delaware decision on a challenge to a flip-over installed by Household International. There has been no definitive or pervasive ruling as yet on flip-ins, but courts in specific cases have limited their applications. A pill was not allowed to block Grand Met's hostile acquisition of Pillsbury Co., and in another decision Interco Inc. was told that its pill could not be used to protect the company while it executed a leveraged recapitalization. Pills that lacked provisions for redemption also have been killed.

In a new guise, pills have become bargaining chips to appease unhappy shareholders. K-mart Corp. agreed to phase out a pill after its shareholders registered strong opposition to the purchase rights, and Westinghouse Electric, seeking an improved image in the face of poor performance, rescinded its pill.

POISON SECURITIES

Like poison pills, poison securities take on a new and deterring character when the company is under siege.

Poison Shares

During periods of tranquility, these shares, usually in the preferred stock class, may be nonvoting or have just one vote per share. Triggered by attack, they become supervoting securities with as much power as, say, 10 votes a share. A variation is to sell an outside investor shares with ordinary voting rights that increase in voting power if the company is attacked.

Poison Puts

Poison puts are attachments to bonds, debentures, notes, and other debt securities. Debt issues with them become callable if control of the issuing company changes hands and the new owner is required to pay them immediately. The first generation of puts make the debt securities immediately callable if the change in control is hostile. A later generation, called superpoison puts, makes the securities immediately callable on any change in control. These originally were not designed as antitakeover weapons but sprang from fears by debtholders that new owners might not be able to pay the attachments off.

CHARTER AND BY-LAW AMENDMENTS

Vehement institutional opposition has torpedoed new attachments of shark repellents to corporate charters and by-laws in the late 1980s and early 1990s, since they require shareholder approval. An exception has been the companies that reach the public markets through IPOs and spin-offs with several of these provisions already on board. The menu includes the following.

Staggered Boards

Known legally as classified boards, these exist at companies that provide directors with three-year terms and put only a third of the board up for election by stockholders annually. The aim is to prevent a hostile acquirer that gains all or most of the shares from kayoing the board, the primary controller of company policy, with one blow. In practice, however, most boards will step out if a hostile bidder wins the battle.

Fair Price

The company in effect sets a minimum price that it considers acceptable and that has also been ratified by stockholders. The price generally is pegged to historical trading levels of the company's shares—that is, the average price over the previous five years or three years. Many fair-price provisions demand that if the offered price falls short of the mandated level, the acquisition must be approved by a supermajority vote (66⅔ percent, 75 percent, or more) of stockholders.

Supermajority Votes

Any hostile bid, again not cleared by the board, must be okayed by a specified supermajority to take effect. Some companies require a supermajority vote even if the offer is friendly.

Stockholder Meetings and Written Consents

Under the once-obscure written consents procedure, shareholders may petition the company for special meetings to vote on issues or may even amend the charter or by-laws if they get enough votes by soliciting them from shareholders. Since this back-channel approach traditionally was too difficult and circuitous to succeed, many companies moved to knock it out. Either they specifically barred written consents or they required that shareholders present specific proposals only at regular annual and special meetings, and then only after giving the company notice. Moreover, many of these companies give the board sole authority to call meetings.

Ironically, written consents, as a by-product of communications technology and institutionalization of shareholders, have become an increased threat to incumbent managers and directors. Using electronic mail and fax machines, hostile acquirers are able to get enough votes to force special meetings simply by signing up a relatively few investors. This happened when Great Northern Nekoosa, which did not eliminate written consents, resisted Georgia-Pacific's acquisition offer. When Georgia-Pacific obtained enough written consents from institutional holders to press for a special meeting so it could present its bid to shareholders, Great Northern gave up the fight.

Directors Duties

Adopting what has been nicknamed the McDonald's amendment, some companies allow directors to consider a wide range of issues beyond purchase price in fielding acquisition bids. They include the impact of the deal on employees, customers, suppliers, relevant communities, and the environment, among other issues.

Antigreenmail

Intended to deter the common 1980s practice of fending off raiders by buying their shares at above-market prices, antigreenmail provisions are on the periphery of antitakeover devices. In the main, they require a board to get shareholder approval to repurchase a significant block of stock, such as 5 percent or more, at a premium. But this is a time-consuming process that can slow raiders who are really trying a quick hit aimed at greenmailing. The theory is that time is the enemy of a hot-money raider. But it may be irrelevant, since Congress has imposed an excise tax on greenmail to discourage the practice.

Director Status

Directors may be removed only for cause, and sometimes only by a supermajority vote. If vacancies on the board occur between annual meetings, they can be filled only by the board itself.

Reincorporation

Some companies reincorporate in a state with stiff antitakeover laws to ward off takeover threats.

CAPITALIZATION CHANGES

The company may erect defenses by inserting them in their capital structures. Most defenses deal with voting powers of stock and usually require stockholder approval.

Multiple Classes of Common

Takeover defense mavens claim that the only truly bulletproofed companies are those with two or more classes of common stock, each of which has different voting privileges. This arrangement is the device most detested by heavyweight investors.

Multiclass common cements voting power in the hands of insiders, and it is sufficient to repel any hostile bid. One class is superior to the other. For example, regular common stock may have 1 vote per share while another class may dominate with 10 votes per share. Or the common may not have any votes while the superior class is the only one that votes.

Companies installing a second class of common may sweeten the deal by boosting the cash dividend for the lower-powered shares. But this is still the hardest sell of all. At the companies that have managed to get inferior voting classes past shareholders—such as Hershey Foods, Playboy, and Strawbridge & Clothier—there was enough insider voting clout to put the proposals across. These firms would seem to need an extreme defense the least. But many planned to use stock for acquisitions or new equity offerings and they feared their hammerlock control would be loosened. With a similar eye on the future, companies going public often start with a two-class equity structure.

Multivoting common remains highly controversial with a debate that ranges into governance issues and has drawn strong regulatory reactions. Congressional legislation is introduced every session to mandate "one share, one vote" for all public companies. The Securities and Exchange Commission tried to erase multivoting common but was aborted by a U.S. Appeals Court in Washington that ruled the SEC overstepped its authority. The SEC's rule would have prevented trading of multiple-class common shares in established public markets.

Phased-Voting Common

Voting power of the common stock increases with the amount of time it is held by an owner. When the investor originally buys the stock, it has one vote per share. But that is gradually increased—up to a maximum of four votes a share—over time, usually up to four years. The idea is that the long-term shareholder is least receptive to a hostile acquisition offer.

Blank-Check Stock

Directors vote a new issue of common or preferred stock with the terms and voting power to be filled in later. Presumably the blank-check shares can be kept in reserve and given enough power to thwart a hostile bid if needed.

FINANCIAL ENGINEERING

Financial engineering techniques may produce changes in the capital structure but they may not be permanent. They also may go beyond the capital structure in effecting change.

Leverage

Boosting a company's leverage is considered a time-honored way of fending off a raider. A debt-strapped firm is less attractive on the face and new owners get saddled with the bills.

There are a number of ways to increase debt. The most extreme is the leveraged recapitalization, which overhauls the capital structure so that it is top-heavy with debt as compared with equity. Usually, shareholders trade existing common stock for a package that includes interest-yielding debt securities and new (stub) common. Special cash dividends also may be included in the deal. Theoretical supporters hold that leveraged capitalizations can offer stockholders superior value to the acquisition offer.

The leveraged recap straddles the line between pure financial engineering and structural change because the debt-heavy company usually has to sell assets to accelerate repayments.

Although widely publicized, recaps have been done by relatively few companies, most of which were trying to beat back unwanted acquisition offers. Some firms, including Owens-Illinois, CBS, and Kroger Co., have been successful. Others, notably Interco Inc., which was driven into bankruptcy, were dismal failures.

Short of a full or partial recap, a company may jack up its leverage by launching an ambitious debt-financed capital spending program or by borrowing to pay for a hefty special cash dividend.

Self-Tenders

Large-scale share repurchases, called self-tenders, have been frequent responses to hostile offers. They can channel cash to shareholders who accept the offers, usually priced at a premium to market; and by shrinking the number of outstanding shares, they can provide a boost for the stock price. They are also leveraged plays, since the company often borrows heavily to pay shareholders. Indeed, if the self-tender is large enough, its impact on the capital structure can resemble a leveraged recap.

In-House ESOPs

An employee stock ownership plan (ESOP), functioning as part of the company's pension and benefits program, holds a significant percentage of the shares—and sets up a blocking position to prevent an unwanted bidder from getting 100 percent control. The rationale is that employees, fearing loss of their jobs, will vote against acquisition. ESOPs of this type have been upheld by the Delaware courts, in a case involving a hostile offer for Polaroid Corp., with the proviso that they provide genuine economic benefits—such as lower overall benefit costs and better worker incentives—for the firm and its shareholders. However, some of their appeal was dimmed when Congress voted to provide traditional tax benefits only to ESOPs used to buy majority control of an operating business.

Pension Parachutes

Many target companies were attractive to buyers in the 1980s because they enjoyed overfunded pension plans. That could mean instant cash for the acquirer skilled in maneuvering within U.S. pension laws. The buyer can terminate the plan and harvest the excess funds as long as it provides an adequate substitute for covered employees.

Corporate responses effectively erased the economic allure of the well-heeled pension plan. One provision specifically barred the acquirer from getting its hands on the fund. Another triggered an immediate boost in benefits for retired and existing employees if control of the company changed in hostile fashion. Congress later joined the parade by imposing a tax on any excess cash reverted to acquirers from termination of pension funds.

Severance Parachutes

The best-known and most controversial of severance payments is the golden parachute, which provides benefits to top executives losing their jobs if their companies are acquired. Extensions include silver parachutes for middle managers and tin parachutes for employees below the managerial ranks. (See Chapter 43.)

STRATEGIC AND STRUCTURAL DEFENSES

Strategic and structural defenses represent a catchall category involving a wide range of initiatives, many of which play on opportunities presented by the M&A market itself. A significant change in the company's looks, operations, or status usually results. Previously mentioned moves like leveraged recapitalizations and self-tenders also can be classified within structural change.

One common technique is to seek a white knight buyer, a more compatible buyer that will pay a higher price than the hostile bidder. A key variation is a management-led LBO of the target, in which management becomes its own white knight. Companies that prefer to remain independent, publicly owned concerns may opt for the white squire approach, in which an outside investor—a company, an investment fund, or a wealthy individual—buys a significant minority interest and agrees to side with management in opposing unwanted offers. The white squire thus gains a blocking position, and in many cases the investment also can be a source of cash for the company.

Steps that gut company operations to make them unattractive are more the stuff of fables than of actual usage. In fact, they have been rarely employed. Under the "crown jewel" strategy, the company sells at least one, and perhaps more, of its best businesses to keep them away from the hostile acquirer. A "scorched earth" policy, a near-liquidation, dramatically widens the divestiture mode by selling virtually all the company's operations and leaving a shell.

At the other end of the spectrum, the besieged company can use acquisitions as defensive tactics, although their effectiveness is dubious. With the "ugly duckling" acquisition, the target purchases a money-losing or poorly performing company to make itself look worse. Or the target can buy a business that competes with the acquirer to set up a possible antitrust conflict.

Perhaps the most romantic of all is the Pac-man defense, in which the target counterattacks the raider by launching a tender offer for its shares. This is a nice ploy for novelists but is seldom used on the M&A battlefield.

PART 8

International Acquisitions and Globalization

49
The Global M&A Market: Europe

S. J. Taqi
*President, IMC Communications,
Geneva, Switzerland*

Garrick Holmes
Geneva, Switzerland

Viewed from an American acquirer's perspective, the European business environment is bewilderingly complex—a mosaic of national markets with different languages and commercial cultures, each with its own set of company laws, accounting practices, corporate tax structures, banking and financial systems, competition rules, and takeover regulations (if any).

It is also an environment undergoing rapid evolution. The changes are most dramatic in the former Communist countries of central and eastern Europe. But those in the west are also being profoundly transformed by the European Community's drive toward a single market that embraces 340 million consumers—with many millions more pounding at the doors.

Once business executives had awakened to the implications of the so-called 1992 program, aimed at dismantling the regulatory barriers that long sheltered many European industries from the full blast of regional and global competition, the result was an unprecedented avalanche of mergers and acquisitions. Most of them were straightforward horizontal deals as companies scrambled to reinforce their home bases and stake out strategic positions in neighboring markets.

The EC Commission, which tracks concentration moves among the Community's largest industrial and service firms, counted 1,122 mergers or majority acquisitions in 1989—more than double the 1987 figure. Of these, 42 percent were purely national, 38 percent occurred between companies from different member states, and the remaining 20 percent involved American, Swiss, Swedish, Japanese, or other non-EC acquirers. In addition, there were 273 purchases of minority holdings and 183 joint ventures.

Since mid-1990 the pace has slowed somewhat, though less drastically than in the United States. The value of cross-border deals slipped to roughly $40 billion in 1991, from a peak of $60 billion the year before. But the pressures of accelerating technological innovation, the succession problems facing many thousands of post–World War II European entrepreneurs, and the ongoing corporate struggle for market leadership—in markets that are themselves being redefined in pan-European or global terms—ensure that industrial concentration will continue apace long after the 1992 milestone is passed.

One factor behind this shakeout is that, in sector after sector, Europe's fragmented markets now support many more companies than can coexist comfortably in the post-1992 competitive arena. Percy Barnevik, chief executive of Swedish-Swiss electrical giant ABB, pointed out that, as of 1989, there were 13 locomotive builders in western Europe, whose number will have to be reduced if Europe is going to compete with the two in the United States and three to four in Japan. Similarly, Europe had 40-odd suppliers of car batteries against 4 in the United States, 11 manufacturers of public telephone exchanges against 4 in North America, and so on.

A comparison of industry concentration levels in the EC and U.S. markets reinforces this contrast, suggesting that further cross-border restructuring and consolidation will be needed if European companies are to remain competitive on a global level.

EC HARMONIZATION MOVES

The wave of industrial concentration touched off by the approach of 1992 gave fresh urgency to the EC Commission's bid for control over large mergers and acquisitions that affect the competitive structure of Community markets. A merger control regulation, first proposed as far back as 1973, finally gained approval from the member states at the end of 1989, giving the trustbusters at Brussels headquarters exclusive authority to approve, reject, or force modifications in deals with "Community dimension."

For the present, the rule applies only to the very largest transactions—those in which the companies' combined worldwide group turnover exceeds 5 billion European Currency Units (ECUs), or approximately $6 billion, and two of them each have sales within the Community of at least 250 million ECUs ($300 million), unless two-thirds of the latter are in the same country. These thresholds, under review in 1993, could well be lowered to catch more deals. Where the criteria are not met, member states still may apply national antitrust laws through their own enforcement agencies.

In effect, these turnover tests mean that any sizable takeover by a major multinational will fall into Brussels' net, regardless of whether the target is based in the EC. Through mid-1992 the Commission's merger task force had dealt with 90 notifications, of which the great majority were waved through within 30 days as posing no threat to competition. A handful were subjected to more rigorous three-month inquiry, which in some cases led to negotiated changes designed to safeguard competition. Only one deal—the proposed joint takeover of Boeing's Canadian offshoot De Havilland by Aerospatiale of France and Italy's Alenia—was blocked outright.

In the field of corporate taxation, two long-pending directives (dating back to 1969) finally were passed in 1990. One extends the same tax privileges to cross-border stock swaps that long have been enjoyed by domestic mergers, notably on the treatment of capital gains. The other aims at avoiding double taxation on dividends from a subsidiary to a parent in another EC country. Taken together, these directives will go some way to level the playing field between companies trying to build a pan-European business and their stay-at-home or host country competitors. Other proposals now in the hopper will deal with double taxation on intragroup interest and royalties, as well as the deductibility by a parent of losses incurred by subsidiaries in other EC countries.

By contrast, little headway has been made in harmonizing national takeover regulations and defensive tactics—another area where the EC playing field is far from level. A proposed directive laying down common procedures for takeover bids was submitted by the Commission in 1988, aimed at increasing the transparency of public offers while protecting the rights of minority shareholders. For example, partial bids no longer would be permitted, and an investor acquiring one-third of a company's voting rights would be obliged to launch a bid for the remaining shares.

Although these and other provisions are modeled on the British takeover code, the proposal has been sidelined largely because of opposition from the United Kingdom, which is unwilling to abandon its well-developed system of voluntary self-regulation in favor of the less flexible statutory approach embodied in the draft directive. However, several other member states, such as France, Belgium, Spain, and Italy, have introduced takeover regulations more or less in line with the EC principles.

A further set of proposals was put forward in 1990, intended to complement the takeover directive by curtailing the legal devices used by managements to repel unwanted bids. Among these are unequal or restricted voting rights, cross-ownership with subsidiaries, and the powers of directors to dispose of key assets or issue new shares during a bid. Such technical barriers are commonplace in Germany and Holland and to a lesser degree in France. Elsewhere on the Continent, there are a few public companies with broad enough shareholdings to make them vulnerable to uninvited takeovers.

In presenting these proposals, the Commission aligned itself firmly with the advocates of an Anglo-American style open market for corporate control. Hostile takeover bids, it noted approvingly, "encourage the selection by market forces of the most competitive companies and the restructuring of European companies which is indispensable to meet international competition."

Many bankers agree, adding that common rules are necessary if a single market is to materialize. However, industrialists on the Continent are understandably reluctant to expose themselves to foreign predators (and not just those of EC origin) by dismantling their defensive ramparts.

At bottom, such divergent perceptions reflect the traditional conflict between shareholders and managers that has been given a new edge by the recent upsurge in takeover activity. In the EC context, this cleavage takes on a political aspect, as the regulatory systems of member states represent differences in the apportioning of power. At one extreme is the U.K. model, where shareholder power is in the ascendance, while industrialists complain bitterly of "short-termism in the City." At the other pole is the Netherlands, where shareholders in large public companies have been virtually disfranchised.

Given these deep national divergencies, it is hardly surprising that the Commission's plan to remove takeover barriers has bogged down in the EC's cumbersome legislative machinery. Adding to the difficulty is that its proposals do not form a stand-alone directive but a series of riders to existing draft proposals, including the stalled 1988 takeover directive and the notorious fifth directive on company laws— first proposed back in 1972, and still hung up over the controversial issue of worker participation in management.

Even if the Commission somehow should succeed in eliminating the technical obstacles to cross-border takeovers, formidable structural barriers would remain. Achieving the hoped-for level playing field across the Community would entail major structural changes in domestic capital markets on the Continent. They include increasing the number of listed firms, expanding the breadth of share ownership, strengthening of local stock exchanges, and development of pan-European trading.

MANY MARKETS, MANY MODELS

A closer look at the various national M&A arenas within Europe reveals the constraints still faced by cross-border deal makers, but also the fact that attitudes in certain countries are evolving toward a climate that is at once more liberal and more shareholder-oriented.

United Kingdom. With its large population of public companies, easy access to corporate information, and technically sophisticated financial markets, the U.K. is the most active hunting ground for foreign acquirers, typically accounting for up to a quarter of cross-border M&A traffic in Europe. Takeovers, both friendly and hostile, are a normal part of the local business culture. And the government, which in the past occasionally stepped in to maintain British ownership of key industries such as cars and banking, has become studiously neutral. Prime examples of this noninterventionist stance are Ford Motor Co.'s takeover of Jaguar PLC, the luxury carmaker; the sale of ICL PLC, the U.K.'s national champion computer firm, to Fujitsu Ltd. of Japan; and the green light to Hong Kong & Shanghai Bank's takeover of Midland Bank PLC while a counterbid from domestic rival Lloyds Bank PLC was referred to the antitrust authorities.

Liberalism also has caught on in France, where governments of both left and right were once known for their ardor in fending off would-be foreign acquirers while cooking up an alternative "French solution." The old approval system no longer applies to buyers of EC origin, and even for others it is seldom a real hurdle. Swiss food giant Nestle SA (non-EC) found this in its epic battle with Italy's Agnelli family (EC) for control of Source Perrier SA, the flagship French mineral water group.

In recent years, in fact, France has become the Continent's most lively M&A market, with activity ranging from a few high-profile takeover contests to a great many private sales to foreign buyers. The main constraint is that many of the largest French companies are state-controlled and, hence, off limits to deal makers, although some of them—Elf Aquitaine, Rhone Poulenc, and St. Gobain—are aggressive international acquirers in their own right. Of late, however, the Socialist government has allowed some blurring of the boundaries between state and private ownership. This development enabled state car maker Renault to link up with Swedish Volvo through a complex of cross-shareholdings that point toward an eventual merger, while ailing state computer firm Machines Bull recruited NEC Ltd. of Japan and International Business Machines Corp. as minority owners and technological backers.

In the private sector, only a handful of listed companies are vulnerable to bids, since many are controlled by family groups or supportive institutions (*"noyaux durs"*). Moreover, a variety of defense measures are available to French companies, including voting limits, double voting rights, and defensive cross-holdings.

Germany. The country has a reputation as a difficult market for foreign acquirers, although in fact the number of in-bound transactions has been increasing steadily. The great majority are friendly mid-sized deals, for, as noted already, the larger German companies are well entrenched behind legal barriers that effectively deter raiders. These often take the form of restrictions on voting rights that limit any shareholder to 5–10 percent of the votes, regardless of its actual holding. Such a provision enabled tire maker Continental AG to withstand a prolonged siege by Italy's Pirelli SpA—though similar defenses were overridden when Swedish paper giant Stora captured more than 75 percent of Feldmuehle Nobel AG, and when Krupp AG launched a market raid on fellow steel maker Hoesch AG that ended in a shotgun merger.

Public takeovers in Germany are further impeded by the close ties between industry and the major banks, which often hold equity stakes in the companies to which they lend, exercise proxy votes for other shareholders, and are represented on the companies' supervisory boards. The bankers' support was crucial in Krupp's victory over Hoesch.

In any case, Germany has relatively few public corporations, and even fewer with widely spread shares. Most German businesses are organized as limited liability companies (GmbH) or partnerships, in which ownership is not freely transferable. Audited accounts theoretically are available for all but the smallest firms, but these are frequently out of date. And in Germany's close-knit business circles, an owner that decides to sell often will prefer a quiet deal with a friendly local competitor rather than turn to the international M&A market.

The Netherlands.   Yet more formidable is the defensive armory of public companies in The Netherlands. They can draw on up to eight different antitakeover repellents—though the Amsterdam Stock Exchange now requires newly listed firms to limit themselves to no more than two. Among the most effective weapons are voting limits, shareholder restrictions, control by a friendly foundation, and issuing new shares to dilute a bidder's stake. In addition, the codetermination system for governance of all sizable companies (in which the supervisory board co-opts its own members) can make it impossible for a predator to exert control.

Not surprisingly, bids for listed Dutch companies are rare, and successful hostile takeovers nonexistent. Minority stake building is possible however, and regularly occurs. Cross-border M&A activity in Holland consists almost entirely of small to mid-sized deals for private companies. Information on Dutch companies, both listed and unlisted, is very good by continental standards, though identifying shareholders may be difficult and accounts are often out of date.

Italy.   The family-owned business tradition has led to a highly concentrated ownership structure, reinforced by shareholder voting pacts, so that even the biggest Italian companies usually are controlled by one of the major family groups, if not by the state. The number and value of foreign acquisitions, though rising, are still low relative to the size of the Italian economy. Mid-sized deals for unlisted family-owned firms are the norm.

Spain.   The country has been a more popular target for cross-border acquirers attracted by Spain's rapid economic growth and relatively low labor costs. Since Spain's EC entry in 1986, government controls on foreign investment have been greatly relaxed and a new takeover law has been put in place. But the once feverish M&A climate cooled considerably by 1992, partly because of sellers' inflated price expectations. As in Italy, most transactions are small to medium private deals, since listed companies are usually tightly controlled by a few major shareholders and the scope for hostile bids is narrow—though some have taken place.

Scandinavia.   M&A markets, traditionally sheltered from outside acquirers, are opening up as Sweden, Finland, and Norway prepare for the new European Economic Area (EEA)—a halfway house toward full EC membership. Official controls on foreign investment, administered more flexibly in recent years, are being eliminated in most sectors, and Sweden's system of free and restricted shares, by which foreigners are limited to 40 percent of equity and 20 percent of voting rights in a company, vanished at the start of 1993. But multiple voting structures, which enable groups like the Wallenbergs in Sweden to maintain control over their empire with small equity stakes, will remain in place until the EC itself adopts the principle of one-share, one-vote. Even in Denmark, an EC member since 1973, many companies are controlled through tax-privileged family foundations holding multiple-vote shares.

Switzerland.   Liberalization also has begun in Switzerland, where a new company law no longer allows directors to refuse to register shares (thus conferring enhanced voting power) on the grounds that their owners are foreign. But companies remain free to impose tight limits (sometimes as low as 2 percent) on the voting rights of any shareholder. The main regulatory hurdle is the so-called Lex Friedrich, a federal law that prevents foreign control of companies with extensive holdings of Swiss real estate; this discrimination is to be lifted for EC/EEA nationals, but not until 1998.

Eastern Europe.   M&A activity in Eastern Europe is driven by privatization programs which differ in each country. Of the three most active markets, Hungary favors a slow case-by-case approach, while Czechoslovakia has opted for rapid mass privatization incorporating a voucher scheme, and Poland is working out its own model based on mutual investment funds managed by western advisers. Still another system prevails in the former East Germany, where a huge agency, the Treuhandanstalt, has been charged with selling or liquidating former state enterprises as expeditiously as possible. And the embryonic scheme in Russia puts the emphasis on preferential distribution of shares to employees and management.

For western acquirers, the common thread among these various privatization systems is that deals usually are initiated at the enterprise level and must then be renegotiated with the relevant supervisory authority and its (western) advisers. Valuations are problematical at best, and the purchase price is often a less critical factor than the western partner's commitment to invest in developing the business.

OUTLOOK FOR THE 1990s

The slowdown in European M&A activity in the early 1990s already may be over. In the first six months of 1992, cross-border spending picked up sharply to $33 billion—almost double the year-earlier total. But even if this proves a false dawn, it seems safe to predict that the next wave of corporate dealmaking cannot be far distant, and that its magnitude will exceed that of the late 1980s.

The strategic pressures that drive most deals in Europe have not gone away, and will resurface more strongly than ever as economies start recovering and interest rates come down. The fundamental needs and motivations that will fuel a new takeoff include:

- Further restructuring in many industries, which are not yet attuned to the broader markets and competition that is unfolding in Europe
- Pressures on many large European firms to continue their globalization efforts, and for small and medium-sized players to enter into alliances
- Privatizations in eastern Europe and the former Soviet republics, where all sectors of the economy will have to be completely rebuilt
- Demands on American and Japanese companies to establish or strengthen their footholds in the emerging European single market

With increasing numbers of firms bent on creating larger pan-European groups, cross-border transactions will be the biggest segment of M&A activity in the 1990s.

Strategic rather than financial buyers will be in the driver's seat. The U.S. frenzy of the 1980s, with its high-risk LBOs and junk bonds, never reached Europe—and is not going to with the troubles overtaking leveraged acquirers at home. Leverage will be used, but with moderation. Share exchanges, cross-holdings, asset swaps, joint ventures, and alliances will proliferate, but cash will continue to be the primary mode of payment in cross-border acquisitions.

The continental climate will become less inhospitable toward public takeovers, with more hostile deals and greater attention to the rights of minority shareholders developing. As in the past, however, friendly private negotiations will remain the rule. For the foreseeable future, the vast majority of acquisitions in Europe will be of private family companies—thousands of which now are coming on the market as the post–World War II generation of entrepreneurs reaches retirement age—or of units being divested by public companies as they seek to jettison excess baggage and strengthen their core businesses.

50

The Global M&A Market: North America

Robert S. Schwartz

Partner, McDermott, Will & Emery,
Washington, D.C.

Bennett A. Caplan

Partner, McDermott, Will & Emery,
Washington, D.C.

The North American Free Trade Agreement (NAFTA) will establish tenets governing investment in North America. These rules will facilitate mergers and acquisitions throughout North America. Mexico, Canada, and the United States concluded this comprehensive trade agreement in August 1992, subject to ratification.

Former President George Bush viewed NAFTA as a first step in his "Enterprise for the Americas Initiative"—a plan that would ultimately provide for free trade agreements, based on NAFTA, throughout the Americas. He said that Chile would be the next country to be invited into this free trade arrangement. The NAFTA investment chapter thus could ultimately apply throughout the Western hemisphere.

President Bill Clinton has announced his support for NAFTA and has said he will present it to Congress for ratification. But Clinton has added that certain areas in the agreement (e.g., the environment, workers' rights) will have to be subject to further "parallel" negotiations.

Clinton has not indicated that the relatively noncontroversial investment chapter would be in need of renegotiation. He has expressed support for the "Americas Initiative," despite opposition from labor, in keeping with the trend toward regional trading blocs.

TYPES OF INVESTORS

NAFTA is primarily addressed to "NAFTA investors," companies established as corporate entities in one of the three largest North American countries. The agreement grants key preferences to NAFTA investors, generally enhancing conditions for investment in North America.

NAFTA is not entirely silent as to "non-NAFTA investors." The agreement extends some of the benefits granted to NAFTA investors to "non-NAFTA investors" as well. Conversely, it imposes some conditions on both NAFTA and non-NAFTA investors alike.

NAFTA Companies

A NAFTA "enterprise" is "any entity constituted or organized under applicable law, whether profit making or not-for-profit, and whether privately owned or governmentally owned, including any corporation, trust partnership, sole proprietorship, joint venture or other association."

"Enterprises of a party" are enterprises "constituted or organized" under the law of one of the three North American countries. These will qualify for NAFTA *preferences*. All NAFTA enterprises, whether North American or foreign-owned, will benefit from the establishment of certain underlying principles. The definition of a NAFTA investor generally is not tied to whether the stock of a company is owned by foreign or North American citizens. NAFTA enterprises include companies and branches *organized* under the laws of a North American country. Consequently, a foreign-owned, U.S.-incorporated entity will qualify as a "NAFTA investor" of the United States on the same terms as a domestically owned American company. There are some qualifications, however, as discussed below.

Non-NAFTA Companies

Non-NAFTA investors will not receive NAFTA preferences, but may receive other benefits and be subject to conditions established under NAFTA. Non-NAFTA investors can include foreign companies that are not incorporated nor doing business in one of the North American countries and even U.S., Canadian, and Mexican-owned companies that are incorporated in other countries and doing business exclusively outside of the North American continent.

Foreign-Owned NAFTA Companies

In limited circumstances, the NAFTA agreement imposes additional qualifications for a foreign-owned company of a NAFTA country to be a "NAFTA enterprise." These conditions are restricted, in keeping with the agreement's intent to encourage non-NAFTA companies to invest and manufacture products in North America.

Each NAFTA country may deny preferences to an entity owned or controlled by non-NAFTA nationals if the company does not have "substantial business activities" in the territory of the NAFTA country under whose laws it is organized. This provision, often included in U.S. bilateral investment treaties, enables NAFTA countries to prevent foreign entities from establishing NAFTA "shell" companies solely to obtain NAFTA preferences.

NAFTA preferences also can be denied to enterprises shown to be owned or controlled by nationals of a non-NAFTA country in the following situations:

- The denying NAFTA country does not maintain normal diplomatic relations with the country of the parent company (e.g., the United States and Cuba).
- The foreign-owned enterprise seeks to violate or circumvent NAFTA investment rules.

Those conditions are, in fact, quite limited in scope.

The text also allows a NAFTA country to require that the majority of the board of a company be of domestic nationality, provided this does not impair the ability of the investor to exercise control over its investment. This provision deals mainly with the "boardroom" control of the company, rather than actual equity ownership. This means, for example, that Mexico can require that a Hong Kong-owned company have Mexican citizens on the board of its Mexican subsidiary.

There are limits on what NAFTA countries can require of non-NAFTA-owned enterprises. No NAFTA country can require that a minimum level of equity in an enterprise in that country be held by that country's nationals, other than certain nominal qualifying shares for directors or incorporators. Nor can a NAFTA country require that an investor from another NAFTA country sell or dispose of an investment in its territory solely on the basis of the investor's nationality.

EXCLUSIVE PREFERENCES FOR NAFTA INVESTORS

The NAFTA investment chapter sets forth the conditions under which investors of the countries party to the agreement—"NAFTA investors"—may invest in one another's countries. The investment text broadly covers the establishment, acquisition, operation, and sale of business enterprises within each country. Each NAFTA country must grant the most favorable treatment possible to investments of enterprises of one of the other NAFTA countries.

Favorable treatment is assured by the acceptance of the principle of "national treatment" for all NAFTA investors. This means that a NAFTA country must grant qualifying investors from other NAFTA countries *no less favorable treatment than investors from its own country.*

In addition, NAFTA embraces the concept of most-favored-nation (MFN) treatment—that is, enterprises from NAFTA countries will receive treatment *no less favorable than companies from non-NAFTA countries*—as a cornerstone principle for investment. Companies from NAFTA countries will receive whatever is more favorable for them—national treatment or MFN treatment.

In connection with their investments, NAFTA investors will be able to convert local currency into foreign currency at the market exchange rate. They will be able to exchange freely such international payments as profits, dividends, interest, capital gains, royalty payments, management fees, returns in kind, and proceeds from the sale of the investment. NAFTA countries cannot require investors from their country to repatriate income, earnings, or profits attributable to an investment in the territory of another NAFTA country.

A NAFTA country cannot expropriate, directly or indirectly, investments of NAFTA investors, except for public policy purposes, and then only on a nondiscriminatory basis. Expropriations must follow due process of law, and fair market value compensation must be paid on a timely basis.

The NAFTA countries may require NAFTA investors to register and submit investment information. However, these requirements cannot undermine NAFTA's investment preferences.

Legal Redress for NAFTA Companies

The investment provisions establish a dispute settlement mechanism for alleged breaches of the NAFTA rules by the United States, Canada, or Mexico. NAFTA investors may bring an action on behalf of themselves or the enterprise. Dispute settlement is through binding arbitration primarily under the 1965 Convention on the Settlement of Investment Disputes Between States and Nationals of other States (ICSID) or the 1976 United Nations Commission on International Trade Law (UNCITRAL). Prior to submitting a claim, a NAFTA investor must notify the other government of its intent to press the action. The claim itself may not be submitted until six months after the loss was incurred.

The tribunal consists of three arbitrators—the disputing parties each choose one and then agree upon the third. The arbitrators may award monetary damages or restitution of property, but cannot order punitive damages. The arbitrators also may require the injured party to accept monetary damages instead of restitution. If a party does not abide by the terms of the arbitral award, a NAFTA dispute settlement panel can mandate compliance. A NAFTA investor also can seek to enforce the award under other permissible means.

For investments in Mexico, the NAFTA investor must choose whether to pursue its claim under NAFTA arbitration or through the Mexican courts or administrative tribunals. The investor cannot pursue both avenues. A NAFTA investor may not bring acquisitions subject to review in Canada and Mexico before a NAFTA dispute settlement panel if the investment or acquisition is denied.

In Canada, no proposed investment ever has been denied under the Investment Canada Act. However, potentially objectionable investments have been withdrawn. Prospective investors may not appeal adverse decisions under Canadian law.

BENEFITS AND CONDITIONS

The investment chapter prohibits investment "performance requirements" (mandating specific domestic sourcing or content levels, requiring companies to export a certain percentage of exports, etc.) from being imposed on either NAFTA or non-

NAFTA investors. The limited exceptions to this rule apply in the cases of government procurement, export promotion, and foreign aid programs. Generally, however, even non-NAFTA investors will be confident of not being subject to performance requirements on projects in North America.

The agreement provides for limited exemptions from its open investment principles. These apply equally to NAFTA and non-NAFTA investors. For example, Mexico will preserve the exclusive right for the government of Mexico and its citizens to invest in certain energy sectors. The Law to Promote Mexican Investment and Regulate Foreign Investment has sought to ensure that Mexican citizens retained control of Mexican corporations since 1973. However, the Mexican authorities more recently have become increasingly flexible in allowing foreign ownership of Mexican corporations.

Canada will maintain its restrictions on foreign investment by either NAFTA or non-NAFTA investors in so-called cultural enterprises, which include the publishing, film, music, recording, broadcasting, and cable TV industries.

Procurement contracts and some subsidies, such as government-supported loans and guarantees granted to domestic companies, are exempt from national and most-favored-nation treatment conditions under NAFTA's investment provisions.

The NAFTA investment chapter also permits NAFTA countries to prohibit investment activities that would harm the environment. A NAFTA country may not lower its environmental standards to encourage investments by NAFTA or non-NAFTA investors.

The NAFTA countries also can screen investments by NAFTA and non-NAFTA investors that raise national security concerns. The United States thus may continue to apply its Exon-Florio law, which allows the U.S. government to prohibit acquisitions of U.S. companies by foreign entities for reasons of national security.

Canada retains its investment screening provisions, permitted under the 1988 U.S.–Canada Free Trade Agreement, for investments of more than $150 million.

Investment Canada, the government agency charged with overseeing foreign investment in Canada, automatically screens investments reaching the threshold dollar amount. Investment Canada reviews investments under a set of criteria set out in the Investment Canada Act to ensure that the investment will "be of a net benefit" to Canada.

Mexico initially will be allowed to screen acquisitions involving more than $25 million. The Mexican dollar amount that triggers screening will rise to $150 million over 10 years. Lower dollar amounts than $150 million apply to the uranium production, oil and gas, financial services, transportation services, and cultural enterprise sectors. The Foreign Investment Commission, the Mexican agency that oversees investments, automatically will screen prospective foreign investments that reach the threshold dollar amount.

TOWARD UNIFICATION

NAFTA seeks to create a unified trading market by eventually eliminating tariffs on products traded between the three North American countries. The NAFTA "rules of origin" give preferential treatment to "North American" products in the form of lower duties, thereby influencing procurement decisions. This ultimately encourages and even can force companies to invest and produce in North America.

Overall, the investment chapter will contribute to the climate of confidence for investment in NAFTA countries. NAFTA's investment principles make the traditionally closed Mexican market more attractive. Investors also may seek to enter the traditionally open U.S. and Canadian markets, where cheap labor is less of a concern.

51

The Global M&A Market: Japan and the Pacific Rim

Stanley Ginsberg

*Daiwa Securities America Inc.,
New York, New York*

For almost all of Japan's recorded history, three hard realities have shaped its economic and political organization—geographic isolation, scarce natural resources, and near-chronic labor surplus. Over the centuries, these factors interacted to produce a highly integrated and interdependent political economy based on resource conservation; patterns of production and consumption founded on strategic collaboration rather than competition; and a system of corporate governance that gives priority to the interests of producers rather than owners. This system has given rise to a uniquely Japanese approach to business combinations—one based on strategic alliances among a large number of entities, rather than on the diversification and/or integration of a single corporate entity.

For this reason, the industrial group or conglomerate (keiretsu)—a large and diverse collection of trading and manufacturing companies and their suppliers, typically centered around a city (money-center) bank—has played a key role in Japanese economic organization and development. Through such groupings and through an informal, highly collaborative method of ministerial intervention called "administrative guidance" (gyosei shido), the Japanese government has been able

507

to implement and direct a comprehensive industrial policy, in which business combination by merger and acquisition is but one of many tools.

In response to the increasing globalization of Japan's markets, Japanese economic organization has undergone significant change in the past 20 years. Government control over the keiretsu was weakened by dramatic increases in Japanese financial liquidity during the mid-1970s. Meanwhile, expanding access to the increasingly globalized capital markets during the "bubble economy" years of the late 1980s began to erode the financial ties between the city banks and their old-line industrial clients, bringing about fundamental changes in the market for control of both domestic Japanese and overseas corporations. In the wake of the Japanese stock market crash of 1990–1992, moreover, deteriorating corporate profitability and balance sheets appeared to be ushering in a new phase of industrial consolidation and corporate restructuring in which merger and acquisition will play an increasingly prominent role.

INDUSTRIAL GROUPS AND MANAGERIAL CONTROL

Modern Japanese political and economic organization assumed its broad outlines under the Tokugawa shoguns. A system of top-down government, based on enforced consensus and strict allocation of resources according to the relative strength of the contending parties, replaced warfare as the primary means of settling competition over control of resources. Complex formal networks of reciprocity between suppliers and consumers—which persist to this day in the supplier networks of giant manufacturing companies like Toyota, Matsushita Electric Industrial Ltd., and Hitachi Ltd.—played a primary role in the Japanese political economy. Competition remained fierce, but it was carefully concealed behind a public façade of harmonious consensus. After the 1868 Meiji Restoration overthrew the Tokugawa, closely held industrial combines (zaibatsu) formed around the biggest and most powerful merchant and banking houses—Mitsui, Mitsubishi, Sumitomo, and Yasuda. The zaibatsu continued to dominate the Japanese economy until the end of World War II.

Following Japan's defeat in 1945, the U.S. Occupation forces carried out a conscious policy of deconcentration. The old zaibatsu families were stripped of their ownership of the holding companies that formed the centers of the industrial combinations, and attempts were made to create a broad base of popular shareholders that mirrored the U.S. model. This policy was not to last, however. With the end of the Occupation, the old zaibatsu companies quickly reconstituted themselves into industrial groups (guruppu)—clustered around their own banks, together with real-estate agencies, insurance firms, and the flagship trading houses that typically bear the group name. Japan's six largest bank-centered guruppu are affiliated with Mitsubishi, Mitsui, Sumitomo, Fuji, Dai Ichi Kangyo, and Sanwa banks. In addition, a second tier of integrated transportation, leisure, and retailing guruppu appeared—those built around railway companies like Tokyu, Seibu, Tobu, and Hankyo.

In the early postwar years, when Japan was experiencing a chronic capital shortage of major proportions, the banks created a powerful and pervasive financial infrastructure, through which the Bank of Japan, the Ministry of Finance (MoF), and Ministry of International Trade and Industry (MITI) could exert close supervision over the rebuilding of the Japanese economy. Rather than doing away with industrial concentration, the Occupation actually laid the groundwork for its reemergence after the war in a more streamlined and efficient form.

Unlike Western corporations, in which equity ownership confers a degree of control over management, Japanese firms make a clear distinction between equity ownership and managerial control. Members of a guruppu tend to own each other. The banks in particular generally hold large interests in their clients' stocks; and Japanese banks have entirely different priorities from Western stockholders. Company presidents in Japan, instead of being bothered by major stockholders breathing over their shoulders and forcing them to watch the profit charts, have to worry about expansion schemes they and their bankers have agreed on. These conglomerates, known as "corporate groups," contain highly diversified industrial companies.

The entire structure in each case is tied together by interlocking directorates and a tightly integrated system of cross-shareholding. This system has placed about two-thirds of all shares outstanding on the Japanese stock exchanges under the direct control of guruppu corporations and financial institutions. A company's "stable" shareholders also can block a takeover, thanks to certain articles of the Commercial Code that give veto power to shareholders that control one-third of a firm's shares. On average, the top 10 shareholders control almost 40 percent of the outstanding shares of all listed companies. Furthermore, because these holdings are considered "political" shares rather than investments, they are rarely, if ever, sold—in effect, creating a system that is virtually immune from unwanted takeovers by outside parties.

Hostile takeover is made even more difficult by virtue of the simple fact that no single individual is in charge of a guruppu, and no one is ultimately responsible for it. The shachokai, or presidents' council, which meets regularly, is an institution for mutual control. Participating presidents of all the major firms in a corporate group attend not as stockholders of their own companies, but as representatives of the stocks their company holds in all the other member companies. One of the functions of these meetings is to discuss joint investments and the creation of new sister companies in new industries.

Cooperation with or control over firms outside the group is largely based on the system of affiliation called keiretsu. Through this arrangement, a firm secures the services of a whole string of otherwise independent enterprises on a permanent basis. The usual aim of this arrangement lies in the direction of vertical integration, ranging from the supply of raw materials and parts to distribution and sales outlets. Usually, the affiliates are small firms that receive orders, capital, credit, materials, and often management personnel from the larger companies—which thus secure the services of reliable subcontractors or a constant supply of parts. The precise organization and degree of control over members vary from group to group, but the obligation to extend mutual aid and to keep as much business as possible within the group is taken for granted.

JAPANESE MERGERS AND ACQUISITIONS

It is probably more accurate to say that until the late 1980s the objective of the vast majority of Japanese mergers and acquisitions was the solution to an industry problem rather than the exploitation of a competitive opportunity. Most business combinations came about in response to clear and specific needs related as much to preserving the fabric of Japanese society as to producing immediate competitive advantage. These needs typically include conformity with government policy, strengthening of industrial groupings, and/or absorption of financially strapped companies with a minimum of social dislocation. In keeping with the broader implications of Japanese business combinations, acquiring companies rarely take the initiative. Rather, the targets most often move first by approaching third parties such as ministry officials, senior managers of their lead banks or securities underwriters, or influential business leaders. The company to be acquired seeks business or financial assistance from the acquiring company.

According to the Japanese Fair Trade Commission, the pace of domestic merger and acquisition has risen steadily, from an average of 500 per year during the 1950s and 1960s, to more than 1000 annually during the 1970s, and double that in the 1980s. The trend peaked in 1987, when Japanese corporations consummated a record 2299 domestic business combinations. The vast majority take place within an industry. During the 1970s and early 1980s, more than a third occurred in the wholesale and retail sectors, where small enterprises predominate. With the coming of the "bubble economy" of the late 1980s, real estate and leisure companies became hot properties.

The relative handful of mega-transactions involving Japanese acquirers—for example, Bridgestone's acquisition of Firestone and the Sony-Columbia Pictures and Matsushita Electric–MCA deals—has given many foreigners a somewhat distorted view of Japanese M&A activity. According to Carl Kester, author of *Japanese Takeovers,* "Most of the 2000 or more mergers occurring annually in Japan today are small, privately negotiated deals. Fully 80 percent of those taking place between 1981 and 1985 were transactions resulting in companies with total book equity capital of 5 billion yen (about $20 million at prevailing exchange rates) or less. Sixty percent produced companies with book capital of less than 1 billion yen ($8 million). Based on a sample of 186 combinations publicly announced between 1982 and 1987 for which actual purchase prices were disclosed, the average price paid for a Japanese company was a mere 520 million yen (less than $4 million at prevailing exchange rates)." Furthermore, the pace of Japanese M&A pales beside that of the United States.

The evolution of Japanese M&A has followed a clear and logical course. The earliest postwar wave of merger and acquisition was brought about during a period of severe capital shortage by the powerful Ministry of International Trade and Investment, which supervised reindustrialization. MITI kept Japanese industry under close control, allocating scarce capital, raw materials, and export licenses to the industries and companies that complied with its "administrative guidance" (gyosei shido). In broad terms, MITI's mandate was to prioritize and rationalize Japanese postwar industrial growth by eliminating duplicate investment, realizing economies of scale, and amortizing past losses by future earnings from expanded operations. During the early postwar years, leading banks involved themselves actively in the consolidation by helping with mergers in the trading, chemical, and textile industries. A decade later, in 1966, MITI gave its blessing to the merger of Prince Motors and Nissan Motors.

A year later, MITI convened the Industrial Problems Research Association, a high-level panel of business leaders and government officials. This cross-section panel of Japanese producers issued a report that recommended widespread mergers or "cooperation" aimed at ending "excessive competition" in several key industries—steel, automobiles, machine tools, computers, petroleum refining, petrochemicals, and synthetic textiles. This effort directly led to the 1969 merger of Yawata Steel and Fuji Steel—products of the Occupation's breakup of wartime giant Nippon Steel—into New Japan Steel. The Industrial Bank of Japan played the role of go-between, as it did in the earlier Prince–Nissan deal. Although most of the recommended consolidations failed to take place, the later successes of the targeted industries underscore the seriousness with which MITI viewed the association's recommendations. In fact, MITI continued to promote industry- concentrating mergers as late as April 1986, when two domestic oil companies, Daikyo and Maruzen, merged to form Cosmo Oil with capital of 27 billion yen.

Shifts in the 1970s and 1980s

Toward the end of the 1970s, however, a new trend started to surface. While most earlier mergers were arranged through third parties, an increasing number resulted from direct discussion between the companies involved—i.e., 52 percent of the mergers in 1985 versus 10 percent in 1975 resulted from direct negotiations. In September 1985, a Nihon Keizai Shimbun survey of the top 100 companies listed on the First Section of the Tokyo Stock Exchange revealed that nearly half believed acquisitions would become an important corporate strategy for two reasons: acquisition of new technologies, and diversification of product lines. Another survey conducted in January 1990 found that one-third of more than 600 major companies, especially those in manufacturing industries, already had engaged in some type of M&A activity. Sixty percent believed M&A would be necessary in the future.

During the late 1980s, further important changes occurred. Huge and persistent trade surpluses, combined with easy monetary policy, slowing economic growth, and the forced run-up of the yen following the September 1985 Plaza Agreement, created a vast pool of excess purchasing power. Balance sheets were bloated with cash, while easy access to the global capital markets gave Japanese corporations opportunities for virtually unlimited financing. The ease with which U.S. companies could be bought changed the attitudes of Japanese managers toward M&A from general disapproval to wild approbation. The need to diversify and to move production overseas in order to bypass proliferating trade barriers suddenly sent Japanese corporations actively looking for foreign acquisitions.

There was little concern that the M&A flow would be reversed. Tokyo-based financial analyst Robert Zielinski has pointed out that the structure of Japan's cross-shareholding system helps defend companies from predators by making them too expensive. At the end of 1988, there were 209 Japanese companies among the world's top 500 in terms of market capitalization. It was difficult to justify the purchase of a Japanese firm on the basis of expected cash flow alone, the usual method for valuing a takeover target, because, at 60 or 70 time earnings, share prices were prohibitively high. By contrast, it was cheap for a Japanese company to acquire another Japanese company by exchanging shares. The implied cost of Mitsui Bank's acquisition of Taiyo Kobe Bank was 3.5 trillion yen ($26.9 billion). No company would have paid this amount of money in cash for Taiyo Kobe Bank. Instead, the deal was done at no out-of-pocket cost—by exchanging eight Mitsui Bank shares for ten of Taiyo Kobe Bank. Similarly, it would have cost $14 billion to buy Mitsubishi Estate, Japan's major commercial real estate owner. Yet it cost Mitsubishi Estate only $846 million to buy half of the Rockefeller Group, owner of New York's Rockefeller Center in the United States.

Within the limits of the tax and commercial codes, merger in Japan resembles the unification of two companies through a pooling of interests. Both managements remain in the combined company, but shares in the surviving company are exchanged for outstanding shares of the liquidating companies. The fate of an acquired company largely depends on its profitability at the time of acquisition. Since tax regulations prohibited the successor company until recently from using acquired tax losses to offset future earnings, mergers sometimes entailed absorption of a profitable company by an unprofitable one.

ALTERNATIVES TO M&A

Even under the best of circumstances, the strategic combination of two independent businesses is a complex and demanding task. In most cases, companies protect their autonomy by assigning stakeholder priority to employees. Through lifetime employment and remuneration based on seniority rather than merit, Japanese corporations secure their employees' loyalty while guaranteeing their own continuity through the severe restriction of labor mobility. Any change in corporate structure that jeopardizes established seniority relationships in executive ranks can result in erosion of employee morale and threaten to destabilize a business combination. At the same time, business combinations can create tremendous headaches when labor unions—which generally restrict membership to permanent employees of a company—find it necessary to integrate.

To surmount this organizational obstacle, the Japanese have developed a highly imperfect compromise. In order to ensure that the management and employees of both companies receive equal treatment, directors from each side retain their positions and relative seniority. Normally, the older senior executive becomes chairman (kaicho), while the younger becomes president (shacho) of the merged enterprise. This arrangement may continue through several management layers. Over time, all of the older managers eventually retire, to be replaced by a new generation of unified corporate leadership.

The enormous difficulty inherent in Japanese-style merger and acquisition has prompted a large number of Japanese corporations to follow alternate paths to diversification. These may involve the affiliation of an existing company by means of a keiretsu relationship, or the creation of an entirely new guruppu-affiliated subsidiary empowered to pursue some additional line of business. Besides simplifying the financial and operational management of the new business line, addition of another subsidiary creates new jobs and provides a convenient landing zone for senior executives who are passed over for promotion. The examples of subsidiary creation are countless. Toshiba and Hitachi, for example, are major manufacturers of machinery whose subsidiaries and associates produce a wide range of electrical machinery and ceramic products. In addition to its securities brokerage, asset management, and research divisions, the Daiwa Securities Group has subsidiaries in the venture capital, real estate, software research, telecommunications, precious metals, business services, and travel and tourism businesses.

In either case, affiliation is less disruptive and easier to manage than merger or acquisition. With unions and seniority intact, affiliates find it easier to work with the parent company as quasi-independent entities that nonetheless enjoy access to the services and benefits of the parent.

The sheer size and complexity of the guruppu, as well as the decentralized nature of Japanese decision making, have worked together to create diversified industrial organizations that differ significantly from their U.S. counterparts. Because Japanese financial reporting regulations did not require corporations to consolidate financial results until 1977, subsidiaries created before then had considerable freedom from supervision by the parent corporation—a situation that continues to this day, despite the introduction of mandatory consolidation. Japanese subsidiaries typically belong to different industrial associations from their parents, enjoy separate relations with other companies and banks, recruit different types of people, maintain their own labor unions, and establish their own personnel policies. Furthermore, subsidiaries are expected to become even more independent of the parent as its own business matures. Unlike Western-style subsidiaries, which, when successful, are drawn ever closer into the corporate net, Japanese subsidiaries normally borrow money and conclude contracts without guarantees from the parent, and even can issue shares to third parties, that dilute the parent company's interest.

AFTER THE BUBBLE

The collapse of the great Tokyo bull market after 1989 turned back the clock for many of Japan's largest corporations. A 60 percent drop in Tokyo share prices, along with the associated slump in corporate earnings and the unraveling of many corporations' highly leveraged speculative investment (zaiteku) positions, led to a credit crunch and crisis of confidence reminiscent of the mid-1960s, when excessive speculation brought the Japanese financial economy to its knees. The crisis accelerated a longer-term move away from Japanese companies' traditional focus on market share. The worst slowdown since 1974 increased talk of rationalization—and with it, the need for more restructuring through M&A. Ironically, when companies found themselves in financial difficulties, Japanese banks suddenly became unwilling to play their traditional matchmaker roles. Instead, faced with their own capital pressures, many just want their money back as soon as possible—even if that means selling to a foreign company.

As in the past, most of the deals are likely to take place between domestic firms within the same guruppu, and will follow historic logic—consolidation of cost centers, elimination of "excessive competition," and realization of economies of scale. However, foreign buyers also are likely to become increasingly active. With price-to-earnings multiples of Japanese companies becoming roughly comparable with those in other major equity markets, the cost of acquiring such companies has come back to earth. Even blue chips like Hitachi, Matsushita, and Nissan were selling for less than their net asset value in late 1992. At the same time, large-scale shifts in liquidity away from Japan created pools of investment-hungry offshore capital, while concern about the growing friction between Japan and its trading partners prompted MITI to take a more favorable position on foreign investment. In early 1992, the Diet passed a bill providing a variety of incentives to foreign investors, including accelerated depreciation and tax loss carryforwards for companies with at least one-third foreign ownership.

For their part, Japanese owners found themselves increasingly motivated to sell. The collapse of the zaiteku-driven investment trusts and fund trusts, as well as the squeeze on corporate and bank capital, have begun to weaken the cross-shareholding system. As early as 1986, financial institutions came under pressure to sell in the face of a December 1987 deadline for reducing their shareholdings in any given company to a maximum of 5 percent. At around that same time, several large manufacturing companies—including Nippon Steel—coped with the beginnings of the manufacturing recession by unloading shares of group companies to raise cash.

The market for closely held small and medium-sized companies also began to open up as aging founder-owners suddenly found themselves without successors. A 1989 change in the tax law that substantially reduced the tax penalty for such sales also added to the appeal of selling. By early 1992, it was reported that foreign M&A specialists resident in Japan were spending most of their time advising foreign companies about Japanese acquisitions and helping Japanese companies sell the overseas businesses purchased at the height of the overseas acquisition boom.

According to Daiwa Securities Co., foreigners made 13 acquisitions worth $1.4 billion in Japan during 1991, with some bankers expecting the total to double or triple in 1992. By contrast, foreign buyers acquired majority ownership of only 30 Japanese companies between 1981 and 1987—or twice that of all prior years.

Much of the activity involves food, pharmaceutical, and chemical companies, sectors of the world's second-largest consumer market in which Japanese competition is relatively weak. In March 1992, Pfizer Inc. acquired Koshin Medical, an Osaka medical equipment distributor, for about $23 million. During the same period, Lion Corp., a household products company with annual sales of $2.3 billion, sold its 74.5 percent share of a money-losing insecticide subsidiary to S. C. Johnson Co.'s Japanese subsidiary. Activity also began heating up in other industries. In March 1992, 19 percent of Japan Systems Corp. was acquired for $28.9 million by Electronic Data Systems, a unit of General Motors Corp., which also got an option to buy up to 51 percent over three years.

IN FLUX

Japan's relationship with western-style M&A clearly is still evolving. As the Japanese economy continues to globalize, thereby losing much of its built-in protections and rigidities, the market for corporate control will continue to liberalize. The dramatic growth of Japanese ownership of international assets during the 1980s may well be matched by an equally dramatic internationalization of Japanese corporate control. Mergers and acquisitions are likely to play an increasingly prominent role in Japan, as they do elsewhere in the world.

52

The Global
M&A Market:
Eastern Europe

John Lindquist

Partner, Boston Consulting Group,
London

Starting up a new business through joint ventures with Eastern Bloc partners has been the traditional entry strategy into eastern Europe. Western companies have been much more hesitant about acquiring major equity stakes in existing enterprises and assets.

WHY HAVE THERE BEEN RELATIVELY FEW ACQUISITIONS?

First and foremost, the laws in most eastern European countries until recently have been too restrictive to make acquisitions possible. While the legal framework for joint ventures and acquisitions has been rapidly evolving in the 1990s, the problem lies in the small print.

In Poland, the laws on privatization and foreign investment allow 100 percent ownership, subject to government authorization, but it is still not clear whether a buyer can own the land underneath the company. The legal quandaries are compounded by a number of other problems. Some countries have been restrictive about the convertibility or repatriation of profits, making the payback on investment highly uncertain.

There are also issues about what to do with the legacies of the Communist era that are inherited with acquired companies. Many eastern European companies are saddled with a stock of "social assets," such as apartments and sporting facilities and a bloated workforce. Divesting the social assets and trimming the workforce can prove to be a difficult endeavor. There is uncertainty regarding liability for past environmental damage.

Another complication is the complete breakup of the COMECON (Council for Mutual Economic Assistance) trade structure. Leading state industrial companies used to tie up a third or more of production capacity in COMECON's five-year specialization agreements for ruble-based exports to the former USSR and other Eastern Bloc countries. Now that the system has been dismantled, it is unclear as to where a large portion of future sales will come from.

Finally, there is the issue of valuation. Existing accounting data can be very misleading. Often, prices are regulated, and key cost inputs subsidized, and differ significantly from international prices; balance sheets often do not recognize basic conventions like bad debt, obsolete stock, and depreciation. Moreover, the absence up to now of functioning stock markets or previous equity transactions means there are few comparable market prices.

On the other side, eastern European governments have their own reasons to be cautious about acquisitions. They too are concerned about valuation and fear that the state may underprice its assets. A major stumbling block in Poland's negotiations to sell the Gdansk shipyards was the lengthy independent valuation. Likewise, valuation has proved to be a problem for Hungary. Some Hungarians thought that the state sold Hungarian Hotels too cheaply, so they nullified the agreement and gave the Swedish company, Quintus, its money back. Such sentiment may affect coming amendments to foreign investment laws and may reinforce some eastern European governments that would rather promote joint ventures than acquisitions.

WILL THE ENVIRONMENT IMPROVE FOR ACQUISITIONS?

Definitely so. Eastern Europe has a great need for investment—any investment. It is saddled with debt, its technology is obsolete, and its standard of living is suffering. To recover and to successfully introduce market economies, these countries must make Western capital and technology feel welcome.

Hungary, with the largest debt burden per capita in eastern Europe, has been the first to respond to this message. The new government is committed to accelerating the privatization program. It has floated shares in 20 companies, including such important ones as Ibusz and Centrum stores. The government also is providing tax incentives and investment guarantees, and allowing profit repatriation.

Poland is accelerating its privatization program. On a trip to the United States in 1990, Lech Walesa announced that 80 percent of the country's industry would be for sale to foreigners.

Like Poland, other eastern European countries are changing investment laws monthly, or even daily. Even the former Soviet Union now allows majority foreign ownership of existing state enterprises.

The development of embryonic stock markets in Hungary, Poland, and the Czech Republic will progressively provide signals to valuations of companies.

In the long run, Eastern European governments all will have to be less restrictive on foreign investment in order to survive. Not only do they need help from Western investors, but also there will be increasing competition among the different Eastern European countries to attract the limited pool of foreign investment. Barring major political reversals, more acquisition opportunities can be expected through all of Eastern Europe.

WHY WOULD A WESTERN COMPANY WANT TO MAKE ACQUISITIONS IN EASTERN EUROPE?

There are sound strategic reasons for Western companies to make acquisitions in Eastern Europe, plus the fact that there are potentially high returns to be made for small investments. Although in the United States and Western Europe it is getting increasingly difficult for companies to add significant value to acquisitions to justify the substantial premium required, in Eastern Europe it is a different story. Assets are very cheap, and the need for change is so strong that it is possible to make very small cash investments if a buyer can offer Western technology, management know-how, or access to foreign markets. It is also possible to operate at a much lower cost. The wage rates are significantly lower, yet the skill level is as high as in many Western countries.

Obviously, investing in newly and partially reformed markets poses very significant risks, but there have been enough examples of successful acquisitions for both strategic and financial reasons to make it worth a closer look.

The most notable example of a strategic investment oriented toward exports was General Electric's purchase of 50 percent and a controlling interest in Hungarian light bulb manufacturer Tungsram. GE bought a company with $300 million of sales, a majority of which were in hard-currency exports, for $150 million. The purchase increased GE's European market share significantly, from 3 percent to 10 percent, just in time for the unification of the European Community. GE effectively bought Western European market share at Eastern European prices. The company also shielded its investment from risk by insuring $100 million of it against expropriation, nationalization, and inconvertibility of currency, through the U.S. Overseas Private Investment Corp.'s new Eastern European Program.

The British manufacturing firm Hunslet, which acquired 51 percent of Hungary's Ganz Railway Engineering for $3 million cash, as well as know-how, training, and technology valued at $16 million, also falls into this category. In addition to structuring the deal so it paid very little cash, Hunslet gained a low-cost way to double its capacity at a time when it had a number of major locomotive contracts on the horizon.

Another case is that of Kvaerner, a Norwegian group with shipbuilding, engineering, and ship-owning interest, which recently reached a provisional agreement to acquire one of its suppliers, the Gdynia shipyard of Poland. Kvaerner has had a business relationship with Gdynia as a licensor of gas-carrier technology since the

1970s. This acquisition makes strategic sense for Kvaerner because it locks in low-cost capacity at a time when many observers are predicting a worldwide shortage of shipbuilding capacity in the mid-1990s.

Another strategic rationale is to buy companies that offer access to the markets within their countries. In eastern Europe, there is a population of 395 million and a GNP equivalent to nearly two-thirds that of the European Community, in terms of purchasing parity.

Some of the first Western companies to tap the eastern European market through acquisitions have been newspaper publishers. In November 1989, Maxwell Communications Corp. PLC acquired 40 percent of *Maygar Hirlap,* the Hungarian government newspaper (and traditionally the main party organ).

Rupert Murdoch's News Corp. also was bold, acquiring more than 50 percent control of the *Reform* newspaper, a Hungarian daily. It was started by Hungarian entrepreneurs with an initial investment of $1.25 million and sold in less than a year for four times that amount. These early moves set off a scramble among publishers to buy the remaining assets. Other leading players include Bertelsmann (stakes in Hungary and eastern Germany), Axel Springer (Hungary and eastern Germany), and Eurexpansion of France (Hungary, the Czech Republic, and Poland).

Similarly, Allianz and Colonia, the leading German insurance companies, bought up all the major insurance companies in both Hungary and eastern Germany.

While compelling strategic reasons motivate some acquisitions, purely financial reasons motivate others. There are significant profit opportunities for those companies that want to take only a passive investment position. The Austrian bank Girozentrale, along with the Hungarian Credit Bank, took a short-term position in Tungsram before selling it to GE for a net profit of $40 million. Girozentrale also took a position several years ago in Novotrade, a Hungarian software firm. In September 1989, it floated Novotrade on the over-the-counter market in Austria at 150 times its initial investment. Girozentrale also purchased 40 percent of Ibusz, a Hungarian travel agency, which it floated on the Vienna Stock Exchange in May 1990. This offering tripled in value on its first day of trading before leveling off at more than double its flotation value.

THE FUTURE

Taken collectively, the investments cited above signal a promising future for acquisitions in eastern Europe. It is likely that the laws throughout eastern Europe will be modified further to make acquisition of equity states more attractive and to eliminate remaining areas of uncertainty.

The choices available to Western investors will also expand. Strategic investors will have real choice in either making new investments through joint ventures or buying into existing market positions and assets.

Watch for bellwether sales—similar to the GE acquisition of Tungsram—in the other eastern European economies to see how serious the different governments are about privatization. These will send a clear signal to the West regarding the range of choices that will be available.

Risks will abound. In addition to the possibilities of major political reversals, there remain the risks of economic collapse, rampant inflation, and wild currency fluctuations and continued inconvertibility. Some new leaders in Poland, Hungary, Slovakia, Romania, and Bulgaria may be bent on correcting some of the recent excesses of capitalism in their countries and protecting the national industrial jewels.

Yet, in spite of the very large downside risk, eastern Europe represents an opportunity for high returns. The lack of information, legal ambiguity, price distortions, inefficient markets, and fast pace of change all prove an extraordinary upside possibility for those Western companies bold enough to seize the opportunities.

Appendix A

Intermac

Cheryl A. Cade

*International Association of Merger and
Acquisition Consultants, Burr Ridge, Illinois*

The International Association of Merger and Acquisition Consultants (INTER-MAC) was founded to enhance the art and science of mergers and acquisitions and to support and encourage transactional activity among its members. The organization promotes professional and ethical conduct of the highest standard. Headquartered in the Chicago area, INTERMAC members are located in most major North American cities. Each office is staffed with full-time M&A professionals who specialize in representing businesses in the $5–$100 million range.

The association was founded in 1973 by seven M&A consultants and originally was named the National Association of Merger and Acquisition Consultants (NAMAC). The name was changed to International Association of Merger and Acquisition Consultants as membership and activities grew worldwide in scope. Approximately 40 member firms serve clients in principal cities in North America.

M&A services provided by INTERMAC members include, but are not limited to:

- Purchase or sale of private companies, including the critical "once in a lifetime" sale of the entrepreneur's family business
- Purchase or sale of product lines
- Divestitures of divisions or subsidiaries of diversified companies
- Acquisition search projects on behalf of national and international companies
- Arranging for financing packages

INTERMAC members have broad experience in retailing, manufacturing, aerospace, insurance, banking, broadcasting, publishing, and many other commercial and industrial fields in addition to M&A experience.

All INTERMAC members adhere to these membership policies:

- Members shall exercise independent professional judgment on behalf of clients and shall act only in their best interests.
- Members shall protect and preserve the confidences and secrets of clients and will disclose them to others only with the prior consent of the client.
- Members subscribe to and operate under a code of ethics of the highest professional standards.
- Members do not practice law or accounting but are available for consultation with the client's accountant and/or attorney in concluding agreements.

Individuals or firms interested in INTERMAC membership should contact Cheryl Cade at headquarters. The telephone number is (708) 323-0233 and the fax number is (708) 323-0237. Or write to 200 South Frontage Road, Suite 103, Bull Ridge, Illinois 60521.

Association for Corporate Growth

Carl A. Wangman

*Executive Director, Association
for Corporate Growth, Glenview, Illinois*

•

The Association for Corporate Growth (ACG) was founded in 1954 by a group of growth-oriented executives and provides a forum for ideas relating to both external and internal growth—through acquisitions, divestitures, joint ventures, and new or expanded products and services. ACG's mission is promotion of the professional interests of its members who have leadership roles in strategic corporate growth. Members have the opportunity to:

■ Gain new ideas from speakers, seminars, and discussions with people working in the field of corporate growth

■ Develop additional skills and techniques that will contribute to the growth of their respective organization

■ Meet other corporate growth professionals who can provide counsel and valuable contacts

MEMBERSHIP

ACG grants membership on an individual basis to people involved in corporate growth. Current membership of nearly 3000 includes representatives of 2000 companies that manufacture a wide range of consumer and industrial products, as well as firms that supply services related to these companies such as accounting firms, financial intermediaries, and related service businesses that facilitate deals.

MEMBERSHIP DIRECTORY

The ACG Membership Directory lists all members by chapter and company. Each member may include up to five categories of areas of expertise and five categories of industry familiarity which facilitates networking across the country for any specific need. ACG offers both members and nonmembers the opportunity to access the skills inventory data base of the ACG membership.

CHAPTER ACTIVITIES

The association's programming centers around monthly chapter meetings and an annual conference. Featured guest speakers include experts in corporate planning, growth, diversification and divestiture, government leaders, and specialists in economics and finance. Other activities include:

- Workshops and seminars
- Reports to members on new techniques for acquisitions, new accounting practices and techniques for valuation and appraisal, new product screening and introduction, and current practices and experiences in international business development
- Liaison with other professional and trade associations

INTERGROWTH

InterGrowth, ACG's annual conference, brings to the membership and others a sampling of the finest business minds in an environment that allows the exchange of ideas through workshops, panels, and speakers.

GROWTH AWARDS

Each year ACG presents two awards. The Founder's Award for Corporate Growth, in memory of Peter Hilson, a founder of ACG, is given to an organization that has demonstrated outstanding growth performance. The ACG Emerging Company Award is presented to the company that has annual sales of less than $1 billion and has demonstrated outstanding growth for the previous three years.

CRITERIA FOR MEMBERSHIP

Applications for membership in ACG are evaluated and processed by the 25 chapters in the United States and Canada. Information is available by contacting International Headquarters, 4350 DiPaolo Center, Suite C, Dearlove Road, Glenview, IL, 60025-5212. The telephone number is (708) 699-1331 and the fax number is (708) 699-1703.

Appendix **C**

The
Planning
Forum

THE INTERNATIONAL
SOCIETY FOR STRATEGIC
MANAGEMENT AND PLANNING

The Planning Forum is the world's leading international business organization focused on advancing the understanding and practice of strategic management as the integrating force for improving organizational performance and achieving global competitiveness. As a nonprofit organization, The Planning Forum accomplishes its mission through a variety of knowledge-based services: the annual International Strategic Management Conference, showcasing best practices in all areas of strategic management; the Research & Education Foundation, seeking practical approaches in strategic management; *Planning Review,* a bimonthly business journal; *Network,* a monthly executive briefing; audiotapes and videotapes of conference presentations; books and monographs representing the cutting edge in the field of strategic management; a 2000-plus volume strategic management library; and the programs and networking opportunities offered by 44 chapters across North America. The address is P.O. Box 70, 5500 College Corner Pike, Oxford, Ohio 45056. The telephone number is (513) 523-4185 and the fax number is (513) 523-7539.

National Association of Corporate Directors

John M. Nash

President, National Association of Corporate Directors, Washington, D.C.

Founded in 1977, the National Association of Corporate Directors (NACD) is a not-for-profit organization focused on serving the needs of individuals serving on corporate boards of directors at both *Fortune* 500 companies and privately held companies. More than 1500 chairpersons, chief executive officers, chief financial officers, presidents, and other professionals that serve on, or deal with, corporate boards are members. NACD is the only national organization developed exclusively for providing information and executive-level education for inside and independent outside corporate directors. Services include:

- *Director's Monthly* newsletter, containing articles by leaders in corporate governance
- Access to special educational monographs, surveys, and reports on current governance concerns
- Opportunity to interact with peers serving on and working with corporate boards
- Discounts on all NACD educational programs and materials

- Access to the NACD Directors Register of experienced individuals to serve on corporate boards
- Local chapter memberships, which offer local networking and educational programs

PROFESSIONAL EXCELLENCE

The members of NACD strive for professional excellence in corporate leadership and encourage self-improvement in the boardroom. NACD members share a commitment to conscientious corporate governance in the companies they lead and serve. In recognition of this commitment, NACD selects a Corporate Director of the Year every fall and honors this individual during its annual Corporate Governance Review.

DIRECTORS REGISTER

The Directors Register is a data bank of NACD members who are experienced professionals and are available for board service. The register is available free to members of NACD. Nonmember organizations may use the register for a nominal fee.

CONSULTATIVE SERVICES

NACD makes available its combined resources of experience, knowledge, research, and dedication to corporate concerns in a broad range of consulting services on specific board issues and processes. NACD conducts a confidential board assessment and in-house director training program tailored to specific company needs.

NACD CENTER FOR CONTINUING CORPORATE GOVERNANCE EDUCATION

The NACD Center holds more than 20 courses across the nation each year, covering all aspects of corporate governance, such as: The Role of the Board of Directors in Publicly Held Companies; CEO–Board Relations Forum; The Role of the Board in Private and Closely Held Companies; and The Role of the Audit, Compensation, Executive, and Nominating Committees.

For information on programs and membership, contact NACD at 1707 L Street, NW, Suite 560, Washington, DC 20036. The telephone number is (202) 775-0509 and the fax number is (202) 775-4857.

The Regulatory Lineup for Mergers and Acquisitions

The U.S. government is divided into three main branches, each of which has several different divisions. The following "blue pages" section organizes these divisions into a general category of interest to all M&A professionals, followed by industry categories that have a bearing on M&A in specific sectors, such as energy and financial services. In all cases, the number of the highest officer (chairman, secretary) is given. If a general information telephone number is available, it is provided.

EXECUTIVE BRANCH

The President of the United States
The White House
1600 Pennsylvania Avenue, NW
Washington, DC 20500
President, Room 1 (202) 456-1414
Chief of Staff (202) 456-6797

Council of Economic Advisers
Old Executive Office Building
17th Street and Pennsylvania Avenue
Washington, DC 20500
Chairman, Room 314 (202) 395-5042

National Security Council
The White House
1600 Pennsylvania Avenue, NW
Washington, DC 20500
Assistant to the President for National
  Security Affairs, Room 1 (202) 456-2255

United States Trade Representative
Winder Building
600 17th Street, NW
Washington, DC 20506
USTR, Room 209 (202) 395-3204

Executive Departments

Department of Commerce
Herbert C. Hoover Building
14th Street and Constitution Avenue, NW
Washington, DC 20230
Main number (202) 377-2000
Secretary, Room 5854 (202) 377-2112

Antitrust Division
Department of Justice
Main Justice Building
10th Street and Constitution Avenue, NW
Washington, DC 20530
Main number (202) 514-2000
Assistant Attorney General for Antitrust,
  Room 3101 (202) 514-2401

Pension and Welfare Benefits
  Administration
Department of Labor
Frances Perkins Building
200 Constitution Avenue, NW
Washington, DC 20210
Main DOL number (202) 523-6666
Assistant Secretary for PWBA, Room
  S2524 (202) 219-8233

Internal Revenue Service
Department of the Treasury
1111 Constitution Avenue, NW
Washington, DC 20224
Main Treasury number (202) 622-2111
Main IRS number (202) 622-6370
IRS Commissioner, Room 3000
  (202) 566-4115

Energy

Federal Energy Regulatory Commission
Department of Energy
825 North Capitol Street, NE
Washington, DC 20426
Main DOE number (202) 586-5000
Chairman of the FERC (202) 208-0550

Financial Services

Comptroller of the Currency
Department of Treasury
250 E Street, SW
Washington, DC 20219
Main number (202) 874-4700
Comptroller, Room 9-1 (202) 874-4900

Office of Thrift Supervision
Department of Treasury
1700 G Street, NW
Washington, DC 20552
Main OTS number (202) 906-6000
Director, Room 1700 G (202) 906-6280

Transportation

Department of Transportation
Nassif Building
400 7th Street, SW
Washington, DC 20590
Main number (202) 366-4000
Secretary, Room 10200 (202) 366-1111

INDEPENDENT AGENCIES

Federal Trade Commission
FTC Building
Sixth Street and Pennsylvania Avenue,
  NW
Washington, DC 20580
Main number (202) 326-2000
Chairman, Room 440 (202) 326-2100

Securities and exchange Commission
450 5th Street, NW
Washington, DC 20549
Main number (202) 272-3100
Chairman, Room 6010 (202) 272-2000

Communications

Federal Communications Commission
FCC Building
1919 M Street, NW
Washington, DC 20554
Main number (202) 632-7000
Chairman, Room 814 (202) 632-6600

Energy

Nuclear Regulatory Commission
East-West Towers Building
4350 East-West Highway
Bethesda, MD 20555
Main number (301) 492-7000
Chairman and Commissioner,
  Room 17-D-1 (301) 492-1759

Financial Services

Federal Deposit Insurance Corp.
FDIC Building
550 17th Street, NW
Washington, DC 20429
Main number (202) 393-8400
Chairperson, Room 6028 (202) 898-3888

FDIC Regional Directors

FDIC–Atlanta
Marquis One Building, Suite 1200
245 Peach Street Center Avenue NE
Atlanta, GA 30303
Regional Director (404) 525-0308

FDIC–Boston
160 Gould Street
Needham, MA 02194
Regional Director (617) 449-9080

FDIC–Chicago
Suite 3100
30 South Wacker Drive
Chicago, IL 60606
Regional Director (312) 207-0210

FDIC–Dallas
Suite 1900
1910 Pacific Avenue
Dallas, TX 75201
Regional Director (214) 220-3342

FDIC–Kansas City
2345 Grand Avenue, Suite 1500
Kansas City, MO 64108
Regional Director (816) 234-8000

FDIC–Memphis
Clark Tower, Suite 1900
5100 Poplar Avenue
Memphis, TN 38137
Regional Director (901) 685-1603

FDIC–New York
452 5th Avenue, 21st Floor
New York, NY 10018
Regional Director (212) 704-1200

FDIC–San Francisco
25 Ecker Street, Suite 2300
San Francisco, CA 94105
Regional Director (415) 546-0160

Federal Reserve System
Marriner S. Eccles Federal Reserve
  Board Building
20th & C Streets, NW
Washington, DC 20551
Main number (202) 452-3000
Chairman and Governor, Room B-2046
  (202) 452-3201

Federal Reserve Banks

District 1
600 Atlantic Avenue
Boston, MA 02106
Main number (617) 973-3000

District 2
33 Liberty Street
Federal Reserve Postal Station
New York, New York 10045
Main number (202) 720-5000

District 3
Ten Independence Mall
PO Box 66
Philadelphia, PA 19105
Main number (215) 574-6000

District 4
1455 East 6th Street
PO Box 6387
Cleveland, OH 44101
Main number (216) 579-2000

District 5
701 East Byrd Avenue
PO Box 27622
Richmond, VA 23219
Main number (804) 643-1250

District 6
104 Marietta Street NW
Atlanta, GA 30303
Main number (404) 521-8500

District 7
230 South LaSalle Street
PO Box 834
Chicago, IL 60690
Main number (312) 322-5322

District 8
411 Locust Street
PO Box 442
St. Louis, MO 63166
Main number (314) 444-8444

District 9
250 Marquette Avenue
Minneapolis, MN 55480
Main number (612) 340-2345

District 10
925 Grand Avenue
Federal Reserve Station
Kansas City, MO 64198
Main number (816) 881-2000

District 11
2200 N. Pearl St.
Dallas, TX 75201
Main number (214) 922-6000

District 12
101 Market Street
PO Box 7702
San Francisco, CA 94120
Main number (415) 974-2000

Resolution Trust Corporation
801 17th Street, NW
Washington, DC 20434
Main number (202) 416-6900
President and Chief Executive Officer,
 Room 1001 (202) 416-4000

Transportation

Interstate Commerce Commission
ICC Building
12th Street and Constitution Avenue, NW
Washington, DC 20423
Main number (202) 927-5885
Chairman and Commissioner, Room
 4126 (202) 927-6000

Federal Maritime Commission
800 North Capitol Street, NW
Washington, DC 20573
Chairman, Room 12313 (202) 523-5911

LEGISLATIVE BRANCH

Write to a House member or staffer care of the U.S. House of Representatives, Washington, DC 20515.

Write to a Senate member or staffer care of the U.S. Senate, Washington, DC 20510.

To reach any member of the House or Senate, or to reach any staff member, call the main switchboard at (202) 224-3121.

Or you may contact legislators directly at the addresses and telephone numbers provided below.

Antitrust

House Judiciary Committee
Rayburn House Office Building
Washington, DC 20515
General Counsel, Room 2138
 (202) 225-3951
Minority Chief Counsel, Room B-351C
 (202) 225-6906

House Economic and Commercial Law
 Subcommittee
Rayburn House Office Building
Washington, DC 20515
Counsel, Room B-353 (202) 225-2825
Minority Chief Counsel (202) 225-2825

Senate Judiciary Committee
Dirksen Senate Office Building
Washington, DC 20510
Counsel, Room 224 (202) 224-5225
Minority Chief Counsel and Staff
Director, Room 147 (202) 224-7703

Senate Antitrust, Monopolies, and
Business Rights Subcommittee
Dirksen Senate Office Building
Washington, D.C. 20510
Chief Counsel (202) 224-5701
Minority Chief Counsel and Staff
Director (202) 224-9494

Securities

House Energy and Commerce
Committee
Rayburn House Office Building
Washington, DC 20515
Staff Director and Chief Counsel,
Room 2125 (202) 225-2927
Minority Chief Counsel and Staff
Director, Room 316 (202) 226-2424
Minority Chief Counsel and Staff
Director, Room 2322 (202) 225-3641

House Telecommunications and
Finance Subcommittee
Ford House Office Building
Washington, DC 20515
Staff Director and Senior Counsel,
Room 316
Minority Counsel, Room 564 Rayburn
(202) 226-3400

Senate Banking, Housing, and Urban
Affairs Committee
Dirksen Senate Office Building
Washington, DC 20510
Chief Counsels and Staff Directors
(Minority and Majority), Room 534
(202) 224-7391

Senate Securities Subcommittee
Dirksen Senate Office Building
Washington, DC 20510
Chief Counsels (Minority and Majority),
Room 534 (202) 224-7391

Taxes

House Ways and Means Committee
Longworth House Office Building
Washington, DC 20515
Chief Counsel and Staff Director,
Room 1102 (202) 225-3625
Minority Chief of Staff, Room 1106
(202) 225-4201

House Select Revenue Measures
Subcommittee
Longworth House Office Building
Washington, DC 20515
Chief Tax Counsel and Staff Director,
Room 1105 (202) 225-6649

Senate Finance Committee
Dirksen Senate Office Building
Washington, DC 20510
Staff Director and Chief Counsel, Room
205 (202) 224-4515
Minority Chief of Staff, Room 5315
(202) 224-5315

Banking

House Banking, Finance, and Urban
Affairs Committee
Rayburn House Office Building
Washington, DC 20515
General Counsel, Room 2129
(202) 225-3548
Minority Staff Director and General
Counsel, Room B-301-C
(202) 225 7509

Senate Banking, Housing, and Urban
Affairs Committee
Dirksen Senate Office Building
Washington, DC 20515
Chief Counsels and Staff Directors,
Room 534 (202) 224-7391

Senate Commerce, Science, and
Transportation Committee
Russell Senate Office Building
Washington, DC 20510
Chief Counsel and Staff Director,
Room 254 (202) 224-0427
Minority Senior Counsel, Room 554
(202) 224-1251

Energy

House Energy and Commerce
Committee (see above)

Other

House Small Business Committee
Rayburn House Office Building
Washington, DC 20515
Staff Director, Room 2361 (202) 225-5821
Minority Staff Director, Room 559 Ford
(202) 226-3420

Senate Small Business Committee
Russell Senate Office Building
Washington, DC 20510
Staff Directors and Chief Counsels
(Majority and Minority), Room 428-A
(202) 224-5175

Senate Budget Committee
Dirksen Senate Office Building
Washington, DC 20510
Staff Director, Room 602A
(202) 224-0553
Minority Staff Director, Room 634A
(202) 224-8769

Joint Economic Committee
Dirksen Senate Office Building
Washington, DC 20510
Executive Director, Room G01
(202) 224-5171

Joint Taxation Committee
Longworth House Office Building
Washington, DC 20515
Chief of Staff, Room 1015 (202) 225-3621

JUDICIAL BRANCH

United States Supreme Court
1 First Street, NE
Washington, DC 20543
Main number (202) 479-3000

U.S. Tax Court
400 2nd Street, NW
Washington, DC 20217
Main number (202) 479-3000

U.S. Courts of Appeal

Federal Circuit
Court of Appeals
Clerk's Office
Washington, DC 20439
(202) 633-6550

District of Columbia
Court of Appeals
Clerk's Office
Washington, DC 20001

First Circuit
Court of Appeals
Clerk's Office
Boston, MA 02109

Second Circuit
Court of Appeals
Clerk's Office
New York, New York 10007

Third Circuit
Court of Appeals
Clerk's Office
Philadelphia, PA 19106

Fourth Circuit
Court of Appeals
Clerk's Office
Richmond, VA 23219

Fifth Circuit
Court of Appeals
Clerk's Office
New Orleans, LA 70130

Sixth Circuit
Court of Appeals
Clerk's Office
Cincinnati, OH 45202

Seventh Circuit
Court of Appeals
Clerk's Office
Chicago, IL 60604

Eighth Circuit
Court of Appeals
Clerk's Office
St. Louis, MO 63101

Ninth Circuit
Court of Appeals
Clerk's Office
San Francisco, CA 94101

Tenth Circuit
Court of Appeals
Clerk's Office
Denver, CO 80294

Eleventh Circuit
Court of Appeals
Clerk's Office
Atlanta, GA 30303

Temporary Emergency
Court of Appeals
Clerk's Office
Washington, DC 20001

Index